Human Communication: Theory and Research

Human Communication: Theory and Research

GORDON L. DAHNKE
Michigan State University

GLEN W. CLATTERBUCK
Butler University

Wadsworth Publishing Company
Belmont, California
A Division of Wadsworth, Inc.

Communications Editor: Kristine M. Clerkin
Editorial Assistant: Tamiko Verkler/Nancy
    Spellman
Production Editor: Carol L. Dondrea/Bookman
    Productions
Print Buyer: Randy Hurst
Designer: MaryEllen Podgorski/R. Kharibian/
    Judith Levinson
Copy Editor: Anne Montague
Technical Illustrator: Judith Levinson
Compositor: Weimer Typesetting Company
Cover: Vargas/Williams/Design

Printed in the United States of America

1 2 3 4 5 6 7 8 9 10---94 93 92 91 90

Library of Congress Cataloging-in-Publication
Data

Human communication : theory and research /
    editors, Gordon L. Dahnke, Glen W.
    Clatterbuck.

        p. cm.
    Includes bibliographical references.
    ISBN 0-534-12396-1
    1. Communication.   I. Dahnke, Gordon
L.   II. Clatterbuck, Glen W.
P90.H77   1990
302.2--dc20   89-24776
                                        CIP

Contents

PART THREE
PERSUASIVE FUNCTIONS OF COMMUNICATION 227

PART FOUR
METHODS OF COMMUNICATION INQUIRY 307

Preface

By common consent, useful textbooks cannot be all things to all people. This one is no exception, despite the wide range of topics addressed. The book proposes to provide a broadly representative survey of current developments in the communications discipline from an empirical research perspective. No claim is made for this school of thought as either the sole or supreme answer regarding communication inquiry in our time. Rather, it represents one viable system of knowledge generation commonly called the scientific method. The principal part of the book offers a digest of what has been learned to date about human communication by way of this approach. A basic orientation to the method itself is also presented so as to enhance the reader's understanding and critical assessment of knowledge claims made throughout the book.

TARGET AUDIENCE AND USE

This text is addressed specifically to college and university students majoring in communication studies. Accordingly, it presupposes the following reader characteristics:

1. A basic familiarity with the terms, concepts, and principles used generally in introductory texts to describe a broad range of communication phenomena.

2. An acute interest in the quantitative methods of social science as currently applied to the study of human interaction.

3. An informed appreciation for the role of theory as a means of generating new knowledge in virtually every existing academic discipline.

Regarding the general utility of a survey text, one caveat deserves early attention. The communications discipline has developed a high degree of specialization over the past two or three decades. On that account, each content area addressed in this volume now represents an extensive, sophisticated body of information in its own right. So much so, it is no longer considered feasible for the student to effectively master all, or even several, of these content areas in a normal four-year program. As a result, communication majors typically begin to receive specialized training, in perhaps two or three substantive areas, immediately following their exposure to a basic skills-oriented, introductory course. This volume addresses the void, as we see it, between preliminary instruction and specialized training; it presents a comprehensive, yet manageable, overview of current theory and research across major subdivisions of the discipline. In brief, we contend that the informed, well-rounded communication major needs exposure to the broad base of information synthesized in Parts One, Two, and Three of this text. Indeed, given the discipline's diverse state, a broad background in the field is now virtually unattainable apart from well-integrated summary reviews such as these chapters contain.

This book, then, is designed to serve as a core text in survey courses seeking to integrate prevailing principles, current theory, and related research within specific content areas. In contrast to other texts, which examine theory types or the research process in relatively abstract terms, this text aligns specific theory with the actual practice of research and its results. Accordingly, the more significant studies and research advances to date within particular contexts such as interpersonal, small group, or organizational communication are reviewed by prominent scholars in their own areas of expertise.

Although the level of reading difficulty varies unavoidably to some extent from chapter to chapter, we believe it is quite compatible with the level of difficulty to which undergraduates are commonly exposed in other science-oriented subjects. We also believe the book is sufficiently challenging and informative to serve the needs of certain survey courses at the graduate level.

THE AUTHORSHIP

One unique feature of this book is the uncommon number of premier scholars it hosts under a single cover. They were selected systematically with the following concerns in mind. We were determined to enlist the best-qualified authorities interested in, and available to, the project. They were collectively to represent a broad spectrum of training and experience, clearly identified with the empirical approach. They were to be widely recognized among their peers for recent advances or mainstay contributions to the discipline. And finally, we sought a balance of scholarly commitment to theory development coupled with active involvement in the conduct of substantive research. The resulting roster of author-researchers speaks for itself.

Along with the potential for incorporating a broad spectrum of ideas and expertise, multi-author texts invariably inherit their own peculiar liabilities and limitations. From chapter to chapter, diverse writing styles, inconsistent or even incompatible definitions, and imbalances in the level of information presented are among the more troublesome problems with texts of this type for users and editors alike. In particular, heavy demands are placed on the reader, who must adapt constantly to a steady stream of new ideas, styles, and perspectives in rapid succession. Understandably, then, most students and many instructors prefer the conceptual consistency and stylistic uniformity achieved more typically in single- or dual-author texts. Those who expect a similar level of congruity in this book will likely be disappointed, despite our concerted efforts to minimize these problems.

But there are at least two compelling reasons for using multiple authors in a survey text. First, the problems noted above are multiplied many times over for the inexpert student attempting to assimilate a comparable body of literature from primary sources. In this regard, the present volume renders a yeoman's service to the reader. Although we would prefer even greater balance and consistency across its diverse subject matter, the book does substantially organize and synthesize an otherwise unwieldy maze of complex information. Second, as desirable as single- or dual-author texts may be, we seriously doubt that a broad survey text of this caliber could have been produced by one or two individuals. The combined breadth and depth of information presented in this volume required the cooperative efforts of a team of experts.

THE SCOPE

This text has little to do with the development of performance skills, save for the extent to which effective practice usually derives from sound theory in any discipline. As noted earlier, the book's spinal cord is the ongoing reciprocal relationship between theoretical ideas and research outcomes, for the purpose of generating new information. We asked the authors to report current knowledge claims resulting from that interplay. They were to identify important theoretical developments and review related research findings, each within his or her own area of expertise. The content areas selected have generally been recognized as focal points of scholarly attention over the last two or three decades; they represent foundations of the discipline from which many other more recent specializations have drawn their impetus, such as family, legal, and health-care communication. Moreover, the book makes no pretense of presenting the "latest fashions" in the communication field. Most of the ideas reported in this volume have been around for a while, tried and tested over time. They are solidly current without claiming to be state-of-the-art.

THE FORMAT

Following a conventional classification scheme, the book is subdivided into four parts, preceded by a single introductory chapter designed to es-

tablish some common ground between authors and readers before broaching the diverse array of topics that follow. Chapter 1 is an enlightening history of human communication inquiry, beginning with the early influences of classical Greek thought. Three mainstream schools of thought inspired by Aristotle, Plato, and the Sophists are traced through more than 1,500 years of development down to the present decade. This chapter sheds new light on the evolution of our discipline in the 20th century and beyond. Its broad historical perspective is an invaluable resource for assessing the significance of scientific research on human interaction in our time. Thus the authors offer the reader one viable yardstick by which the balance of this book can be evaluated.

Each of the four parts is preceded by an introductory section explaining our rationale for including it in the book and a chapter-by-chapter synopsis of its content. In turn, each chapter begins with an agenda of specific learning objectives to guide the reader, followed by the chapter's main text and an editor's summary To serve a variety of pedagogical purposes of interest to instructors and students alike, a list of in-depth review and discussion questions is provided at the end of each chapter unit.

Part One, "Channels of Communication," contains three chapters. Use of the term *channel* in this context extends its conventional meaning beyond sound and light waves or electronic media to include all the physical tools and operations people use to produce verbal and nonverbal messages. Accordingly, Chapter 2 focuses on the central communication process as it comes to expression through the verbal or linguistic channel. Similarly, Chapter 3 is an overview of that process as it comes to fruition through the nonverbal channel. In line with the traditional concept of *channel*, Chapter 4 examines contemporary emphases on electronic technology as a means of extending our verbal and nonverbal capabilities beyond their natural limits in time and space.

Part Two, "Contexts of Communication," addresses five specialized areas of study. Their inclusion in this text should require little justification. Representing progressively larger boundaries and numbers of communicators, Chapters 5 through 9 survey basic theory and research germane to our current understanding of interpersonal, small group, organizational, mass, and intercultural communication, respectively.

The next three units, Chapters 10 through 12, might also have been included appropriately in Part Two. However, they are set apart as "Persuasive Functions of Communication" in Part Three to underscore the importance of communication as a means of influencing others across all five contexts represented in Part Two. Indeed, some scholars argue that all human communication per se has its persuasive element.

Chapter 10 is a comprehensive overview of persuasion as a distinct type of communication, in contrast with other types of interaction serving different purposes. The next two chapters are specialized cases of the general model presented in Chapter 10. Chapter 11 focuses on persuasive communication as a means of implementing innovation and social change in broad cultural contexts. Application of persuasive strategies in the political arena is the particular interest of Chapter 12. The latter unit offers a unique comparative analysis of political communication in the United States and Latin America.

Part Four, "Methods of Communication Inquiry," addresses the common complaint of our students regarding the proverbial "forest versus trees" problem in the area of research methodology. Our experience suggests that communication majors are often exposed to a maze of methodological issues, couched in terms and examples borrowed from other disciplines, in lieu of an adequate organizational framework. Chapters 13 and 14 provide the broad superstructure, a general map of the research process into which finer details can be assimilated as the student's expertise develops over time. Because these two chapters are quite technical and were expected to be among the more difficult units in the book for our readers, we encountered some difference of opinion regarding their placement in the text. Some instructors prefer to expose students to methodology at the outset, to enhance their understanding of subsequent content areas; others find students more amenable to methodology following their exposure to substantive content. We see no compelling reason to discourage the use of Part Four prior to Parts One, Two, and Three, to accommodate a preference for that order. Given its present placement, the methodology in Part Four can also be omitted conveniently to meet specific classroom needs and requirements.

Gordon L. Dahnke
Glen W. Clatterbuck

1

The Historical Context of Communication as a Science

W. Barnett Pearce
University of Massachusetts

Karen A. Foss
Humboldt State University

*W. **Barnett Pearce** is Professor and Chair of the Department of Communication at the University of Massachusetts, Amherst. He earned the Ph.D. degree at Ohio University in 1969. Dr. Pearce is well known for his central contribution to the development of the theory of the "coordinated management of meaning," a communication perspective precipitating research on a wide array of topics. He has authored or co-authored several books, including* Communicating Personally; Communication, Action and Meaning; The Construction of Social Realities; Development as Communication. A Perspective on India; *and* Communication and the Human Condition. *Dr. Pearce has served as president of the Eastern Communication Association and held various offices within the International Communication and Speech Communication Associations.*

***Karen A. Foss** received her Ph.D. in speech communication from the University of Iowa in 1976. She is Professor of Speech Communication at Humboldt State University, where she also serves as Director of Women's Studies and of the Honors program. Her research areas include rhetorical theory and criticism, contemporary social movements, gender and communication, and communication apprehension.*

LEARNING OBJECTIVES

After studying this chapter you should be able to:

• Understand why putting the social science investigation of communication into historical context is necessary and useful.

1

- Identify the differences among the three most important theorists on the study of communication in classical times: the Sophistic philosophers, Plato, and Aristotle.
- Trace the reasons for decline of interest in the study of communication between the classical Greeks and the 20th century.
- Explain the importance of the difference between the Midwestern school's emphasis on "speech" and the Cornell school's emphasis on "rhetoric" in their approaches to the study of communication.
- Understand the significance of each of the seven new trends or directions in the study of communication discussed in this chapter.

Social science is a relatively recent invention, but the scientific study of communication is not. The prevailing myth portrays the scientific study of human communication as beginning only a few decades ago, in the 1940s, and as replacing with objective data a long tradition of relatively unproductive prescientific thought that combined speculation and personal value judgments under the guises of "humanism."

Both aspects of this myth are incorrect. Aristotle's *Rhetoric* can be considered the first research report of the empirical study of communication. Some might not accept Aristotle's claim to be a scientist because the scientific method, as we know it today, was not developed until the work of Francis Bacon and Galileo in the early 17th century. Bacon himself called for scientific studies of communication, and in 1644 John Bulwer responded with *Chirologia,* a study of the nonverbal expression of ideas and emotions. However one keeps score, the scientific study of communication is at least as old as the scientific study of anything.

As we shall discuss, the proper research methods, the most useful conceptualization, and the role of communication in the larger scheme of things have always been matters of tension. On several occasions, the tension has taken the form

of a "science" versus "humanism" controversy, but at other times, the issues have cut quite differently, and to say that one way of thinking about communication is younger or older than another is impossible. Rather than replacing an earlier, allegedly inferior way of thinking, the scientific study of communication has always coexisted with other approaches as one strand among others in a convoluted, intertwined history.

This book surveys the work and findings of social scientists in the 20th century. The purpose of this introductory chapter is to provide a frame in which the significance of that work can be assessed. A brief survey of three systems of thought about communication, each of which originated in the classical period in Greece and has continued in various forms to the present, is followed by a review of the development of the discipline of communication in the United States in the 20th century, with particular attention to the role of social scientific research. The final section describes a pattern of changes that we see coming in the discipline of communication.

One function of a historical context is to establish a baseline for evaluating contemporary activity. The communication technology available to ordinary citizens has undergone tremendous changes in this century. Within the lifetime of people now living, telephones have gone from a novelty to a necessity, and we have seen the development of "wireless" radios, videodiscs, and television transmissions from the surface of Mars and the rings of Saturn. But are these merely changes in the surface of society, or have they materially affected our way of life? Wilson Dizard (1982) says that they are "not simply a linear extension of what has gone on before. We are experiencing a qualitative shift in the thrust and purpose of American society" (p. 2). Claims like Dizard's can only be made and evaluated based on a knowledge of what has gone before as well as a knowledge of the communication technologies that have been introduced.

The systematic application of the methods of social science to the phenomenon of communication is itself a contemporary practice that requires historical context. "The communications revolution" has generated new questions about communication, employed novel research methods, and produced massive amounts of information about it. But how has the net effect been evaluated, and how does that evaluation compare with the composite of observations, intuitions, and experiences of the women and men who have thought about communication for thousands of years? Have the practices and institutions that characterize the current social scientific study of communication *extended* traditional knowledge, *revolutionized* it, or *trivialized* it? Without knowing the history of the tradition, it is impossible to say.

A more important reason for locating social scientific studies of communication in their historical context is that it illuminates the nature of the knowledge produced by scientific studies. Specifically, three surprises about the relation between social science and other forms of communication theory become apparent.

The first surprise is that social science is not nearly so different from humanistic studies as is commonly thought. A heated controversy between humanists and scientists has raged through this century, as reflected in C. P. Snow's (1962) famous analysis of the "two cultures" (scientists and humanists) who are similar in race, nationality, amount of education, intelligence, and socioeconomic class but live in such different intellectual worlds that each is illiterate in the speech and writings of the other.

The reason for the controversy is not hard to understand. The characteristic method of scientific inquiry is to put the most cherished traditional theories and beliefs to the test of empirical verification. To the custodians of a tradition, such tests sometimes seemed a brash dismissal of the wisdom of the ancients and a trivialization of the fundamental concerns that have sustained a discipline throughout its history.

This controversy suggests that science and humanism occupy extreme ends of some continuum that represents the various modes of human inquiry. We argue to the contrary that scientific

and humanistic approaches to communication in this century have been intramural squabbles within what we call Aristotelianism, one of three major traditions in the history of thought about communication (the other two are Platonic and Sophistic).

Second, the way scientists think about communication has changed as a result of research. Scientists are much more sophisticated now than they were in the first two-thirds of this century. Their sophistication has been the hard-won consequence of the often painful process of having to confront and abandon—on the basis of their own research—their own assumptions and working principles. Many of these assumptions dealt with communication as it is used in conducting scientific research as well as communication as the object of scientific study. The surprise is how differently scientists think about communication now than they did only a few decades ago.

Third, the direction in which the social scientific study of human communication is moving aligns it with the oldest extant form of thought about communication, which we refer to as Sophistic. The science-versus-humanism struggles that so unproductively preoccupied researchers in the first half of the 20th century seem increasingly irrelevant as both move away from their Aristotelian basis and toward something which, surprisingly, resembles the Sophists.

We will elaborate on these ideas as we turn to the origins of the study of communication in the West. We hope this history will function as a first step in understanding the social scientific tradition within the discipline.

THREE PATTERNS OF THOUGHT ABOUT COMMUNICATION

The formal study of communication in the West began in the fifth century B.C. in Greece, in both practical and conceptual forms. The conceptual approach was taken by the pre-Socratic philosophers who debated the nature of reality, the nature of knowledge, and the nature of language.

Some argued that reality was timeless, changeless, and perfect; others that it was all in flux. Notions of knowledge, language, and communication ultimately derived from these differing philosophical positions.[1]

The practical approach was shaped by political events and the economic self-interest of the Greek citizenry. The overthrow of a tyrant on the island of Syracuse left a legal morass of conflicting claims on the land. Because Greek citizens were required to argue their own cases in court, Corax, a specialist in forensic rhetoric from Syracuse, started a thriving business teaching plaintiffs and defendants how to argue effectively. Corax's teachings were carried to mainland Greece by his student Tisias, and the teaching of principles of public speaking became an accepted part of Greek culture.

The Sophistic Tradition

Corax and Tisias were first among a group of teachers and practitioners of rhetoric known as Sophists (from the Greek word meaning "wisdom" or "knowledge"). The Sophists were interested in the role of *logos,* or the power of language in the human world. They recognized that language is by its very nature inaccurate in its descriptions of the world, ambiguous and metaphorical. Rather than treating these characteristics as flaws impeding a mirrorlike knowledge of reality, they celebrated the capacity of language to create possibilities in the world. They believed that two characteristics of language confer great power: the ability to name the unseen and the ability to conceal as well as reveal aspects of reality.

The Sophists have been maligned throughout Western history. The word *sophist* has come to mean a speaker who uses clever arguments in an attempt to deceive the audience; sophistry consists of a set of tricks by which one may make the worse appear to be the better. This judgment merely repeats that of the Sophists' primary enemy, Plato. Like the Sophists, Plato wrote well and prolifically; unlike them, much of Plato's work

survived the ravages of time and the Vandals' sacking of Rome in A.D. 455. Filtered through Plato's dialogs, the Sophists seem to have little of importance to say about communication. If Plato's judgments are suspended, however, the Sophists can be seen as making a bold and provocative argument similar to that now known as the social construction of reality (Berger & Luckmann, 1966; Gergen & Davis, 1985).

The Platonic Tradition

Plato espoused a concept of communication quite different from that of the Sophists. In his dialogs, Plato set his friend Socrates against the Sophists Gorgias and Timaeus to argue for a theory of communication based on knowledge of a true reality. He believed that reality consisted of timeless, changeless forms that lie beyond the variable, changing world of appearances and can be known only by trained philosophers. Through proper use of dialectic, philosophers can be enlightened and attain true knowledge, of which the perceptions of the everyday world are mere shadows.

Disparaging the Sophists' seeming relativism, Plato suggested—but did not work out the details of—a rhetoric based on true knowledge, not just argumentative tricks. A philosophical rhetorician could present the truth rather than mere opinions to an audience in such a way that they, too, could intuitively grasp divine wisdom. In contrast to this ideal, the teachings of the Sophists were considered a mere "knack" like cookery, not an art; they were based on comparisons among mere opinions, not presentations of knowledge gained through philosophic insight.

The Sophists and Plato, then, stand as endpoints of a continuum about the function and significance of language. For the Sophists, language was a powerful force that constructed the possibilities for the human world. For Plato, language was a necessary evil—an imperfect means of expression that could only distort true reality whenever it was used. These concepts, of course, led to very different practices. The Sophists delighted in paradoxes and rhetorical stratagems and hired themselves out to teach ordinary people to argue more skillfully. Plato established an academy for the training of an intellectual elite, set himself up as an opponent of the Sophists, and, in *The Republic,* envisioned censoring those who used language irresponsibly. The Sophists developed a curriculum centered on the study of rhetoric, because they believed that truth and rhetorical effectiveness were inherently intertwined. Believing that the sorry state of the audience often made rhetorical effectiveness unrelated to knowledge, Plato separated rhetoric from what he considered more important topics—a distinction that has recurred often through the centuries.

The Aristotelian Tradition

An alternative position in the vigorous debate between the Sophists and Plato was provided by Plato's former student Aristotle. Aristotle believed that a combination of careful observation of the world and meticulous reasoning according to the standards of logic would provide true knowledge of the natural world and good judgment in contingent human affairs in which certainty is not possible. Following his own ethical principle of moderation in all things, he combined the Sophists' attention to the actual world of human affairs and Plato's quest for certainty, although arguing that certainty could only be approximated in human affairs.

Aristotle's *Rhetoric* was based on empirical observations of the practices of speakers and the responses of audiences and was designed to help a rhetorician discover all the available means of persuasion in any given situation. Whether as a practical handbook or as a model of empirical method, Aristotle's *Rhetoric* was a fundamental influence on the study of communication during the Roman Empire and has been the single most influential work in the history of Western thought about communication.

The study of communication faced new challenges when Christianity became the official religion of the Roman Empire in the early fourth century A.D. The endorsement of Christian doctrine by Emperor Constantine subordinated pagan writings about rhetoric to Christian Scriptures. A compromise was offered by Augustine, the Bishop of Hippo in North Africa, at the end of the fourth century. Heavily influenced by Plato's writings, Augustine treated Christian doctrine as the knowledge that could not be attained through rhetoric (something like philosophic enlightenment in Plato's thought) but that might be made more effective in presentation to particular audiences through rhetoric. Knowledge is gained, Augustine wrote in *On Christian Doctrine,* by the interpretation of Scripture. Once edified, however, the Christian minister was free to use pagan rhetorical theories to make his sermons more effective.

Although the writers on communication in the next few centuries were heavily influenced by Augustine, they tended to overlook the theoretical aspects of his work and to reduce it to a set of prescriptive speaking techniques. Augustine argued for the integration of secular and divine subject matters, but lost.

The Middle Ages In the Middle Ages, secular and religious studies were separated in a rigid curriculum. The liberal arts were composed of the *trivium,* consisting of grammar, rhetoric, and dialectic, and the *quadrivium;* arithmetic, music, geometry, and astronomy. The *trivium* (from which we get the word "trivial") dealt with those inferior matters in which certainty was not possible; the *quadrivium* was considered preferable because it allowed for exact demonstrations. Theological studies followed and were considered superior to these seven liberal arts.

The 16th-century French philosopher Petrus Ramus completed the medieval separation of rhetoric from the more important concerns of education by fragmenting the traditional canons of rhetoric—invention, disposition, elocution, pronunciation, and memory—into different specializations. Invention and disposition were assigned to dialectic; memory was simply deemphasized.

Rhetoric was considered to deal only with elocution and pronunciation, and these were treated as if they were composed only of figures of speech and gestures. All these fields seemed trivial in comparison with the exciting new developments in the physical sciences, in the arts, and in the study of classical documents.

The educational curriculum of the Middle Ages institutionalized the commonality between Aristotle and Plato, both of whom separated rhetoric from the process of achieving knowledge. Further, this curriculum reproduced Aristotle and Plato's disagreement about whether to place the emphasis on observable certainties or on an absolute, transcendent world. Essentially, medieval teachers agreed with Plato by making theological studies the culmination of an education, although they incorporated Aristotle's logical and rhetorical teachings as useful in the inferior world of mere appearances. Finally, this curriculum institutionalized rhetoric as the mere sophistry Plato considered it. It was about as far as one could get from the Sophists' own theory of communication that placed the creative powers of language at the center of the curriculum, and it incorporated little, if any, of Aristotle's belief in the importance of careful observation of the practices of actual rhetoricians.

The Humanist Revival   Although clearly overshadowed by other traditions, the Sophistic way of thinking about communication found expression in the revival of humanism in the 15th century. Several factors combined to create a rich intellectual tradition that had new access to the Greek classical texts, a belief in the dignity of individuals as the product of culture, and a mastery of the techniques of philology as a means of research.

The Italian humanists in particular made an effort to give renewed prominence to the notion that the world is not a factual one to be discovered and then talked about but one that comes into being as it is constructed through language. The humanists saw literature as a form of philosophizing because it is a way of constructing meaning without losing the particulars and emotions of an event. Thus metaphors, irony, and other rhetorical figures can be forms of philosophizing. The 16th-century Dutch humanist Erasmus is an excellent example of this tradition. Erasmus's *Praise of Folly* (1509) is often dismissed as a playful and hastily written treatise without serious purpose (Grassi & Lorch, 1986). It should be read, however, as a witty, sarcastic complement to his careful linguistic study of the Christian Scriptures, in which he pointed out flaws and inconsistencies, much to the discomfort of the religious authorities. In both works, Erasmus cites forms of expression as the means of creating the institutions and beliefs in which people live. Giambattista Vico, an 18th-century scholar whose work often is considered the culmination of humanist thought, argued that efforts to understand the world cannot be separated from the forms of expression of that knowledge, since the choices one makes about what name or label to give an experience will determine what that experience is.

The Scientific Age   Just as Plato and Aristotle overshadowed the Sophists in the fifth century B.C., the perspective of the Italian humanists was obscured by the excitement generated by the development of modern science. Ironically, the fascination the humanists felt for the classics that liberated them from the scholasticism of the medieval period made them vulnerable to the criticisms of the new scientists, who—in the spirit but not the language of Aristotle—demanded an empirical analysis of the physical world.

In the early 17th century, Francis Bacon offered the structure for a "new science" based on inductive reasoning and empirical observations. Claiming that what was needed was not wings but chains for the imagination, Bacon claimed that the scientific method enabled his contemporaries to be vastly superior to the ancients in the physical sciences and the arts. At about the same time, Galileo argued that the language of the cosmos is mathematics, not—in a blatant criticism of the humanists—Latin or Greek. Galileo and Bacon's polemics institutionalized a new way of thinking about the nature of the world that was highly structured, mechanical, and scientific in orientation. The growing interest in science, then, and the continuing dominance of the Aristotelian and Platonic traditions overwhelmed the voices of the humanists.

The Elocutionists The scientific studies of communication in the 17th century sowed the seeds of the elocutionist movement, which became the essence of the study of communication in the United States in the late 1800s. Recall that under the influence of Ramus, rhetoric had been reduced to the narrow domain of elocution and pronunciation. Furthermore, as part of Francis Bacon's claim that all knowledge was his province, Bacon suggested that the scientific method be applied to rhetoric as he knew it, which meant the gestures that orators used as embellishments. Bulwer's *Chirologia* in 1644 was the first of a series of studies of the physical, nonverbal expression of ideas and emotions.

The elocutionists who drew upon this literature limited their interests to the vocal and bodily movements that would augment the oral reading of speeches. Thomas Sheridan (1719–1788), a former actor in London, found in the writings of John Locke a basis for studying words as the signs of ideas and tones of voice as the signs of passions. The major alternative to elocution was found in the works of Hugh Blair, George Campbell, and Richard Whately—all 18th- and 19th-century Protestant ministers influenced by the Enlightenment's faith in reason. By basing their theories on the best available psychological concepts, these rhetoricians recaptured some of the richness that had been lost in Ramus's fragmentation into mere elocution, but they were unable to overcome the strength of the elocutionary tradition.

Although the study of elocution dominated the field in the United States, it was not highly respected. At the start of the 20th century, colleges were not replacing professors of oratory when they retired, and their positions often were given to English departments, where the rhetoric of writing was taught. When public speaking was taught at all, it usually was done by a professor of English who was more interested in poetry and literature than oratory.

THE DEVELOPMENT OF THE DISCIPLINE IN THE 20TH CENTURY

The study of communication has been reborn three times in this century: once as the speech profession, then as the field of communication, and finally as the discipline of communication. We will discuss each of these phases in order to provide a context for the contemporary study of communication as social science.

The Reestablishment of the Speech Profession

The development of the Midwestern school of speech marks the beginning of the contemporary study of communication. In 1914 a group of speech teachers withdrew from the National Association of English Teachers to establish a new professional association for teachers of public speaking. These teachers wanted to return to classical texts in rhetoric and to make use of the experimental research methods of psychology in order to give renewed substance to the study of communication. James Winans and Charles Woolbert, at the universities of Wisconsin and Illinois, respectively, were major instigators of what would come to be called the Midwestern school of speech.

The Cornell school of rhetoric was spawned in the 1920s when a group of scholars, led by Everett Hunt and Alexander Drummond, rediscovered the classical texts of rhetoric. They differed from the Midwestern school in their conceptualization of the nature of the act of communication, the nature of the substance of instruction, and the nature of research that guided instruction. The controversy about these issues shaped and limited the study of communication for half a century.

The Midwestern tradition defined *speaking* as the act with which they were concerned, while the Cornell group emphasized *public* speaking, or oratory. The significance of this distinction was evident in the curricular differences between the two schools. Departments influenced by the Midwestern approach offered courses in dramatics, voice and diction, oral interpretation, radio speaking, debate, and small-group discussion as well as public speaking. Many departments offered courses in the psychology of speech, which examined the development of oral language skills; the physical process of sound-making; and the development of dialects and speech defects. Students were encouraged to take courses outside the department in psychology and in the physiology of the speaking process.[2] In contrast, the departments influenced by the Cornell school offered courses in classical, medieval, and modern rhetorical theory; rhetorical criticism; and British and American public address. Students usually took courses outside the department in history or political science.[3]

Both schools were concerned with capturing the substance of communication, but they disagreed on what that substance was. Members of the Midwestern school focused on equipping speakers to make the best possible case for whatever content position was chosen, an emphasis on form that derived from their faith in science. They thought that the "content" of their discipline was a series of "true" statements about the form of effective speech. The Cornell school, on the other hand, emphasized the discovery and evaluation of "good reasons" for belief and action in uncertain situations. The members of this school sought to prepare students to exercise good judgment in situations in which truth was unknown and perhaps unknowable. Rather than teaching students empirically grounded generalizations about the variables most highly correlated with effective speaking, the Cornell school led students to a critical appraisal of rhetorical discourse in order to offer guide-

lines that would serve them in their own rhetorical encounters.

Their research orientations also distinguished these traditions. The Cornell school endorsed humanistic values, whereas the Midwestern school adhered to scientific procedures and goals. The Midwestern school assumed that the relationships among the variables that accounted for the effectiveness of speeches were sufficiently robust to apply to a wide variety of specific historical occasions. The Cornell school assumed that although particular rhetorical situations were deeply embedded in historical contexts and the response of a rhetorician could be guided by good judgment based on precedent, ultimately communication has to be adapted to the present moment. In short, the Cornell school assumed that rhetorical situations were contingent, with no set formula to guide speakers; the Midwestern school had a more mechanical model implicit in its approach.

The interaction, then, between the Midwestern and Cornell schools dominated the study of communication in the first part of the 20th century. In general, the Midwestern school argued that not enough scientific research had been done; that more rigorous applications of sophisticated methods would produce a body of knowledge about what makes speech effective; and that the study of historical speeches and rhetorical theory was at best not useful and at worst prevented differentiation between mere opinionated moralizing and scientifically established facts. Those in the Cornell school argued that scientific research was inherently incapable of guiding the good judgment required to adapt to a rhetorical situation; that the pursuit of scientific research trivialized the demands placed on a rhetorician and suggested the substitution of knowledge of mere formula for good judgment; and that increased humanistic understanding of rhetoric could equip students to respond creatively and eloquently to the speaking situations they would encounter.

This argument between rhetoric and speech was never resolved. Rather, the impasse was broken by the entrance into the profession of people and ideas unrelated to either school.

The Development of the Field of Communication

Communication became one of the great intellectual buzz words in the period after World War II, and an autonomous but unintegrated field emerged whose principal subspecialties were communication theory and mass communication. These groups drew from journalists, political scientists, sociologists, and information theorists rather than from speech teachers. Their pantheon of heroes included Carl Hovland, Harold Lasswell, Paul Lazarsfeld, Wilbur Schramm, Bruce Westley, Elihu Katz, Theodor Adorno, Kurt Lang and Gladys Lang, and Kurt Lewin. James Carey (1979) summarized this growing field:

The phrases "communication research" and "mass communication" achieved sufficient identity in the postwar years that they entered the vocabulary. There were now options to studying journalism or the newspaper or the magazine— one could study mass communications. There were now options to studying speech, or rhetoric, or drama—one could now study communications. (p. 285)

Many communication theorists and mass communication researchers had disciplinary homes of their own; others established interdisciplinary communication research centers. In 1959—the same year that Oliver and Bauer celebrated the 50th anniversary of the reestablishment of the speech profession—Wilbur Schramm (1964) characterized communication as a "field, not a discipline," calling it a "great crossroads where many pass but few tarry" (p. 511). The idea of communication and the research methods and interests of the mass communication scholars, however, began to influence the speech profession. The conversation between rhetoric and speech was ripe for a fresh voice, and the notion of communication was ideally situated to assume a position of dominance. Within 20 years—by 1975—most of the journals and associations in the discipline had changed their names to include *communication.*[4]

The Emergence of the Discipline of Communication

The invasion of communication broke the impasse between rhetoric and speech, opening the way for new insights and perspectives about the subject. It also intensified the field's commitment to research in addition to teaching and compounded the field's preoccupation with the effects rather than with the processes of communication.[5] Ultimately, the union of the speech profession and the field of communication produced a discipline of communication, characterized by research interests and methods of its own. This new discipline harmonized in some ways with both rhetoric and speech, although there was by far more affinity with the Midwestern school's emphasis on scientific research and its orientation to effects of speeches (rather than to the exigencies and strategies of speakers).

The marriage of speech and communication was formalized in 1969, with the publication of *Conceptual Frontiers in Speech-Communication,* edited by Kibler and Barker. This book was a report of the New Orleans Conference on Research and Instructional Development. The conference participants clearly thought that although the hybrid phrase "speech-communication" was not entirely satisfactory as a label for the discipline, at least it encompassed a growing theme in it and one they hoped would characterize its future.

This is not to say that the rhetorical tradition in the discipline died or that it no longer is important. On the contrary, there is today more convergence between the humanist and scientific approaches to communication than in times past, as both social scientists and rhetoricians explore such themes as the process of inquiry, the "rhetoric" of science, and the nature of knowledge. In fact, the social science and humanistic traditions together are producing some exciting developments in the study of communication.

FUTURE PROJECTIONS

Physicists know that the more accurately the velocity of a moving object is described, the less accurately its position can be specified and vice versa. The velocity with which thinking about communication is changing is extraordinarily high; therefore, any efforts to make accurate projections about the future directions of the discipline necessarily will be fuzzy and even controversial. The following seven characteristics, however, seem to capture the current state of the discipline in its ongoing evolution.

An Expanded Concept of Communication

Communication usually has been thought of as occurring in a relatively narrow range of situations. Until recently, rhetoricians were preoccupied with public speaking, whereas those in the field of communication focused on the mass media and on effects of communication processes. An expanded concept of communication is evolving, however, because researchers realize that important things happen even in apparently mundane forms of communication. The private talk among friends, the patterns of daily talk in families, and the normal patterns of official and unofficial talk in organizations are all important social processes, in which personal identities are forged and people develop and test their ideas about what is real and what is good.

Further, the evolution of this view of communication has been fueled by the discovery that communication occurs in ways that extend beyond the obvious forms of talk. Some theorists examine machine technology for what it says about and how it alters human communication. Other researchers have found that animals and even plants communicate with one another and with their environment; thus ecology has supplemented genetics and nutrition as the framework through which such researchers understand the nonhuman world. Still others have focused on how human beings use nonverbal channels of communication more than verbal signals to exchange certain kinds of information. All these findings have led to an expanded concept of communication throughout the discipline, and researchers now can study communication in virtually any form and context.

A More Complex Concept of Communication

Communication has traditionally been viewed as an important but essentially straightforward process, the apparent complexities of which could be penetrated if the correct concepts could be identified. In the early 20th century, the leaders of the new discipline of communication felt a need to find a model of the communication process that would be consensually accepted, could help organize and guide research, and could be referred to when they explained the discipline to outsiders. Their enthusiasm for this project was stimulated by the successes of the natural sciences, such as physics and chemistry, in which models of the atom, molecules, and other fundamental components feature prominently.

One of the most influential communication models, developed by Harold Lasswell (1964), consisted of a series of questions. According to Lasswell, a communication researcher seeks to know: Who? Says what? To whom? Through what channel? With what effect? Some of the major assumptions of the whole effort to produce a consensual model are embodied in Lasswell's formula. Communication is identified as the intentional act of one person directed toward another, and the model follows the movement of that message from sender to receiver.

The form of Claude Shannon and Warren Weaver's (1949) mathematical model of communication made the strategy of "following the message" even more explicit. The arrows trace the path of the message as depicted in their model:

source → transmitter → message → receiver → destination
↑
noise

The addition of a feedback loop from destination to source made the process circular in that it showed sources could also be receivers and vice versa, but the model is analogous to Lasswell's in its basic linearity: It follows messages from one source to another.

Wilbur Schramm's (1954) model in Figure 1.1 put the source and receiver on equal ground, but in other respects duplicated Lasswell's and Shannon and Weaver's work. The arrows still depict the movement of messages from one person to another.

In the 1960s, numerous models and definitions of communication followed in a bewildering, frustrating sequence. Each successive model was based on a convincing demonstration of the inadequacies of its predecessor and was in turn shown inadequate by its successor. The titles of articles in scholarly journals, such as "On Defining Communication: Another Stab" (Miller, 1966) and "On Defining Communication: Still Another View" (Gerbner, 1966), revealed the authors' frustrations with this approach. The effort to produce a definitive model was abandoned more than declared a failure. In 1970 Frank Dance urged the discipline to accept a family of models

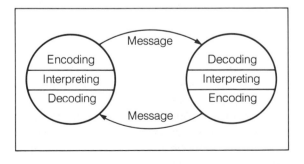

Figure 1.1 Wilbur Schramm's model of communication.

and definitions, each of which might be useful in some situations but not in others.

The attempt to understand communication by finding a model that would simplify it is consistent with one of the most basic forms of Western thought: analysis. To analyze something means to take it apart, identifying and describing the smallest possible components of a complex whole. Behind the passion for analysis is the belief that irreducible elements are more fundamental or more real than composite elements or than the relations among elements, and that a sufficiently rich description of the smallest possible units of analysis provides the best possible understanding of any phenomenon.

Applied to communication, this analytic approach resulted in a series of categorizations of communication acts. Mass communication was differentiated from interpersonal communication, oratory from literature, small-group communication from public communication, and so on. Public speaking occasions were divided into persuasive, deliberative, and ceremonial categories, each with a different purpose and method. Audiences were differentiated by such characteristics as age, sex, and predisposition to believe the speaker. Speakers were categorized on the basis of their credibility, for example, or according to the types of persuasive strategies employed.

Despite the unquestionable success of the analytical approach in certain natural sciences, social scientists began to wonder whether it was the best conceptual approach to communication. Some argued that the biological sciences provided a better model, and the emergence of general systems theory provided a vocabulary capable of capturing the complexity of the process rather than attempting to cut through it to its constituent parts. The value of systemic models has been easier to see, however, than to incorporate into research programs. Nonetheless, virtually all current research envisions communication as more complex than early models indicated.

A Primary Rather Than a Secondary Process

Following either Plato or Aristotle, many have believed that physical objects and human intentions are real and that communication is a process used in the service of these realities. For those who take this perspective, communication can express reality or can be used to discover good reasons for choosing one policy rather than another, but it is not involved in the ontological creation of those objects or reasons. In this view, communication is considered central to the human condition but not basic; it is important but not crucial.

In a manner reminiscent of the Sophists, many social scientists now argue that communication is both basic and important. For example, George Herbert Mead (1934) made the development and use of significant symbols the cornerstone of his theory of symbolic interactionism. Kenneth Burke's (1969) dramatistic analysis of the human condition characterizes human beings as symbol-using animals. Peter Berger and Thomas Luckmann (1966) show that selves, intentions, and objects do not exist for human beings per se; they achieve their existence from the process of social construction. Gaye Tuchman (1973) has shown how this process works in the news media, and Barnett Pearce and Vernon Cronen (1980) have described it in face-to-face talk.

Action Rather Than Mere Referent

If communication is a secondary social process, it occurs in a world that is relatively unaffected by how it is used. But if communication is the primary social process, then it creates the world in which it occurs. To say something is not simply to describe it but to do something. Bronislaw Malinowski (1945) came to this understanding of communication as a result of his problem in interpreting "magic" among the Melanesians. He first understood them as simply doing "bad science." In other words, they attributed particular events to the effects of their magic, when any scientifically literate person could see natural causes at work. But Malinowski came to understand that some important things were happening when they did magic talk quite irrespective of the scientific accuracy of what they were saying. They were telling themselves stories that made their world understandable and gave them a sense of efficacy in it; they were defining themselves as a people who believed in certain ways and not in others. This form of talk was a way of "doing" something more than it was a way of "referring" to something.

Malinowski's work was paralleled by Ludwig Wittgenstein's (1953) analysis of language games. Language games, Wittgenstein argued, have their own rules and construct the world in which their users live. For example, the language game of science may be particularly useful for developing a technology and explaining the world around us, but it is inherently deficient for dealing with questions of beauty and ethics—subjects that require different language games. To talk scientifically about ethics, Wittgenstein argued, makes no more sense than to evaluate what the Melanesians are doing in their magic talk by treating it as a description of the physical universe.

More recently, J. L. Austin (1962) introduced the concept of "speech acts" to talk about speech as a process of doing. One category of speech acts is "performatives": those events or objects that come into being by virtue of their being said or "performed." For example, when a minister says, "I now pronounce you husband and wife," it makes no sense to ask whether the statement is true or false. The minister either performs the act or does not.

The implications of the notion that communication is a primary process of doing something, rather than a secondary process of referring to something not materially affected by it, are staggering. Paul Watzlawick (1976) said:

Communication creates what we call reality. At first glance this may seem a most peculiar statement, for surely reality is what is, and communi-

cation is merely a way of expressing or explain-ing it.

Not at all. . . . our everyday, traditional ideas of reality are delusions which we spend substan-tial parts of our daily lives shoring up, even at the considerable risk of trying to force facts to fit our definition of reality instead of vice versa. And the most dangerous delusion of all is that there is only one reality. What there are, in fact, are many different versions of reality, some of which are contradictory, but all of which are the results of communication and not reflections of eternal, objective truths. (pp. 141–142)

A Process of Achieving Coordination Rather Than Producing Effects

The Romans envisioned Mercury as the messen-ger of the gods and depicted him with wings on his heels and carrying a spear. The traditional way of thinking about communication in the first half of the 20th century was not that different from this image of Mercury: Communication was con-ceptualized as the physical movement from one place to another of a message that was then thrust or jabbed into the audience, much as Mercury's spear might have been.

This view of communication is now known as the "bullet theory" or the "hypodermic model" of communication. The source of the message is considered active in a way the recipient is not, and the message "contains" that which accounts for its effects, just as the effect of an injection is determined by the solution in the syringe. This way of thinking about communication leads inex-orably to a preoccupation with the intended ef-fects of messages.

One of the earliest signs that the bullet theory was not adequate to fully describe the process of communication came in 1960, with the publica-tion of Joseph Klapper's *The Effects of Mass Com-munication*. Klapper surveyed the extensive research literature produced by those who sought to determine what the impact of bulletlike messages might be and reached the startling con-

clusion that mass mediated messages normally have no effect whatsoever. When they do have an effect, it is usually to strengthen existing attitudes and behaviors rather than to change them. When mass mediated messages do produce attitude or behavioral change, it almost always occurs when other conditions already have impelled the per-son toward change.

These were discouraging results for several decades of sophisticated work in which research-ers tried to assess the potential of the media for good or ill. What conclusion should be drawn? Some, like network executives, were happy to take the results at face value: Klapper's findings appeared to exonerate them from the charges that they were corrupting the young, polluting the culture, and wasting the power of the me-dium by broadcasting lucrative game shows and situation comedies. Another response was to as-sume that Klapper's surprising results were the product of asking the wrong question, or of seek-ing an answer in the wrong vocabulary. Rather than focusing on the simple effects one person can achieve in the attitudes and behavior of oth-ers by hurling messages at them, communication researchers now are asking the broader question of how people *coordinate* their behaviors with each other to produce patterns in which various sorts of effects may occur.

Some communication theorists ask how the behaviors of message producers and message users connect. They assume that all messages emerge from unacknowledged constraints and lead to unanticipated consequences. From this perspective, mass communication can be seen as the means of producing cultural artifacts such as movie stars, television programs, and slang. These artifacts, in turn, expose the social, political, and economic structures in which the media function. Other theorists focus on the audience's intentional behavior in selecting and interpreting the messages produced by others. People are not passive receivers of information, so this line of thinking goes, but deliberate users of the media in ways which gratify partic-ular needs.

This emphasis on coordination is more than simply a shift in attention from messages to sources or receivers; it is a shift from thinking about communicators one at a time to looking at the patterns among multiple communicators. Even so small a communicative act as insult or compliment is accomplished by the coordinated activity of two or more people. More complex acts, such as having dinner with friends or electing a president, entail coordination on a far greater scale. The emphasis on coordination, then, shows that messages do not have meanings in themselves; rather, they derive their meanings from the social context in which they are uttered and from the responses to them.

A Process of Telling Stories Rather Than Achieving Understanding

Understanding each other implies a comparison of what is "in the head" of one person to that which is "in the head" of another. Attempts to scientifically measure the notion of understanding were not successful, however, and whether understanding ever occurs remains very much a subjective evaluation. Researchers began to suspect that they were conceptualizing the process of communication wrongly in their efforts to achieve and understand the processes involved in sharing meanings.

One model that began to move away from a strict focus on understanding is Jack McLeod and Stephen Chaffee's coorientation model (1973), which depicts the extent to which two people or groups have the same orientation to the events and objects in their environment. The model sought to define three relationships: agreement, congruence, and accuracy. *Agreement* describes the extent to which two persons' orientations to an object are the same; *congruence* describes the extent to which they believe that they agree; and *accuracy* describes the extent to which their perception of the others' orientation matches that orientation. By defining *relations* among ori-

entations rather than attitudes or behaviors themselves as the objects of interest, the coorientational model represented a more sophisticated concept of communication.

Another line of research found that understanding or accuracy is not necessary for good coordination or coherence, and that the persistent search for understanding and accuracy may be dysfunctional. A study of the communication between two college students, pseudonymed Jan and Dave, found a recurring pattern important to their relationship (Cronen & McNamee, 1980). Jan was, by her own admission, lazy and had to be urged to do what she needed to do; Dave was, by his own description, a laid-back person who would not demand or insist that the other person do something. One of the perennial problems the couple faced was earning sufficient money to stay in school. They had decided that Jan needed to get a job, but she had made no effort to do so. Finally, this became an issue that threatened their relationship. In a pivotal moment, Jan performed speech acts intended to get Dave to insist that she take a more aggressive approach to looking for work, and Dave performed speech acts intended to tell her that he refused to accept responsibility for her life. Dave finally said something that *he* interpreted in the context of the argument as a refusal to tell her what to do; *she* interpreted it as an ultimatum in which he did tell her what to do. The next day, she assertively sought and found a job. Each achieved a coherent story about what happened, and the stories they told themselves were in accordance with their important concepts of self and of the relationship—but only because they misunderstood each other.

The point here is that understanding is not necessarily bad, only that the persistent search for it is not necessarily always good. Some people fight because they misunderstand each other, others because they understand each other all too well. Despite the value of understanding, the more potent process is to tell a story that enables each of us to understand ourselves, the world around us, and other people coherently. Clifford Geertz (1983) summarizes:

Life . . . always involves at the centre of it, a search for at least some level of coherence of meaning, for the significance of what's going on. A sense that we know who we are, that we know what the world is like, and that we have some purchase on what's going on; that it isn't just one damn thing after another. That it isn't chaos. We have to think we have an understanding, however partial, of what's happening to us. And that "have to" will never go away, because there's no way in which instrumental activity can alto-gether satisfy us. . . . People can stand not know-ing or not understanding this or that; but they can't or at least not for very long stand the no-tion that the world is absurd, *that you can't un-derstand it at all, that there's no meaning to it at all. (pp. 208–209)*

A Process That Allows for Mystery

Echoing Aristotle's preference for logical means of persuasion and the Enlightenment's faith in rationality, communication theorists have usually assumed that clarity and precision are the desired ends of communication. If the world consists of events and objects unaffected by communica-tion, and the function of communication is to de-scribe it or to convey meanings from one place to another within it, then clarity and precision are the appropriate criteria for communication. Lack of clarity indicates that a speaker is lazy or devious; vague, imprecise messages can and should be improved by adding qualification, details, or clarification. Although the ideal of a totally clear, precise, and "noiseless" mes-sage may never be reached, there is nothing in principle that precludes the attainment of these goals.

The aptness of clarity and precision, however, as criteria for evaluating communication has been challenged. A respectful tolerance for—if not appreciation of—mystery derives from the concept of communication as a complex, primary process of constructing events and objects in the service of coherence and coordination. Give this understanding of what communication is and what it does, the events and objects of the world as they are perceived are open-ended, and the very meaning of clarity and precision is trans-muted. A precise statement about an ambiguous, fluid phenomenon must reflect that ambiguity and fluidity, not try to make it more concrete and discrete than it is. "If reality is largely fluid and half-paradoxical," Philip Wheelwright warned, "steel nets are not the best instruments for taking samples of it" (1962, p. 128).

Events and objects do not come prepackaged with their own interpretations, and they mean nothing until they are interpreted. Further, inter-pretation is an act by the interpreter, not an attri-bute of the event or object interpreted. As a result, an infinite number of interpretations is possible (that is, given any number of interpreta-tions, an imaginative person always can supply one more), and there is no criterion by which one interpretation can be shown to be the correct one.

Family therapists are all too familiar with a syndrome in which one party nags and the other withdraws from interaction, but each punctuates the sequence of cause and effect differently. Take the case of a parent who nags a child about doing homework. The parent claims to nag because the child withdraws; the child says she withdraws be-cause the parent nags. They agree about the facts, but disagree about which comes first and which comes second. So which one is right? The parent? The child? Both? Neither? The question depends on a special definition that communication schol-ars assign to the term *punctuation*. It refers to the different perceptions communicators often have of how their interaction episodes should be divided or sequenced. For example, the child and parent in this case both see the problem as hav-ing begun with the other person's behavior. It is not a useful question because there is no crite-rion by which correctness in punctuation can be assessed. The facts of life may be put together in many ways, each of which is a legitimate act of interpretation.

CONCLUSION

The history of the study of communication is one of short-term discontinuities and long-term continuities. In narrow focus, the differences between various forms of research seem unbridgeable and the changes from one period to the next abrupt and disjointed. There seems to be, for instance, little in common between the scientific and humanistic traditions or any coherence between the *trivium,* the Italian humanists, and the Midwestern or Cornell schools that formed the basis of the contemporary discipline. A broader focus, however, shows the resiliency of three intertwined patterns of thought, which we have called the Aristotelian, Platonic, and Sophistic.

The Aristotelian tradition has been dominant and, in fact, fueled both the scientific and human-istic research programs in the 20th century. Thus the often heated controversy about the legitimacy of either tradition focused attention on differences that were rather minor when compared with either the Platonic or Sophistic traditions. In recent years, the discipline of communication has developed in ways that have moved away from its Aristotelian roots. Indeed, the new ways of looking at communication that characterize the contemporary era show much affinity with the Sophistic tradition.

The chapters that follow provide an authoritative report of the social scientific study of communication at this point in history. As you read the remaining chapters, we encourage you to look for the diverse themes and perspectives present within the social science tradition and to connect these themes to the larger history of which this tradition is a part.

SUMMARY

The formal study of human communication has been going on for more than 2,500 years. Many of the same issues raised by such classical theorists as Plato, Aristotle, and the Sophistic philosophers remain important questions for today's communication scholars. Two major approaches to the study of communication emerged during the first part of this century: the Cornell and the Midwestern schools. The former emphasized public communication, whereas the latter investigated speech generally. These two approaches in turn were broadened and fused during the second half of this century into the communication discipline we see today.

Seven broad propositions or assumptions characterize the new direction of the discipline of communication today, including: an expanded and more complex concept of communication; viewing communication as a primary process; studying communication as action; and investigating the coordination, narrative, and mystery functions of communication.

REVIEW AND DISCUSSION QUESTIONS

1. The history of the study of communication seems to show a cycle between an emphasis on studying the process of communication and an emphasis on the out-comes of communication. Is this cycle important to understanding the field? Which is the more useful approach (or are there other approaches of greater value), and why?

2. Various opinions exist about the term *speech-communication* as a description of this discipline. Is it redundant? Is it too limiting, since many forms of communication exist besides speech? Does it provide a focus by distinguishing the study of human communication from the study of other types of communication, and if so, is that good? Is there a better title to describe what we do in this discipline?

3. Historically, the scholars studying communication have been described as dividing into informal groups or camps, reflecting different theoretical and methodological approaches. Is that division a sign of health (reflecting active and competitive scholars attacking a problem from various angles) or illness (reflecting discord and a fundamental lack of agreement on basic premises and goals) for the field? Will additional study and theorizing tend to bring unity or additional divisions within the discipline, and why?

4. What does communication research have to contribute to the social sciences that is unique? Among the seven major propositions outlined at the end of the chapter as representing the new direction of the field, which justify the study of communication as a separate discipline (as opposed to blending communication into traditional disciplines such as psychology or sociology) and why?

NOTES

1. We have not provided specific references for each of the historical sources to which we refer in this first section. Instead, we encourage you to seek out various histories of the study of communication. See, for example, Harper (1979) and Golden, Berquist, and Coleman (1983).

2. Gary Cronkhite's *Persuasion: Speech and Behavioral Change* (1969) provides one of the best examples of the way the mature Midwestern school framed its thinking about communication. Cronkhite defined persuasion as "the act of manipulating symbols so as to produce changes in the evaluative or approach-avoidance behavior of those who interpret the symbols." The explanation he offered of his title, with its focus on *oral* persuasion, also was typical of the Midwestern school: "The remainder of the title, 'Speech and Behavioral Change,' should be taken to mean that the primary concern will be with oral persuasion" (p. 15). Cronkhite differentiated his behavioral approach from what he called "the early writings on the topic of 'rhetoric.'" His work emphasized "*observable* phenomena and *testable* predictions," while virtually everything written before the 18th century "dealt with *classification* of the factors involved in persuasion and with the *morality* of these factors and the morality of persuasion or rhetoric as a whole. Such considerations, while they may be of interest, do not qualify as theoretical considerations in the present sense" (p. 18) [italics his].

The final chapter of Cronkhite's book contains the kind of knowledge claims that the Midwestern school viewed as ideal: summaries of research results about the variables that differentiate effective from ineffective speaking performances. These summaries address three questions: (1) What choices must be made by the person who seeks to persuade a listener? (2) What are the available alternatives in each case? (3) Under what circumstances should each alternative be chosen?

Raymond G. Smith's *Speech-Communication: Theory and Models* (1970) also exemplifies the Midwestern school's concept of communication as the act of speaking that is to be studied scientifically. In a section titled "A Proper Domain for Speech Research," Smith offered this definition: "*Speech-communication is the study of component properties in the formation, transmission, and interaction stages of oral-visual messages as these alternate between speaker and audience*" (p. 21) [italics his].

3. Robert T. Oliver's *History of Public Speaking in America* (1965) is a good example of the Cornell school's approach to communication. Oliver makes public oratory "a central core around which to depict the general flow of the history itself" (p. xviii) and discusses the important speeches of each historical era from the days of the American Revolution to Woodrow Wilson's presidency.

Lester Thonssen and A. Craig Baird's *Speech Criticism: The Development of Standards for Rhetorical Appraisal* (1948) exemplifies the Cornell school's interest in the development of standards of criticism. Thonssen and Baird sought to articulate critical standards for understanding public speaking, which then could serve as models for students when confronted with similar rhetorical choices:

> The reader should understand that we offer no set formula for critical evaluation. When it is considered that a speech may be devoted to practically any subject . . . , that the background or setting of the speech is equally variable and possibly even more influential in determining its effectiveness, and, finally, that speeches in themselves are of many different types and have greatly varying objectives, it is apparent that no formula can be fitted into even a majority of speech situations. What we do offer is a starting point, a conception of rhetorical criticism as an intellectual enterprise: announced principles are simply statements of theory to be applied to particular cases and are designed to aid the critic in discharging his obligation to relate his criticism to the larger pattern of ideas and ideals in oratorical history. (p. vi)

4. Shifts away from the use of the term *speech* are evident in the name changes of the associations and journals within the discipline. What was once the National Council of Teachers of Public Speaking became the Speech Association of America, and in 1970 it changed its name to the Speech Communication Association (SCA). A proposal to change the name to the American Communication Association received a majority vote but failed to reach the required two-thirds plurality in 1985. The titles of three of the four journals published by the SCA also are indications of this trend: What is now the *Quarterly Journal of Speech* was at first called the *Quarterly Journal of Public Speaking* and then became the *Quarterly Journal of Speech Education; Communication Monographs* was once called *Speech Monographs;* and *Communication Education* was the *Speech Teacher*. Similar shifts have occurred in the regional associations as well. The journal of the Eastern Communication Association formerly was titled *Today's Speech;* it now is known as *Communication Quarterly.*

5. James Carey (1979) describes the kinds of communication studies produced at the end of the war—studies that naturally were oriented toward "effects":

The first major scientific studies of mass communication were published at the end of the war, and the war itself produced progress in a new area known as communication theory. *The People's Choice* was based on research done in 1940, though it did not appear until 1944. *Studies in Social Psychology in World War II,* which contained the important third volume reporting experiments in mass communication, was published in 1949. The group that had carried forward these studies, partially reformed at Yale under Carl Hovland, constituted perhaps the second center of communications research. The first, Paul Lazarsfeld's Office of Radio Research, transformed into the Bureau of Applied Social Research at Columbia, was a principal contractor of research for the Office of War Information as well as for commercial organizations and continued to make mass communication research a principal focus of activity both during the war and in the years immediately thereafter. (p. 284)

REFERENCES

Austin, J. L. (1962). *How to do things with words.* Cambridge: Harvard University Press.

Berger, P., & Luckmann, T. (1966). *The social construction of reality.* Garden City, NY: Doubleday.

Burke, K. B. (1969). *A rhetoric of motives.* Berkeley: University of California Press.

Carey, J. (1979). Graduate education in mass communication. *Communication Education, 28,* 282–293.

Cronen, V. E., & McNamee, S. (1980, May). Coorientation, observer coding, and the analysis of overt patterns of talk: A case study and a challenge to three "idols" of communication research. Paper presented at the meeting of the International Communication Association, Acapulco, Mexico.

Cronkhite, G. (1969). *Persuasion: Speech and behavioral change.* Indianapolis: Bobbs-Merrill.

Dance, F. E. X. (1970). The "concept" of communication. *Journal of Communication, 20,* 201–210.

Dizard, W. P. (1982). *The coming information age: An overview of technology, economics, and politics* (2nd ed.). New York: Longman.

Geertz, C. (1983). Notions of primitive thought: Dialogue with Clifford Geertz. In J. Miller, *States of mind* (pp. 192–210). New York: Pantheon.

Gerbner, G. (1966). On defining communication: Still another view. *Journal of Communication, 16,* 99–103.

Gergen, K. J., & Davis, K. E. (1985). *The social construction of the person.* New York: Springer-Verlag.

Golden, J. L., Berquist, G. F., & Coleman, W. E. (1983). *The rhetoric of Western thought* (3rd ed.). Dubuque, IA: Kendall/Hunt.

Grassi, E., & Lorch, M. (1986). *Folly and insanity in renaissance literature.* Binghamton, NY: Medieval & Renaissance Texts & Studies.

Harper, N. (1979). *Human communication theory: The history of a paradigm.* Rochelle Park, NJ: Hayden.

Kibler, R. J., & Barker, L. L. (Eds.). (1969). *Conceptual frontiers in speech-communication.* New York: Speech Association of America.

Klapper, J. T. (1960). *The effects of mass communication.* Glencoe, IL: Free Press.

Lasswell, H. (1964). The structure and function of communication in society. In L. Bryson (Ed.), *The communication of ideas* (pp. 37–51). New York: Cooper Square. (Original work published 1948)

Malinowski, B. (1945). The problem of meaning in primitive languages. In C. K. Ogden & I. A. Richards (Eds.), *The meaning of meaning* (pp. 296–336). New York: Harcourt, Brace & World. (Original work published 1923)

McLeod, J. M., & Chaffee, S. H. (1973). Interpersonal approaches to communication research. *American Behavioral Scientist, 16,* 469–499.

Mead, G. H. (1934). *Mind, self, and society.* Chicago: University of Chicago Press.

Miller, G. R. (1966). On defining communication: Another stab. *Journal of Communication, 16,* 88–98.

Oliver, R. T. (1965). *The history of public speaking in America.* Boston: Allyn and Bacon.

Oliver, R. T., & Bauer, M. G. (Eds.). (1959). *Re-establishing the speech profession: The first fifty years* (15th ed.). New York: Speech Association of the Eastern States.

Pearce, W. B., & Cronen, V. (1980). *Communication, action and meaning.* New York: Praeger.

Rogers, E. M. (1976). Communication and development: The passing of the dominant paradigm. In E. M. Rogers (Ed.), *Communication and development: Critical perspectives* (pp. 121–148). Beverly Hills: Sage.

Schramm, W. (1954). How communication works. In W. Schramm (Ed.), *The processes and effects of mass communication* (pp. 3–26). Urbana: University of Illinois Press.

Schramm, W. (1964). Comments by Wilbur Schramm. In L. A. Dexter & D. M. White (Eds.), *People, society, and mass communication* (pp. 509–512). New York: Free Press of Glencoe.

Schramm, W. (1971). The nature of communication between humans. In W. Schramm & D. F. Roberts (Eds.), *The processes and effects of mass communi-*

cation (rev. ed.) (pp. 3–53). Urbana: University of Illinois Press.

Shannon, C. E., & Weaver, W. (1949). *The mathematical theory of communication.* Urbana: University of Illinois Press.

Smith, R. G. (1970). *Speech-communication: Theory and models.* New York: Harper & Row.

Snow, C. P. (1962). *Two cultures and the scientific revolution.* New York: Cambridge.

Thonssen, L., & Baird, A. C. (1948). *Speech criticism: The development of standards for rhetorical appraisal.* New York: Ronald Press.

Tuchman, G. (1973). Making news by doing work: Routinizing the unexpected. *American Journal of Sociology, 79,* 110–131.

Watzlawick, P. (1976). *How real is real?: Confusion, disinformation, communication.* New York: Random House.

Wheelwright, P. (1962). *Metaphor and reality.* Bloomington: Indiana University Press.

Williams, F. (1982). *The communications revolution.* Beverly Hills: Sage.

Wittgenstein, L. (1953). *Philosophical investigations* (G. E. M. Anscombe, Trans.). New York: Macmillan.

PART ONE

Channels of Communication

Human beings use two major symbol systems, verbal and nonverbal, in their efforts to communicate. Accordingly, our review of communication science begins with fundamental operations involved in the exchange of verbal and nonverbal messages. These basic symbol systems, including their respective encoding, transmission, and decoding processes, are viewed collectively in Part One as channels of communication. Our broad use of the term *channel* in this regard underscores the idea that symbolic behavior is an ever-present medium of exchange between communicators, whether or not they are "connected" by other external means.

In Chapter 2, "Language and Communication," Barbara O'Keefe and Jesse Delia review 60 years of theory development and research into the complexities of verbal communication. Their essay is organized around three primary themes: (1) the nature of language as a means of encoding ideas; (2) the notion that human communication can be understood and explained adequately in terms of language skills alone; and (3) a comprehensive general framework for the study of communication, known as the constructivist approach. This chapter offers insightful emphasis on the deep-seated interplay between individual thought processes, social and cultural influences, and the development of language skills. This perspective has contributed significantly to our current understanding of human interaction, as the perceptive reader will recognize throughout this text.

In Chapter 3, Mark Knapp examines the role of nonverbal communication in human interaction. He first explains why the study of nonverbal behavior is crucial for an understanding of most ordinary communication situations, then traces the history of nonverbal inquiry from Darwin's classic work in 1872 to trends of the 1980s. Next, Knapp addresses six fundamental questions regarding the nature of nonverbal inquiry, including: How is nonverbal communication defined? Are all nonverbal behaviors learned? Can nonverbal behavior be controlled? Finally, he reviews the common functions served by nonverbal cues in everyday human interaction. Overall, Knapp offers the reader a broad historical perspective, a solid theoretical foundation, and a practical understanding of the nonverbal area.

Chapter 4 is an appropriate finale for Part One, since "Technologies of Communication" are generally viewed as tools for extending the verbal and nonverbal capabilities of humankind in time and space. Whereas the two prior essays are predominantly theory-oriented, Chapter 4 is unique in this text for its focus on the application of communication theory to specific problems and practical use. The relevant science, in this case, involves the invention and development of technical equipment or technology for use in storing, transmitting, retrieving, and altering messages of many different types. As social scientists, the authors of Chapter 4 are also centrally interested in the individual, societal, cultural, and international consequences, positive or negative, that may result from the adoption of such technologies.

Concentrating on recent developments in electronic technology termed the *new media,* Williams, Hudson, and Strover disclose what many students of communication theory have "always wanted to know, but were afraid to ask" (lest they appear uninformed). Following an introduction to the area as a viable subject for scientific research, communication technologies of three major types are reviewed: *interactive systems,* including advances in two-way text services, teleconferencing, and innovative use of fiber optic telephone networks; *television technologies,* covering the development of cable service, research findings on its use, and the growing popularity of videocassette machines; and *satellite communication,* with its global implications for national and international information systems, as well as the potential for cooperation or conflict. The importance of the electronic computer is discussed relative to its role within each of these primary systems. Finally, through a fascinating look into the future, the reader is tantalized with prospects of worldwide cellular telephones, briefcase antennas, advanced microwave communication, and lifelong educational opportunities via satellite.

2

Language and Communication

Barbara J. O'Keefe
University of Illinois

Jesse G. Delia
University of Illinois

Barbara J. O'Keefe is Associate Professor of Speech Communication at the University of Illinois, Urbana-Champaign, where she received her Ph.D. in speech communication. Her research interests are in language and communication theory, social cognition and communication, and processes of social interaction; she has contributed to the development of a general constructivist approach to communication.

Jesse G. Delia is Professor and Head of the Department of Speech Communication and a Research Professor in the Institute of Communications Research at the University of Illinois, Urbana-Champaign. He has contributed to the development of the constructivist approach to communication and to its applications to problems in social cognition, communication development, and interaction processes.

LEARNING OBJECTIVES

After studying this chapter you should be able to:

- Understand what is meant by linguistic competence and how that concept relates to the theory that language is a code system.

- Distinguish between surface order and deep structure in language.

- Know the basic limitations of using the linguistic-competence approach to the study of all language.

- Understand the implications of the distinction between semantic knowledge and pragmatic knowledge in the use of language.

- Know why social context is essential to the understanding of language.
- Understand what is meant by describing language as communicative action.
- Recognize that the use of language is heavily influenced by historical, cultural, and functional factors as well as individual factors.
- Identify the various relationships among symbols, thought, and language.
- Describe the link between cognitive psychological or constructivist theories and the use of language.
- Explain how social-cognitive processes influence language behaviors.
- Discuss developmental changes in language behaviors and link those changes to social-cognitive processes.

Like most 20th-century communication theorists, we begin with the recognition that human beings live in a world of symbolic meaning; that is, the human world is a world that is defined and organized through symbolic communication among individuals. And so we take the central task of communication theory to be explicating the processes through which individuals and societies develop and use systems for sharing meaning. Our ultimate aim is to provide a framework for integrating the roles of individual cognitive processes, sociocultural knowledge, and linguistic processes within a general understanding of communication and the development of communication skills.

In this chapter we provide an overview of work on verbal communication processes, highlighting some of the central issues that any communication theory must face in its attempt to explain communication processes involving language. Our discussion is organized in three major sections. The first discusses language and its characteristics as a system for coding and expressing meaning. The second section then offers a critique of an understanding of communication

as resting solely on a theory of linguistic competence; we argue that language is not an isolable system in communication, but is deeply interconnected with other kinds of psychological processes and cultural practices. The final major section then discusses the role of psychological processes and social knowledge in communication, developing a conception of communication as a reciprocal interpretative process. Throughout the chapter we make reference to aspects of communication development in children to clarify and illustrate our general points.

LANGUAGE AND LINGUISTIC COMPETENCE

One common view of communication holds that it is a process in which a message producer puts thoughts or feelings into words and transmits those words to a hearer who then gets the information from them. The central concept in this view is the concept of a code: a system for associating thoughts or feelings with verbal expressions. Contemporary thinking about the nature of communication codes has been deeply influenced by the fact that everyday language is taken as the paradigm case of a communication code.

A view of communication as reflecting the operation of codes, and codes as essentially being like language, has a number of important consequences for the way communication processes are analyzed. When communication is viewed as a process in which encoded ideas are transmitted from a sender to a receiver, the only competence required for interaction is code competence. Utterances are given structure only in terms of the code, and meanings are seen as transmitted via the coded message, rather than created in an ongoing process of interpretation.

This view is represented by DeVito (1970), who explains that "the code . . . refers to the rules or grammar of communication which override or govern the form of the various messages. In the case where source and receiver are native speakers of English and communicating orally, the code is the grammar of English" (p. 86). Under this view, communication will be successful to the extent that the codes of the interactants overlap. When the interactants violate the rules of the code or employ different codes, miscommunication and misunderstanding occur.

Communicative Competence as Linguistic Competence

The tendency to view communication as involving just code competence has resulted, in part, from the reliance of many contemporary theorists on the conception of linguistic competence forwarded by Noam Chomsky (1965) (although Chomsky himself never took his theory of linguistic competence to apply to communicative competence). Chomsky (1972) sought to isolate purely linguistic competence from what he terms performance factors:

. . . the actual observed use of language—actual performance—does not simply reflect the intrinsic sound-meaning connections established by the system of linguistic rules. Performance involves many other factors as well. We do not interpret what is said in our presence simply by application of the linguistic principles that determine the phonetic and semantic properties of utterances. Extralinguistic beliefs concerning the speaker and the situation play a fundamental role in determining how speech is produced, identified, and understood. Linguistic performance is, furthermore, governed by principles of cognitive structure (for example, by memory restrictions) that are not, properly speaking, aspects of language.

To study a language, then, we must attempt to disassociate a variety of factors that interact with underlying competence to determine actual performance: the technical term "competence" refers to the ability of the idealized speaker-hearer to associate sounds and meanings strictly in accordance with the rules of his language. The grammar of a language, as a model for idealized competence, establishes a certain relation between sound and meaning—between

phonetic and semantic representations. . . . To discover this grammar is the primary goal of the linguistic investigation of a particular language. (pp. 115–116)

Thus the linguistic knowledge of the idealized speaker-hearer of a language consists primarily of the grammatical knowledge that allows him or her to link underlying meanings with sounds.

The Nature of Linguistic Competence

The genius of Chomsky's analysis was to show that a language is more than a simple collection of symbols—it is an organized, generative system that is acquired and controlled as a set of rules for formulating interpretable utterances. Even if you listed all the words in a language, you would not have a complete description of that language. When we use language to describe or represent ideas, objects, or events, the order in which we use words is as important as the words we use. "The cat bit the dog" is obviously not equivalent to "The dog bit the cat." In human languages, the ordering of words in sentences is an integral part of describing or representing.

Suppose you were to try to give a complete description of a language by listing all the *sentences* in a language. You would find that this is an impossible task, since one startling fact about languages is that one can construct an infinite number of sentences in any human language. Consider the following examples:

(1) John likes Mary.

(2) John likes Mary and Mary likes Paul.

(3) John likes Mary and Mary likes Paul and Paul likes Sue.

The principle here is clear: We could go on forever adding to the original sentence. There is no longest sentence in English; for every sentence produced, one can always find a longer one, if only by adding "and . . ." There are, however, other ways to add to the sentence. Consider examples (4) through (6) and (7) through (9):

(4) The boy was running.

(5) The boy who hit the dog was running.

(6) The boy who hit the dog that bit the cat was running.

(7) The man was tall.

(8) The man the woman saw was tall.

(9) The man the woman saw the dog bite was tall.

Thus the collection of sentences in a language is open-ended; as a result, it is impossible to describe a language by listing all its sentences.

These examples show that language cannot be treated simply as a list of words or sentences. But suppose we were to try to describe language as a list of words (vocabulary) and a list of *principles* of order (grammar or syntax). There is certainly a sense in which sentences have an order or structure that is independent of the words in them.

(10) Colorless green ideas sleep furiously.

(11) Furiously sleep ideas green colorless.

As Chomsky pointed out, these two strings of words are both nonsensical, but example (10) follows a recognizably acceptable order for a sentence; example (11) does not. Obviously, there must be some set of principles that governs the structure of sentences. Example (10) follows these rules, even though the words themselves do not make sense.

Chomsky (1957) offered an approach to describing the principles of order that underlie sentences, one of the most influential views of language in the 20th century. He argued that a number of important features of language had been overlooked or underemphasized in previous work. One of these is the fact mentioned above: that in any language, the number of theoretically possible sentences is infinite. Therefore, it is not possible to describe language by listing all the forms that sentences can take; like the list of possible sentences, the list of possible sentence structures is infinite. To describe the rules of order that sentences follow, the theorist must find a finite set of principles that can generate an infinite set of sentences.

Chomsky pointed to another important fact about sentences: Every sentence really has two levels of structure. It has a surface order—the actual apparent order of its words or elements. It also has a "deep structure." To understand what Chomsky means by deep structure, consider the following sentence:

The shooting of the hunters was terrible.

This sentence has more than one meaning. The ambiguity is produced by the fact that the sentence can be interpreted as having more than one deep structure. The sentence could be interpreted as "The hunters were lousy shots" or as "It was terrible that the hunters were shot." These two interpretations are paraphrases of the two different deep structures that can share this one surface structure. Chomsky argued that every sentence has both these levels of structure; his theory was an attempt to describe the deep structures of sentences and the rules that connect deep to surface structures. Such a theory describes the grammar or syntax of a language. Chomsky believed that a good theory of syntax would describe the principles of order that could generate all the possible sentences in a language.

The Acquisition of Linguistic Competence

Applied to the question of communicative development, this view results in a focus on language acquisition. Language acquisition has received considerable attention since the early 1960s, owing mainly to the promise of Chomskyan theory as providing a framework for research. Not surprisingly, during the 1960s most "researchers took a primarily linguistic approach by studying language acquisition without serious consideration of the development of other faculties" (Smith, 1975, p. 303). Language acquisition was studied in terms of the stages in attaining grammatical knowledge (linguistic rules) against the backdrop of the adult language system as described in Chomskyan theory.

A variety of perspectives were pursued (see Brown, 1973), all of which proved inadequate for accounting for the child's linguistic performance. The particulars of these various efforts need not concern us here, but considering briefly some of the limitations of a purely linguistic code analysis of communication and linguistic competence is essential to appreciating the factors other than language acquisition that are central to communication.

LANGUAGE, CULTURE, AND COMMUNICATIVE COMPETENCE

Many critics have argued that even a powerful syntactic theory such as Chomsky's cannot adequately describe principles of linguistic order. (Although much of contemporary linguistic theory still reflects Chomsky's original program, even Chomsky's own ideas have moved away from the kind of simple model outlined above.) A number of theorists maintain that language cannot be adequately modeled as an abstract system, independent of cultural norms governing the use of language in everyday life.

Semantic and Pragmatic Constraints on Sentences

Some theorists have pointed out the important ways in which *semantic* knowledge (that is, knowledge about meaning) and *pragmatic* knowledge (that is, knowledge about uses) influence the construction of sentences.

To see the importance of such knowledge to the construction of sentences, consider the following simple examples:

(12) John: I just saw Mary and she was going to the store.

(13) John: I just saw Mary.
   Joe: She was going to the store.

Now, it is fairly obvious why John and Joe use the word *she* in these examples. In both cases, the person to whom *she* refers (namely, Mary) was already mentioned, so in subsequent reference to Mary the pronoun *she* is appropriate. It would be most peculiar if in example (12) John said "I just saw Mary and Mary was going to the store" or if in (13) Joe said "Mary was going to the store." One problem with Chomsky's linguistic theory was the restriction that it be a theory of sentences; such a theory cannot effectively take account of processes (like pronoun reference) that operate across speakers or across sentences.

A theory of sentences is forced to treat a case of pronominalization such as (12) differently from (13), when common sense tells us they are the same. In (12), John says *she* because he believes Joe has listened to the first part of the sentence; since they both understand who is being referred to, he uses *she* instead of saying *Mary* twice. The same analysis applies to (13): Because John mentioned Mary, Joe believes that John will understand that Mary is being referred to by *she*. Thus in both cases the use of *she* is determined by what the speaker thinks the listener knows, as well as by what meaning he intends to convey. Chomsky's theory treats these two cases as different phenomena explained by different rules; but in fact the use of the pronoun in both cases follows from a single principle. The structure of sentence (12) depends on John's knowledge and the knowledge he thinks Joe has, not just an abstract principle of order.

Many of Chomsky's critics have argued that, in general, to understand the structure of sentences one must understand what the speaker intends to convey and the way a speaker structures sentences to fit the listener's knowledge. In short, sentence structure cannot be explained except by considering the meaning and use of an expression. As a result, even if you listed the words in a language and described its syntax, you would still not have a complete description of the language.

Because of such realizations among those working in linguistics and language acquisition, by the early 1970s there was a growing awareness that a purely grammatical analysis of the processes involved in language and language development would be inadequate. The major shift in research was in the direction of considering the dependency of language and language acquisition both general cognitive processes and on cultural knowledge. As Wells (1974) suggests, "The child's task is seen as being to match the organization of language with the cognitive organization that he has already imposed upon his experience" (p. 243). Hence, to really describe mastery of a language it would be necessary to describe a culture and the psychological processes through which the individual represents it.

This is true because, in the first place, the meaning of words and sentences depends on the knowledge speakers have in general and the knowledge they think their listeners possess. The example just discussed illustrates one way that people take such knowledge into account in constructing their utterances. In the second place, utterances have meaning not simply as sentences but as acts. For example, a supervisor could say to an employee, "Drop by when you have a minute" or "Can you stop by my office when you get a second?" These two sentences have very different forms, but the employee will interpret them both as commands to appear in the boss's office. Neither looks like a command, but they both function as commands. The meaning of these utterances as acts can be explained only when the relationship between supervisor and employee is considered. Thus to really understand the meaning of utterances, one must consider not just the meaning of words but also the meaning of acts; to understand the meaning of acts, one must understand the roles and norms and ways of behaving that define a culture. Therefore, meaning cannot really be separated from the body of culturally shared knowledge; nor can it be separated from the complex web of relationships and ways

of behaving that make up the everyday life of a social group (see Kempson, 1977).

The Sociolinguistic Analysis of Communicative Competence

The line of analysis in the previous section has been given its most elaborate and forceful presentation by sociolinguists—particularly Dell Hymes (1972)—in arguing against a narrow view of linguistic competence. Sociolinguistics is a branch of linguistics that is concerned with the social organization and uses of language; consideration of the sociolinguistic critique of narrow views of linguistic competence can broaden understanding of the nature of language and communication.

First, sociolinguists have argued that the narrow sense of linguistic competence oversimplifies the nature of language by ignoring linguistic diversity. In any language community, many varieties of that language are employed systematically according to situation and participants. A speaker may use one dialect at work and another at home; will speak formally in some situations and informally in others; will respond to status and role with changes in forms of address. Many sociolinguists have stated that linguistic theory must, in order to adequately describe linguistic competence, explicate the knowledge that allows speakers to vary their linguistic choices (see Hymes, 1972).

A second sociolinguistic objection to the narrow view of linguistic competence is based on the idea that speaking involves more than formulating sentences. In fact, it has been argued that Chomsky's ideal speaker-hearer would be a conversational monster, lacking the everyday knowledge that any competent member of a speech community possesses: namely, how to structure an utterance and coordinate it within a larger interaction (Fillmore, 1973). Interaction is governed by community understandings regarding how to begin speaking, how to gain or retain the floor, when to speak and when to remain silent, and so on (see Sacks, 1972; Schegloff, 1968). To become a competent member of a speech community, one must learn the rules of interaction as well as the rules of syntax. As Hymes (1972, 1974) has argued, development of the child's ability to communicate is influenced as such by his or her sensitivity to communicative demands of the speech situation as by his increasing linguistic knowledge.

A third objection to the narrow view of linguistic competence raised by sociolinguists and others centers on the fact that speaking is part of an interaction. A speaker must know not only how to form sentences, but how to construct utterances that take the preceding utterance into account. For example, Clark and Haviland (1977) have argued that utterances are structured to reflect the contrast between "given" and "new" information. Given information is information that has already been passed between speaker and hearer and thus functions as a background for new information that is being shared. When people construct sentences in conversation, they do so in a way that highlights the new information. For example, a speaker would stress different words in saying the sentence "The dog bit Joe" to convey that the dog (not the cat) bit Joe ("The *dog* bit Joe") or that the dog bit Joe rather than Joan ("The dog bit *Joe*"). The case of using pronouns (discussed earlier) also shows how given and new information is encoded systematically in utterances. The important point these examples illustrate is that the process of fitting sentences to their communicative task and context exerts systematic and theoretically significant influence on sentence construction. It is unlikely, then, that one can construct a legitimate theory of language if language is perceived as independent of the process of communication.

Although sociolinguists have offered other critiques of Chomsky's views, the objections sketched here call for a broader view of linguistic competence. This broader view holds that a speaker's competence includes knowledge of linguistic variation, knowledge of the structure of speaking situations, and the ability to construct utterances taking account of previous interaction. Hymes and other sociolinguists have called this broad view of linguistic competence "communicative competence" (Hymes, 1972, 1974).

Language as Communicative Action

The arguments raised by sociolinguists and by those emphasizing cognitive processes and developments in language and language acquisition have spurred recent interest in analyses of linguistic phenomena as speech acts (see Cole & Morgan, 1975; Searle, 1969). This general shift in linguistic theory has been accompanied by attention to the role of the child's social development in the acquisition of linguistic and communicative competence.

To argue that linguistic knowledge is intertwined with a variety of social factors (such as knowledge of the rule structure on conversation), of course, does not move one beyond a code conception of communication. In both the narrow view of linguistic competence and its recent expanded versions, communication is typically seen to be message transmission, and competence is knowing a code (albeit a highly expanded code that includes a wide range of extralinguistic knowledge and depends on particular cognitive abilities).

In contrast, Glucksberg, Krauss, and Higgins (1975) emphasize that "in learning and using language one's real concern is to learn how to most effectively engage in communications with those one comes into contact with" (p. 339). Language acquisition is thus only one part of what Halliday (1975) has called the process of "learning to mean." Language and communication must be considered within the framework of their purpose. In such a view, as Rommetveit (1974) stresses, analysis of functional message structure rather than syntactic or other formal linguistic structures represents a more promising framework for understanding language behavior. "The name of the game is," in Glucksberg, Krauss, and

Higgins's (1975) terms, "messages, not words, sentences, or paragraphs" (p. 339).

A number of theorists have directly applied this kind of view to the problem of language acquisition. They conceive of language as a mode of action rather than as a countersign of thought. Schmidt (1974), in summarizing Halliday's indebtedness to Malinowski, explains:

Though language may be and often is used to convey thoughts and information, this function is derivative. [Moreover,] . . . since language is a mode of behaviour, meaning in language is derived from the context of concurrent human activity, and language can be analyzed only within the general "context of culture" and the specific "context of situation" in which it occurs. (pp. 358–359)

Greenfield, Smith, and Laufer (1976) have argued, for instance, that analyzing early childhood language using the rules of adult language can be accomplished only by either underestimating the child's competence or positing abilities corresponding to later stages of development, beyond the child's current performance. They go on to show that first word utterances can best be understood when seen as part of a contextually embedded communication process.

This general line of argument has been forcefully advanced recently by Bruner (1975). He suggests that instead of communication emerging from the acquisition of language, language is acquired in an already existing prelinguistic structure of communication binding the child and his or her caregivers. Bruner maintains that the inference of communicative intent, early reference, the use of language in the regulation of joint action, early forms of predication, and, perhaps, grammar itself can be seen as emerging out of prelinguistic communication. As he says:

Neither the syntactic nor the semantic approach to language acquisition takes sufficiently into account what the child is trying to do by communicating. As linguistic philosophers remind us, utterances are used for different ends and use is a powerful determinant of rule structures. The brunt of my argument has been that one cannot understand the transition from prelinguistic to linguistic communication without taking into account the uses of communication as speech acts. I have, accordingly, placed greater emphasis on the importance of pragmatics in this transition—the directive function of speech through which speakers affect the behavior of others in trying to carry out their intentions. I find myself in sympathy with Dore's effort . . . to understand the process whereby "primitive forces" or "orectic intentions" are gradually conventionalized and "grammaticalized" so that they can be reformed into communications with illocutionary force. (p. 283)

Bruner is thus suggesting, as have Glucksberg, Krauss, and Higgins (1975), that "the demands of interpersonal communication, not some idealized rule system, [are] . . . the most likely source of motivation and information for language acquisition" (p. 339). The child's first year of life is spent in elaborating prelinguistic systems of communication and social interaction. Before the child utters a single word, he or she has learned to respond to the social overtures of others (see Escanola, 1973) and has, as Friedlander (1970) has shown, developed significant receptive ability.

Furthermore, prior to the productive control of language, the child "is able to engage in reciprocal games, such as peekaboo (after five months), to comply with requests and/or to answer questions (eleventh month) and independently initiate interactions by expressing a wish or demand, by showing or giving things to people" (Keenan, 1974, p. 163). As Keenan (1974) emphasizes along with Bruner, "The emergence of speech in a child must be seen in the context of these social skills" (p. 163). The child must learn to speak within the parameters imposed by culture in order to achieve interpersonal aims.

Although we subscribe to this general view, it is important, we believe, that some crucial features of the interrelationship of language, culture, and communication be clearly recognized as encompassed within this general discussion. In particular, in going beyond the simple view that language use be considered within the structure of the pragmatic functions that communication serves for the interactants, we want to emphasize the extent to which language must also be treated as an organized system, the role of cultural definitions in defining speech acts, and the importance of analysis at the functional, strategic level to a full understanding of language usage.

Thus while we are suggesting that language use must be understood through giving attention to pragmatic communicative aims, we recognize that such a stance on language acquisition and language use frequently fails to adequately emphasize the "grammaticalization" of utterances. We have argued that language cannot be decontextualized and treated as a formal system. However, it must be recognized at the same time that language is characterized by strong regularity. A child does not simply learn to achieve pragmatic social ends through communication; the child also learns to achieve this through the conventionalized system of language used within his or her speech community. Language is historically preserved as an organized system; the child confronts this system and must accommodate to it; hence, an essential part of communicative competence should be understood as the development of purely linguistic knowledge. As the child's communication is channeled into the historically preserved structures of language, he or she acquires the corresponding modes of conceptualization permitting spontaneous organization of semantic and pragmatic intentions in accommodation to the structure of language. In other words, the analysis of language use cannot be divorced either from the structure of communicative aims or from the structure of language as an organized system for the public expression of intentions.

The second general point we wish to emphasize is the deep connection between language use as the production of speech acts and the cultural context. We think it is important in thinking about language and communication to recognize that language is tied to action and that many events of speaking are organized by cultural knowledge. Thus a child, in learning to communicate, faces a historically preserved system specifying boundaries around any event of speaking: what forms it is to take, when it is appropriate, with whom, in what way, on what topics (see Hymes, 1972). That is, in learning to speak, one must not only learn to express semantic and pragmatic intentions through the grammaticalized and conventionalized system of language, one must learn as well to articulate those intentions within the cultural constraints governing the event of communication. Learning to talk is but a part of learning to communicate, to participate in the culturally framed process of accomplishing one's task through language and action.

Our argument here is similar to that of Silverstein (1976), who emphasizes that within any culture, an "implicit communication theory" is acquired; each culture sets limits on the forms and functions of speech. Hence, any speech act simultaneously actualizes the speaker's personal intentions and the sociocultural definitions of the event of communication. "Having a conversation," "making a speech," "rhyming while playing jump rope," "talking like a man," "joking," and an endless variety of other potential communication events are defined with particular forms and functions by various cultures. Each communicative episode is framed or organized within alternative systems of deeply tacit expectations and beliefs acquired in acculturation. It is in just this sense that, as Malinowski recognized, language cannot be severed from "the context of culture." Hence, analyses of communication must encompass an ethnography of communication.

The third general point we wish to emphasize is that functional strategic control over communication is acquired at increasingly abstract levels all across the course of development. This has been argued indirectly by Weinstein (1969) in his claim that competence for interaction implies not simply knowledge of a code, but also the ability to employ interpersonal strategies to accomplish interpersonal tasks. In any interaction, the competent actor adapts his or her behavior strategically in order to elicit desired responses from the other. The actor's strategies are guided by a definition of the situation, his or her best guess as to the nature of the reality with which he or she is currently engaged, and his or her answer to the question, "What's going on here?"

From the definition of the situation, the actor can draw inferences concerning the other's probable behavior and expectations. He or she can formulate a strategy for self-presentations and for casting the other into a desired role. All this obviously depends on the ability to tacitly recognize exactly what the socioculturally common understandings are in a given situation (so that interaction can proceed smoothly) and the ability to anticipate the other's reactions to alternative tactics (so that strategies designed to influence the other's view of the situation or self can be selected). In learning to organize and articulate complex communicative strategies, one must learn to coordinate communicative choices within a given speech event and adapt them together toward some end. In order to do this, one must both tacitly understand the shared cultural constraints on communication and be able to erect, sustain, and adapt a cognitive assessment of the message recipient across interaction sequences.

This analysis of current thinking about language and communication thus suggests that communication involves a complex nexus of cognitive, linguistic, sociocultural, and behavioral achievements. It also involves interpretative abilities (particularly those involved in social perception) and behavioral strategies for accomplishing personally defined goals.

INTERPRETATIVE PROCESSES AND LANGUAGE BEHAVIOR

In developing as a communicator, one must progressively master three main levels of behavioral skills: constructing sentences, fitting sentences into an interactional context, and organizing utterances into integrated, goal-directed strategies. The mastery of these skills can be seen as the progressive development of interpretative and behavioral control over the organization of communication at increasingly abstract levels. This section considers these developments and their importance to understanding language and communication.

Symbols, Thought, and Language

To understand the role of interpretation in language behavior and communication requires considering the relationship of language and thought. This relationship has been the object of considerable discussion and analysis in the disciplines concerned with language and communication. One important approach to the relationship is that offered early in this century by the pragmatist social philosopher George Herbert Mead (1934). Mead focused his analysis on the symbol as the key concept for understanding the language-thought relationship.

Mead argued that thought originates in the process of creating and acquiring socially shared symbols. He believed that language distinguishes human beings from other animals, which engage in a kind of communication fundamentally different from human symbolic communication. He frequently pointed to the dog fight as an example of this animal kind of communication. Dogs approaching each other in a hostile attitude use what Mead called "a language of gestures." In a dog fight, the animals will circle and growl; one dog may spring at the other, causing the second dog to shift his position and perhaps to leap at the other in response. Mead called this "a conversation of gestures," a reciprocal shifting of the dogs' positions and attitudes.

Mead saw human communication as similar to the dogs' conversation of gestures. Human beings, however, rely on the word, the "vocal gesture." And human beings do not simply respond to gestures the way other animals do—unlike other animals, they recognize the meaning of their own gestures. This is true because for humans, the vocal gesture becomes a "significant symbol." A significant symbol is a gesture that produces the same response in its maker as it does in others. Words are significant symbols because they produce related responses (their meaning) in all members of a social group. Mead thought that only human beings were capable of creating significant symbols (his views on this issue and the ones discussed below are laid out particularly clearly in the supplementary essays in *Mind, Self, and Society,* his classic social-behaviorist analysis of human action).

This special capacity for symbolic communication results, in part, from the use of the vocal gesture (speech). A person cannot, in interacting with someone else, actually observe his or her own facial expressions and body movements. A person *can* hear and respond to his or her own speech. Because of this, people can produce responses in themselves parallel to those they produce in others.

According to Mead, it is the transformation of the vocal gesture into a significant symbol that creates human beings and their unique cognitive and social skills. In short, when a person acquires language, a mind is acquired. As a child learns language, the child learns the set of symbolic gestures and actions his or her social group uses and the responses the gestures and actions produce. In doing this, the child internalizes the perspective of the social group, including the historically constituted perspective of the cultural "generalized other" that crystallizes the shared worldview of a speech community. This knowledge of other people's responses produces a new mental process in the individual, a process Mead calls "taking the role of the other" (often shortened to "role taking"). Human beings can take each other's roles in their imagination to produce an internal conversation of gestures. This internalized conversation of gestures is thought. Thus Mead argued that thought is an internal dialog that arises through the acquisition of significant symbols.

We now know that Mead's theory was not quite correct. First, Mead placed too much emphasis on the vocal gesture as the foundation of language. If his arguments were strictly true, deaf children would never learn language and thus never be able to think. Yet deaf children obviously do think and do learn both signed and spoken language. The first researchers who tried to teach language to chimpanzees were misled by a similar assumption about language. Like Mead, they believed that language is necessarily tied to vocalization. For years, researchers tried to teach chimpanzees to talk, with very little success. It was finally discovered that a chimpanzee's nervous system does not contain the kind of connections between brain and speech-producing organs that would allow them to learn to talk.

But this does not necessarily mean that they cannot learn language. Recently, a number of researchers appear to have successfully taught chimpanzees to use a limited sign language. Perhaps the most famous of these is the Gardners' (1969) chimpanzee Washoe. The Gardners raised Washoe from infancy and taught the chimp aspects of American Sign Language, a manual linguistic system used by many deaf people. Washoe not only learned a large number of signs but put them together in sentencelike combinations. Exhibiting some linguistic creativity, Washoe put words together in new combinations to name new things; for example, upon seeing a duck, the chimp signed, "water bird." All these facts indicate that Mead overemphasized the role of vocalization in language.

The second problem in Mead's analysis lies in his conception of language. Mead treated language as identical to speech; the language of a social group is just the set of "gestures" or symbolic actions that the community employs. The meanings of such gestures are just the responses they call out in self and other. But as we noted earlier, language is more than a set of gestures with fixed meanings. It is an abstract and flexible system, capable of producing an infinite number of potential utterances. Moreover, the meaning of utterances is not just the response they call out. Linguistic meanings are multilayered, open-ended, and characterized by intrinsic indefiniteness.

Finally, Mead failed to recognize the character of intelligence in prelinguistic humans and in other species. In Mead's theory, mind develops with the acquisition of significant symbols (language). Mead believed that because other animals lacked language, they lacked thought and reasoning abilities. Jane Van Lawick-Goodall's (1968) impressive work with chimps in Africa is a striking refutation of Mead's views. She found chimpanzees using tools and engaging in complex social behavior, even though chimps have no historically transmitted symbolic systems in Mead's sense.

Just as he underestimated the cognitive abilities of other species, Mead underestimated the cognitive capacities of human infants. Even before they learn language, small children engage in complex social behavior. They have strategies for getting attention; they know how to follow eye movements to infer what someone is looking at and how to coordinate their behavior to the rhythm of conversation (see Stern, 1977). Even more important, though, children just learning language seem to know what they want to communicate before they have the linguistic capability to do so precisely.

Lois Bloom (1973) recorded a now-famous example, in which a child used the expression "Mommy sock" to mean two very different things. The first time, the expression was used to mean "Mommy puts on my sock." The second time, the expression was used to mean "Mommy has a sock." This is an important example because it shows that the child's intentions to communicate and the meaning he or she wants to convey are more complex than the language the child has available to communicate it. If the child simply learned meanings in learning the words used by the community, he would not have communicative intentions that were more complex than his vocabulary. It is just this kind of realization that led to the shift from the purely linguistic to the pragmatic analyses of language we summarized earlier.

It is also important to recognize that children learning language do not simply imitate the people around them. Children, like adults, are constantly producing novel utterances, sentences no one has ever heard before or will hear again. Very few of the things children say can be regarded as mere imitations of the things they hear. Children often make systematic errors that an adult would never make. For example, it is not unusual for children at a certain stage to say "I goed" rather than "I went." The reasons behind this are complex, but the fact that they do make regular errors of this kind indicates that they are not simply imitating adults.

Now, if children do not simply absorb the system of language used by the social group and if they have complex meanings to communicate before they have words to communicate with, then Mead's theory cannot possibly be right. That is, mind exists independent of language, so Mead's argument that language creates mind cannot be accurate.

The problems in Mead's analysis point to the delicate relation between language and thought, between mind and symbol. Mead argued—erroneously—that symbols create mind. But the available evidence indicates that while human mind develops *in* a social and symbolic context, it does not develop *from* the acquisition of symbols. This evidence, of course, in no way suggests that language is unnecessary to the content of human thought or the maintenance of human society and culture; on the contrary, without such a sophisticated communication system, human cognition would have had no outlet and would have been unable to express its potential. The fact remains, however, that it is not language per se that creates mind; rather, mind, expressing itself through systems of shared meaning, can generate more and more elaborate symbolic and social systems.

As symbolist theorists such as Kenneth Burke (1968) and Ernst Cassirer (1962) have pointed out, having elaborate symbolic systems provides human beings with a special way of approaching the world. We come to experience with a special kind of attention, an attention guided by our symbolic forms. We have categories into which we classify events; we know which characteristics of things are relevant to us and which can be ignored. We have expectations about the world that guide what we see.

Language and Perception

A number of theorists have argued that language supplies us with all our categories and expectations and thereby determines our perceptions. This argument is commonly referred to as the strong version of the Whorf-Sapir hypothesis. Benjamin Whorf (1956) and Edward Sapir (1949) both forwarded the hypothesis that perception is structured by language.

Whorf, in particular, pointed to many interesting cases in which the label applied to a situation seemed to guide people's perceptions of it. Whorf worked for an insurance company; in the course of his work he analyzed many reports of fires and explosions. On one occasion he noticed that whereas people are very careful around stored gasoline drums, they tend to be very careless around empty gasoline drums. When drums are empty of gasoline, people will smoke and even toss cigarette stubs into them. Yet the empty drums are often more hazardous than the full drums, because they can contain explosive vapor. Whorf argued that because the drums are labeled "empty" (meaning empty of gasoline), people perceive them as empty of anything dangerous. This is because the word *empty* suggests a lack of hazard. As a result, people act as though the supposedly empty drums are not dangerous and fail to take appropriate precautions. People perceive and act in terms of the label applied to the situation.

The strong version of the Whorf-Sapir hypothesis asserts that people actually see reality in terms of the categories their language provides.

If this strong relationship between language and perception existed, we would be unable to perceive anything that did not fit the categories of our language. Thus if a language had only one term for the textures we classify as rough and smooth, the people who use that language would not be able to distinguish and experience the difference between rough and smooth surfaces. A large number of investigators have tried to test this intriguing hypothesis. However, the results of such studies have been, for the most part, negative.

A study by Greenfield and Childs (see Bates et al., 1977) provides a nice example of this research. They studied the color terms used by the Chiapas people in southern Mexico. The language spoken by Chiapas weavers does not distinguish among red, pink, and orange; only one word is used to code these colors. These weavers generally fail to distinguish among these colors in making red-and-white patterned weavings, using pink and orange in the pattern as though they were red. But when asked to sort red, orange, and pink objects into separate piles, they can do so with very little difficulty. They can *see* three different colors, even though their language has only one term for all three shades. Lenneberg (1967) summarizes a large number of similar studies. In general, this research shows two things. First, it shows that language does not structure perception, at least not in any strongly deterministic way. Speakers of a language can almost always sort things along new dimensions that are not provided in their language. But, second, language does seem to have some effect on memory. Distinctions that are *codable* are easier to remember. It is easier to remember different colors when one's language has distinct labels for them than when the colors are called by the same name.

Why should language have this effect on memory but not on perception? One explanation would be that rather than language influencing perception, perception determines language; we develop words to code distinctions we habitually make in perceiving. Thus we can perceive any distinction we want, but it is easier to remember distinctions we use habitually. We just happen to have words for these frequently used distinctions. The problem with this explanation is that all members of a culture tend to make the same habitual distinctions, and people from different cultures, as the example of the Chiapas shows, make different distinctions. Somehow, *culture* has an impact on the habitual ways we see reality.

The Influence of Culture

The best way to explain how culture has this impact is to recognize that in learning a language, an individual learns the distinctions that the language encodes. Roger Brown (1973) has pointed to one of the ways a child learns these distinctions. He found that at a particular stage in learning language, children omit a particular class of words from their speech. These words, called *functors,* are prepositions, articles, and so on. This omission of nonessential words makes the speech of small children sound rather like a telegram. Brown noticed that mothers will often repeat and expand their children's utterances, fitting the appropriate functors into their expansions. He argues that the mothers' expanded utterances help teach the child about the world as well as about language:

The mother's expansion encodes aspects of reality that are not coded by the child's telegraphic utterance. Functors have meaning but it is meaning that accrues to them in context rather than in isolation. The meanings that are added by functors seem to be nothing less than the basic terms in which we construe reality: the time of an action, whether it is ongoing or completed, whether it is presently relevant or not; the concept of possession and such relational concepts as are coded by in, on, up, down, *and the like; the difference between a particular instance of a class (*"Has anybody seen the *paper?") and any instance of a class (*"Has anybody seen a

paper?"); the difference between extended substances given shape and size by an "accidental" container (*sand, water, syrup, etc.) *and countable things having a characteristic fixed shape and size (*a cup, a man, a tree, etc.). *It seems to us that a mother in expanding speech may be teaching more than a grammar, she may be teaching something like a world view. (pp. 88–89)*

This example illustrates an important point. Language is a structured system that is built on a particular way of categorizing and organizing experience. In order to learn a language, the child has to learn the perceptual distinctions implied in the language. These distinctions are made in both the vocabulary of a language and in its grammar (as Brown's analysis shows). The distinctions coded in the language are central to the way of life followed by members of a cultural group; linguistically coded discriminations are the only perceptual distinctions that are important enough to communicate about. Thus language reflects the way of life and view of reality shared by members of a culture. It is not surprising, then, that codable distinctions are easier to perceive and remember than uncoded discriminations.

In summary, the relations between symbolic systems and individual processes like thought, perception, and memory are complex and delicate. Language does not create or determine thought, but does serve as an important medium for representing or communicating thought. Language alone does not determine perception; language does, however, imply a set of perceptual discriminations. As a result, to learn to use a language, one must learn to make just those discriminations implied in it. Language does not limit memory, but experiences that are codable are easier to remember than those that are not. In short, language does not determine or govern other cognitive processes, but is a vitally important medium for representing and communicating knowledge and, as a result, has a profound impact on the ways we think about and look at our world.

Interpretation and Communication

Recognition of the interrelationship of thought, language, and culture leads to an interpretative understanding of language and communication that is consistent with that outlined earlier in noting the shift away from narrow linguistic models. As we saw, communication involves more than the mere transmission of messages in some code. Although alternative interpretative approaches to language and communication vary in their central concepts and details, all accept that communication involves thought and action through which human social reality is constituted. However, in line with the foregoing discussion, most interpretative orientations also recognize that communication is accomplished within sociohistorical constraints. In fact, Grossberg (1976) defines the essential structure of interpretative understandings of communication as the dialectic of creativity and tradition—the social reconstruction of reality is seen to involve an interplay of individual and socially constituted processes and contexts. Delia and Grossberg (1977) put it this way:

While the individual's approach to reality is defined within ongoing processes of interpretation, the everyday world with which he or she is confronted is already meaningful. Social reality is predefined, presented as an already-meaningful whole. Thus, the individual, in the process of socialization, does more than simply coordinate his or her idiosyncratic beliefs about the world with those of the larger sociocultural group . . . ; one embraces an entire universe of shared meaning and acquires a range of socially and historically constituted vehicles (a common language, shared cultural understandings, typical modes of interpreting expressions and experiences) for interpretation and communication.

However, communication always involves individuals with their own personal interpretive perspectives and projects acting in concrete situations. (p. 36)

The interpretative process that links the partially shared social perspectives of individuals has most often been referred to, following Mead's analysis, as "role taking." Through role taking or taking others' perspectives, individuals interpret one another's actions. As we saw earlier, for Mead the ability to take the perspectives of others arises directly from the internalization of anticipated responses in the acquisition of social meanings.

The basis for more differentiated role taking lies in the history of relationships. As individuals interact within a social group, they develop a system of terms and gestures unique to that group. Thus they internalize understandings shared with specific individuals; these shared meanings form the basis for more individuated role taking.

This conception of role taking is fundamental to interaction- or culture-centered interpretative views of communication. In our estimation, however, there are a number of difficulties with this approach that follow from the analysis offered earlier of the language-thought relationship. More important for the present discussion are the difficulties stemming from the fact that such a view makes role taking act- and situation-specific. Because actors are seen to construct acts only in terms of the history of the social group in which they act, only the content of that history, a collection of shared beliefs, is seen to structure interaction. The result of this analysis is an inability to generate cross-situational understanding of role taking and interaction. However, there are important continuities in an individual's social perceptions across situations and continuities in underlying changes in social perception processes that run across the span of the individual's development. The consequent failure of Mead's followers to recognize the extent to which social interaction is structured by the stabilities in the interpretative and behavioral practices of individuals represents a serious inadequacy in their approach.

A variety of cognitive psychological theories represent and recognize stabilities in the way individuals construe social processes. One such theory integrates aspects of George Kelly's (1955) theory of personal constructs with aspects of Heinz Werner's (1957; Wapner, Kaplan, & Cohen, 1973) organismic-developmental psychological theory. This perspective, which is part of a more general constructivist approach to communication (see Delia, 1977; Delia, O'Keefe, & O'Keefe, 1982; O'Keefe & Delia, 1982, 1985), focuses on general processes of social inference and personal perception. It emphasizes that understanding of others is always in terms of images or impressions. Another's intentions, inner qualities, or attitudes are never apprehended directly; rather, the perceiver constructs an impression of the actions, qualities, or attitudes of the other. Impressions are formed within the cognitive structures the perceiver brings to interpersonal situations.

According to Kelly's theory, these cognitive structures are conceptualized as personal constructs—dimensions of judgment within which events, objects, or persons are interpreted or given meaning. Personal constructs undergo systematic development with social experience, becoming more differentiated, more abstract, and more complexly organized. Over time and with experience, each individual comes to have a relatively stable system of cognitive structures that channel social perceptions and organize knowledge about other people and social situations.

In the following section, we illustrate the deep interconnection between interpretative processes and linguistic behavior by discussing the role of stable (particularly developmental) social perception processes in language use at the linguistic, sociolinguistic, and strategic levels. Such a discussion will serve, we hope, to show that language and communication are interpretative activities whose understanding requires integration of psychological, sociocultural, and behavioral structures and processes.

Social Cognition and Communication at Linguistic, Sociolinguistic, and Strategic Levels

Social Perception and the Construction of Sentences Understanding and producing sentences involves more than knowledge of a grammar and a lexicon. In most conversations, as Garfinkel (1967) has argued,

Expressions are such that their sense cannot be decided by an auditor unless he knows or assumes something about the biography and the purposes of the speaker, the circumstances of the utterance, the previous course of the conversation, or the particular relationship of actual or potential interaction that exists between user and auditor. The expressions do not have a sense that remains identical through the changing occasions of their use. (p. 4)

Thus in order to understand sentences in context, the hearer must rely on certain extralinguistic data. This argument has been made cogently by Uhlenbeck (1963), who notes that sentences are interpreted in light of "(1) the situation in which the sentence is spoken; (2) the preceding sentences, if any; (3) the hearer's knowledge of the speaker and the topics which might be discussed by him; in other words, the hearer must know the frame of reference of the speaker in order to arrive at the correct interpretation, that is the interpretation intended by the speaker" (p. 11). The speaker similarly must rely on an understanding of the context and hearer in formulating utterances. Such understandings underlying the production and comprehension of utterances are gained through social-cognitive skills.

Children, in particular, often fail to produce standard sentences not because of any purely linguistic restrictions, but because of inadequate social-cognitive skills. As Brown (1973) has argued:

[The child just beginning to learn language] . . . operates as if all major sentence constituents

were optional, and this does not seem to be because of some absolute ceiling on sentence complexity. . . . He operates, often for long periods, as if grammatical morphemes were optional. Furthermore, the child's omissions are by no means limited to the relatively lawful omissions which also occur in adult speech. This suggests to me that the child expects to be understood if he produces any appropriate words at all. . . . The child who is going to move out into the world, as children do, must learn to make his speech broadly and flexibly adaptive. (p. 245)

The child's first real accomplishment in terms of listener adaptation is acquisition of the ability to construct sentences supplying all grammatically relevant features.

Children acquire the ability to adjust the size and complexity of their utterances relatively early. For example, Shatz and Gelman (1973) asked four-year-old children to explain the workings of two toys to both the experimenter and to a two-year-old child. They found that the mean length of utterances (MLU) of the four-year-olds when talking to the adult was much larger than the MLU when talking to the two-year-old. Moreover, these researchers found that when they scored the speech for frequency of certain complex grammatical forms (for example, coordinate and subordinate constructions), use of these forms differed significantly between talk to adults and talk to younger children. Only two forms were not used differently: relative clauses and predicate complements. However, these forms were used much less frequently than other forms.

A second study Shatz and Gelman (1973) report showed that four-year-old children make no such differential use of grammatical forms or adjustments in MLU when addressing peers and adults. The reason for this is fairly obvious when one considers the nature of the strategy available to a child of this age. Children of four have certain abilities that can be most fully utilized when dealing with people of equal or greater ability (peers or adults); they cannot exceed their own level of linguistic control in attempting to adapt

to an adult. On the other hand, the children can adjust to less competent individuals (the two-year-olds) by employing a strategy of simplification. It should be noted that this strategy is a gross and undirected one, for while simplifications in grammatical structure may help the younger child to comprehend each sentence better, they may not necessarily help in understanding the workings of the toy. Given that two-year-olds have less experience of the world, one would expect that a good explanation would take the form of much more talk with simpler sentences, because the younger child would require more information. In fact, the four-year-olds talked about twice as much to adults as they did to younger children. Moving beyond a rigid strategy such as this requires that the child come to see the other not simply as a less linguistically skilled person but as a person with less complete knowledge and a particular perspective on the world.

It is not until substantially later in development that children employ the full resources of language in order to supply all the requisite information to a listener. Shatz and Gelman's finding that relative clauses and predicate complements were used much less frequently than other complex grammatical forms is suggestive in this regard, since these forms seem to be functionally related to listener adaptation (Limber, 1973). When a simple, unmodified noun phrase exhausts the meaning to be expressed in a subject or object, no complex clause or modifier is likely to be employed. Only when the speaker feels that a simple expression would fail to represent an intended meaning would he or she employ such an elaboration. For example, one needs to use a modifying phrase like "who has the dog" to modify a noun (for example, "man") when speaking in a context where the unmodified referent would be unclear (for example, a circumstance involving two or more men whose identities are unknown to one's interlocutor). The recognition of the need for using such further clarification and specification within an utterance should be strongly related to the development of social perspective-taking abilities.

The fact is that infrequency in the use of these particular forms adaptively cannot be explained in terms of the lack of linguistic understanding. Research by Limber (1973) and by Slobin and Welsh (1973) suggests that by the age of three, most children are able to understand sentences with these forms and reproduce them given adult prodding (younger children find the task of repeating such sentences difficult; they either garble the sentence or transform the sentence into a simple conjunction of clauses that roughly preserves the meaning). Menyuk (1969) further suggests that although children in first and second grade do produce relative-clause constructions, they use them in questions and in forms that suggest the clause construction is serving simply to conjoin ideas. Menyuk argues that this tendency to avoid certain uses of relative clauses is due to some hypothesized syntactic complexity. It seems more reasonable, however, to assume that the child fails to use relative clauses in more flexible ways because of an inadequate ability to infer just when the listener requires additional information. Later developments in the way social processes occurring during middle childhood are construed allow the child to realize the full functional possibilities of these syntactic forms.

We could give a host of other examples, but that would belabor the point. We are suggesting that many aspects of sentence construction, heretofore seen only as aspects of syntax, may best be understood as wedded to the pragmatics of communication and to underlying developments in interpretative abilities. Many syntactic forms emerge to serve the end of listener adaptation and, hence, appear in situated communication only after levels of social-cognitive development that afford the requisite conceptualization of the listener and the social context have been achieved.

Social Perception and Sociolinguistic Understanding We argued earlier that an integral part of learning a language is gaining the ability to control language in accordance with socio-cultural constraints on communication. Many sociolinguists have made this argument, stressing that in learning a language, we learn not only the code but also the sociocultural rules for its use. Within middle-class Western culture, these rules take the form of shared understandings as to who is to be called what under what circumstances, who has the floor in a conversation, how speaker switching is to be accomplished, how one makes a comment relevant to the previous utterance, how topic switching is to be conducted, and so on.

Although very little research has investigated the relationship between sociolinguistic abilities and interpretative processes, some inquiry has been made into two significant issues that can be used to extend our analysis: (1) the point at which the child comes to differentiate various styles or codes for speaking and to use them appropriately and (2) the point at which the child demonstrates understanding of the fact that conversation is a stream of connected discourse.

Berko-Gleason (1973) has shown, for example, that children as young as four years of age employ at least two different code varieties: one for peers and adults and one for younger children. For purposes of speaking to very young children and infants, many cultures have developed a discrete linguistic variety, "baby talk." In these cultures, baby talk is a structured system, in no way a direct reflection of the actual speech or sounds of infants. Rather, the system is an elaboration of the full adult system in particular directions (see Ferguson, 1964). When the four-year-old children in Berko-Gleason's study used this second code, they displayed their ability to differentiate among hearers along at least one simple dimension and make culturally appropriate code choices. As we saw above, the same sort of adaptation was shown by Shatz and Gelman.

Research on the ability to maintain and control conversation has been more extensive. One in-depth investigation in this area is that of Steven Taylor (1976), who observed four-, six-, and eight-year-olds' conversational practices in both naturalistic and controlled laboratory settings. He reports that several developmental features of children's talk reflect a steadily emerging understanding of conversation as an organized form of talk:

First, . . . younger children tended to use talk as an accompaniment to their "world of action," while older children were more inclined to "talk for the sake of talk"; second, . . . younger children displayed more egocentric talk (neglecting to take into consideration the presence and characteristics of listeners), while older children were more apt to make their talk appropriately social; and third, . . . younger children were less likely than older ones to overtly respond to attempts by others to initiate conversation. (p. 131)

At the same time, children as young as age four appear to follow a rule of turn taking, "one speaker at a time." Taylor observed, however, that "this general finding was mediated by two factors, the setting for conversation and the number of parties involved. . . . The younger children were less likely to speak one at a time in play areas or when the number of parties involved in the interaction was increased" (pp. 132–133). Moreover, with reference to how turn taking was accomplished, "the means of stimulating the next speaker varied from physical means for four-year-olds, to direct address terms for six-year-olds, to nonverbal means for eight-year-olds" (p. 133).

In regard to overlapped speech, Taylor found a clear correspondence between age and the use of permissible timing practices. An awareness of appropriate timing in conversation is reflected, for example, in simultaneous starts (in that both speakers recognize a transitional opening) and in joint sentence production (in that speakers coordinate timing to produce a single idea). Taylor reports that four-year-olds' conversational practices only infrequently reflected these two features, whereas older children used both procedures to some extent. Furthermore, in the course of analyzing how children initiate, sustain, or change topics of talk, Taylor observed that four-year-olds tended to initiate and change topics quite abruptly, whereas the older age groups

were more likely to make some attempt to indicate the relevance of a topic to the listeners. Only the eight-year-olds were observed to make clear attempts to bridge utterances with appropriate transitions.

Narrower research efforts by several other investigators have yielded results consistent with various aspects of Taylor's findings. For example, in modification of Piaget's early view that the interactions of very young children are essentially dual monologues, several researchers (for example, Butt, 1973; Garvey, 1975; Hogan & Garvey, 1973; Keenan, 1974; Keenan & Klein, 1975) have shown that children tend from a very early age (two and a half to three and a half) to take turns in conversation and, hence, to maintain some sequential coherence in their interactional talk.

Observations of a number of researchers suggest, in fact, that a reciprocal structure to social interaction is present in very early caregiver-infant interaction and in the spontaneous play activity of babies between ages one and two (see Stern, 1977). Baker (1942), Dittman (1972), and Mueller (1972; Mueller & Lucas, 1975), furthermore, have all shown that with age, children progressively come to be able to manage their participation in conversation. Dittman observed (as did Taylor) that as they get older, children come to make more "listener responses" ("uh-huh," "yeah") which serve to inform the speaker that he or she has the listener's sustained attention and understanding. Mueller observed an analogous phenomenon with reference to speakers' behavior: Young speakers who successfully manage conversation tend to be more effective in their use of eye contact and other nonverbal means to secure and hold the attention of their listener. Baker undertook an analysis of free-flowing discussions of elementary-school children and coded their utterances into three types of responses: those unrelated to the previous utterance, those introducing new topics suggested by previous responses, and those logically continuing previous topics. He found that in grade two, 87 percent of the responses were unrelated, 8 percent were suggested by a previous utterance, and only 4 percent were logical continuations of previous statements. In grade four the percentages were 33, 24, and 43, respectively; for grade six they were 23, 33, and 44, respectively. Thus the older the child, the better he or she is able to articulate utterances within a conversational structure.

Unfortunately, no research has yet been undertaken directly relating the social-cognitive abilities to make appropriate sociolinguistic choices. However, the ability to maintain and control conversation and to participate effectively within the community understandings that govern social interaction can be seen to depend heavily on the ability to construe the other's knowledge and to anticipate his or her view of the situation. As we observed above, to learn to organize communication within their community's rules of speech, children must learn not only how to speak formally, colloquially, or with baby talk, but how to recognize the conditions for the use of these code varieties; they must learn not only how to construct a sentence, but also how to fit that sentence to the preceding one and into the context of interaction; they must learn not only the rules governing the assignment of titles and honorifics, but also how to use and interpret violations of these rules.

They must also be able to recognize and sustain another's perspective on the situation in order to understand the other's characteristics and/or to see how the other defines the situation (and thus what code is appropriate), to see how the other expects the conversation to progress (and thus what utterances and topics are appropriate), to represent the other's knowledge as it is similar and different from their own (and thus what conversational transitions are necessary to maintain the connectedness of discourse), to recognize the social role of the other and to understand the other's self-perceptions (and thus what title or name is appropriate).

Finally, to maintain the orderliness of talk in situations requiring the accomplishment of socially defined joint tasks, a child must learn to coordinate a set of communicative choices and adapt them together toward the defined goal. In order to do this, the child must be able not simply to make a cognitive assessment of the other and the context but to give detailed and sustained consideration to the assessment.

Although there has been no direct research testing such interrelations among social-cognitive and sociolinguistic developments, Taylor (1976) was able to interpret his results within the general framework of cognitive-developmental theory, with its emphasis on the general transformations in the child's mode of interpreting the physical and social world. For instance, the shift with age in children's conversational talk from administration of ongoing activities to abstract, symbolically represented topics appears to reflect a general feature of social-cognitive development observed by Werner (1948), namely, that the course of cognitive development involves a shift from a concrete, thing-oriented view of the world to a more abstract, symbol-oriented view. With developmental changes in modes of interpreting the social world, social reality comes more and more to be organized through talk rather than overt action.

Other social-cognitive developments of a more restricted nature can be seen to underlie specific aspects of sociolinguistic development. To take a single example, one striking feature of Baker's (1942) results is the developmental progression in the increase in numbers of topic-maintaining responses, with the predominant change occurring between grades two and four. As is noted below, this pattern of results closely parallels the results of those investigating general developmental progressions in social-cognitive and strategic communication performance. Flavell et al. (1968) found, for instance, that second and third graders could not construct and maintain another's perspective in a structured situation, while fourth graders had no difficulty with the task and did not differ appreciably from older children. Thus it seems worthwhile to consider as a working hypothesis the idea that the appropriate use of sociolinguistic rules directing the forms and functions of speech in various situations is contingent on developments in interpretative abilities involved in social perception.

Social Perception and Strategic Communication The ability to construct and organize goal-directed strategies in communication is, we will argue, fundamentally dependent on developments in social perception capacities. This point was first made by Jean Piaget (1926) in *The Language and Thought of the Child;* in that work he articulated his conception of communicative development as a progression from egocentric to social (listener-adapted) speech. Piaget's initial statement stimulated considerable research, which is now of primarily historical interest. Considerable recent research, however, is germane to our argument for the dependence of developments in strategic communication ability on particular developments in interpretative social perception processes. Rather than discussing all this research, we will summarize a line of work in this area conducted by members of our own research group.

One study by Delia and Clark (1977) clearly shows the role of social perception abilities in the use of strategies for adaptation to differing listeners. The study was based on an earlier investigation conducted by Alvy (1973), in which children were shown pairs of pictures that depicted potential audiences. The two pictures in a pair differed along one significant dimension. For example, one pair of pictures showed a boy playing with several toys. The boy in the first picture was smiling and obviously friendly; in the second, the boy was frowning and clutching the toys in a possessive posture. The difference in the "listeners" (in the present example, the boys in the pictures) was pointed out to the child, who was then asked to indicate how he would approach the person depicted in each pair of pictures given a certain communicative goal. For example, the child was asked to indicate how he would ask first the smiling boy and then the frowning boy if he could play with some of his toys. Alvy found that younger children did not employ different strategies to be used in the different circumstances

each pair represented; most older children, however, outlined alternative strategies for each listener in a pair.

In extending Alvy's study, Delia and Clark (1977) had boys ages 6, 8, 10, and 12 complete a series of tasks similar to those employed in Alvy's research. However, where Alvy indicated to the child how each pair of listeners differed, Delia and Clark first asked the children to spontaneously describe each of the 12 figures in six paired situations and then spontaneously to construct a message aimed at each figure and designed to accomplish the same interpersonal tasks set for each pair of figures by Alvy (for example, asking to play with the toys).

They found the following: (1) In every case involving the construction of messages spontaneously adapted to the listener, the child first spontaneously represented the communication-relevant characteristic in the listener. In other words, making communication-relevant attributions of the listener characteristics was a necessary condition for communicative adaptation.

(2) However, attributing potentially relevant characteristics to the listeners alone was not sufficient to produce listener-adapted communications. In fact, in the cases where the communication-relevant characteristics of the listeners were represented, listener-adapted communications were constructed in only 36 percent of the cases among 6-year-olds, 50 percent among 8- and 10-year-olds, and 69 percent among 12-year-olds.

(3) Analyses of children's spontaneously constructed messages and of their explanations of the effect of listener characteristics on message choices suggested that social perception and listener-adapted communication show interrelated development through a series of stages: (a) the ability to identify in (attribute to) listeners characteristics potentially relevant to particular communicative tasks develops first and precedes recognition of the relevance of those characteristics to communicative adaptation; (b) subsequently, the relevance of particular listener characteristics to the outcome of the child's com-

municative efforts is understood but the communication code is not controlled by the child, so that the child can predict the outcomes of communicative efforts but cannot adapt messages; (c) finally, behavioral control over strategic communication is achieved, first through global, undifferentiated adaptation strategies and then through differentiated and refined strategies that reflect abstract, dispositional understandings of listeners.

(4) All along the developmental course, children of a given age who possessed relatively more interpersonal constructs for perceiving individuals exceeded the performance of those with fewer constructs. Thus children with more differentiated constructs for interpreting other people's actions better understood the relevance of personal attributes to communication earlier and developed strategies for adapting to such qualities sooner than did children with sparse sets of constructs for perceiving others.

This study shows the role of social-cognitive abilities in making listener-adapted message choices. We also have argued recently for considering other roles that the development of interpersonal cognition might play in communicative behavior, including, in particular, the role of social cognition in generating the intentions that organize receiver-focused message production (O'Keefe & Delia, 1982, 1985). Specifically, we advance the thesis that variations in social-cognitive development lead to differences in the perception of obstacles and subsidiary objectives that must be addressed in the pursuit of a dominant situational goal.

The line of research we interpret as supporting this conclusion is based on the hierarchic ordering of message structures in terms of the degree to which multiple dimensions (obstacles and aims) of complex communication situations are recognized and reconciled in messages. Most of this research involves coding schemes derived from the work of Clark and Delia (1976) and Applegate and Delia (1980).

Clark and Delia's (1976) message classification system defines general types of messages that might be produced when a child is asked to make a request of a listener. Each message type reflects one possible response to an influence situation in which the persuadee is presumed to be reluctant to grant the request. Clark and Delia identified four basic message strategies: simple request; elaborated requests (in which the needs of the persuader are stressed); counterarguing (in which the objections of the persuadee are anticipated and refuted); and advantage to other (in which the advantages of compliance to the persuadee are stressed). In research on the development of persuasive message production, Clark and Delia (1976) and Delia, Kline, and Burleson (1979) have shown that these four message types appear to be developmentally ordered. As children develop, they first process simple requests, then elaborated requests, then counterarguments, and finally messages emphasizing advantages to the persuadee. Moreover, in both developmental research (for example, Delia, Kline, & Burleson, 1979) and research with adults (for example, Applegate, 1982; Burke, 1979), the production of strategies higher in this hierarchy has been found to be positively correlated with individual differences in interpersonal construct differentiation in both role-play situations where there is no physically present listener and in actual interaction.

In interpreting these results, the relationship of the message hierarchy to the structure of the persuasion situation should be considered. Persuasion occurs when one person wants something from another person who is presumably unwilling to satisfy the want. Thus the essential structure of a persuasion situation implies two people, persuader and persuadee, with competing agendas. Approached in this way, the ordering of Clark and Delia's four message strategies can be explained as a function of increasing success in reconciling the needs of persuader and persuadee in the message, from emphasizing one's own agenda, to denying the validity of the persuadee's agenda, to manufacturing a common agenda. Clark and Delia's message strategies thus represent four alternative actions that make up a set of generalized options for dealing with the competing wants of persuader and persuadee. The strategies are not simply ways of adapting messages to listeners, nor are the strategies ordered by increasing listener-adaptedness, although individual differences in social-cognitive schemes clearly play a central role in the perception of situational obstacles and issues.

Research on situations requiring regulative and comforting communication even more clearly demonstrate the role of social-cognitive development in the recognition of obstacles, the possession of multiple aims, and the reconciliation of primary aims with perceived obstacles and with subsidiary aims. For example, the analysis system used to categorize messages in which the communicator must modify another's behavior involves a set of nine hierarchically ordered categories, which can be seen as reflecting variations in attempts to accomplish multiple aims in messages (see Applegate & Delia, 1980; O'Keefe & Delia, 1982). The first three categories (physical punishment, commands, and rule giving) all involve messages produced with a single aim, the primary aim of the subject's assigned task: Modify the message recipient's behavior. The next three categories involve messages that address the obstacle of gaining the message recipient's compliance (offering reasons for rules, discussing consequences of noncompliance, and discussing general principles behind appropriate behavior). The final three categories involve messages in which the communicator simultaneously corrects the behavior, offers reasons for compliance, and encourages the message recipient to be empathic in his or her social conduct (describing feelings produced by inappropriate behavior, encouraging the recipient to see multiple aspects of the situation in terms of feelings, helping the recipient make an empathic response through analogy, leading the recipient to reason through the situation, and so on).

Messages produced in response to comforting situations (in which conflicts in feelings figure prominently) have been classified using a coding system that essentially reflects the degree to which a communicator increasingly deals with multiple dimensions of interpersonal conflicts, including hurt feelings, the reasons for and consequences of hurt feelings, and the message recipient's ability to understand and empathize in conflict situations (see Applegate & Delia, 1980; Burleson, 1984). Thus the lowest-level strategies deal with the immediate situation without regard to the message recipient's need for support; strategies at the intermediate levels deal with the situation through acknowledging feelings and providing psychological support; strategies coded at the highest levels deal with the immediate situation, provide psychological support, and help the message recipient reason through the situation and to learn from it.

The findings of this series of investigations parallel those of investigations of persuasive communication skills using Clark and Delia's message analysis system: For both role-played and realistic interaction situations, within age-homogeneous groups of adults and children, and across the age span from early childhood to young adulthood, interpersonal construct differentiation is significantly related to performance on message construction tasks. Taken as a whole, this research suggests that developments in the constructs employed in interpreting people's actions and social situations play a central role in the perception of communication-relevant objectives and obstacles and in the use of communicative strategies to organize dominant and subsidiary intentions in situations.

Social Cognition, Communication, and the Social Context of Development

Earlier we noted that individuals acquire many of their interpretative schemes in common with others through socialization. In interaction itself, socializing agents force particular differentiations on the child's worldview by the ways they make manifest in their actions and speech particular domains of experience. This idea has served as the basis for socialization studies in which we have attempted to investigate the influence of mothers' communication on their children (Applegate, Burke, Burleson, Delia, & Kline, 1985; Applegate & Delia, 1980; Delia, Burleson, & Kline, 1979; Jones, Delia, & Clark, 1981).

In undertaking these studies, we reasoned that mothers who control their children's behavior and deal with their interpersonal problems through discussing consequences, giving reasons, and elaborating on perspectives (as opposed to using commands, rules, and so on) present to the child a social world that includes the psychological domain of experience as a manifest feature of reality. Over time, children raised by a mother using highly psychologically centered strategies should come to develop a more differentiated and abstract (psychologically centered) set of constructs for understanding people and social situations. As communicative situations are represented within such constructs, the wants, needs, and perspectives of others should be a more salient aspect of the relevant structure by which the child defines the situation. Moreover, since the psychological domain of experience should be more clearly manifest in the child's world, the child of such a parent should gradually develop communicative strategies taking the wants, needs, and interests of the listeners into account.

Our research has directly supported this expectation. Jones, Delia, and Clark (1981) found greater receiver focus in maternal communication to be a significant predictor of both the development of the children's interpersonal construct system and of their use of more receiver-focused persuasive appeals. Interestingly, this relationship was stronger among seventh-grade than second-grade children. In a longitudinal study, a similar pattern of results has been obtained, showing that receiver-centered maternal communication becomes an increasingly strong force in shaping the child's interpersonal construct system and communicative strategies from early into middle childhood (see Applegate & Delia, 1980, and Delia, Burleson, & Kline, 1979, for initial reports of this work; also see Applegate et al., 1985).

A CONCLUDING NOTE

The general approach to communication outlined here emphasizes the reciprocal creation of meaning in communication as the joint product of socially shared codes for the public expression of thought (langauge and culture) and the individual processes of interpretation and control of language. Accordingly, we have stressed the processes by which individuals define situations and understand the perspectives of others in using and interpreting language and in following social rules to make the adaptations needed for social interaction. What we have provided, we hope, is a framework in which interpretative practices and the structures that organize them can be related to language in understanding how communication works.

SUMMARY

Developing a comprehensive theory of how people acquire and learn to use language is an indispensable part of understanding the whole communication process. Several traditional theoretical approaches to the study of language, such as linguistic theories, sociolinguistic theories, and speech-act theories help describe the process of "learning to mean," but none of them individually tell the whole story of language acquisition and use. "Learning to mean" includes, but is more than, acquiring a historical language rule system, as embedded in a particular culture, and applying it to various ends.

A social-cognition approach to the study of language and its role in communication helps to pull together various theories as well as to provide a link between language behaviors and interpretation of those behaviors. An active relationship exists between language and thought, between language and perception, and between interpretation and communication when these phenomena are described in terms of cognitive psychological theories. These theories of social-cognitive processes in communication help reconcile and integrate the findings of traditional linguistic, sociolinguistic, and psychological approaches to studying language by showing the communicator to be doing more than responding automatically to signals or triggers.

REVIEW AND DISCUSSION QUESTIONS

1. The linguistic view of language treats it as a code or rule system that can be acquired. Discuss whether "knowing the rules" is sufficient to use language effectively.

2. It is argued in this chapter that language acquisition follows from the desire to communicate, rather than vice versa. If "learning to mean" is the motivation for language acquisition and use, does that imply that all communication is directed toward some practical goal? What other functions of communication are discussed in other chapters that would not be included in this pragmatic view of communication?

3. Various relationships between language, thought, perception, and interpretation have been proposed, even to the extreme that thought and perception are a product of language. How strong are the relationships among these processes and how frequently do their influences actually occur?

4. Social-cognition theories suggest that our mental processing helps shape reality as we communicate. Are there some contexts of communication (see Chapters 6 through 10) in which cognitive processing is relatively more active, or conversely, some contexts in which the situational structure and rules make such processing less active or influential? Can you as a communicator influence the degree of mental processing involved in a transaction, and how would you achieve that outcome?

REFERENCES

Alvy, K. T. (1973). The development of listener adapted communication in grade school children from different social class backgrounds. *Genetic Psychology Monographs, 87,* 33–104.

Applegate, J. L. (1982). Construct system development and identity-management skills in persuasive contexts. Paper presented at the annual meeting of the Western Speech Communication Association, Denver, CO.

Applegate, J. L., Burke, J. A., Burleson, B. R., Delia, J. G., & Kline, S. L. (1985). Reflection-enhancing parental communication. In I. E. Sigel (Ed.), *Parental belief systems: The psychological consequences for children* (pp. 107–142). Hillsdale, NJ: Erlbaum.

Applegate, J. L., & Delia, J. G. (1980). Person-centered speech, psychological development, and the contexts of language usage. In R. St. Clair & H. Giles (Eds.), *The social and psychological contexts of language* (pp. 245–282). Hillsdale, NJ: Erlbaum.

Baker, H. V. (1942). Children's contributions in elementary school general discussion. *Child Development Monographs,* Monograph No. 29, 1–150.

Bates, E., Binigni, L., Bretherton, I., Camaioni, L., & Volterra, V. (1977). On cognitive and social prerequisites. In M. Lewis & L. A. Rosenblum (Eds.), *Interaction, conversation, and the development of language* (pp. 247–307). New York: Wiley.

Berko-Gleason, J. (1973). Code switching in children's language. In T. E. Moore (Ed.), *Cognitive development and the acquisition of language* (pp. 159–168). New York: Academic Press.

Bloom, L. (1973). *One word at a time.* The Hague: Mouton.

Brewer, W. F. (1974). The problem of meaning and the interrelations of higher mental processes. In W. B. Weimer & D. S. Palermo (Eds.), *Cognition and the symbolic processes* (pp. 1–42). Hillsdale, NJ: Erlbaum.

Brown, R. (1973). *A first language: The early stages.* Cambridge, MA: Harvard University Press.

Bruner, J. S. (1975). The ontogenesis of speech acts. *Journal of Child Language, 2,* 1–19.

Burke, J. A. (1979). The relationship of interpersonal cognitive development to the adaptation of persuasive strategies in adults. Paper presented at the annual meeting of the Central States Speech Association, St. Louis, MO.

Burke, K. (1968). *Language as symbolic action.* Berkeley: University of California Press.

Burleson, B. R. (1984). Comforting communication. In H. E. Sypher & J. L. Applegate (Eds.), *Understanding interpersonal communication: Social cognitive and strategic processes in children and adults* (pp. 63–105). Beverly Hills: Sage.

Butt, D. E. (1973). The child's development of communicative patterns during the course of socialization. Paper presented at the annual convention of the International Communication Association, Montreal, Quebec, Canada.

Cassirer, E. (1962). *Essay on man.* New Haven, CT: Yale University Press.

Chomsky, N. (1957). *Syntactic structures.* The Hague: Mouton.

Chomsky, N. (1965). *Aspects of the theory of syntax.* Cambridge, MA: MIT Press.

Chomsky, N. (1972). *Language and mind* (enlarged ed.). New York: Harcourt Brace Jovanovich.

Clark, H. H., & Haviland, S. E. (1977). Comprehension and the given-new contract. In R. O. Freedle (Ed.), *Discourse production and comprehension* (pp. 1–40). Norwood, NJ: Ablex.

Clark, R. A., & Delia, J. G. (1976). The development of functional persuasive skills in childhood and early adolescence. *Child Development, 47,* 1008–1014.

Cole, P., & Morgan, J. L. (Eds.). (1975). *Syntax and semantics: Vol. 3, speech acts.* New York: Academic Press.

Delia, J. G. (1977). Constructivism and the study of human communication. *Quarterly Journal of Speech, 63,* 66–83.

Delia, J. G., Burleson, B. R., & Kline, S. L. (1979). Person-centered parental communication and the development of social-cognitive and communicative abilities. Paper presented at the annual meeting of the Central States Speech Association, St. Louis.

Delia, J. G., & Clark, R. A. (1977). Cognitive complexity, social perception, and the development of listener-adapted communication in six-, eight-, ten-, and twelve-year-old boys. *Communication Monographs, 44,* 326–345.

Delia, J. G., & Grossberg, L. (1977). Interpretation and evidence. *Western Journal of Speech Communication, 41,* 32–42.

Delia, J. G., Kline, S. L., & Burleson, B. R. (1979). The development of persuasive communication strategies in kindergartners through twelfth-graders. *Communication Monographs, 40,* 241–256.

Delia, J. G., O'Keefe, B. J., & O'Keefe, D. J. (1982). The constructivist approach to communication. In F. E. X. Dance (Ed.), *Comparative human communication theory* (pp. 147–191). New York: Harper & Row.

DeVito, J. (1970). *The psychology of speech and language.* New York: Random House.

Dittman, A. T. (1972). Developmental factors in conversational behavior. *Journal of Communication, 22,* 404–423.

Escanola, S. K. (1973). Basic modes of social interaction: Their emergence and patterning during the first two years of life. *Merrill-Palmer Quarterly, 19,* 205–232.

Ferguson, C. A. (1964). Baby talk in six languages. *American Anthropologist, 66*(6), 103–114.

Fillmore, C. J. (1973). A grammarian looks to sociolinguistics. In R. W. Shuy (Ed.), *Report of the twenty-third annual round table meeting on linguistics and language studies: Sociolinguistics* (pp. 273–288). Washington, DC: Georgetown University Press.

Flavell, J. H., Botkin, P. T., Fry, C. L., Wright, J. W., & Jarvis, P. E. (1968). *Role-taking and communication skills in children.* New York: Wiley.

Friedlander, B. Z. (1970). Receptive language development in infancy: Issues and problems. *Merrill-Palmer Quarterly, 16,* 7–51.

Gardner, R. A., & Gardner, B. J. (1969). Teaching signs to a chimpanzee. *Science, 165,* 664–672.

Garfinkel, H. (1967). *Studies in ethnomethodology.* Englewood Cliffs, NJ: Prentice-Hall.

Garvey, C. (1975). Requests and responses in children's speech. *Journal of Child Language, 2,* 41–63.

Glucksberg, S., Krauss, R., & Higgins, E. T. (1975). The development of referential communication skills. In T. D. Horowitz (Ed.), *Review of child development research, vol. 4* (pp. 305–346). Chicago: University of Chicago Press.

Greenfield, P. M., Smith, J. H., & Laufer, B. (1976). *Communication and the beginnings of language: The development of semantic structure in one-word speech and beyond.* New York: Academic Press.

Grossberg, L. (1976). Immanent and transcendent aspects of meaning. Unpublished manuscript, University of Illinois, Urbana-Champaign.

Halliday, M. A. K. (1975). *Learning how to mean.* London: Edward Arnold.

Hogan, R., & Garvey, C. (1973). Social speech and social interaction: Egocentrism revisited. *Child Development, 44,* 562–568.

Hymes, D. (1972). Models of the interaction of language and social life. In J. J. Gumpertz & D. Hymes (Eds.), *Directions in sociolinguistics: The ethnography of communication* (pp. 35–71). New York: Holt.

Hymes, D. (1974). Linguistics, language, and communication. *Communication, 1,* 37–53.

Jones, J., Delia, J. G., & Clark, R. A. (1981). Person-centered parental communication and the development of communication in children. Paper presented at the annual convention of the International Communication Association, Minneapolis, MN.

Keenan, E. O. (1974). Conversational competence in children. *Journal of Child Language, 1,* 163–183.

Keenan, E. O., & Klein, E. (1975). Coherency in children's discourse. *Journal of Psycholinguistic Research, 4,* 365–380.

Kelly, G. A. (1955). *The psychology of personal constructs.* New York: W. W. Norton.

Kempson, R. M. (1977). *Semantic theory.* Cambridge: Cambridge University Press.

Lenneberg, E. H. (1967). *Biological foundations of language.* New York: Academic Press.

Limber, J. (1973). The genesis of complex sentences. In T. E. Moore (Ed.), *Cognitive development and the acquisition of language* (pp. 169–186). New York: Academic Press.

Mead, G. H. (1934). *Mind, self, and society.* Chicago: University of Chicago Press.

Menyuk, P. (1969). *Sentences children use.* Cambridge, MA: MIT Press.

Mueller, E. (1972). The maintenance of verbal exchanges between children. *Child Development, 43,* 930–938.

Mueller, E., & Lucas, T. (1975). A developmental analysis of peer interaction among toddlers. In M. Lewis & L. A. Rosenblum (Eds.), *Friendship and peer relations* (pp. 223–258). New York: Wiley.

O'Keefe, B. J., & Delia, J. G. (1982). Impression formation and message production. In M. E. Roloff & C. R. Berger (Eds.), *Social cognition and communication* (pp. 32–72). Beverly Hills: Sage.

O'Keefe, B. J., & Delia, J. G. (1985). Psychological and interactional dimensions of communicative development. In H. Giles & R. St. Clair (Eds.), *Recent advances in language, communication, and social psychology* (pp. 41–85). London: Erlbaum.

Piaget, J. (1926). *The language and thought of a child.* New York: World Publishing.

Rommetveit, R. (1974). *On message structure.* New York: Wiley.

Sacks, H. (1972). On the analyzability of stories by children. In J. J. Gumpertz & D. Hymes (Eds.), *Directions in sociolinguistics: The ethnography of communication* (pp. 325–345). New York: Holt.

Sapir, E. (1949). *Language.* New York: Harcourt, Brace & World.

Schegloff, E. A. (1968). Sequencing in conversational openings. *American Anthropologist, 70,* 1075–1095.

Schmidt, R. W. (1974). The functional development of language in a child of two and a half years. *Language and Speech, 17,* 358–359.

Searle, J. R. (1969). *Speech acts: An essay in the philosophy of language.* Cambridge: Cambridge University Press.

Shatz, M., & Gelman, R. (1973). The development of communication skills in the speech of young children as a function of the listener. *Monographs of the Society for Research in Child Development, 38* (5, serial no. 152).

Silverstein, M. (1976). Shifters, linguistic categories, and cultural description. In K. H. Basso & H. A. Selby (Eds.), *Meaning in anthropology* (pp. 11–56). Albuquerque: University of New Mexico Press.

Slobin, D. I., & Welsh, C. A. (1973). Elicited imitation as a research tool in developmental psycholinguistics. In C. A. Ferguson & D. I Slobin (Eds.), *Studies of child language development* (pp. 485–496). New York: Holt.

Smith, C. (1975). Review of T. Moore: Cognitive development and acquisition of language. *Journal of Child Language, 2,* 303–305.

Stern, D. (1977). *The first relationship: Infant and mother.* Cambridge, MA: Harvard University Press.

Taylor, S. A. (1976). The development of conversational rules in four-, six-, and eight-year-old children: An investigation with naturalistic and controlled methodologies. Unpublished doctoral dissertation, University of Illinois, Urbana-Champaign.

Uhlenbeck, E. M. (1963). An appraisal of transformation theory. *Lingua, 12,* 1–15.

Van Lawick-Goodall, J. (1968). A preliminary report on expressive movements and communication in the Gambe stream chimpanzees. In P. Jay (Ed.), *Primates: Studies in adaptation and variability* (pp. 313–374). New York: Holt.

Wapner, S., Kaplan, B., & Cohen, S. B. (1973). An organismic-developmental perspective for understanding transactions of man and environments. *Environment and Behavior, 5,* 255–289.

Weinstein, E. A. (1969). The development of interpersonal competence. In D. A. Goslin (Ed.), *Handbook of socialization theory and research* (pp. 753–778). Chicago: Rand McNally.

Wells, G. (1974). Learning to code experience through language. *Journal of Child Language, 1,* 243–253.

Werner, H. (1948). *The comparative psychology of mental development.* New York: International Universities Press.

Werner, H. (1957). The concept of development from a comparative organismic point of view. In D. B. Harris (Ed.), *The concept of development* (pp. 125–148). Minneapolis: University of Minnesota Press.

Whorf, B. L. (1956). Science and linguistics. In J. B. Carroll (Ed.), *Language, thought and reality: Selected writings of Benjamin Lee Whorf.* Cambridge, MA: MIT Press.

3

Nonverbal Communication

Mark L. Knapp
University of Texas, Austin

Mark L. Knapp *is Professor of Speech Communication at the University of Texas at Austin. His teaching and research interests focus on interpersonal and nonverbal communication. Dr. Knapp is a past president of the International Communication Association and former editor of the journal* Human Communication Research. *He is author of* Nonverbal Communication in Human Interaction *and* Interpersonal Communication in Human Relationships.

LEARNING OBJECTIVES

After studying this chapter you should be able to:

- Indicate why the study of nonverbal communication is important.
- Trace briefly the early development of the study of nonverbal communication and discuss current trends in research.
- Define nonverbal communication.
- Explain how meaning is assigned to nonverbal communication.
- Discuss the extent to which nonverbal communication is controllable.
- List and give examples of five major types of nonverbal behavior.
- Differentiate types of communicators who are more or less skillful than others at nonverbal communication.
- Explain how nonverbal communication systems are acquired.
- Specify six major uses of nonverbal communication.

Can people identify their spouses and children by smelling their clothing? Can we tell when someone is lying to us by the way he or she moves? Does the weather affect our communication behavior? In conversation, how do we know when it is our turn to talk? How do people react in crowded situations? What messages do we convey when we touch other people? These are only a few of the many fascinating questions that have been explored by researchers interested in systems of communication that accompany and sometimes replace verbal behavior—commonly known as *nonverbal* communication.

Nonverbal communication typically includes such things as: (1) how we look (physical features and clothes); (2) how we sound (tone of voice); (3) how we smell; (4) how we move—individually and in conjunction with others (gestures, postures, glances, facial expressions, touching, and proximity); and (5) how the environment (furniture arrangement, temperature, other people, noises, and so on) affects and is affected by people interacting. It is the purpose of this chapter to provide a basic understanding of the theory and research findings pertinent to the study of nonverbal communication.

THE IMPORTANCE OF NONVERBAL BEHAVIOR

It would be neither accurate nor helpful for understanding the total communication process to argue that nonverbal behavior is *more* important than verbal behavior. Although in any given situation we may attribute primary responsibility to nonverbal or verbal behavior, an understanding of each system is necessary in order to successfully analyze most communication situations. But verbal communication has received far more scientific attention and study. The following should serve to remind us that in both quantity and impact, nonverbal signals often play a critical role in the process of communicating.

First, the potential sources of nonverbal information during conversation are plentiful. E. T. Hall (1959) outlines ten separate kinds of human activity which he calls "primary message systems." He says only one involves language. Ruesch and Kees (1956) indicate that human communication involves at least seven different systems: personal appearance and dress, gestures or deliberate movements, random action, traces of action, vocal sounds, spoken words, and written words. Only two of the seven involve the overt use of words. Ray Birdwhistell (1970), generally agreed to be one of the foremost authorities in the study of nonverbal behavior, says that probably no more than 30 to 35 percent of the social meaning derived from a conversation is carried by words alone (pp. 157–158). Several empirical studies also confirm a general preeminence of nonverbal signals for determining meaning in interpersonal transactions (Argyle, Alkema, & Gilmour, 1971; Argyle, Salter, Nicholson, Williams, & Burgess, 1970; Philpott, 1983).

In situations where constraints are imposed on the use of spoken language, nonverbal signals may become especially important. Sometimes these constraints stem from environmental factors—for example, underwater divers or people who work in noisy factories. Sometimes the constraints on language are self-imposed, as in the desire to communicate romantic involvement with minimal conversation. And sometimes the constraints are embedded in cultural ceremonies and rituals. Funerals, weddings, religious rituals, and the Christmas celebration are examples of ceremonies that rely on an abundance of nonverbal symbolism to carry the verbalizations.

Some occupations put occasional constraints on talking—for example, TV production personnel during a live broadcast or doctors and nurses wearing masks during surgery. Artists often rely on nonverbal communication exclusively in their work. People who are physically unable or who experience great difficulty talking will naturally rely more heavily on nonverbal channels for communicating. And people who speak their native language perfectly but do not speak or understand any other language will revert to nonverbal signals when communicating with a person whose language is unknown. Usually, this situation arises in intercultural encounters, but it can also occur when individuals from two distinct subcultural groups meet.

In some situations, words are suspect. In such situations, nonverbal messages may not take priority over verbal messages, but they are likely to receive more credence than normally would be the case. For example, interrogating a prisoner or questioning a witness in the courtroom requires careful attention to nonverbal signals because of the likelihood of verbal deception (Peskin, 1980; Pryor & Buchanan, 1984; Starr & McCormick, 1985). Words are also suspected of telling only part of the story in many therapeutic encounters as well—patients, for various reasons, may tell one story verbally ("I don't feel guilty") and another nonverbally (frequent eye cover gestures with the hands).

The preceding examples remind us that a listener may pay careful attention to nonverbal signals when he or she perceives an incongruity between a verbal message and the nonverbal signals accompanying it. In order to reduce the ambiguity created by two seemingly incongruent messages, we search for information we can believe (Leathers, 1979). Most often, adults tend to give more credence to the nonverbal signals they perceive because they seem to be more spontaneous, harder to fake, and less apt to be manipulated than verbal behavior (Burgoon, 1980). Obviously, some nonverbal signals are harder to fake than others, and some people are more proficient than others at nonverbal deception.

In addition to the preceding situations in which nonverbal behavior assumes added significance, the long-term, sustained impact of nonverbal signals comes from their frequent use during the course of our everyday communication activities—at home, at work (Cooper, 1979; Heilman & Saruwatari, 1979; McCaskey, 1979), at school (Smith, 1979; Woolfolk & Brooks, 1983), and at play. Whether we are forming an impression of a person we've just met, assessing the mood of a person we've known for a long time, seeking to understand what somebody is saying, or trying to persuade an employer to hire us,

nonverbal signals will play an important role. Although the preceding may appear to be "obvious" or "common sense" to us today, the scientific study of nonverbal communication in human transactions was largely neglected prior to 1950.

THE DEVELOPMENT OF A FIELD OF STUDY

Before 1950, most communication studies focused almost exclusively on analyses of written and spoken words. There were, however, some important exceptions, which have exerted an influence on current research. For example, the observations and ideas in Darwin's *Expression of Emotions in Man and Animals* (1872) have provided guidance for the contemporary study of facial expressions. A centennial tribute to Darwin that included recent research on facial expressions of emotion said that "many of Darwin's observations, and a large part of his theoretical explanations and forecasts, are substantiated by current knowledge" (Ekman, 1973b, p. ix).

Another important contribution during this period was David Efron's 1941 classic, *Gesture and Environment*. Efron, like Darwin, was an astute observer who kept detailed records. Darwin's work suggested the possibility that human beings in all cultural contexts have some elements of expression in common, whereas Efron's work established the important role of culture in shaping many of our gestures. Efron also introduced innovative ways of studying gestures, and his framework for classifying nonverbal behaviors still permeates current theory and research. The republication of Efron's work 30 years after it originally appeared is a tribute to its lasting influence.

Two other pre-1950 books continue to influence researchers who are interested in whether certain personality characteristics are associated with body shapes: Kretschmer's *Physique and Character* (1925) and Sheldon's *Varieties of Human Physique* (1940).

The 1950s

In the United States, the 1950s was a decade of awakening consciousness for all areas of human communication. In the nonverbal area, at least three important events occurred. In 1952, anthropologist Ray Birdwhistell published *Introduction to Kinesics,* which explored the possibility that body movement may be organized in a way similar to the structure of language. His efforts to microscopically examine human behavior through the use of film had a profound influence and provided a new label for the study of body movement and gestures: *kinesics.*

Another anthropologist, Edward Hall, provided the stimulus for many years of research into the human use of space when he published his 1959 classic, *The Silent Language.* Hall used the word *proxemics* to refer to this area of study and further detailed his ideas a few years later in *The Hidden Dimension* (1966). In 1956 the first book to use the term *nonverbal communication* was published. *Nonverbal Communication: Notes on the Visual Perception of Human Relations* by psychiatrist Jurgen Ruesch and photographer Weldon Kees provided additional insights into the origins, use, and coding of nonverbal behavior, as well as extensive visual documentation.

The '60s and '70s

During the 1960s and 1970s, individual researchers established systematic research programs in various areas of nonverbal behavior. For example, Sommer (1969) continued to work in proxemics, while Kendon (1970), Scheflen and Scheflen (1972), and Duncan and Fiske (1977) further examined the structure and organization of body movement and posture. Expressions of emotion were studied as facial (Ekman, 1982; Ekman, Friesen, & Ellsworth, 1972) and vocal (Davitz, 1964) signals.

In addition, new areas of investigation were pursued. These included eye behavior (Argyle & Cook, 1976; Exline, 1971); pauses (Goldman-Eisler, 1968); pupil dilation (Hess, 1975); physical attractiveness (Berscheid & Walster, 1974); and the ability to accurately send and receive nonverbal signals (Rosenthal, 1979; Rosenthal, Hall, DiMatteo, Rogers, & Archer, 1979). Mehrabian (1972) sought to understand what various clusters of nonverbal behaviors meant to the interactants.

Other related developments during this period included the growth of research into environmental psychology (Prohansky, Ittleson, & Rivlin, 1970); Montagu's (1971) book which summarized the diverse literature on touching behavior; and several scientific efforts to study the role of clothing, jewelry, and cosmetics in communication (Roach & Eicher, 1965).

Two important, but very different, events occurred during the years 1969 and 1970. In 1969 Ekman and Friesen published what is probably one of the most important theoretical statements in recent times concerning the origins, use, and coding of nonverbal behavior. In 1970 a journalist published a book that summarized the research of Birdwhistell, Hall, Scheflen, and a few others (Fast, 1970). It became a best-seller and brought the fascinating but relatively unknown world of nonverbal behavior to the attention of the American public. It was not long thereafter that colleges, followed by high schools and elementary schools, began to offer courses in nonverbal communication, and a spate of textbooks were published. And although the work of nonverbal-communication researchers is published in nearly all areas of the social sciences, a journal specifically devoted to nonverbal study was established in 1976. Originally called the *Journal of Environmental Psychology and Nonverbal Behavior* it is now simply the *Journal of Nonverbal Behavior.*

The Present

It is difficult to talk about the present from a historical perspective, but some trends do seem to characterize today's study of nonverbal behavior. Emphasis on studying parts of the body (eyes, face, voice) seems to be decreasing, with more interest in determining how various parts of the body combine to accomplish certain communicative goals (Burgoon & Saine, 1978; LaFrance & Mayo, 1978; Patterson, 1983). As a result, there seem to be fewer studies that examine a single nonverbal signal.

The immediate past has also been heavily influenced by experimental research designs. Although such designs continue to be useful for some research questions, an increasing number of studies rely on other research strategies as well, such as observation of people in natural settings. Much of our research in the immediate past was devoted to an intense examination of individual behaviors, isolated from their complex interconnections with the whole. Currently, however, more and more efforts are being made to understand how individual parts (for example, vocal signals of emphasis) function in relation to other parts (for example, gestural signals of emphasis), and how the nonverbal signals of each communicator influence the other communicator (Cappella, 1981). But whatever advances we are currently making, it is clear that our understanding of nonverbal behavior results from a science of relatively recent origin.

THE NATURE OF NONVERBAL COMMUNICATION

The six questions that follow are frequently asked by those seeking a greater understanding of nonverbal communication. The questions address several fundamental issues about the nature of nonverbal communication.

How Is Nonverbal Communication Defined?

The most popular referent for the phrase *nonverbal communication* is communication effected by means other than words. Although this definition seems adequate for a general understanding,

some important qualifications also need to be noted. For example, some gestures have many of the same features that words do. Emblematic gestures, by definition, are virtually direct translations of single words or phrases (see Figure 3.1), and American Sign Language, used by the deaf, has entire gestural sequences that are word substitutes. In such cases, the signal and the interpretation of the signal are closely interwoven with words.

In addition, some spoken words do not seem to be clearly or singularly verbal. Onomatopoetic words like *buzz* and *murmur,* and the speech of auctioneers, which often relies on rhythm and vocal tone for understanding because the words

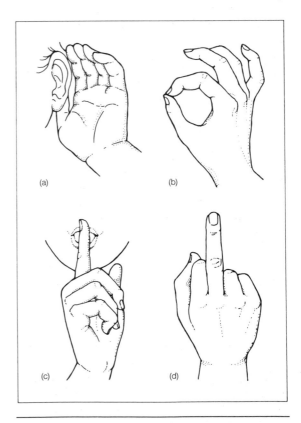

Figure 3.1 Emblems used in the United States for: (a) "I can't hear you," or "Speak up"; (b) "OK," "Correct," or "Good"; (c) "Be quiet"; and (d) "Fuck you."

are unintelligible, are two examples. The line dividing verbal and nonverbal is sometimes fuzzy.

To illustrate the interdependence of verbal and nonverbal signals, consider this classroom exercise. Two students are told to engage in a conversation while standing. One student has been privately told to slowly move toward the other person—trying to get the other to back up without realizing what is happening. To further distract the person whose personal space is being invaded, the teacher has privately told the invader, "Gradually make it clear that you disagree with what your partner is saying, and observe his or her gestures." Instead of making the invader's task easier, some people, especially those who express their verbal disagreements with more intensity, do not back up when their partner moves closer. They have literally and figuratively "taken a stand." This exercise also shows how some people make intrusions on the other's speech in the form of interruptions while they are simultaneously trying to make intrusions on the other's personal space with feet and body. Kendon (1983) makes the following observation on the relationships of verbal and nonverbal systems in everyday interaction:

It is a common observation that, when a person speaks, muscular systems besides those of the lips, tongue, and jaws often become active . . . gesticulation is organized as part of the same overall unit of action by which speech is organized . . . gesture and speech are available as two separate modes of representation and are coordinate because both are being guided by the same overall aim. That aim is to produce a pattern of action that will accomplish the representation of a meaning. (pp. 17, 20)

In an effort to avoid the pitfalls of a single definition, some people define nonverbal communication by listing the areas typically studied: gaze, facial expressions, odor, physical appearance, gestures, postures, vocalizations, distance, clothing, body adornment, touching, and environmental factors such as architecture, furniture, color, lighting, and temperature.

In summary, nonverbal communication can be defined as communication involving signals "other than words" as long as it is understood that the distinction between words and "other" signals is sometimes unclear and overlapping. Researchers are usually more concerned that they agree on a definition of their particular area of study (such as gaze or posture) than they are about the more abstract label used to describe the entire field of study.

Does Every Nonverbal Behavior Have a Meaning of Its Own?

We do tend to associate certain meanings with certain nonverbal behaviors, but as with verbal behaviors, each nonverbal behavior may have many possible meanings, depending on the context in which it occurs. If I asked you to write down the meaning for *fast,* you might legitimately argue that the meaning depends on who is using it, what was said before the person used it, what other words were used in the sentence, and so on. We should apply the same reasoning to nonverbal behavior, too. Gazing into another person's eyes may mean you are in love with him or very hostile toward him; a smile may mean you are happy or even anxious; clearing your throat may be a warning to a child or an attention-getting signal. Sometimes two very different meanings may be communicated simultaneously by the same signal. For example, when you reprimand a child and tightly grip her shoulder, you may communicate "remember what I'm saying" as well as "I don't mind hurting you in order to get you to obey me." Sometimes the same behavior will mean different things with different people or even with the same person. An act of affection can become an act of aggression with the same person when the relationship loses intimacy.

When you make minor changes in the spelling of a word, the meaning can sometimes dramatically change. This is also true of nonverbal signals as well. Nodding can signal agreement with the speaker, a desire to leave the conversation, or a desire to speak. The meaning is partly dependent on the characteristics of the behavior itself. The frequency, speed, and vertical sweep of the head are likely to increase when signaling leave-taking or a desire for a turn rather than agreement with the speaker. In addition, the placement of the behavior in the stream of interaction will give clues to meaning. Nods of agreement and supportiveness occur at natural junctures in the speaker's speech; turn-requesting and leave-taking nods are more likely to occur randomly, without much regard for placement in the speech stream.

It is also important to assess other behaviors that occur with the nodding—for example, was the posture relaxed or tense? Did the person look at his or her watch? The participants may also give clues to meaning. Was the speaker known to be a person who monopolized conversations? And the environment may also influence our attributions of meaning. These and other contextual factors are used to assess the meaning of nonverbal signals.

Some nonverbal signals, like those pictured in Figure 3.1, may elicit similar meanings from many people without any contextual information. But as soon as the gesture is placed in an interaction context, the context-free meaning may or may not apply. For example, the circle formed with the index finger and thumb may, without any particular context, mean "A-OK" to many people. But as a response in specific situations, it could be "zero" or "he has no brains" or a multitude of other meanings. In some countries this emblem is also used as a sexual gesture.

Like words, some nonverbal cues are abstract and embrace many meanings; some are more concrete and have a narrower range of meanings. And nonverbal signals can also evolve new meanings, as with the V sign (made with the index and middle fingers), which signaled "victory" during World War II and "peace in Vietnam" during the 1960s.

Can People Control Their Nonverbal Behavior?

In daily interaction, some behaviors are very much within our control and some seem to be more habitually performed. With the proper kind and amount of feedback, we could probably bring more of these habitual behaviors under conscious control.

Ekman and Friesen (1969a) discussed five types of nonverbal behaviors and the extent to which we are aware of performing them:

1. *Emblems* are nonverbal acts that have a direct verbal translation (see Figure 3.1). We are very aware of performing these acts, and they are probably as much within our control as is word choice.

2. *Illustrators* are gestures that accompany and illustrate our speech. Although we seem to be aware of and able to control these movements, the level of awareness and control is less than it is for emblems.

3. *Affect displays* are expressions of emotion—normally displayed by the face. Once the expression appears on the face, we seem to have a great deal of awareness, but the expressions can occur without any awareness of control. Ekman and Friesen (1969b) believe that we generally do a pretty good job of controlling our facial expressions, so it is an inappropriate place to search for tipoffs that a person may not be telling you the truth.

4. *Regulators* are those behaviors that help to maintain the back-and-forth flow of speaking and listening. We generally have little awareness of performing these actions, but we seem to be very aware of them in other people. These are the signals that say hurry up, stop talking, elaborate, repeat, and so on.

5. *Adaptors* are those behaviors we often call nervous mannerisms: picking one's fingernails, twirl-

ing one's hair with a finger, scratching oneself. These behaviors apparently develop in conjunction with our early experiences in learning social, emotional, and instrumental tasks. Normally, we have little awareness of such acts.

Thus we are sometimes very conscious of and exert a lot of control over our nonverbal behavior, as in case of a political candidate planning his or her appearance and movements very carefully for a television broadcast. In addition, we often take control of the interaction environment when we choose to meet in one place rather than another, when we adjust the lighting and furniture to the purposes of our meeting, and so on.

But sometimes we seem to have very little control, like the teachers in a study conducted by Rosenthal and Jacobson (1968). Intelligence tests were given to elementary school pupils before the school year started. *Randomly* (not according to test scores), these pupils were sent to different teachers. Some teachers were told they had students who had made high scores and should show much improvement during the year. These students showed a sharp increase on intelligence tests taken at the end of the year. Among other things, the researchers believe that the nonverbal behavior of these teachers contributed significantly to the students' learning—touch, facial expressions, tone of voice, and so on, conveyed expectations of success, even though the teachers weren't consciously trying to manipulate such behaviors.

Despite the fact that we seem to have more control over some areas of nonverbal behavior than others, people tend to believe that nonverbal signals are not generally under control. As speakers, we rely on this assumption when we try to escape responsibility for communicating a particular message—for example, "Well, I didn't mean for it to sound sarcastic." As listeners, we use this assumption when we say to ourselves, "He may have said he agreed with me, but the way he said it and his lack of eye contact with me make me skeptical." Naturally, the more people

learn about nonverbal behavior, the more likely it is that some behaviors which have been beyond our control may come well within our control.

Who Are the Most Skilled Nonverbal Communicators?

This question has been the focus for a number of researchers in recent years (Buck, 1976, 1983, 1984; Rosenthal, 1979; Rosenthal et al., 1979). Most findings about individual differences in sending and receiving nonverbal signals are derived from Rosenthal's Profile of Nonverbal Sensitivity (PONS) test and Buck's Communication of Affect-Receiving Ability Test (CARAT). The PONS test is a film composed of segments that communicate different messages—dominance, negativity, and so on. Each message can also be administered in such a way as to measure a person's ability to accurately decode nonverbal messages in a particular channel or combination of channels—for example, the face, the body, and the voice. CARAT measures sensitivity to nonverbal messages by asking people to identify which slide a person is viewing by looking at the slide-viewing person's face. There are 32 slides involving four themes designed to produce emotion: scenic, sexual, unpleasant, and unusual. The results of these tests, which have been administered to thousands of people, plus the results of other studies suggest the following conclusions.

Women, as a group, tend to score better than men on tests that measure both the sending and receiving of nonverbal messages (J. A. Hall, 1984; LaFrance & Mayo, 1979; Rosenthal, 1979). Women seem to be particularly adept at perceiving negative nonverbal signals. Some researchers believe that the female ability in general is rooted in the fact that women are often trained to be more attentive to others and sensitive to the nature of interpersonal relationships. Other groups that have shown skill in decoding nonverbal signals are actors, students studying nonverbal communication, and students studying visual arts. But anyone who is independently rated as excellent at performing his or her job also tends to score well on measures of nonverbal sensitivity. Even though men as a group do not do well, for instance, other evidence suggests that in happily married couples, husbands are much more sensitive to their wives' nonverbal signals than husbands in less happy couples (Gottman, 1979).

Personality characteristics of effective nonverbal decoders seem to include extroversion, popularity, and high self-monitoring. Self-monitoring people (Snyder, 1974) are sensitive to and exert strong control over their own behavior, but they are also sensitive to the behaviors of others, using these cues as guidelines for monitoring their own self-presentation. Scores on standard intelligence tests do not seem to be strongly related to nonverbal skills.

Rosenthal's (1979) work with PONS suggests that people who are skilled decoders are generally skilled encoders; people who are skilled at decoding one channel also seem to demonstrate skills in other channels; and people who do well at sending and receiving messages spontaneously also seem to do well when posed expressions are involved.

Receiving ability, says Buck (1983), does not appear to be a transsituational skill like sending ability. Instead, the ability to read nonverbal signals seems to vary. This may be due to the fact that each of us is educated to attend to nonverbal signals differently in different situations, which, in turn, affects our knowledge of the rules for decoding signals in various contexts.

It should also be noted that these tests are almost entirely based on one's skill in accurately decoding signals expressed by strangers. We have much to learn about nonverbal sending and receiving skills with friends and intimates. Finally, it should be noted that one's skill in sending and receiving has *not* usually been conceptualized and measured from an interaction standpoint. For example, one's skill in sending accurate nonverbal signals may affect the manner in which one's partner responds—thereby affecting the sender's ability to accurately decode his or her partner's signals.

Are All Nonverbal Behaviors Learned?

From others in our environment, we learn certain rules of behavior (men shouldn't cry; don't stand too close to people you don't know; and so on). We also learn how to react to certain stimuli by watching others. If people around us show fear, rather than happiness, at seeing a snake, we are likely to display an expression of fear in future encounters with snakes. Our environment is also instrumental in determining when a behavior first occurs and how often it occurs after that. Some behaviors we learn and share with one other person; others are shared with larger groups like families or an entire culture. Indeed, much of our nonverbal behavior is learned (LaBarre, 1964). As a result, it is not surprising to find people from different cultures reacting very differently to the same events or stimuli.

But some of our behavior seems to have a biological foundation as well. There is evidence that inherited neurological programs form the basis for some of our nonverbal behavior. This evidence of a hereditary basis for our nonverbal behavior has accumulated from three different types of research. First, Eibl-Eibesfeldt (1973) has compared the facial expressions of children who were blind and deaf from birth, as well as some who were limbless, blind, and deaf, with those of normal children. Although some differences were noted, the expressions of these children who could not have learned them by watching, hearing, or touching others were strikingly similar to those of children born without such limitations.

Second, Ekman (1973a, 1982) found similarities in the display and meaning of facial expressions across literate and preliterate cultures around the world. Even people who had been almost totally isolated from contact with other cultures responded similarly to faces showing happiness, fear, surprise, sadness, anger, and disgust/contempt.

The third type of research used to support the idea that some of our behavior has a genetic basis comes from the study of our closest nonhuman primate relatives. If similarities in facial expressions of humans and nonhuman primates can be demonstrated, this further attests to the possibility of an evolutionary development. Chevalier-Skolnikoff (1973) has noted evolutionary paths for facial displays of anger in four living primates. Similar developmental patterns have also been found for happiness (smiling, laughter) and sadness (with or without crying). Even though most of the evidence for the proposition that some of our nonverbal behavior is inherited is linked to facial expressions of emotion, other behaviors are under investigation. Pitcairn and Eibl-Eibesfeldt (1976) have, for example, noted similar patterns of head movements in greeting rituals among adults, infants, nonhuman primates, and visually deprived people.

We are, as a species born with the capacity to learn verbal language (Lennenberg, 1969). But without proper environmental stimuli and teaching, we will not develop linguistic competence. Children isolated from human contact do not learn to use language. Similarly, we seem to be born with the predisposition or capacity to learn certain nonverbal behaviors. The extent to which these behaviors develop and the peculiarities of display will, however, be determined by our environment.

Isn't an Understanding of Nonverbal Behavior the Key to Success in Interpersonal Relations?

Yes and no. Yes, an understanding of nonverbal behavior is bound to increase your proficiency as a communicator, but no, it will not guarantee success or mastery over others. Nonverbal behavior is only a part of the total process of communication—sometimes it is very important; sometimes it is much less important to the outcome of the conversation.

Some people feel that an understanding of these often ignored behaviors will somehow enable them to exert greater control over others.

This may be true for *some* people on *some* occasions. Those who are skilled at verbal interaction have similar advantages on *some* occasions, too. But widespread abuse of such knowledge is inhibited by two factors: (1) We are never finished learning about nonverbal communication. Situations and people change. In recent years, a considerable amount of research has been devoted to the nonverbal behaviors liars exhibit (Ekman, 1985; Knapp & Comadena, 1979; Zuckerman & Driver, 1985). This information will be useful for a time, but eventually liars will learn to change and control those behaviors others are looking for. (2) No matter how skilled or knowledgeable we are, we are still subject to human perceptual frailties. We will still be misled by stereotypes, see things that aren't there, project our own needs and qualities onto others, selectively perceive what we want to, and miss seeing behaviors that happen too quickly or occur when we are distracted. We should learn as much as we can about nonverbal behavior and encourage others to do so. We needn't fear that we or others are learning too much. Rhetoricians have been studying speeches for over 2,500 years, but we don't worry that too many people will learn the secrets of the perfect speech and manipulate audience members as they please.

Having offered a historical and theoretical perspective for the study of nonverbal communication, we will now focus on how we use these nonverbal signals in everyday interaction to accomplish six common and practical goals: communicating our identity, our relationship, and our emotions to others; trying to exert influence over others and ourselves; trying to achieve understanding, and managing the interaction.

NONVERBAL BEHAVIOR IN DAILY COMMUNICATION

Nonverbal behavior is used to communicate in a variety of ways. The following are some of the most common objectives we seek to accomplish in daily encounters.

Communicating Our Identity

There are many ways we communicate to others who we are. Our sex, age, personality, socioeconomic status, occupation, geographical background, group membership, and social attitudes can all be communicated through nonverbal signals. Sometimes these signals are accurate reflections of characteristics associated with your identity—for example, a Southern accent suggesting you were born or currently live in the southern region of the United States. But sometimes we manipulate nonverbal signals in order to communicate a special part of our identity—for example, a person who normally dresses casually will often put on more formal attire for a job interview. There are also times when people will associate our clothes, voice, or behavior with a stereotype that may or may not be accurate. If others constantly treat you as if the stereotype were true, your own self-perception is likely to be affected accordingly.

Some aspects of a person's identity are more likely to be judged accurately than others. A person's sex, age, and socioeconomic status are often accurately assessed from photographs or voice samples (Knapp, 1978). There are signals associated with body movement that may distinguish these groups as well. For example, women, when compared with men, seem to gaze at their partner more during interaction, gesture closer to their bodies, maintain less relaxed postures and smile on more occasions (Bull, 1983; J. A. Hall, 1984, 1985; Henley & LaFrance, 1984).

Other identity signals may be judged with great accuracy on some occasions, but reliable indicators are not always present. A person's geographical background may be easily identified if the person's accent or dialect is strong or if the person is wearing clothes unique to a particular region. In the absence of such clues, however, a person's place of birth or residence may be very difficult to judge. Occupation may be clearly designated by a uniform, style of clothing, or a special vocal style. But many occupations are not clearly distinguished by dress or voice, so the degree of accuracy in judging occupation depends on the occupation being assessed.

This is also the case in judging a person's group membership and social attitudes. Sometimes these indicators will be quite obvious from a person's appearance and demeanor and sometimes they are well-hidden. We do tend to associate extreme political and social attitudes with people who reflect extremes in hair style and attire. For example, long hair and unconventional dress are more often associated with liberal ideology than are short hair and conventional dress.

Personality characteristics are the most difficult to judge, although sometimes judgments are quite accurate. Some characteristics are easier to judge from nonverbal signals than others. You may be able to judge a person's neatness, conformity, practicality, and need for attention from the way he or she dresses, but certain other characteristics may be more difficult. And some personality characteristics are easily assessed in one context and not in another. For instance, the extent to which a person wants to dominate a situation may be clearly shown by his or her selection of a seat at the head of the table or by the person arranging an environment so he or she has the most territory. Vocal cues may give us a more accurate reading of a person's general activity level (energetic/lazy) but may be a poor indicator of his or her independence/dependence (Scherer, 1979).

And, right or wrong, we do tend to associate certain personality characteristics with certain body shapes. Thin people with extremely lean features are commonly perceived as withdrawn, tense, suspicious, and sensitive; fat people with soft and round features are often seen as sympathetic, dependent, sociable, and sluggish; and muscular, athletic body types are frequently assumed to be assertive, active, adventurous, and determined (Cortes & Gatti, 1965; Wells & Siegel, 1961).

Communicating Our Relationship to Others

From a distance, an observer can detect what Morris (1977) calls "tie-signs," nonverbal signals indicating that two people have some type of personal relationship with one another. Positioning yourself close to another person, shaking hands, patting another on the back, holding hands, embracing, linking arms—all indicate some type of relationship. Usually, however, determining the exact nature of the relationship will depend on observing other simultaneously occurring signals, further details of the tie-sign (a kiss may indicate a romantic attachment or a polite ritual among acquaintances, depending on how it is performed), and further knowledge of the context.

We have many types of relationships, but the important descriptive features common to most of them concern the extent to which they are positive or negative and the extent to which there are differences in power, dominance, or status (Ellyson & Dovidio, 1985). Mehrabian's (1969) experiments tried to identify nonverbal behaviors associated with these dimensions. He found that liking for another was communicated primarily by the following signals: more leaning toward the other, more touching of the other, more openness of arms and legs, closer proximity to the other, more gazing toward the other, a more direct body orientation toward the other, more postural relaxation, and more positive facial and vocal expressions. Dislike is most often revealed in the opposites of the liking behaviors. Mehrabian was examining casual, get-acquainted conversations, so many nonverbal acts of more intense liking or disliking (hugging, obscene gestures, and so on) are not included. The behavior he identified may also be less applicable as liking indicators in relationships between close friends and intimates than between acquaintances. Intimates are more likely to reveal unique patterns of affection and liking with their partners. Sometimes intimate couples will show a considerable amount of synchrony in their postures and movements.

Mehrabian also found several behaviors that were associated with status or dominance in conversation. More-dominant interactants needed more space or territory, gazed at the other person less than nondominant interactants, used more expansive movements and postures, were relaxed in posture, spoke more loudly, displayed the arms akimbo (hands on hips) more often, and sought a position of height.

Different patterns for indicating the liking/disliking and dominance/submissiveness nature of a relationship will occur in other cultures. In addition, the pattern for *achieving* intimacy or power may be very different than that necessary for *maintaining* it. Even though people who like each other tend to gaze at each other a lot, we may find that in long-term relationships, daily gazing patterns decline substantially except on those occasions when one wants to explicitly reiterate the closeness of the relationship. Similarly, a powerful person may gaze a great deal at his or her partner in an effort *to establish dominance,* but once the other person grants dominance, gazing may decrease. But threats to a person's power will likely bring about renewed visual vigilance, staring, and body tenseness.

Communicating Our Feelings and Emotions

Our emotional states are primarily communicated through facial and vocal cues. Body movements such as nail biting, excessive scratching, or playing nervously with jewelry, matches, or cigarettes may indicate a feeling such as anxiety or frustration. But generally, body movements are more likely to act as an indicator of the intensity of the emotion rather than an indicator of the type of emotion felt.

Although we experience many emotions, the expression of these emotions on the face seems to be mainly variations on six primary affect displays: surprise, fear, anger, disgust, happiness, and sadness. These facial expressions have been carefully analyzed and precise muscle movements have been recorded (Ekman, 1982; Ekman & Friesen, 1975; Ekman, Friesen, & Ellsworth, 1972). For example, the pure or full expression of surprise is displayed as follows: (1) The brows are raised, so that they are curved and high. (2) The skin below the brow is stretched. (3) Horizontal wrinkles often go across the forehead. (4) The eyelids are opened; the upper lid is raised and the lower lid drawn down; the white of the eye, the sclera, shows above the iris, and often below as well. (5) The jaw drops open so that the lips and teeth are parted, but there is no tension or stretching of the mouth.

But we don't always exhibit the complete or pure expression. Sometimes we experience several feelings, and these are revealed on our face in the form of affect *blends*. A blend combines features of the emotions felt. For example, you may find out that you got a passing grade on a test you thought you had failed. Your face may show a blend of happiness (smile) and surprise (raised eyebrows and slight dropping of jaw).

Each emotion seems to rely on a particular part of the face to carry key identifying information. For disgust, the nose wrinkle is a key feature; for sadness, the eyes and eyebrows give critical information. Ordinarily, facial expressions of emotion indicate how a person feels at a particular moment in time. But they sometimes predict subsequent behavior as well. In one study, boys who had pleasant expressions while watching a violent television program tended to engage in more aggressive play behavior following the program than those who had unpleasant expressions (Ekman, Liebert, et al., 1971).

The components of vocal expressions of emotion have been analyzed in less detail than those of facial expressions, but one researcher (Davitz, 1964) used the characteristics in Table 3.1 to identify two common emotions.

Influencing Others and Ourselves

Obviously, the extent to which we are persuaded to do something for another person is partly the result of the message content and partly the result of the context in which the message is delivered. But nonverbal signals may also play an important role in persuading others.

One of the reasons we are persuaded to believe or act as others ask is that we perceive them to be likable. Thus signals that convey liking and approval of others may prove to be useful in some persuasive situations. Mehrabian and Williams (1969) conducted several experiments in which people gave speeches designed to persuade others. The findings generally support the idea that more liking cues and fewer cues associated with dominance are associated with greater persuasiveness.

There are some exceptions, however, depending on the sex of the persuader. It seems men need to decrease the possibility that their persuasive efforts will be seen as threatening—by facing their partner with a more indirect body orientation than females, being careful not to gaze too much at their partners, and so on.

Table 3.1 Characteristics of Vocal Expressions of Emotion (Davitz, 1964, p. 63)

Feeling	Loudness	Pitch	Timbre	Rate	Inflection	Rhythm	Enunciation
Anger	Loud	High	Blaring	Fast	Irregular up and down	Irregular	Clipped
Sadness	Soft	Low	Resonant	Slow	Downward	Irregular pauses	Slurred

Women, on the other hand, were able to use high amounts of gaze, direct body orientation, and body tenseness as signals of involvement for the persuasive advantage.

Another common explanation for the ability of one person to influence another is related to perceptions of expertise. Does the persuader know what he or she is talking about? Physical attractiveness has been shown to be an important factor during the initial stages of a persuasive effort in achieving higher credibility and eliciting expectations for a skilled performance (Horai, Naccari, & Faloultah, 1974; Mills & Aronson, 1965; Widgery, 1974). Skilled performance, in this case, concerned the style with which the persuasive message was delivered. Research shows that effective delivery communicates confidence, poise, and energy. Behaviorally, an effective delivery includes such things as fluent speech (few speech errors), speaking at a fairly rapid rate, speaking at a volume level that communicates an authoritative tone, maintaining a slightly relaxed posture, gazing often at your audience, and displaying variations in intonation, gestures, and facial expressions.

Sometimes we comply with another's request because we perceive that person to have power over us. Nonverbally, this message may be communicated by a person's appearance—for example, body size, a policeman's uniform (Bickman, 1974).

When we perceive similarities between our own appearance and behavior and those of the persuader, we may have a tendency to trust the persuader more. Once a person is trusted, his or her ability to influence others is greatly enhanced.

Influencing others sometimes involves deception. In recent years, the subject of lying and deception has been of particular interest to social scientists—particularly nonverbal communication researchers (Ekman, 1985; Knapp & Comadena, 1979; Zuckerman, DePaulo, & Rosenthal, 1981). A liar's desire to control his or her behavior may make it seem too planned, stilted, or rehearsed; the arousal liars often feel may produce speech errors, more pupil dilation, and increases in pitch; a cluster of disliking cues may be associated with the negative affect experienced by the liar; or the liar's behavior may be associated with the fact that lying is a cognitively more demanding task, causing more speech hesitations or pupil dilation. Generally, liars do well at controlling their facial expressions, so few clues to deception are found in this region of the body. Although most of the research shows that untrained observers can accurately identify unknown liars at or slightly above what would be expected by chance alone, detection rates may be higher when the liar is a person you know well, when you have reason to suspect deception, or if you are exceptionally skilled at reading nonverbal signals.

Our nonverbal activities and qualities have an effect in changing our own behavior as well as that of others. We sometimes gesture emphatically when talking on the phone. This "self-priming" behavior often creates more vocal and verbal animation, even though the receiver cannot see the gestures. We also know that physically attractive people typically have higher levels of self-esteem and that improved appearance through the use of cosmetics has made hospital patients feel healthier (Graham & Kligman, 1985).

Thus clusters of nonverbal signals in the process of persuasion tend to reflect liking, dominance/power, expertise, and similarity. Most of this work, however, focuses on initial impressions and effects. Getting a persuasive effort off on the right foot is unquestionably important, but we need to know more about the role of nonverbal signals that occur through the duration of persuasive sequences and campaigns.

Achieving Accuracy and Understanding

Nonverbal signals also play an important role in determining how accurately a verbal message is performed and how accurately it is received. Verbal and nonverbal signals interrelate in many ways. Sometimes these interrelationships make messages easier to understand; sometimes they make the message more ambiguous. The same behavior that was a useful attention-getter at one point may later become a distracting mannerism that impedes understanding.

Nonverbal behavior reinforces speech in at least two ways. First, it can simply repeat what is said—for example, pointing north when you are talking about going north. Second, nonverbal behavior can complement or support speech. That is, when you are expressing affection for another person verbally, your nonverbal behavior also tends to show affection. It is presumed that messages supported by both verbal and nonverbal channels will be the most likely to be clearly understood.

Nonverbal behavior also works in contrasting ways with speech. Sometimes, for instance, you wish to accent or tone down the verbal message. You can add emphasis by pounding your fist on the table, squeezing a person's arm while discussing an important matter, raising your voice, and so on. Toning-down or deemphasis occurs when you open a present and say, "I'm really happy you got me this," with little variation in the vocal pitch and with a smile that shows moderate (but not extreme) happiness.

Sometimes we contrast verbal and nonverbal behavior in extreme ways so that the message communicated in one channel contradicts the message communicated in the other. We do this when we are trying to communicate sarcasm— for example, "I think you're the most athletic person I've ever met" said with a tone that indicates you really think the person is not very athletic at all. But we can also communicate contradictory messages in verbal and nonverbal channels unintentionally—usually as a result of truly ambivalent feelings toward the topic or person or an imperfect job of lying. As we noted earlier, the nonverbal message is often the one others will consider valid if further communication does not clarify the discrepancy.

We also use nonverbal signals to organize our spoken messages so comprehension will be increased. This is done in a variety of ways. Pauses organize spoken information into units; a series of three chopping gestures may indicate you intend to discuss these three points separately, or a single chopping gesture following the verbalization of all three points is likely to indicate that all three points will be discussed together; and we sometimes demarcate topic changes by major shifts in posture (Erickson, 1975).

Managing Interaction

Interaction management refers to the process of regulating the back-and-forth flow of speaking and listening. It also includes the initiation and termination of our encounters.

We initiate our encounters with others in a variety of ways, but since greetings are primarily designed for making contact and providing a smooth transition to a conversation, many greetings have similar behavior elements. In fact, the eyebrow flash (a rapid up-and-down movement of the eyebrows) has been noted in most cultures throughout the world (Eibl-Eibesfeldt, 1975). Making eye contact with the other person is a common method of signaling that the communication channels are open and that the two parties are now obligated to say something to each other (Rutter, 1984). Smiles and a variety of open hand movements indicate that the beginning of the encounter will be pleasant and friendly.

Saying goodbye requires its own signals. Sometimes these signals precede actual termination by a long time—for example, a person may look at his or her watch shortly after initiating a conversation. In our research, several nonverbal cues served to signal impending leave-taking: decreased gazing at the other person; body oriented toward an exit; rapid nodding, indicating the listener wanted the speaker to hurry up and finish talking; and getting one's possessions (books, umbrellas, and so on) organized for carrying (Knapp, Hart, Friedrich, & Shulman, 1973).

The smooth exchange of speaking turns in daily conversation requires each participant to signal his or her interaction intentions (Cappella,

1985; Duncan & Fiske, 1977). Speakers can yield their turn or maintain it; listeners can request a speaking turn or deny it when it is offered. Wiemann and Knapp (1975) summarized some of the signals frequently reported in the research. Turn yielding, or giving up one's turn, may be indicated by a slowed speaking tempo; rising (questions) or lowered (statements) pitch; gestures that come to rest; an extended pause; and/or gazing at the other person. Sometimes, if the other person does not pick up the speaking turn, the speaker will add a "trailer," such as ". . . so ah . . ." Turn maintaining requires the speaker to continue gesturing; fill speaking pauses with "uhs" or other vocalizations; increase loudness when turn-requesting signals are observed; and sometimes use a polite form of a "stop" gesture— either in midair or by lightly touching the other person.

When listeners want to request a turn, common signals include: an upraised and pointed index finger; an audible inhaling of breath; self-grooming to indicate preparation for a new interaction role; rapid and almost random head nodding accompanied by vocalizations of pseudo-agreement such as "yes . . . uh-huh . . ." to encourage the speaker to complete his or her turn; and stutter starts such as "I . . . I . . . I . . . wa . . ." In order to forgo a turn, listeners may gaze away from the speaker; maintain a relaxed posture; or ask the speaker to clarify his or her remarks.

CONCLUSION

In the long history of communication research, the systematic study of nonverbal communication is of relatively recent origin. Much of the research to date has focused on individual behavior, although current efforts tend to emphasize interpersonal transactions. We know relatively little about the roles played by nonverbal signals in group/organizational and mass communication contexts (Knapp, Cody, & Reardon, in press). There is much to learn, and it should be clear that our understanding of human communication will suffer greatly without continued efforts to further our knowledge of nonverbal behavior.

Even though nonverbal behavior was described as all those signaling systems other than words, nonverbal signals do share some important similarities, as well as differences, with spoken language. Nonverbal behavior, like verbal, seems to have a biological as well as learned foundation; and, like words, some nonverbal behaviors are very much under our conscious control and some are less so. Words have multiple meanings and depend on the communication context for final clarification—as do nonverbal signals. Nonverbal signals also operate in conjunction with verbal signals to communicate who we are, how we feel, how we feel about others, and how we get others to understand us and do what we want.

Although some of the questions posed at the beginning of this chapter were answered, others were not. For all who feel the need for closure: (1) Yes, people do seem to be able to identify spouses and children by smelling their clothing (Hopson, 1979; Porter & Moore, 1981). (2) Although we don't know how to make specific predictions yet, temperature, barometric pressure, and other weather-related factors do seem to influence our moods and communication behavior (Moos, 1976). (3) People react differently to highly populated situations depending on whether they chose to be there, whether they have to have a lot of social contact with the people surrounding them, and whether they have plenty of needed resources (Altman, 1975).

SUMMARY

Nonverbal communication is the network of channels for a major portion of the messages communicated in most interactions. Although a limited awareness of nonverbal elements of communication existed for many years, the systematic study of nonverbal communication is relatively new.

Major questions now being answered by research into nonverbal communication include how meaning is assigned to nonverbal behaviors, how much control we have over the various types of nonverbal behavior, who is most effective in dealing with nonverbal communication, how nonverbal communication systems are acquired, and the various uses of nonverbal communication in social interaction.

REVIEW AND DISCUSSION QUESTIONS

1. Verbal and nonverbal communication systems often operate simultaneously in many interactions. There is dispute over how much each system is relied on and how much meaning each carries, because the relative weight borne by each system changes from interaction to interaction. What are some social situations in which one system (verbal or nonverbal) will dominate the other, and why?

2. Compare the discussion of language acquisition in Chapter 2 to the discussion here of the acquisition of nonverbal communication systems. What role does the influence of social learning play in the acquisition of each of these systems, as compared to innate communicative abilities?

3. Are the processes of interpreting nonverbal messages more or less subject to social-cognitive processes (see Chapter 2) than the interpretation of verbal messages? Why?

4. How do the uses given for nonverbal communication compare to the uses one might describe for verbal communication systems? Are there any functions that are better done, or can only be done, in verbal or nonverbal communication? Why would someone elect to use (or unconsciously use) one system in preference to another if both were equally effective?

REFERENCES

Altman, I. (1975). *The environment and social behavior.* Belmont, CA: Wadsworth.

Argyle, M., Alkema, F., & Gilmour, R. (1971). The communication of friendly and hostile attitudes by verbal and non-verbal signals. *European Journal of Social Psychology, 1,* 385–402.

Argyle, M., & Cook, M. (1976). *Gaze and mutual gaze.* Cambridge: Cambridge University Press.

Argyle, M., Salter, V., Nicholson, H., Williams, M., & Burgess, P. (1970). The communication of inferior and superior attitudes by verbal and nonverbal signals. *British Journal of Social and Clinical Psychology, 9,* 221–231.

Berscheid, E., & Walster, E. H. (1974). Physical attractiveness. In L. Berkowitz (Ed.), *Advances in experimental social psychology* (Vol. 7). New York: Academic Press.

Bickman, L. (1974). The social power of a uniform. *Journal of Applied Social Psychology, 4,* 47–61.

Birdwhistell, R. L. (1952). *Introduction to kinesics.* Louisville, KY: University of Louisville Press. (Now available on microfilm only. Ann Arbor, MI: University Microfilms).

Birdwhistell, R. L. (1970). *Kinesics and context.* Philadelphia: University of Pennsylvania Press.

Buck, R. (1976). A test of nonverbal receiving ability: Preliminary studies. *Human Communication Research, 2,* 162–171.

Buck, R. (1983). Recent approaches to the study of nonverbal receiving ability. In J. M. Wiemann & R. P. Harrison (Eds.), *Nonverbal interaction.* Beverly Hills: Sage.

Buck, R. (1984). *The communication of emotion.* New York: Guilford Press.

Bull, P. (1983). *Body movement and interpersonal communication.* New York: Wiley.

Burgoon, J. K. (1980). Nonverbal communication research in the 1970s: An overview. In D. Nimo (Ed.), *Communication Yearbook 4.* New Brunswick, NJ: Transaction.

Burgoon, J. K. (1985). Nonverbal signals. In M. L. Knapp & G. R. Miller (Eds.), *Handbook of interpersonal communication.* Beverly Hills: Sage.

Burgoon, J. K., & Saine, T. J. (1978). *The unspoken dialogue: An introduction to nonverbal communication.* Boston: Houghton Mifflin.

Cappella, J. N. (1981). Mutual influence in expressive behavior: Adult-adult and infant-adult interaction. *Psychological Bulletin, 89,* 101–132.

Cappella, J. N. (1985). Controlling the floor in conversation. in A. W. Siegman & S. Feldstein (Eds.), *Multichannel integrations of nonverbal behavior.* Hillsdale, NJ: Erlbaum.

Chevalier-Skolnikoff, S. (1973). Facial expression of emotion in nonhuman primates. In P. Ekman (Ed.), *Darwin and facial expression.* New York: Academic Press.

Cooper, K. (1979). *Nonverbal communication for business success.* New York: Amacom.

Cortes, J. B., & Gatti, F. M. (1965). Physique and self-description of temperament. *Journal of Consulting Psychology, 29,* 432–439.

Darwin, C. (1965). *The expression of emotions in man and animals.* Chicago: University of Chicago Press. (Original work published 1872)

Davis, M. (1979). The state of the art: Past and present trends in body movement research. In A. Wolfgang (Ed.), *Nonverbal behavior: Applications and cultural implications.* New York: Academic Press.

Davitz, J. R. (1964). *The communication of emotional meaning.* New York: McGraw-Hill.

Duncan, S., & Fiske, D. W. (1977). *Face-to-face interaction: Research, methods, and theory.* Hillsdale, NJ: Erlbaum.

Efron, D. (1941). *Gesture and environment.* New York: King's Crown Press. Reissued as *Gesture, race and culture.* The Hague: Mouton, 1972.

Eibl-Eibesfeldt, I. (1973). The expressive behavior of the deaf-and-blind-born. In M. von Cranach & I. Vine (Eds.), *Social communication and movement.* New York: Academic Press.

Eibl-Eibesfeldt, I. (1975). *Ethology· The biology of behavior* (2nd ed.) New York: Holt, Rinehart & Winston.

Ekman, P. (1973a). Cross-cultural studies of facial expression. In P. Ekman (Ed.), *Darwin and facial expression.* New York: Academic Press.

Ekman, P. (1973b). *Darwin and facial expression.* New York: Academic Press.

Ekman, P. (Ed.) (1982). *Emotion in the human face* (2nd ed.). New York: Cambridge University Press.

Ekman, P. (1985). *Telling lies.* New York: W. W. Norton.

Ekman, P., & Friesen, W. V. (1969a). The repertoire of nonverbal behavior: Categories, origins, usage, and coding. *Semiotica, 1,* 49–98.

Ekman, P., & Friesen, W. V. (1969b). Nonverbal leakage and clues to deception. *Psychiatry, 32,* 88–106.

Ekman, P., & Friesen, W. V. (1975). *Unmasking the face.* Englewood Cliffs, NJ: Prentice-Hall.

Ekman, P., Friesen, W. V., & Ellsworth, P. (1972). *Emotion in the human face.* Elmsford, NY: Pergamon.

Ekman, P., Liebert, R. M., Friesen, W. V., Harrison, R. P., Zlatchin, C., Malmstrom, E. J., & Baron, R. A. (1971, June). *Facial expressions of emotion while watching televised violence as predictors of subsequent aggression.* Report to the Surgeon General's Scientific Advisory Committee on Television and Social Behavior.

Ellyson, S. L., & Dovidio, J. F. (Eds.). (1985). *Power, dominance and nonverbal behavior.* New York: Springer-Verlag.

Erickson, F. (1975). One function of proxemic shifts in face-to-face interaction. In A. Kendon, R. M. Harris, & M. R. Key (Eds.), *Organization of behavior in face-to-face interaction.* The Hague: Mouton.

Exline, R. (1971). Visual interaction: The glances of power and preference. In J. K. Cole (Ed.), *Nebraska symposium on motivation 1971.* Lincoln: University of Nebraska Press.

Fast, J. (1970). *Body language.* New York: M. Evans

Goldman-Eisler, F. (1968). *Psycholinguistics: Experiments in spontaneous speech.* New York: Academic Press.

Gottman, J. M. (1979). *Marital interaction: Experimental investigations.* New York: Academic Press.

Graham, J. A., & Kligman, A. M. (Eds.). (1985). *The psychology of cosmetic treatments.* New York: Praeger.

Hall, E. T. (1959). *The silent language.* Garden City, NY: Doubleday.

Hall, E. T. (1966). *The hidden dimension.* Garden City, NY: Doubleday.

Hall, J. A. (1984). *Nonverbal sex differences: Communication accuracy and expressive style.* Baltimore: Johns Hopkins University Press.

Hall, J. A. (1985). Male and female nonverbal behavior. In A. W. Siegman and S. Feldstein (Eds.), *Multichannel integrations of nonverbal behavior.* Hillsdale, NJ: Erlbaum.

Harper, R. G., Weins, A. N., & Matarazzo, J. D. (1978). *Nonverbal communication: The state of the art.* New York: Wiley.

Heilman, M. E., & Saruwatari, L. F. (1979). When beauty is beastly. The effects of appearance and sex on evaluations of job applicants for managerial and nonmanagerial jobs. *Organizational Behavior and Human Performance, 22,* 360–372.

Henley, N., & LaFrance, M. (1984). Gender as culture: Difference and dominance in nonverbal behavior. In A. Wolfgang (Ed.), *Nonverbal behavior: Perspectives, applications, and intercultural insights.* New York: Hogrefe.

Hess, E. H. (1975). *The tell-tale eye.* New York: Van Nostrand Reinhold.

Hopson, J. L. (1979). *Scent signals.* New York: William Morrow.

Horai, J., Naccari, N., & Faloultah, E. (1974). The effects of expertise and physical attractiveness upon opinion agreement and liking. *Sociometry, 37,* 601–606.

Kendon, A. (1970). Movement coordination in social interaction: Some examples described. *Acta Psychologica, 32,* 101–125.

Kendon, A. (1983). Gesture and speech: How they interact. In J. M. Wiemann & R. P. Harrison (Eds.), *Nonverbal interaction.* Beverly Hills: Sage.

Knapp, M. L. (1978). *Nonverbal communication in human interaction.* New York: Holt, Rinehart & Winston.

Knapp, M. L. (1984). The study of nonverbal behavior vis-à-vis human communication theory. In A. Wolfgang (Ed.), *Nonverbal behavior: Perspectives, applications, and intercultural insights.* New York: Hogrefe.

Knapp, M. L. (1985). The study of physical appearance and cosmetics in Western culture. In J. A. Graham & A. M. Kligman (Eds.), *The psychology of cosmetic treatments.* New York: Praeger.

Knapp, M. L., Cody, M. J., & Reardon, K. (in press). Viewing nonverbal signals from multi-level perspectives. In S. Chaffee & C. Berger (Eds.), *Handbook of communication science.* Newbury Park, CA: Sage.

Knapp, M. L., & Comadena, M. E. (1979). Telling it like it isn't: A review of theory and research on deceptive communications. *Human Communication Research, 5,* 270–285.

Knapp, M. L., Hart, R. P., Friedrich, G. W., & Shulman, G. M. (1973). The rhetoric of goodbye: Verbal and nonverbal correlates of human leave-taking. *Speech Monographs, 40,* 182–198.

Kretschmer, E. (1925). *Physique and character.* New York: Cooper Square.

LaBarre, W. (1964). Paralinguistics, kinesics, and cultural anthropology. In T. A. Sebeok, A. S. Hayes, & M. C. Bateson (Eds.), *Approaches to semiotics.* The Hague: Mouton.

LaFrance, M., & Mayo, C. (1978). *Moving bodies.* Monterey, CA: Brooks/Cole.

LaFrance, M., & Mayo, C. (1979). A review of nonverbal behaviors of women and men. *Western Journal of Speech Communication, 43,* 96–107.

Leathers, D. G. (1979). The impact of multichannel message inconsistency on verbal and nonverbal decoding behaviors. *Communication Monographs, 46,* 88–100.

Lenneberg, E. (1969). *Biological foundations of language.* New York: Wiley.

McCaskey, M. B. (1979, November-December). The hidden messages managers send. *Harvard Business Review,* pp. 137–148.

Mehrabian, A. (1969). Significance of posture and position in the communication of attitude and status relationships. *Psychological Bulletin, 71,* 359–372.

Mehrabian, A. (1972). *Nonverbal communication.* Chicago: Aldine-Atherton.

Mehrabian, A., & Williams, M. (1969). Nonverbal concomitants of perceived and intended persuasiveness. *Journal of Personality and Social Psychology, 13,* 37–58.

Mills, J., & Aronson, E. (1965). Opinion change as a function of the communicator's attractiveness and desire to influence. *Journal of Personality and Social Psychology, 61,* 73–77.

Montagu, M. F. A. (1971). *Touching: The human significance of the skin.* New York: Columbia University Press.

Moos, R. H. (1976). *The human context: Environmental determinants of behavior.* New York: Wiley.

Morris, D. (1977). *Manwatching: A field guide to human behavior.* New York: Harry N. Abrams.

Patterson, M. L. (1983). *Nonverbal behavior: A functional perspective.* New York: Springer-Verlag.

Peskin, S. H. (1980). Nonverbal communication in the courtroom. *Trial Diplomacy Journal, 3,* Spring, 8–9, and *3,* Summer, 6–7, 55.

Philpott, J. S. (1983). The relative contribution to meaning of verbal and nonverbal channels of communication: A meta-analysis. Unpublished master's thesis, University of Nebraska, Lincoln.

Pitcairn, T. K., & Eibl-Eibesfeldt, I. (1976). Concerning the evolution of nonverbal communication in man. In M. E. Hahn & E. C. Simmel (Eds.), *Communicative behavior and evolution.* New York: Academic Press.

Porter, R. H., & Moore, J. D. (1981). Human kin recognition by olfactory cues. *Physiology and Behavior, 27,* 493–495.

Prohansky, H. M., Ittleson, W. H., & Rivlin, L. G. (Eds.). (1970). *Environmental psychology: Man and his physical setting.* New York: Holt, Rinehart & Winston.

Pryor, B., & Buchanan, R. W. (1984). The effects of a defendant's demeanor on juror perceptions of credibility and guilt. *Journal of Communication, 34,* 92–99.

Roach, M. E., & Eicher, J. B. (Eds.). (1965). *Dress, adornment and the social order.* New York: Wiley.

Rosenthal, R. (Ed.). (1979). *Skill in nonverbal communication: Individual differences.* Cambridge, MA: Oelgeschlager, Gunn, & Hain.

Rosenthal, R. (1985). Nonverbal cues in the mediation of interperson expectancy effects. In A. W. Siegman & S. Feldstein (Eds.), *Multichannel integrations of nonverbal behavior.* Hillsdale, NJ: Erlbaum.

Rosenthal, R., Hall, J. A., DiMatteo, M. R., Rogers, P. L., & Archer, D. (1979). *Sensitivity to nonverbal communication: The PONS test.* Baltimore: Johns Hopkins University Press.

Rosenthal, R., & Jacobson, L. (1968). *Pygmalion in the classroom.* New York: Holt, Rinehart & Winston.

Ruesch, J., & Kees, W. (1956). *Nonverbal communication: Notes on the visual perception of human relations.* Berkeley and Los Angeles: University of California Press.

Rutter, D. R. (1984). *Looking and seeing.* New York: Wiley.

Scheflen, A. E., & Scheflen, A. (1972). *Body language and the social order.* Englewood Cliffs, NJ: Prentice-Hall.

Scherer, K. R. (1979). Personality markers in speech. In K. R. Scherer & H. Giles (Eds.), *Social markers in speech*. New York: Cambridge University Press.

Sheldon, W. H. (1940). *The varieties of human physique*. New York: Harper & Row.

Smith, H. A. (1979). Nonverbal communication in teaching. *Review of Educational Research, 49,* 631–672.

Snyder, M. (1974). Self-monitoring of expressive behavior. *Journal of Personality and Social Psychology, 30,* 526–537.

Sommer, R. (1979). *Personal space*. Englewood Cliffs, NJ: Prentice-Hall.

Starr, V. H., & McCormick, M. (1985). *Jury selection: An attorney's guide to jury law and methods*. Boston: Little, Brown.

Wells, W., & Siegel, B. (1961). Stereotyped somotypes. *Psychological Reports, 8,* 77–78.

Widgery, R. N. (1974). Sex of receiver and physical attractiveness of source as determinants of initial credibility perception. *Western Speech, 38,* 13–17.

Wiemann, J. M., & Knapp, M. L. (1975). Turn-taking in conversations. *Journal of Communication, 25,* 75–92.

Woolfolk, A. W., & Brooks, D. M. (1983). Nonverbal communication in teaching. In E. Gordon (Ed.), *Review of Research in Education* (Vol. X). Washington, DC: American Educational Research Association.

Zuckerman, M., DePaulo, B. M., & Rosenthal, R. (1981). Verbal and nonverbal communication of deception. In L. Berkowitz (Ed.), *Advances in experimental social psychology* (Vol. 14). New York: Academic Press.

Zuckerman, M., & Driver, R. E. (1985). Telling lies: Verbal and nonverbal correlates of deception. In A. W. Siegman & S. Feldstein (Eds.), *Multichannel integrations of nonverbal behavior*. Hillsdale, NJ: Erlbaum.

4

Communication Technologies

Frederick Williams
University of Texas, Austin

Heather E. Hudson
University of Texas, Austin

Sharon Stover
University of Texas, Austin

*Frederick **Williams** is Director of the Center for Research on Communication Technology and Society at the University of Texas at Austin, where he also occupies the Mary Gibbs Jones Centennial Chair in Communication. He has written numerous articles and books on modern communication, including* The Communications Revolution, Communication Technology and Behavior, The New Communications, *and two management books,* The Executive's Guide to Information Technology *and* Innovative Management Using Telecommunications *(the latter two with Herbert Dordick). Williams has also received international recognition for his work on the content of the "Spaceship Earth" pavilion at Epcot Center near Walt Disney World. He is a former president of the International Communication Association.*

*Heather E. **Hudson** is Associate Professor in the Department of Radio-Television-Film at the University of Texas at Austin. She has extensive research experience in many international applications of communication, and was for a number of years a staff member of the Academy for Educational Development in Washington, D.C. Dr. Hudson is the editor of the book* New Directions in Satellite Communication: Challenges for North and South, *and author of* When Telephones Reach the Village: The Role of Telecommunications in Rural Development. *Among her major research interests are rural applications of telecommunications.*

Sharon Stover *is an Assistant Professor in the Radio-Television-Film Department at the University of Texas at Austin. Her research and teaching interests are in new information technologies and their social effects, the economic and competitive structure of communication industries, and U.S. information and communication policy. She recently completed a major paper on the cable television industry,* Issues Facing Cable Television. *She received her advanced degrees from Stanford University.*

LEARNING OBJECTIVES

After studying this chapter you should be able to:

- List examples of new media to move signals, store information, and interact with users.
- Outline briefly the basic theories used to understand technologies and their effects on communication.
- Describe interactive technologies such as text services and teleconferencing in terms of their impact on communication.
- Explain how cable television and videocassettes have changed the nature of the audience for the electronic mass media.
- Trace a brief history of satellite communication technology and give examples of research conducted on this method of distribution.
- Discuss some of the major new issues in theory and research that are raised by these new technologies.

Communication technologies are not really as "new" as people think. Yet the term can conjure up images of satellites, computers, lasers, and other electronic media. Most communications media are a technology in themselves. That is, they involve the use of something that human beings have crafted from the environment in order to facilitate their communication exchanges. From papyrus scrolls to video display terminals, all media are essentially extensions of the human

capability for communication. That these extensions have many social consequences which can be researched is the theme of this chapter.

Social research into communication technologies may involve consideration of what new capabilities a technology offers, how people may or may not adopt a technology, the consequences for individuals or organizations when they adopt a technology, and methods for evaluating longer-range effects. This chapter examines three clusters of technology, after a preliminary discussion of the nature of communication technologies as "new media" and as a topic of social scientific inquiry. First, interactive technologies are considered, including advances in text services, teleconferencing, and new uses of the telephone. The second cluster focuses on technologies associated with everyday uses of cable television and cassettes, two of the most popular developments in America. Finally, satellite technologies are discussed. Among the more important consequences are the implications for international communication, including simultaneous challenges of cooperation and conflict. The chapter closes with a review of some important concerns for social research, such as the impact of new technology on traditional areas of study: interpersonal, small group, and mass communication.

COMMUNICATION TECHNOLOGY AS NEW MEDIA

In its broadest application, *technology* refers to the applied science of developing tools, instruments, and other components for practical use. Inventions resulting from scientific or technical progress are often referred to as technologies. A "communication" or "information" technology (the terms are often used interchangeably) is anything we have invented to extend the process of human communication or information handling. These inventions range from the clay writing tablets of 6000 B.C. to today's supercomputers.

Most communication technologies are extensions of the various forms of communication media. That is, they are the means we use to store, transport, transmit, or alter various message forms. When we refer to the "new technologies," we are describing recent developments in communication media, such as the communication satellite or the electronic computer. Sometimes, however, we are as equally concerned with new uses of older media, such as innovations in telephone services.

Some of us writing on modern communication have come to call the new technologies of media simply "new media." More of these developments have taken place within our lifetime than in all human history. Most of these developments are the result of an electronic boom that began during World War II and was further accelerated by space exploration programs. Such technologies include the communication satellite, advances in the land distribution of messages via wire and microwave, vast improvements in television, new forms of radio broadcasting, videotape and videodisc machines, cable television distribution systems, and, of course, the electronic computer. The most striking current development of this revolution is the convergence of telecommunications and computer technologies.

Most advances in electronic communication have taken place along three major lines. One is in moving signals from one place to another via telecommunications systems—for example, by satellite. A second major application is in storing information in highly compact, efficient, and easily retrievable forms, such as computer disks. The networking capability of electronic computers represents the third line of development.

Computers

But most important is the convergence of these technologies. The ability to combine a powerful transmission system with a powerful computer system implies that the data of the latter system can be distributed anywhere on the communication network. That is, when you use telephone lines to tap into a computer in a remote location, you can transport much of the power of the computer across the distance involved. Generally, this is known as a "computer network system," which has been one of the directions of largest growth for computer power in advanced societies.

Convergence can also be seen in how computing systems have enabled us to vastly increase the efficiency of telecommunications systems. For example, in most modern telephone systems, human switchboard operators are no longer required. When we dial a telephone, you are sending instructions to computers for routing your call to its intended destination.

Computerlike components improve the operation of many other everyday communication technologies. They are what allow modern television sets and radios to fine-tune themselves. They are important in videotape and videodisc machines. In many modern countries, computer components enable telephones to "remember" numbers, to repeat dialing, and to forward calls to a designated location. Many are examples of "intelligent" communication technologies, where computer components automate parts of the operations.

Finally, we can consider computers themselves as a communication technology. They can receive, store, and send messages, and act in all ways like communication devices. They can also act on our messages. For example, we can give a computer a set of instructions (a program) for performing certain calculations. When the computer is given data, it performs operations that in effect represent the application of human direction to the machine's operation.

TECHNOLOGY AND SOCIAL SCIENTIFIC INQUIRY

In the social sciences we are interested less in the details of technology than in how technologies both affect and are affected by the human condition. For example, what human capabilities are enhanced by technology? What are the circumstances of the development and adoption of new media? What are the impacts on the individual, on groups or organizations, or on an entire society? The range of research topics is broad, extending, for example, from "human factors" studies of the best fit between the human hand and a keyboard to such general topics as the nature of a society that depends heavily on information technologies the so-called information society.

Researchers studying the effects of communication technologies typically draw from social science theory and methodology. For example, the work of Short, Williams, and Christie (1976) on the personalness of communication via telephone draws from interpersonal-communication theory. Rogers's (1983) theory of the diffusion of innovations is an apt starting point to speculate about how groups adopt new communication technologies, such as word processors in office environments. Other researchers, such as Williams (1986), consider uses-and-gratifications theory applicable to studying the rewards individuals expect from different media technologies. There are even broader perspectives, as in Hudson's (1984) research into how the coming of the telephone affects village life. Studies of this latter type often incorporate economic variables, as in Porat's (1977) studies of the growth of the "information economy" in the United States.

In the next sections of this chapter, we review several examples of new media and the social research they have, or will, stimulate. These examples include interactive technologies, technologies of television, and communication satellites.

INTERACTIVE TECHNOLOGIES

Text Services

Interactive technologies of current interest include two-way cable (for example, the Warner-Amex "Qube" system) and various forms of text services, both broadcast and cable transmitted or available via telephone networks. *Videotext* (or *videotex*) is the generic term used to describe interactive systems in which the user can send and receive information (usually via phone line or television cable); *teletext* is a one-way broadcast system where "pages" are sent for users to read on their TV screen. Some two-way text systems are the basis for remote home services such as shopping, banking, asking questions of different vendors, or sending "electronic mail" to other users.

It is now clear that interactive television services such as Qube have not become as popular as was originally envisaged. A reason frequently given is that the American television audience has come to expect mainly entertainment; television offers escape rather than involvement. Another reason is that for interactive services to hold longer-range customers, they must offer combined advantages of efficiency, convenience, and cost.

But although there has been little growth of interactive television on a mass media scale, specialized information services such as Dow Jones News Retrieval and CompuServe have seen steady growth. For many years, it has been possible to link multiple users simultaneously to a large computer. Computers operate so quickly that they can move back and forth between users without the users ever knowing the difference. Imagine, then, such a service connected via telephone to computer terminals in subscribers' homes. An individual need only dial a computer number by phone, request a particular information service, and in effect, draw information out of the computer. This is the basis for the well-known Prestel system used in Great Britain. Prestel is displayed on a television monitor that is connected to special equipment for communicating the textual messages to and from the telephone lines. Computer-aided networks such as electronic bulletin boards and on-line data bases (for example, The Source) are becoming more publicly accessible as people purchase home computers.

Hiltz and Turoff (1978) suggest that an affective dimension is present in computer communication. People may anthropomorphize computers as they use them in roles ranging from psychiatrists to partners in crime.

In one study of interactive services, Dozier and Ledingham (1982) identified two key dimensions in use of interactive banking, shopping, and home security in San Diego: surveillance and transaction. The surveillance mode, a "read-only" status, was found to be more attractive to users than the interactive transaction ("read-write") mode. This finding prompted the researchers to conclude that all other factors being equal, the surveillance function of this information utility will be adopted more rapidly than the transaction function.

Information retrieval systems are sometimes associated with depersonalization. Consider, for example, interactive systems used mainly for electronic banking, computerized shopping, and home security. Dozier and Ledingham (1982) found that although advantages such as efficiency and convenience are perceived, these services are often viewed as not being worth the loss of social interaction. The desire for convenience is fulfilled, but the need for getting out of the house and experiencing social contact is not.

Electronic Mail Some of the computer-based systems discussed above have the same characteristics as electronic mail. Messages are sent to a central computer, where they can be retrieved at the receiver's request. For several years, the U.S. Postal Service offered a service called ECOM, whereby computer-originated mail was electronically distributed to post offices nearest addresses, then printed and mailed first class. Although that service has now been discontinued, similar forms are offered, for example, by Western Union and MCI.

Computer networks within organizations sometimes offer messaging systems also referred to as electronic mail. In a study of one such system, Steinfield (1983) found that the mail system was used for a wide variety of purposes, grouped mainly in "task" and "socioemotional" clusters. The former were self-evident, mostly the act of transferring or obtaining information. The latter, however, related to the maintaining of personal relationships, feeling a part of the organization, and being "in touch." Social uses were reported almost as frequently as were task-oriented ones.

Teleconferencing

Communication technologies have various applications for long-distance group communication. Although audio conferencing has long been available through U.S. public telephone services, its use has been surprisingly modest, given all the attention paid to modern teleconferencing. Current applications of teleconferencing include not only audio, but video, facsimile, data, and computer-text links, as well as combinations of them. Most studies of teleconferencing have centered on message effectiveness, conference procedures, or costs. Many studies (for example, Dutton, Fulk, & Steinfield, 1982) have shown that with proper management, teleconferencing can be highly effective for meeting situation-specific communication needs of corporations. Computer teleconferencing has grown in recent years, especially in organizations where messages can be stored for forwarding—as in "asynchronous" conferencing.

The decision to use conferencing systems seems to reflect various motives. In addition to accomplishing specific tasks, reasons include the desire to establish and maintain contacts outside one's own geographic areas, the need for access to schedules, and the like. The degree to which the communicative restrictions of a text exchange affect the personalness of the message is a subject of debate. Both Hiltz (1978) and Phillips (1983) found that people actively attempt to use computers for socioemotional ends, such as working out problems and employing face-saving tactics or stream-of-consciousness thinking, even when the conference involved is task-oriented. Accordingly, the electronic medium is viewed as suspect regarding the full satisfaction of users' socioemotional and interpersonal needs. However, Hiemstra (1982) and Rice (1980) suggest that some types of computer conferencing do not depend on interpersonal involvement; hence, the technical restrictions of the medium do not impede effectiveness so much.

As conferencing and computer bulletin boards become increasingly popular for meeting new friends, developing relationships, and exchanging personal opinions, this medium may become an important topic for extensions of interpersonal communication research.

New Considerations of the Telephone

Although the telephone has been with us for well over a century, we will consider many of its new uses as comparable to the questions we raise for new media. The telephone network is all the interconnections, or possibilities for them, among individuals or stations via a communications system that started with wire but now uses many additional transmission technologies. Microwave links assist over long or intermediate distances. Through this specialized broadcasting system, voice and data signals can be retransmitted by line of sight from one receiver to another. In the last 30 years, additional wired communication systems using coaxial cable have evolved. Today, the major advance in telephone transmission is fiber optic networks that are far less expensive than copper wire and have a much greater message capacity.

Our local telephones are connected to switching stations, which, in turn, are connected by main (trunk) lines, all as a "switched" network. Computers now play a major role in the operation of these switching systems.

We have chosen to consider the telephone in this chapter because for years it has provided interactive services that are highly accepted in all modern societies. Ironically, the telephone has received little attention from social scientists. Studying its past as well as current changes can contribute to our understanding of the uses of new technologies.

Keller (1976) has postulated that telephone use has two dimensions, the instrumental (accomplishing a given message task) and the intrinsic (talking on the telephone for its own sake). The concept of the telephone's intrinsic uses was further borne out in Wurtzel and Turner's (1977) study of New York City residents whose telephone service was temporarily cut off. Contrary to the expectation that other forms of communication would be substituted for the telephone, it was found that certain uses of the telephone, particularly for making social calls, were not substitutable.

An ethnographic study of telephone uses (Phillips, Lum, & Lawrence, 1983) showed that people tend to differentiate most between business and pleasure calls. Business-related calls and some types of social calls to certain people in various relationships to the caller are thought to be more appropriate for the workplace, while social calls and some business calls are more appropriate for the home. Use appears to be associated with location and relationship among the business-pleasure dimension.

Lum (1984), in conducting a series of in-depth interviews about phone use with senior citizens in Hawaii, found two major needs dimensions satisfied via the telephone. The convenience dimension was divided into social calls and informational calls, which included the needs to "get information and get things done." The second category was that of contact calls, and included social-obligation calls (perceived as necessary to uphold the notion of one's social role) and "I care" calls meant to "brighten one's day," say "I love you," or to lift morale. Another important observation was that respondents did not consider their telephone use similar to the singular use of other communications media. Instead, its content and use were seen as an interdependent part of everyday life. Lum found that other media, such as television, were brought up as being important, especially when respondents were asked to imagine what would happen if their phone were taken away. But television could not substitute for telephone use. Further commentary on social uses of the telephone can be found in a research report by Williams and Dordick (1985).

TELEVISION TECHNOLOGIES

Development of Cable Services

Cable television in the United States dates from the 1950s. These first cable systems were generally in isolated rural regions where getting a television signal was a problem. Cable technology solved that problem by setting up receiving antennas on high hills and then delivering the television signal through wires to the locations that ordinarily would be unable to get off-air signals, mainly communities in valleys or blocked by mountains. Beginning in the 1960s, cable systems gradually spread to suburban areas and other small cities.

In the late 1970s, satellite-delivered television signals brought new programming and efficient signal distribution possibilities. Alongside satellite technology in importance was a new government attitude toward cable. The earliest government response to this industry was to try to mold it as something that would not compete with broadcasting. Regulation of cable television, or CATV (community antenna television) systems, as they were then called, was used to promote localism and diversity. By localism, the government meant that cable television should offer distinctively local media and not compete with broadcast fare that was more national in its orientation. Having the cable operator provide local programming and offer access channels for community-based programming contributed to localism and hence were mandatory for a period of time. Similarly, diversity was promoted by limiting a cable operator's ability to get the same type of programming already available over the air. Several rules prohibited the operator from nonlocal "import" signals and from rebroadcasting programs that were available at different times of day on regular affiliate stations. However, these attempts to confine the cable industry to a cir-

cumscribed role were tested in several court cases.

Ultimately, the courts and the government regulators, particularly the Federal Communications Commission, decided to unleash the technology. By the late 1970s, prohibitions on nonlocal programming were lifted, along with several other requirements that maintained the industry's local identity. Communication satellites also emerged as a cost-effective technology for delivering programming simultaneously to several sites around the nation, fostering alternative national programming networks. The FCC and the courts agreed that cable systems should offer an alternative to broadcasting, and allowing satellite-delivered programming to reach more homes via cable was one way it could do so.

The earlier protectionist or "trusteeship" model of regulating cable television as well as conventional broadcasting is gradually wearing down. The current federal philosophy of media increasingly advocates deregulation, allowing market forces to determine which systems will survive or thrive. It advocates that government retreat as much as possible from putting any restrictions or obligations on media systems and simply let the "best" system win.

To date, broadcasters have lost a sizable portion of their audience to cable; conventional programming is currently attracting 68–70 percent of the viewership, an all-time low, down from 90 percent at the inception of cable television. But the broadcast networks remain extremely successful and still offer the most programming. Cable, too, is extremely successful. There appears to be room for both kinds of systems.

Toward the end of the 1970s, cable operators pushed hard to wire the remainder of the country. With satellite delivery of diverse programming now available and favorable government rulings, even large cities with decent over-the-air television reception seemed like attractive places for cable. Twenty-four-hour movie channels were a particular draw. Cable subscription skyrocketed to about 45 percent of all television households in 1986; current estimates indicate that 70–80 percent of the country is now wired for cable. Moreover, a first-ever test of high-definition TV programming on a typical cable system was sponsored recently by the National Cable Television Association in Maryland. The successful trial was hailed as the harbinger of a whole new generation of electronics. The most isolated rural homes will probably never get cable television, but the remainder of the country has or will have it available.

Currently, about 7,300 cable systems operate in the United States. Most have at least 20 channels of programming; many are upgrading to about 54 channels, and a few have over 100. A subscriber pays about $12–$15 a month for basic service, which usually consists of local over-the-air broadcast signals, locally produced programming known as "access programming," and specialized channels for sports, news, weather, music videos, religion, public affairs, and minority-oriented programming. Many of the channels beyond the basic level in the expanded tier are specialized channels. A few others aim for a larger, more generalized audience. Another $10 added to the fee for basic and expanded service will purchase a movie service such as Home Box Office, Showtime, or The Movie Channel, which airs movies, both old and new, 24 hours a day.

When cable was more regulated, the government imposed a strict system of controls on its programming and on its rates. Many of these restrictions no longer stand. By 1987, cable systems in most regions of the United States were able to charge whatever they desired for service. Furthermore, recent legislation makes it much easier for cable systems to maintain their virtual monopoly position within communities. Rarely does more than one cable system choose to locate in a given city. The amount of money a cable system pays a city to lay its cable (to use public right-of-way and easements) has also been capped by federal law. It can go no higher than 5 percent of a system's total revenues.

Some observers are becoming alarmed about the power of the cable industry. Many large cable operators (the largest serves nearly 4 million households nationally) are financially linked to programming services, creating a situation in which they offer the television fare they themselves own and produce over the systems they also own and operate. This necessarily shrinks the program variety a cable system is supposed to offer. Although vertical integration has been a regulatory target in other contexts (notably the film industry in the 1940s), the current deregulatory mood seems to be a bit more tolerant.

Some cable operators are so large that they serve well over 50 percent of all subscribers in some states, which some claim is a dangerous level of control. Many cable systems are owned by other media corporations, such as large newspaper chains and broadcasters. Cross-ownership is barely monitored by the government, prompting more fears about the concentration of power among a few large companies. Whether these relationships will continue to go unchecked remains to be seen.

Research into Cable Use   To date, research on the social consequences of cable television has been limited. Most critics view cable as "just more television," and therefore ignore its distinctive qualities. What we do know can be summarized as follows. Households with cable television do tend to watch more television than their noncable counterparts. They spend less time with network programming, although well over half their viewing time is still with the three oldest networks, ABC, NBC, and CBS. Cable households tend to be middle class, arguably because the service costs additional money and therefore is not affordable among the lower class, and because upper-class people simply do not watch much television and therefore do not feel they need cable. Cable households also tend to have children.

Most studies of cable television have focused on the individual, particularly the factors differentiating the cable subscriber from the nonsubscriber. In areas where substantial over-the-air television is available, cable will not be heavily subscribed (perhaps 30 to 40 percent of households will subscribe). On the other hand, in regions where there is little over-the-air television, cable is welcomed and a higher percentage of people subscribe.

Researchers generally conclude that cable subscribers watch more television than nonsubscribers (Becker, Dunwoody, & Rafaeli, 1983; Robinson, 1981; Rothe, Harvey, & Michael, 1983; Sparkes, 1983). Others, such as Agostino (1980), find that cable households watch more channels, although not necessarily for a longer period of time. What may be happening is that people watch some of the new channels while not completely abandoning their previous network television viewing habits.

Krugman and Eckrich (1982) report pay cable subscribers shift their viewing to pay channels rather than simply viewing more conventional (network) television overall. They also found that pay cable subscribers value entertainment from television more than basic subscribers (who more often value simply better reception) and that they tend to be younger, more affluent, and more permissive. Heeter, D'Alessio, and Greenberg (1983) state that the special cable programming channels that have proliferated over the past decade drew half the cable audience, along with the obvious finding that viewing was spread across many more channels in cable households than in noncable ones.

Several studies have examined the effects of cable on the appetite for local news, concluding that cable erodes attention to local events (Hill & Dyer, 1981; Webster, 1984). Other survey-based studies have examined cable's effects on movie attendance and concluded that having cable does not affect moviegoing (Kaplan, 1978; McDermott & Medhurst, 1984; Rothe et al., 1983). Unfortunately, nearly all the studies cited above suffer from shortcomings. They usually base their conclusions on one-time survey data, collected either via the telephone or a self-administered mailed questionnaire. Carefully controlled field experiments are lacking.

One recent exception is Sparkes's (1983) longitudinal investigation into the diffusion of cable television. Gathering data from a panel sample over five years, Sparkes concluded that the adoption of cable takes place in phases. In the first phase, cable is seen as "more of the same," just "more TV." In the second phase, more of cable's specialized programming is explored and appreciated. In the third phase, there is even more appreciation for some of the more exotic services cable has to offer. Sparkes underscores the idea that cable's integration into a household and into a community is still an ongoing, dynamic process.

The unique dimensions of cable as a viewing form with distinctive viewing fare are still largely unexplored. As has been the case with other new media, researchers' first impulses have been simply to describe what the medium is and who uses it. Later generations of scholars will undoubtedly investigate the more complex questions of effects and relationships between using cable television and using other media and cultural forms.

For example, questions about the audience for narrowcasting (specialized channels) and whether watching more targeted television channels does indeed produce a qualitatively different feeling of being a member of a viewing "community" could be examined. With 24-hour programming, the television environment has changed dramatically. The audience for late-night/early-morning television, the so-called fringe audience, could be examined: Are these viewers somehow different from prime-time viewers? How and why might they be? Does the heavy diet of news available with cable television influence one's interaction with conventional print media?

One investigation that deals directly with viewer expectations of cable television points out the need for researchers to expand their concept of what types of specific gratifications these may include. Shaver (1983) conducted focus-group interviews and found that the two most frequently mentioned motives for viewing cable television were variety provided by the increased number of channels and control over viewing associated with the abundance of programming. Although the study does not group them in this way, the motives fall into content (religious programs), structural (variety), service (better reception), and psychological needs (companionship) categories. Some of these gratifications have also been associated with traditional broadcast television, but others are linked specifically to the cable medium.

In a study conducted by the Opinion Research Corporation (1983), cable subscribers were loosely classified into user groups. Although better reception was still mentioned as the primary reason for subscribing to cable, certain other distinctions between users were defined. Three groups reflected the following characteristics:

1. Undifferentiated users of the medium, who will watch everything and signed up for cable early on.

2. The "entertain me" group, who primarily seek entertainment and diversion and are likely to be pay-television subscribers.

3. The "basic but . . ." group, who are more discriminating in their use; they want sophisticated, intellectually stimulating, children's, family-oriented, or information programming, and are likely to seek out home services and other special services.

These groups are interesting to researchers because their functional needs are perceived as different, even though they are all users of cable television.

This study shows that functions relating both to the form and to the content of the medium will be associated with a technology. Furthermore, a distinction seems to be evident between people who seek out entertainment or escape and those who seek a variety of specific services.

Videocassette Use

Videocassette recorders (VCRs) allow the audience choice in the time dimension, and perhaps along the qualitative dimension proposed by Levy and Windahl (1984). Specifically, VCRs, which are rapidly growing in popularity and use, offer the audience the opportunity for time-shift viewing (Waterman, 1984). Unlike videodiscs, which except for several expensive new models of player-recorders can be obtained only with prerecorded content, blank videocassettes can be used for recording broadcast or cable television programs for viewing at a later time.

Studies (for example, Waterman, 1984) consistently show that time-shifting and prerecorded theatrical films are the most popular uses of videocassette machines. Further uses include playback of home-produced tapes, self-help programs, educational materials, music videos, and uses coupled with a camera (see also studies by Levy and Fink and by Rue as discussed in Palmgreen, 1984).

These uses of VCRs reflect especially on the psychological consequences of choice, time, and mobility. The program content may often be the same as in television or films, but the additional advantage is now related to circumstances of use. Nor should we overlook that cost may often be reduced, as with the case of viewing films. In all, the implications here are that a new media technology may offer less in the way of new uses itself as it makes traditional gratifications more easily obtainable.

Videocassettes also hold implications for the structure of the film and television industries. One advantage in the production and distribution of videocassettes is that new programs can be economically successful without having to appeal to large audiences. Thus we may see the proliferation of highly specialized cassettes along with those geared to the mass market.

SATELLITE TECHNOLOGIES

Early Developments

In 1945, science fiction author and physicist Arthur C. Clarke described in an article in *Wireless World* a system of "extra terrestrial relays," or repeaters in space. He calculated that an object put into orbit 22,300 miles (36,000 kilometers) above the earth would revolve around the earth in 24 hours, the time it takes for the earth to rotate once on its axis. Thus the repeater would appear motionless from the earth. He pointed out that three such repeaters located 120 degrees apart above the equator would cover the entire globe. This concept of a geostationary satellite is what led to the satellites used for domestic and international communications today.

It took less than 20 years for Clarke's idea to become a reality. In 1957, the Russian *Sputnik* showed the world that people could communicate using space satellites. *Sputnik* was not a geostationary satellite; it was in a low earth orbit and had to be tracked across the sky, and it simply beeped! But it spurred scientists and engineers to develop more-sophisticated satellites for commercial use. In the early 1960s the SYNCOM series of satellites was built; in 1964 the world saw the results of the research, as *SYNCOM 3* transmitted television coverage of the Tokyo Olympics. In 1965, just 20 years after Clarke's article was published, the first international satellite, known as *Early Bird* or *INTELSAT I,* was launched to link North America and Europe.

Changes in satellites since 1965 have been dramatic. *Early Bird* had 480 voice channels; the latest international satellites, the INTELSAT VI series, have 80,000 voice channels each. Satellites that can be launched from the space shuttle are much larger, and the lifetime of commercial satellites has been extended from one and a half years to ten years.

A Period of Experiments

During the late 1960s and 1970s, NASA (the National Aeronautics and Space Administration) launched a series of satellites that were made available for social experiments. The first of the Applied Technology Satellite series, *ATS-1,* was used in Alaska to link health workers in isolated villages with doctors in regional hospitals. The experiment, which involved numerous social science studies, was a success, and led to the installation of satellite earth stations in more than 100 Alaskan villages. Today, RCA's *Aurora* satellite

brings telephone service and commercial and educational television to Alaskan villagers. *ATS-1* also linked countries in the South Pacific through a network known as PEACESAT and an educational network operated by the University of the South Pacific, which serves ten island nations and territories from its main campus in Fiji.

In 1974 the *ATS-6* satellite brought educational television programs to schools and communities in the Rocky Mountain states, continuing-education courses to teachers and doctors in Appalachia, and biomedical as well as educational television programs to Alaskan clinics and schools. The same satellite was moved to a "parking space" over India in 1975, so that it could be used to transmit educational television programs to more than 2,500 villages in a project known as SITE (Satellite Instructional Television Experiment). In 1976–77, *CTS* (the Communications Technology Satellite), a joint program of NASA and the Canadian Department of Communications, was used for experiments in both Canada and the United States, and for links between the two countries.

Many of these experiments led to services available today. In Alaska, children in village schools watch educational television programs and adults participate in seminars over the LEARN/ALASKA network. In British Columbia, students in mining and logging towns in the interior take courses over the Knowledge Network on Canada's *ANIK-C* satellite. The successor to the Appalachian experiments is the Learning Channel, which now offers courses for credit delivered by satellite to cable systems around the country. And India now has its own INSAT system to deliver public and educational television to thousands of villages.

National and International Services

The first major service on U.S. commercial satellites was pay cable. Home Box Office (HBO) began transmissions in 1975 on RCA's *SATCOM I* to cable stations around the country. HBO realized that the satellite could be used to beam feature movies to every cable system in the country. Satellites helped spur the growth of cable television in major markets as they brought programs not available on broadcast channels. Satellites also led to the development of narrowcasting, programming aimed at specific target audiences, no matter where they live. Today, the *SATCOM, GALAXY, WESTAR,* and *TELSTAR* satellites deliver specialized news, sports, music, movie, and educational channels to cable systems throughout the country.

The television networks use satellites to distribute their programming to affiliates, and independent distributors also transmit syndicated programs to subscribing stations. Satellites play an increasingly important role in news programming. INTELSAT's international satellites transmit eyewitness coverage of foreign news, sports events such as the Olympics and World Cup, and special events such as fund-raising concerts to viewers worldwide.

Even small television stations can now transmit stories using portable satellite antennas. Satellites also transmit data for business users. Wire services and stock market reports are captured by satellite dish at newspapers and brokers' offices around the country. Large corporations use rooftop antennas to transmit data from one office to another. Others transmit their data to large teleports in major cities that are equipped to communicate with many satellites. Now smaller users can also communicate via satellite with small aperture terminals that can transmit and receive data from microcomputers and individual computer terminals.

Organizations also turn to satellites for video teleconferencing, or "business television." Some companies have in-house networks for communicating from headquarters to field staff. Others use portable antennas (uplinks) for occasional conferences. Hotels, public television stations, and many universities now offer teleconferencing facilities.

The INTELSAT system, which began offering international satellite services in 1965, now provides 110 member countries with international telephone, data, and video communications. More than 25 countries now also use INTELSAT for domestic communications, to bring telephone and television services to cities and towns that would be too difficult and expensive to serve with terrestrial networks.

In addition to the United States, several other countries have their own satellite systems. Canada, the U.S.S.R., and Australia use satellites to reach remote communities as well as for national networks. Japan, France, and Germany are beginning to use satellites for direct broadcasting to homes and for business communications. The first developing country to have its own satellite was Indonesia in 1976; its *PALAPA* satellite now covers other Southeast Asian nations as well. India, Mexico, and Brazil have their own domestic satellites, and 22 Arab countries are members of the regional ARABSAT system. China intends to have its own satellite, and several other countries are at various stages of planning.

In the future, we will undoubtedly see many new developments in satellite technology. Intersatellite links could enable one satellite to communicate directly with another, without retransmitting its signals to earth. Multiple antennas with switchable spot beams could make possible the equivalent of global cellular telephone service. High-powered satellites at higher frequencies could make rooftop and suitcase antennas commonplace, and perhaps one day, Dick Tracy–style wristwatch communication by satellite as well.

Meanwhile, developments in other technologies will give users more choices in selecting the most appropriate and least expensive means of transmitting information. Fiber optic networks will link major cities, but satellites will still be important for communication among large numbers of sites (multipoint networks) and for service to remote areas. "Smart buildings" designed for voice and data communications will communicate with other smart buildings through rooftop antennas or fiber optic links to city teleports.

Satellite services are now commonplace. Mobile satellites allow trucking companies to keep track of their fleets through satellite links direct to antennas on each truck. Automatic teller machines and point-of-sale terminals in stores transmit data from your plastic card via satellite to national host computers. Broadcasters use satellites for on-the-spot coverage from anywhere in the world.

Research Agenda

There is much still to learn about the effects of this new technology (Hudson, 1985). Satellites have the potential to eliminate the barriers of distance. We will need to study how they affect rural residents' access to information and how they can be used to increase productivity in agriculture and rural industries. It will also be important to examine the extent to which the availability of satellite communications combined with computers can enable other industries to decentralize away from the cities.

Researchers will be able to evaluate the impact of satellites on education, not only in the classroom but in the home and workplace. Satellites can bring specialized courses to small schools to help upgrade and enrich their curricula. Employees can take job-related courses at the workplace, delivered by satellite from universities around the country. Courses delivered by satellite and cable to homes offer lifelong learning opportunities to all. We will need to learn how to use satellites most effectively to meet the needs of these diverse student populations.

Internationally, satellites are truly creating the "global village" as cable networks are partnering increasingly with overseas companies to produce quality, low-cost programming. Clearly, the trend is toward the globalization of television. We have much to learn about the impact of global television on the knowledge and attitudes of viewers in the United States and other countries. Perhaps the most dramatic contribution of satellites will be to bring basic communications to people in developing countries. How the extension of tele-phone and broadcast services can contribute to social and economic development is an important research question for the 1990s.

PERSPECTIVES ON RESEARCH AND THEORY

Although there are economic barriers to consider, the new media have vastly increased the availability of nearly every form of communication, and with this, the need for new applications of social research.

On a personal level of communication, modern telephone networks make it possible to communicate with individuals in nearly any part of the world, often by simply dialing a number. The telephone has also been found to be important in economic activities for planning and managing businesses, linking suppliers and markets, and providing access to resource people for consultation. The telephone line harnessed to the computer is now an important organizational communication tool.

Further, more of the world's population has an expanding variety of personal entertainment available to them through inexpensive audiocassettes, powerful but inexpensive radios, and a growing number of alternative radio stations. Film and television entertainment also increases in availability as more television services are mounted, as cable and satellite systems distribute these services, and as audiovisual entertainment becomes available in videotape and videodisc. Usually, this expansion of services offers increased opportunity for personal choice, a phenomenon called "demassification."

What are the social consequences of new technologies on group communication? In a general view, a major effect is that spatial or geographic barriers among members of a group may be reduced or eliminated altogether. Individuals can interact as a group over telecommunication links, thus avoiding the need to meet in the same physical space. Another overall generalization linked to the previous one is that the new technologies present many opportunities for individuals to easily share information and to exchange messages about that information. A popular example is the new "integrated office," in which individuals working in an organization have common access to centralized information and messaging systems regardless of their spatial location.

In the largest view, we can examine the social effects of new technologies on public or mass communication. For example, technological advances have greatly increased the availability and variety of mass media forms in the last half-century. The costs of publishing have been substantially reduced by such innovations as the offset press, improvements in the typesetting machine, and of course, the widespread adoption of computer editing and typesetting equipment of contemporary times. Radio's penetration in societies was vastly increased by the invention of the transistor in the late 1940s and the manufacture of inexpensive, palm-sized transistor radios in the 1950s and '60s. The mass manufacture of television sets and the recognition by most governments of the world of television's power in society has led to rapid penetration of television in any society where it is sanctioned by government. The development of sophisticated land transmission systems (microwave and television cable) coupled with the development of the communication satellite is rapidly bringing broadcast services to nearly every square inch of the earth's surface. The earlier described convergence of computing and telecommunications technologies may bring the greatest advance to date in the development of communication networks underlying large social structures. There is a convergence of all new media, from computers through mass media, that is the basis for new communication services. This trend, which we shall see grow in the future, will create new needs for social research.

SUMMARY

Advances in communication technology such as teleconferencing, communication satellites, computers, cable, and videocassettes are changing communication behaviors. These technologies are making the classical distinctions between mass or mediated communication and direct, face-to-face communication less and less clear.

The new technologies have created new ways of moving signals, new methods of storing information, and new methods of interacting with messages. Most significant is that these technologies are converging to create new channels of intelligent communication. Theories and research methods to deal with these advances are only now beginning to emerge.

In the field of interactive technology, the newest advances are represented by text-based services, teleconferencing, and innovations in phone systems. In television, the spread of cable and videocassettes has changed both methods of distribution information and the media content consumed. Satellite distribution of information has both national and global impact. Early social experiments in satellite distribution of information have set the stage for advances in this field.

All of these technologies represent challenges to apply existing theory, develop new theory, and conduct research to observe their effects.

REVIEW AND DISCUSSION QUESTIONS

1. To what extent does the use of a mechanical channel for person-to-person communication (telephone, computer network, teleconference) require changes in interaction style as compared to face-to-face encounters? What influence do these changes have on the interactions and their content?

2. It has been observed that such communication media as radio and TV have changed the way people interact socially, even when they are not using the media (for example, the theory that family members talk less because of TV). To what extent do changes in technology really change the interaction patterns of society? What changes in social interaction patterns might result from the technological advances described in this chapter if these advances come into widespread use?

3. One simple definition of "artificial intelligence" has been that a person interacting with such an intelligent communication system cannot tell the difference between that interaction and one with a human being. What differentiates interaction between two people and interaction between a person and a machine? What principles of human communication have not yet been simulated on machines? What are the prospects for doing so?

4. The increasing use of cable, videocassette, and satellite technology to spread information will obviously give people more access to information, but that information itself is frequently in traditional forms. Will the increasing availability of information in these new channels change the way information is organized and presented?

REFERENCES

Agostino, D. (1980). Cable television's impact on the audience of public television. *Journal of Broadcasting, 24*(3), 347–365.

Becker, L., Dunwoody, S., & Rafaeli, S. (1983). Cable's impact on use of other news media. *Journal of Broadcasting, 27*(2), 127–140.

Dozier, D. M., & Ledingham, J. A. (1982, May). Perceived attributes of interactive cable services among potential adopters. Paper presented at the annual meeting of the International Communication Association, Boston.

Dutton, W. H., Fulk, J., & Steinfield, C. (1982). Utilization of video conferencing. *Telecommunications Policy, 6*(3), 164–178.

Heeter, C., D'Alessio, D., & Greenberg, B. (1983, May). Cableviewing. Paper presented at the annual meeting of the International Communication Association, Dallas.

Hiemstra, G. (1982). Teleconferencing, concern for face, and organizational culture. In M. Burgoon (Ed.), *Communication Yearbook 6* (pp. 874–904). Beverly Hills: Sage.

Hill, D., & Dyer, J. (1981). Extent of diversion to newscasts from distant stations by cable viewers. *Journalism Quarterly, 58*(4), 552–555.

Hiltz, S. R. (1978). Controlled experiments with computerized conferencing: Results of a pilot study. *Bulletin of the American Society for Information Science, 4,* 11–12.

Hiltz, S. R., & Turoff, M. (1978). *The network nation: Human communication via computer.* Reading, MA: Addison-Wesley.

Hudson, H. E. (1984). *When telephones reach the village: The role of telecommunications in rural development.* Norwood, NJ: Ablex.

Hudson, H. E. (Ed.). (1985). *New directions in satellite communications: Challenges for North and South.* Norwood, MA: Artech.

Kaplan, S. (1978). The impact of cable television services on the use of competing media. *Journal of Broadcasting, 22*(2), 155–166.

Keller, S. (1976). The telephone in new (and old) communities. In I. Pool (Ed.), *The social impact of the telephone* (pp. 281–298). Cambridge, MA: MIT Press.

Krugman, D., & Eckrich, D. (1982). Differences in cable and pay cable audiences. *Journal of Advertising Research, 22*(4), 23–30.

Levy, M. R., & Windahl, S. (1984). Audience activity and gratifications: A conceptual clarification and exploration. *Communication Research, 11,* 51–78.

Lum, P. (1984). Telephone use by senior citizens: Community snapshot. Unpublished manuscript, Annenberg School of Communications, University of Southern California, Los Angeles.

McDermott, S., & Medhurst, M. J. (1984, May). Reasons for subscribing to cable television. Paper presented at the annual meeting of the International Communication Association, San Francisco.

Opinion Research Corporation. (1983). *Segmentation study of the urban/suburban cable television market.* Princeton, NJ: Opinion Research Corporation.

Palmgreen, P. (1984). The uses and gratifications approach: A theoretical perspective. In R. N. Bostrom (Ed.), *Communication Yearbook 8* (pp. 20–55). Beverly Hills: Sage.

Phillips, A. F. (1983). Computer conferences: Success or failure? In R. N. Bostrom (Ed.), *Communication Yearbook 7* (pp. 837–856). Beverly Hills: Sage.

Phillips, A. F., Lum, P., & Lawrence, D. (1983, March). An ethnographic study of telephone use. Paper presented at the fifth annual Conference on Culture and Communication, Philadelphia.

Porat, M. (1977). *The information economy: Definition and measurement.* Washington, DC: U.S. Government Printing Office.

Rice, R. E. (1980). The impacts of computer-mediated organizational and interpersonal communication. *Annual Review of Information Science and Technology, 15,* 221–249.

Robinson, J. (1981). Television and leisure time: A new scenario. *Journal of Communication, 31*(1), 120–130.

Rogers, E. M. (1983). *Diffusion of innovation.* New York: Free Press.

Rothe, E. M., Harvey, M. G., & Michael, G. C. (1983). The impact of cable television on subscriber and nonsubscriber behavior. *Journal of Advertising Research, 23*(4), 15–24.

Shaver, T. L. (1983). The uses of cable TV. Unpublished master's thesis, University of Kentucky, Lexington.

Short, J., Williams, E., & Christie, B. (1976). *The social psychology of telecommunications.* New York: Wiley.

Sparkes, V. (1983). Public perception of and reaction to multichannel cable television service. *Journal of Broadcasting, 27*(2), 1963–1975.

Steinfield, C. S. (1983). Communicating via electronic mail: Patterns and predictions of use in organizations. Unpublished doctoral dissertation, Annenberg School of Communications, University of Southern California, Los Angeles.

Waterman, D. (1984, April). The prerecorded home video and the distribution of theatrical feature films. Paper presented at the Arden House Conference of Rivalry Among Video Media, Harriman, NY.

Webster, J. (1984). Cable television's impact on audience for local news. *Journalism Quarterly, 61*(2), 419–421.

Williams, F. (1986). *Technology and communication behavior.* Belmont, CA: Wadsworth.

Williams, F., & Dordick, H. S. (1985). Social research and the telephone. Unpublished manuscript, Annenberg School of Communications, University of Southern California, Los Angeles.

Wurtzel, A. H., & Turner, C. (1977). What missing the telephone means. *Journal of Communication, 27,* 48–57.

PART TWO

Contexts of Communication

Over time, every science stakes its claim on a particular domain of study. Eventually, it will subdivide itself, establish internal boundaries, and develop a relatively standard map of its territory. Like the invisible lines that define city limits and state borders, the boundaries around various specializations within a given discipline are somewhat arbitrary and often difficult to locate precisely. They are usually established by first possession, fierce debate, and, ultimately, conventional use. The science of communication is typical in these regards. Collectively, the substantive areas of study examined in Part Two represent an early, now conventional map of the discipline.

A single map, of course, never tells the whole story. Depending on its specific purpose, it will accentuate certain features of the terrain, omitting other details. Part Two calls particular attention to five contexts in which communication can occur; they are typically labeled *interpersonal, small group, organizational, mass,* and *intercultural communication.* These specializations are called *contexts of communication* because their subject matters are defined and differentiated largely on the basis of contextual (or situational) variables. Conventional variables of this type, such as the number of participants in a communicative event and their physical proximity, are discussed in Chapter 5.

Since their lines of demarcation are not hard and fast, the five types of communication included in Part Two often occur simultaneously. Picture these types as represented by a series of progressively larger concentric circles. That is, each successive type (or context), from interpersonal to intercultural communication, can be conceptualized as involving a larger circle of communicators, within a larger space, than the preceding type. Communication in small groups, for example, typically involves more participants in a larger spatial arrangement than interpersonal communication; in turn, organizational contexts ordinarily exceed the two preceding types in space and numbers.

In addition, our circular model indicates that the five contexts of interest are, properly understood, cumulative in nature. Each succeeding context, represented by a larger outer circle, includes the preceding context(s), represented by one or more inner circles. Thus the model suggests, for example, that although organizational communication focuses on properties and processes unique to organizations, interpersonal and small group events are present and do contribute to the organizational operation as a whole. Specific reference to these lower-level influences in organizations is made in Chapter 7. However, neither the ascending order of their presentation in Part Two nor the cumulative nature of these contexts should be interpreted as an assignment of rank or importance. Each of the five areas of study represents a body of knowledge in its own right; each represents an alternate focus, directing our attention to different features of essentially the same phenomenon: human communication.

Gerald Miller introduces perhaps the most common, pervasive form of interaction in Chapter 5, "Interpersonal Communication." Unlike many of his colleagues, Miller adopts a single theoretical perspective as a basis for analyzing interpersonal events and then presses his viewpoint to its logical and practical limits. A unique feature of this article is its thorough explication of the *developmental approach*. In contrast to the situational view (emphasizing external characteristics of the situation), which draws no interpersonal distinction between, for example, casual friends and intimate lovers, the developmental view specifies qualitative changes

that commonly occur within such relationships over time.

Along with its strong theoretical roots, Miller's treatise is intensely practical. With or without academic interests in this area, the reader will gain substantial insight into his or her own most valuable links with other human beings, such as marital, parent-child, social, and professional relationships. Supported by solid research (unlike much of the popular folklore peddled at corner drugstores), Miller's essay addresses the critical questions we commonly ask. Why do people pursue certain relational options and avoid others? How do healthy interpersonal relationships develop, and how is their vitality maintained? Which communication strategies are likely to be most effective in interpersonal contexts? How can decaying relationships be dissolved with minimal pain and punishment? Established principles, as opposed to transparent advice, characterize Miller's discussion of these and other basic issues.

Among the social sciences, psychology in particular has been keenly interested in group behavior since the first quarter of this century. The seminal influence of the field of psychology on the study of small groups is represented in Chapter 6, "Group Dynamics and Communication," by coauthor Marvin Shaw. More recently, relying on social-psychological foundations, scholars in the communication discipline have focused on the distinctive role of communication in small group processes. Coauthor Dennis Gouran brings the latter interest to bear on this essay.

Because an enormous body of relevant literature is available on group dynamics, the emphasis in Chapter 6 is on information gleaned from empirical studies spanning nearly 50 years of research. Even so, the review is necessarily representative, rather than exhaustive. Moreover, it is not devoid of theory; many variables that influence small group behavior are examined, not as isolated phenomena, but as integral and interrelated components of a complex dynamic process. With particular attention to communicative issues, Shaw and Gouran guide us through the activities of small groups, underscoring basic factors that influence their formation, evolution, structure, leadership, performance, and, ultimately, their achievements.

In Chapter 7, "Organizational Communication," Fredric Jablin introduces the reader to one of the most rapidly expanding contexts of communication research and formal instruction. Following a brief discussion of the nature of organizational communication, the essay addresses two major topics of interest that epitomize the central concerns of this text, theory development and the results of empirical research. Adopting a historical perspective, the author first traces the evolution of organizational theory (as related to communication in organizations) from its classical roots, through humanistic advances and the development of a general systems approach, to its current accent on contingency theory.

In a parallel chronological pattern, Jablin then classifies the major research questions addressed and representative studies designed to address them, in the five decades from the 1940s to the 1980s. The latter segment of the survey, "The Early 1980s and Beyond," is a solid review of up-to-the-minute trends, as well as a perceptive look at what lies ahead, in organizational communication research. Jablin's conclusion gives a straightforward assessment of what has and has not been accomplished in 50 years of organizational research; he also explains why certain long-standing questions of import to scholars and practitioners alike remain largely unanswered.

The all-pervasive impact of mass communication on modern life is reviewed by Bradley Greenberg. Most readers of Chapter 8 will acknowledge their keen interest in mass media; few are likely to realize how much time they commit to media activities every day, according to national averages. Greenberg offers several plausible reasons for our preoccupation with the media and explains why it is practically impossible to escape their influence. Next, we learn how the primary media—radio, television and newspa-

pers—permeate virtually every nook and cranny of our society as a function of their organization and structure.

The larger contribution of this essay, however, is its digest of current research on a series of pragmatic issues for both producers and consumers of the media. How is information about news events gathered, then selectively disseminated to the public? How are social perceptions and expectations (for example, regarding the role of women in society) influenced by media entertainment? Which environmental variables contribute to social learning outcomes from television viewing? How much sexual content actually appears on TV; does it really matter in terms of impact on the viewer? And finally, what motives do consumers report for their extensive use of the mass media?

Supplementing the broad futuristic discussion of new technologies in Chapter 4, Greenberg concludes his essay by focusing on new trends in the three traditional media. He expects mass communications to become increasingly non-mass in nature, as individual consumers assume an even more active-interactive role in determining what media services will be offered and in conducting a variety of daily activities from in-home communication centers.

The final selection in Part Two, "Intercultural Communication," addresses perhaps the most recent and least familiar context of inquiry represented in this volume. According to author Nobleza Asuncion-Lande, although people have been practicing cross-cultural interaction for centuries, serious academic interest in this area emerged largely as a function of new challenges confronting the world community during the last two decades. One such global challenge is a frantic human race scrambling to survive impending nuclear destruction. Even as I write, international news services are monitoring diplomatic movements, moment by moment, toward a superpower summit to help resolve the accelerating arms race controversy—perhaps the ultimate exercise in intercultural communication.

Choosing not to belabor the obvious, Asuncion-Lande concentrates initially on *what* we study in cross-cultural contexts, rather than *why* we study it. She identifies the conceptual foundations of intercultural communication inquiry and defines its subject matter, drawing on principles of communication explicated in preceding chapters. This is necessarily the case because, as noted earlier, the series of contexts presented in Part Two is cumulative in nature. On this account, intercultural communication may and often does involve, for example, an even more complex form of interpersonal communication than one ordinarily encounters within his or her own culture.

Not surprisingly, then, the author's discussion of key variables influencing the success or failure of cross-cultural exchanges also extends to other segments of this text, including issues of language and nonverbal codes. Moreover, the complexity of intercultural communication and its relatively brief history as a scientific endeavor make the area especially difficult to research. Accordingly, Asuncion-Lande devotes a major portion of her essay to the current state of theory and methodological developments, as well as unanswered questions of import, bearing on intercultural communication inquiry. To meet the practical needs of students (and instructors), she also provides a useful review of skill-oriented techniques and current approaches to more formal cross-cultural instruction.

5

Interpersonal Communication

Gerald R. Miller
Michigan State University

Gerald R. Miller is Distinguished Professor and Head of the Department of Communication at Michigan State University. He holds B.A. and M.A. degrees in political science as well as a Ph.D. degree in communication, all from the University of Iowa. His research and teaching interests include communication theory, interpersonal communication, persuasion, and communication in legal settings. Dr. Miller has authored or edited nine books and written numerous chapters as well as journal articles in communication, psychology, and law. He was the first editor of the journal Human Communication Research *and is a former editor of* Communication Monographs. *He is also a past president of the International Communication Association. Additional honors include: four-time recipient of the Speech Communication Association's Golden Anniversary Award for Outstanding Scholarship, designation as a Fellow of the International Communication Association and the American Psychological Association, the Distinguished Faculty Award and* Centennial Review *lectureship from Michigan State University.*

LEARNING OBJECTIVES

After studying this chapter you should be able to:

- Define interpersonal communication from several perspectives.
- Distinguish between interpersonal communication and interpersonal relationship development.
- Discuss three basic prerequisites or beginning steps in relationship development.

91

- Explain the importance of uncertainty reduction in relationship development.
- Describe three basic strategies for eliciting information in a developing relationship.
- Interpret the role of self-disclosure in developing interpersonal relationships.
- Define empathy in the context of interpersonal communication.
- Understand the role of interpersonal communication in the process of mutually defining a relationship.
- Distinguish between the contributions of complementarity and similarity to relational development.
- Discuss the role of interpersonal communication in relational deescalation.

If yours is a typical life, much of it will be spent communicating with others in informal settings. During your preschool years, most of your time was probably devoted to message exchanges with your immediate family—indeed, a great deal of your communication during this period centered on learning the rudimentary verbal and nonverbal vocabulary of communication. After you began school, you developed friendships with classmates, and you continued to polish your communicative skills, delving into increasingly complex aspects of syntax and grammar. As you moved into young adulthood, intimate, romantic relationships assumed greater significance. For some of you, such a relationship may have already culminated in marriage and assuming the role of wife or husband; for others, this step may still await you. In either event, you are keenly aware of the time your romantic partner and you spend communicating about immediate relational outcomes and long-term relational goals. Those of you who elect to have children will inherit the same communicative roles your parents played with you. At the same time, as you pass from young adulthood through middle age and on to retirement, most of you will be exchanging innumerable messages with co-workers in your chosen profession or vocation. Finally, if you are fortunate in choosing close friends and marital partners and if your choices receive the gifts of good health and long life, you will spend your postretirement years conversing with these valued intimates.

This brief, hypothetical journey through your life seeks to underscore the personal and social significance of interpersonal communication. Consider again the amount of time you have spent and will spend communicating with one person or more in informal settings. Moreover, reflect for a moment on how important some of the relationships mentioned in the preceding paragraph are to you: Marital relationships, parent-child bondings, and close friendships are the most vital links with other human beings most persons ever experience. Thus interpersonal communication is not just one of our most frequent social activities, it is also a principal ingredient of those few key relationships that largely determine our perceptions of the quality of our lives.

The vital significance of interpersonal communication has not escaped the eye of the communication scientist, the student of other social sciences such as psychology or sociology, the helping professional in areas such as clinical psychology or marriage counseling, or the popular writer who cautions us about our "intimate enemies" (Bach & Wyden, 1968), the "games" people play (Berne, 1964), and the meanings conveyed by our "body language" (Fast, 1971). As this chapter reveals, a good deal of theoretical speculation and a substantial body of research have addressed problems relating to interpersonal communication. These insights and findings should enhance your understanding of interpersonal communication and enable you to practice it more effectively. Before proceeding further, however, it is necessary to arrive at a definition of the term *interpersonal communication,* in order to differentiate it from the other kinds of communication discussed in this volume.

SOME DEFINING CHARACTERISTICS OF THE TERM *INTERPERSONAL COMMUNICATION*

Situational Characteristics

One way of defining interpersonal communication is from a *situational perspective* (Miller, 1978), which holds that interpersonal communication can be distinguished from other kinds of communication by specifying the social milieu in which interpersonal messages are exchanged. Until relatively recently, most theorizing and research dealing with interpersonal communication have been grounded in a situational perspective.

Probably the most crucial situational determinant of interpersonal communication is the number of communicators involved. As Figure 5.1 reveals, the entire communicative "pie," ranging from intrapersonal to mass communication, can

be carved up in terms of a set of situational measures. Of the four measures found in Figure 5.1, it is no accident that *number of communicators* is listed first, since, to a large extent, this characteristic determines the applicability of the other three measures. Thus if a communicator wishes to transmit messages to millions of people, as is true with mass media such as television, it stands to reason that physical proximity is limited, available sensory channels are reduced (for example, of the five senses, television relies only on seeing and hearing), and feedback from message receivers is often delayed (for example, letters to newspaper editors received and printed days or weeks after the initial message) and/or indirect (such as television ratings that tell the communicator only approximately how many viewers were exposed to the program and provide no information about what portions of the program were attended to or how viewers interpreted and responded to those portions). By contrast, a conversation between two friends permits close physical prox-

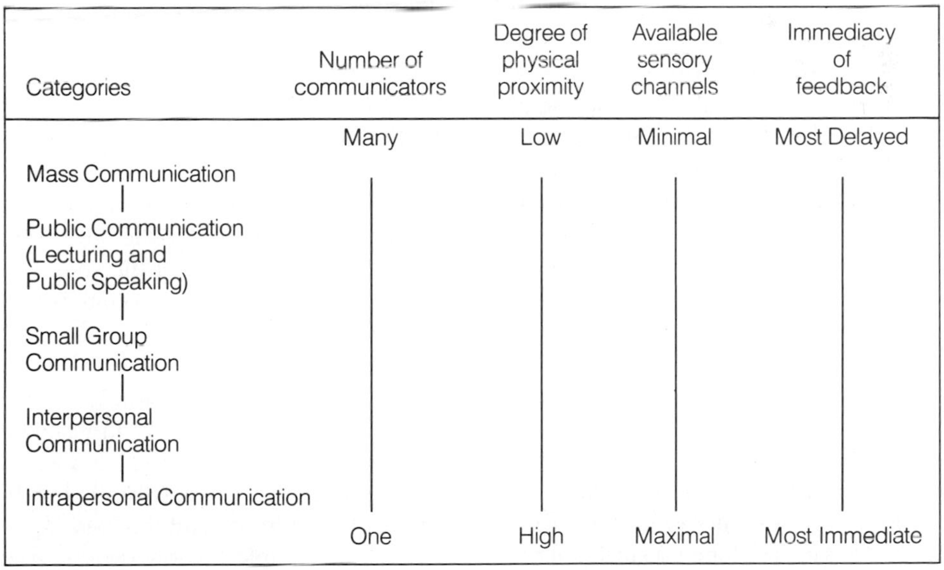

Categories	Number of communicators	Degree of physical proximity	Available sensory channels	Immediacy of feedback
	Many	Low	Minimal	Most Delayed
Mass Communication | Public Communication (Lecturing and Public Speaking) | Small Group Communication | Interpersonal Communication | Intrapersonal Communication				
	One	High	Maximal	Most Immediate

Figure 5.1 A set of categories frequently employed in the situational approach to distinguishing interpersonal communication.
Source: Miller, 1978, p. 165.

imity, allows the conversants to employ all or most of the five sensory channels, and yields immediate feedback for both communicators.

Clearly, an element of ambiguity is associated with the number-of-communicators measure, for only the most rigid, dogmatic individual would demand that an advocate of the situational perspective specify the precise number of communicators who must be participating before a transaction ceases to be interpersonal and becomes instead impersonal, or noninterpersonal. A discussion involving a group of ten friends or acquaintances is somehow "more interpersonal" than a network television program beamed to millions of viewers; but at the same time, it is somehow "less interpersonal" than a conversation between two friends. Thus a situational perspective places communicative relationships on a continuum ranging from very interpersonal to very impersonal, rather than providing two mutually exclusive, distinct categories: interpersonal versus impersonal communication.

But if we were to argue that the number of communicators is irrelevant, *interpersonal communication* would be in danger of becoming synonymous with *communication,* in which case the modifier *interpersonal* would serve no useful defining function. Moreover, in terms of how people use language in everyday discourse, it would seem odd to talk about network newscasters communicating interpersonally with all their viewers or to characterize a speech by a government leader broadcast to the entire populace of a country as an instance of interpersonal communication. Indeed, most of the research commonly labeled "interpersonal communication research" by communication scholars deals with *dyadic* exchanges: communication between two persons.

Though indispensable when attempting to make sense of the term *interpersonal communication,* situational criteria alone are inadequate; as argued earlier, such measures are necessary but not sufficient ingredients of an optimally useful definition. To understand why, consider two problems arising from sole reliance on a situational definition of interpersonal communication.

The first problem may be called the *one-among-many situation,* in which a communicator, while ostensibly communicating with a large audience, simultaneously transmits messages intended for only a small subset of that audience—in some cases, just one or two persons. Television comedienne Carol Burnett always reached up and tugged her ear while saying good night to her viewing audience. This nonverbal message communicated a special "good night" to certain family members, symbolizing her love and affection for them. A message apparently directed at an audience of hundreds may be laced with numerous allusions and references intended for but a single audience member. Some years ago, a prominent communication educator was a candidate for a major administrative position at a state university. At a critical point in the selection process, this person presented a speech dealing with his philosophy of education to a large group of colleagues attending an international conference on communication. Also present in the audience was the chairperson of the committee charged with recommending a candidate for the administrative post. Following the speech, several people who knew of the chairperson's presence opined that the speech, though undoubtedly relevant to all audience members, was primarily aimed at this individual and was intended to enhance the speaker's candidacy for the administrative post. Although it is hard to assess the precise impact of the speech on the selection process, it is worth noting that the speaker got the job.

Total reliance on a situational perspective would prompt the conclusion that neither of the above examples qualifies as an instance of interpersonal communication, since a large number of communicators are apparently involved in the transaction. More careful analysis suggests, however, that complex subnetworks exist within the overall social milieu of the communicative transaction. Furthermore, as the example of the communication educator emphasizes, many communicators often may be unaware of the existence of these subnetworks and may remain blissfully ignorant of the fact that communication is occurring at more than one level. Indeed, to anticipate a concept discussed below, these listeners usually lack knowledge of the *rules* guiding subnetwork transactions; for example, someone viewing the Carol Burnett program for the first time would have been likely to interpret her ear tugging as a nervous gesture rather than a meaningful message to her relatives. Even a regular viewer who had figured out that the ear tugging meant something was destined to remain ignorant of what it meant unless provided with information by Burnett herself or by another party who was privy to the rule.

Skeptics still may contend that the one-among-many situation is not an indictment of the situational perspective per se, but rather a testimony to the care that must be exercised when analyzing complex communicative exchanges. As will become clear later, certain elements of the subnetwork situations described above—for example, the special meaning rules existing between Carol Burnett and her relatives—transcend a situational definition of interpersonal communication and render it inadequate. Nevertheless, a second problem constitutes a more convincing indictment of sole recourse to situational defining criteria: the *intimacy-transcends-distance phenomenon.*

To illustrate the thrust of this problem, consider again the Carol Burnett example. In the circumstances described, her relatives were not in close physical contact with her; on the contrary, they were far from her television studio location. Since this situation fails to meet the criterion of close physical proximity, are we to conclude that Burnett was communicating impersonally with her relatives? Such a conclusion seems not only arbitrary but also intuitively wrongheaded, for its acceptance implies that only when two close friends or romantic partners exchange messages in face-to-face surroundings are they communicating interpersonally. Moreover, when the communicators are eyeball to eyeball, a greeting exchange between two strangers and a mutual pledge of undying devotion by two lovers are,

from a strictly situational perspective, equally interpersonal transactions. The duration or quality of a relationship has no bearing on its interpersonalness; situational characteristics alone affect the definitional judgment.

Obviously, this position seems seriously wanting. In addition to situational factors, a useful definition of interpersonal communication must also take into account certain developmental processes associated with the relationship; it must consider how the communicators relate to and "see" each other and how they plan and regulate their communicative exchanges. A sketch of this developmental perspective will reveal several qualitative factors that bear on the interpersonalness of the relationship and contribute to an adequate definition of the term *interpersonal communication.*

Developmental Characteristics

A *developmental perspective* assumes that initial messages between strangers are, of necessity, impersonal. When individuals meet and communicate with each other for the first time, they are relating primarily as social role occupants (Peters, 1974), not as individuals. Consequently, little differentiation occurs; the communicators perceive each other merely as a member of a particular social or cultural group and attribute traits and characteristics to each other rightly or wrongly perceived to be held in common by all members of these groups. For example, you have now met the authors of this book through the pages of their chapters, so you are likely to think of and relate to them as members of some professional groups such as "university professors" or "authors of communication textbooks," despite the fact that they differ in many ways. Conversely, some authors have adopted the strategy of addressing readers by the pronoun *you,* but they do not possess information that permits them to transform that plural, collective *you* to the singular, unique *you.* Instead, *you* are university students who are either voluntary or captive readers of this chapter, and their mental picture of *you* is restricted to traits and characteristics they perceive to be shared by most university students.

Once the initial communicative exchanges have occurred, several outcomes are possible. The communicators may decide, either individually or mutually, to quickly end the relationship. Though figures on how many potential dating relationships end after the first date are not readily available, the percentage is probably substantial. Similarly, when 30 applicants interview for a job, 29 are destined to have little or no further relationship with the employer. Many potential relationships just never get off the ground.

But suppose the relationship does continue, either because the participants choose to continue it or because they are cast into a situation that forces them to—for example, convicts seldom have a choice about their cellmates, and for that matter, university students frequently have little voice in the assignment of their dormitory roommates. In some cases, the participants may continue the relationship for a long time without getting to "know" each other as individuals; that is, they may establish and maintain a relatively impersonal communicative relationship. Almost everyone has a number of these relationships with casual acquaintances. We meet and greet the other person, exchange conversation about the weather, the latest international crisis, or last weekend's football scores, and go on our way. These pleasant interludes may continue for months or years without yielding much personal knowledge about the other, or without what Altman and Taylor (1973) label as *social penetration* taking place.

If the parties decide to continue the relationship, if they are strongly motivated to expend the effort, and if their interpersonal skills permit, their relationship may undergo certain qualitative changes. When these changes do occur, the communicative relationship becomes increasingly interpersonal. Like the situational perspective, the developmental perspective conceives of relationships as varying on a continuum from very interpersonal to very impersonal, but unlike

the situational viewpoint, the developmental perspective sees these variations as resulting from certain qualitative characteristics of the relationship, not from the situational context in which communication occurs. Figure 5.2 depicts several possible paths a relationship may follow, including the relatively impersonal path discussed earlier.

What are some of the qualitative changes that may occur, and how do these changes affect the relationship? The second question can be answered more succinctly than the first: The changes of greatest import to a developmental perspective of interpersonal communication are those producing a greater degree of differentiation in the relationship. They are changes that cause the communicators to relate to each other more as individuals than as undifferentiated role occupants or cultural entities. Changes in the quality of communicative transactions are both a

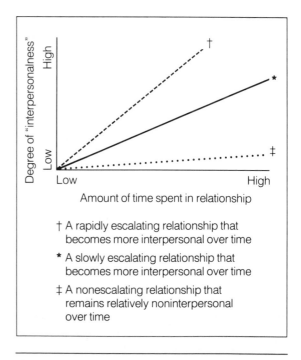

Figure 5.2 Continuum of relational development showing several possible alternatives.
Source: Miller, 1978, p. 168.

cause and an effect of this relational transformation. Hence, the first question raised at the beginning of this paragraph can be answered by examining several possible changes in greater detail, particularly changes that are tied to the communicative behaviors of relational partners.

Changes in the Type of Information Used for Making Predictions about Message Outcomes   One of the most frequently cited (Andersen, 1982) qualitative changes that may occur as a relationship progresses was first suggested by Miller (1975), and was later extended in collaboration with two colleagues (Miller & Steinberg, 1975; Miller & Sunnafrank, 1982). This kind of change rests on the assumption that communication is a prediction-making activity: When people communicate with others, they make predictions about the probable outcomes, or consequences, of differing message strategies, or alternative message selections. In instances involving very significant objectives, such as a job interview, an oral examination, or a marriage proposal, the prediction-making process is highly cognitive and is often accompanied by considerable overt rehearsal; the communicator actually inventories available alternative messages and anticipates probable responses to each. In most routine exchanges, however, prediction making occurs at a low level of consciousness; thus it is closely akin to perception or to what some writers have termed "mindlessness" (Berger & Douglas, 1982; Langer, 1978).

Nevertheless, even in highly scripted exchanges (Ableson, 1976)—routinized, habitual activities such as greeting and leave-taking—when we are not aware of our predictions, we still make them implicitly. Furthermore, we are made aware of our implicit predictions once they are disconfirmed. Thus a casual "Hello, how are you?" followed by "Fine, thanks, and yourself?" masks or minimizes the role of prediction in communication, but the same greeting followed by "None of your damn business!" awakens the greeting initiator to his or her response expectations, causing considerable consternation or even

prompting a defensive reaction such as "Well, excuse me!" uttered in a sarcastic tone.

Unless we assume that prediction making is a random activity (a virtual contradiction in terms), it follows that communicators must base predictions on some kind of information. We contend that this information takes one of three broad forms and, even more important, that a communicator's relative reliance on each of the three forms determines the relative interpersonalness of the relationship (Miller, 1975; Miller & Steinberg, 1975; Miller & Sunnafrank, 1982).

Cultural information is a minimum prerequisite for prediction making; indeed, in the absence of such information, communication becomes a random, trial-and-error process. People sometimes speculate about how they would communicate with creatures from other planets; in the movie *E.T.,* the earthlings spend considerable time experimenting with ways of communicating with their extraterrestrial visitor. Cultural information pertains to a person's native language, myths and folklore, societal norms, and prevailing ideology. For example, knowledge about general greeting exchanges qualifies as cultural information, since every culture has a reasonably standardized set of verbal and nonverbal messages used to acknowledge awareness of another's presence. These messages vary between cultures (Hall, 1959) and may also change over time within a particular culture. At one time, it was considered desirable among members of the white, middle-class culture of the United States for a gentleman to tip his hat when greeting a lady. A sharp reduction in the number of male hat wearers, the quest for women's equality, and various other factors have rendered male hat tipping a quaint, albeit acceptable, greeting custom.

The numerous modifiers used in the preceding paragraph to describe one cultural group suggest, however, that specifying the exact boundaries of a culture is often difficult to do. The vast majority of politically defined nations are culturally diverse, numbering within their borders a variety of cultures, each distinguished by its own language, heritage, norms, and ideology.

Knowledge about these factors assists a communicator in the prediction-making process.

Helpful as it is in prediction making, cultural information embraces a limited number of situations. *Sociological information* adds to the communicator's predictive power. This information pertains to people's *membership groups* and to the *reference groups* they value (positive reference groups) or renounce (negative reference groups). Membership in some groups is involuntary and all but inevitable; for example, genetic laws determine whether a person is a member of the sociological group labeled *men* or *women,* and stages in the aging cycle consign people to groups such as *teenagers* and *senior citizens.* Membership in other groups is thought to be more under the individual's control; for example, people supposedly choose to be Democrats or Republicans, Catholics or Presbyterians, and married or single. The word *supposedly* in the preceding sentence reminds us that the concept of freedom of choice varies itself from one culture to another, depending on the prevailing ideology. Most Western democracies embrace this concept as a central ideological tenet; by contrast, the ideological posture of most communist states is decidedly more deterministic.

Membership groups and reference groups are not always synonymous; indeed, many people may view some of their own membership groups negatively and yearn to achieve membership in other, positively valued groups. The notion of upward mobility, commonly viewed as a strong motivating force in so-called modern societies, posits that people aspire to move into more prestigious, higher-status social and economic membership groups. Knowledge about a person's negative reference groups also increases predictive power, since the communicator may presume that the person will respond negatively to messages supporting the beliefs, attitudes, and values of these groups and will react favorably to communications rejecting their views.

Sociological information comes into play in a wide variety of communicative situations. In the classroom and on the campus, partners in the educational process relate to each other as teachers and students; lawyers and doctors see clients, who in turn respond on the basis of their knowledge about occupants of these professional roles; salespeople gear their sales pitches to cultural and sociological generalizations about an amorphous group called consumers; even some married couples communicate as husbands and wives.

Prediction making grounded in cultural and sociological information is frequent, particularly during initial stages of a relationship. This process, illustrated in Table 5.1, results in very little differentiation, since the predictive target is viewed as a cultural entity or a role occupant, rather than an individual. The prediction maker looks for sameness among other communicators and necessarily ignores the characteristics that distinguish people and events.

An important consequence of prediction making based on cultural and/or sociological information is the inevitability of predictive error. Frequency or magnitude of error, of course, depends on the relative accuracy of the cultural and/or sociological generalizations used in arriving at predictions. At best, cultural and sociological generalizations seldom, if ever, apply to all members of the particular group; at worst, they are grossly inaccurate and therefore apply to few members of the relevant group. Even if most members of the white, middle-class, United States culture are aggressive and competitive, Jones may be retiring and cooperative; even if most professors are of liberal or radical political persuasion, Jones may be a conservative. Furthermore, note in Table 5.1 that cultural and sociological generalizations sometimes conflict: the "cultural Jones" is likely to think practically and pragmatically, but the "sociological Jones" is likely to think theoretically and abstractly.

To minimize individual error, communicators must rely on a third kind of information for predicting message outcomes. *Psychological information* enables communicators to distinguish an individual from other members of his or her cultural and sociological groups. Such information

Table 5.1 An Example of Communicative Prediction Making Based on Cultural and Sociological Information

Cultural Generalizations	Sociological Generalizations
Members of white, middle-class, U.S. culture are:	Professors are:
aggressive and competitive	politically liberal or radical
economically motivated	socially unskilled
practical and pragmatic	theoretical and abstract
individualistic	irreligious
Specific Instance	*Specific Instance*
Jones is a member of white, middle-class, U.S. culture	Jones is a professor
Specific Predictions	*Specific Predictions*
Jones is:	Jones is:
aggressive and competitive	politically liberal or radical
economically motivated	socially unskilled
practical and pragmatic	theoretical and abstract
individualistic	irreligious

focuses on differences instead of similarities: The relevant question becomes "How is Jones different from other professors?" rather than "How is Jones similar to other professors?" In principle, error could be eliminated entirely by relying exclusively on psychological information; practically, though, it is doubtful that anyone could gather enough psychological information about another to achieve predictive perfection.

During the initial stages of a relationship, communicators seldom have much psychological information about each other. But if the relationship continues, the communicators may obtain ever larger stores of psychological information (though as emphasized earlier, such increases in knowledge are not inevitable). As communicators reduce their use of cultural and sociological information and increase their use of psychological information, the relationship will become more interpersonal. The communicators come to relate to each other as differentiated individuals, rather than as undifferentiated cultural entities or role occupants.

It should be apparent how this qualitative change fits a developmental view of interpersonal communication. Gathering psychological information is often difficult and tedious. Moreover, it requires persons to spend time communicating with each other. Although people vary in ability to amass psychological information, even exceptionally skilled communicators must expend some time and effort to get to know their relational partners as individuals.

Changes in the Level of "Knowing" the Other Relational Participants In everyday discourse, people commonly assert that they "know" someone else. Still, the assertion "I know

Jane Smith" means various things depending on the nature of the relationship between Jane Smith and the party making the assertion. Differing levels of knowing another imply differing amounts and types of information about the other; we know some people better than others. As a relationship progresses, participants may come to know each other more intimately, though such increased intimacy need not necessarily occur. If relational progress is marked by a qualitative change in levels of knowing other relational participants, the relationship becomes more interpersonal (Berger, Gardner, Parks, Schulman, & Miller, 1976; Miller, 1980).

Superficial impersonal relationships are marked by *descriptive level* knowledge about others. To know someone descriptively is merely to know his or her outward physical characteristics sufficiently to discriminate him from other persons. Most of us have nodding acquaintanceships with persons we know only at the descriptive level: They may ride the same bus to work, frequent the same building on campus, or stop at the same bar for a drink. Sometimes we are even ignorant of their names, responding "Oh, that's the fellow who rides the same bus I take every morning" when another party asks about the person's identity. Loyal sports fans know all the members of their favorite teams at the descriptive level, familiarizing themselves with each player's number, position on the field or court, and unique style of movement and play. Acquiring descriptive-level knowledge is usually relatively simple, with one or two encounters serving to fix the other's physical characteristics in our minds.

As people continue to interact, they may advance to a *predictive level* of knowledge. To know others predictively is to possess some valid information about the ways they behave and the things they believe. If accurate, the statements "Professor Miller will give a short-answer essay examination" and "Professor Miller will penalize you if you miss class" are examples of knowing Professor Miller at the predictive level. Moreover, they reflect a more advanced level of knowledge

than the descriptive assertion "That is Professor Miller, my communication professor"; in addition, they are the product of a more difficult information search, as Berger et al. (1976) emphasize:

Predictive knowledge is more difficult to attain than descriptive knowledge, for while the statement "Mary is tall" can be verified relatively easily by observation, the statement "Mary believes that abortion on demand should be extended to all women" is less subject to direct verification. In the first case, others can determine Mary's "tallness" by unobtrusively observing her. Moreover, it is relatively difficult for Mary to hide her height from view. However, even if others hear Mary assert that she endorses abortion on demand for all women, they cannot be certain that she is telling the truth. In other words, they can never know with complete certainty what Mary "really" thinks. (p. 150)

Many ongoing, relatively impersonal relationships are characterized by mutual predictive-level knowledge. Such knowledge forms the cornerstone of most commercial, marketplace relationships. I know my butcher is concerned about obtaining good cuts of meat for me. He, in turn, knows: (1) I will not object to paying a fair price for them. (2) I will not order special cuts and then fail to pick them up. (3) My check will not bounce. Neither of us spends much time speculating on the reasons that the other behaves predictably. So long as our behavioral expectations are confirmed, the relationship remains cordial and mutually rewarding.

Sometimes, however, knowing another at the predictive level is perceived as insufficient, and relational participants seek to know each other at the *explanatory level*. To know someone at this level is to believe you understand the reasons for his or her behaviors and beliefs. Explanatory-level knowledge transcends both the descriptive and predictive levels. "The predictive level deals with how a person will behave in certain situations, while the explanatory level deals with why a person behaves that way" (Miller, 1980, p. 120). Thus when individuals believe they know another person at the explanatory level, they are confident they know the person intimately, that "they are really inside the person's head" and "know what makes the person tick."

Clearly, however, explanatory knowledge is both difficult to come by and inherently uncertain. People's motives are always hidden from view and must, of necessity, be inferred. Consider the following exchange:

Ruth: "Why is Gail so antagonistic toward Sam?"

Fred: "Because she thinks Sam is dishonest and untrustworthy."

Ruth: "How do you know that's the reason?"

Fred: "Because she told me. Besides, I've known Gail for a long time and she's always detested dishonest people."

Obviously, Fred is certain that he knows Gail at the explanatory level, that he understands her reasons for reacting to Sam antagonistically. His confidence stems from Gail's reported reasons for disliking Sam and from his observations of Gail's past reactions to certain individuals. But though he may be supremely confident, Fred can never directly observe the actual reasons for Gail's behavior. Perhaps Gail is consciously or unconsciously masking her real reasons for disliking Sam. Perhaps Gail does not even dislike Sam, but is feigning antagonism because of Sam's indifference toward her. Perhaps Fred thinks so highly of Gail that he is distorting her reasons for reacting negatively to particular persons in the past. The possibilities are numerous; the "correct answer" is unattainable. Indeed, Fred may choose to interpret Gail's assertion "I dislike Sam because he is dishonest and untrustworthy" as an item of explanatory information, but it is, in strictly logical terms, more closely akin to predictive information: Fred can predict that if he asks Gail why she dislikes Sam, she will say it is because of dishonesty, whether or not her answer reflects her actual feelings.

Despite the inherent uncertainty of explanatory knowledge, people are strongly motivated to acquire it. Attribution theorists (Jones & Davis, 1965; Kelley, 1967; Shaver, 1975; Sillars, 1982) contend that individuals operate like naive social scientists in their daily social activities, constantly raising "why" questions and seeking the causes of others' behavior. This zeal for explanatory knowledge becomes keener as people establish increasingly intimate relationships. Miller (1980) suggests two reasons why concern for such knowledge provides a reliable marker of a relationship that is becoming increasingly interpersonal. First, people in close relationships are expected to discover as much as possible about each other. Acquisition of explanatory knowledge is thus seen as an important relational goal and a public signal that the parties are heavily committed to maintaining and expanding their relationship. Second, as a relationship becomes more interpersonal, the participants become concerned about more and more areas of each other's behavior and strive to establish wider spans of prediction and control. Indeed, the span is often so wide that observing all relevant behaviors becomes impossible.

The thirst for explanatory knowledge in close relationships is so pervasive that it constitutes a crucial ingredient of mutual trust. In impersonal relationships, where concern is typically restricted to a small domain of activities, trust is equated with the performance of expected behaviors; returning to an earlier example, the assertion "I trust my butcher" means that I anticipate he will deliver good cuts of meat at fair prices. His precise reasons for behaving this way are unimportant as long as he acts appropriately: Accurate predictive knowledge is usually sufficient to produce impersonal trust. In sharp contrast, participants in interpersonal relationships are concerned not only with behaviors (predictive-level knowledge) but with the causes for them (explanatory-level knowledge). To illustrate this point, consider the probable relational consequences of this exchange:

Romantic Partner 1: "Darling, I can't tell you how much it means to me that I can always trust you to be faithful to me!"

Romantic Partner 2: "Well, to tell you the truth, I've never felt as if I had much choice about the matter, because I was always afraid that if I strayed, you'd find out about it."

Partner 1 is likely to explode, not because of something Partner 2 has done, but rather because of the implied reasons for not doing it. In other words, Partner 1 is not satisfied solely because Partner 2 has always behaved faithfully; Partner 2 must be perceived as behaving faithfully for relationally appropriate reasons. Fear of discovery is not an acceptable reason. Partner 1 prefers reasons that center on Partner 2's love and respect for Partner 1. As a result of this unexpected disclosure, Partner 1's trust in Partner 2 will probably be diminished.

Although the two qualitative relational changes discussed thus far are partially distinctive, they obviously overlap to an extent. Predictive and explanatory knowledge are often linked to cultural and sociological generalizations about people's behavior. In some instances, such generalizations may even be invoked as explanations for a predicted behavior; for example, it may be predicted that professors will encourage controversy and disagreement with their viewpoints because they are taught to value scholarly controversy and disagreement. This example underscores the fact that some explanatory knowledge is itself impersonal in its informational foundations; the next professor encountered may actually dislike people who challenge his or her views and may punish these challenges.

Changes in the Locus of Rules Governing the Relationship Most writers have traditionally treated communication as primarily a law-governed process, but recently a number have argued for the advantages of conceptualizing communication as rule-governed (Cushman & Craig, 1976; Cushman & Florence, 1974; Cushman & Pearce, 1977; Cushman, Valentinsen, & Die-

trich, 1982; Cushman & Whiting, 1972; Harré & Secord, 1973; Pearce & Cronen, 1980; Reardon, 1981; Smith, 1982). Without becoming embroiled in the many issues surrounding the relative advantages of laws versus rules, it can safely be said that many communicative transactions are guided by externally imposed or internally negotiated rules. As the influence of externally imposed rules decreases and the influence of internally negotiated rules increases, the relationship becomes more interpersonal.

To illustrate how this change takes place, let us begin by stipulating a definition of the concept *communication rules:* "Statements which express consensus, shared at varying levels of generality, concerning the structure, procedures, and content of communicative relationships" (Miller, 1978, p. 175).

The phrase "which express consensus" emphasizes that, like doing the tango, creating and following rules are activities requiring, at a minimum, two persons. A communication rule cannot be operative unless at least two persons agree to accept it as a guiding principle of their relationship. Of course, as the phrase "shared at varying levels of generality" implies, the number of people conforming to a specific communication rule or rule set may vary from two to millions.

Finally, the terms "structure," "procedures," and "content" differ in this way: The first term refers to differences in factors such as the relative status or power of the relational participants; the second to the initiation, sequencing, and frequency of communicative exchanges; and the third to the actual verbal and nonverbal content of messages. Thus a supervisor and an employee may reach consensus on these rules: The supervisor has more relational status and power than the employee (structure); the supervisor initiates communicative exchanges and the employee responds (procedures); and the supervisor issues orders and the employee obeys them (content).

Structural, procedural, and content rules vary in their relative rigidity depending on the specific communicative situation. In formal, stylized environments, rules are precisely articulated and slavishly followed; in more informal settings, rules are defined less exactly and permit wider latitudes of exchange. A formal state dinner follows strictly defined protocol; an informal luncheon meeting of a government leader and several advisers, while also rule-guided, is likely to permit greater communicative flexibility. A formal Mass and a discussion between the priest and members of the church finance committee are both rule-governed events, but the former operates under more precise, defined rules. Meetings guided by parliamentary rules provide a familiar example of a formal, stylized communicative environment. The best-known, most widely used rule book, *Robert's Rules of Order,* prescribes the structure, procedures, and content of appropriate meeting communication. When all members of the body understand these rules and are guided by them, efficiency is enhanced; when members are ignorant of the rules or refuse to abide by them, chaos often reigns.

Knowledge of externally imposed rules constitutes cultural and sociological information that permits communicators to behave appropriately and to anticipate probable responses to their messages. Typically, little negotiation ensues about these rules; they are simply there at the outset of the relationship. When these externally imposed rules are primary guideposts, the relationship is relatively impersonal.

In an ongoing relationship, however, communicators may achieve consensus on certain rules that apply solely to that relationship. These rules, emerging from the continuing negotiations of the participants rather than being imposed from the outset, reflect a qualitative change that gradually increases the interpersonalness of the relationship.

The negotiation and definition of these idiosyncratic rules confer a sense of intimacy and uniqueness on interpersonal relationships. Parties to the relationship share numerous communicative secrets; they are able to exchange private messages in a roomful of strangers. They are like people who at social gatherings converse in a

foreign language that others cannot comprehend. . . . But unlike speakers of a foreign tongue, parties who rely on an idiosyncratic rule structure can communicate without others even being aware of their exchanges. (Miller, 1980, pp. 118–119)

As the shift from externally imposed to internally negotiated rules takes place, the relationship becomes increasingly interpersonal. As was true for the two previous qualitative changes, such a shift is not inevitable; in fact, a substantial set of intrinsically negotiated rules probably emerges in only a few particularly significant relationships. Relatively impersonal relationships make up most of people's everyday social commerce.

Interpersonal Communicators Versus Interpersonal Relationships

Earlier it was noted that for a rule to operate, relational partners must share consensus regarding it. Thus a qualitative change from externally imposed to internally negotiated rules is, of necessity, reciprocal. Relationships cannot be guided by intrinsic rules unless the partners agree to accept them. In the case of the other two qualitative changes discussed above, however, considerable disparity may exist between communicators. One individual may be basing a number of predictions on psychological information, while the other is relying almost exclusively on cultural and sociological information. Similarly, one party may know the other at the explanatory level, but the other may have acquired only descriptive or predictive knowledge about the first.

When such changes occur at roughly the same pace for both participants, the relationship can be described as becoming increasingly interpersonal. If large disparities exist between the participants, it makes better sense to say that one person is communicating more interpersonally than the other. Miller and Steinberg (1975) have characterized this latter situation as a *mixed-level relationship*. Typically, persons communicating interpersonally will exert more relational power, since they will be able to make more accurate predictions about message choices and will better understand the motives and reasons for the other's behavior. Consequently, the probability of achieving certain goals is enhanced by being capable of communicating interpersonally. Such an edge is not always ethically desirable, for an unscrupulous communicator can use it to manipulate and to exploit as well as to provide support and to show understanding.

BEGINNING STEPS IN RELATIONAL DEVELOPMENT

According to an old proverb, "A journey of a thousand miles begins with the first step." Though relational journeys are not usually clocked on speedometers, participants must log considerable informational mileage if the relationship is to develop. This section first considers some of the factors that predispose individuals to choose certain relationships over others and then examines some communicative strategies for acquiring information during the initial stages of a relationship.

Some Factors Contributing to Relational Choices

Students of human social behavior have always been intrigued by people's reasons for entering into relationships; in fact, Chapter 6 looks briefly at this question as it pertains to the formation of groups. Even with relational formation taken as a given, it is interesting to speculate why persons choose certain relational opportunities over others: What factors predispose individuals to explore certain relational options and to ignore others? Researchers have identified several important variables.

Propinquity Not surprisingly, physical proximity, or propinquity, plays an important role in

relationship formation. People who live in New York City are not equally likely to form relationships with all others who live in New York City; rather, it is necessary to think in terms of smaller geographical units. Thus persons living in the Bronx are more apt to date other Bronx residents than to date persons living in Brooklyn. In terms of more modest distances, college students will probably make friends among fellow dormitory residents, not among students housed across campus. For that matter, a student taking a seat in a classroom of strangers will probably strike up acquaintanceships with those seated nearby, rather than with students on the other side of the room.

More intriguing are the subtle influences of propinquity in relatively confined spatial quarters. For example, research by Festinger, Schachter, and Back (1950) indicates that some residents in multiple-occupancy dwellings have propinquitous advantage over others in terms of social contacts, and hence in forming relationships: Persons living in rooms near the center of a dormitory or apartment floor have more social contacts with other residents of that floor than residents of rooms at the ends of the halls.

Of course, other factors may diminish or even negate the impact of physical distance. A study conducted using residents of sorority houses in a large university revealed that members of lower-status sororities reported many social contacts with residents of higher-status houses, even though the latter houses were located in a different part of campus (Barnlund, 1968). Interestingly, these reported contacts were not reciprocated by higher-status sorority members, who said most of their social transactions were with social peers and reported few contacts with lower-status members. Since the investigators did not actually observe socializing patterns, it is impossible to tell which set of reports is more accurate. Indeed, both sets may be largely valid: Lower-status sorority members may have sought social contacts with their higher-status counterparts, but the latter may have ignored or rebuffed these approaches. Regardless of how the findings are interpreted, it seems reasonable to assume that if someone is sufficiently important, likable, or compatible, people will more likely accept the costs imposed by distance to form relationships with the attractive party. To use an extreme example, many persons would travel hundreds of miles to have dinner with an important government official, an athletic hero, a movie star, or a financial tycoon.

Attitude Similarity   Thus after recognizing the impact of propinquity on relationships, the question remains as to why some people are perceived as potentially more attractive partners than others. One extensive body of research (for example, Byrne, 1969, 1971) suggests that attitude similarity strongly influences relationship formation. Stated simply, people find others attractive if they share similar social, political, and economic views; if they disagree attitudinally, they are seen as less attractive. It follows, then, that Catholics should form relationships with Catholics rather than Protestants, Democrats with Democrats rather than Republicans, and so on. Though perhaps disquieting in its implications, the attitude-similarity hypothesis holds that people are drawn to ideological clones and are repelled by ideological opposites.

Most research concerning the effects of attitudinal similarity on initial attraction has not involved communication between persons with similar and dissimilar views; for that matter, it has not even required participants to make actual contact with other persons. After assessing the participants' attitudes about a number of issues, the researcher uses a gambit known as the "bogus stranger" procedure (Byrne, 1969, 1971). Participants are told they will soon be meeting with another person, and to set the stage for the meeting, they will receive some biographical information about the stranger. This information includes items indicating the stranger's attitudes are either in harmony or at odds with the participant's. After perusing the information, partici-

pants fill out forms asking for their impressions of the stranger. The forms contain items for measuring perceived attractiveness, and almost invariably, ratings of the attitudinally similar stranger are more positive than those of the dissimilar counterpart. There are some disagreements about interpretation, for while Byrne and his colleagues attribute the difference primarily to the attractiveness of the attitudinally similar stranger, Rosenbaum (1986) argues that aversion to the attitudinally dissimilar stranger is the main reason for the difference.

Regardless of how they are interpreted, these findings have limited import for students of communication. Often, persons who establish contact do not possess much information about each other's attitudes. To be sure, the situational context sometimes provides helpful clues about attitudinal "goodness of fit": If a Republican meets someone at a fund-raising party for a GOP candidate, both individuals probably assume they share similar political attitudes. Furthermore, on encountering a stranger, individuals probably arrive at some inferences about the stranger's attitudes by scrutinizing his or her physical appearance. As noted in Chapter 3, a young man in blue jeans sporting long hair and a beard usually will receive a different attitudinal appraisal than a middle-aged, clean-shaven man in a three-piece business suit, for these appearance and dress cues provide sociological information that allows at least tentative predictions. Seldom, however, are people provided with a catalog of another's attitudes before communicating with the person.

Moreover, even if a stranger is known to have discrepant attitudes, the mere exchange of introductory messages may sometimes overcome the negative impact of this knowledge. Persons' initial dialogs do not often concern areas of attitudinal controversy; instead, the communicators usually trade biographical information and make small talk about the weather, the stock market, or the baseball scores. Assuming that the communicators impress each other as decent, congenial persons, the rapport established may temper the negative effect of dissimilar attitudes.

To test this possibility, Sunnafrank and Miller (1981) conducted a study using an approach different from the "bogus stranger" technique. Participants' attitudes were tested, and dyads of persons with similar or dissimilar attitudes were formed. Groups of eight participants reported to a common site and were immediately sent to separate rooms. They were told that the study involved exchanging information about their attitudes with another student and that after the exchange they would be studying their partner's attitudes and making some predictions about him or her. All participants then indicated their attitudes on two issues, and the forms were exchanged. Attitudinally similar dyads received information revealing they agreed on two issues, while attitudinally dissimilar dyads received information revealing disagreement.

After studying the partner's attitudes, half of the attitudinally similar and half of the attitudinally dissimilar dyads were asked to "spend a few minutes conversing in order to make some tapes of initial interactions to be used in another study." Each dyad then interacted for five minutes, with the sessions actually being taped. In every instance, the conversations followed the typical path of initial interactions: Participants exchanged biographical summaries and chatted about commonplace topics; in no instance did they explore their areas of attitudinal harmony or discord. Members of noninteracting similar and dissimilar dyads stayed in their rooms and did not communicate with each other.

Next, all participants evaluated the attractiveness of their partners. Results for the noninteracting dyads confirmed the attitude similarity hypothesis: Similar partners were rated more attractive than dissimilar partners. By contrast, there was no difference between the attractiveness ratings for similar and dissimilar dyads who interacted, and both sets of ratings did not differ from those of noninteracting similar dyads. The effects of a simple, five-minute "getting acquainted" exchange blunted the impact of atti-

tude dissimilarity, with only attitudinally dissimilar, noninteracting dyads reporting significantly lower ratings of their partners' attractiveness. Thus even though attitude similarity influences initial perceptions of attractiveness, the effect is sometimes ephemeral and may be largely erased by a congenial initial conversation.

Need Complementarity A third variable that predisposes individuals to prefer certain partners over others is need complementarity (Winch, 1958). This construct describes a situation where a particular need of one person psychologically fits a need of the other. For example, dominant persons are expected to be drawn to submissive persons, and vice versa. Whereas attitude similarity conforms to the old cliché "Birds of a feather flock together," need complementarity supports "Opposites attract."

Actually, the two concepts are not so inconsistent as they may first appear. Attitude similarity refers to agreement on social, political, and economic issues; need complementarity pertains to situations where diverse motivational characteristics of two individuals fit together in the relationship. Given this distinction, it is not hard to imagine a dominant Presbyterian Republican forming a relationship with a submissive Presbyterian Republican, or a nurturant Catholic Democrat pairing up with a succorant Catholic Democrat. Perhaps it is the pervasiveness of need complementarity—the fact that it is involved in a wide variety of attitudes and behaviors—that led Winch and his colleagues (1958) to center their research on the highly involving, heavily committed relationship of marriage.

Propinquity, attitude similarity, and need complementarity, as well as other variables, contribute to the formation and subsequent maintenance of relationships. Undoubtedly, the surface has only been scratched in isolating factors that cause individuals to single out particular partners. Nevertheless, the first steps in cementing an acquaintanceship occur when the parties begin communicating. Moreover, these initial exchanges provide helpful clues about some communicative strategies used in this important phase of the relationship.

Strategies for Eliciting Information in Initial Interactions

Berger and his colleagues (Berger & Calabrese, 1975; Berger et al., 1976) have argued persuasively that the chief objective of initial dialog is *uncertainty reduction*. When strangers are face to face, they are unsure about how to proceed. To reduce uncertainty, they seek information that will place them on solid communicative ground. This quest for information and subsequent uncertainty reduction explains the common place form of initial interactions noted earlier. The communicators solicit and exchange biographical tidbits: home towns, occupations or courses of study, interests and hobbies. So habitual are these initial "interactive dances" that people find it difficult if not impossible to deviate from them (Berger, 1973). Moreover, when conversational topics are markedly out of sync with the temporal pace of the interaction, as when a communicator supplies or requests highly personal data during the early stages of an initial exchange, the offender is usually perceived by others as socially incompetent and unattractive, rather than interesting and intriguing (Berger et al., 1976). Despite some conventional wisdom regarding the value of striving for striking first impressions, a cautious, conservative approach to initial exchanges generally yields the ripest fruits.

This quest for uncertainty reduction is closely linked to the first two qualitative changes in relationships discussed earlier. Biographical information provides the substance for cultural and sociological predictions. As information is gained, communicators begin to feel less uncertain; they perceive they are beginning to know each other predictively, not just descriptively. These mutual personal inventories are not merely a social device for filling early communicative time and space, they are powerful tools for speeding the process of relationship development.

Interrogation Interrogation is the most common strategy used to solicit information in initial interactions. Consider this hypothetical conversation, including the parenthesized mental inferences that occur as the conversation proceeds:

Fred: "Hi, guess we'll be sitting next to each other in this class. What's your name?"

Tony: "Tony Castellani."

Fred: ("Oh, an Italian." And perhaps some other inferences, such as "a Catholic" and "maybe some Mafia connections.") "Where you from, Tony?"

Tony: "I've lived in the Detroit area all my life."

Fred: ("Definitely a big-city guy, but still hard to figure.") "What part of Detroit do you live in?

Tony: "Well, I've lived in Grosse Point for the last five years."

Fred: ("Definitely not hurting for money if he lives in Grosse Pointe.") "What's your major here at State?"

Tony: "I'm getting a B.A. in multidisciplinary social science. Hope to go to law school when I graduate."

Fred: ("Probably one of those limousine liberals from a wealthy family.") "Tony . . ."

This kind of conversation is familiar to every one. For simplicity's sake, the example consists of a series of questions raised by Fred and answered by Tony. Actually, in most beginning dialogs, the parties alternate the roles of interrogator and respondent. Thus, after volunteering his name, Tony would normally ask Fred to supply his. Such informational parity is grounded in the *norm of reciprocity* (Gouldner, 1960), which holds that people who supply information can justifiably expect the other party to return information in similar quantity and of comparable intimacy. If Tony requests Fred's name in return but Fred refuses to give it, the budding relationship will quickly wither on the vine. Conversely, if Tony asks Fred how much money he has in the bank or whether he is gay, Fred may refuse to answer on the grounds that the requested information is much more personal than the information Tony has offered Fred.

Clearly, there is no guarantee that Tony has answered all of Fred's questions candidly. Perhaps Tony actually lives in East Detroit rather than Grosse Pointe, for people sometimes distort information to make positive first impressions. But more obvious is the risk of inferential error on Fred's part. In particular, the inference about possible Mafia ties stems from an erroneous social stereotype of Italians; few Italians are Mafia members. Uncertainty reduction does not necessarily produce a completely accurate picture of the interactants, a fact that again underlines the potential error of predictions based on cultural and sociological information.

Self-Description   A glance at the hypothetical conversation reveals that continued questioning can transform a casual conversation into a semiformal interview. Since such a format is likely to prove awkward for the participants, interrogation should be used prudently. A second strategy, self-description, offers the advantages of interrogation while avoiding the problem of turning the conversation into a "twenty questions" exercise. When using the self-description strategy, a communicator offers information to the other person, rather than quizzing the other about himself or herself. As noted earlier, the norm of reciprocity socially obligates the other person to return similar information. Thus, rather than requesting Tony's name, Fred supplies his own, assuming that Tony will reciprocate, either in kind or by supplying additional data. If Tony responds, "Hi, I'm Tony Castellani from Grosse Point," the obligation shifts to Fred; if Tony offers only his name, Fred can continue with another self-descriptive item or he can terminate the conversation with the social ledger balanced.

This information-gaining strategy has previously been labeled *self-disclosure* (Berger et al., 1976; Miller, 1980). The decision to abandon this label for *self-description* is based on a distinction between the two concepts suggested by Culbert (1967):

Self-description designates self-data that an individual is likely to feel comfortable in revealing to most others. Additionally, self-description includes information that an individual knows about himself that is readily perceivable by others, and by which he agrees to be known. Self-description is likely to include an individual's physical characteristics, his occupation, marital status, and so on. Self-disclosure refers to an individual explicitly communicating to one or more others personal information that he believes these others would be unlikely to acquire unless he himself discloses it. Moreover, this information must be "personally private"; that is, it must be of such a nature that it is not something the individual would disclose to everyone who might inquire about it. (p. 2)

Not only are most persons reluctant to disclose genuinely personal information with relative strangers, but as noted earlier, such information is typically considered out of place in initial interactions, thus fostering the perception that the information giver is socially inept and/or interpersonally unattractive (Berger et al., 1976). Information shared in the early stages of a relationship is therefore likely to be self-descriptive. In terms of the qualitative changes in relationships outlined above, it is largely cultural and sociological data that help the recipient to know the other partner at the descriptive, or at best, predictive level. This limitation, however, does not deny the utility of such information in reducing uncertainty and moving the relationship along the path of added understanding.

Environmental Structuring   Although interrogation and self-description are the most frequently used strategies, information can be acquired by other means. Environmental structuring sometimes yields rich information returns: This strategy rests on the individual's ability to structure the communicative context so as to en hance the probability of eliciting certain kinds of information. For instance, a couple's first date is often carefully planned to capitalize on a specific type of environment. Dinner at an excellent restaurant, with candlelight, flowers, and a fine wine, provides an excellent opportunity for a person to assess his or her partner's feelings about their relationship. During a social occasion involving a group of people, such as a dinner party, the host may seat herself or himself within hearing distance of the object of the information search and monitor the conversation between that person and his or her immediate dinner companions. This example of environmental structuring may seem a bit devious. It provides a reminder, however, that information is often acquired indirectly, either by availing oneself of eavesdropping opportunities or by interrogating third parties. Indeed, many persons place greater confidence in indirectly gained information, rightly or wrongly believing that deception is less probable than if information is sought directly.

Deception Detection The issue of potential deviousness and deceit brings us to the strategy of deception detection. Sometimes a new acquaintance may be suspected of attempting to curry favor, of using ingratiation (Jones, 1975) to create favorable impressions. Communicators who use this deceptive tactic readily agree with the other's opinions, engage in flattery, or offer favors. Deception detection seeks to unmask insincerity. If the suspected ingratiator has agreed with a stated opinion, the skeptical party may "clarify" his or her statement so that it contradicts the original opinion. If the other party expresses agreement with the "clarified" position, there are solid grounds for assuming deceit. Similarly, when the sincerity of a compliment is doubted— for example, "That was really a delicious meal!" —the skeptical party may engage in self-derogation—"Oh, I don't know, it didn't seem as good as several meals I've fixed lately." If the dinner guests persists in praising the meal, an inference of sincere appreciation and enjoyment is more warranted. If the compliment is not reinforced, flattery becomes a distinct possibility. In fact, if engaged in ingratiation, the guest may be reluctant to disagree with the cook's negative evaluation of the meal, since such a move would constitute opinion disagreement with the target of the ingratiation attempt.

Deviation Testing Sometimes communicators in a budding relationship want to test the waters, particularly to determine whether the other party wishes to begin moving from externally imposed to internally negotiated rules. In such situations the strategy of deviation testing may yield information about the other person's attitude about the relationship. To illustrate, consider the extrinsic rules of address accompanying relationships between college professors and students. Though somewhat variable, these rules suggest that formality is the safest approach: The student addresses the professor by an appropriate title such as "Professor (or "Doctor") Jones" and the professor addresses the student as "Mr (or "Ms.") Smith." In seeking to negotiate a less formal address rule, the student may deviate from externally imposed expectations and call the professor by first name. A response in kind indicates willingness to be guided by the intrinsically modified rule, but if the professor continues to address the student formally, it suggests a preference for the externally imposed rule. Deviation testing should be used judiciously, for an abrupt and radical departure from the extrinsic rules guiding the relationship often results in social censure.

This brief inventory surely does not exhaust the strategies available to communicators for gathering information in a relationship's initial stages. Although verbal strategies have been stressed, the importance of scrutinizing nonverbal behaviors should be apparent—for example, if the professor addresses the student by first name but in a sarcastic or angry tone, the latter is likely to think twice about continuing on a first-name basis. Verbal and nonverbal information function collectively to reduce uncertainty and thus create greater familiarity. As indicated, however, these initial moves are halting and the relationship remains relatively impersonal. Further initiatives must occur if interpersonalness is to increase markedly, and the next step is to examine these initiatives.

IMPORTANT FACTORS IN DEVELOPING INTERPERSONAL RELATIONSHIPS

If initial communicative exchanges mark the start of a relationship, the relationship, as noted earlier, will follow one of numerous possible developmental paths. This section considers several factors associated with relational escalation and that result in increasingly interpersonal relationships. The fact that relationships that remain relatively impersonal are not discussed extensively does not imply they are either undesirable or unimportant. Rather, these relationships are largely ignored here for two reasons: First, previous sections have identified many of the tools needed to forge impersonal relationships; second, and perhaps more important, some basic characteristics of impersonal relationships are identified indirectly in the following pages. Stated differently, if a relationship is not marked by such changes as mutually accelerating patterns of self-disclosure, emergence of strong empathic bonds, and compatibility of relationship definition across a wide band of beliefs and behaviors, it is destined to remain impersonal. Thus individuals who understand the vital ingredients of interpersonal relationships will be able to regulate relational escalation and exert control over the relative interpersonalness of their various relationships.

Self-Disclosure

Whereas self-description is important in initial encounters, self-disclosure is especially vital for the relationship to escalate. If self-disclosure takes place, it is usually in gradual, halting steps as the relationship progresses temporally. As the term is used here, self-disclosure involves shar-

ing *personally private* information—information hidden from the eyes and ears of others and that the potential discloser is reluctant to share indiscriminately (Miller & Steinberg, 1975). Two closely related terms characterizing genuine self-disclosure are *risk* and *vulnerability*. Personally private information is shared with the knowledge that the listener conceivably could use it to harm and embarrass the discloser; this is the risk associated with self-disclosing messages. A corollary consideration lies in the fact that making sensitive information available to others increases their power over the discloser; that is where vulnerability enters into the relational equation. Thus if much self-disclosure is to occur, the potential discloser must feel confident that the listener will treat the information with integrity and compassion. Most individuals rebel against the thought that their revelations may be used to taunt and torment them or that they may be passed along to others whose possession of the information might well trigger harmful consequences for the discloser.

Some other writers seem to look on self-disclosure as an unqualifiedly positive activity. Miller and Steinberg (1975) summarize this view thus:

It is generally considered "good" to self-disclose and "bad" to be unable or unwilling to self-disclose—i.e., to self-conceal. The two terms seem to have acquired the following associations:

People who self-disclose are open, honest, authentic, warm, friendly, free, together, strong, trusting and to be trusted, and maturing personally and interpersonally.

People who self-conceal are phony, dishonest, unauthentic, hung up, fearful, manipulative, distrustful and not to be trusted, cold, and stunted personally and interpersonally. (p. 309)

Obviously, total unwillingness to self-disclose severely limits one's relational horizons. On the other hand, people who practice self-disclosure prudently and discriminatingly are acting in their relational self-interests. Just as the social world is not completely hostile and brutal, neither is it totally benign and compassionate. To paraphrase an old saw about marriage, those who self-disclose in haste often repent in leisure. Although people must determine their own limits of openness, the position taken here holds that genuine self-disclosure should be reserved for those relationships with strong interpersonal potential.

Indeed, many compatible, functional impersonal relationships may be severely burdened by the weight of excessive self-disclosure. Sharing personally private information imposes mutual restrictions and obligations: Not only do disclosers engage in a risky communicative step, they also impose a social obligation on listeners, who are now saddled with information that must be treated wisely and consciously concealed from others. Unless the appropriate role behaviors prescribe such a relationship—as in the case of a priest and a penitent or a lawyer and a client—it is unfair to impose this obligation on impersonal partners. My butcher has no need nor desire to know my most intimate secrets, nor do I wish to be privy to his, unless, of course, we decide to expand radically the boundaries of our relationship.

The modifier *genuine* has been attached to the term *self-disclosure* to underscore the frequent difficulty of determining when one has actually witnessed the sharing of personally private information. Such information is psychological in nature; it acquaints the listener with events and feelings the individual discloser regards as intimate and significant. In order to discuss self-disclosure generally, however, it is necessary to resort to cultural and sociological generalizations regarding the topics most people would probably regard as self-disclosing. For instance, matters such as sexual fears, inadequacies, and perversions, economic problems and dishonest practices, and hostile or ambivalent feelings toward parents or other immediate family members are regarded by most members of our society as private. To recognize the culturally imposed intimacy of these topics does not deny that some persons may be willing to share truthful or fabricated information about them with almost anyone. In fact, an unscrupulous or exploitive

communicator may parlay his or her willingness to talk freely about matters most people consider private into an unfair relational advantage. Miller and Steinberg (1975) have labeled this Machiavellian communication strategy *apparent self-disclosure.*

Apparent self-disclosure involves sharing information most people would be reluctant or embarrassed to share, but which the communicator does not consider personally private. Such a ruse potentially confers two relational advantages on the apparent discloser. First, because of his or her seeming willingness to get down to "gut-level feelings" early in the relationship, the apparent discloser is likely to be perceived as open, accepting, authentic, and honest, even though such impressions are 180 degrees from the truth. Second, the previously mentioned norm of reciprocity dictates that the beneficiary of this supposedly intimate information should respond in kind. If the naive party has been duped into accepting the authenticity of the "self-disclosing" messages, he or she will probably reciprocate with some genuine self-disclosure. What may superficially appear a relationship of information equals actually becomes a situation where the apparent discloser has much more relational power than the duped partner.

In the hands of motivated and sincere communicators, genuine self-disclosure moves a relationship along the path to greater interpersonalness. Psychological information contained in self-disclosing messages increases predictive accuracy. As relational partners share personal information, they come to know each other at the explanatory level. Finally, self-disclosure, when pursued with integrity, fosters trust and confidence between the parties.

Although self-disclosure thus far has been viewed primarily as a verbal activity, even participants in attractive, potentially interpersonal relationships are often reluctant or embarrassed to unveil particularly poignant private portraits. Sometimes a sensitive communicator can detect this reluctance by noticing revealing nonverbal cues and can then encourage subsequent disclosive messages. Consider this hypothetical dialog:

Sally: "Even though you say your childhood relationship with your parents was great, you seem to be a little uncomfortable talking about it. Is there anything else you want to tell me? You know I'll be glad to help you in any way I can."

Gerry: "It's amazing how you're always on my wavelength! To be truthful, I was ashamed of my parents when I was little because we never had as much money or as nice a place to live as a lot of my friends. As I've grown older, I've come to realize that my folks did everything they could to help me, and I've regretted that I didn't do more to show them how much I loved them before it was too late. When they were killed in that car accident, I felt guilty as hell for not having demonstrated more consistently how much they meant to me."

As with other kinds of psychological information, amassing personal information demands motivation, time, and expenditure of physical and psychic energy.

Some critics may contend this examination of the role of self-disclosure in relationship development has unduly accentuated the negative. In particular, since most writers distinguish between positive and negative self-disclosure (Chelune & Associates, 1979; Gilbert, 1976), it may seem curious that this section has focused on negative disclosure content. Keep in mind that this chapter is itself impersonal; it seeks to impart ideas to a large, heterogeneous audience concerning effective ways of communicating interpersonally with most people. The decision to exclude positive disclosure content rests on the following generalization: For most persons, sharing positive information about the self is more closely akin to self-description than to self-disclosure. In other words, "good news" about the self is not usually private; it is information individuals are willing, and often eager, to share with almost anyone. In initial encounters, people strive to create favorable impressions, to put their best foot (and face) forward. Furthermore, research demonstrates

that people initially respond more favorably to positive than to negative information about the self (Gilbert, 1976, 1977). To be sure, a few individuals may be embarrassed or reluctant to sing their own praises to others—to disclose that they are Congressional Medal of Honor winners, that they were voted the most popular person in their graduating class, or that they spent the entire summer as a volunteer worker for a worthy charitable cause. Such modesty is the exception rather than the rule. The most difficult information to divulge and to discover concerns real or imagined weaknesses.

Empathy

A second highly prized and lavishly praised communicative skill affecting relationship development is empathy. Although almost everyone agrees empathy is a good thing, there is less apparent consensus regarding its definition. The empathic process is frequently described in figurative language: People speak of "putting themselves in the other person's shoes" or "getting inside the other person's head." Stated less figuratively, a key step in the empathic process involves accurate prediction of the moods and feelings of others. The prospective empathizer observes the situational circumstances and the overt behaviors of others, and based on these observations, makes an inference about their feelings. Like other predictions, this inference may be based on impersonal or interpersonal reasoning. For instance, if someone is faced with the circumstance of death in the family, it is almost always safe to infer the individual is sad and depressed. The grounds for this inference can be highly impersonal; it would usually be made even in the case of relative strangers, since most cultures mandate that people should feel sad when a family member dies. On rare occasions, the inference may be erroneous: The bereaved may actually despise the departed relative, or religious faith may be so strong that there is sincere rejoicing about the relative's passage to an ideal existence.

If the empathizer has psychological information about the bereaved, the same inference could be highly interpersonal. The empathizer may know a particularly strong bond of affection existed between the grieving friend and the dead relative. Furthermore, he or she may be aware that the friend's religious beliefs will not cushion this personal blow. This latter possibility again underscores the greater predictive power inherent in interpersonal relationships: To be able to interpret and to analyze feelings from the individual's viewpoint, rather than relying on cultural and sociological generalizations, is bound to sharpen empathic accuracy.

The preceding example is somewhat atypical because of the extreme circumstances. Of course individuals who have recently lost a close friend or immediate relative are usually sad and depressed, just as those who have recently won large lottery prizes are usually excited and elated. Most of the time, precise situational circumstances are much more ambiguous. The empathizer senses the other is experiencing some kind of feeling or mood state, but the causes of this state and the precise label for the emotion are difficult to define. Is Brad somber or contemplative? Is Kathleen smarting because of a colleague's remarks or because of a lovers' quarrel with Greg? The successful empathizer must sort out these conflicting possibilities and arrive at accurate predictions.

For some students of social behavior, accurate prediction of others' feelings is synonymous with effective empathizing (Dymond, 1949; Katz, 1963). A communication perspective requires an additional step. If a relational partner is to be perceived as empathic, she or he must be able not only to predict the other's feelings, but also to respond in ways perceived as positively reinforcing (Miller & Steinberg, 1975). The statement "He (or she) is a very empathic person" translates "He (or she) understands how I feel *and* communicates with me in a sympathetic, rewarding manner."

There are at least two reasons why a communicator may not be able to achieve the second step of "reaching" another person symbolically, even though he or she can accurately predict the other's feelings. First, the individual may simply not know how to communicate effectively with the other. Everyone has experienced the frustration of knowing how someone else feels but being at a loss about what to say, either because of ignorance or embarrassment. Usually, several communicative alternatives are available, and the best choice is often unclear. To illustrate, let us return to the self-disclosing dialog between Sally and Gerry. Recall Gerry has disclosed that he was ashamed of his parents as a child and that since their death he had felt guilty about not showing more affection for them:

Sally: (Alternative 1) "I don't think you should lay a heavy guilt trip on yourself. I'm certain your parents knew you cared for them a great deal. The kinds of feelings you're having are experienced by everyone when a loved one dies."

Sally: (Alternative 2) "You probably have good reason for feeling guilty, for it sounds as if you treated your folks pretty shabbily. Hopefully, though, you've learned something about dealing with important people in your life and won't repeat your mistake."

Certainly, the first alternative is more commonly employed, and when in doubt, most people would probably opt for it. At first glance, the second seems heartless and unsympathetic; it resembles some of the advice and counsel Lucy proffers to Charlie Brown in the comic strip "Peanuts." Still, depending on his attitudinal and motivational posture, Gerry may find the second approach more rewarding—"At last, someone who's willing to tell me I erred badly in my relationship with my parents"—than the first—"I've heard this song before; no matter what she says, I know my conduct toward my parents was terrible." Though choosing the most empathic response to make is seldom easy, psychological information and explanatory-level knowledge enhance predictive accuracy, suggesting that greater empathy is both a cause and an effect of increasingly interpersonal relationships.

People may also respond inappropriately out of sheer perversity or manipulativeness. In other words, they may understand how the other feels, but their own needs may drive them to communicate in punishing ways. Most of us have known individuals who delighted in exacerbating others' miseries instead of being helpful and supportive. This fact underscores the importance of the second communicative step in the empathic process, for although such persons have a handle on the other's feelings, they will not be seen as empathic. Quite the opposite: people who interpret another's feelings accurately and then prey on these emotions in a communicative cat-and-mouse game are likely to be viewed as sadistic, heartless, and cruel—in short, as the least empathic communicator imaginable.

Mutuality of Relational Definition

Among other things, impersonal relationships are characterized by a narrow breadth and shallow depth of social penetration (Altman & Taylor, 1973). Participants relate concerning a relatively few behaviors and beliefs of minimal intimacy. As relationships grow more interpersonal, partners become concerned with a wider band of behaviors and beliefs (breadth), many of which are quite central and intimate (depth). In both types of relationships, participants are concerned about *mutuality of relational definition* (Morton, Alexander, & Altman, 1976); but in interpersonal relationships, issues associated with this concept become more complex because of the wider and deeper behavioral domains.

Simply stated, mutuality of relational definition means the partners agree on the ways they are to relate to each other: the structure of the relationship, their respective roles and obligations, and so on. Cognitive consistency theories (Festinger, 1957; Osgood & Tannenbaum, 1955) provide one useful way of conceptualizing this agreement. In particular, Newcomb's (1953) the-

ory of interpersonal balance deals with the ways relational partners coorient toward issues, objects, and events and how varying coorientational postures affect the relationship.

Figure 5.3a depicts a balanced, harmoniously defined impersonal relationship between a milkman and a customer. Note that the two participants are positively oriented toward each other. In addition, each perceives that the other is positively oriented toward the salient aspects of the relationship (*X*s). These salient aspects are few in number, the three crucial aspects being fresh products, prompt service, and prompt payment, and the two peripheral ones being superficial cordiality and occasional tipping. Should either party perceive a lack of mutuality of relational definition on the three crucial aspects, the relationship would be severely threatened (Figure 5.3b). Disagreement on the peripheral aspects could create minor relational strains but probably would not endanger the relationship (Figure 5.3c).

A balanced, harmoniously defined interpersonal relationship between a husband and wife is depicted in Figure 5.4a, with only a few of the salient aspects of the relationship listed. As noted earlier, the participants must coorient toward numerous *X*s, many involving fundamental values. Indeed, partners achieve mutuality of relational definition hierarchically; apparent imbalance toward specific *X*s is often resolved by agreement on more abstract *X*s. Thus Figure 5.4b indicates disagreement over a particular acquaintance, Ray; the husband likes Ray but the wife dislikes him. Viewed in isolation, this disagreement might be expected to spark conflict. But as Figure 5.4c reveals, the partners coorient positively toward the more abstract, relational *X*, "mutual freedom to select our own friends." The relationship is therefore balanced at this more abstract relational level, and unless Ray begins to demand inordinate time from the husband or violates the wife's expectations in other ways, the couple should adjust nicely to their differing evaluations of him.

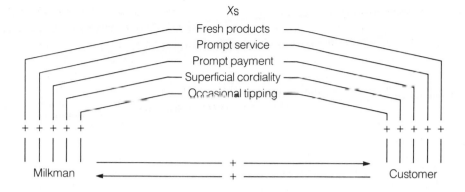

a. A balanced impersonal relationship.

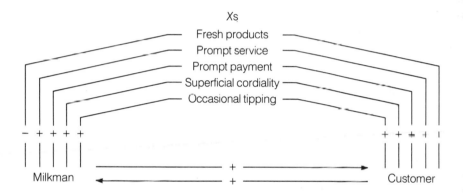

b. An imbalanced impersonal relationship, crucial aspect.

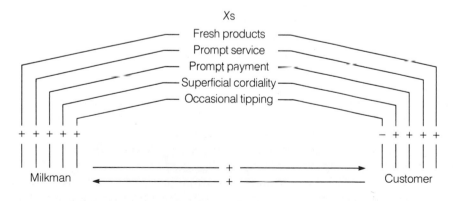

c. An imbalanced impersonal relationship, peripheral aspect.

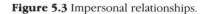

Figure 5.3 Impersonal relationships.

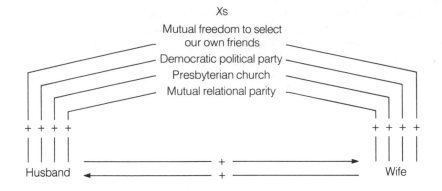

a. A balanced interpersonal relationship.

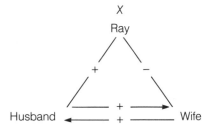

b. An apparently imbalanced interpersonal relationship.

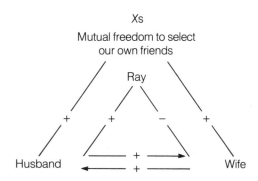

c. Balance on more abstract X subsumes disagreement on specific X.

Figure 5.4 Interpersonal relationships.

As the preceding paragraph suggests, relational Xs are probably the most important objects of coorientation in interpersonal relationships. If the parties' definitions of the relationship match, other specific Xs are likely to be subsumed harmoniously. For example, if the participants accept a definition of absolute relational parity—all options available to one partner must be available to the other—division of numerous social and economic resources has been solved. If one person spends about $100 monthly on recreation, the other person is entitled to spend the same amount, or if one person spends time away from the other with friends, the other person is granted the same social option. Of course, some actions may fall outside the purview of the parity rule, thereby requiring separate negotiation. For instance, one person may not want the option of developing other romantic relationships, preferring instead that both participants reserve romantic attachments for each other. If so, "romantic exclusivity" becomes another relational X requiring negotiation and agreement. The key point remains: Mutuality of relational definition, reflected by coordination toward relational Xs, is a crucial ingredient of harmonious interpersonal relationships.

Whereas mutuality of relational definition is usually imposed on impersonal relationships, agreement is usually internally negotiated in interpersonal relationships. The salient aspects of the milkman-customer relationship mirror the factors imposed by society on all impersonal, marketplace transactions. When entering into commercial exchanges, customers and merchants assume that quality goods and services will be issued promptly and paid for promptly. By contrast, society does not mandate how much time marital partners can spend apart from each other with friends, nor does it dictate whether one partner should be allowed more than the other. These rules must be negotiated by the partners; they illustrate the intrinsic locus of rules governing the relationship, a qualitative relational dimension discussed earlier in this chapter.

Dominance and Submissiveness

A particularly important dimension of most relationships is the relative dominance and submissiveness of the partners. *Symmetrical* relationships are characterized by equality; *complementary* relationships are based on apparent inequality (Watzlawick, Beavin, & Jackson, 1967). In the latter type of relationship, one participant occupies the one-up, or dominant, position and the other occupies the one-down, or submissive, role. This type of relationship is illustrated by the following dialog:

Ruth: "On your way over, stop at the store to pick up some coffee."

Noel: "OK. Do you need anything else?"

Ruth: "No, that should handle dinner. Be sure to be here by 6:30 so we can get started for the party by 8."

Noel: "I will."

Ruth: "Oh, and don't forget that you have to take my car to the garage tomorrow. I told them you'd have it there when they open."

Noel: "I won't forget. See you at 6:30."

Ruth: "Good. Don't be late."

Note that Ruth's communicative behavior is consistently dominant while Noel's is submissive. That both seem satisfied with their roles suggests this definition of the relationship coincides with their expectations and is mutually rewarding. Even though Ruth dominates and Noel submits, this does not mean Ruth has more power and control than Noel. Noel's submissive behavior reinforces Ruth's dominance, and if Noel chooses to withdraw reinforcement by rebelling or by ignoring Ruth's requests, he can cause Ruth considerable consternation. The relationship thus entails elements of mutual control; each participant would be severely handicapped without the other.

Symmetrical relationships, on the other hand, reflect a sense of communicative equality, with neither party clearly seizing a one-up position. Consider the following conversation between two professors at a convention:

Professor 1: "Yes, I've been at the University of Massachusetts for the last five years. I teach a couple of graduate courses and a couple of undergrad courses in interpersonal communication and do research on developing relationships."

Professor 2: "I've got an interest in that area; in fact, I've got a series of studies coming out in the next issue of *Human Communication Research.*"

Professor 1: "Great, I'll watch for your paper. I have a couple of things accepted by *Communication Monographs,* but they won't be out for a while."

Professor 2: "Yeah, those journals take forever to get something out. I've been thinking about doing a book on relationships."

Professor 1: "Really? I was just talking the other day to Wadsworth about an idea I had for a book like that."

Although the two professors seem comfortable in their relationship, symmetrical exchanges often become unstable, with both parties striving to seize the one-up position. The process of escalating symmetry is illustrated by a whimsical expansion of our preceding dialog:

Professor 2: "I like to publish my research in books because I can get them out fast. It's not uncommon for me to crank out 25 or 30 pages a day."

Professor 1: "Let me tell you, I once wrote 50 pages a day for eight days running."

Professor 2: "That's great, but once I went up to my cottage for a week to write and I averaged 80 pages daily and still caught my limit of bass every day."

Professor 1: "Let me tell you, with this new word processing equipment . . ."

Clearly, neither party is willing to accept relational parity, yet neither is willing to grant the other the one-up position. The exchange has settled into a "Can you top this?" contest that appears to be going nowhere. One suspects the professors will soon terminate the conversation and that each will rush off to tell friends about an "unbelievable encounter with a colossal liar." Because of this escalatory potential, symmetrical relationships are often difficult to maintain for long.

In the impersonal arena, extrinsic factors typically dictate whether a relationship will be complementary or symmetrical. Task-oriented transactions involving superiors and subordinates are almost invariably complementary, as are exchanges between individuals of widely varying status. Conversely, relationships between professional or social equals can better proceed symmetrically, although such equality does not guarantee that either participant will refrain, to paraphrase Orwell, from trying to become "more equal than the other."

Complementarity and symmetry are internally negotiated in interpersonal relationships; the parties strive to reach agreement on the structure of their communicative encounters. Because interpersonal relationships are characterized by wide and deep social penetration, they are frequently a subtle blend of parity and inequality: At one moment, the two parties are relating symmetrically; at the next, one party has assumed the dominant position; at yet a third moment, the other party has taken the one-up role. Such orchestrated changes underscore the complexity of interpersonal relationships and indicate why the search for mutuality of relational definition requires the commitment and the energy of both partners.

DEESCALATION AND DISENGAGEMENT

Among students of human behavior, many more words have been written about relational highs than lows. Until recently, almost all discussions of relationships focused on the joys and mysteries of escalation, with only lip service paid to deescalation and disengagement. "Getting to know you" has been praised as a delightful activity; the other side of the record reminds us that "breaking up is hard to do."

The traditional preoccupation with relational escalation is easily understood. Not only is it more pleasant to contemplate relationships in harmony than relationships in trouble, the conventional wisdom of our society reinforces the view that "every day, in every way, close relationships should get better and better." The beautiful princess and the handsome prince are married and live happily ever after. People who have maintained close relationships for most of their life span are pointed to as examples of relational successes, often with the implication that their lengthy relationship has been an idyllic journey through time, each succeeding year becoming more utopian. As Miller and Parks (1982) have pointed out, even the language used to describe deescalation and disengagement—for example, "relational decay," "relational disintegration," "the death of a relationship"—smacks of despair and failure.

Despite conventional wisdom and cultural myth, realistic reflection reveals that the best relationships periodically fall on hard times. Certain tension points are wired into the normal life cycle: the birth of the first child, the youngest child's departure from home, the shift from work to retirement. In addition to these predictable happenings, numerous unforeseen events may cast a pall on the relationship. At best, such negative occurrences trigger a period of deescalation and withdrawal, followed by an escalatory rebound; at worst, they result in disengagement and subsequent radical redefinition of the relationship.

Disengagement from impersonal relationships

is relatively easy. By contrast, withdrawal from interpersonal relationships is often traumatic and psychologically damaging. Heavy commitment, manifested in intense ego involvement and extreme energy expenditure, translates into perceptions of failure once it is clear the relationship is in trouble. Not only do the intrinsic costs of disengagement frequently seem exorbitant, extrinsic factors such as real or imagined criticism by acquaintances and loss of joint friendship networks add to the pain of disengagement.

In such circumstances the existence of an interpersonal relationship may be either an asset or a liability, depending on the needs and motivations of the partners. If both participants view disengagement as a persuasive activity that seeks radical redefinition of the relationship with minimum punishment and personal trauma, the added information and knowledge found in interpersonal relationships can cushion the blow of disengagement (Miller & Parks, 1982). On the other hand, if either participant is bent on exacting a pound of relational flesh, interpersonal communication with the disengaging partner enhances destructive potential; the keenest barbs and sharpest arrows can be hurled in the closest relationships. As with other areas discussed in this chapter, the option lies with the partners. The developmental view of interpersonal communication mandates both individual freedom and responsibility in communicative transactions; hence, it squares with the two major cornerstones of democratic ideology. Such correspondence strikes us as both realistic and optimistic. The underlying message of this entire chapter stresses the individual's opportunity to define the nature of particular communicative relationships and the individual's responsibility to invest the energy and commitment needed to make these relationships work.

SUMMARY

Communicating with other individuals in informal settings makes up a significant part of all the communica-

tion in anyone's life. Interpersonal communication has been defined from a variety of perspectives, including definitions based on situational characteristics and definitions based on studying developmental characteristics of such communication. These definitions illustrate the complexity of interpersonal communication and the many elements involved in studying it completely.

The development of interpersonal relationships is not the same as interpersonal communication, although there is a significant connection between the two. Some of the basic elements contributing to the beginning of an interpersonal relationship are discussed, including propinquity, similarity, and needs of the persons interacting.

The need for information to reduce uncertainty about the other and strategies for collecting information figure prominently in the communication behaviors in a developing relationship. Other elements of communication behavior that become important in the development of a relationship include self-disclosure, empathy, and the mutual definition of relational rules.

Communication is also involved in relationships that do not develop and in relationships that deescalate or disengage, but much less is known about the termination of relationships than about the forming of relationships.

REVIEW AND DISCUSSION QUESTIONS

1. There are strengths and weaknesses of each of the methods of defining interpersonal communication. Some definitions are easy to study because they rely on external elements, and some definitions rely on internal processes, which are difficult to observe. Some definitions are broad enough to apply to many situations, but others are very narrow. Discuss the advantages and disadvantages of each of the definitions described in this chapter.

2. The study of relationship development implies that regularities or patterns of development exist. Yet the individual differences of the members of each relationship and the individualized rules of relationship that each member agrees to suggest that each relationship is a unique entity. Are there more regularities or individual differences in defining relationships? How much can a given relationship deviate from the normal pattern of development and still be considered a typical example of that type of relationship?

3. The question of how conscious the members of an interpersonal transaction are of such processes as uncertainty reduction, eliciting information, self-disclosure, or defining relational rules was raised in the chapter. Why would it matter whether these processes were done consciously or unconsciously? What changes would it make in the communication of a person who was trying consciously to perform one of these functions?

4. Informal social communication often occurs in a variety of settings, including groups (Chapter 6), organizations (Chapter 7), and other settings in which other activities besides social relationships are the predominant goal. To what extent does the setting influence the process of relationship development? How important (or harmful) is the development of good interpersonal relationships to good performance of these other tasks?

REFERENCES

Abelson, R. P. (1976). Script processing in attitude formation and decision making. In J. S. Carroll & J. W. Payne (Eds.), *Cognition and social behavior* (pp. 33–45). Hillsdale, NJ: Erlbaum.

Altman, I., & Taylor, D. A. (1973). *Social penetration: The development of interpersonal relationships.* New York: Holt, Rinehart & Winston.

Andersen, P. A. (1982). Interpersonal communication research across three decades. Paper presented at the annual meeting of the Speech Communication Association, Louisville, KY.

Bach, G. R., & Wyden, P. (1968). *The intimate enemy.* New York: Avon.

Barnlund, D. C. (1968). *Interpersonal communication: Survey and studies.* New York: Houghton Mifflin.

Berger, C. R. (1973). The acquaintance process revisited. Paper presented at the annual meeting of the Speech Communication Association, New York.

Berger, C. R., & Calabrese, R. J. (1975). Some explorations in initial interaction and beyond: Toward a developmental theory of interpersonal communication. *Human Communication Research, 1,* 99–112.

Berger, C. R., & Douglas, W. (1982). Thought and talk: Excuse me, but have I been talking to myself? In F. E. X. Dance (Ed.), *Human communication theory* (pp. 42–60). New York: Harper & Row.

Berger, C. R., Gardner, R. R., Parks, M. R., Schulman, L., & Miller, G. R. (1976). Interpersonal epistemology and interpersonal communication. In G. R. Miller (Ed.), *Explorations in interpersonal communication* (pp. 149–171). Beverly Hills: Sage.

Berne, E. (1964). *Games people play.* New York: Grove.

Byrne, D. (1969). Attitudes and attraction. In L. Berkowitz (Ed.), *Advances in experimental social psychology* (Vol. 4, pp. 35–89). New York: Academic Press.

Byrne, D. (1971). *The attraction paradigm.* New York: Academic Press.

Chelune, G. J., & Associates. (1979). *Self-disclosure.* San Francisco: Jossey-Bass.

Culbert, S. A. (1967). *Interpersonal process of self-disclosure: It takes two to see one*. Washington, DC: N.T.L. Institute for Applied Behavioral Science.

Cushman, D. P., & Craig, R. T. (1976). Communication systems: Interpersonal implications. In G. R. Miller (Ed.), *Explorations in interpersonal communication* (pp. 37–58). Beverly Hills: Sage.

Cushman, D. P., & Florence, B. T. (1974). The development of interpersonal communication theory. *Today's Speech, 22,* 11–15.

Cushman, D. P., & Pearce, W. B. (1977). Generality and necessity in three types of theory about human communication, with special attention to rules theory. *Human Communication Research, 3,* 344–353.

Cushman, D. P., Valentinsen, B., & Dietrich, D. (1982). A rules theory of interpersonal relationships. In F. E. X. Dance (Ed.), *Human communication theory* (pp. 90–119). New York: Harper & Row.

Cushman, D. P., & Whiting, G. (1972). An approach to communication theory: Towards consensus on rules. *Journal of Communication, 22,* 217–238.

Dymond, R. F. (1949). A scale for the measurement of empathic ability. *Journal of Consulting Psychology, 8,* 127–133.

Fast, J. (1971). *Body language*. New York: Pocket Books.

Festinger, L. (1957). *A theory of cognitive dissonance*. Stanford, CA: Stanford University Press.

Festinger, L., Schachter, S., & Back, K. (1950). *Social pressures in informal groups*. New York: Harper.

Gilbert, S. J. (1976). Empirical and theoretical extensions of self-disclosure. In G. R. Miller (Ed.), *Explorations in interpersonal communication* (pp. 197–215). Beverly Hills: Sage.

Gilbert, S. J. (1977). Differential effects of unanticipated self-disclosure on recipients of varying levels of self-esteem: A research note. *Human Communication Research, 3,* 368–371.

Gouldner, A. W. (1960). The norm of reciprocity: A preliminary statement. *American Sociological Review, 25,* 161–178.

Hall, E. T. (1959). *The silent language*. New York: Doubleday.

Harré, R., & Secord, P. F. (1973). *The explanation of social behavior*. Totowa, NJ: Littlefield, Adams.

Jones, E. E. (1975). *Ingratiation*. New York: Irvington.

Jones, E. E., & Davis, K. E. (1965). From acts to dispositions: The attribution process in person perception. In L. Berkowitz (Ed.), *Advances in experimental social psychology* (Vol. 2, pp. 219–266). New York: Academic Press.

Katz, R. L. (1963). *Empathy: Its nature and uses*. New York: Free Press.

Kelley, H. H. (1967). Attribution theory in social psychology. In D. Levine (Ed.), *Nebraska symposium on motivation* (Vol. 15, pp. 192–238). Lincoln: University of Nebraska Press.

Langer, E. J. (1978). Rethinking the role of thought in social interaction. In J. H. Harvey, W. Ickes, & R. F. Kidd (Eds.), *New directions in attribution research* (Vol. 2, pp. 35–58). New York: Wiley.

Miller, G. R. (1975). Interpersonal communication: A conceptual perspective. *Communication, 2,* 93–105.

Miller, G. R. (1978). The current status of theory and research in interpersonal communication. *Human Communication Research, 4,* 164–178.

Miller, G. R. (1980). Interpersonal communication. In C. L. Book (Ed.), *Human communication: Principles, contexts and skills* (pp. 107–139). New York: St. Martin's.

Miller, G. R. (1986). A neglected connection: Mass media exposure and interpersonal communication competency. In G. Gumpert & R. Cathcart (Eds.), *Intermedia: Interpersonal communication in a media world* (3rd ed., pp. 132–139). New York: Oxford University Press.

Miller, G. R., & Parks, M. R. (1982). Communication in dissolving relationships. In S. Duck (Ed.), *Personal relationships 4: Dissolving relationships*. (pp. 127–154). New York: Academic Press.

Miller, G. R., & Steinberg, M. (1975). *Between people: A new analysis of interpersonal communication*. Chicago: Science Research Associates.

Miller, G. R., & Sunnafrank, M. J. (1982). All is for one but one is not for all: A conceptual perspective of interpersonal communication. In F. E. X. Dance (Ed.), *Human communication theory* (pp. 220–242). New York: Harper & Row.

Morton, T. L., Alexander, J. F., & Altman, I. (1976). Communication and relationship definition. In G. R. Miller (Ed.), *Explorations in interpersonal communication* (pp. 105–125). Beverly Hills: Sage.

Newcomb, T. M. (1953). An approach to the study of communicative acts. *Psychological Review, 60,* 393–404.

Osgood, C., & Tannenbaum, P. H. (1955). The principle of congruity in the prediction of attitude change. *Psychological Review, 62,* 42–55.

Pearce, W. B., & Cronen, V. E. (1980). *Communication, action, and meaning: The creation of social realities*. New York: Praeger.

Peters, R. S. (1974). Personal understanding and personal relationships. In T. Mischel (Ed.), *Understanding other persons* (pp. 37–65). Oxford: Basil Blackwell.

Reardon, K. K. (1981). *Persuasion theory and context*. Beverly Hills: Sage.

Rosenbaum, M. R. (1986). The repulsion hypothesis: On the nondevelopment of relationships. *Journal* of *Personality and Social Psychology, 51,* 1156–1166.

Shaver, K. G. (1975). *An introduction to attribution processes.* Cambridge, MA: Winthrop, 1975.

Sillars, A. L. (1982). Attribution and communication: Are people "naive scientists" or just naive? In M. E. Roloff & C. R. Berger (Eds.), *Social cognition and communication* (pp. 73–106). Beverly Hills: Sage.

Smith, M. J. (1982). *Persuasion and human action: A review and critique of social influence theories.* Belmont, CA: Wadsworth.

Sunnafrank, M. J., & Miller, G. R. (1981). The role of initial conversations in determining attraction to similar and dissimilar strangers. *Human Communication Research, 8,* 16–25.

Watzlawick, P., Beavin, J., & Jackson, D. D. (1967). *Pragmatics of human communication.* New York: W. W. Norton.

Winch, R. F. (1958). *Mate selection: A study of complementary needs.* New York: Harper.

6

Group Dynamics and Communication

Marvin E. Shaw
University of Florida

Dennis S. Gouran
The Pennsylvania State University

Marvin E. Shaw is Professor Emeritus in the Department of Psychology at the University of Florida. He has contributed to research and theory in several areas of social psychology including communication networks, attitudes, attribution, leadership, and group decision making. He is author of Group Dynamics: The Psychology of Small Group Behavior *and coauthor of* Scales for the Measurement of Attitudes *and* Theories of Social Psychology.

Dennis S. Gouran is Professor and Head of the Department of Speech Communication at The Pennsylvania State University. He holds B.S. and M.S. degrees in speech from Illinois State University and a Ph.D. degree in speech and dramatic art from the University of Iowa. Gouran's research and teaching interests lie in the area of group communication, with particular attention to decision-making processes. He is author of numerous publications dealing with this subject, including Making Decisions in Groups: Choices and Consequences. *He is past editor of the* Central States Speech Journal *and a former president of the Central States Speech Association. He is currently president-elect of the Speech Communication Association.*

LEARNING OBJECTIVES

After studying this chapter you should be able to:

• Differentiate primary and secondary groups, formal and informal groups, and task versus experiential groups.

- List four basic reasons why individuals join groups.

- Discuss the basic stages of development in a group.

- Identify examples of individual characteristics that affect an individual's behavior in a group.

- Explain how group size and group homogeneity are related to group performance and participation.

- Discuss why cohesiveness is regarded as an important factor in group performance.

- Describe what group status is and what influence it has on group behavior.

- Analyze why communication networks influence group success.

- Define leadership and discuss various theories explaining why some leaders are more successful than others.

- Differentiate various types of group tasks and discuss the relationship between type of task, leadership style, and group effectiveness.

- List various types of experiential groups and explain what makes them different from other groups.

Participating in groups can range from being completely rewarding and positive to being completely frustrating and negative. Indeed, most of us have had the opportunity to experience both extremes. Whether participation has been predominantly rewarding or costly, however, it is a fact of life that none of us can escape the necessity of being a member of groups a significant part of the time. For this reason alone, it is useful to understand something of the ways in which groups function and the factors that influence the interaction among members, as well as the outcomes they achieve.

Since the 1930s, when Kurt Lewin first demonstrated that groups could be studied in a systematic and rigorous fashion, an enormous literature has developed. Although much about groups and the behavior of their members re-

mains a mystery, we have learned a good deal about their formation, evolution, and performance. Of particular interest in this chapter is the body of information that deals directly or indirectly with the interaction of group members, the factors that affect it, and its consequences for the outcomes that groups achieve.

George Homans (1963) once observed that "groups are not *what* we study, but *where* we often study it" (p. 165). The "it" in our case represents the verbal and nonverbal messages that individuals in groups exchange. Such messages are constrained by the characteristics of the individuals who produce them, the ends toward which they are directed, and the producers' relationships to other individuals who constitute the social entity we call the small group. Messages, in turn, have effects on relationships and the outcomes groups achieve. This type of reciprocity and the continuously evolving character of groups is suggested in the title of this chapter. Our aim is to create a better understanding of how this dynamic interplay manifests itself in the performance of groups.

An introductory essay of this type cannot provide an exhaustive review of all relevant research on small group communicative processes. It can, however, point to some of the significant data that have been accumulated and thereby illuminate the more salient influences in the interaction of individuals who form groups. In so doing, we hope not only to provide summary knowledge, but to develop an understanding of the complexity of group life and thus a deeper appreciation of the functions, successes, and failures of groups. Someone who possesses such understandings and appreciations can become a more sensitive, and possibly more effective, participant, or at least a better informed one.

THE NATURE OF GROUPS

The Definition of a Group

The term *group* has been defined in many different ways by students of the subject. Some definitions require that the collectivity have an organizational structure—accepted standards of conduct (norms), established roles, and so on—before a group can be said to exist. Others suggest that common goals must exist or that members must perceive that they constitute a group. Nearly all definitions, however, involve the concept of interdependence and interaction. Members of all groups are to some extent dependent on each other and must, therefore, interact with each other. Given these essential characteristics, we can define a group as a collection of two or more persons who are interacting with each other so that each person influences and is influenced by each other person (Shaw, 1981).

Our definition does not imply that motivations, goals, and organizational structure are unimportant aspects of groups, but only that they are unnecessary for a group to exist. Motivations are important for the formation of groups and may affect a person's decision to join one once it has formed; goals usually emerge either before the group is established or during the course of interaction; and interaction among participants may, and usually does, lead to organizational structure. But any one of these factors can be absent and a group still exists.

Types of Groups

Small group theorists and scholars classify groups according to various criteria, such as number of persons involved, degree of cohesiveness, and level of intimacy. When this approach is taken, groups are often dichotomized as primary-secondary, formal-informal, large-small, temporary–long term, or in similar ways. Probably the most common dichotomous classifications are primary-secondary and formal-informal.

Primary and Secondary Groups A *primary group,* as conceived by Cooley (1909), is an intimate face-to-face association of two or more individuals. Members are cooperatively related and are characterized by mutual sympathy and identification. Such groups are primary in that they

are instrumental in forming the social nature and ideals of individual members. Families, children's play groups, and intimate adult work and play groups are examples. In contrast, *secondary groups* are typically large, and their members may have only intermittent contact. Communication in the group is often indirect and carried on through written messages rather than through verbal exchanges. Relations among members of secondary groups are relatively formal, impersonal, and socially distant. Professional groups, formal work groups, and bureaucratic organizations are just a few examples of such entities.[1]

Formal and Informal Groups The formal-informal classification has much in common with the primary-secondary typology. *Formal groups* have a well-established social structure that is often imposed by external authority. Norms are formally stated, roles are explicit, and members are aware of relationships within the group. In *informal groups,* the structure has emerged through the interaction process, and norms, roles, and relationships are usually implicit. Such groups typically are smaller and more intimate than formal groups.

Task-Oriented and Experiential Groups Groups may also be classified according to their objectives or activities. Thus one thinks of work groups, therapy groups, social groups, and the like. Perhaps the most general distinction deriving from this approach is task-oriented versus experiential groups. *Task-oriented groups* are formed and exist for the express purpose of achieving some goal outside the group—for example, solving a problem, arriving at a decision, creating a product, or resolving a controversial issue. *Experiential groups* consist of members who wish to benefit from the group experience itself (Lakin, 1972). Members seek to learn about group processes, to rid themselves of undesirable personal characteristics, or to achieve greater freedom to express feelings and emotions. Decision-making and problem-solving groups are task-oriented, whereas therapy groups, sensitivity training groups, and encounter groups are examples of experiential groups.

In addition to the criteria of objectives and activities, some writers include the setting in which the group functions. Thus groups may be sorted into committees, gangs, clubs, teams, juries, and the like.

Such classification systems are useful for showing the great variety of groups that exist in our society and may be necessary for special purposes. In general, however, they contribute relatively little to our understanding of groups or how they function. At least, generic classifications and their relationship to the performance of groups have not been the object of much scholarly attention. The exception appears to be in the task-oriented/experiential group distinction. And the overwhelming amount of inquiry has focused on the task-oriented group. In this essay, therefore, we are concerned primarily with small, task-oriented groups, with some attention to experiential groups.

GROUP FORMATION AND DEVELOPMENT

Groups are formed when two or more persons perceive or believe that something can be accomplished through joint action that cannot be achieved by one person acting alone. The list is almost endless: a task completed, a problem solved, interaction with others, the election of a political candidate—even the overthrow of a hated government. Once a group is established, other people join for many of the same reasons that the group was established in the first place. It may be helpful to consider some of these reasons in greater detail.

Why People Join Groups

Among the many factors that influence a person's decision to join a group, the following are probably the most powerful ones: attraction to others who are members, commitment to the goals of the group, enjoyment of the activities of the

group, need for affiliation, and perceived instrumental value.

As noted in Chapter 5, interpersonal *attraction,* one of the most important reasons for joining a group, is influenced by several factors, such as proximity, physical attributes, similarity, and perceived ability of others. The role of proximity in interpersonal attraction has been observed in many situations (see, for example, Festinger, Schachter, & Back, 1950; Maissonneuve, Palmade, & Fourment, 1952; Sommer, 1959; Sykes, Larntz, & Fox, 1976). Similarity of attitudes is another powerful determinant of interpersonal attraction (see, for instance, Byrne, 1961; Byrne, London, & Griffitt, 1968; Byrne & Nelson, 1964, 1965; Newcomb, 1961). Interpersonal attraction is also affected by similarity of personality (Griffitt, 1966), economic similarity (Byrne, Clore, & Worchel, 1966), and similarity of sex and race (Kandel, 1978; Lumsden, Brown, Lumsden, & Hill, 1974; C. R. Smith, Williams, & Willis, 1967).

In addition to their attraction to members of a group, individuals may join for several other reasons. For example, a person who believes that protecting the environment is important might join the Sierra Club; a person who is committed to improving public education could be attracted to a parent-teacher association (see Reckman & Goethals, 1973; Sherif & Sherif, 1953). Thus an individual often joins a particular group because he or she finds the *goals* of the group worthwhile or because he or she enjoys the activities engaged in by group members.

Sometimes joining a group satisfies one's *need for affiliation* (McClelland, Atkinson, Clark, & Lowell, 1953; Schachter, 1959). Several studies show that deprivation of social interaction influences subsequent behaviors in social situations (for example, Gerwirtz & Baer, 1958a, 1958b; Stevenson & Odom, 1962). Group membership is a way of generating social contact.

Finally, people join groups because they perceive that group membership will be *useful* for achieving goals outside the group itself. A businessman or woman, for instance, may join the Chamber of Commerce because it is a source of business contacts, or college students may join a sorority or fraternity to enhance their prestige on campus (Willerman & Swanson, 1953).

Whatever the specific reason for joining a group, the decision to do so depends in part on what one's interactions with others have revealed about the group and how it will seemingly satisfy one's needs, desires, and interests. Similarly, the invitation to join a group is partially a result of what interaction with a prospective member has indicated about his or her ability to contribute to the group's purposes and to the relationships among its members (see Zander, 1976). These mutual expectations will, in turn, affect subsequent interaction among the members of a group and its peculiar evolution.

Group Development

When a number of persons meet as a group for the first time, they typically begin to talk with one another. An observer will notice that there appears to be much uncertainty about what the group is supposed to be doing, how it should be organized, and what kinds of interpersonal relationships should exist. If this same observer were to watch the interaction after the group had met several times, he or she would probably be impressed by the changes that had occurred. It is likely that the uncertainty would be much less evident, members would relate to each other with greater assurance, and the group would appear to be working in unison to achieve some goal. In short, group development would have taken place. The nature and degree of such development, however, vary from group to group.

To understand the process of development, researchers commonly make systematic observations of several groups, usually groups of a particular type, such as encounter groups, sensitivity training groups, or task-oriented groups. They then analyze the observations and identify and label the various stages in group development. The particular stages identified are influenced not only by the kinds of groups observed, but also by the person who conducts the analysis.

The content of group interaction may be reasonably classified in several different ways, so it is not surprising that different analysts find somewhat different stages of development. Table 6.1 outlines the stages that several researchers have reported. Differences exist with respect to the kinds of groups analyzed, the number of stages identified, the labels applied to the stages, and the descriptions of the dominant themes during each stage of development.

For instance, Bales and Strodtbeck (1951) analyzed task-oriented groups and found three stages of development, whereas B. A. Fisher (1970) identified four. Although differences may seem great, closer examination reveals significant commonalities. Tuckman (1965) reviewed several studies of group development and concluded that the typical sequence could be described adequately in terms of four phases, which he labeled forming, storming, norming, and performing. In the forming stage, groups are concerned with orientation; in the storming stage, conflicts and polarization arise; in the norming stage, the group begins to resolve conflicts and establish new standards of conduct and social roles; and in the performing stage, the recently developed interpersonal structure facilitates the achievement of group goals (cf. Poole, 1981).

A good deal of the early research on group development focused on relationships among participants as characterized by the phases through which they typically pass. Parallel patterns, however, have been detected in the task dimension of group process. Bales and Strodtbeck (1951) and B. A. Fisher (1970) are among the earlier studies not concerned with relationships so much as with stages of problem solving. More recent research has been supportive of phase development (see, for example, Ellis & Fisher, 1975; B. A. Fisher, 1979; Mabry, 1975).[2]

Despite differences in specific analyses, group development seems to proceed in an orderly and reasonably consistent manner. Most groups initially experience uncertainty and require time for orientation, experience a stage of conflict regarding personal and authority relations among

Table 6.1 Results of Representative Analyses of Stages in Group Development

---

Bales & Strodtbeck (1951): Analysis of Task-Oriented Groups

Stage 1. Orientation: Primary concern with distribution of task-relevant information among group members.
Stage 2. Evaluation: Group members judge the information relative to the problem or task; evaluate alternative solutions.
Stage 3. Control: Concern with intermember control and environmental control, including the task.

Bennis & Shepard (1956): Analysis of Sensitivity Training Groups

---

Stage 1. Authority: Preoccupation with authority relations.
Subphase a. Preoccupation with submission.
Subphase b. Preoccupation with rebellion.
Subphase c. Resolution of problems with authority.
Stage 2. Personal: Preoccupation with personal relations.
Subphase d. Preoccupation with intermember identification.
Subphase e. Preoccupation with individual identity.
Subphase f. Resolution of the interdependence problem.

B. A. Fisher (1970): Analysis of Task-Oriented Groups

Stage 1. Orientation: Characterized by clarification and agreement; members search tentatively for ideas and direction relative to decision making.
Stage 2. Conflict: Characterized by disagreement; opinions become more definite, attitudes polarize, and comments become less ambiguous.
Stage 3. Emergence: Characterized by dissipation of conflict; ambiguity of comments recurs.
Stage 4. Reinforcement: Characterized by harmony; arguments decrease, comments favoring decision proposals are reinforced, and dissent almost disappears.

Winter (1976): Analysis of Self-Analytic Groups

Stage 1. Encounter: Characterized by uncertainty, concerns with acceptance and inclusion in the group.
Stage 2. Differentiation, Conflict, Norm Building: Characterized by concerns about accommodating individual differences, roles, and leadership.
Stage 3. Production: Group norms and roles are well established; focus is on the task.
Stage 4. Separation: Characterized by concerns about what happens after the group disbands.

Caple (1978): Analysis of Counseling, Facilitating, and Task-Oriented Groups

---

Stage 1. Orientation: Characterized by ambiguity, tentative actions, and uncoordinated behavior.

Table 6.1 *continued*

Stage 2. Conflict: There is much dissension, disagreement, and impatience among group.
Stage 3. Integration: A period of reconciliation and consensus seeking; polarization decreases.
Stage 4. Achievement: Group has reached a functional level; norms and roles well established; relations good.
Stage 5. Order: Members are satisfied with the group, but show concern about the future of the group.

Near (1978): Analysis of Self-Analytic Groups

Stage 1. Leader abdication: Confusion reigns, resulting from trainer's refusal to accept the leadership role.
Stage 2. Affectivity: Members are concerned about norm expression and about accepting responsibility for the group.
Stage 3. Control: Some members assume control of group, leading to discussions of roles of institutional and peer leaders.
Stage 4. Affectivity: A period of equalization; characterized by affective reactions to leadership structure.
Stage 5. Inclusion: Attention shifts to role differentiations; some members want to be included in elite group, others want autonomy.

group members, resolve these conflicts, and eventually reach a productive state in which members work toward achieving group goals. Obviously, not all groups go through all stages. In some groups, some phases may be greatly attenuated; other groups may disband before their development is complete. On the whole, however, the phase pattern described is more frequently in evidence than not.

GROUP COMPOSITION

As the preceding discussion emphasized, group formation and development are influenced by many factors, not the least of which are the types of communicative exchanges in which members engage. Once a group has reached a relatively stable stage of development, the members' performance continues to be affected by numerous variables. These include, at minimum, composition, structure, the type of communication net-

work, leadership, goals, and task requirements. Each of these concepts, of course, refers to a class or set of factors that partially determine the characteristics of a group's interaction.

The term *composition* refers to the individuals who constitute a group, their personal characteristics and idiosyncrasies, their manner of behaving, their skills and abilities, their typical reactions to others, and the like. Group processes are influenced by at least two aspects of composition. First, the characteristics of group members, to some degree, influence their own behavior and how others in the group react to them. Second, the particular combination of individual characteristics has an important effect on the entire group's ability to perform as a unit. In the first case, an attribute such as high intelligence may influence interaction regardless of the intelligence of others in the group; in the second case, the effect that a particular quality has on the group's functioning depends on the characteristics of others in the same group. It is represented by variables such as group size, cohesiveness, and the homogeneity-heterogeneity of the participants.

Personal Characteristics and Group Behavior

Personal characteristics important to group interaction include variables such as age, gender, ability, and personality attributes. Our knowledge about the relative impact of each of these types of variables is rather uneven, however.

Age Chronological age appears to influence several aspects of the individual group member's behavior, especially his or her communicative behavior. Early studies (Beaver, 1932; Parten, 1932) revealed that the number of interactions increases with age, and more recent studies have shown that interaction patterns change with increasing age. For instance, H. W. Smith (1977) observed that simultaneous talking and interruptions of others decrease in frequency from age 5 to age 20. Similarly, Newman (1976) noted that egocentric behavior decreased as the individual developed language skills and the ability to comprehend social rules. The person who emerges as leader is often older than others in the group (Stogdill, 1974).

Sex The gender of group members also affects group process. Traditional sex roles in American society imply that males should be assertive, aggressive, domineering, and task-oriented, whereas females should be nurturant, passive, submissive, and person-oriented (Wiley, 1973). Until recently, observations of groups tended to reveal such differential patterns of behavior. Men react more negatively to uninvited face-to-face approach (Fisher & Byrne, 1975) and respond more quickly to close approach (Krail & Leventhal, 1976) than women do. McGuire (1973) observed aggressive behavior in natural settings and found that men were more aggressive than women, but highly aggressive women were more popular than less aggressive women. The oppo-

site was true for men. However, the belief that women are typically less aggressive than men has been questioned by the results of a study of norm violations (de Gloria & de Ridder, 1979). These investigators found that when norm violation was relatively infrequent, men responded more aggressively than women, but women responded more aggressively than men when violations were frequent. Perhaps women are less easily aroused to aggression than men but respond more strongly when stimulated to aggress.

Women and men have also revealed differences in other facets of communication. Women talk more than men (Ickes & Barnes, 1977), and they socialize more intensely in new environments than men (Wheeler & Nezlek, 1977). Women also make more eye contact than men (Exline, 1963).

Differences in the communicative behavior of male and female group members no longer appear to be the rule. Mabry (1985) found virtually no differences in the frequency of occurrence of the 12 categories of Bales's (1950) Interaction Process Analysis scheme as a function of the gender composition of problem-solving groups. Bunyi and Andrews (1985) similarly failed to detect consistent differences in the interaction characteristics of male and female participants or in the likelihood of their emerging as group leaders. Spillman, Spillman, and Reinking (1981), moreover, discovered that even when differences in leadership emergence among males and females were present, they diminished over time. When gender is viewed as a psychological rather than biological attribute, male-female comparisons show less differentiation in communicative behavior than earlier research has suggested.

Abilities It is probably quite obvious that the members' abilities, skills, and knowledge have an effect on their behavior in the group. Several studies have shown that intelligence is positively related to general activity, including amount of participation, in the group (Bass, McGehee, Hawkins, Young, & Gebel, 1953), leadership emergence (Bass & Wurster, 1953; Hollander,

1954), and popularity (Mann, 1959; Mill, 1953). Reflective thinking ability, moreover, has been shown to increase one's potential for influencing group decisions as well as the quality of ideas generated (Pyron, 1964; Pyron & Sharp, 1963).

The group's ability to draw appropriate inferences from the information it consults can be important in determining the quality of decisions the group reaches (see, for example, Hirokawa & Pace, 1983; Martz, 1986). Gouran (1984a), in an examination of the Watergate transcripts, found consistent evidence of inferential shortcomings of those responsible for the decisions to conceal White House involvement in the 1972 break-in at Democratic National Committee headquarters. In addition, it appears that communication, rather than serving as a corrective for inferential errors, often exacerbates the problem and, hence, increases the likelihood that such misjudgments will affect the choice a group makes (Gouran, 1986).

Abilities and knowledge specifically relevant to a task or group goal may have even greater effects on group interaction than a general aptitude. For instance, task-related abilities were found to correlate 0.66 with influence on the group's decision and 0.83 with effective leadership (Palmer, 1962a, 1962b). The leader who knows the correct solution to a problem is generally more successful in communicating the wisdom of his or her choice than one who does not know the correct solution (Maier, 1950, 1953), and the possession of expert knowledge induces more attempts to lead and higher status in the group (Shevitz, 1955). When a group member has special task-related information, he or she has more influence on a group's decisions, and those decisions are of higher quality if other members perceive the information as valid (Shaw & Penrod, 1962a, 1962b). An exception to this general premise was noted by Riecken (1958), who discovered that talkativeness may be more important than knowledge of a correct solution in gaining its acceptance or influencing decisions. At least, knowledge alone appears to be an insufficient condition for influencing decisions.

Personality Finally, the personality characteristics of participants strongly influence their behavior in groups, not unexpectedly, since personality traits supposedly represent relatively stable ways of behaving. Thus the findings in this area are to some extent merely validations of traits. For example, socially sensitive persons behave in ways that enhance their acceptance in the group (Cattell & Stice, 1960; Greer, 1955). The anxious member inhibits effective group functioning (Beckwith, Iverson, & Render, 1965), presumably by making his or her anxieties an object of attention. The well-adjusted member, on the other hand, contributes to effective group functioning (Greer, 1955; Haythorn, 1953). Numerous other investigations could be cited (see Mann, 1959), but the general conclusion is that socially desirable traits facilitate group functioning, whereas socially undesirable characteristics impede effective group functioning (Shaw, 1981).

Group Size

The contributions a member can make often depends on how many other persons are present. Thus size can affect the range of talents available to the group, the degree of participation of the members, the relationships between the leader and other participants, the feelings of the members about the group, and, often, the outcome of a group's interaction.

As the size of the group increases, the range of abilities, skills, and knowledge also increases. The advantages of this increase in resources for problem solving and decision making may appear to be self-evident. However, realizing these advantages depends in part on the kind of task the group faces. In some cases, increased group size may be disadvantageous, especially if it limits the participation of the most competent members, makes coordination of a task more difficult, or increases the likelihood of irrelevant input. We will explore this facet of group size in more depth when we consider group goals and tasks.

One of the more significant effects of group size is its impact on participation in group discussions. As the size of the group increases, the proportion of time available to each participant decreases. For most members, this means that the larger the group, the less opportunity they will have to be involved, to express beliefs and opinions, to provide necessary information, or to engage in the critical examination of ideas. In addition, members often feel more inhibited in larger than in smaller groups. The total amount of talking is usually less in larger than in smaller groups (Indik, 1965). More important, the distribution of participation varies with the group size: As the number of participants increases, a few members may dominate discussion, with others contributing little or not at all (Bales, Strodtbeck, Mills, & Rosenborough, 1951). Poole, McPhee, and Seibold (1982), in their examination of how communication processes influence decision making and other aspects of group behavior, found that communication's effect on decision outcomes will diminish as group size increases. Group members are more likely to make decisions on the basis of such producers as majority vote or delegation of responsibility to key members, such as the acknowledged leader. After studying leadership behavior in groups of varying sizes, Hemphill (1950) concluded that as groups become larger, the demands on the leader become greater, and tolerance for leader-centered direction of group activities increases.

Increasing group size appears to have adverse effects on members' reactions to the group and toward other participants. An early study by Katz (1949) demonstrated that members of smaller groups are better satisfied than members of larger groups, a finding supported by another study revealing that members of smaller groups express significantly more positive evaluations of their group than members of larger groups (Slater, 1958). These unfavorable reactions to larger groups are reflected in members' behaviors during the course of their interaction. An analysis of the content of group discussions about ways of reducing automobile accidents, for example, indicated that as size increased from two to five members, group members showed greater dis-

agreement, greater antagonism toward others, and greater tension release (O'Dell, 1968). Such reactions may also account for the fact that consensus is more difficult to achieve in larger than in smaller groups (Hare, 1952).

Group Cohesiveness

In addition to the effects that we have discussed above, member characteristics and group size affect the degree to which the group holds together. This characteristic of groups is usually referred to as *cohesiveness*. Definitions of cohesiveness vary, but perhaps the most widely accepted one is that offered by Festinger (1950): the result of all those forces acting on the members to remain in or to leave the group.

Cohesiveness is a complex phenomenon influenced by numerous factors, including those we discussed as determinants of group formation. For example, groups composed of persons with similar attitudes are more cohesive than groups whose members have dissimilar attitudes (Terborg, Castore, & DeNinno, 1976). Successful groups, moreover, tend to be more cohesive than unsuccessful groups (Blanchard, Weigel, & Cook, 1975). In addition, cohesiveness is affected by the communicative exchanges that occur in groups. Deutsch (1968) reviewed research on cohesiveness and concluded that it is associated with the types of sentiments group members express, their readiness to be influenced by others in the group, and the individual's tendency to respond positively to the behaviors of others in the group.

Conversely, the degree of cohesiveness that exists in a group clearly affects the interaction process, member satisfaction, social influence of members, and overall productivity. Lott and Lott (1961) determined that cohesiveness and amount of communication in the group are moderately to strongly correlated. Level of communication and cohesiveness were also positively associated in a study of industrial training groups (Moran, 1966).

The pattern of communication in cohesive groups is different from the pattern in noncohesive groups. In laboratory discussion groups, Back (1951) found that members of noncohesive groups tended to act independently, whereas cohesive-group members worked together in seeking information and in striving to reach agreement. Similarly, highly cohesive and noncohesive groups of second graders assigned the task of learning to spell lists of words revealed different patterns of interaction (Shaw & Shaw, 1962). Members of cohesive groups engaged in planning prior to attempting to learn to spell the words, and once they formed a plan, they usually followed it; nonconhesive-group members began testing one another at once with seemingly no specific plan of study. Members of cohesive groups were friendly, cooperative, and praised each other for successes; members of noncohesive groups were hostile, aggressive, and often complained to the teacher about the behavior of fellow group members.

Perhaps because of these differences in interaction, cohesive-group members have more influence over others in the group (Back, 1951; Lott & Lott, 1961) and experience greater satisfaction both with the group and its progress (Exline, 1957; Gross, 1954).

One might anticipate that the positive effects of cohesiveness described above would have a direct effect on productivity, as well as an indirect effect via increased member motivation to work toward group goals. Research generally supports these expectations. For example, a field study of 12 six-man squads in the United States Army yielded correlations between measures of cohesiveness and scores on assigned military problems ranging from $+0.61$ to $+0.78$ (Goodacre, 1951). Positive correlations between cohesiveness and productivity were also reported by Van Zelst (1952) for teams of bricklayers and carpenters. Other investigations of natural groups yielded similar findings (such as Hemphill & Sechrest, 1952; Strupp & Hausman, 1953).

Results of laboratory studies are less consistent. Berkowitz (1954) and Hoogstraten and Vorst (1978) reported a positive relationship; Schachter, Ellertson, McBride, and Gregory (1951) found

no relationship; and Shaw and Shaw (1962) discovered both positive and negative relationships between cohesiveness and productivity. Analysis of the circumstances in which these studies were conducted suggests that cohesive groups are more effective in achieving those goals that they accept as goals for the group, but are not necessarily more effective on assigned tasks.

On the face of it, cohesiveness appears to be a highly desirable quality for a group to possess. The attribute, however, has its dark side. Schachter (1951), for instance, found that cohesiveness promotes an expressed intolerance for deviant opinion, even when such opinions may have constructive value. Janis (1982), moreover, has shown cohesiveness and the resulting tendency to promote concurrence that it fosters to be at the base of a number of disastrous foreign policy and domestic decisions in his celebrated work on groupthink.[3] McKinney (1985) detected several symptoms of groupthink in the deliberations of the Warren Commission, a group whose conclusions concerning the 1963 assassination of President John F. Kennedy were thrown into serious question by a congressional inquiry nearly 15 years after the original report. Among the communicative behaviors to which cohesiveness may lead are concurrence seeking, selective dismissal of potentially relevant information, and the censure of discrepant or unwanted opinions.

Homogeneity-Heterogeneity of Group Members

Up to this point, we have been discussing various combinations of persons that produce some group characteristics which, in turn, influence group process and output. A somewhat different group-composition variable receiving attention is the extent to which the members of a group have similar or dissimilar personal characteristics, such as intelligence (Goldman, 1965), gender (Mabry, 1985), or racial background (Lumsden et al., 1974). Of greater relevance to the subject of this chapter, however, is a concept we may refer to as *profile homogeneity,* the extent to which the members of groups are similar across a range of personality and attitude characteristics.

Groups that are heterogeneous with respect to personality characteristics appear to be more effective than homogeneous groups. For example, Hoffman (1959) and Hoffman and Maier (1961) found that groups whose members had similar profiles on the Guilford-Zimmerman Temperament Survey were less adept at solving problems than groups whose members had dissimilar profiles. Other research (for example, Triandis, Hall, & Ewen, 1965) supports these findings.

In general, heterogeneity of membership appears to facilitate group effectiveness because of the increased range of abilities, skills, knowledge, and other resources that it brings. In contrast, similarity in group members' personality profiles, while conducive to consensus and agreement, also appears to contribute to shared misconceptions and the reinforcement of misjudgment. This tendency was clearly evident, for example, in the discussions of President Nixon and his associates as they attempted to manage the Watergate crisis (see Gouran, 1976, 1986). Heterogeneity can provide a necessary safeguard against such possibilities.

GROUP STRUCTURE

In our discussion of group development, we used such terms as *role, authority relations,* and *norms,* all of which refer to aspects of group structure. The reader might infer (correctly) that group structure emerges through a process of group development.[4] When a number of persons interact for the first time, differentiations begin to occur. Some talk more than others and, thereby, may have more influence in the group. Some attempt to dominate and may succeed. Standard ways of behaving in the group develop, and relationships among group members are established. As a result, the group becomes divided into parts or positions. The pattern of relationships among these differentiated parts of the group is called *group structure.*

Depending on what differentiations have taken place during its development, within any particular group there may exist many or only a few positions. We speak of the positions of leader and follower in a general way. But we also think in more specific terms, such as chairperson, secretary, and treasurer, when positions have been specifically designated. A *position,* then, is the particular part one takes (or is given) in a group as distinguished from parts taken by (or given to) other group members.

Roles

In addition, a *social role* (or merely *role*) is associated with each position in the group. Whereas a position represents the distinctive part one has as a group member and is identified by a label, the concept of *role* refers to behavior related to a position. There are actually three types of roles we can identify: expected roles, perceived roles, and enacted roles. An *expected role* is a set of behaviors that group members desire the occupant of the position to enact; a *perceived role* is the set of behaviors that the occupant believes he or she should enact; and an *enacted role* is the set of behaviors the occupant actually exhibits. Unless otherwise specified, the term *role* ordinarily refers to other group members' expectations for a given position. We should also note that expected roles and perceived roles represent behaviors deriving solely from a position in a group, whereas an enacted role derives from both the position and the occupant's idiosyncrasies.

Figure 6.1 shows a hypothetical group structure for the Administrative Council of a small college. The president's position at the top of the diagram indicates that the occupant has the highest status in the group. Vice presidents have the next-highest status, followed by the supervisor, registrar, bursar, and deans. Figure 6.1 also shows that the roles associated with different positions vary considerably. The president is expected to assume responsibility for the entire college, to set major policies, to chair meetings of the Ad-

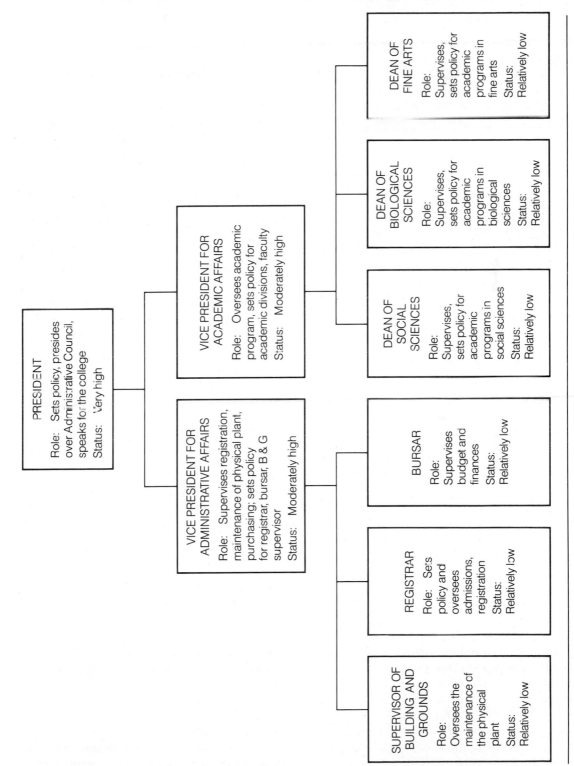

Figure 6.1 Hypothetical structure of the administrative group for a small college.

ministrative Council, and so on. The vice president for administrative affairs is expected to supervise those responsible for maintenance and support services for the college, and the vice president for academic affairs is concerned with the educational and instructional programs in the college. Other roles in the group are equally distinctive.

Roles often come into conflict. This can occur, for example, when one is enacting a role differently from the way other group members expect, or when one crosses role boundaries and begins performing functions assumed to be the prerogative of other group members. Such conflicts, according to Gross, Mason, and McEachern (1957), are typically managed by reference either to perceived personal costs or to one's standards of morality. These points of reference, in turn, affect the manner and content of one's exchanges with other group members. Whereas an individual perceiving high costs for continuing to violate role expectations might comply with others' insistence that he/she "keep his/her place," a morally driven group member might well develop a defensive reaction to comments about his or her alleged infraction.

A rigid observance of role expectations will sometimes prevent one from communicating honestly with other group members or, at least, cause one to refrain from comments that could be construed as exceeding one's legitimate freedoms. Gouran, Hirokawa, and Martz (1986) found this to be the case in a study of the decision-making processes involved in the *Challenger* accident, when a number of people opposed to the launch of the space shuttle nevertheless refused to bypass their superiors. As we shall show momentarily, however, the likelihood of a particular response to role conflict and role observance is affected by a group member's status.

Norms and Conformity

In addition to social roles that specify appropriate behaviors for the occupants of particular positions, members typically establish a set of general rules of conduct that apply to everyone in the group, called *norms*. Norms are formed with respect to those behaviors that are important to the group. They vary in relation to the number of participants who agree with them (although presumably more than 50 percent of group members must accept a rule in order for it to become a norm), the degree to which members conform, and the range of permissible deviation. Depending on the extent to which they have internalized the values that norms represent, group members conform to some norms most of the time, whereas they often deviate from the behavior specified by some other norms. Similarly, members may deviate markedly from some norms without sanction, but even minor deviations from others elicit strong negative responses.

Although most participants have some degree of freedom to violate role requirements and other group norms, such behavior is not likely to be tolerated indefinitely. Hollander (1958) has coined the term *idiosyncratic credit* to refer to the freedom one has to deviate from a group's expectations. As in the case of other types of credit, one can exhaust the supply rather quickly. When a member has little freedom to violate a group's norms, the typical response to even a threatened infraction is pressure for uniformity. The amount of pressure is likely to be proportional to the severity of the deviation and the importance of the norm.

Schachter's (1951) classic study of deviation, communication, and rejection revealed a pattern in which the majority initially directs a great deal of communication to a member holding a deviant opinion. If conformity does not result, communication is reduced sharply, with the deviant's becoming a virtual social isolate. Communication is also affected in other ways. Taylor (1970), for example, found that comments directed at deviants showed higher levels of hostility and were less reasonable than comments made to other group members.

Begin the target of hostile communication and facing rejection are not pleasant prospects, especially if one values one's membership in a group. As a result, many group members succumb to majority pressure with very little resistance. There is, however, some evidence of deviant influence in situations involving pressure for uniformity (see, for example, Bradley, Hamon, & Harris, 1976; Harnack, 1963). When a person taking a deviant position on an issue has superior arguments and communicates in nonhostile ways, he or she can apparently sometimes sway an initially opposed majority to the deviant point of view (Valentine & Fisher, 1974).

Conformity to group norms varies with many conditions. When a high degree of conformity exists, the consequences for the group may be either desirable (Berkowitz & Daniels, 1963) or undesirable (Milgram, 1963). Some conformity is necessary if the group is to function as a social unit, but blind conformity to majority opinion may lead to faulty group decisions. For the individual, conformity is usually rewarded and deviation punished (Levine, Saxe, & Harris, 1976; Schachter, 1951), but as we have also noted, a great deal depends on how the deviant communicates his or her position and responds to majority pressure.

Status

Each of the positions in the group is usually evaluated by the members in terms of its prestige, value, or importance to the group. This evaluation is called *social status,* or merely *status.* The status ascribed to a position is also credited to any person who occupies that position. However, status may be conferred on a person for other reasons; hence, two individuals who occupy the same position at different times may be of quite different value to the group.

The status accorded a group member has major effects on both the person's behavior and that of others with whom he or she interacts. However, status is almost inextricably related to social power. Therefore, when we are discussing the effects of status, remember that these same effects occur in respect to power differences and that

power may actually be the critical variable (see Bradley, 1978).

The most pervasive effects of status differences relate to the pattern and content of communication in the group. In general, more communication is initiated and received by those of high status than by those of low status; moreover, the content of messages directed upward in the status hierarchy tends to be more positive than the content of messages directed downward in the hierarchy.

In an early study, Kelley (1951) analyzed the communication output of group members in high- and low-status positions, with and without the possibility that the positions would be changed during the course of the experiment. Several effects were observed: (1) Low-status members communicated more task-irrelevant information than high-status members. (2) High-status members appeared to be restrained from communicating criticisms of their own jobs to those in lower-status positions. (3) Communication with those of high status apparently served as a substitute for real upward movement for those low-status members who had no possibility of attaining a higher-status position.

In another study, investigators found that group members received more communication from those at their own status level than from those occupying either higher- or lower-status positions (Barnlund & Harland, 1963). Further evidence concerning the effects of the status hierarchy on communication was provided by a study of rumor transmissions (Back et al., 1950). Rumors were planted at five status levels in an industrial organization, and selected members of the organization reported from whom they first heard the rumors. Of 17 communications, 11 were upward, 4 were at the same level, and only 2 were downward. These researchers also found that rumors critical of high-status persons were infrequently communicated to others.

High status can protect group members from severe sanctions when they deviate from group norms. A study of fraternity and sorority members' assignment of sanctions revealed that less severe censure was recommended for high-status deviants than for those of low status (Wahrman, 1977). Studies by Gerson (1967), Gouran, Ketrow, Spear, and Metzger (1984), and Gouran and Andrews (1984) further support the notion that high status affords certain protections against verbal and other kinds of censure. As Gouran, et al. found, communication involving the infractions of high-status individuals functions to portray the infractions as less serious than when they are attributed to those of low status. In addition, group members seem to rationalize the misconduct of high-status individuals on the grounds that their behavior is the result of circumstantial factors.

High status does not always protect against censure, however. A study of destructive obedience based on the My Lai massacre of civilians during the Vietnam War (a military officer carries out orders from a superior officer, with disastrous consequences) indicated that the officer who gave the order was held more responsible than the person who implemented it (Hamilton, 1978). In such cases, the role requirements of the higher-status positions supersede the protective effects of status: Military officers are expected to accept responsibility for those under their command.

Relative status also affects other behaviors in the group. For example, high-status individuals apparently feel free to approach closely or to stand apart when interacting with a low-status person, but the low-status person feels constrained to an "appropriate interperson distance" (Dean, Willis, & Hewitt, 1975). If high- and low-status persons perform equally well on easy tasks, those with high status are seen as having greater skill than ones having low status (Zimmer & Sheposh, 1975). A study of nonverbal behaviors in a simulated teaching situation indicated that individuals having high status (teachers) claimed more space with their bodies, talked more, and attempted more interruptions than their lower-status counterparts (students) (Leffler, Gillespie, & Conaty, 1982).

COMMUNICATION NETWORKS

The arrangement of communication channels among the members of the group could be viewed as an aspect of group structure. However, it differs from the other aspects of structure discussed above, in that they have to do with personal relationships among participants. The concept of a network has to do with how group members are related to one another in terms of opportunities for interaction. A communication network in a group may be either formal (imposed by external authority) or informal (derived from group interaction processes). *Network* (or *net*) refers to who communicates with whom, either as consequence of communication channel availability or the perceived freedom to use available channels. Research on the effects of communication nets on group processes and outcomes has been limited almost entirely to the study of imposed nets (experiments in which the investigator determines the arrangements of communication channels among group members).

The flow of information in the interaction of a group determines to a significant degree its efficiency and the satisfaction of its members. Years ago, Bavelas (1950) suggested that in groups free of outside direction, interaction patterns that emerge and stabilize are products of social processes within the group. However, when groups are embedded in larger organizations, interaction processes do not completely determine the communication pattern.

This fact raises the question of how fixed communication patterns affect group behavior and output. Working with Bavelas, Leavitt (1951) devised a methodology for investigating this problem. Group members were placed in cubicles interconnected by means of slots in the walls. Written messages could be exchanged by simply pushing them through the slots. Any desired communication channel could be imposed on a group by closing the appropriate slots. Figure 6.2

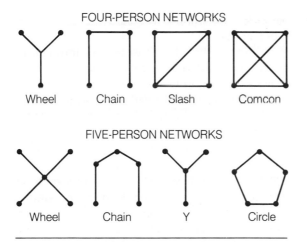

FOUR-PERSON NETWORKS

Wheel   Chain   Slash   Comcon

FIVE-PERSON NETWORKS

Wheel   Chain   Y   Circle

Figure 6.2 Examples of communication networks in four- and five-person groups. Dots represent positions in the group and lines represent two-way communication channels between positions.

shows examples of the kinds of communication patterns that can be created by this technique. In these diagrams, dots represent positions in the group, and lines represent two-way communication channels between positions. Of course, one-way channels can be established, but most investigations have employed two-way channels. We should point out that spatial arrangements are of no consequence; it is the relationships among positions, in terms of communication channels, that are of interest.

Centralized Versus Decentralized Networks

Leavitt (1951) conducted an experiment using the five-person networks shown in Figure 6.2. Five groups in each network were given 15 trials on a simple symbol-identification task. For each trial, each member in the group was given a card containing a number of symbols, such as a diamond, a square, an asterisk, and so on. Only one symbol appeared on every card. The task was to identify this common symbol. The data gathered suggested that centralized networks (that is, those in

which one position is distinctly more central than others, such as the wheel, Y, and chain) are more efficient on symbol-identification tasks than decentralized networks (those in which all members are the same or nearly the same in centrality, such as the circle and the comcon). The data also indicated that leaders emerge more frequently in centralized nets, whereas members send more messages and are better satisfied in decentralized nets.

Subsequent investigations of network effects using the same or similar kinds of tasks generally support Leavitt's findings (for example, Guetzkow & Simon, 1955; Kano, 1971; Lawson, 1964). When more complex tasks have been used (for example, arithmetic tasks, sentence completion tasks, and discussion problems), findings agree with Leavitt's with respect to member satisfaction, leadership emergence, and number of messages sent. However, very different results are obtained for performance: Groups in decentralized nets require less time to solve problems and make fewer errors than groups in centralized nets (for a review of network studies, see Shaw, 1964).

Independence and Saturation

The differential effects of communication nets on group performance and member satisfaction are at least partially accounted for by two explanatory concepts: independence and saturation. The concept of independence was first proposed by Leavitt (1951) and later revised by Shaw (1964). According to the later formulation, *independence* refers to the degree of freedom a member has to function in the group. Those who are free from restrictions on their behavior are better satisfied, perhaps because of culturally supported needs for autonomy. Although freedom of action may be influenced by situational factors, such as the actions of others in the group and one's own perceptions of the situation, one's position in a network exerts a strong effect on independence through its effect on access to information.

The concept of *saturation,* first proposed by Gilchrist, Shaw, and Walker (1954), refers to communication overload that frequently occurs in the central positions in centralized communication nets. When the number of messages that the person occupying a central position must handle exceeds his or her capacity to process them, the communication requirements begin to counteract the positive effects of a favorable network position. When this happens, the position is said to be saturated. In general, the greater the saturation, the less efficient the group and the less satisfied the group members. The effect on satisfaction is not so great as the effect on group efficiency, however.

As a number of studies show, the negative consequences of position saturation on group performance are greater for centralized networks than for decentralized networks. For example, Macy, Christie, and Luce (1953) found that groups were less successful in identifying a "noisy" marble (a marble having many different colors) in a centralized than in a decentralized network; Shaw (1958) discovered that centralized nets were disrupted more than decentralized nets by irrelevant information; Kano (1977) determined that the amount of information relevant to a Leavitt-type symbol-identification task (11 symbols versus 6) had little effect on performance in the circle, but groups in a wheel network performed less effectively when required to process more information; and Moore, Johnson, and Arnold (1972) produced evidence showing that the number of messages sent to the central position in centralized nets correlated with several measures of group efficiency in ways predicted by the saturation hypothesis (for example, +0.59 with mean time to solution, +0.67 with total number of errors, and +0.47 with total number of failures). In short, anything that increases saturation has greater negative effects on performance by groups in centralized nets as compared with groups in decentralized nets.

In brief summary, centralized networks in comparison to decentralized networks enhance leadership emergence and performance on sim-

ple tasks, but impede the solution of complex problems and reduce member satisfaction. These effects are mediated, at least in part, through independence and saturation processes.

Network studies have been criticized for their artificiality and lack of relationship to the conditions under which most groups function. As a result, interest in them began to wane in the 1960s. In an important sense, however, this line of research may have been ahead of its time. The 1970s and 1980s have been witness to significant developments in computer technology. Among these developments has been the rise of decision support systems and the recognition of computers as a communication device (see, for example, Conrath & Bair, 1974; DeSanctis & Gallupe, 1984; Rohrbaugh & McCartt, 1986). The increasingly widespread use of such electronic technology places many groups in network arrangements not unlike those being investigated in the 1950s and early 1960s. The findings regarding quality of solutions to problems, efficiency, leadership emergence, and group member satisfaction, therefore, may have much greater relevance today than they did at the time they were originally produced.

LEADERSHIP

Leadership is another aspect of group process that may be considered an element of group structure. There is often a part in a group identified as the leader position, along with the associated leader's role. However, leadership is more frequently treated as an independent aspect of groups, perhaps because it is viewed as a particularly significant phenomenon. It has also been studied more extensively than perhaps any other variable.

Definition of Leadership

If someone asked if you know what leadership is, you probably would not hesitate to say, "Yes, of course I know what leadership is." But if several persons were asked to define leadership, different definitions would undoubtedly be given—even if those questioned were "experts" in leadership research. For example, in a review of the literature on leadership, Stogdill (1974) identified no fewer than 11 fundamentally different definitions of leadership. For our purposes, we will adopt the definition of leadership proposed by Tannenbaum and Massarik (1957): interpersonal influence exercised in a situation and directed, through the communication process, toward the attainment of a specified goal or goals. A leader, then, is a person who exerts such influence.

Approaches to Leadership

Early researchers assumed that persons who were successful in achieving a position of leadership possessed traits that distinguished them from nonleaders or followers. Thus it seemed reasonable to try to identify these traits so that they could be measured and used in selecting leaders. Data from hundreds of studies using this approach revealed that in order for a person to be a leader, he or she must have the necessary goal-related abilities, be able to relate to others effectively, and *want* to be a leader (Stogdill, 1974). These conclusions are of theoretical interest, but are of little practical value in identifying potential leaders.

As it became increasingly clear that the trait approach was inadequate, students of leadership shifted to two relatively independent lines of inquiry: the study of situational factors and leadership styles. These approaches revealed that both situational factors and leadership styles are significant variables and contributed greatly to contingency models of leadership. These aspects of leadership will be discussed more fully as we consider leader emergence and leadership effectiveness.

Leadership Emergence

Which member of a group emerges as the leader is not, of course, a matter of chance, but is a function of several aspects of the group and the situation, not the least of which is how one communicates. One of the most significant variables appears to be the extent to which a person participates in group activities. Bass (1981) reviewed the numerous studies that indicated the member who participates most actively in a group is also most likely to emerge as the leader (assuming no leader has been appointed by external authority). Most of this participation involves talking with others. Talking calls attention to the speaker and permits him or her to reveal knowledge and abilities to others (Riecken, 1958). Active nonverbal participation also contributes to leadership emergence (Baird, 1977), or at least appears to be correlated with it.

Although the quantity of participation is important, the quality and timing of communication also help determine who emerges as a leader. Quality of participation simply means how accurate, relevant, or helpful one's comments are to the group. For example, trained confederates in one study varied the quality of their participation. The higher the quality of participation, the more likely it was that the person would emerge as the leader (Sorrentino & Boutillier, 1975). The person who participates early in the group discussion, moreover, has a better chance of emerging as the leader (Hollander, 1978).

Several studies suggest that individuals who concentrate on maintaining a good interpersonal climate and who provide direction to group members have improved chances for emerging as leaders. For instance, both Lumsden (1974) and Russell (1970) found agreeableness to be a quality more frequently characteristic of those judged most influential in group discussions than those judged relatively noninfluential. Hill (1976) discovered that neutrality and objectivity were important attributes in assessments of influence and the ability of a member to help a group achieve consensus. Finally, Knutson (1972) and Holdridge (1975) both detected a strong relationship between the guidance functions a group member performs (orientation) and his or her impact on the outcome of decision-making discussions.

Despite its brevity, this review reveals that leadership emergence is influenced by numerous factors. Clearly, if one wishes to become a leader, one must participate actively in the group's activities, communicate early, and preferably have those personal characteristics that are related to leadership attainment. It also helps to have a position in the group that facilitates communication with others in the group. Finally, providing reinforcement to other group members while remaining relatively neutral on matters of substance appears to be important. Leaders emerge more as a result of their skills in managing communication than because of their positions on issues.

Leadership Effectiveness

Once a person has achieved a position of leadership, either through appointment or emergence, his or her performance is of considerable importance to the group. Many attempts have been made to identify the characteristics of effective leaders (the trait approach) and to explain the processes that facilitate or impede effective leadership. An early attempt in this direction was the study of leadership styles. The archetypal example is the Lewin, Lippitt, and White (1939) study of "social climates." Groups of five boys (age 10) were exposed to adult leaders who played either an autocratic, democratic, or laissez-faire leadership role. The autocrat determined all policy for the group, dictated techniques and actions, and was impersonal and aloof. The democrat allowed group members to determine policy and work with whomever they wanted, and gave praise and criticism that were objective rather than personal. The laissez-faire leader essentially abdicated his position and allowed members to make their own decisions. He provided information and materials when asked, but otherwise did not participate in group activities.

The major effects of leadership style were on the socioemotional aspects of the group process. Thirty times as much hostility was expressed in the autocratic groups as in the democratic ones,

and overt aggressive acts were eight times as frequent in the autocratic as in the democratic groups. Laissez-faire groups were intermediate. Ninety percent of the boys liked the democrat and 70 percent liked the laissez-faire leader better than the autocrat. There was no reliable difference in the number of products created by the groups, although the autocratic groups produced slightly more than the other groups.

The findings regarding socioemotional reactions to autocratic and democratic leadership styles have been replicated many times, although the labels are often different (see, for example, Morse & Reimer, 1956; Preston & Heintz, 1949; Shaw, 1955). The effects of leadership styles on productivity are not so clear, however. In general, either no differences in productivity are found, or the autocratic style results in greater productivity than the democratic style.[5] One reason for this inconsistency seems to be the difficulty in effectively enacting the democratic leadership role. For instance, it has been observed that both the most and least effective groups are those with democratic leaders (Shaw, 1955).

The Contingency Model   More recently, emphasis has shifted to theoretical models of leadership. Fiedler's (1964, 1967) contingency model of leadership effectiveness is a notable example. The basic hypothesis is that the most effective style of leadership depends on the favorability of the task situation for the leader. Fiedler assumed that interpersonal perception reflects attitudes that influence leadership effectiveness. Therefore, leadership styles may be inferred from measures of interpersonal perception. The measure he used, the LPC (Least Preferred Co-worker) score, is determined by asking the individual (usually the leader) to rate his or her preferred co-worker on a series of evaluative scales. The person who scores high on this scale perceives the least preferred co-worker in a relatively favorable manner; the low scorer sees the co-worker unfavorably. The high-LPC leader is primarily concerned with interpersonal relations and only secondarily concerned with task completion, whereas the low-LPC leader is primarily concerned with the task and secondarily with interpersonal relations. Consequently, the high-LPC leader tends to be considerate, permissive, nondirective; the low-LPC leader tends to be managing, controlling, and directive. Both the person-oriented (high LPC) leader and the task-oriented (low-LPC) leader concern themselves with the task and interpersonal relations, but do so for different reasons and under different circumstances.

The favorability of the task situation is said to depend on three dimensions: the affective relations between the leader and his or her followers, the degree to which the task is structured, and the power inherent in the leadership position.

Affective relations refer to the degree to which the leader is liked and accepted by followers: *task structure* refers to the degree to which there is a demonstrably correct solution, the number of possible solutions, and the clarity of the goal and path to the goal; and *position power* refers to the degree to which his or her position in the group structure enables the leader to induce others to comply with his or her wishes. The most favorable task situation for the leader is one in which the leader-member relations are good, the task is structured, and the position power is strong. The most unfavorable situation is one in which the leader-member relations are poor, the task is unstructured, and the position power is weak. Intermediate favorabilities are determined by various combinations of the three dimensions, with leader-member relations making the greatest contribution and position power the least contribution.

According to the contingency model, a task-oriented (low-LPC) leader will be most effective when the task situation is either very favorable or very unfavorable for the leader, whereas a person-oriented (high-LPC) leader will be most effective when the task situation is in the intermediate range of favorability. Numerous investigations provide evidence that supports this proposition (for example, Chemers &

Skrzypek, 1972; Fiedler, 1967; Koch, 1978; Saha, 1979).

Despite the generally supportive nature of research testing the contingency model, other contingency theorists have held that leadership effectiveness is a function of adaptability—that is, the extent to which a person is able to produce the behavior a particular situation requires (for example, see Hunt & Larson, 1974). Gouran (1984b) and Gouran and Hirokawa (1983) have taken a similar position in characterizing leadership as the art of counteractive influence. From this perspective, leadership consists of communicative acts appropriate to any incident or event that has the potential consequence of diverting a group from its goal path. Leadership effectiveness, therefore, is assessed in terms of the extent to which such communicative acts prevent unwanted diversions.

Transactional Theories Transactional theories represent still another perspective on leadership. The model proposed by Hollander (1978) is representative of the related theories. As the label implies, leadership is viewed as a transaction between the leader and his or her followers. It is a two-way influence process involving a social exchange between leaders and followers in which both give and receive rewards or benefits. The leader provides goal direction, reduces uncertainty arising from ambiguous situations and events, and helps resolve conflicts. This is much the same behavior we referred to previously as orientation. In exchange, followers accord the leader high status, esteem, and similar benefits. The most effective situation is one that is perceived as equitable by both the leader and followers. In such situations, the leader performs efficiently and is perceived as deserving the esteem and status accorded him or her. Hollander cites several investigations that are congruent with this analysis.

This necessarily limited survey of leadership effectiveness (there are literally thousands of leadership studies) indicates the complexity of the process. In fact, one scholar (Fisher, 1985) has defined leadership as the management of complexity. Who becomes a leader and the effectiveness of the leader once in position depend on a variety of personal and situational factors. Contingency models provide an explanation of how personal and situational variables are interrelated. Transactional approaches contribute to our understanding of leadership as a communicative process. Whether one is concerned with emergence or effectiveness, it should be clear that leadership and communication in the context of small groups are inextricably intertwined. So interrelated are they that one could even entertain the hypothesis that leadership is completely reducible to communication.

GROUP GOALS AND TASKS

Groups ordinarily arise because some person or persons perceives a desirable goal or a task to be completed that can be achieved only or most efficiently through collective action. Such goals or tasks may be assigned by an external authority, or they may emerge from interactions of potential group members. Whatever their source, these goals and tasks obviously have important ramifications for group behavior. The terms *goal* and *task* are sometimes used interchangeably, but technically, they refer to different things. A group goal is an end state desired by a majority of group members (Shaw, 1981), whereas a group task is what must be done in order to achieve the goal (Hackman, 1968). For example, a committee formed to raise money to help needy families might have as its goal the collection of $50,000. To achieve this goal, several tasks must be carried out, such as preparing brochures, making public appeals, and soliciting funds from business organizations. In some cases, task completion may be the only goal of the group, as in many decision-making situations. Both group goals and tasks affect group behavior and performance, but most of the research has been devoted to task effects.

Task Characteristics and Group Performance

Task characteristics have been described in a variety of ways, ranging from simple typologies to attempts to specify dimensions. One interesting typology has been described by Steiner (1972). Although he identifies several types, for our purposes the most significant ones are conjunctive and disjunctive tasks.

Conjunctive and Disjunctive Tasks A *conjunctive task* is one that cannot be considered completed unless the members of a group have, as a whole, completed it. The example given by Steiner is a group of Boy Scouts trying to climb a mountain. They cannot be said to have completed this task until all members have reached the top. On such tasks, group performance depends on the least competent group member. As size increases, so does the probability that the group will have at least one member who cannot complete the task or requires an unduly long time to complete it. Therefore, assuming no assembly-effect bonus (no contribution deriving from group interaction), as the size of the group increases, the performance of the group is likely to decrease.

A *disjunctive task* is one that requires an either-or decision or a choice among two or more alternatives. On this type of task, if one group member can complete the task, the group can complete it. For example, suppose a group must compute the projected earnings of a company for the fiscal year, using a complex formula. (The choice here is among an almost unlimited number of possible alternative projected earnings.) If one member is able to apply the formula and compute the predicted earnings, the group can do so. It follows, therefore, that as the size increases, the probability that a group will have one member who can complete such a task also increases. In general, group performance improves with increasing group size.

Research concerning group performance on conjunctive and disjunctive tasks as a function of group size generally supports these hypotheses. However, there are some variations. On conjunctive tasks, performance decreases with group size, but not as much as expected on the basis of individual performances (Frank & Anderson, 1971). This suggests that interaction effects may have enhanced group performance. On disjunctive tasks, however, group performance appears to increase with group size as expected (Bray, Kerr, & Atkin, 1978; Egerbladh, 1976; Ziller, 1957).

The relationship of this task typology to communication in groups has not been explored. However, it is reasonable to assume that in the case of conjunctive tasks involving the need for consensus, communication plays a central role. As size increases, groups performing such a task will be faced with the prospect of having one or more disruptive or otherwise ineffective contributors. Limiting their impact is an important function of leadership. In addition, input by the most knowledgeable members is likely to be reduced in bigger groups, the amount of irrelevant input may rise substantially, and the opportunity for the phenomenon of pluralistic ignorance—a tendency for group members to acquiesce in decisions with which they do not concur (see Harvey, 1974; Schanck, 1932)—to set in is increased. Such possibilities are in need of more systematic inquiry.

Production, Discussion, and Problem-Solving Tasks Other typologies have been introduced that consider the type of activities required to complete the task. For example, Hackman (1968) refers to production tasks, discussion tasks, and problem-solving tasks. *Production tasks* require production and presentation of ideas, images, or arrangements, such as writing a story about the eruption of a volcano. *Discussion tasks* involve evaluations of issues, such as defending the proposition that the government of one country should help defend another country from internal dissidents. *Problem-solving tasks* demand that a group determine a course of ac-

tion to be followed in order to resolve some problem.

Hackman's research indicates that, in general, production tasks influence group members to engage in actions characterized by high originality, discussion tasks prompt actions that indicate high involvement with the issue, and problem-solving tasks lead to orientation toward much activity. Other studies suggest that production tasks lead to an emphasis by the group on task completion, discussion tasks elicit more process-oriented activity (such as defending, clarifying, explaining), and problem-solving tasks induce both types of activity (see Hackman & Vidmar, 1970; Morris, 1965).

It should be clear from the preceding discussion that the type of task significantly affects small group behavior. For instance, we noted in our discussion of leadership that the task's structure is a situational factor that strongly influences the leadership process. In addition, many other investigations have pointed to the effects that the task has on groups. The interested reader may wish to consult other reports (such as Lanzetta & Roby, 1957; Raven & Rietsema, 1957; Shaw, 1973).

EXPERIENTIAL GROUPS

In the preceding pages, we have been concerned primarily with task-oriented groups—groups that are formed to solve a problem or problems, to make decisions, or to produce something. But there is a different kind of group that is of some importance. We refer to these as *experiential groups,* or groups in which members expect to benefit from participation itself (Lakin, 1972). Experiential groups have a long history, dating back at least to the 1930s (Back, 1973). Groups similar to those now called experiential groups were used in a variety of settings, such as industry (Roethlisberger & Dickson, 1939) and psychotherapy (Moreno, 1946). Experiential groups occur in many forms and have various purposes, but they also share characteristics and processes. We will examine several types of experiential groups, their common characteristics and processes, and some evidence concerning their effectiveness.

Types of Experiential Groups

Experiential groups are variously labeled and differ in the kinds of benefits that members hope to attain. All of them can be reasonably classified into three categories based primarily on the motivations of participants: learning, therapeutic, and expressive groups (Lakin, 1972).

Learning groups are established to help participants gain an understanding of group influences on their own behavior, to help them obtain feedback about the consequences of their behavior on others, and to facilitate communication. Examples include human-relations groups, sensitivity training groups, and T-groups.

Therapeutic groups are intended to help participants repair something in themselves—to eliminate disvalued aspects of personality, to change personality styles, to overcome unfortunate emotional experiences, and the like. In other words, participants in therapeutic groups seek to change their perceived selves to make them more congruent with their ideal selves. Encounter groups, psychotherapy groups, confrontation groups, and marathon groups are common examples.

Expressive groups are based on participants' desires to achieve greater emotional expressiveness for its sake. These persons believe that socialization has led to inhibition of emotional expression, and that this inhibition reduces the quality of life. Thus they want to learn to express their emotions more freely and completely, and they believe that group participation will help them achieve this goal. Personal-growth and personal-awareness groups are representative of this category.

Experiential Group Processes

Experiential groups are not radically different from task-oriented groups: Members talk to each other, structure emerges, and norms are formed. Group process is influenced by this structure and by the group's composition. However, they differ from task-oriented groups in at least three ways: (1) There is no easily identifiable task, and the goal may be unclear. (2) Some of the norms that are formed are unique. (3) The interaction is personally oriented.

Lakin (1972) noted certain processes common to all three types of experiential groups:

Facilitating emotional expressiveness. In experiential groups, the ideal atmosphere is one that encourages participants to express their feelings openly.

Generating feelings of belongingness. Experiential groups enhance members' feelings of being an important part of the group.

Fostering norms of self-disclosure. There is usually a clearly recognized norm or "social rule" that requires participants to disclose information about themselves that they might be unwilling to disclose under ordinary conditions.

Sampling personal behaviors. Members are encouraged to try new behaviors and to examine the personal behaviors of others.

Making interpersonal comparisons. In experiential groups, it is entirely acceptable to make comparisons among group members, without fear of disapproval.

Sharing responsibility for leadership and direction with the appointed leader. The "appointed leader" is usually a trainer, a facilitator, or a therapist. Since this person does not assume the leadership role that participants expect on the basis of past experiences, they must assume many of the leadership functions themselves.

Probably other processes are common to all or most experiential groups, but these are the most readily identifiable ones. The function of these processes, of course, is to facilitate achievement of the personal goals of the members.

Effectiveness of Experiential Groups

An important question for those involved with experiential groups is whether and to what extent these sorts of groups achieve their goals. Despite numerous attempts to evaluate their effectiveness, many difficulties are inherent in the conditions surrounding the use of such groups. For example, it is often not completely clear just what changes the group experiences are supposed to produce. If expected effects are not precisely indicated, designing a study to determine whether such effects have occurred is difficult. If effects are precisely identified, then the problem of how to measure them reliably and validly arises. Finally, even if we have adequate measuring devices, there is still the problem of determining exactly what has produced any observed effects. Finding a comparable control group is almost impossible, since assignment to experiential groups ordinarily is not random (for example, participants volunteer or are selected by superiors) and other persons with whom they associate know that they have participated in experiential groups, which may affect how these colleagues perceive and treat them. Research findings must be interpreted with these difficulties in mind.

Three general approaches to evaluating the effects of experiential groups may be employed: self-report, reports by associates, and observed behavior change. Self-report studies require participants to reveal their perceptions of the experience's effect on them, either directly or via standard psychological tests. Studies of this type have yielded mixed results, with some finding evidence of significant change as a function of participation in experiential groups and others finding little or no evidence of change (for example, Friedlander, 1967; Harrison, 1966; McLeish & Park, 1972; Page & Kubiak, 1978; Ware & Barr, 1977).

Investigations using the reports-by-associates approach rely on the observations and perceptions of those who work with or are otherwise associated with the experiential-group partici-

pants. In most instances, associates report that changes have occurred, but they often disagree about what these changes are, and the kinds of changes noted vary from study to study (for example, Bunker, 1965; Lieberman, Yalom, & Miles, 1973; Miles, 1965; Valiquet, 1968).

Few attempts have been made to record actual behavior before and after participation in experiential groups. Cooper (1972a, 1972b) examined the records of a university health center and found that students who had participated in T-groups did not visit the infirmary significantly more frequently than a group of control students. However, this study appears to be an attempt to demonstrate that participation does not have undesirable effects on those who participate rather than to show that it has desirable ones.

After an extensive review of studies concerning the effectiveness of sensitivity training and encounter groups, P. B. Smith (1980) concluded that measurable change does occur after participation in these groups but that these effects fade substantially after a few months. This is probably the most reasonable conclusion that can be drawn concerning the effectiveness of experiential groups in general.[6]

CONCLUSION

Participation in groups represents a significant dimension of the lives of most individuals. How such groups function is largely determined by the interaction of their members. People form and join groups because they perceive that interaction and collective action can satisfy some need or help them achieve some desirable goal. They may join a group because its members are attractive, because the goals are perceived as worthwhile, because they enjoy the activities of the group, because membership is seen as a means of achieving some external goal, or for a variety of other reasons. Once a group has been established, it typically develops in an orderly fashion. Initially, there is a period of uncertainty about what the group should be doing, how it should function, and the like. Members are concerned with orientation. This is often followed by a conflict stage, in which members disagree about the group's structure and norms. If the members are successful, these conflicts are resolved, and the group reaches a productive stage in which energies are directed toward goal achievement.

Members bring with them a variety of personal characteristics that have major effects on interaction. Some of these characteristics facilitate group functioning, whereas others interfere. Which effects are most likely depends on whether the particular combination of characteristics induces compatibility and cohesiveness or incompatibility and noncohesiveness. Socially desirable characteristics facilitate and socially undesirable ones impede the effectiveness of groups. Heterogeneity of personal characteristics of group members usually increases effectiveness.

As group members interact, a social structure emerges. Different positions emerge, with associated roles that specify appropriate behavior for persons in those positions. Each position is evaluated by group members, and the status assigned the position is accorded to the person who occupies it. These structural variables influence communication patterns in the group, the emergence of leadership, satisfaction of members, performance and other aspects of group process.

Goals established by the members or assigned by external authority and the tasks faced are closely related to the interaction and performance of groups. Task requirements determine to a large extent the kinds of personal characteristics that participants need for effective action, and structural factors operate in conjunction with task characteristics to determine group effectiveness.

Finally, there are some groups that are not task-oriented, but are designed to help participants achieve personal goals. These experiential groups may be designed to help members learn about interpersonal processes, to help them change or eliminate some disvalued aspect of the personality, or to facilitate emotional expressiveness. Research evidence suggests that such groups have measurable effects on participants, although such effects appear to be temporary.

SUMMARY

Groups are one of the most frequent communication contexts encountered by most persons. Various types of groups exist, although most of the research discussed in this chapter has been collected on task groups. Persons join groups for a variety of reasons, but once assembled, a group will frequently develop in a fairly predictable series of stages.

The composition of a group will have a significant effect on the group's performance. The characteristics of members, the size of the group, the cohesiveness of the group, and the communication network among members all influence performance of the group. The roles of the group's members will affect their status and in turn their behavior in the group.

Leadership is a subject that has been frequently studied. A number of theories of leadership have been developed, and a number of factors such as the group's tasks or goals influence which type of leadership works best. In general, there is no one best type of leader nor one best style of leadership.

Various types of experiential groups are increasingly common. These groups have been studied less than task groups, but they do appear to have different characteristics from task groups. Evaluation of the outcomes of experiential groups is also different and difficult.

REVIEW AND DISCUSSION QUESTIONS

1. There are various types of groups and various reasons that individuals join groups. Does there appear to be a relationship between the type of group and the reasons people join?

2. All the major factors in group composition (personal characteristics, size, cohesiveness, homogeneity, structure, networks) are at work simultaneously in any group. Rank each of these factors by relative importance to the success of the group. Which of these factors can be controlled in putting together a group? Which can be dealt with during the operation of the group to improve its performance?

3. The chances of success for various types or styles of leadership differ depending on the characteristics of the group and the characteristics of the task. If you wanted to create an ideal group, does it make more sense to build a group around a proven leader (choose members to fit the leader's style and task at hand) or to select a leader from the group to fit the type of task and group? Why?

4. Communication is often described as a system, in which all the processes are related and cannot be studied in isolation. For example, group communication as discussed in this chapter is influenced by interpersonal communication (Chapter 5) among its members and by the larger setting in which the group occurs, such as the organization (Chapter 7). In that context, how important are internal processes of the group to its success, relative to outside influences on group members? Would these outside influences tend to improve or harm group interaction processes? What can group members do to insulate the group from outside influences that would hinder its performance?

NOTES

1. Developments in electronic communication may at some point in the near future begin to change our conception of primary and secondary groups—at least so far as face-to-face association as a distinguishing characteristic is concerned. Recent work with microcomputer-assisted communication, for example, has removed the necessity of physical propinquity for members of groups to carry on effective interaction (see, for example, Conrath & Bair, 1974).

2. It should be noted here that evidence for stable phases in the execution of decision-making and problem-solving tasks has been challenged by both Hewes (1979) and Poole (1981, 1985). Nevertheless, there is reason to believe that some degree of consistency can be found in the ways groups develop and in the ways they perform particular sorts of tasks.

3. A condition similar to groupthink and also traceable to a group's cohesiveness has been referred to as "freeze-think." According to Kruglanski (1986), freeze-think is a condition in which decision makers are locked into thinking that past successes are a sufficient index of probable success in present and future actions. Such thinking appears to have been involved in the actions of NASA officials responsible for the ill-fated

launch of the *Challenger* space shuttle in January 1986 (see also Freund, Kruglanski, & Shipitajzen, 1985).

4. Of course, it is possible for a group structure to be imposed by external authority, as when an official appoints a committee and specifies the positions and roles in the group. Even in those cases, however, some developmental processes and informal changes are made in the imposed structure.

5. We should note here that sustained productivity appears to require continuous monitoring by an autocratic leader. When such leaders are not present, productivity may decline sharply.

6. A word of caution: Participation in experiential groups can be an intensely emotional experience and there is some evidence that participation affects some persons adversely. Experiential groups should be led only by those who are trained to deal with emotional disorders.

REFERENCES

Back, K. W. (1951). Influence through social communication. *Journal of Abnormal and Social Psychology, 46,* 9–23.

Back, K. W. (1973). *Beyond words: The story of sensitivity training and the encounter movement.* Baltimore: Penguin.

Back, K. W., Festinger, L., Hymovitch, B., Kelley, H. H., Shachter, S., & Thibaut, J. W. (1950). The methodology of studying rumor transmission. *Human Relations, 3,* 307–312.

Baird, J. E., Jr. (1977). Some nonverbal elements of leadership emergence. *Southern Speech Communication Journal, 42,* 352–361.

Bales, R. F. (1950). *Interaction process analysis: A method for the study of small groups.* Cambridge, MA: Addison-Wesley.

Bales, R. F., & Strodtbeck, F. L. (1951). Phases in group problem solving. *Journal of Abnormal and Social Psychology, 46,* 485–495.

Bales, R. F., Strodtbeck, F. L., Mills, T. M., & Rosenborough, M. E. (1951). Channels of communication in small groups. *American Sociological Review, 16,* 461–468.

Barnlund, D. C., & Harland, C. (1963). Propinquity and prestige as determinants of communication networks. *Sociometry, 26,* 467–479.

Bass, B. M. (1981). *Stogdill's handbook of leadership.* New York: Free Press.

Bass, B. M., McGehee, C. R., Hawkins, W. C., Young, P. C., & Gebel, A. S. (1953). Personality variables related to leaderless group discussion. *Journal of Abnormal and Social Psychology, 48,* 120–128.

Bass, B. M., & Wurster, C. R. (1953). Effects of company rank on LGD performance of oil refinery supervisors. *Journal of Applied Psychology, 37,* 100–104.

Bravelas, A. (1950). Communication patterns in task-oriented groups. *Journal of the Acoustical Society of America, 22,* 725–730.

Beaver, A. P. (1932). The initiation of social contacts by pre-school children. *Child Development Monograph,* No. 7.

Beckwith, J., Iverson, M. A., & Render, M. E. (1965). Test anxiety, task relevance of group experience, and change in level of aspiration. *Journal of Personality and Social Psychology, 1,* 579–588.

Bennis, W. G., & Shepard, H. A. (1956). A theory of group development. *Human Relations, 9,* 415–437.

Berkowitz, L. (1954). Group standards, cohesiveness, and productivity. *Human Relations, 7,* 509–519.

Berkowitz, L., & Daniels, L. R. (1963). Responsibility and dependency. *Journal of Abnormal and Social Psychology, 66,* 429–436.

Blanchard, F. A., Weigel, R. H., & Cook, S. W. (1975). The effect of relative competence of group members upon interpersonal attraction in cooperating interracial groups. *Journal of Personality and Social Psychology, 32,* 519–530.

Bradley, P. H. (1978). Power, status, and upward communication in small decision-making groups. *Communication Monographs, 45,* 33–43.

Bradley, P. H., Hamon, C. M., & Harris, A. M. (1976, Autumn). Dissent in small groups. *Journal of Communication, 26,* 155–159.

Bray, R. M., Kerr, N. L., & Atkin, R. S. (1978). Effects of group size, problem difficulty, and sex on group performance and member reactions. *Journal of Personality and Social Psychology, 36,* 1224–1240.

Bunker, D. R. (1965). Individual applications of laboratory training. *Journal of Applied Behavioral Science, 1,* 131–148.

Bunyi, J. M., & Andrews, P. H. (1985). Gender and leadership emergence: An experimental study. *Southern Speech Communication Journal, 50,* 246–260.

Byrne, D. (1961). Interpersonal attraction and attitude similarity. *Journal of Abnormal and Social Psychology, 62,* 713–715.

Byrne, D., Clore, J. L., Jr., & Worchel, P. (1966). Effect of economic similarity-dissimilarity on interpersonal attraction. *Journal of Personality and Social Psychology, 4,* 220–224.

Byrne, D., London, O., & Griffitt, W. (1968). The effect of topic importance and attitude similarity-dissimilarity on attraction in an intrastranger design. *Psychonomic Science, 11,* 303–304.

Byrne, D., & Nelson, D. (1964). Attraction as a function of attitude similarity-dissimilarity: The effect of topic importance. *Psychonomic Science, 1,* 93–94.

Byrne, D., & Nelson, D. (1965). The effect of topic importance and attitude similarity-dissimilarity on attraction in a multi-stranger design. *Psychonomic Science, 3,* 449–450.

Caple, R. B. (1978). The sequential stages of group development. *Small Group Behavior, 9,* 470–476.

Cattell, R. B., & Stice, G. F. (1960). *The dimensions of groups and their relations to the behavior of members.* Champaign, IL: Institute for Personality and Ability Testing.

Chemers, M. M., & Skrzypek, G. J. (1972). Experimental test of the contingency model of leadership effectiveness. *Journal of Personality and Social Psychology, 24,* 172–177.

Conrath, D. W., & Bair, J. H. (1974, August). The computer as an interpersonal communication device: A study of augmentation technology and its apparent impact on organizational communication. Paper presented at the Second International Conference on Computer Communications, Stockholm.

Cooley, C. H. (1909). *Social organization.* New York: Charles Scribner's.

Cooper, C. L. (1972a). An attempt to assess the psychologically disturbing effects of T-group training. *British Journal of Social and Clinical Psychology, 11,* 342–345.

Cooper, C. L. (1972b). Coping with life stress after sensitivity training. *Psychological Reports, 31,* 602.

Dean, L. M., Willis, F. N., & Hewitt, J. (1975). Initial interaction distance among individuals equal and unequal in military rank. *Journal of Personality and Social Psychology, 32,* 294–299.

de Gloria, J., & de Ridder, R. (1979). Sex differences in aggression: Are current notions misleading? *European Journal of Social Psychology, 9,* 49–66.

DeSanctis, G., & Gallupe, R. B. (1984). Group decision support systems: A new frontier. Unpublished manuscript, University of Minnesota, Department of Management Sciences, Minneapolis.

Deutsch, M. (1968). Field theory in social psychology. In G. Lindzey & E. Aronson (Eds.), *The handbook of social psychology* (2nd ed.) (pp. 412–487). Reading, MA: Addison-Wesley.

Egerbladh, T. (1976). The function of group size and ability level on solving a multidimensional and complementary task. *Journal of Personality and Social Psychology, 34,* 805–808.

Ellis, D. G., & Fisher, B. A. (1975). Phases of conflict in small group development: A Markov analysis. *Human Communication Research, 1,* 195–212.

Exline, R. V. (1957). Group climate as a factor in the relevance and accuracy of social perception. *Journal of Abnormal and Social Psychology, 55,* 382–388.

Exline, R. V. (1963). Explorations in the process of person perception: Visual interaction in relation to completion, sex, and need for affiliation. *Journal of Personality, 31,* 1–20.

Festinger, L. (1950). Informal social communication. *Psychological Review, 57,* 271–282.

Festinger, L., Schachter, S., & Back, K. W. (1950). *Social pressure in informal groups.* New York: Harper.

Fiedler, F. E. (1964). A contingency model of leadership effectiveness. In L. Berkowitz (Ed.), *Advances in experimental social psychology* (Vol. 1, pp. 149–190). New York: Academic Press.

Fiedler, F. E. (1967). *A theory of leadership effectiveness.* New York: McGraw-Hill.

Fisher, B. A. (1970). Decision emergence: Phases in group decision-making. *Speech Monographs, 37,* 53–66.

Fisher, B. A. (1979, Fall). Content and relationship dimensions of communication in decision-making groups. *Communication Quarterly, 27,* 3–11.

Fisher, B. A. (1985). Leadership as medium: Treating complexity in group communication research. *Small Group Behavior, 16,* 167–196.

Fisher, J. D., & Byrne, D. (1975). Too close for comfort: Sex differences in response to invasions of personal space. *Journal of Personality and Social Psychology, 32,* 15–21.

Frank, F., & Anderson, L. R. (1971). Effects of task and group size upon group productivity and member satisfaction. *Sociometry, 34,* 135–149.

Freund, T., Kruglanski, A. W., & Shipitajzen, A. (1985). The freezing and unfreezing of impressional primacy: Effects of the need for structure and the fear of invalidity. *Personality and Social Psychology Bulletin, 11,* 479–487.

Friedlander, F. (1967). The impact of organizational training upon the effectiveness and interaction of ongoing work groups. *Personnel Psychology, 20,* 289–309.

Gerson, L. W. (1967). Punishment and position: The sanctioning of deviants in small groups. *Case Western Reserve Journal of Sociology, 1,* 54–62.

Gerwitz, J. L., & Baer, D. M. (1958a). The effect of brief social deprivation on behaviors for a social reinforcer. *Journal of Abnormal and Social Psychology, 56,* 49–56.

Gerwitz, J. L., & Baer, D. M. (1958b). Deprivation and satiation of social reinforcers as drive conditions. *Journal of Abnormal and Social Psychology, 57,* 165–172.

Gilchrist, J. C., Shaw, M. E., & Walker, L. C. (1954). Some effects of unequal distribution of information in a wheel group structure. *Journal of Abnormal and Social Psychology, 49,* 554–556.

Goldman, M. (1965). A comparison of individual and group performance for varying combinations of initial ability. *Journal of Personality and Social Psychology, 1,* 210–216.

Goodacre, D. M. III (1951). The use of a sociometric test as a predictor of combat unit effectiveness. *Sociometry, 14,* 148–152.

Gouran, D. S. (1976). The Watergate coverup: Its dynamics and its implications. *Communication Monographs, 43,* 176–186.

Gouran, D. S. (1984a). Communicative influences on decisions related to the Watergate coverup: The failure of collective judgment. *Central States Speech Journal, 35,* 260–268.

Gouran, D. S. (1984b). Principles of counteractive influence in decision-making and problem-solving groups. In R. S. Cathcart & L. A. Samovar (Eds.), *Small group communication: A reader* (4th ed.) (pp. 166–181). Dubuque, IA: Wm. C. Brown.

Gouran, D. S. (1986). Inferential errors, interaction, and group decision-making. In R. Y. Hirokawa & M. S. Poole (Eds.), *Communication and group decision-making* (pp. 93–112). Beverly Hills. Sage.

Gouran, D. S., & Andrews, P. H. (1984). Seriousness, attribution of responsibility, and status of the offender. *Small Group Behavior, 15,* 525–543.

Gouran, D. S., & Hirokawa, R. Y. (1983). The role of communication in decision-making groups: A functional perspective. In M. S. Mander (Ed.), *Communications in transition: Issues and debates in current research* (pp. 168–185). New York: Praeger.

Gouran, D. S., Hirokawa, R. Y., & Martz, A. E. (1986). A critical analysis of factors related to decisional processes involved in the Challenger disaster. Manuscript submitted for publication.

Gouran, D. S., Ketrow, S. M., Spear, S., & Metzger, J. (1984). Social deviance and occupational status: Group assessment of penalties. *Small Group Behavior, 15,* 63–86.

Greer, F. L. (1955). Small group effectiveness. Institute Rept. No. 6, contract Nonr-1229(00), Institute for Research in Human Relations.

Griffitt, W. (1966). Interpersonal attraction as a function of self-concept and personality similarity-dissimilarity. *Journal of Personality and Social Psychology, 4,* 581–584.

Gross, E. (1954). Primary functions of the small group. *American Journal of Sociology, 60,* 24–30.

Gross, N., Mason, W. S., & McEachern, A. W. (1957). *Explorations in role analysis: Studies of the school superintendency role.* New York: Wiley.

Guetzkow, H., & Simon, H. A. (1955). The impact of certain communication nets upon organization and performance in task-oriented groups. *Management Science, 1,* 233–250.

Hackman, J. R. (1968). Effects of task characteristics on group products. *Journal of Experimental Social Psychology, 4,* 162–187.

Hackman, J. R., & Vidmar, N. (1970). Effects of size and task type on group performance and member reactions. *Sociometry, 33,* 37–54.

Hamilton, V. L. (1978). Obedience and responsibility: A jury simulation. *Journal of Personality and Social Psychology, 36,* 126–146.

Hare, A. P. (1952). Interaction and consensus in different sized groups. *American Sociological Review, 17,* 261–267.

Harnack, R. G. (1963). A study of the effects of an organized minority upon a discussion group. *Journal of Communication, 13,* 12–24.

Harrison, R. (1966). Cognitive change and participation in a sensitivity training laboratory. *Journal of Consulting Psychology, 30,* 517–520.

Harvey, J. B. (1974). The Abilene paradox: The management of agreement. *Organizational Dynamics, 3,* 63–80.

Haythorn, W. (1953). The influence of individual members on the characteristics of small groups. *Journal of Abnormal and Social Psychology, 48,* 276–284.

Hemphill, J. K. (1950). Relations between the size of the group and the behavior of "superior" leaders. *Journal of Social Psychology, 32,* 11–22.

Hemphill, J. K., & Sechrest, L. (1952). A comparison of three criteria of air crew effectiveness in combat over Korea. *American Psychologist, 7,* 391.

Hewes, D. E. (1979). The sequential analysis of social interaction. *Quarterly Journal of Speech, 65,* 56–73.

Hill, T. A. (1976). An experimental study of the relationship between opinionated leadership and small group consensus. *Communication Monographs, 43,* 246–257.

Hirokawa, R. Y., & Pace, R. C. (1983). A descriptive investigation of the possible communication-based reasons for effective and ineffective group decision-making. *Communication Monographs, 50,* 363–379.

Hoffman, L. R. (1959). Homogeneity of member personality and its effect on group problem-solving. *Journal of Abnormal and Social Psychology, 58,* 27–32.

Hoffman, L. R., & Maier, N. R. F. (1961). Quality and acceptance of problem solutions by members of homogeneous and heterogeneous groups. *Journal of Abnormal and Social Psychology, 62,* 401–407.

Hollander, E. P. (1954). Authoritarianism and leadership choice in a military setting. *Journal of Abnormal and Social Psychology, 49,* 365–376.

Hollander, E. P. (1958). Conformity, status, and idiosyncrasy credit. *Psychological Review, 65,* 117–127.

Hollander, E. P. (1978). *Leadership dynamics.* New York: Free Press.

Homans, G. C. (1963). Small groups. In B. Berelson (Ed.), *The behavioral sciences today* (pp. 165–175). New York: Harper Torch Books.

Hoogstraten, J., & Vorst, H. C. M. (1978). Groups cohesion, task performance, and the experimenter expectancy effect. *Human Relations, 31,* 939–956.

Hunt, J. G., & Larson, L. L. (Eds.). (1974). *Contingency approaches to leadership.* Carbondale: Southern Illinois University Press.

Ickes, W., & Barnes, R. D. (1977). The role of sex and self-monitoring in unstructured dyadic interactions. *Journal of Personality and Social Psychology, 35,* 315–330.

Indik, B. P. (1965). Organization size and member participation: Some empirical tests of alternatives. *Human Relations, 18,* 339–350.

Janis, I. L. (1982). *Groupthink* (2nd ed.). Boston: Houghton Mifflin.

Kandel, D. B. (1978). Similarity in real-life adolescent friendship pairs. *Journal of Personality and Social Psychology, 36,* 306–312.

Kano, S. (1971). Task characteristics and network. *Japanese Journal of Experimental Social Psychology, 10,* 55–66.

Kano, S. (1977). A change of effectiveness of communication networks under different amounts of information. *Japanese Journal of Experimental Social Psychology, 17,* 50–59.

Katz, D. (1949). Morale and motivation in industry. In W. Dennis (Ed.), *Current trends in industrial psychology* (pp. 145–171). Pittsburgh: University of Pittsburgh Press.

Kelley, H. H. (1951). Communication in experimentally created hierarchies. *Human Relations, 4,* 39–56.

Knutson, T. J. (1972). An experimental study of the effects of orientation behavior on small group consensus. *Speech Monographs, 39,* 159–165.

Knutson, T. J., & Holdridge, U. E. (1975). Orientation behavior, leadership, and consensus: A possible functional relationship. *Speech Monographs, 42,* 107–114.

Koch, J. L. (1978). Managerial succession in a factory and changes in supervisory patterns: A field study. *Human Relations, 31,* 49–58.

Krail, K. A., & Leventhal, G. (1976). The sex variable in the intrusion of personal space. *Sociometry, 39,* 170–173.

Kruglanski, A. W. (1986, August). Freeze-think and the Challenger. *Psychology Today,* pp. 48–49.

Lakin, M. (1972). *Experiential groups: The uses of interpersonal encounter, psychotherapy groups, and sen-*

sitivity training. Morristown, NJ: General Learning Press

Lanzetta, J. T., & Roby, T. B. (1957). Group learning and communication as a function of task and structure "demands." *Journal of Abnormal and Social Psychology, 55,* 121–131.

Lawson, E. D. (1964). Reinforced and non-reinforced four-man communication nets. *Psychological Reports, 14,* 287–296.

Leavitt, H. J. (1951). Some effects of certain communication patterns on group performance. *Journal of Abnormal and Social Psychology, 46,* 38–50.

Leffler, A., Gillespie, D. L., & Conaty, J. C. (1982). The effect of status differentiation on nonverbal behavior. *Social Psychology Quarterly, 45,* 153–161.

Levine, J. M., Saxe, L., & Harris, H. J. (1976). Reaction to attitudinal deviance: Impact of deviate's direction and distance of movement. *Sociometry, 39,* 97–107.

Lewin, K., Lippitt, R., & White, R. K. (1939). Patterns of aggressive behavior in experimentally created "social climates." *Journal of Science Psychology, 10,* 271–299.

Lieberman, M. A., Yalom, I. D., & Miles, M. B. (1973). *Encounter groups: First facts.* New York: Basic Books.

Lott, A. J., & Lott, B. E. (1961). Group cohesiveness, communication level, and conformity. *Journal of Abnormal and Social Psychology, 62,* 408–412.

Lumsden, G. (1974). An experimental study of the effect of verbal agreement on leadership maintenance in problem-solving discussion. *Central States Speech Journal, 25,* 270–276.

Lumsden, G., Brown, D. R., Lumsden, D., & Hill, T. A. (1974, Fall). An investigation of differences in verbal behavior between black and white informal peer group discussions. *Today's Speech, 22,* 31–36.

Mabry, E. A. (1975). Sequential structure of interaction in encounter groups. *Human Communication Research, 1,* 302–307.

Mabry, E. A. (1985). The effects of gender composition and task structure on small group interaction. *Small Group Behavior, 16,* 75–96.

Macy, J., Jr., Christie, L. S., & Luce, R. D. (1953). Coding noise in a task-oriented group. *Journal of Abnormal and Social Psychology, 48,* 401–409.

Maier, N. R. F. (1950). The quality of group decisions as influenced by the discussion leader. *Human Relations, 3,* 155–174.

Maier, N. R. F. (1953). An experimental test of the effect of training on discussion leadership. *Human Relations, 6,* 161–173.

Maissonneuve, J., Palmade, G., & Fourment, C. (1952). Selective choices and propinquity. *Sociometry, 15,* 135–140.

Mann, R. D. (1959). A review of the relationships between personality and performance in small groups. *Psychological Bulletin, 56,* 241–270.

Martz, A. E. (1986). An investigation of communication in the production and acceptance of unwarranted inferences by members of decision-making groups. Unpublished master's thesis, Pennsylvania State University, University Park.

McClelland, D. C., Atkinson, J. W., Clark, R. A., & Lowell, E. L. (1953). *The achievement motive.* New York: Appleton-Century-Crofts.

McGuire, J. M. (1973). Aggression and sociometric status with preschool children. *Sociometry, 36,* 542–549.

McKinney, B. C. (1985). Decision-making in the president's commission on the assassination of President Kennedy: A descriptive analysis employing Irving Janis' groupthink hypothesis. Unpublished doctoral dissertation, Pennsylvania State University, University Park.

McLeish, J., & Park, J. (1972). Outcomes associated with direct and vicarious experience in training groups: I. Personality changes. *British Journal of Social and Clinical Psychology, 11,* 333–341.

Miles, M. B. (1965). Changes during and following laboratory training: A clinical-experimental study. *Journal of Applied Behavioral Science, 1,* 215–242.

Milgram, S. (1963). Behavioral study of obedience. *Journal of Abnormal and Social Psychology, 67,* 371–378.

Mill, C. R. (1953). Personality patterns of sociometrically selected and sociometrically rejected male college students. *Sociometry, 16,* 151–167.

Moore, J. C., Jr., Johnson, E. B., & Arnold, M. S. C. (1972). Status congruence and equity in communication networks. *Sociometry, 35,* 519–537.

Moran, G. (1966). Dyadic attraction and orientational consensus. *Journal of Personality and Social Psychology, 4,* 94–99.

Moreno, J. L. (1946). *Psychodrama.* New York: Beacon House.

Morris, C. G. (1965). *Effects of task characteristics on group process.* Technical Report No. 2, AFOSR Contract AF 49 (638)-1291, University of Illinois.

Morse, N. C., & Reimer, E. (1956). The experimental change of a major organizational variable. *Journal of Abnormal and Social Psychology, 52,* 120–129.

Near, J. P. (1978). Comparison of developmental patterns in groups. *Small Group Behavior, 9,* 493–506.

Newcomb, T. M. (1961). *The acquaintance process.* New York: Holt.

Newman, B. M. (1976). The development of social interaction from infancy through adolescence. *Small Group Behavior, 7,* 19–32.

O'Dell, J. W. (1968). Group size and emotional interaction. *Journal of Personality and Social Psychology, 8,* 75–78.

Page, R. C., & Kubiak, L. (1978). Marathon groups: Facilitating personal growth of imprisoned, black female heroin abusers. *Small Group Behavior, 9,* 409–416.

Palmer, G. J., Jr. (1962a). *Task ability and effective leadership.* Tech. Report No. 4, Contract Nonr 1575(05), Louisiana State University.

Palmer, G. J., Jr. (1962b). *Task ability and successful and effective leadership.* Tech. Report. No. 6, Contract Nonr 1575(05), Louisiana State University.

Parten, M. B. (1932). Social participation among preschool children. *Journal of Abnormal and Social Psychology, 27,* 243–269.

Poole, M. S. (1981). Decision development in small groups I: A comparison of two models. *Speech Monographs, 48,* 1–24.

Poole, M. S. (1985). Task and interaction sequences: A theory of coherence in group decision-making interaction. In R. L. Street & J. N. Cappella (Eds.), *Sequence and pattern in communicative behaviour* (pp. 206–224). London: Edward Arnold.

Poole, M. S., McPhee, R. D., & Seibold, D. R. (1982). A comparison of normative and interactional explanations of group decision-making: Social decision schemas versus valence distributions. *Speech Monographs, 49,* 1–19.

Preston, M. G., & Heintz, R. K. (1949). Effects of participatory vs. supervisory leadership on group judgment. *Journal of Abnormal and Social Psychology, 44,* 345–355.

Pyron, H. C. (1964). An experimental study of the role of reflective thinking in business and professional conferences and discussions. *Speech Monographs, 31,* 157–161.

Pyron, H. C., & Sharp, H., Jr. (1963). A quantitative study of reflective thinking and performance in problem-solving discussion. *Journal of Communication, 13,* 46–53.

Raven, B. H., & Rietsema, J. (1957). The effects of varied clarity of group goal and group path upon the individual and his relation to the group. *Human Relations, 10,* 29–44.

Reckman, R. F., & Goethals, G. R. (1973). Deviancy and group orientation as determinants of group composition preferences. *Sociometry, 36,* 419–423.

Riecken, H. W. (1958). The effect of talkativeness on ability to influence group solutions of problems. *Sociometry, 21,* 309–321.

Roethlisberger, F. J., & Dickson, W. J. (1939). *Management and the worker.* Cambridge, MA: Harvard University Press.

Rohrbaugh, J., & McCartt, A. J. (Eds.). (1986). *Applying decision support systems in higher education.* San Francisco: Jossey-Bass.

Russell, H. C. (1970). *An investigation of leadership maintenance behavior.* Unpublished doctoral dissertation, Indiana University, Bloomington.

Saha, S. K. (1979). Contingency theories of leadership: A study. *Human Relations, 32,* 313–322.

Schachter, S. (1951). Deviation, rejection, and communication. *Journal of Abnormal and Social Psychology, 46,* 190–207.

Schachter, S. (1959). *The psychology of affiliation.* Stanford, CA: Stanford University Press.

Schachter, S., Ellertson, N., McBride, D., & Gregory, D. (1951). An experimental study of cohesiveness and productivity. *Human Relations, 4,* 229–238.

Schanck, R. L. (1932). A study of a community and its groups and institutions conceived of as behaviors of individuals. *Psychological Monographs, 43,* (2, Whole No. 195).

Shaw, M. E. (1955). A comparison of two types of leadership in various communication nets. *Journal of Abnormal and Social Psychology, 50,* 127–134.

Shaw, M. E. (1958). Some effects of irrelevant information upon problem-solving by small groups. *Journal of Social Psychology, 47,* 33–37.

Shaw, M. E. (1964). Communication networks. In L. Berkowitz (Ed.), *Advances in experimental social psychology* (Vol. 1, pp. 111–147). New York: Academic Press.

Shaw, M. E. (1973). Scaling group tasks: A method for dimensional analysis. *JSAS Catalog of Selected Documents in Psychology, 3,* 8 (MS No. 294).

Shaw, M. E. (1981). *Group dynamics: The psychology of small group behavior.* (3rd ed.). New York: McGraw-Hill.

Shaw, M. E., & Penrod, W. T., Jr. (1962a). Validity of information, attempted influence, and quality of group decisions. *Psychological Reports, 10,* 19–23.

Shaw, M. E., & Penrod, W. T., Jr. (1962b). Does more information available to a group always improve group performance? *Sociometry, 25,* 377–390.

Shaw, M. E., & Shaw, L. M. (1962). Some effects of sociometric grouping upon learning in a second grade classroom. *Journal of Social Psychology, 57,* 453–458.

Sherif, M., & Sherif, C. W. (1953). *Groups in harmony and tension.* New York: Harper.

Shevitz, R. N. (1955). *Leadership acts: IV. An investigation of the relation between exclusive possession of information and attempts to lead.* Columbus: Ohio State University Research Foundation.

Slater, P. E. (1958). Contrasting correlates of group size. *Sociometry, 21,* 129–139.

Smith, C. R., Williams, L., & Willis, R. H. (1967). Race, sex and belief as determinants of friendship acceptance. *Journal of Personality and Social Psychology, 5,* 127–137.

Smith, H. W. (1977). Small group interaction at various ages: Simultaneous talking and interruptions of others. *Small Group Behavior, 8,* 65–74.

Smith, P. B. (1980). The outcome of sensitivity training and encounter. In P. B. Smith (Ed.), *Small groups and personal change.* London: Methuen, pp. 25–55.

Sommer, R. (1959). Studies in personal space. *Sociometry, 22,* 247–260.

Sorrentino, R. M., & Boutillier, R. G. (1975). The effect of quantity and quality of verbal interaction on ratings of leadership ability. *Journal of Experimental Social Psychology, 11,* 403–411.

Spillman, B., Spillman, R., & Reinking, K. (1981). Leadership emergence: Dynamic analysis of the effects of sex and androgyny. *Small Group Behavior, 12,* 139–158.

Steiner, I. D. (1972). *Group process and productivity.* New York: Academic Press.

Stevenson, H. W., & Odom, R. D. (1962). The effectiveness of social reinforcement following two conditions of social deprivation. *Journal of Abnormal and Social Psychology, 65,* 429–431.

Stogdill, R. M. (1974). *Handbook of leadership.* New York: Free Press

Strupp, H. H., & Hausman, H. J. (1953). Some correlates of group productivity. *American Psychologist, 8,* 443–444.

Sykes, R. E., Larntz, K., & Fox, J. C. (1976). Proximity and similarity effects on frequency of interaction in a class of naval recruits. *Sociometry, 39,* 263–269.

Tannenbaum, R., & Massarik, F. (1957). Leadership: A frame of reference. *Management Science, 4,* 1–19.

Taylor, K. P. (1970). An investigation of majority verbal behavior toward opinions of deviant members in group discussions of policy. Unpublished doctoral dissertation, Indiana University, Bloomington.

Terborg, J. R., Castore, C., & DeNinno, J. A. (1976). A longitudinal field investigation of the impact of group composition on group performance and cohesion. *Journal of Personality and Social Psychology, 34,* 782–790.

Triandis, H. E., Hall, E. R., & Ewen, R. B. (1965). Member heterogeneity and dyadic creativity. *Human Relations, 18,* 33–55.

Tuckman, B. W. (1965). Developmental sequences in small groups. *Psychological Bulletin, 63,* 384–399.

Valentine, K. B., & Fisher, B. A. (1974). An interaction analysis of verbal innovative deviance in small groups. *Speech Monographs, 41,* 413–420.

Valiquet, M. I. (1968). Individual change in a management development program. *Journal of Applied Behavioral Science, 4,* 313–325.

Van Zelst, R. H. (1952). Sociometrically selected work teams increase production. *Personnel Psychology, 5,* 175–186.

Wahrman, R. (1977). Status, deviance, sanctions, and group discussion. *Small Group Behavior, 8,* 147–168.

Ware, J. R., & Barr, J. E. (1977). Effects of a nine-week structured and unstructured group experience on measures of self-concept and self-actualization. *Small Group Behavior, 8,* 93–100.

Wheeler, L., & Nezlek, J. (1977). Sex differences in social participation. *Journal of Personality and Social Psychology, 35,* 742–754.

Wiley, M. G. (1973). Sex roles in games. *Sociometry, 36,* 526–541.

Willerman, B., & Swanson, L. (1953). Group prestige in voluntary organizations. *Human Relations, 6,* 57–77.

Winter, S. K. (1976). Developmental stages in the roles and concerns of group co-leaders. *Small Group Behavior, 7,* 349–362.

Zander, A. (1976). The psychology of removing group members and recruiting new ones. *Human Relations, 29,* 969–987.

Ziller, R. C. (1957). Group size: A determinant of the quality and stability of group decisions. *Sociometry, 20,* 165–173.

Zimmer, J. L., & Sheposh, J. P. (1975). Effects of high-status and low-status actors' performance on observers' attributions of causality and behavioral intentions. *Sociometry, 38,* 395–407.

7

Organizational Communication

Fredric M. Jablin
University of Texas, Austin

Fredric M. Jablin is Associate Professor of Speech Communication at the University of Texas at Austin. He received a Ph.D. degree in organizational communication from Purdue University. His research interests include superior-subordinate communication, influence processes in organizations, and the role of communication in the organizational assimilation process. Dr. Jablin has published research in a wide variety of communication, psychology, and management journals. Currently, he is co-editing the Handbook of Organizational Communication.

LEARNING OBJECTIVES

After studying this chapter you should be able to:

- Define organizational communication.
- List the four major schools of organizational theory.
- Discuss the role played by organizational communication within each of the four major schools of organizational theory.
- Explain the importance to organizational communication of concepts such as unity of direction and the scalar chain in classical theory.
- Distinguish between open and closed systems.
- Trace briefly the development of organizational communication research from the 1940s through the 1980s.
- Know the key research issues or questions being asked during each decade and some of the key findings that answer those questions.

- See the relationship between the changes in organizational theory from classical through contingency approaches and the changes in research on organizational communication.

In recent years organizational communication has increasingly become a focus of investigation for communication researchers. A handbook summarizing research and theory in the area has been published (Jablin, Putnam, Roberts, & Porter, 1987), and a large number of undergraduate texts have been written on the subject (for example, Conrad, 1985; Gibson & Hodgetts, 1986; Goldhaber, 1986; Kreps, 1986). Surveys suggest that organizational communication is growing in popularity as a course of study at American colleges and universities (for example, Downs & Larimer, 1974). Yet, despite its exponential growth as an area of social science research and instruction, the study of communication in organizations remains a relatively new one, and consequently a field that is still experiencing many of the growing pains of an "infant" area of scientific inquiry. Given this state of the art, the purpose of this chapter is to provide a general overview of the historical origins of research and theory on organizational communication, describe major topics of study and prominent research findings, and discuss the directions the field seems to be headed in.

More specifically, this chapter will introduce the study of organizational communication from an *evolutionary perspective*. After a brief description of the basic properties and characteristics of organizational communication, a historical review of organizational theories that have influenced the development of the field is provided, followed by an overview of the major questions that organizational communication researchers have attempted to answer in their empirical studies. The chapter then concludes with an analysis of the directions organizational communication research and theory seem to be headed in the future.

ORGANIZATIONAL COMMUNICATION: THE NATURE OF THE PHENOMENON

Even a cursory examination of research and theory in the area of organizational communication suggests there are just about as many definitions of the phenomenon as there are persons writing on the subject. But almost all these definitions attribute a number of similar elemental properties or characteristics to communication in organizations.

First, organizational communication is typically viewed as a *process* occurring within (or between) members of social collectivities, or *systems*. As a process, communication within organizations is a dynamic activity, to some extent constantly in flux, but still maintaining an identifiable degree of structure. However, this structure changes or adjusts as the organization evolves over time.

An organizational system is composed of a set of interdependent activities which when completed achieve some specific set of objectives. Consequently, organizational communication is considered to be a process occurring within a purposive system of interrelated activities. Finally, communication between members of organizations involves the creating, sending and receiving, processing, and storing of *messages*. Simply put, a message is any kind of stimulus which when received and interpreted by a member of an organization causes the individual to attribute meaning to the stimulus. Thus at a very basic level we may think of organizational communication as the *process of creating, exchanging, interpreting and storing of messages within purposive systems*.

Organizational communication is somewhat distinct qualitatively and quantitatively from communication in other contexts (for example, family, friends) because of the constraints (positive and negative) that organizing and organization place on communication. For example, organizations typically contain formal divisions of labor (job specialization), status hierarchies (superiors and subordinates), formal and informal communication networks (in fact, organizations can be thought of as "networks of networks"), groups of groups interacting with one another, coalitions, a wide variety of technologies, and so forth (for a complete discussion of basic constraints and properties of organizations, see Redding, 1972). These factors, as well as constraints contained within an organization's relevant environments (such as government, community, and markets), shape and in turn are shaped by the nature of communication in the organization. Thus when studying communication in organizations, we need to explore relationships between message behaviors (at individual, group, and organizational levels) and characteristics of organizations, as well as properties of organizational environments.

ORGANIZATIONAL THEORY AND ORGANIZATIONAL COMMUNICATION

Despite the fact that organizations have existed in one form or another since biblical times, it was not until the early 20th century that formal theories of organizations were developed and widely disseminated. Most of these theories have either explicitly stated principles about communication in organizations or have made implicit assumptions about the role of communication in "effective" organizations (for example, Tompkins, 1984). Before reviewing empirical research that has been conducted in the area of organizational communication, it is important to have a basic understanding of the organizational theories on which much of the research is founded. Though numerous approaches or theories of organizations exist, most can be placed in four basic categories, which emerged in the following chronological order: (1) classical theories, (2) humanistic theories, (3) systems theories, and (4) contingency theories. Each of these "theories" really represents a school of thought, which to some degree has affected the study and practice of communication in organizations.

Classical Theory

To a large extent, classical theories of organization evolved in response to the massive industrialization of the European and American economic systems in the late 19th and early 20th centuries. Prior to classical statements of organizational theory, most managers and workers within industrial organizations selected for themselves the "best" methods for completing their assigned tasks and coordinating activities with others. A major goal of classical theories was to systematize organizing activity by determining the one "best" way to structure and operate organizations. The classical theories and their general perspective on communication in organizations is perhaps best represented in the writings of Taylor (1911), Fayol (1929), and Weber (1947).

"Scientific Management"   Frederick Taylor, in his book *The Principles of Scientific Management* (1911), attempted to set forth a series of tenets by which managers could determine the most efficient or scientific methods for blue-collar work. By scientifically considering human physiology and the specialization or functionalization of tasks, as well as a number of assumptions about human motivation, Taylor maintained he could determine the one "best" way to organize any particular type of work. By applying scientific management principles in the steel plant in which he worked, Taylor became one of the earliest proponents of what is known today as industrial engineering.

Taylor's assumptions about human motivation, though, had the most impact on the theory and practice of communication in organizations. In basic terms, scientific management viewed workers almost entirely from an economic perspective; workers were seen as motivated almost solely by the opportunity for higher wages. Moreover, Taylor perceived the average worker to be "mentally sluggish" (p. 46), and thus incapable of determining the best way to complete his or her job. Thus Taylor maintained that managers needed to induce the cooperation of workers in order to "develop each individual man to his highest state of efficiency and prosperity" (p. 43). Specifically, Taylor advised managers when communicating with workers to emphasize material rewards (wages), to use "rough" or authoritarian talk to accomplish this, and not to tolerate any "back talk" from workers (p. 46).

Although such a linear, one-way approach to communication may seem harsh, Taylor believed that it was in the mutual interest of management and workers to enact this model of communication. For Taylor, the outcomes of scientific management, higher profits for the organization and higher wages for workers, justified the means.

The Structuring of Tasks and Authority
Scientific management concepts focused more on the functions of the worker than on the manager. Taylor's principles said little about the more general problem of how management relationships should be organized. Another classicist, Henry Fayol, in his book *General and Industrial Management* (1929), filled this void in Taylor's work by stating 14 "universal" principles of management. These principles, based on Fayol's experiences as a manager in a coal mining company in France, explicitly and implicitly suggest several principles of organizational communication.

Probably the principles that most directly relate to the study and practice of communication in organizations are those concerned with the structuring of tasks and authority. In particular, three related principles stand out in importance: unity of direction, the scalar chain, and unity of command. Each of these principles is concerned with vertical communication in organizations, though the scalar chain has implications as well for horizontal communication.

In simple terms, the principle of unity of direction argues that task functions should be departmentalized and their operations directed by only one manager. The scalar chain suggests that within an organization a "graded chain of superiors" from those with highest to those with lowest authority should exist, and that this chain should

be the route for all upward and downward communication. This principle was supplemented, however, with what has become known as "Fayol's Bridge," which allowed for direct horizontal communication between managers of equal rank in situations deemed appropriate by top management, such as crisis situations. Finally, the principle of unity of command posits that a manager should never violate the chain of command by bypassing a subordinate's superior in dealing with a subordinate. Taken together, Fayol's principles argue for highly differentiated (functionalized) and hierarchical organizational structures in which communication is closely controlled and follows the organization's decision-making chain of command.

Weber's Theory of Bureaucracy Probably most would agree that Max Weber's *Theory of Social and Economic Organization,* first published in 1922, represents the culmination of the tenets of classical organizational theory. In a fully articulated theory of authority structure in organizations, Weber outlines his well-known theory of bureaucracy. His theory, in addition to reiterating many of the principles of other classical theorists (such as job specialization, unity of command, scalar chain), also suggests that organizations be governed by "consistent sets of abstract rules" designed to assure predictability of performance and coordination of tasks. Officials are advised to manage their offices through "written documents ('the files')," and to separate "official activity" from private life (Gerth & Mills, 1946). In bureaucracies, relationships with subordinates, superiors, and peers follow the specific rules of the organization, and "impersonality, as contrasted to personal relationships, regulates activity" (Tausky, 1970, p. 32).

As Tompkins (1984) observes, however, the use of "formal, impartial rules leads to a kind of impersonal communicative behavior" that often results in feelings of alienation among workers and clients (p. 670). Thus maintaining "social distance" with workers and enacting impersonal communication behaviors have costs associated with them, but they also have potential benefits—ideally, they should lead to fewer interpersonal problems among employees and result in more rational, efficient organizational operations.

To summarize, classical organizational theory can be characterized as promoting highly differentiated and pyramidal organizational structures, restricted interaction among organization members, vertical communication processes (particularly oriented toward the downward flow of information), centralized control and decision processes, the proliferation of rules and regulations, and an orientation toward employee motivation based primarily on economic need. In addition, it should be noted that the classical perspective showed little concern for the effects organizational environments have on the internal functioning of organizations, since at the time this perspective was developed, organizational environments tended to be quite stable and homogeneous (for example, supplies of labor, raw materials, and markets for products were abundant, and government regulations were few).

Humanistic Theory

Somewhat in response to the classical approach to organizations, the humanistic or human-relations school of organizational theory emerged in the mid-1930s. Most scholars agree that the Hawthorne studies (Mayo, 1933; Roethlisberger & Dickson, 1939) inaugurated the movement. These studies, conducted over a five-year period at the Hawthorne plant of the Western Electric Company, were originally designed to explore several scientific management principles. For example, one of the first studies conducted was concerned with determining the effects varying intensities of illumination had on the productivity of workers. However, the results of this study as well as several others led the research team to conclude that the productivity of workers was not merely a function of the physical conditions of work, the physiology of the workers, and monetary incentives, but that interpersonal relationships among the workers, group norms, and

supervisory style of leadership also affected productivity.

In essence, the results of the Hawthorne studies revealed that in order to fully understand the nature of organizations, it is necessary to view them as *social* collectivities, containing formal and informal structures and relationships (rather than just formal, as the classical theories claimed). In addition, findings from the investigations suggested that levels of job performance are to some degree affected by workers' feelings of job satisfaction and morale. The classicists' assumption that employees are primarily motivated by economic concerns was seriously brought into question. In fact, the Hawthorne data were interpreted as indicating that social and psychological factors could influence worker motivation as strongly as, if not more than, economic ones.

Although the Hawthorne studies have received considerable criticism with respect to methodology and data interpretation (for example, Carey, 1967), there is no question that they have had an enormous impact on the study of communication in organizations. Because the findings were interpreted as indicating that organizational performance is closely tied to management's understanding of and concern about the needs and ideas of workers, advocates of the incipient "human relations" movement argued for greater attention to a *two-way* flow of communication between workers and management. Specifically, results of the Hawthorne and related studies (such as Coch & French, 1948; Lewin, Lippitt, & White, 1939) were construed as supporting increased worker participation in decision making and consequently more attention to upward communication processes in organizations, greater trust and openness in communication between management and workers, and cultivation of interpersonal communication skills of managers in group and dyadic settings. Typical of the human-relations approach are the theories of McGregor (1960), Argyris (1957), and Likert (1961, 1967).

Douglas McGregor, in his now classic book *The Human Side of Enterprise* (1960), posits two theories of human nature, "Theory X" and "Theory Y." Theory X is comparable to the classicists' view of the nature of worker motivation: Employees dislike work, need to be coerced, directed, and threatened to perform adequately, lack ambition, tend to avoid responsibility, and are driven primarily by needs for security. In contrast, Theory Y, founded on Abraham Maslow's (1955) theory of human motivation, argues that work is as natural as play, employees desire responsibility and opportunities to be creative and use their intelligence, and are motivated by chances to satisfy their needs for personal growth and self-actualization (the maximization of one's potential). According to McGregor (1960), "Theory Y assumes that people will exercise self-direction and self-control in the achievement of organizational objectives *to the degree that they are committed to those objectives*" (p. 56). Consequently, McGregor believed that by opening up channels of communication between workers and management, mutually shared goals could be established (the "integration" of individual and organizational needs), which would result in greater work commitment and higher levels of job performance and satisfaction.

Somewhat similar to McGregor, Chris Argyris (1957) maintains that there is an incongruency between the needs of a healthy personality and the requirements or restrictions organizations place on human behavior. Argyris argues that the typical individual in a formal organization is frustrated, because the organization thwarts his or her self-development by encouraging dependency, limited utilization of abilities, passivity, and a short time perspective. He concludes that this situation can be corrected by encouraging more worker participation in decision making, employee-centered leadership, and job enrichment, among other approaches.

In turn, Rensis Likert (1961, 1967) has suggested that management styles in organizations fall into one of four "systems." Likert's "System 1" ("exploitive-authoritative") is similar to McGregor's Theory X in its managerial assumptions, while "System 4" ("participative") parallels Theory Y. Systems 2 ("benevolent-authoritative") and

3 ("consultative") are considered gradients between these two extremes. From a communication perspective, as one moves from System 1 to System 4 there is supposed to be an increase in superior and subordinate trust, confidence in communication, a sharing of decision making, open flow of communication (up, down, and across the organization), accurate feedback, and candid questioning of organizational policies and decisions. According to Likert, organizations that adopt a System 4 managerial style will be more effective than organizations utilizing any of the other systems.

In summary, humanistic approaches to organizational theory have argued for the participation of lower-level employees in organizational decision making; increased openness and trust among organization members; multiple, free-flowing channels of communication; the integration of individual and organization goals; greater interest in and consideration for the development and self-actualization of workers; employee-centered styles of leadership; and in general, extensive interaction processes. In contrast to the classical theorists, humanists have also called for organizations with fewer hierarchical levels, with a corresponding emphasis on a high state of organizational integration (collaboration) versus differentiation (functionalization). On the other hand, similar to the classicists, human-relations proponents consider their approach to be universally applicable to all organizations and show little consideration for the effects organizations' environments have on their operations.

Systems Theory

As noted earlier, organizations are considered to be systems, since they are composed of interdependent activities and possess (at least on an abstract level) identifiable boundaries. When we refer to an organization as a system, we can consider it to be either a "closed" system or an "open" system. The classical theorists, as well as many of those advocating the human-relations approach, generally viewed organizations in closed-system terms: Organizations are self-contained systems that operate in rational, deterministic ways, independent of their environments. An open-system view regards organizations as transformation systems that are in dynamic relationship with their environments. Internal organizational activities and relationships are considered less predictable, since the organization is in a constant state of proactive and reactive adaptation to its environment.

Although some notable early theorists (such as Barnard, 1938; Follett, 1946) maintained that organizations should be considered open systems, this perspective was not widely accepted until the mid-20th century. Applying many of the principles of general systems theory (see Von Bertalanffy, 1950), Katz and Kahn in *The Social Psychology of Organizations* (1966) provide one of the most comprehensive and influential statements of the application of open-systems theory to the operation of organizations. In basic terms they suggest that:

- Organizations are composed of interdependent parts whose operations cannot be fully understood without looking at the total organizational system—problems in the marketing department may be related to activities of the production and delivery departments, for example.
- In order to survive, organizations must exchange (import-transform-export) "energy" (products, information, materials) with their environments.
- In order to survive, organizations must acquire "negative entropy": maximize their ratios of imported to exported energy so they possess sufficient resources to operate on a daily basis, and to fall back on during difficult economic periods.
- Organizations should be viewed as systems in dynamic equilibrium (steady-state) with their environments, in a constant process of adapting.
- Organizations maintain equilibrium with their

environments through the positive and negative feedback they receive from those environments, such as orders for products or services.
- Organizations move in the direction of greater versus less differentiation (or elaboration).
- Organizations possess multiple goals or purposes.
- Organizations can achieve the same final results from various initial conditions and by differing paths (the principle of "equifinality").

In essence, an open-systems approach to organizations really combines the strengths of both the classical and human-relations perspectives to organizations, but unites them in a flexible, heuristic manner. Open-systems theory recognizes that organizations are composed of both functional subsystems (classical emphasis) and social systems (humanistic emphasis), and that these are dynamically interrelated. Moreover, the open-systems approach acknowledges that organizations are dependent on their environments, and that to a large degree their survival is a function of their ability to develop and understand environmental feedback. From the open-systems perspective, the successful organization is one that is effective in managing relationships within and between its own internal subsystems (departments or divisions), as well as relationships with its suprasystems (suppliers, markets, local community). Further, it should be noted that an implication of open-systems theory is that there is probably no one "best" way to organize in general, or operate an organization's communication system in particular.

Contingency Theory

Most contemporary organizational theories are contingency theories, and are a direct outgrowth of viewing organizations as open systems. In fact, one could consider contingency theory to be the research operationalization of the abstract principles of open-systems theory. Rather than assume that there is one "best" way in which to organize, a contingency perspective attempts to identify and understand the patterns or configurations that exist among an organization's subsystems and with the environment. According to Lorsch and Lawrence (1970), "Underlying this new approach is the idea that the internal functioning of organizations must be consistent with the demands of the organization task, technology, or external environment, and the needs of its members if the organization is to be effective" (p. 1). In other words, contingency theory suggests that what is effective in one organization may not be effective in another organization, since the configuration of task, people, and structural and environmental subsystems may vary. Consequently, the goal of the contingency theorist is to identify the most effective forms of organization for various configurations.

Environmental Stability   Some examples of actual research based on contingency theory may help clarify the approach. Burns and Stalker (1961) investigated 20 different British organizations and identified two basic forms of management systems, each of which was effective under different conditions of *environmental stability*. The "mechanistic" system, found to be effective for organizations in *stable* economic and technical environments, was characterized by a high degree of functional differentiation, precise rules and regulations, vertical patterns of communication, and rather strict control of work behavior. In contrast, these researchers discovered that an "organic" system was more appropriate in *changing* economic and technical environments. Organic organizational forms were characterized by a wide sharing of knowledge, experience, and decision making among members, a network structure of communication, a lateral versus vertical flow of messages, messages typically in the form of advice rather than instructions or decisions, and ad hoc centers of control and authority. Thus Burns and Stalker's research suggests that the degree of change or stability in an organization's environment affects the type of management and communication system that will be effective.

Form of Technology   Joan Woodward's (1965) research has demonstrated that an organization's modal (basic) *technology* is also important to consider in determining how to structure and manage an organization. As a byproduct of her studies, she has identified three basic types of technologies found in industrial organizations: (1) unit or small-batch production of typically complex, custom-made items; (2) mass or large-batch production (most typically assembly-line production); and (3) process production (continuous-flow manufacturing, of chemicals, for example). In general, her findings indicate that the attitudes and behaviors of organization members vary depending on their organizations' modal technologies. For example, with respect to communication variables, she has discovered that the total amount of *oral* communication is higher in unit and process technologies than in mass-production technologies, and that in mass-production technologies there is more *written* communication than in the other types of technologies.

Level of Integration   Finally, Lawrence and Lorsch (1967), expanding on the work of Burns and Stalker, explored the effects that various environments have on the structural differentiation and integration of organizations. Their results suggest that successful organizations adapt their structures to the amount of uncertainty in their environments, but that regardless of degree of uncertainty, successful organizations are highly integrated. Yet their findings indicate that the mechanisms necessary to achieve a high state of integration vary depending on the type of environment in which an organization is located. Essentially, they discovered that the more uncertain the environment, the more effort (in terms of time, personnel, procedures) an organization has to expend to achieve an effective amount of collaboration and communication among departments and individuals.

To conclude, a contingency approach to organizational design and behavior is founded on principles of open-system theory, and posits that effectiveness depends on the degree to which an organization can match its structure, policy, and so on to the configuration of its situational variables (such as technology, environment, people, culture). Consequently, this perspective assumes that there is no one "best" design for an organization's communication system, and that when conducting empirical research concerning communication in organizations, one must consider numerous situational factors.

Summary

This very basic introduction to the evolution of organizational theory has suggested how the development of organizational theory has affected the study and practice of communication in organizations. Originating with a very static, functional view of organizations (classical approach), these theories have evolved into increasing concern for organizations as social-psychological collectivities (humanistic approach), and as open systems interacting dynamically with their environments (systems approach). These developments have culminated in the major current approach to the study of organizations: contingency theory. A contingency perspective assumes that there may not be one "best" way in which to organize, and consequently seeks to determine the effects situational or subsystem variables have on organizational effectiveness.

As organizational theory has evolved, so has its perspective on the roles and functions of communication in organizations. From initially viewing communication in very linear, formal, downward-message-sending terms, these theories have evolved into recognizing the importance of two-way formal and informal communication in organizations, and increasingly the multichannel nature of complex communication systems. Organization theory has provided the foundations on which much of the empirical research into communication in organizations (to be reviewed in the following section) is based.

RESEARCH TRENDS IN ORGANIZATIONAL COMMUNICATION

Modern research into organizational communication is somewhat arbitrarily defined as research in organizations where communication has explicitly been the focus of study, and in which empirical, qualitative or quantitative scientific techniques of data collection have been employed. Roughly speaking, the era of modern organizational communication research emerged about the time of the Second World War. This section attempts to outline the major research questions and trends that have dominated the study of organizational communication since the 1940s. This is not a complete review of the literature, however, and many other specific research areas were also explored in this period (see Jablin, 1979, 1980; Porter & Roberts, 1976; Putnam & Cheney, 1985; Redding, 1972, 1985; Richetto, 1977; Tompkins, 1984).

The 1940s

From an organizational communication perspective, this decade has been labeled the "Era of Information" (Dover, 1959). During this period the human-relations movement was gaining in popularity, and the catchword of the day was, "An informed employee is a happy and productive employee." Organizations devoted a great deal of time and resources to providing employees with increased information about such areas as organizational growth, market position, and financial status. The primary vehicle for the transmission of such information was employee publications, such as handbooks and newsletters.

Several studies attempted to ascertain the effectiveness of these downward-directed media (for example, Baker, Ballantine, & True, 1949; Peterson & Jenkins, 1948). These investigations focused primarily on issues related to the readability of internal company publications and employee attitudes toward downward corporate communication. Studies typically used objective "tests of knowledge" (prepared by management) as indicators of employees' levels of information adequacy. Results of these studies generally showed employees to be seriously *un*informed about information that management considered essential for them to know. In addition, explorations of the readability of company publications indicated that most were too difficult in vocabulary and style for the average high school–educated employee to understand. Contrary to the position of the human-relations advocates, several studies conducted during this period revealed little association between levels of employees' information adequacy and their job satisfaction and morale (Redding, 1972).

Clearly, for this decade the major priority of both researchers and practitioners was to determine ways to improve downward-directed mass communication to employees. Researchers were trying to discover how to better impart information that would instill in workers a sense of their organization's mission and ideology (for example, Katz & Kahn, 1966). Thus the most pressing research questions of this decade appear to have been: (1) What effects do downward-directed mass communications have on employees? and (2) Is an informed employee a productive employee?

The 1950s

In the 1950s the studies of downward-directed communication initiated in the preceding decade continued. In addition, general systems theory, and in particular the open-systems approach to organizational communication, started to appear in the theoretical research literature. Furthermore, three new directions of research emerged. These studies focused on: (1) analysis of small group and organization networks; (2) perceptions of communication climate; and (3) impediments to upward organizational communication.

One of the more important lines of research that reached prominence during this period in-volved small group studies (see Chapter 6). These investigations (including Bavelas & Barrett, 1951; Leavitt, 1951) laid the foundation for later large-scale network analyses of complex organizational systems. Studies of small group networks were typically conducted in laboratory settings and focused on determining the effects of various network configurations (such as wheel, chain, circle) on leadership emergence, member satisfaction or morale, adaptability, performance speed and accuracy, and communication patterns. With respect to group performance, results of these studies generally showed that group "centrality" (the degree to which communication in a group revolved around a single group member) and the nature of a group's task or problem were extremely important. At the same time, the effects of network shape on performance were typically found to be temporary; that is, after a period of time, regardless of network shape, most groups reached the same performance levels.

The applicability of the results from these studies to actual organizations has often been questioned, however, since the great majority of research was conducted with groups pulled together by the researchers in artificial laboratory settings (for example, Cohen, Robinson, & Edwards, 1969; Guetzkow, 1965). Nevertheless, most would agree that these investigations provided a strong impetus for the later development of methodologies capable of measuring the communication networks of actual large, complex organizations.

Several other significant approaches to the analysis of communication networks in complex systems were also developed during the 1950s. In particular, the research of Jacobson and Seashore (1951) and Weiss and Jacobson (1955) is of interest. Questioning whether actual communication in organizations follows formal organization structures, these investigators developed techniques to map the *emergent* communication structures of organizations. By obtaining self-reports of the regular dyadic communication contacts of organization members (for example,

Burns, 1954), and then arraying these links in who-talks-to-whom matrices, Jacobson and his colleagues were able to identify a number of very specific communication *network roles:* group members (individuals who communicate more with other group members than with persons outside their groups), liaison roles (individuals who link together two groups other than their own groups), and isolates (individuals who have no reciprocated links with other organization members). The characteristics of communication network roles remains, even now, a major focus of communication research in organizations.

Keith Davis (1953) also developed his ECCO (Episodic Communication Channels in Organizations) network analysis technique during this decade. By tracing how individuals learned about *particular* items of information, ECCO analysis showed the sequences or patterns through which selected messages flowed in an organization. The method has proved especially useful in the mapping of employee "grapevine" networks (Davis, 1969; Sutton & Porter, 1968).

The 1950s also marked the inception of the Purdue University "climate" studies, which focused on collecting communication-related attitudinal and perceptual data from employees. Richetto (1977) succinctly summarizes this first decade of climate research:

[T]he Purdue group investigated alternative communication modes and their effects (Dahle, 1953), attitudes of corporate managers toward correlates of communication and productivity (Funk, 1956), perceptions of communication breakdowns in organizations (Ross, 1954), the role of organizational communication practices among first-line supervisors (Piersol, 1955), information flow within the banking industry (Level, 1959), and other communication variables operating within formal organizations. (p. 334)

These studies are noteworthy in that they initiated a research paradigm directed at discriminating the communication behaviors and attitudes of

effective versus ineffective leaders or supervisors (as determined by upper-level management sources), which was to dominate a considerable amount of future organizational-climate research.

Closely associated with the climate research of the Purdue group were several studies examining interpersonal feedback processes within organizations. Primarily using laboratory settings, these investigations focused on the effects of varying degrees of feedback (open, restricted, one-way, two-way) on sender and receiver perceptions of accuracy of communication, confidence, satisfaction, and perceived and actual performance (Leavitt & Mueller, 1951; Smith & Kight, 1959; Zajonc, 1962). Results of these and later studies (such as Brown, 1967; Cook, 1968; Haney, 1964) generally showed that open (bilateral), specific feedback from receiver to sender (and vice versa) increased the accuracy of task performance as well as one's perception that the task was completed correctly. Findings also suggested that the more supportive versus ego-threatening or derogatory the feedback, the more likely the recipient would be to accept it (Gibb, 1961).

A third direction of organizational communication research during this period explored impediments to upward communication in organizations. Several eminent studies associated with the Institute for Social Research at the University of Michigan examined such issues as the distortion of upward-communicated messages, the effects of superiors' hierarchical influence on their subordinates' upward communication, and various moderators of subordinate-to-superior communication (Jackson, 1953; Maier, Read, & Hooven, 1959; Mellinger, 1956; Pelz, 1952; Planty & Machaver, 1952). Like the Purdue studies of the same period, these investigations focused primarily on collecting perceptual or "climate" data from actual organization members.

The findings of these upward-communication studies resulted in an interesting set of conclusions. With respect to upward distortion in subordinate-to-superior communication, results indicated that the greater a subordinate's desire to advance in the organization and the lower the subordinate's trust in his or her superior, the more likely the subordinate would be to distort messages sent upward to the superior. Further, Pelz's (1952) research on upward influence revealed that subordinates who perceived their supervisors as supportive leaders and possessing considerable influence with higher-level bosses were more satisfied with their supervisors than subordinates who worked for supervisors who were supportive leaders but who possessed limited amounts of upward influence in their organizations.

In addition, the research tradition begun in the 1940s that examined the effects of downward-directed communication on employees' attitudes continued. The study of the relationship between the adequacy of downward communication and employee morale and satisfaction often produced equivocal or contradictory findings (for example, Browne & Neitzel, 1952; Level, 1959). In fact, the results of these studies, as well as those conducted in the preceding decade, led Redding (1972) to conclude in his review of the literature that "no automatic relationship should be assumed between mere quantity of information understood by employees and the over-all morale of those employees" (p. 449). More recent research (such as Driver, 1979; Holley & Ingram, 1973), which has improved on some of the methodological weaknesses of earlier studies, also supports Redding's admonition. Yet it should be noted that research conducted during the 1950s did clearly indicate a combination of oral and written methods rather than oral or written alone was more effective in disseminating information within organizations (Dahle, 1953).

Finally, it was during the 1950s that researchers began to realize the importance of studying organizational behavior from a general systems perspective (Von Bertalanffy, 1950), and more specifically from an open-systems approach (Parsons, 1951). Although little empirical research actually employed systems concepts, theories of organizational behavior and communication began to reflect the necessity of using systems approaches in future research.

To summarize, organizational communication research in the 1950s appears to have addressed itself primarily to the following questions: (1) How do communication networks affect organizational performance and member attitudes and behaviors? (2) How can emergent communication networks in organizations be measured? (3) What are the relationships between organization members' attitudes and perceptions of their communication behavior (primarily upward and downward) and their job performance? (4) What is the relationship between the attitudes and performance of workers and the feedback they receive? (5) Is a well-informed employee a satisfied employee?

The 1960s

The 1960s might best be described as the "Era of Isolated Variables." As Richetto (1977) has observed, summarizing the theory and research of this period is difficult because investigators made few attempts "to integrate findings into holistic frameworks" (p. 335). However, it is obvious that the trends toward studying communication climates within organizations and analyzing communication networks, which were initiated during the preceding decade, continued to gain momentum in the 1960s.

Climate studies, particularly those conducted at Purdue University, focused on determining the communicative qualities of good supervisors (as perceived by subordinates and bosses). The results of these investigations suggested that an effective supervisor is a person who tends to be communication-minded, is a willing, empathic listener, asks or persuades rather than tells or demands, and generally is fairly open in passing along information to subordinates (see Redding, 1972, pp. 436–446). However, before generalizing this communication profile of the effective supervisor to all organizational contexts, note that research conducted in the 1970s has indicated effective supervisory communication behaviors may be situational and contingent on a variety of factors (for example, Jablin, 1979).

Still other climate studies focused on delineating the nature and effects of "semantic-information distance" (Tompkins, 1962) on superior-subordinate communication. Semantic-information distance "describes the gap in information or understanding that exists between superiors and subordinates (or other groups within an organization) on specified issues" (Jablin, 1979, p. 1207). Building on the findings of pioneering studies of this phenomenon (such as Browne & Neitzel, 1952; Weaver, 1958; Triandis, 1959), research conducted in the 1960s revealed that significant gaps in semantic distance exist not only between superiors and subordinates on such simple issues as basic job duties (Maier, Hoffman, Hooven, & Read, 1961; Rosen, 1961), but also between union members and their leaders (Tompkins, 1962). Data analyses indicated that serious semantic misunderstandings were frequent in superior-subordinate interactions (for example, Minter, 1969), and that even if a superior had previously held his or her subordinate's job, significant amounts of semantic distance existed between them (Maier, Hoffman, & Read, 1963). More recent research seems to support the conclusion that semantic-information distance is a persistent problem in organizations. In fact, in his review of the literature, Jablin (1979) asserts, "Incessantly, we find the existence of semantic-information distance in superior-subordinate relations, often at levels that would appear to seriously obstruct organizational effectiveness" (p. 1208).

In addition to exploring correlates of good supervision and semantic-information distance, climate researchers during the 1960s attempted to ascertain the relationship between workers' perceptions of participation in decision making (PDM) and job-related attitudes and performance (Chaney, 1969; Greiner, 1967; Lowin, 1968; Roche & MacKinnon, 1970; Vroom & Mann, 1960). Typically, these studies measured PDM along a continuum ranging from very little subordinate participation ("boss centered") to almost a complete sharing of power and decision making between superior and subordinate ("subordinate centered") (Tannenbaum & Schmidt, 1958). In general terms, the results of these and later PDM studies (for reviews, see Locke & Schwieger, 1979; Miller & Monge, 1986) have showed equivocal relationships between adoption of participative decision-making approaches and improved productivity and performance. However, a fair amount of research has supported the conclusion that participative versus directive approaches to decision making lead to higher levels of worker morale and satisfaction.

As a result of more sophisticated sociometric measurement techniques, network analyses in the 1960s also advanced considerably. Resurrecting and building the seminal network methodologies of Jacobson and his colleagues, investigators at Michigan State University began to explore communication roles within complex organizational networks, in particular describing the differences between liaison and nonliaison roles (MacDonald, 1970; Schwartz, 1968). These studies were to lend some support to Walton's (1963) "magnetic theory" of organizational communication that was proposed earlier in the decade, in which "centrals" (essentially liaisons) played significant roles. Also during this period, Allen and his associates (Allen, 1966; Allen & Cohen, 1969) at the Massachusetts Institute of Technology were exploring the channels by which information is diffused within organizations, and in particular "gatekeeping" roles within these networks.

Findings from studies exploring the characteristics of liaisons in communication networks suggested that they have more access to information, send more messages, are more influential, and possess broader communication contacts than those in nonliaison roles. Moreover, liaisons were more often found to be initial sources of information about organizational activities and changes than nonliaisons. As Monge, Edwards, and Kirste (1978) observe, "These studies present a remarkably consistent profile of the liaison member as an energetic, dynamic, committed organization member, fulfilling a vital communication service for his[/her] organization" (p. 320).

In brief, organizational communication research during the 1960s appears to have continued research initiated in the 1950s. Generally, researchers maintained their focus on describing the characteristics of communication climates and networks within complex organizations. More specifically, this research concentrated on four key questions: (1) What do organization members perceive to be the communication correlates of good supervision? (2) To what degree is superior-subordinate semantic-information distance a problem in organizations? (3) What is the relationship between subordinates' job-related attitudes and productivity and the extent to which they perceive they participate in decision-making? and (4) In what ways do the actual and perceived communication behaviors of liaison and nonliaison roles within organizational communication networks differ?

The 1970s

Although the directions of organizational communication research in the 1970s are difficult to categorize, there is little doubt that, in comparison to earlier periods, empirical research during this decade grew at almost an exponential rate. While studies still frequently investigated a hodgepodge of isolated variables, research in the area increased considerably in methodological sophistication. At the same time, scholars began to focus on issues associated with the theoretical foundations of their research and the need to build and test conceptual models of organizational communication processes. Consequently, during this period a number of important critiques of research appeared, and several paradigms to follow in studying and theorizing about organizational communication were proposed (Farace & MacDonald, 1974; Redding, 1972, 1979; Roberts, O'Reilly, Bretton, & Porter, 1974).

The number of studies exploring communication climates within organizations grew tremendously in the 1970s. The prime target of climate investigations was superior-subordinate communication. As in the preceding decade, researchers continued to explore the communication correlates of effective superiors, subordinate-to-superior distortion in upward communication, and the nature and functions of feedback in superior-subordinate communication. In addition, research programs were initiated that examined the roles and functions of openness in superior-subordinate communication and the effects personal characteristics such as sex, age, and values of superiors and subordinates have on their respective communication behaviors.

Probably the major impetus for studying openness in superior-subordinate communication was provided by the human-relations theorists, who typically included openness as an essential feature of effective organizations. According to Redding (1972), openness in superior-subordinate communication is composed of two closely related dimensions: openness in message sending and openness in message receiving. He suggests that openness in message sending includes the "candid disclosure of feelings, or 'bad news,' and important company facts"; openness in message receiving involves "encouraging, or at least permitting, the frank expression of views divergent from one's own; the willingness to listen to 'bad news' or discomforting information" (p. 330). The results of openness studies are summarized by Jablin (1979):

[I]n an open communication relationship between superior and subordinate, both parties perceive the other interactant as a willing and receptive listener and refrain from responses that might be perceived as providing negative relational or disconfirming feedback . . . these studies provide strong evidence for the proposition that employees are more satisfied with their jobs when openness of communication exists between superior and subordinate than when the relationship is closed. (p. 1204)

The personal characteristics of superiors and subordinates that mediate their respective communication behaviors and attitudes were also a research focus during the 1970s (for a review of this literature, see Jablin, 1979). For example, studies showed that younger superiors (20–29) tend to possess more authoritarian communication styles than older superiors (30–55), subordinates do not particularly like superiors who are apprehensive communicators, and that a subordinate's perception of his or her superior's communication credibility is associated with the subordinate's satisfaction with the superior.

A number of inquiries focused on differentiating the communication behaviors of male and female superiors. Generally, results of these investigations indicated that subordinates have sex-role stereotypes of the communication behaviors appropriate for superiors of each sex (for a review of the literature, see Fairhurst, 1986). For example, subordinates (regardless of sex) were found to be more satisfied with a "considerate" communication style in female versus male superiors.

As in the 1960s, research in the 1970s, concerned with identifying the communication behaviors of effective leaders, suggested that there may not be one particular communication style that works "best" in all situations. Support for this contingency perspective is considerable and indicates that such factors as task structure, a leader's positional (formal) power, the quality of previous superior-subordinate relations, sex, organizational climate, work-group size, and leader-upward influence may influence the leadership and communication style that will be effective in a given situation (see Jablin, 1979). Thus it would seem, as Redding (1972) observes in his interpretation of the Purdue studies of supervisory communication climate, that "the precise combination of behaviors or attitudes that 'works' in one company is likely to be different from what 'works' in another company or organization" (p. 445).

Investigations exploring message distortion in subordinates' upward communication to superiors generally supported the findings of previous research, though several studies found weaker relationships between subordinates' desire for advancement and their proclivity to distort upward communication (for example, O'Reilly & Roberts, 1974; Roberts & O'Reilly, 1974a). Additional factors were also discovered to be related to a subordinate's propensity to distort upward messages, including the subordinate's security needs and risk-taking disposition, organizational climate, and supervisory leadership style (Athanassiades, 1973, 1974). Research also showed that subordinates tend to distort messages that are negative-unfavorable more than messages that are positive-favorable to themselves (Rosen & Tesser, 1970).

Since "probably one of the most common complaints aired by superiors and subordinates about their communication relationship is that one of the interactants does not provide the other with sufficient and relevant feedback" (Jablin, 1979, p. 1212), it is not surprising that a considerable number of studies explored the characteristics and effects of superior-subordinate feedback processes. Results of investigations showed that subordinates' levels of job satisfaction were related to the feedback they received from their superiors. Moreover, findings from these studies suggested that feedback processes in superior-subordinate relationships are *reciprocally* related, and that attributions posited to explain the other party's performance influence the type and frequency of feedback that is administered. In addition, evidence collected from studies during this period revealed that subordinates' motivational states may be related to the feedback they receive, and that both superiors and subordinates prefer positive relational feedback (Cusella, 1980; Jablin, 1979).

A significant number of studies conducted during the 1970s focused on delineating the interaction patterns that characterize superior-subordinate relationships. Results of these inquiries, as well as those of earlier studies, consistently indicate that superiors spend between one-third and two-thirds of their time interacting in face-to-face discussions with subordinates about task-related issues. Further, findings suggest that superiors and subordinates have different perceptions of how much they communicate with one another and the degree to which they find these interactions satisfactory (Jablin, 1979; Webber, 1970).

In addition to exploring the climate of superior-subordinate communication, researchers during this period attempted to measure or audit the overall communication climate of organizations (Dennis, 1974; Goldhaber & Rogers, 1979; Roberts & O'Reilly, 1974b). Though subtle differences exist between the various instruments constructed to measure the overall climate, most attempted to measure the following types of variables: quality and quantity of downward and upward communication, superior-subordinate communication (particularly openness, trust, and influence), the types of messages that are sent and received between organization members (different sources of communication), the channels through which these messages travel, the timeliness and accuracy of messages, and overall satisfaction with organizational communication.

Results of these studies generally suggest relationships between an individual's perception of the organization's communication climate and facets of job satisfaction. Before generalizing from this research, however, one should be aware that numerous methodological and conceptual questions have been raised about how these investigations measured climate. They have been criticized for combining evaluative and descriptive items in questionnaire scales (climate is generally considered to be a description of the environment), using questionable procedures in aggregating data, focusing on individual or dyadic dimensions of organizational communication while neglecting group, organization, and interorganization communication issues, and treating climate as a static instead of a dynamic entity (Jablin, 1980).

Analyses of organizational communication networks also increased in number and showed greater sophistication in the 1970s. A significant portion of this research continued to focus on identifying or describing the characteristics of key communication roles within networks (Albrecht, 1979; Roberts & O'Reilly, 1978), the distribution of these roles (Farace & Johnson, 1974), and distinguishing the structural characteristics of communication networks (Bernard & Killworth, 1975). Studies also began to consider the characteristics of a communication role closely related to network liaisons, "boundary spanners"—individuals who relate an organization to its environment through outside transactions and the gathering and filtering of extraorganizational information (Adams, 1976, 1980; Tushman, 1977).

Perhaps more than any other area of organizational communication research, network analysis benefited from methodological advances in the 1970s. Computer programs were developed that have proved capable of analyzing hundreds of communication links between members of organizational communication networks (Rice & Richards, 1985; Richards, 1975). Though problems still exist in the conceptualization and measurement of communication networks (Jablin, 1980; Monge, Edwards, & Kirste, 1978; Monge & Eisenberg, 1987), the advances of the 1970s have provided a strong foundation for future progress in this area.

Finally, it should be noted that a considerable amount of research exploring organizational group communication was conducted during the 1970s. In particular, studies examined leadership (traits, styles, sex differences, and conversational strategies), task characteristics (task types and technology), communication networks (in laboratory and field settings), and communication correlates of decision making (trust, consensus, and feedback) in small groups (see Jablin & Sussman, 1983). Results of research exploring task characteristics and group communication deserve special attention. Without question, these findings suggest that the type of task (such as production, discussion, problem solving) on which a group is working affects interaction patterns and performance levels of group members.

Relatedly, investigations of group technology (task variability and analyzability) have revealed that technology affects not only internal group communication patterns but also the communication modes used to coordinate activities between organizational groups (Van de Ven, Delbecq, & Koenig, 1976). Essentially, it appears that groups in organizations attempt to match their communication and information-processing behavior to the demands of their particular tasks and the technologies associated with those tasks (Tushman, 1978).

In summary, organizational communication research grew considerably in scope and depth during the 1970s. Yet it is probably accurate to conclude that the majority of investigations concentrated on delineating the nature, qualities, and characteristics of organizational communication climates and networks. Thus during the 1970s, research priorities appear associated with attempts to answer the following general research questions: (1) What are the components and correlates of superior-subordinate, work-group, and overall organizational communication climates? and (2) What are the characteristics of work-group and organizational communication networks (and in particular, the distribution of key communication roles)?

The Early 1980s and Beyond

Although it is hazardous to offer predictions about the future, current evidence suggests that the trends of the early 1980s are likely to dominate the directions of organizational communication research well into the next decade.

Research conducted through the mid-1980s has shown a greater emphasis than that of previous decades on studying organizations as *systems,* exploring communication as a *process* (versus a static phenomenon; see Monge, Farace, Eisenberg, Miller, & White, 1984) and in determining how organization members create and recreate shared *meaning* through their communication behavior (Putnam & Cheney, 1985; Putnam & Pacanowsky, 1983). These emphases are evident in many traditional lines of organizational

communication research, as well as in several new avenues of inquiry.

As in the 1970s, the study of organizational communication climates (at the dyadic, group, and organizational levels) and networks remained focal points of investigation. Researchers continued to explore many traditional areas of inquiry, including various aspects of superior-subordinate communication (especially feedback and upward influence; see Jablin, 1985) and correlates of network connectivity (Danowski, 1980; Eisenberg, Monge, & Miller, 1983) and network roles (Reynolds & Johnson, 1982; Tushman & Scanlon, 1981).

A shift is beginning to occur, however, in the theoretical and empirical approaches scholars are assuming in their studies. In particular, researchers are focusing on how communication processes shape and are shaped by climates and networks. Extrapolating from "structuration theory" (Giddens, 1981, 1983), McPhee and Poole have argued that through their daily interactions, organization members *produce* and *reproduce* organizational climates and networks (McPhee, 1985; Poole, 1985; Poole & McPhee, 1983). Communication climate is viewed as an intersubjective phenomenon (rather than as either a subjective or objective one) that is continuously being structured and restructured through evolving interaction rules and resources (Falcione, Sussman, & Herden, 1987; Poole, 1985).

Similarly, with respect to networks, structuration theory posits that emergent communication networks and formal organization structures are reciprocally related—organization and communication structures and networks are "continually produced and recreated in interaction and yet shape that interaction" (Ranson, Hinings, & Greenwood, 1980, p. 3). In brief, the structuration perspective is concerned with how meanings are created through communication *and* with how meanings function to constrain communication processes.

Recent research exploring organizational cultures also reflects an emphasis on processes associated with how organization members achieve common meanings, understandings, and goals. Smircich (1983) suggests a number of approaches to the study of organizational cultures, four of which have dominated most investigations to date. Two of the approaches ("culture and comparative management" and "corporate culture") treat culture as an entity or variable that can be discovered and controlled by management. These approaches, which typify the popular-press treatment of the culture construct (Deal & Kennedy, 1982; Ouchi, 1981; Peters & Waterman, 1982), focus on issues associated with "strong" and "weak" cultures, as manifested through stories, myths, ceremonies, symbolism, and the like.

The other two major approaches ("cognitive" and "symbolic") focus on culture in terms of what an organization "is" versus what an organization "has" (Smircich, 1983). These approaches emphasize culture as a way of understanding organizations. Thus, for instance, communication researchers exploring culture from a cognitive approach have attempted to understand how shared rules guide the communication behavior of organization members (Harris & Cronen, 1979), whereas communication researchers adopting the symbolic perspective have examined how organizational reality is created and re-created through shared symbols and language use (Koch & Deetz, 1981); Pacanowsky & O'Donnell-Trujillo, 1982, 1983).

Relatedly, a number of rhetoric-based analyses of shared symbolism and reality construction in organizations have recently been completed. Among other issues, researchers have studied how groups form "rhetorical visions" of their past, present, and future actions (Bormann, 1983), and how "enthymemic" (syllogistic) processes explain the ways organization members learn to identify with their organizations, are influenced by them, and are "unobtrusively controlled" (Cheney, 1983; Tompkins & Cheney, 1985).

The emphasis on studying communicating and organizing as processes is evident at almost every level of analysis in organizational communication research. For example, with respect to one of the most traditional areas of study, superior-subordinate communication, investigations have focused on coding actual sequential message exchanges during feedback episodes and performance appraisals (Fairhust, Green, & Snavely, 1984a, 1984b; Gioia & Sims, 1986; Sims & Manz, 1984). Similarly, research has been initiated exploring message patterns associated with various types of bargaining and conflict in organizations (see Putnam & Poole, 1987). Other studies have been directed at explicating the communication processes by which newcomers are assimilated into organizations (see Jablin, 1987), and how their relationships with superiors and co-workers develop over time (Graen, Liden, & Hoel, 1982; Jablin, 1984). Rather than examining particular message patterns, these studies use longitudinal research designs in which data are gathered over months and even years. In like fashion, researchers have attempted to examine how organizational communication networks change over time (Barnett & Rice, 1985; Danowski, 1986; Rice, 1982), a process that has recently been referred to as "reorganizing" (Monge & Eisenberg, 1987). The manner in which communication processes change over the life cycles of organizations has also become a recent focus of research attention (Jablin & Krone, 1987; Miller & Friesen, 1984; Smith, Mitchell, & Summer, 1985).

Consistent with open-systems and contingency approaches to the study of organizations, researchers have begun to explore the effects that "macro" organizational variables (organizational structures, technologies, and environments; see Miles, 1980) have on communication behavior in organizations. Some of this research has focused on the effects of macro variables on traditional areas of organizational communication research, such as the effects of formal organization structures and technologies on supervisory communication (Jablin, 1982; Klauss & Bass, 1982). However, a considerable amount of this research has adapted an information-processing perspective to the study of organizations (Daft & Lengel,

1986; Galbraith, 1973; Tushman & Nadler, 1978). In basic terms, this approach proposes that organizations be considered as continually adapting their communication systems to the information demands (gathering, interpreting, and sending of messages) associated with "uncertainty" (lack of predictability) in their internal and external environments. From this perspective, an effective organization is one in which there is a dynamic match between "task characteristics and the ability of organizational structure to provide participants with required information" (Daft & Macintosh, 1981, p. 207). For example, research has shown that as task variety (frequency of unexpected events) associated with a work unit's technology increases, information-processing activity increases (Daft & Macintosh, 1981; Van de Ven & Ferry, 1980), and that the greater the work flow interdependence between units, the more they interact with one another (Stech, 1980; Tushman, 1978).

Researchers have also applied the information-processing perspective at the individual level of analysis by exploring how managers process information in decision making (O'Reilly, 1982; Ungson, Braunstein, & Hall, 1981). Whereas most of these investigations have emphasized the effects of information flow and message volume and direction on decision making, other research has considered the manner in which organization members interpret information they receive and use in decision making. In particular, these studies have focused on exploring how individuals reduce information equivocality (multiple meanings of messages; see Weick, 1979), and how message equivocality affects information interpretation and use (Eisenberg, 1984; Feldman & March, 1981; Kreps, 1980; Putnam & Sorenson, 1982). To some extent, these inquiries suggest that the processing and use of information in organizations may not be entirely rational, but rather may serve important symbolic functions— for example, decision makers collect more information than they can process because it symbolizes rational decision making (see Feldman & March, 1981).

In addition, during the early 1980s the potential impact of advanced electronic information and communication technologies (such as computer conferencing, computer mail, and teleconferencing (see Rice & Associates, 1984; Vallee, 1984) on organizational communication processes developed into an important focus of study. Research along these lines typically considers organizations and their members from an information-processing perspective. Among other findings, investigations have shown that electronic media can affect organizational status differentials (Sproull & Kiesler, 1986), result in flatter, more decentralized hierarchies and smaller organizational units (McKenny, 1985; Pfeffer, 1978; Strassmann, 1985), lead to the development of new communication networks (Palme, 1981; Rice & Case, 1983), increase employees' overall communication contacts (Fulk & Dutton, 1984; Hiltz, 1984), and result in greater upward communication in organizations (Lippitt, Miller, & Halamaj, 1980; Rice & Case, 1983). Recent studies have also explored issues associated with the implementation and use of information technologies in organizations, including the effects of the accessibility of media technology on its use by organization members (Culnan & Bair, 1983), and how task-related perceptions affect choice and use of communication media (Steinfeld, 1985a, 1985b).

Finally, interest in how organizational environments are related to organizational processes is apparent in the growing number of studies exploring distinctions in organizational communication systems across cultures (Gudykunst, Stewart, & Ting-Toomey, 1985; Triandis & Albert, 1987). In particular, a considerable amount of study has been stimulated by Hofstede's (1980) investigation of differences in work-related attitudes and values across cultures. Research has attempted to determine whether theories of organization and related communication principles are culturally specific or universally applicable. For example, scholars have attempted to discover whether North American conceptualizations of openness in communication are applicable to

Japanese organizations (Stewart, Gudykunst, Ting-Toomey, & Nishida, 1986). Similarly, numerous studies have examined the usefulness of "quality circles," the Japanese participative decision-making device, in U.S. corporations (for example, Hirokawa, 1981; Stohl, 1986).

To summarize, an inspection of organizational communication research through the middle of the 1980s suggests that scholars are continuing to explore many of the same areas of inquiry as in the preceding decades. However, their studies are showing a greater concern with respect to the following three issues: (1) How are subsystem and suprasystem factors affecting organizational communication phenomena? (2) How are communication phenomena changing over time? (3) How are organizational members creating and re-creating shared meanings through their communication behavior? Inclusion of these issues in studies exploring communication in organizations creates many methodological and theoretical complexities. As a consequence, researchers will likely be exploring these issues well into the 1990s.

CONCLUSION

Having identified the research questions and trends of the last 45 years, it is important to consider how successful investigators have been in obtaining answers to their inquiries. Though many significant questions have been asked and progress has been made in answering them, it is apparent that definitive answers to many of our questions are not yet available. Two research traditions that have evolved over the past five decades illustrate this point. The first concerns the effects of downward-directed written communication on employees' productivity and motivation, and the second the communication characteristics of effective superiors.

Over the years, communication researchers have been concerned with determining the effects management's downward mass media communication has on employees, and more specifically, whether an informed employee is a productive employee. Given the amount of time that has passed since this research tradition began, one would assume that researchers have by now adequately answered these questions. Some examples of the successful effects of print-related downward media campaigns on employee productivity do exist (see Cutlip & Center, 1971), but most studies lack scientific rigor. In other words, we really do not know what effect downward, print, mass communication has on worker productivity or motivation. As Redding (1972) observes, there still appears to be an "urgent need for objective, controlled studies of the real-life effects of print media, as compared to the effects of other modalities" of downward communication on employees (p. 474). In particular, such studies need to compare the effectiveness of traditional print forms of communication to the newer electronic media (Culnan & Markus, 1987).

Similarly, progress has been made in identifying effective communication behaviors of superiors, but a number of problems still exist in this research tradition. Studies conducted in this area have uncovered many of the basic conceptual dimensions of the climate of superior-subordinate communication, but have not done so well in linking perceptions of communication behaviors or *actual* communication behaviors to job performance. One problem has been that "effective" as compared to "ineffective" performance has been determined by higher management evaluations and not by objective performance indexes. Relatedly, most researchers have not examined the relationship between *actual* supervisory communication behavior and performance; rather, they have explored the relationships between *perceptions* of communication and *perceptions* of job performance. Moreover, most recent research has indicated that what may be perceived as "effective" performance in one organization may not be in another. As a consequence, the results of many existing "effectiveness" studies have become suspect and will require replication and further research (probably from a contingency-theory perspective).

In conclusion, organizational communication scholars have made substantial progress in answering the major research questions of the past 45 years, but considerably more study will be necessary before most of these questions are thoroughly answered. This should be of little surprise, given that the study of communication in organizations is a relatively new area of social science research. Thus, although the field has grown rapidly in the last few decades, numerous challenges remain in our efforts to understand the nature of organizational communication.

SUMMARY

Organizational communication deals with communication processes within purposive systems. Many types of communication processes go on within a complex organization, both formally and informally.

The theory of organizations began with a classical approach that emphasized organizational structure. Later, a humanistic approach to organizations put more emphasis on the study of individuals within the organization in attempting to explain organizational performance. Systems theory brought about a shift in focus for studying organizations. Instead of looking at organizations only from the inside as closed systems, systems theory advocated seeing organizations as open systems that react to and interact with the outside world. Contingency theory added to the open-systems perspective and began to study issues such as the fit between an organization and its environment.

The history of organizational communication research decade by decade from the 1940s to the present provides an evolutionary perspective on the study of organizations. Research in each decade asked different questions and studied different issues. The links between early discoveries and later research that either support or change those early findings is made clearer by seeing each researcher in historical context.

REVIEW AND DISCUSSION QUESTIONS

1. Each of the four major schools of organizational theory discusses communication within the organization. How important for the organization is communication, according each theoretical approach? What functions does each theory see communication performing for the organization?

2. To what extent do the research trends described for the decades of the '40s through the '80s parallel changes in the theoretical frameworks from classical theory through contingency theories? Does it seem that change in theory guided research into new areas, or

have the results of research challenged and brought about revised theories? Do all the research results discussed in the text seem to be accounted for within the theoretical frameworks discussed? If not, where might the new findings require change in theories?

3. There are long-standing links between the study of organizations and the study of groups (Chapter 6), interpersonal communication (Chapter 5), and even the study of mass communication (Chapter 8). The relationship between organizations and new technology (Chapter 3) and organizations and intercultural communication (Chapter 9) are also mentioned as new directions in organizational research. Is an organization merely a place where many types of communication occur, or does an organization have unique forms of communication not mentioned in other chapters? Are there unique constraints or opportunities for other types of communication when they occur in organizations that differ from the principles discussed elsewhere in this book?

4. The chapter frequently mentions problems in conducting research on organizational communication. What are some of those problems? How might each of the flaws cause research results to be incomplete, incorrect, or misleading? How can these problems be overcome to produce better research?

REFERENCES

Adams, J. S. (1976). The structure and dynamics of behavior in organizational boundary roles. In M. D. Dunnette (Ed.), *Handbook of industrial and organizational psychology* (pp. 1175–1199). Chicago: Rand McNally.

Adams, J. S. (1980). Interorganizational processes and organization boundary activities. In B. M. Staw & L. L. Cummings (Eds.), *Research in organizational behavior* (Vol. 2, pp. 321–355). Greenwich, CT: JAI Press.

Albrecht, T. L. (1979). The role of communication in perceptions of organizational climate. In D. Nimmo

(Ed.), *Communication Yearbook 3* (pp. 343–357). New Brunswick, NJ: Transaction.

Allen, T. J. (1966). Performance information channels in the transfer of technology. *Industrial Management Review, 8,* 87–98.

Allen, T. J., & Cohen, S. I. (1969). Information flow in research and development laboratories. *Administrative Science Quarterly, 14,* 12–19.

Argyris, C. (1957). *Personality and organization.* New York: Harper.

Athanassiades, J. C. (1973). The distortion of upward communication in hierarchical organizations. *Academy of Management Journal, 16,* 207–226.

Athanassiades, J. C. (1974). An investigation of some communication patterns of female subordinates in hierarchical organizations. *Human Relations, 27,* 195–209.

Baker, H., Ballantine, J. W., & True, J. M. (1949). *Transmitting information through management and union channels: Two case studies.* Princeton, NJ: Princeton University, Industrial Relations Section.

Barnard, C. I. (1938). *The functions of the executive.* Cambridge, MA: Harvard University Press.

Barnett, G. A., & Rice, R. R. (1985). Longitudinal non-Euclidean networks: Applying Galileo. *Social Networks, 7,* 207–322.

Bavelas, A., & Barrett, D. (1951). An experimental approach to organizational communication. *Personnel, 27,* 366–371.

Bernard, H. H., & Killworth, P. D. (1975). *Some formal properties of networks.* Technical report. Arlington, VA: Office of Naval Research.

Bormann, E. G. (1983). Symbolic convergence: Organizational communication and culture. In L. L. Putnam & M. E. Pacanowsky (Eds.), *Communication and organization: An interpretive approach* (pp. 99–122). Beverly Hills: Sage.

Brown, D. S. (1967, January). Some feedback on feedback. *Adult Leadership,* pp. 226–228, 251–252.

Browne, C. G., & Neitzel, B. J. (1952). Communication, supervision and morale. *Journal of Applied Psychology, 36,* 86–91.

Burns, T. (1954). The directions of activity and communication in a departmental executive group. *Human Relations, 7,* 73–97.

Burns, T., & Stalker, G. M. (1961). *The management of innovation.* London: Tavistock.

Carey, A. (1967). The Hawthorne studies: A radical criticism. *American Sociological Review, 32,* 403–416.

Chaney, F. M. (1969). Employee participation in manufacturing job design. *Human Factors, 11,* 101–106.

Cheney, G. (1983). The rhetoric of identification and the study of organizational communication. *Quarterly Journal of Speech, 69,* 143–158.

Coch, L., & French, J. R. P. (1948). Overcoming resistance to change. *Human Relations, 1,* 512–532.

Cohen, A. M., Robinson, E. L., & Edwards, J. L. (1969). Experiments in organizational embeddedness. *Administrative Science Quarterly, 14,* 208–221.

Conrad, C. (1985). *Strategic organizational communication: Cultures, situations, and adaptation.* New York: Holt, Rinehart & Winston.

Cook, D. M. (1968). The impact on managers of frequency of feedback. *Academy of Management Journal, 11,* 263–278.

Culnan, M. J., & Bair, J. H. (1983). Human communication needs and organizational productivity: The potential impact of office automation. *Journal of the American Society for Information Science, 34,* 215–221.

Culnan, M. J., & Markus, M. L. (1987). Information technologies. In F. M. Jablin, L. L. Putnam, K. H. Roberts, & L. W. Porter (Eds.), *Handbook of organizational communication.* Newbury Park, CA: Sage.

Cusella, L. P. (1980). The effects of feedback on intrinsic motivation: A propositional extension of cognitive evaluation theory from an organizational communication perspective. In D. Nimmo (Ed.), *Communication Yearbook 4* (pp. 367–387). New Brunswick, NJ: Transaction.

Cutlip, S. M., & Center, A. H. (1971). *Effective public relations* (4th ed.). Englewood Cliffs, NJ: Prentice-Hall.

Daft, R. D., & Lengel, R. H. (1986). Organizational information requirements, media richness and structural design. *Management Science, 32,* 554–571.

Daft, R., & Macintosh, N. B. (1981). A tentative exploration into the amount and equivocality of information processing in organizational work units. *Administrative Science Quarterly, 26,* 207–224.

Dahle, T. L. (1953). An experimental study of methods of communication in business. Unpublished doctoral dissertation, Purdue University, Lafayette, IN.

Danowski, J. A. (1980). Group attitude-belief uniformity and connectivity of organizational communication networks for production, innovation, and maintenance content. *Human Communication Research, 6,* 299–308.

Danowski, J. A. (1986). Linking an organization's who-to-whom communication networks and message content networks in electronic mail. Paper presented at the annual meeting of the International Communication Association, Chicago.

Davis, K. (1953). A method of studying communication patterns in organizations. *Personnel Psychology, 6,* 301–312.

Davis, K. (1969). Grapevine communication among lower and middle managers. *Personnel Journal, 48,* 269–272.

Deal, T. E., & Kennedy, A. A. (1982). *Corporate culture.* Reading, MA: Addison-Wesley.

Dennis, H. S. (1974). A theoretical and empirical study of managerial communication climate in complex organizations. Unpublished doctoral dissertation, Purdue University, Lafayette, IN.

Dover, C. (1959). The three eras of management communication. *Journal of Communication, 9,* 168–172.

Downs, C. W., & Larimer, M. (1974). Status of organizational communication in speech departments. *Speech Teacher, 23,* 325–329.

Driver, R. W. (1979). The relative efficiency of different methods for communicating benefits: A quasi-experiment in a field setting. Paper presented at the annual convention of the Academy of Management, Atlanta.

Eisenberg, E. M. (1984). Ambiguity as strategy in organizational communication. *Communication Monographs, 51,* 227–242.

Eisenberg, E. M., Monge, P. R., & Miller, K. I. (1983). Involvement in communication networks as a predictor of organization commitment. *Human Communication Research, 10,* 179–201.

Fairhurst, G. T. (1986). Male-female communication on the job: Literature review and commentary. In M. L. McLaughlin (Ed.), *Communication Yearbook 9* (pp. 83–116). Beverly Hills: Sage.

Fairhurst, G. T., Green, S. G., & Snavely, B. K. (1984a). Managerial control and discipline: Whips and chains. In R. N. Bostrom (Ed.), *Communication Yearbook 8* (pp. 558–593). Beverly Hills: Sage.

Fairhurst, G. T., Green, S. G., & Snavely, B. K. (1984b). Face support in controlling poor performance. *Human Communication Research, 11,* 272–295.

Falcione, R. L., Sussman, L., & Herden, R. (1987). Organizational communication climate. In F. M. Jablin, L. L. Putnam, K. H. Roberts, & L. W. Porter (Eds.), *Handbook of organizational communication.* Newbury Park, CA: Sage.

Farace, R. V., & Johnson, J. D. (1974). Comparative analysis of human communication networks in selected formal organizations. Paper presented at the annual meeting of the International Communication Association, New Orleans.

Farace, R. V., & MacDonald, D. (1974). New directions in the study of organizational communication. *Personnel Psychology, 27,* 1–15.

Fayol, H. (1929). *General and industrial management.* (J. A. Conbrough, Trans.). Geneva: International Management Institute.

Feldman, M. S., & March, J. G. (1981). Information in organizations as signal and symbol. *Administrative Science Quarterly, 26,* 171–186.

Follett, M. P. (1946). *Dynamic administration: The collected papers of Mary Parker Follett* (H. S. Metcals & L. Urwick, Eds.). New York: Harper & Row.

Fulk, J., & Dutton, W. (1984). Video conferencing as an organizational information system: Assessing the role of electronic meetings. *Systems, Objectives and Solutions, 4,* 105–118.

Funk, F. E. (1956). Communication attitudes of industrial foremen as related to their productivity. Unpublished doctoral dissertation, Purdue University, Lafayette, IN.

Galbraith, J. (1973). *Organization design.* Reading, MA: Addison-Wesley.

Gerth, H. H., & Mills, C. W. (1946). *From Max Weber: Essays in sociology.* New York: Oxford University Press.

Gibb, J. R. (1961). Defensive communication. *Journal of Communication, 11,* 141–148.

Gibson, J. W., & Hodgetts, R. M. (1986). *Organizational communication: A managerial perspective.* Orlando, FL: Academic Press College Division.

Giddens, A. (1981). *A contemporary critique of historical materialism.* Berkeley: University of California Press.

Giddens, A. (1983). *Profiles and critiques in social theory.* Berkeley: University of California Press.

Gioia, D. A., & Sims, H. P. (1986). Cognition-behavior connections: Attribution and verbal behavior in leader-subordinate interactions. *Organizational Behavior and Human Decision Processes, 37,* 197–229.

Goldhaber, G. M. (1986). *Organizational communication* (4th ed.). Dubuque, IA: Wm. C. Brown.

Goldhaber, G. M., & Rogers, D. P. (1979). *Auditing organizational communication systems: The ICA communication audit.* Dubuque, IA: Kendall/Hunt.

Graen, G. B., Liden, R. C., & Hoel, W. (1982). Role of leadership in the employee withdrawal process. *Journal of Applied Psychology, 67,* 868–872.

Greiner, L. E. (1967). Patterns of organizational change. *Harvard Business Review, 45,* 119–130.

Gudykunst, W. B., Stewart, L. P., & Ting-Toomey, S. (Eds.). (1985). *Communication, culture and organizational processes.* Beverly Hills: Sage.

Guetzkow, H. (1965). Communication in organizations. In J. G. March (Ed.), *Handbook of organizations* (pp. 534—573). Chicago: Rand McNally.

Haney, W. F. (1964). A comparative study of unilateral and bilateral communication. *Academy of Management Journal, 7,* 128–136.

Harris, L., & Cronen, V. (1979). A rules-based model for the analysis and evaluation of organizational communication. *Communication Quarterly, 27,* 12–28.

Hiltz, S. R., (1984). *Online communities: A case study of the office of the future.* Norwood, NJ: Ablex.

Hirokowa, R. Y. (1981). Improving intra-organizational communication: A lesson from Japanese management. *Communication Quarterly, 30,* 35–40.

Hofstede, G. (1980). *Culture's consequences: International differences in work-related values.* Beverly Hills: Sage.

Holley, W. H., & Ingram, F. (1973). Communicating fringe benefits. *Personnel Administrator, 18,* 21–22.

Jablin, F. M. (1979). Superior-subordinate communication: The state of the art. *Psychological Bulletin, 86,* 1201–1222.

Jablin, F. M. (1980). Organizational communication theory and research: An overview of communication climate and network research. In D. Nimmo (Ed.), *Communication Yearbook 4* (pp. 327–347). New Brunswick, NJ: Transaction.

Jablin, F. M. (1982). Formal structural characteristics of organizations and superior-subordinate communication. *Human Communication Research, 8,* 338–347.

Jablin, F. M. (1984). Assimilating new members into organizations. In R. Bostrom (Ed.), *Communication Yearbook 8* (pp. 594–626). Beverly Hills: Sage.

Jablin, F. M. (1985). Task/work relationships: A life-span perspective. In M. L. Knapp & G. R. Miller (Eds.), *Handbook of interpersonal communication* (pp. 615–654). Beverly Hills. Sage.

Jablin, F. M. (1987). Organizational entry, assimilation, and exit. In F. M. Jablin, L. L. Putnam, K. H. Roberts, & L. W. Porter (Eds.), *Handbook of organizational communication* (pp. 679–740). Newbury Park, CA: Sage.

Jablin, F. M., & Krone, K. J. (1987). Organizational communication and organizational assimilation: An intra- and inter-level analysis. In C. Berger & S. H. Chaffee (Eds.), *Handbook of communication science* (pp. 711–746). Newbury Park, CA: Sage.

Jablin, F. M., & Putnam, L. L., Roberts, K. H., & Porter, L. W. (Eds.). (1987). *Handbook of organizational communication.* Newbury Park, CA: Sage.

Jablin, F. M., & Sussman, L. (1983). Organizational group communication: A review of the literature and model of the process. In H. H. Greenbaum, R. L. Falcione, & S. A. Hellweg (Eds.), *Organizational communication: Abstracts, analysis and overview* (Vol. 8, pp. 11–50). Beverly Hills, CA: Sage.

Jackson, J. (1953). Analysis of interpersonal relations in a formal organization. Unpublished doctoral dissertation, University of Michigan, Ann Arbor.

Jacobson, E., & Seashore, S. E. (1951). Communication practices in complex organizations. *Journal of Social Issues, 7,* 28–40.

Katz, D., & Kahn, R. (1966). *The social psychology of organizations.* New York: Wiley.

Klauss, R., & Bass, B. M. (1982). *Interpersonal communication in organizations.* New York: Academic Press.

Koch, S., & Deetz, S. (1981). Metaphor analysis of social reality in organizations. *Journal of Applied Communication Research, 9,* 1–15.

Kreps, G. L. (1980). A field experimental test and reevaluation of Weick's model of organizing. In D. Nimmo (Ed.), *Communication Yearbook 4* (pp. 389–398). New Brunswick, NJ: Transaction.

Kreps, G. L. (1986). *Organizational communication: Theory and practice.* New York: Longman.

Lawrence, P. R., & Lorsch, J. W. (1967). *Organization and environment.* Boston: Harvard Business School, Division of Research.

Leavitt, H. J. (1951). Some effects of certain communication patterns on group performance. *Journal of Abnormal and Social Pscyhology, 46,* 38–50.

Leavitt, H. M., & Mueller, R. (1951). Some effects of feedback on communications. *Human Relations, 4,* 401–410.

Level, D. A. (1959). A case study of human communications in an urban bank. Unpublished doctoral dissertation, Purdue University, Lafayette, IN.

Lewin, K., Lippitt, R., & White, R. K. (1939). Patterns of aggressive behavior in experimentally created "social climates." *Journal of Social Psychology, 10,* 271–299.

Likert, R. (1961). *New patterns of management.* New York: McGraw-Hill.

Likert, R. (1961). *The human organization.* New York: McGraw-Hill.

Lippitt, M. E., Miller, J. P., & Halamaj, J. (1980). Patterns of use and correlates of adoption of an electronic mail system. *Proceedings of the American Institute of Decision Sciences.*

Locke, E. A., & Schweiger, D. M. (1979). Participation in decision-making: One more look. In B. M. Staw (Ed.), *Research in organizational behavior* (Vol. 1, pp. 265–340). Greenwich, CT: JAI Press.

Lorsch, J. W., & Lawrence, P. R. (1970). *Studies in organizational design.* Homewood, IL: Irwin-Dorsey Press.

Lowin, A. (1968). Participative decision-making: A model, literature critique, and prescriptions for research. *Organizational Behavior and Human Performance, 3,* 68–106.

MacDonald, D. (1970). Communication roles and communication content in a bureaucratic setting. Unpublished doctoral dissertation, Michigan State University, East Lansing.

Maier, N. R. F., Hoffman, R. L., Hooven, J. L., & Read, W. H. (1961). Superior-subordinate communication: A statistical research project. *American Management Research Studies, 52,* 9–30.

Maier, N. R. F., Hoffman, R. L., & Read, W. H. (1963). Superior-subordinate communication: The relative effectiveness of managers who held their subordinates' positions. *Personnel Psychology, 16,* 1–11.

Maier, N. R. F., Read, W. H., & Hooven, J. (1959). Breakdowns in boss-subordinate communication. In *Communication in organizations: Some new research findings.* Ann Arbor: University of Michigan, Foundation for Research on Human Behavior.

Maslow, A. H. (1955). *Motivation and personality.* New York: Harper.

Mayo, E. (1933). *The human problems of an industrial civilization.* New York: Macmillan.

McGregor, D. (1960). *The human side of enterprise.* New York: McGraw-Hill.

McKenny, J. (1985). The influence of computer-based communication on the organization. Unpublished working paper 9-785-053, Harvard Business School.

McPhee, R. D. (1985). Formal structure and organizational communication. In R. D. McPhee & P. K. Tompkins (Eds.), *Organizational communication: Traditional themes and new directions* (pp. 149–177). Beverly Hills: Sage.

Mellinger, G. D. (1956). Interpersonal trust as a factor in communication. *Journal of Abnormal and Social Psychology, 52,* 304–309.

Miles, R. H. (1980). *Macro organizational behavior.* Santa Monica, CA: Goodyear Publishing.

Miller, D., & Friesen, P. H. (1984). A longitudinal study of the corporate life cycle. *Management Science, 30,* 1161–1183.

Miller, K. I., & Monge, P. R. (1986). Participation, satisfaction, and productivity: A meta-analytic review. *Academy of Management Journal, 29,* 727–753.

Minter, R. (1969). A comparative analysis of managerial communication in two divisions of a large manufacturing company. Unpublished doctoral dissertation, Purdue University, Lafayette, IN.

Monge, P. R., Edwards, J. A., & Kirste, K. K. (1978). The determinants of communication and structure in large organizations: A review of research. In B. D. Ruben (Ed.), *Communication Yearbook 2* (pp. 311–331). New Brunswick, NJ: Transaction.

Monge, P. R., & Eisenberg, E. M. (1987). Emergent communication networks. In F. M. Jablin, L. L. Putnam, K. H. Roberts, & L. W. Porter (Eds.), *Handbook of organizational communication.* Newbury Park, CA: Sage.

Monge, P. R., Farace, R. V., Eisenberg, E. M., Miller, K. I., & White, L. L. (1984). The process of studying process in organizational communication. *Journal of Communication, 34,* 22–43.

O'Reilly, C. A. (1982). Variations in decision makers' use of information sources: The impact of quality and accessibility of information. *Academy of Management Journal, 25,* 756–771.

O'Reilly, C. A., & Roberts, K. H. (1974). Information filtration in organizations: Three experiments. *Organizational Behavior and Human Performance, 11,* 253–265.

Ouchi, W. G. (1981). *Theory Z.* Reading, MA: Addison-Wesley.

Pacanowsky, M. E., & O'Donnell-Trujillo, N. (1982). Communication and organizational cultures. *Western Journal of Speech Communication, 46,* 115–130.

Pacanowsky, M. E., & O'Donnell-Trujillo, N. (1983). Organizational communication as cultural performance. *Communication Monographs, 50,* 126–147.

Palme, J. (1981). *Experience with the use of the COM computerized conferencing system.* Stockholm: Forsvarets Forskningsanstalt.

Parson, T. (1951). *The social system.* New York: Free Press.

Pelz, D. (1952). Influence: A key to leadership in the first-line supervisor. *Personnel, 29,* 209–217.

Peters, T. J., & Waterman, R. H., Jr. (1982). *In search of excellence.* New York: Harper & Row.

Peterson, D., & Jenkins, J. (1948). Communication between management and workers. *Journal of Applied Psychology, 32,* 71–80.

Pfeffer, J. (1978). *Organizational design.* Arlington Heights, IL: AHM.

Piersol, D. T. (1955). A case study of oral communication practices of foremen in a mid-western corporation. Unpublished doctoral dissertation, Purdue University, Lafayette, IN.

Planty, E., & Machaver, W. (1952). Upward communications: A project in executive development. *Personnel, 28,* 304–318.

Poole, M. S. (1985). Communication and organizational climates: Review, critique, and a new perspective. In R. D. McPhee & P. K. Tompkins (Eds.), *Organizational communication: Traditional themes and new directions* (pp. 79–108). Beverly Hills: Sage.

Poole, M. S., & McPhee, R. D. (1983). A structuration theory of organizational climate. In L. L. Putnam & M. Pacanowsky (Eds.), *Organizational communication: An interpretive approach* (pp. 195–213). Beverly Hills: Sage.

Porter, L. W., & Roberts, K. H. (1976). Communication in organizations. In M. D. Dunnette (Ed.), *Handbook of industrial and organizational psychology* (pp. 1553–1589). Chicago: Rand McNally.

Putnam, L. L., & Cheney, G. (1985). Organizational communication: Historical development and future directions. In T. Benson (Ed.), *Communication in the twentieth century* (pp. 130–156). Carbondale: Southern Illinois University Press.

Putnam, L. L., & Pacanowsky, M. (Eds.) (1983). *Organizational communication: An interpretive approach.* Beverly Hills: Sage.

Putnam, L. L., & Poole, M. S. (1987). Conflict and negotiation. In F. M. Jablin, L. L. Putnam, K. H. Roberts, & L. W. Porter (Eds.), *Handbook of organizational communication.* Newbury Park, CA: Sage.

Putnam, L. L., & Sorenson, R. L. (1982). Equivocal messages in organizations. *Human Communication Research, 8,* 114–132.

Ranson, S., Hinings, R., & Greenwood, R. (1980). The structuring of organizational structures. *Administrative Science Quarterly, 25,* 1–17.

Redding, W. C. (1972). *Communication within the organization: An interpretive review of theory and research.* New York: Industrial Communication Council.

Redding, W. C., (1979). Organizational communication theory and ideology: An overview. In D. Nimmo (Ed.), *Communication Yearbook 3* (pp. 309–342). New Brunswick, NJ: Transaction.

Redding, W. C. (1985). Stumbling toward identity: The emergence of organizational communication as a field of study. In R. D. McPhee & P. K. Tompkins (Eds.), *Organizational communication: Traditional themes and new directions* (pp. 15–54) Beverly Hills: Sage.

Reynolds, E., & Johnson, J. D. (1982). Liaison emergence. Relating theoretical perspectives. *Academy of Management Review, 7,* 551–559.

Rice, R. E. (1982). Communication networking in computer conferencing systems: A longitudinal study of group roles and systems structure. In M. Burgoon (Ed.), *Communication Yearbook 6* (pp. 925–944). Beverly Hills: Sage.

Rice, R. E., & Associates (Eds.) (1984). *The new media: Communication, research and technology.* Beverly Hills: Sage.

Rice, R. E., & Case, D. (1983). Electronic message systems in the university: A description of use and utility. *Journal of Communication, 33,* 131–152.

Rice, R. E., & Richards, W. D. (1985). An overview of network analysis methods and programs. In B. Dervin & M. Voigt (Eds.) *Progress in communication sciences* (Vol. 6, pp. 105–165). New York: Ablex.

Richards, W. (1975). *A manual for network analysis: Using the NEGOPY network analysis program.* Stanford, CA: Stanford University, Institute for Communication Research.

Richetto, G. M. (1977). Organizational communication theory and research: An overview. In B. D. Ruben (Ed.), *Communication Yearbook 1* (pp. 331–346). New Brunswick, NJ: Transaction.

Roberts, K., & O'Reilly, C. (1974a). Failures in upward communication: Three possible culprits. *Academy of Management Journal, 17,* 205–215.

Roberts, K., & O'Reilly, C. (1974b). Measuring organizational communication. *Journal of Applied Psychology, 59,* 321–326.

Roberts, K., & O'Reilly, C. (1978). Organizations as communication structures: An empirical approach. *Human Relations, 4,* 283–293.

Roberts, K., O'Reilly, C., Bretton, G. E., & Porter, L. (1974). Organizational theory and organizational communication: A communication failure. *Human Relations, 27,* 501–524.

Roche, W. J., & MacKinnon, N. L. (1970). Motivating people with meaningful work. *Harvard Business Review, 48,* 97–110.

Roethlisberger, F. J., & Dickson, W. J. (1939). *Management and the worker.* Cambridge, MA: Harvard University Press.

Rosen, H. (1961). Managerial role interaction: A study of three managerial levels. *Journal of Applied Psychology, 45,* 30–34.

Rosen, S., & Tesser, A. (1970). On reluctance to communicate undesirable information: The MUM effect. *Sociometry, 33,* 253–263.

Ross, R. (1954). A case study of communication breakdowns in the General Telephone Company of Indiana, Inc. Unpublished doctoral dissertation, Purdue University, Lafayette, IN.

Schwartz, D. F. (1968). Liaison-communication roles in a formal organization. *Communimetrics Report* (No. 1). Fargo: North Dakota State University.

Sims, H. P., & Manz, C. C. (1984). Observing leader verbal behavior: Toward reciprocal determinism in leadership theory. *Journal of Applied Psychology, 69,* 222–232.

Smircich, L. (1983). Concepts of culture and organizational analysis. *Administrative Science Quarterly, 28,* 339–358.

Smith, E. E., & Kight, S. S. (1959). Effects of feedback on insight and problem solving efficiency in training groups. *Journal of Applied Psychology, 43,* 209–211.

Smith, K. G., Mitchell, T. R., & Summer, C. E. (1985). Top level management priorities in different stages of the organizational life cycle. *Academy of Management Journal, 28,* 799–820.

Sproull, L., & Kiesler, S. (1986). Reducing social context cues: The case of electronic mail. *Management Science, 32,* 1492–1512.

Stech, E. L. (1980). Work group communication modes and assessment of contingency and situational models of leadership. Paper presented at the annual meeting of the Speech Communication Association, New York.

Steinfeld, C. (1985a). Computer-mediated communication: Explaining task and socioemotional uses. In M. L. McLaughlin (Ed.), *Communication Yearbook 9* (pp. 777–804). Beverly Hills: Sage.

Steinfeld, C. (1985b). Dimensions of electronic mail use in an organization setting. *Proceedings of the Academy of Management,* 239–243.

Stewart, L. P., Gudykunst, W. B., Ting-Toomey, S., & Nishida, T. (1986). The effects of decision-making styles on openness and satisfaction within Japanese organizations. *Communication Monographs, 53,* 236–251.

Stohl, C. (1986). Quality circles and changing patterns of communication. In M. L. McLaughlin (Ed.), *Communication Yearbook 9* (pp. 511–531). Beverly Hills: Sage.

Strassmann, P. (1985). *Information payoff: The transformation of work in the electronic age.* New York: Free Press.

Sutton, H., & Porter, L. W. (1968). A study of the grapevine in a governmental organization. *Personnel Psychology, 21,* 223–230.

Tannenbaum, R., & Schmidt, W. H. (1958). How to choose a leadership pattern. *Harvard Business Review, 36,* 95–101.

Tausky, C. (1970). *Work organizations: Major theoretical perspectives.* Itasca, IL: F. E. Peacock.

Taylor, F. W. (1911). *The principles of scientific management.* New York: Harper.

Tompkins, P. K. (1962). An analysis of communication between headquarters and selected units of a national labor union. Unpublished doctoral dissertation, Purdue University, Lafayette, IN.

Tompkins, P. K. (1984). The functions of human communication in organizations. In C. Arnold & J. Bowers (Eds.), *Handbook of rhetorical and communication theory* (pp. 659–719). Boston: Allyn & Bacon.

Tompkins, P. K., & Cheney, G. (1985). Communication and unobtrusive control in contemporary organizations. In R. D. McPhee & P. K. Tompkins (Eds.), *Organizational communication: Traditional themes and new directions* (pp. 179–210). Beverly Hills: Sage.

Triandis, H. C. (1959). Cognitive similarity and interpersonal communications in industry. *Journal of Applied Psychology, 43,* 321–326.

Triandis, H. C., & Albert, R. D. (1987). Cross-cultural perspectives. In F. M. Jablin, L. L. Putnam, K. H. Roberts, & L. W. Porter (Eds.), *Handbook of organizational communication.* Newbury Park, CA: Sage.

Tushman, M. L. (1977). Special boundary roles in the innovation process. *Administrative Science Quarterly, 22,* 587–605.

Tushman, M. L. (1978). Technical communication in research and development laboratories: The impact of task characteristics. *Academy of Management Journal, 21,* 624–645.

Tushman, M. L., & Nadler, D. A. (1978). Information processing as an integrating concept in organization design. *Academy of Management Review, 3,* 613–624.

Tushman, M. L., & Scanlon, T. (1981). Boundary scanning individuals: Their role in information transfer and their antecedents. *Academy of Management Journal, 24,* 289–305.

Ungson, G. R., Braunstein, D. N., & Hall, P. D. (1981). Managerial information processing: A research review. *Administrative Science Quarterly, 26,* 116–134.

Vallee, J. (1984). *Computer message systems.* New York: McGraw-Hill.

Van de Ven, A. H., Delbecq, A. L., & Koenig, R. (1976). Determinants of coordination modes within organizations. *American Sociological Review, 41,* 332–338.

Van de Ven, A. H., & Ferry, D. L. (1980). *Measuring and assessing organizations.* New York: Wiley Interscience.

Von Bertalanffy, L. (1950). The theory of open systems in physics and biology. *Science, 3,* 23–39.

Vroom, V., & Mann, F. (1960). Leader authoritarianism and employee attitudes. *Personnel Psychology, 13,* 125–140.

Walton, E. (1963). A study of organizational communication systems. *Personnel Administration, 26,* 46–49.

Weaver, C. H. (1958). The quantification of the frame of reference in labor-management communication. *Journal of Applied Psychology, 42,* 1–9.

Webber, R. A. (1970). Perceptions of interactions between superiors and subordinates. *Human Relations, 23,* 235–248.

Weber, M. (1947). *The theory of social and economic organization* (A. M. Henderson & T. Parsons, Trans.). New York: Oxford University Press. (Original work published 1922)

Weick, K. E. (1979). *The social psychology of organizing* (2nd ed.). Reading, MA: Addison-Wesley.

Weiss, R. S., & Jacobson, E. H. (1955). Method for the analysis of the structure of complex organizations. *American Sociological Review, 20,* 661–668.

Woodward, J. (1965). *Industrial organization: Theory and practice.* London: Oxford University Press.

Zajonc, R. B. (1962). The effects of feedback and probability of group success on individual and group performance. *Human Relations, 15,* 149–161.

8

Mass Communication

Bradley S. Greenberg
Michigan State University

Bradley S. Greenberg is Professor of Communication and Telecommunication and Chair of Telecommunication at Michigan State University. He completed his graduate degrees in journalism and mass communication at the University of Wisconsin. His current research is on the social uses and impacts of the new media, as a complement to his research on the effects of television and other mass media. Dr. Greenberg is a Fellow of the International Communication Association.

LEARNING OBJECTIVES

After studying this chapter you should be able to:

- List several reasons that mass media are considered to be pervasive.
- Explain the impact of the mass media on everyday time allocation.
- Discuss major factors influencing the diffusion of news.
- Illustrate social role learning in the acquisition of gender roles.
- Summarize research on the effects of the media on minority children.
- Review research on the portrayal of sexual content in the mass media.
- List major motives for mass media use.
- Evaluate the potential impact of new technology on mass media use in the future.

Interest in the mass media extends beyond scholars and students. Government is interested in the mass media because public officials believe the media can be used to promote government stands on key national, state, and local issues. Political candidates are interested in the mass media because they believe the media can make them better known and add voters to their side. Entertainers are interested in the mass media because they believe they live or die by media publicity. It would be hard to find any person or group of people that does not have either a personal or professional interest in the media.

Most people believe that they are very knowledgeable about the media. This belief is probably incorrect, but perhaps this chapter can make you relatively better informed about certain aspects of the media. It will try to enhance your understanding of mass communication by examining the following issues:

- Why is there so much general interest in the media?
- What does a typical media day contain?
- What are the structural features of U.S. mass media?
- What do we know about
  the diffusion of news process?
  the portrayal of women in the media?
  the impact of minority media images?
  the effects of sexual content?
- What motivates media use?
- What does the future of mass communication hold?

THE PERVASIVENESS OF THE MASS MEDIA

Interest in the media is widespread for several reasons. First of all, almost every individual can say "I do it. I use the media."

Second, just about everyone you and I know also uses the media. We may use different media at different times, but there is sufficient overlap to consider it a shared activity that may be national in scope. How often have you turned to someone, perhaps someone you didn't know

well, and begun a conversation by asking if he or she had seen a certain television program, listened to a new record album, or seen a movie you had just seen? Knowledge of media content and the common experience it offers provide a basis for starting and maintaining relationships.

Third, the media are all around us. It is virtually impossible to avoid the mass media in the United States. Two kinds of exercises common in introductory communication classes illustrate this fact. One is to keep a diary of all your media activities for a 24-hour period. The other is to go "cold turkey" and abstain from contact with any of the mass media for at least 24 hours. The former is easy to do and often demonstrates how much of daily life the mass media fill. The second becomes a real chore. Even for a university student away from home and living on a campus, total avoidance of the mass media is difficult. My daughter was given that assignment and had to start over again in four different 24-hour periods, as she either habitually or inadvertently picked up a magazine or turned on the radio or glanced at a newspaper headline. It was not until the fifth day of trying to totally avoid any mass media contact that she succeeded. Many people are media addicts, spending six or seven hours a day with a variety of media, but so few media hermits exist that they have never been sufficiently identified to be studied.

Fourth, the media are easily available, especially in this country. A radio can be obtained for a few dollars, a newspaper for far less than a dollar, and television sets are in 98 percent of U.S. homes. TV sets are inexpensive enough that American households average more than two sets each. This makes consumption of mass media content easy and inexpensive, and the widespread availability and use of the mass media feed the interests that earlier exposure stimulated.

Fifth, media affect people. Some assume that the media are very powerful in teaching and persuading and causing people to change their behavior. Others believe that media effects are relatively limited. Elsewhere in this chapter we will examine some specific areas of media effects.

In this section let me identify two effects that are noncontroversial.

Vicarious Experience

For one, the media provide us with a large set of experiences that we would not be able to get in any other ways. For most of us, trips to foreign lands are few or nonexistent; what we know about China or Russia or Peru or Mexico or Africa comes from news stories in the paper and on television, from fictional TV programming and movies that purport to indicate something about the kinds of people who live there and the lives they lead, from historical novels, and from documentaries. What most of us know about the space program and astronauts and trips to the moon we know only from what we have seen on television or read in the newspaper or obtained from other media. Our experiences with people from ethnic backgrounds other than our own come principally from mass media programs.

Name any topic, think about any public figure or personality and the odds are that you have little if any direct contact or direct experience with it, him, or her. Public figures you think you know, places you think you recognize, ideas you have accepted as your own are likely to have originated through mass media experiences. No study has yet been able to identify how much of what we hold in our head is attributable to direct experiences versus indirect, mediated experiences. Although mediated experiences include being told about things by other people, the best bet is that the largest share comes directly from the mass media and that share is also larger than what personal experience produces.

Time Spent with the Media

A second identifiable effect relates to our allocation of time. We give time to the mass media because we obtain certain pleasures from what occurs in that time. Let me demonstrate just where the mass media fit into our daily lives by talking about the extent of mass media activity from two perspectives: the scope of media time as a primary activity in our daily lives, and a more intensive examination by media researchers of mass media use.

The typical 24-hour day in the United States has been examined in terms of primary activities. Sociologists have counted up the amount of time spent doing different things that are, by their definition, the main activity being pursued at the time. They clearly recognize that people sometimes do more than one thing at a time, but for present purposes we will recount only what has been considered the primary activity. (This may be subject to some quarrel; what's primary if I'm eating while watching television?) That 24-hour day can be broken into "fixed time" and "leisure time" allocations. The former are those things that are unavoidable. For example, most adult Americans sleep about 8 hours a day, work 7½ hours a day, spend a half hour traveling to and from work, give 2½ hours a day to personal care, including cleaning oneself and napping, and about a half hour to taking care of children.

About 5 hours a day remain for leisure, the opportunity to decide what you want to do. Adults in the United States give about 2 hours of that leisure time to various mass media, primarily television; 2 hours to social activities, like talking and partying; about a half hour a day to nonwork travel; and about a half hour to educational or cultural activities.

That amount of leisure time in absolute hours is fairly stable across many, many cultures, ranging from a low of 4 hours each day to perhaps as much as 6 or 6½ hours. In more-developed countries, the mass media provide the primary leisure-time activity.

Media researchers, who do not discount media activities as secondary if other things are going on at the same time, present even stronger evidence of the U.S. dedication to mass media as leisure behavior. They have found that U.S. adults now average about 3½ hours with television every day. Those adults also spend perhaps a half hour with one or more newspapers and complement those media activities by listening to the radio about 1½ hours a day. This amounts to 5½ hours of daily media activity for adults in this country from what is now increasing to perhaps 6 hours of leisure time available each day.

Among teenagers, a similar pattern of media domination of free time is evident. Teenagers give about 3 hours on the average each day to television and 2½ to radio. Although their newspaper reading is negligible on any given day, they do look at a newspaper from some period of time four or five days a week. Children younger than teenagers in this country do even more television watching, and certainly less newspaper reading. Preteens average 4 hours a day with television and 1 to 1½ hours with radio. The media clearly affect the allocation of personal time; how great their effect and to which media people are oriented may be more substantial issues.

Many daily mass media behaviors are independent of each other. Studies consistently show that the amount of time an individual spends with radio is not related to the amount of time spent with television or with newspapers or with magazines. Television behavior does not appear to increase or decrease one's use of newspapers or any other medium. Print media behaviors do tend to be associated; readers are readers, regardless of whether it's newspapers or magazines or books. In particular, radio and television use are unrelated to each other and unrelated to most other media behaviors. You would be hard pressed to find an individual who is an addict across all mass media.

Clearly, the mass media touch every one of us. What do they consist of?

ORGANIZATION AND STRUCTURE OF THE MASS MEDIA

Although one chapter cannot do justice to all the mass media, let us identify the major structural characteristics of three major media: radio, television, and newspapers.

Radio

About 10,500 radio stations operate in the United States; 80 percent are commercial stations. Radio is the most individualistic of these three major media. The typical radio station will define its subaudience very specifically. It can do so because in any given city you will probably have 10 to 20 competing stations from which to choose. Most major formats will be represented to attract the maximum portion of a specific audience. *Format* means the kind of programming provided. Although there are some all-news, religious, and ethnic stations, the music format has come to characterize the great majority of all AM and FM stations. Stations want to be identified on the basis of the kind of music they play. Popular formats include adult contemporary, country-western, and rock. When audience preferences change, some stations in any market will change their formats to take advantage of new trends.

Radio is fully available to the public. You would be hard pressed to find any home or car without a radio. According to a recent estimate, there were 500 million radios belonging to individual people in the United States. A typical household has five or six radios, the majority of which have both AM and FM capabilities.

The Radio Advertising Bureau, a lobbying group for the industry, estimates that Americans average about three hours a day of radio listening. The largest group of listeners is young men ages 18 to 24, who average more than four hours of radio each day.

Many radio stations in the United States, perhaps as many as 2,000 of them, are fully automated. If you visited such a station, you would not find much if anything in the way of announcers or news staffs or disc jockeys. These stations use tapes or receive satellite programming that is fed automatically or electronically to the station. This movement to automation was expected to have doubled by 1990.

Public Radio Of the 10,500 radio stations in this country, about 1,350 are noncommercial or educational stations. Nearly 1,000 of those are quite small, with few broadcast hours and a limited transmission range. But the remaining 350 are members of the National Public Radio system, which provides them with programming and a satellite service that connects them. That national service constitutes about one-fourth of the broadcast day for local public radio stations; most of the remainder is locally produced. The primary content for about 60 percent of public radio stations is music, with news and public affairs as the major format for another 20 percent. A majority of these stations are located at U.S. colleges and universities. The most frequent music formats on public radio stations are classical and jazz, which seldom dominate at commercial stations.

Whereas commercial radio draws most of its funding from selling advertising time, public radio depends on federal, state, and local sources for most of its income. In recent years, local stations have relied more and more on drawing financial donations from its listeners. This trend will continue—the form of public support will be fewer tax dollars and more voluntary donations.

Television

Watching television is the single most pervasive media activity among people of all ages. Currently, the television set is turned on for seven hours a day in each U.S. home. Throughout history, no other single nonwork activity has been so widespread among families in countries where television is fully available.

Peak viewing time, of course, is at night; during the first hour of prime time at 7 or 8 p.m., two-thirds of the households in the United States will be watching television. About one-third watch something in the afternoon, and one-fourth watch television before noon. These viewing averages have grown steadily in the last decade. The typical American watches television an hour longer now than ten years ago.

About 800 commercial television stations are operating in the United States; about three-fourths of these stations are affiliated with one of the three major commercial networks, ABC, CBS, and NBC. The networks provide their affiliates with the majority of their programs and a share in the revenues that come from network advertising. As with radio, ownership of television stations is limited to avoid monopoly control over programming and advertising, or television in general. The networks themselves are permitted to own only 5 stations each, whereas non-network owners are limited to a maximum of 7 television stations, with not more than one in the same viewing area.

About 200 television stations are independent of any network. These stations have been growing in audience penetration. They can concoct their own schedule from among the best programs they can find, and their current mix of movie offerings, reruns of popular old series, and some syndicated programming is challenging the audience domination of network-affiliated stations.

As of mid 1987, 50 percent of all homes in the United States were receiving their primary television programming by cable. In 1990, two-thirds of the homes in this country will have cable. In most communities, homes without cable can receive 4 to 6 television channels. Normally, these would be the three commercial television networks, one public television station, and possibly one or two independent channels as well. Even in the largest cities, homes would not be receiving more than 10 different television channels without cable. Because cable can import signals from so many different sources, there is essentially no limit to the number of channels it can offer. The newest cable systems being developed are bringing from 54 to 108 television channels into American homes.

Programming The most popular programming on the networks consists of situation comedies. Thirty different situation comedies are carried by the networks most seasons, and they typically draw nearly half the network audience share. The other major program preferences are general drama, mystery, and suspense series, and feature films.

Audience preferences for content have changed substantially during the 30 years that television has been widely available. In the early years, Westerns, quiz shows, and variety shows dominated; today, in addition to situation comedies, there is a continuing shift toward feature films, sports programming, and crime shows. The audience is not totally fickle, but the stability of its preference for program content has been found to function in 5-year cycles.

Those interested in the commercial networks' children's programming continue to be disappointed, because that programming is shrinking. Last season there was no weekday children's program on any commercial network on a regularly scheduled basis. In the United States, Saturday-morning cartoons constitute virtually all that is available on commercial TV specifically for children.

If you wanted to expose yourself to a full day of network television in the United States, you could start in most cities at about 6 A.M. For the next two hours you would likely find news, talk, and interviews, with a current emphasis on exercise shows as well. From midmorning until about noon, that program content would be supplemented primarily by the reruns of old television series. From noon until about 4 P.M., network programming consists of soap operas in 30- and 60-minute versions. Alternative programming on the network affiliates would include some quiz shows. From late afternoon until about 6 P.M., there again will be reruns, rented at the option of the local station. These reruns include older syndicated episodes of series still on the air as well as reruns of canceled series. Then comes an hour of both local and network news, and from 7 to 8 P.M. the local station will air syndicated offerings. From 8 to 11 P.M., the prime-time hours of television, network programs are carried. After 11 P.M. and into the early-morning hours, one finds a mixture of news, old movies, variety-interview shows, and some public affairs broadcasts.

Public Television   Currently, about 300 public television stations are operating in the United States. In the past, this has meant television without commercials. However, these stations rely heavily on public support in the form of funds provided by the government, individual citizens, and, increasingly, corporations. The absence of commercials on programs has, to some extent, been offset by the time devoted to membership drives and auctions.

It would be difficult to characterize the sequences of programming on public television as we did for commercial television. Although public television also has a prime period, there is considerably more juggling of broadcast times during a day in order to meet the needs of the local market. However, public television programming is divisible into three general program types: news and public affairs, children's programming, and drama, music, culture, and instructional programs. Only on public television can one find children's programming on a regular weekday basis, with the bulk of it aimed at preschool children.

There is some indication that the audience for public television has been increasing. But that increase has been from a very small base. In the late 1970s, public television overall was watched by about 2.5 percent of viewers, on the average. In the 1980s, this increased to about 5 percent. But it is a distinctly upscale audience segment of high income and high education. Public television penetrates into all demographic groups, but seldom does it find itself competitive with commercial television. The prospect for public television is that with increased reliance on direct public support for funding rather than indirect public support from tax dollars, the programming emphasis may have to appeal to even broader audience segments.

Newspapers

The daily newspaper, and there are about 1,800 of them, primarily serves the community in which it is published. No daily newspaper in the United

States has a circulation greater than 2 million, and only a handful even reach 1 million or more readers. The most recent attempt at a nationally distributed newspaper, *USA Today,* began in 1982 and now circulates 1.5 million copies daily. The typical newspaper in the United States serves a city of 50,000 or fewer people. More than 1,200 papers serve cities of that size; each averages perhaps 15,000 circulation.

Let us contrast these three media. Television content is primarily national in origin, with three networks providing the bulk of early-morning, afternoon, and evening programming to 98 percent of the nation's households. Radio, much more a local entity, is available from so many different stations in any listening area that each station's programming is aimed at a small segment of the local audience. The daily newspaper, on the other hand, is likely to be the only game in town. Fewer than three dozen cities have more than one daily newspaper. These three media are very different in terms of their audience-driven composition.

Daily newspapers in the United States vary in size depending on community size, but their content is remarkably similar. A typical newspaper in a small community will run 20 to 30 pages, in larger communities it will be 40 to 50 pages, and in the largest cities bout 70 pages on any given day. Regardless of overall size, however, one finds about two-fifths of the pages given to display advertising and another fifth to classified advertising. When you buy a newspaper, about one-third of the pages, exclusive of special advertising sections, will consist of news. That "news hole," the space allocated to news, will then be subdivided into soft news (such content as sports, feature columns, social events, leisure time activities, the comics) and hard news (news of government, politics, crime, catastrophe). Soft news will typically fill about twice as much of the news hole as hard news.

The U.S. newspaper industry is not regulated by government. Unlike radio and television stations, a daily newspaper doesn't need a license to operate. This has meant that group ownership is a common feature of the daily newspaper business. About 65 percent of, or approximately 1,200, newspapers are owned by 150 newspaper groups. This masks the fact that a few very large groups are dominant. Two groups own newspapers that have a total daily circulation of 4 million or more, and a dozen other groups have circulations ranging from 1 million to 3 million. Stated differently, there are ten newspaper ownership groups in the United States that cover more than one-third of the total daily newspaper circulation.

The move to group or chain ownership has largely taken place since the end of World War II. Although the total number of daily newspapers has changed little, other outcomes are apparent. The number of competitive newspaper markets has been steadily decreasing and a distinct shift from afternoon to morning newspapers has taken place. There still remain about three afternoon papers for each morning paper, but the circulation difference between those two publication times is shrinking rapidly. Most morning papers are located in major cities with very large circulations, and most afternoon papers are in small communities with small circulations. In the last decade, the daily circulation of 62 million copies has remained relatively stable. On the other hand, Sunday circulation has increased by more than 10 million in the last decade, and the total Sunday circulation is within a few million of the daily circulation total.

Newspapers now strive to increase their penetration into that substantial portion of the market that does not take a newspaper on a regular basis. Penetration of newspapers into U.S. households is somewhere between 50 and 60 percent. This contrasts with what amounts to total penetration of radio and television. The 62 million copies of newspapers circulated daily do not reach that many households, as a substantial number of households take more than one paper. Considerable effort has been invested in trying to identify the characteristics of nonreaders of the newspaper and to decide how to attract them. The evidence to date suggests that nonreaders include a disproportionate share of young adults

(18–34), and those with less education and smaller incomes. For example, only half of those with only a grammar school education read a daily newspaper. However, education levels have been rising for the last decade without a commensurate increase in daily newspaper circulation. Furthermore, population increases in the last decade would suggest an overall rise in newspaper circulation, and that has not occurred. Young adults are a potential reader pool for the newspaper market if they can be attracted in larger quantities.

SOCIAL RESEARCH ON THE MASS MEDIA

This brief introduction to the three major traditional media in the United States has not been able to cover films, magazines, or other media forms. However, the bulk of the social research to date has also concentrated on the three major media. We shall now identify some of the dominant research traditions of the past 30 years that have traced the effects of media content on different segments of the U.S. public.

Diffusion of News

How do people get news about events of the day? That question has interested researchers for about 30 years.

Conceptually, the issue of news diffusion can be characterized by these components:

1. Audience characteristics: their demographic and social characteristics, news interests, and their access to media.

2. Event characteristics: expected and unexpected events; important and less important events; short-term and long-term events.

3. The diffusion process, including: the first source (medium) that informs people; the speed with which they are informed; what they found out; their checking what they found out by going to other media; where they found out; who finds out and who does not; their emotional and cognitive responses to information about the event.

4. The role that interpersonal communication plays as a first source; by telling others who do not know; by discussing what happened with others.

Among the three dozen studies of news diffusion in the United States published in the past 40 years, most have purported to reflect the public diffusion process—the means by which the public becomes aware of breaking news events (for example, Bogart, 1950–51; Funkhouser & McCombs, 1971; Gantz, 1983; Mendelsohn, 1964; Miller, 1945). Unanticipated calamities of one kind or another have been studied often; many of these have been individual calamities befalling personalities, such as Eisenhower's heart attack (Deutschman & Danielson, 1960), the Kennedy assassination (Spitzer, 1964–65), and the assassination attempt on President Reagan (Gantz, 1983).

Looking at findings common to studies done with the public is one means of examining propositions about the diffusion of news. From his examination of 20 studies, Rosengren (1973) proposed that personal communication was relatively more important the higher the rate and amount of diffusion and the more important the event; in such instances, he reasoned, there would be lesser roles for other media, notably newspapers.

Updating those notions from more-current research, several basic lessons can be summarized here:

When the media choose to devote all their resources (time and space) to coverage of a single event, the rate of diffusion intensifies, which means that knowledge of the event spreads more rapidly (Greenberg, 1964a). When the media choose to uniformly maximize their efforts at dissemination of information, there's rarely a person around who would not be informed, either directly by the media or from other people within a very short time. Think of the attempt to assassinate President Reagan, or the explosion of the *Challenger* space shuttle. These events brought immediate coverage by international radio and television. Normal programming was dropped. When the broadcast media choose to do this on virtually all stations, dissemination of the news will be so rapid that most diffusion will have occurred before any surveying can begin. When the broadcast media do decide to turn all their machinery to covering an event as it occurs, it is fair to predict that more than 90 percent of the public will be informed within one hour. That diffusion speed places other media in supplementary roles. For example, the newspaper then becomes a resource for confirming the information received earlier and to get a larger dose of the now available information.

Since the earliest studies, the electronic media have largely usurped print media as a first source of information for major news events (Weaver-Lariscy, Sweeney, & Steinfatt, 1984). Today the first sources of information about most major national and international events will be radio and television, with television tending to be the leader, even when radio is more accessible. One of the first things people do when they get such information from the media is to try to check it out, turning to another television station or another radio station, to see whether the same or additional information is available. Thus the broadcast media play a striking role for most major news events, either as the first source of information or as an immediate supplementary source of information.

Those who find out about a news event from broadcast media tend to go to other media for additional information. Those who find out from print media tend to go to other people for additional information.

Critical news events stimulate interpersonal discussion; people use other people as sources of information (Ostland, 1973). When something really big happens, social diffusion takes place very rapidly. Your own excitement at hearing such a story leads you to find others to ask whether they have heard, or to pick up the telephone and call others for the same purpose. When President John F. Kennedy was assassinated, for example, nearly half the people in the country first heard the news from others. Then there was an immediate and dramatic movement to television sets and radios to become a direct observer of continuing events as they unfolded.

The vast majority of people learn about most news events directly from some mass medium (Greenberg, 1964b). In a study that focused on a series of news events ranging from those of relatively low importance (for example, the results of a local chess tournament) to those of considerable but not catastrophic importance (for example, a local labor strike), the pattern indicated that mass media were the most pervasive first source of information across 17 different news events studied. Overall, more than 93 percent of the informed public learned about these events first from the media. However, for those events that were most and least significant, interpersonal communication of information played a more important role. A full 10 percent of the first sources of information for the most major and least significant news events were other people. This study also revealed that approximately 50 percent of the populace learns of catastrophic events (such as the JFK assassination) through interpersonal channels.

Major events are likely to be covered on television and radio newscasts; average and minor news events are more likely to receive only newspaper coverage. The typical evening television newscast may have 15 to 20 stories in it compared to the 100 or more stories appearing in the daily newspaper. Thus a large portion of news events are available only by reading a newspaper. When a news event is covered by all media, the broadcast media will dominate as the first source of information and the print media will serve a largely supplementary role.

The timing of an event affects the diffusion process (Hill & Bonjean, 1964). Late-night or overnight events are slower to diffuse, with the most dramatic differences observed between midday and overnight events.

What we have described has been the news diffusion pattern for unexpected events, those events the reader, viewer, or listener has no opportunity to anticipate. Some research on news diffusion has also looked at anticipated news events, those that receive some buildup, such as the Olympics, the coronation of a queen, or any major sporting event. The media often generate a good deal of hype (short for *hyperbole*) about these events, attempting to create or reinforce interest and to build on positive attitudes. Hype increases media attention to the event and thereby accelerates the rate of diffusion.

How one becomes aware of an event is functionally related to accessibility to media and interpersonal channels (Gantz, 1983). Typically, people away from home are more likely to hear about an event from other people. Typically, those who find out about major news events from other people are more likely to have gotten the news later than those informed directly through the media. They also tend to be those who are less interested in the event. This is especially true when interpersonal communication is direct and not mediated by the telephone, for example. With major news events, the telephone tends to be used as a personal broadcasting system, and those who get news by telephone get it early.

Few demographic characteristics have differentiated knowers from nonknowers. Often the knowers are somewhat more educated and have higher-status occupations, but those differences tend not to be large. People's interest in the news content area, which may cut across social class lines, appears to be a better predictor both of how soon they will know and what they will know.

Some investigators have asked whether the interpersonal segment of the diffusion process acts as an important source of influence. Perhaps what someone tells you about a major news event biases your attitude toward that event. But since very few people typically learn of such events from others (except in crises such as the JFK assassination), the opportunity for interpersonal influence of any magnitude is negligible.

The Knowledge Gap In addition to these news diffusion studies, a related area has looked at how people accumulate information about news topics. This line of research proposes that a story that unfolds over time or general media information presented over time on particular topics, such as science or politics, is better learned by those of higher education and higher social class. From this research has emerged the "knowledge gap" hypothesis, which says that the gap in knowledge between those who know something and those who don't know something will increase as new information is fed into the social system, and that the primary attribute identifying those who learn more is their current education and/or social status. Early studies used education to predict such things as amount of knowledge about science and found that those who knew something and were better educated were more likely to be even more informed at some later time period: The information-rich get richer and the information-poor get poorer.

Other research suggests, however, that these education discrepancies in predicting who is more or less informed may be offset by interest in the subject matter. Genova and Greenberg (1979) looked at two news events that continued for a long period of time, a professional football players' strike and impeachment proceedings against a United States president. Interest in football and in politics were measured, as well as education and social class. Interest was found to be at least as strong a predictor, and in some cases a stronger predictor, of who learned the most from the time of the initial release of information about these events through several weeks later. There is a knowledge gap in society in most subject matter areas. It is heartening to find it as much a function of personal interests as of overall education.

The dissemination of news and information continues to be an important subject for research. Recall that less than two-thirds of American households receive a newspaper. An even smaller portion watch a television news broadcast on a daily basis. Much information does not diffuse throughout society; if you examined the diffusion of the entire contents of a newspaper, you would find the typical story read by perhaps 10 to 20 percent of the subscribers. Futhermore, if you asked individuals after they had viewed an evening news telecast to identify or recall as many stories as they could, most would recall four or five at most. With the development of all-news programming on radio and on cable television systems, and with the commercial networks offering news and public affairs shows on a daily basis between midnight and sunrise, available news information has increased remarkably over what it was less than a decade ago. In one sense, then, there is much more to learn and it is more available. In another sense, there's also much more news to ignore.

Social Role Learning and Television

News broadcasts and publications are deliberately designed to teach people about current events and public affairs. However, the vast majority of media content is designed primarily to entertain rather than to inform. Such content may also have the effect of teaching people about various kinds of social roles.

For example, to what extent are one's beliefs about doctors or old people or police officers and how they behave a function of their portrayal on television? The most likely expectation is that the receiver will accept such social-role information more if he or she has had minimal personal experience with the real-life occupants of the social roles. In this section we can demonstrate how television portrays one social role from among many possibilities and what current research suggests is the consequence of the portrayal of a sec-

ond social role. Let us first look at the way television portrays women.

Sex Roles The accumulated evidence and argument is that the portrait of women on television is restricted. We are indebted to Barrie Gunter's monograph on sex roles for some of the structure in this section (Gunter, 1986).

First, women have always been and continue to be substantially "underrepresented" on television, if one takes 50-50 as a goal. In each of the last four decades, and regardless of whether the body of shows was adult prime-time programs or Saturday-morning cartoons, males have outnumbered females by about a 3–1 ratio (Signorielli, 1984). Deviations from this count can be found in different program types. The most dominant male province is the action-adventure program, where the male-female ratio is 6–1; greatest equivalence is found in the afternoon soaps (1–1 ratio) and in situation comedies (2–1) (Barcus, 1983). The lesson implied by this measure of sheer television presence, whether in major, supporting, or minor roles, is that women are a less significant part of the populace, that counting fewer of them must make them count less.

Second, there remains substantial evidence that women on television are limited to a narrow range of roles, those primarily of wives and/or mothers (Downing, 1974). The range of female roles has expanded during the past 10–15 years. Yet marriage (or divorce) and parenthood are still of greater significance in the television lives of women than of men. This observation is supported by the relative confinement of television women to a home life centering on family and personal relationships and interests. Even when cast or seen in out-of-home contexts, the women's expressed concerns focus more often on family and personal matters than on professional ones. This phenomenon is buttressed by the larger presence of women in the program genres of soaps and situation comedies, whose settings are primarily domestic and whose major action is conversation—about romance, family matters, and other interpersonal relationships. This emphasis is also made manifest in the women's relative lack of employment, an underrepresentation in professional occupations when shown as employed, and the lesser likelihood of combining marriage and any job (McNeil, 1975). Traditional outlooks as to the role of women emerge from these studies. More recently, programs such as *L.A. Law, Designing Women, Murphy Brown, Thirtysomething,* and *The Cosby Show* have been altering the traditional motif by presenting women in a variety of professional roles.

Third is a small set of sex traits consistently found among television women studied in this manner. One heralded trait is that women on television are more emotional and more in need of emotional support than men, who in turn are more physical and more in need of physical support (Greenberg, Richards, & Henderson, 1980). Another is the dominance of men over women in personal relationships, which has been approached in terms of men's greater competence, authority, order giving, plan making, and the eventual more positive outcomes that men enjoy in all these acts (Turow, 1974). Filling out this personality syndrome of television women is the finding that they typically appear less likely to be in control of events in their lives and that they are more likely to be controlled primarily by forces external to themselves over which they have little if any influence (Hodges, Brandt, & Kline, 1981).

The employment status of women filters through both the sex-role and sex-trait studies. For roles, they are less employed; for traits, even when employed, they are in lesser occupations, less likely to be married, less likely to be successfully married, and ten times as likely to be unsuccessful in marriage as housewives (Manes & Melnyk, 1974).

The consistency of this imagery over time needs one quite specific example. Kalisch, Kalisch, and Scobey (1983) looked at nurses in all U.S. television series and series pilots from the 1950s to 1982. They report that apart from changing from cotton to synthetic uniforms, the only change television nurses have undergone in 30 years has been the addition of one new stereo-type—the sexually promiscuous nurse—to the traditional role as nurturing listener-girlfriend. The cancellation in 1989 of NBC's *Nightingales* series in the wake of heavy criticism for its portrayal of promiscuous nursing students is perhaps a positive omen.

These general findings apply to children's television as well as to prime time. In two studies, Barcus (1978, 1983) analyzed some 2,000 characters on children's programs and found that males outnumbered females 3–1. Schechtman (1978) examined occupation portrayals in such children's favorites as *Batman, The Flintstones,* and *Happy Days* and concluded that women were underrepresented as employed, and where employed were generally portrayed in inferior occupational roles. Women on children's programs emphasized youth and attractiveness, according to Long and Simon (1974).

This distortion of women occurs even more intensively in television advertising content than in programming. Knill and colleagues determined that men provided over 90 percent of the casts of commercials in the daytime and in prime time and that 80 percent of the female product representatives were shown in family or household situations, whereas 70 percent of the men were portrayed in upper-echelon occupations (Knill, Pesch, Parsey, Giltin, & Perloff, 1981).

These studies were all concerned with U.S. television. There is, however, more to the world of television than is contained within these borders. In July 1985, a report was presented in Nairobi, Kenya, to the World Conference to Review and Appraise the Achievements of the United Nations Decade for Women. The report was based on responses from 95 countries, and a portion of it dealt with media images as of 1980 (UNESCO, 1985). The conclusion from these pre-1980 studies is similar to those of U.S. research reports:

A consistent picture emerges from these research studies which have investigated the media's portrayal of women. At the very best, that portrayal is narrow; at worst it is unrealistic, demeaning and damaging. There are no notable differences between the mass media in this respect. (p. 50)

All these findings were obtained from studies five years before the 1985 conference. So the conference examined the extent to which the conclusions were the same or different in 1985:

- From Malaysia, Korea, and mainland China, studies of television drama found the conventional image pattern: Women were less crucial to plot development, marriage and parenthood more important to women than to men, employed women subordinate to men, and women more passive (Siu, 1981).

- In India, a trend toward more negative portrayals of women was reported. This trend featured increases in violence toward women, in offensive advertising, and an increasing availability of pornography (Agarwal & Bhasin, 1984).

- From Canada, a similar refrain to that of India: "Sexism has taken on more subtle forms. Visual and written pornography have become a source of grave concern, with themes of violence and humiliation aimed against women sharply on the increase" (UNESCO, 1985, p. 38).

From various countries, studies of advertising show a particularly pernicious continuation of the use of women as either a household drudge or a sex object. In a British study, Manstead and McCulloch (1981) concluded that British commercials use more sex-role stereotypes in portraying adults than American commercials. A Jamaican study (Royale, 1981) directly compared men and women as sex objects. The score was 5–1 in favor of women.

The Indian report seems to sum up the situation best: "Today our ads project the worst of Indian sexist attitudes . . . On the one hand, the kitchen-confined-housewife stereotype and on the other the women spread-eagled over a carpet in transparent underwear with the copy reading: Don't be a wallflower, use Peter Pan underwear" (Agarwal & Bhasin, 1984). This observation was echoed by Hoffman's (1984) study in Hungary, which found that the majority of advertisements were peopled by young women, whose sexual attractiveness was emphasized by picturing them sprawled on beds, floors, grass, and so on.

Minority Roles   Rather than examine the general portrayal of the races in the media, this section will begin with the assertions that black Americans and Hispanics have been underrepresented; a trend toward their increased visibility has developed; stereotyping and negative connotations of blacks continue; and blacks typically appear in minor roles, for brief periods of time, and in low-status occupations on television (Poindexter & Stroman, 1981). The question to be examined here is what minority and nonminority viewers do with the minority programming and characters that are available. The findings summarized here are from projects examining the responses of children and adolescents.

Dates (1980) verified that black high school students had a stronger preference for black television shows than did white youngsters. The viewing of white situation comedies did not differ by race. The major focus of her study was the extent to which black and white youngsters identified with, thought favorably of, and perceived greater realism in black and/or white television characters. The black youngsters consistently rated black characters more positively; they rated white characters equally with white students. The same finding held for the other two variables; perceived reality and personal identification. Blacks exceeded nonblack students in both estimates for black television characters, with no stable differences between black and white responses to white characters.

Elementary-school children exhibit the same tendency to select same-race characters as their favorites. When limited to identifying one favorite television character (during a season in which 85 percent of all characters were Anglo), 96 percent of the Anglo youngsters chose same-race characters, compared to 75 percent of the black and 80 percent of the Hispanic youth (Eastman & Liss, 1980). When limited to one favorite television program, the minority youth cited a minority-dominant show.

When not limited to a single character, the pattern of same-race selection becomes even more striking. Blacks and whites are equally likely to identify with white television characters. Across 26 white TV characters, only 17 percent of the black youths and 16 percent of the white youths said they wanted to be like the character; relatively few white or black children wanted to be like most of the white models available to them on television. But black youths are more than three times as likely to identify with black characters. Note these findings from Greenberg and Atkin (1982):

Percentage Wanting to Be Like:	Blacks	Whites
Freddy Washington	57%	27%
Lamont Sanford	45	13
J. J. Evans	45	19
Bill Cosby	43	15
Thelma Evans	43	7
George Jefferson	41	8
Dee Thomas	37	17
Louise Jefferson	30	6
Roger Thomas	28	11
James Evans	29	4
Mrs. Thomas	22	5
Florida Evans	21	3
Average	(37%)	(11%)

Even the few black female characters on television draw strong identification scores (31 percent versus 7 percent) among the black youth.

Experimental work supports minority role models in television programs as an effective means of enhancing interracial perceptions. Allsopp (1982) experimentally introduced two situation comedies, one with a predesignated negative black portrayal and another with a positive portrayal. The negative portrayal induced more positive attitudes among fourth- and fifth-grade black and white children. One plausible explanation for this finding is that negative portrayal tends to confirm predispositions or acquired negative stereotypes. The positive portrayal decreased negative stereotyping among black youngsters. It is unclear whether any portrayal is better than none or whether distinctively positive portrayals are necessary.

Experimental work also supports the ratings data that show minority viewers watch more minority programming, when available. Liss (1981) made two 10-minute excerpts from situation comedies, one black-dominant and one white-dominant, simultaneously available to third and sixth graders. Blacks watched the black situation comedy for 7.5 of the 10 minutes; whites watched the same-race show for 8 of 10 minutes.

Media content perceptions for Hispanic and Anglo youngsters in the fifth and tenth grades are reported by Greenberg, Heeter, Burgoon, Burgoon, and Korzenny (1983). Hispanic youngsters believed more strongly that the portrayals of both Mexican Americans and blacks on television were more realistic than did Anglo youth, and they were far more likely to believe that local media and network television portrayed Mexican Americans more often doing good things than did the Anglos. Studies among blacks confirm this reality perception (Greenberg & Atkin, 1982). Black youths consistently believe that the television portrayals of blacks and nonblacks are more true-to-life. Typically, 40 percent of the blacks would agree that television's presentation of black men, women, teenagers, dress, and language are realistic, compared to 30 percent for whites.

Furthermore, black youngsters approach television more vigorously with the stated motivation to learn something they can apply in their daily lives. An early study (Greenberg, 1972) indicated that white youngsters depended on television as a major source of information about black youth. In a study ten years later, several hundred black preteens and teens claimed that television taught them most of what they know about jobs (47 percent), how men and women solve problems (42 percent), how parents and children interact (57 percent), how husbands and wives interact (45 percent), and how teenagers act (48 percent). Corresponding percentages for white respondents averaged 33 percent (Greenberg & Atkin, 1982). Whites learn more about blacks from television; blacks claim to learn about both whites and themselves.

In turn, the impact of black programs on the self-esteem in general and the racial self-esteem in particular of black fourth and fifth graders has been assessed by McDermott and Greenberg (1985). Parental communication and the regularity of watching black shows were both related to the black students' self-esteem; parental and peer communication were related to racial esteem, with exposure falling just short of significance. On the other hand, when respondents were subdivided into those with more and less positive attitudes toward black television characters, the correlations between exposure and both self- and racial esteem were significantly larger for those with more favorable perceptions. Strong correlations were also found between program exposure and attitudes toward both black adult and child television characters. Thus black youngsters used the televised portrayals to reflect on themselves.

What do white youth who choose to watch black television programs on a regular basis learn? From a sample of white fourth, sixth, and eight graders, Atkin, Greenberg, and McDermott (1983) explored the effects of black program exposure on a variety of belief areas. Frequent exposure to programs starring blacks was significantly associated with the motivation to watch television to find out how different people talk, dress, behave, and look, with higher estimates of the numbers of blacks to be seen in various roles in the real world, and with self-reports that television teaches them most of what they know about blacks. Show exposure was not related to real-life evaluations of black people in terms of attractiveness, strength, activity, or to discrepancies in these attributes between black and whites.

The white youngsters' interpretation of black television character traits is closely related to parallel beliefs about the real world. Television serves both to reinforce what is learned outside the television situation and offers the possibility of new information, where little or none was available. Finally, direct contact with blacks in real life did not diminish or enhance any of these findings. The combination of mediated and direct interactions with minority-group members has yet to be clarified in any reported research.

A Model of Social Learning from Television

The first part of this section dealt with television's social-role portrayals of women (and men by inference), and the second dealt with viewer choices and responses to social-role portrayals of minority character. Both these approaches can be considered part of a model of key variables in social-role learning from television.

Our conceptualization of the general process of acquiring social-role orientations from television is derived primarily from Bandura's (1977) social-learning theory. This perspective posits imitative performance of vicariously reinforced stimuli observed directly or via television. According to Bandura, many role models presented on television are highly effective in attracting children's attention because they are relevant, powerful, competent, distinctive, attractive, and readily accessible. Since these models are featured frequently and pervasively, children's retention of images and symbols is also enhanced. The learned messages are likely to be acted out to the extent that the programs provide cues indicating the context in which the learned behavior is likely to be rewarded.

Three modeling functions constitute significant mechanisms for learning from television:

- *Observational learning* is the absorption of information about ways of organizing responses into new patterns of behavior; observers acquire novel responses by watching the performances of televised models. The pictorial demonstrations available on television are particularly powerful for younger viewers with less-developed conceptual skills and less motivation to learn from verbal sources.

- *Strengthening or weakening inhibitions* that govern the expression of previously learned responses. Observing reinforcement to a model helps determine how behavioral restraints are modified; vicariously punished responses tend to inhibit expression, whereas normally prohibited responses that are rewarded or merely ignored reduce inhibitory constraints.

• *Response facilitation* occurs when the model performs a socially approved behavior that serves as an external reminder, eliciting the performance of the viewer's existing responses in the same general class.

A large amount of research evidence compiled since 1960 has demonstrated that television has significant effects on young viewers; hundreds of these studies have been reviewed in annotated bibliographies by Atkin, Murray, and Nayman (1971) and Comstock, Lindsey, and Fisher (1975). The research yields a very complex picture of these effects. The characteristics that youth bring to television interact with the attributes of the television content to produce varying types of attitudinal and behavioral consequences. The social context of viewers has important implications for their predisposition and their responses to television. The general proposition that consumption of televised messages will produce corresponding changes in the role orientations of adolescents is contingent on the juxtaposition of television content factors, viewer characteristics, social influences, and patterns of exposure and interpretation. A schematic outline of the key variables is in Figure 8.1.

A comprehensive and sensitive analysis of television effects must consider the components of this model. It stipulates that television effects occur in a social nexus of family and peers. Who they are, how they behave, what they have to say about the social roles (gender, race, occupation) presented on TV all may interact with the young person's viewing experience. That is what the left-hand set of boxes in Figure 8.1 poses.

Young viewers approach their television experiences with their personal slate of experiences. They may have had direct experience with social-role occupants, such as talking with police officers in school or seeing their grandparents as old folks, or they may have been otherwise "in-formed" about social-role occupants, as in "what blacks are really like." These experiences may have already affected their attitudes and beliefs.

Next, the content of programming viewed regularly by the target viewing group must be systematically analyzed both quantitatively and qualitatively. Major themes that appear often must be isolated if these are to form the core for what is expected to be learned. What are the specific attributes of the role occupants of interest—their age, sex, job? How do they interact with others—with prosocial or antisocial behavior? How do they talk about and what is their interpersonal style? Are there characters displayed with whom identification is strong?

The exposure situation provides another subset of variables. How attentive is the viewer? What is the context of viewing—with others or alone? In a bedroom or a den?

What interpretation does the young viewer make of the story and its players? Is it an interpretation that corresponds to an "expert" interpretation of the meanings presented? How realistic is it judged to be; is it understood; and is it accepted?

When these elements are considered (or discarded), then the researcher may examine the effects of television viewing on social-role attitudes:

1. *Cognitions about a particular role.* What does the viewer believe to be true about that social role, and why? How much variance does the youngster perceive to exist or to be permitted for a special social role?

2. *Valuations of role and role attributes.* What role attributes or behaviors does the youngster value, and for what reasons? What preferences develop?

3. *Development of role aspirations.* What roles are aspired to through anticipatory socialization? Why?

4. *Expectations about role-appropriate behaviors.* How is a role occupant expected to behave? How is this expectation affected by the discrep-

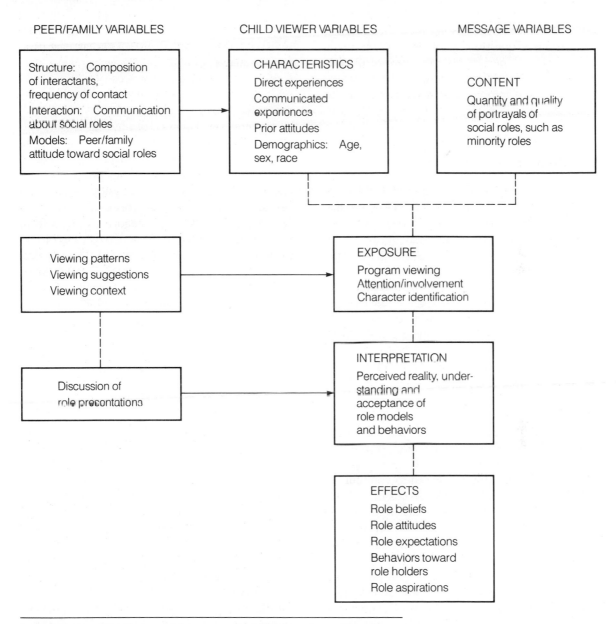

PEER/FAMILY VARIABLES CHILD VIEWER VARIABLES MESSAGE VARIABLES

Structure: Composition
of interactants,
frequency of contact
Interaction: Communication
about social roles
Models: Peer/family
attitude toward social roles

CHARACTERISTICS
Direct experiences
Communicated
experiences
Prior attitudes
Demographics: Age,
sex, race

CONTENT
Quantity and quality
of portrayals of
social roles, such as
minority roles

Viewing patterns
Viewing suggestions
Viewing context

EXPOSURE
Program viewing
Attention/involvement
Character identification

Discussion of
role presentations

INTERPRETATION
Perceived reality, under-
standing and
acceptance of
role models
and behaviors

EFFECTS
Role beliefs
Role attitudes
Role expectations
Behaviors toward
role holders
Role aspirations

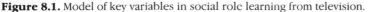

Figure 8.1. Model of key variables in social role learning from television.

ancy between the TV role occupant and the role occupants who are experienced directly?

5. *Behavior toward role occupants.* In what ways does the youngster behave differently toward

role occupants because of images shaped by television?

In this manner, we have moved from subareas of research—describing role portrayals and viewers' preferences from among them—to locating those kinds of questions in a more general framework, one that permits us to see more broadly the intersection of the multiple factors which must be taken into account when attempting to study such social issues.

Televised Sex and Its Effects

As a further demonstration of these ideas and approaches, we turn to a contemporary examination of the impact of sexual content in the media, principally television, on viewers.

Social science researchers have expressed the idea that certain media portrayals of sex are modeling influences for young people and adults, although these ideas are not backed up by content-specific research. Bandura and Walters (1963) pointed out that American children and adolescents are not given the opportunity to observe actual sexual behavior in real life, due to our norms of privacy prohibiting exposure to all but very peripheral forms of sexual activity. Because of this scarcity of real-life observational learning opportunities, they argued, the child is forced into dependence on media models for sexual learning (Baran, 1976b).

This idea need not be limited to youthful observers. Adult Americans are also customarily excluded from observing the sexual behaviors of others. If, night after night, they are invited into the TV bedroom of other adults and observe, for example, sexual intercourse between unmarried partners as the norm, they may incorporate that information and later use it in confronting relevant situations. They may approve of extramarital cohabitation for other family members, expect sexual activity to take place between co-workers, or be more receptive to sexual overtures from other adults to whom they are not married. In fact, as "functional value" is one of the characteristics of the modeling stimuli important to social learning, an adult may be more likely to engage in observational learning from sex on TV than would a child.

Is sexual content present on TV, and if so, what is its frequency and nature? Whereas early systematic analyses of TV content were mainly concerned with itemizing instances of violence and sex-role behaviors, more-recent studies have begun to quantify sexual behaviors.

A quantitative analysis of physical contact and sexual behavior during the 1977–78 prime-time season was conducted by Silverman, Sprafkin, and Rubinstein (1979). Sixty-four programs were coded for 12 categories of physical contact and sexual behavior and 11 categories of discouraged sexual practices. These categories ranged from nonsexual touching (such as handshakes) to affection displays (such as kissing), from typical sexual behaviors (such as heterosexual intercourse) to atypical or deviant sexual behaviors (such as transvestism and prostitution).

In this analysis, nonsexual touching and aggression occurred much more frequently than any sexual behaviors. For this season the researchers did find multiple instances of implied intercourse, in contrast to their 1975 study, in which they reported no incidents, explicit or implicit, of intercourse.

Reeves and Garramone (1979) looked for statements that could be interpreted as references to intimate sexual behaviors. These behaviors included sexual intercourse, prostitution, homosexuality, and other intimate acts aside from kissing and embracing. Two episodes of each of the top-rated 24 prime-time programs were coded. "Euphemisms for sexual behavior" were quantified, as were demographics for the source of the statement and the context of the statement. The researchers found 3.7 references per hour, on the average; 6.3 per hour in sitcoms, 2.3 per hour in action/adventure shows, and 1.2 per hour in family drama. The behaviors referred to were largely premarital (63 percent) and heterosexual (96 percent). Overall, the study showed a clear increase in the frequency of verbal references to sex over previous studies.

Lowry, Love, and Kirby (1981), Greenberg, Abelman, and Neuendorf (1981), and Greenberg and D'Alessio (1985) each focused specifically on content analysis of sex acts on soap operas. Lowry et al. coded one week (50 hours) of soaps in 1979, counting 329 codable sex acts (6.58 per hour). Their coding system treated multiple occurrences of an ongoing sex act or discussion as separate acts—for example, "an erotic kiss that also involved an embrace counted as two instances of erotic touching if both acts met the basic requirements" (p. 92). In both Greenberg studies, a sex act or reference "began with a physical or verbal display of a category and ended with the completion of the act category, a new character entering the scene, or a change of scene" (p. 85). Thus fewer acts per hour were found. Greenberg et al. counted 2.0, 2.28 and 1.80 in 1976, 1979, and 1980, respectively. Greenberg and D'Alessio found approximately 4 sexual acts or references per hour in 1982.

There is a strong agreement across all three studies that more sex acts occur between people not married to each other than between marital partners by a 4–1 ratio. Lowry et al. reported 18 percent of the acts of erotic touching and 32 percent of the acts of heterosexual intercourse occurred between marital partners. Greenberg et al. found 35 percent of all petting and 6 percent of heterosexual intercourse to occur between marital partners. Greenberg and D'Alessio report 20 percent of heterosexual intercourse occurring between marital partners; 20 percent of intercourse partners were married to someone else.

What are the effects of exposure? In one of the more sobering studies of sex and the media, Zillman and Bryant (1982) demonstrated that "massive" exposure to pornography (4 hours and 48 minutes over six weeks) resulted in subjects recommending significantly shorter prison terms for rapists, indicating less support for the women's liberation movement, and, among males, increased "sexual callousness" toward women. In addition, the controlled exposure to pornography in three experimental conditions (massive, intermediate, and no exposure) resulted in significant positive linear relationships between exposure and estimates of the percentage of adults practicing common and uncommon sexual be-

haviors, including group sex and sadomasochism, as well as perceptions of general levels of adult sexual activity. Exposure was also related to finding pornography less offensive and recommending fewer broadcast restrictions, including access by minors.

Most media sex falls short of pornography, but the dramatic demonstration of pornography's impact on sexual perceptions and attitudes suggests the possibility of impact from less explicit content. Some impacts have been demonstrated.

In his study of adolescents, Baran (1976a) was concerned with the question of whether portrayals in the media form images and create "great expectations" in the minds of adolescents, resulting in disappointment and dissatisfaction with first coital experiences. Questionnaires were completed by 202 high school students from Cleveland. Significant negative correlations were found between initial coital satisfaction and perceptions of TV characters' sexual prowess and pleasure. A significant positive relationship was also found between initial coital satisfaction and perception of the reality of TV sex.

In his study of college students, Baran (1976b) again investigated whether coital satisfaction was related to media exposure with this older age group. The questionnaire was completed by 207 undergraduate college students. Findings similar to those of the adolescent study were achieved: a significant negative correlation between perceived sexual prowess of TV characters and initial coital satisfaction, as well as a significant positive relationship between perceived reality of TV sex portrayals and initial coital satisfaction.

Southwest Educational Development Laboratory conducted a pilot study on the influence of TV on adolescent girls' attitudes toward love, sex, and marriage ("Impact of TV," 1980). Interviews were completed with teenage girls who were either pregnant and enrolled in a program for unwed mothers or enrolled in a youth program, never having been pregnant. A comparison of the two found certain differences in their TV viewing habits and attitudes. Pregnant teens reported watching TV an average of 20 hours a week; those never pregnant reported watching an average of 13 hours a week. Although such a difference is easily attributable to a third factor, such as loneliness, other differences are not so easily explained. Seventy percent of the pregnant group reported that adult heterosexual relationships shown on TV were similar to real-life relationships; only 33 percent of the never-pregnant group reported such a belief. Additional analyses indicated that the teens who identified more with romantic TV characters were pregnant, and that those who reported that their favorite TV character would not use birth control if involved in a premarital sexual relationship were 2.4 times as likely to be pregnant.

Two studies addressed the impact of soap opera viewing on estimates of real occurrences of sex relationships and their accompanying complications. Buerkel-Rothfuss and Mayes (1981) tested 290 college students, finding that soap viewers estimated more occurrences of divorce, illegitimate children, and abortions than did nonviewers. Sipes (1984) found that avid high school viewers of daytime soap operas were far more likely to make larger estimates of the occurrences of illegitimate pregnancies, of marriages resulting from pregnancies, and the occurrences of rape. She replicated her findings among high school fans of nighttime soap operas.

Motives for Mass Media Use

Much of the research discussed proceeds from the perspective of trying to determine the effects mass media experiences have on individuals. Some believe that media cause such effects, others that individuals with certain predispositions seek out content corresponding to those predispositions. This second perspective has been examined in the framework of the uses and gratifications of mass media. Here the question revolves around what individuals do with the media rather than what the media do to individuals.

Studies have asked "Why do you watch TV, read newspapers, and so on?" Although the an-

swers differ somewhat among different age and social groups, and the reasons vary somewhat from medium to medium, some general findings have emerged.

Learning   A major motive for watching television (and most other media) is to learn something, to gain information. When expressed by young people, this learning tends to have two subgoals. One is to learn the kind of information that can be obtained from news programming or other forms of educational content, to learn what is going on in the world, to try to understand the things that happen in society, to learn new ideas, and to learn about things they have not yet experienced. A second part of this learning motive is to find out what is expected of them in society, to learn how to act and dress, to learn about things that could happen, and to see how other people deal with common and uncommon situations.

Excitement and Relaxation   Two commonly expressed motives seem competitive with each other. One is that media content is exciting and thrilling. The contradictory motive that receives equivalent emphasis is relaxation. The counterbalance of these two strongly suggests that the mood of the individual before using media may be a strong indicator of the motive most prominent in that particular media-seeking activity.

Another well-defined motive is to fill time. Individuals who are bored and can find nothing better to do use the media because it passes the time and gives them something to do. This motive probably can be satisfied as easily by sheer media use as from seeking any specific kinds of content. A related motive for using the media is because it has become a habit. Other motives–for example, seeking arousal—may better be satisfied by certain kinds of content—for example, aggressive content.

Companionship and Escape   A final pair of motives points out that opposite motives may be operating at different times for the same individnal. One is the seeking of companionship. Talking back to the television set, answering questions along with quiz contestants, cheering during sports events, or just wanting to hear others talk all indicate the companionship motive. If you don't want to be alone or there's no one to talk with at the time or you're feeling lonely, the media are there for a vicarious partnership. On the other hand, real-life difficulties with others may well prompt one to escape via the media.

Dominant motives for using different media will differ to some extent. For example, if the question were, Why do you read a newspaper? the responses would focus more heavily on the learning or informational purposes of that medium and weakly if at all on escape or passing time. Asking about contemporary radio would probably draw answers such as habit, relaxation, and perhaps arousal.

In identifying alternative motives for media use, we must ask another fundamental question: What conditions led to these particular motives? Motives may be transient, coming and going depending on particular mood states of the individual just prior to using the media, including anger or tiredness or boredom. More-general states of the individual can also orient media motives. For example, individuals whose work environment tends to be low in social stimulation and high in solitary activity may seek to satisfy a consistent need for social stimulation through media. Those who are constantly interacting with people may be oriented toward media use that offsets or balances their real-life activity. Little has been done to try to identify the relative extent of either temporary or long-term needs being satisfied through the media.

As new and additional media resources became available, the traditional view of major media and how they are used to satisfy individual motives may undergo substantial change. The increase in media resources requires that some of the trends in media development be identified. The next section introduces some of these possibilities.

WHAT OF THE FUTURE IN MASS COMMUNICATIONS?

To a considerable extent, the future in mass communication is *now*. Developments occur so rapidly that by the time writings about future technologies are in print, the information may be outdated if not obsolete. An entire chapter of this book, Chapter 4, is devoted to new communication technologies. Much of this discussion focuses on those technologies that will significantly alter our orientations to the more traditional media.

Cable has significant implications for research in the field of mass communications. Consider a household in which viewers have normally had 4 or 5 channel offerings to choose from and now face 30 or more options. How are those decisions made? Does it lead to increased conflict? Or to the cabling of multiple sets in the household so that different family members can isolate themselves and view what they prefer? Would a sports fan become a sports addict and devote himself or herself entirely to two or three cable channels that provide day and night sports programming? Will there be more or less diversity of viewing in cable homes? What can we project about the process by which these decisions are made?

Most research on television has examined only traditional network television. The programming of the three commercial networks was sufficiently similar that one could make claims about violence or prosocial behavior or sexual content available on television and not be overly concerned about relatively small differences between networks. That's not the case with cable, where a sea of varied programming content could dilute the social impacts of commercial network programming. That assumes, of course, that network viewing will be sharply reduced in cable homes.

Recent data support that proposition. People with cable television watch more total television than those without, as was likely the case for those particular people before they had cable.

However, the portion of cable viewing of network TV is now at about 70 to 80 percent. A large chunk of the remainder goes to pay channels and some few basic channels. Commercial network viewing constitutes a smaller portion of the daily diet of cable television.

To what extent will it be necessary to reassess the social effects claimed to result from viewing experiences with network television? One interesting research area is news content. Cable TV offers 24-hour all-news channels of at least two kinds. One is the Cable News Network, which provides continuous coverage of national and international events. Typically, an all-text news channel in which most recent happenings can be read off the screen will also be available, plus business news and sports news channels. This cable brand of television news may alter patterns of news seeking and news diffusion.

Several alternatives to cable are being marketed and tested. These alternatives have some attractive features, particularly for those countries largely without cable. One competitor is direct broadcast satellite services (DBS). High-powered satellite transmissions can be received on a small home dish. As few as a half-dozen channels may be available, but if they offer very popular content, such as movies, this limited system may be an acceptable option. The signals coming from the satellite are scrambled; homeowners must subscribe to the service in order to receive a special device to unscramble them.

The Computerization of Newspaper Production

New communication technologies are having a major impact on the newspaper industry. Visit the newsroom of any daily newspaper in this country and you will find stories being composed on word processors rather than typewriters. Those newspapers are compiling massive amounts of information into computer data banks for immediate retrieval by reporters as they assemble stories. Newspapers can be plugged into computerized data banks from around the country and from around the world to supplement the information they have immediately available. Different newspapers operating under the same owner can be interconnected to share information immediately and without someone having to answer a phone at the other end. Reporters are equipped with portable typing terminals so that they can write their stories on-site.

The Home Communication Center

In what context will mass communication research be designed by the beginning of the 21st century? The home will be a central communication center. Your television set will pick up dozens of channels, whether it is a tabletop unit or the whole wall of a room used as a huge television screen. The incoming offerings will be informational, educational, entertaining, persuasive, and whatever other functions you may choose. You also will be sending messages from the home, responding to inquiries made of you and initiating transactions yourself. A home telecommunications system will be linked to a personal computer and a printer; you will be able to request general and specialized news on a minute-by-minute basis and have it printed out for you.

A newspaper will still be delivered to your home in the traditional way; however, the printing of that newspaper will have been achieved by satellite transmission of the pages to a nearby printing site so that home delivery will be even more current. Satellites will bring you more sensitive and better audio reception, and much of that music and/or aural information will have a video counterpart. The home communication center will have a video recording system so that you need not be physically present to receive mass communication messages.

Your VCR will store information that you can retrieve when convenient. This home communication system will be linked to your home computer and through telephone lines or satellites to information bases around the world. It's reasonable to expect to research papers and reports by tapping into both local and remote library sources, looking up information in a video version of an encyclopedia, and eventually composing and editing your effort on the system's word processor. The new mix of media for the home blurs the distinction between mass and nonmass communication. More clear, perhaps, may be the recognition that all the activities described involve mediated communication.

This mass communication system of the future will provide a radical opportunity to shift from reactive to active uses of mass media. The new media increase our choices, even though the specification of the options begins elsewhere. Adding new services such as computer-accessed information and videotext material will allow for more initiative from individual users. Passive use of mass communication will still be possible, but the kind of new services identified here require far more active inputs from the user. The implications of this for learning, for enjoying, and for potential social effects have yet to be specified.

SUMMARY

Mass media are of great interest because they are so pervasive in our society. A quick review of the structure of the media today reveals their importance and their wide availability.

Many social effects of the mass media have been studied, but several effects stand out as relatively well established. A number of media effects are interesting but relatively noncontroversial, from providing expanded experiences and influencing how people allocate their time to spreading news. More complex are social-learning effects in areas such as sex roles and minority roles. The effects of the media portrayal of sexual conduct are another example of such social learning. A sound model of social-role learning provides an explanation of a wide range of media effects.

A new line of research on the mass media asks why people consume mass communication. Identifying the motives for mass media use puts an emphasis on the media consumers. It is easier to determine the effects the media will have if the motives of the audience for consuming the messages are known.

As new media become available in society, the effects of the media on society can be expected to change. Such new technologies as cable television, satellites, computers, videocassettes, and videotext will bring new classes of effects from the mass media.

REVIEW AND DISCUSSION QUESTIONS

1. The structure of the mass media can have an influence on the content carried by the media (see Chapter 12 on political communication). How does the structure of the major media today (newspapers, radio, television) influence what each medium carries?

2. The social learning that takes place through the mass media affects many kinds of role learning. To what extent do the media mirror society for us and to what extent does learning from the media change society? What effect does this circular relationship between the media and its audience have on changes in society?

3. How much relationship is there between the reasons that people give for consuming mass media messages and the kinds of effects that are found for the media? Can the media influence a person if he or she is not seeking out the media for that particular reason?

4. Are the new forms of mass communication technology now being developed (Chapter 4) designed to meet the same needs as the current media? Will people find new uses for the new media, or will the new technologies be accepted only to the extent that they perform a function people expect of the mass media?

REFERENCES

Agarwal, B., & Bhasin, K. (1984, August). Action for change. *Seminar,* pp. 38–42.

Allsopp, R. N. (1982). Portrayals of black people on network television and the racial attitudes of elementary school children: An experimental study. Unpublished doctoral dissertation, New York University.

Atkin, C., & Greenberg, B. (1980). Effects of the mass media. In C. Book (Ed.), *Human communication.* New York: St. Martin's.

Atkin, C. K., Greenberg, B., & McDermott, S. (1983). Television and race role socialization. *Journalism Quarterly, 60,* 407–414.

Atkin, C. K., Murray, J., & Nayman, O. (1971). *Television and social behavior: An annotated bibliography of research focusing on television's impact on children.* Washington, DC: U.S. Government Printing Office.

Baldwin, T., & McVoy, S. (1983). *Cable communication.* Englewood Cliffs, NJ: Prentice-Hall.

Bandura, A. (1977). *Social learning theory.* Englewood Cliffs, NJ: Prentice-Hall.

Bandura, A., & Walters, R. H. (1963). *Social learning and personality development.* New York: Holt, Rinehart & Winston.

Baran, S. (1976a). How TV and film portrayals affect sexual satisfaction in college students. *Journalism Quarterly, 53,* 468–473.

Baran, S. (1976b). Sex on TV and adolescent sexual self-image. *Journal of Broadcasting, 20*(1), 61–68.

Barcus, F. E. (1978). *Commercial children's television on weekend and weekday afternoons.* Newtonville, MA: Action for Children's Television.

Barcus, F. E. (1983). *Images of life on children's television: Sex roles, minorities and families.* New York: Praeger.

Bogart, L. (1950–51). The spread of news on a local event: A case history. *Public Opinion Quarterly, 14,* 769–772.

Buerkel-Rothfuss, N., & Mayes, S. (1981). Soap opera viewing: The cultivation effect. *Journal of Communication, 31*(3), 108–115.

Comstock, G. (1982). Violence in television content. In *Television and behavior.* Washington, DC: National Institute of Mental Health.

Comstock, G., Lindsey, G., & Fisher, M. (1975). *Television and human behavior.* Santa Monica, CA: Rand Corporation.

Dates, J. (1980). Race, racial attitudes and adolescent perceptions of black characters. *Journal of Broadcasting, 24,* 549–560.

Deutschman, P., & Danielson, W. (1960). Diffusion of knowledge of the major news story. *Journalism Quarterly, 37,* 345–355.

Downing, M. (1974). Heroine of the daytime serial. *Journal of Communication, 24*(2), 130–139.

Eastman, H., & Liss, M. (1980). Ethnicity and children's preferences. *Journalism Quarterly, 57,* 277–280.

Funkhouser, G. R., and McCombs, M. (1971). The rise and fall of news diffusion. *Public Opinion Quarterly, 35,* 107–113.

Gantz, W. (1983). The diffusion of news about the attempted Reagan assassination. *Journal of Communication, 33*(1), 56–66.

Genova, B. K., & Greenberg, B. S. (1979). Interests in news and the knowledge gap. *Public Opinion Quarterly, 43,* 79–91.

Greenberg, B. S. (1964a). Diffusion of the news about the Kennedy assassination. *Public Opinion Quarterly, 28,* 225–232.

Greenberg, B. S. (1964b). Person-to-person communication in the diffusion of a news event. *Journalism Quarterly, 41,* 489–494.

Greenberg, B. S. (1972). Children's reactions to TV blacks. *Journalism Quarterly, 49,* 5–14.

Greenberg, B. S. (1982). Television and role socialization: An overview. In *Television and behavior.* Washington, DC: National Institute of Mental Health.

Greenberg, B. S. (1985). Mass media in the U.S. in the 1980s. In E. Rogers & F. Balle (Eds.), *Mass communication in the United States and Western Europe.* Norwood, NJ: Ablex.

Greenberg, B. S., Abelman, R., & Neuendorf, K. (1981). Sex on the soap opera: Afternoon delight. *Journal of Communication, 31*(3), 83–89.

Greenberg, B., & Atkin, C. (1982). Learning about minorities from television: A research agenda. In G. Berry & C. Mitchell-Kearnan (Eds.), *Television and the socialization of the minority child.* New York: Academic Press.

Greenberg, B. S., & D'Alessio, D. (1985). The quantity and quality of sex in the soaps. *Journal of Broadcasting and Electronic Media, 29,* 309–321.

Greenberg, B., Heeter, C., Burgoon, M., Burgoon, J., & Korzenny, F. (1983). Mass media use, preferences and attitudes among young people. In B. Greenberg, M. Burgoon, J. Burgoon, & F. Korzenny (Eds.), *Mexican Americans and the mass media.* Norwood, NJ: Ablex.

Greenberg, B., Richards, M., & Henderson, L. (1980). Trends in sex-role portrayals on television. In B. Greenberg (Ed.), *Life on television: Content analyses of U.S. TV drama.* Norwood, NJ: Ablex.

Gunter, B. (1986). *Television and sex role stereotyping.* London: John Libbey and the Independent Broadcasting Authority.

Hill, R. J., & Bonjean, C. M. (1964). News diffusion: A test of the regularity hypothesis. *Journalism Quarterly, 41,* 336–342.

Hodges, K. K., Brandt, D. A., & Kline, J. (1981). Competence, guilt and victimization: Sex differences in ambition of causality in television drama. *Sex Roles, 7,* 537–546.

Hoffman, M. (1984). Gender advertisements in Hungary. Paper presented at the 14th conference of the International Association for Mass Communication Research, Prague.

Impact of TV on adolescent girls' sexual attitudes and behavior. (1980, February 14). *TV Viewer,* No. 13, pp. 1–2.

Kalisch, P. A., Kalisch, B. J., & Scobey, M. (1983). *Images of nurses on television.* New York: Springer.

Knill, B. J., Pesch, M., Parsey, G., Giltin, P., & Perloff, R. M. (1981). Still typecast after all these years: Sex role portrayals in television advertising. *International Journal of Women's Studies, 4,* 497–506.

Liss, M. (1981). Children's television selections: A study of indicators of same-race preference. *Journal of Cross-cultural Psychology, 12*(1), 103–11^

Long, M., & Simon, R. (1974). The roles and statuses of women and children on family TV programs. *Journalism Quarterly, 51,* 107–110.

Lowry, D., Love, G., & Kirby, M. (1981). Sex on the soap operas: Patterns of intimacy. *Journal of Communication, 31*(3), 90–96.

Manes, A. L., & Melnyk, P. (1974). Televised models of female achievement. *Journal of Applied Social Psychology, 4,* 365–374.

Manstead, A. S. R., & McCulloch, C. (1981). Sex-role stereotyping in British television advertisements. *British Journal of Social Psychology, 20,* 171–180.

McDermott, S., & Greenberg, B. (1985). Parents, peers and television as determinants of black children's esteem. In R. Bostrom (Ed.), *Communication Yearbook 8.* Beverly Hills: Sage.

NcNeil, J. (1975). Feminism, femininity and the television shows: A content analysis. *Journal of Broadcasting, 19,* 259–269.

Mendelsohn, H. (1964). Broadcast vs. personal sources of information in emergent public crises: The presidential assassination. *Journal of Broadcasting, 8,* 147–156.

Miller, D. C. (1945). A research note on mass communication. *American Sociological Review, 10,* 691–694.

Ostland, L. E. (1973). Interpersonal communication following McGovern's Eagleton decision. *Public Opinion Quarterly, 37,* 601–610.

Poindexter, P. M., & Stroman, C. (1981). Blacks and television: A review of the research literature. *Journal of Broadcasting, 25,* 103–122.

Reeves, B. (1979). Children's understanding of television people. In E. Wartella (Ed.), *Children communicating: Media and development of thought, speech, understanding.* Beverly Hills: Sage.

Reeves, B., & Garramone, G. (1979). Sex on television: Euphemisms for intimate sexual behavior. Paper presented to the Association for Education in Journalism, Houston.

Rosengren, K. E. (1973). News diffusion: An overview. *Journalism Quarterly, 50,* 83–91.

Royale, G. (1981). Images of women in Caribbean TV ads: A case study. Paper presented at the regional seminar on women and media decision-making, Kingston, Jamaica.

Schechtman, S. A. (1978). Occupational portrayal of men and women on the most frequently mentioned television shows of pre-school children. *Resource in Education* (ERIC document reproduction service).

Signorielli, N. (1984). The demography of the television world. In G. Melischeck, K. E. Rosengren, & J. Stappers (Eds.), *Cultural indicators: An international symposium.* Vienna: Austrian Academy of Sciences.

Silverman, L., Sprafkin, J., & Rubinstein, E. (1979). Physical contact and sexual behavior on primetime TV. *Journal of Communication, 29*(1), 33–43.

Sipes, S., (1984). Teens, soaps and social perceptions. Unpublished master's thesis, Michigan State University, East Lansing.

Siu, Y. (1981, Winter). TV images of Chinese women. *Asian Messenger,* pp. 39–42.

Spitzer, S. (1964–65). Mass media vs. personal sources of information about the presidential assassination: A comparison of six investigations. *Journal of Broadcasting, 9,* 45–50.

Sterling, C., & Kittross, J. (1978). *Stay tuned: A concise history of American broadcasting,* Belmont CA: Wadsworth.

Turow, J. (1974). Advising and ordering: Daytime, prime time. *Journal of Communication, 24*(2), 138–141.

UNESCO (1985). *Communication in the service of women: A report on action and research programmes.* Paris: UNESCO.

Weaver-Lariscy, R., Sweeney, B., & Steinfatt, T. (1984). Communication during assassination attempts: Diffusion of information in attacks on President Reagan and the pope. *Southern Speech Communication Journal, 49,* 258–276.

Zillman, D., & Bryant, J. (1982). Pornography, sexual callousness and the trivialization of rape. *Journal of Communication, 32*(4), 10–21.

9

Intercultural Communication

Nobleza C. Asuncion-Lande
University of Kansas

Nobleza C. Asuncion-Lande is Professor of Communication Studies at the University of Kansas. She has published numerous articles and edited several books on intercultural communication, development communication, and sociolinguistics. Dr. Asuncion-Lande has been Visiting Professor of Communication at the Sheffield Polytechnic in England. She also recently served the International Communication Association as chairperson for the Division of Intercultural and Development Communication.

LEARNING OBJECTIVES

After studying this chapter you should be able to:

- Explain the importance of intercultural communication.
- Define intercultural communication.
- List major variables that differ among cultures.
- Discuss basic issues that affect theory construction and research in intercultural communication.
- Define culture shock and explain its relevance to intercultural communication.
- Identify five basic guidelines for more effective intercultural communication.
- Differentiate between a culture-general and culture-specific approach to intercultural communication training.
- Give examples of experiential methods of learning intercultural communication.
- Explain the value of cultural synergy.

The practice of intercultural communication is not new. Encounters between peoples of different cultures have taken place throughout history. Earlier encounters, however, were usually limited in scope, involved few people, and were far less complicated than they are today.

In recent years, the nature of intercultural encounters has change dramatically. An increasing number of people travel to more foreign countries as tourists, students, business people, soldiers, refugees, diplomats, or employees of multinational organizations. Whether they stay for a short or a long period, they all have to cope with problems of adjustment. Members of the host culture, likewise, face difficulties of accommodating their visitors.

Events occurring in one corner of the globe become known almost instantly in other parts of the world as news is flashed electronically through satellite systems that were unknown only a few decades ago. A new set of understandings is needed in order to comprehend the effects of such events on our daily lives.

Government attempts at social engineering, such as the enforcement of civil rights legislation, have increased contact between persons of diverse cultural, racial, and ethnic backgrounds. Even if individuals might have preferred otherwise, the political, social, and economic developments of the past few years have made it almost impossible to restrict one's choices of neighbors and schoolmates.

These complex developments have brought the widespread realization that *all* peoples and cultures are interdependent. They have also deepened an awareness of the immense diversity of interests and expectations that make up a world community.

As members of this world community interact with increasing frequency, the possibilities for tension and rivalry increase (Asuncion-Lande, 1981; Korzenny & Griffis Korzenny, 1980). At the same time, they also present opportunities for cooperation and understanding (Bochner, 1982; Condon & Saito, 1976; Samovar & Porter, 1985). Knowledge of intercultural

communication would be helpful in such situations.

THE PARADOX OF INTERCULTURAL COMMUNICATION

The student of intercultural communication is specially trained in skills to become a competent intercultural communicator, and to contribute to cross-cultural understanding. The skills necessary for intercultural communication include sensitivity to cultural differences, an appreciation of cultural uniqueness, tolerance for ambiguous communication behavior, willingness to accept the unexpected, responsiveness to change, flexibility in adopting new alternatives, and lowered expectations for effective communication (Harris & Moran, 1979, 1987; Ruben, 1985). Intercultural competence is the ability to demonstrate or use these skills in such a way that the other people in the cross-cultural encounter are able to accept and use them.

This is not to say that knowledge of intercultural communication will solve all the problems inherent in the communication between peoples of the world. Some research on contact situations has concluded that when individuals from diverse cultures interact, the differences that divide them tend to become important. Such differences often become exaggerated or distorted to provide mutually negative images or stereotypes (Bochner, 1982; Brislin, 1981).

This paradox of intercultural communication has been the subject of a number of investigations on intercultural contacts and perceptions by psychologists and communication scholars. Their findings have indicated that several variables are at work when persons with differing orientations interact. When these variables are taken into account, increased interpersonal communication may lead to greater familiarity between members of different cultures. Such familiarity may lead to a perception of similarity of orientations between the participants, which can sustain the interpersonal encounter (Bochner, 1982; Brislin, 1981; Sarbaugh, 1979).

INTERCULTURAL COMMUNICATION AS A DISCIPLINE

Intercultural communication developed out of practical needs, but its emergence as an academic area of inquiry was partly a consequence of the intellectual ferment of the 1960s. The "Communication Revolution," as some have called it, brought about a rethinking of the term *communication,* and with it a new genre of communication study taking a social science approach (Schramm, 1983). This development resulted in a new type of scholar, who made communication the central variable of his or her research. As the research emphasis passed from disciplines to communication problems per se, the new social science of communication began to compartmentalize into interpersonal, small group, organizational, intercultural, and development communication (Rogers & Chaffee, 1983; Schramm, 1983).

The study of intercultural communication in the United States has expanded rapidly in the past two decades. The first courses in intercultural communication were taught in the mid-'60s at a few universities and colleges. The number of institutions of higher learning that offer introductory courses in the subject has increased dramatically since then. Several universities in the United States, among them the University of Kansas, the University of Minnesota, the State University of New York at Buffalo, and the University of Hawaii in conjunction with the East-West Center in Honolulu, offer graduate courses. Intercultural communication courses are also being taught at institutions of higher learning in Japan, Korea, Australia, the Philippines, Mexico, India, and Nigeria.

Governments, multinational organizations, and business enterprises are providing cross-cultural training components in management programs for their personnel. Several organizations and consulting firms have been established to provide cross-cultural briefings, training programs, workshops, and seminars for the private and public sectors (Harris & Moran, 1987).

A growing body of publications is also available on this subject. In the past ten years, several textbooks on intercultural communication and handbooks on cross-cultural training have been published. Some are listed in the reference section at the end of this chapter. Three major journals now publish articles exclusively on intercultural communication or cross-cultural contacts: the *International and Intercultural Communication Annual,* published by the Speech Communication Association; the *International Journal of Intercultural Relations;* and the *Journal of Cross-Cultural Psychology.* Articles on intercultural communication also appear regularly in major professional, trade, and general-interest journals.

Some professional organizations have also recognized the intercultural component of their membership by establishing divisions or interest groups on intercultural communication. Among them are the International Communication Association; the Speech Communication Association and its regional counterparts: the Eastern Communication Association, the Western Communication Association, and the Southern Speech Communication Association; and the Academy of Management. A special association established to serve the needs and interests of practitioners and academics in intercultural communication is the Society for Intercultural Education, Training and Research. All these organizations sponsor seminars, workshops, programs, and conferences on intercultural communication on a regular basis.

With this brief chronological history of intercultural communication, we are now ready to examine what it is that we study. The purpose of this chapter is to provide an overview of intercultural communication. The first section will discuss the major objectives, the core content, the conceptual foundations, and the characteristics that distinguish intercultural communication from other subareas of communication study. The second section will briefly discuss research findings and issues in intercultural communication which have contributed to the development of the field. The third section will suggest some guidelines for improving intercultural communication skills and briefly explain some of the training methodologies that have been employed for intercultural effectiveness.

WHAT DO WE STUDY IN INTERCULTURAL COMMUNICATION?

The study of intercultural communication as it has currently evolved from its uncertain beginnings focuses on the cultural aspects of interpersonal communication, and on the effects of cultural differences on communication patterns. Intercultural communication begins with the assumption of cultural differences, which are viewed not simply as barriers to communication, but as the matrix in which communication takes place. Knowing that differences exist and recognizing their potential effects on the communication process will enable the participants to be more sensitive to the fact that nothing in their communication behavior should be taken for granted and that accommodations should be made for perceived differences. As cultural differences become more apparent, they are easier to control and correct (Asuncion-Lande, 1981; Brislin, 1981).

The principle of cultural difference suggests certain aspects of culture that regularly affect the degree of communicative effectiveness. These aspects are hierarchically ordered; some may have a greater effect than others (Samovar, Porter, & Jain, 1981; Sarbaugh, 1979). The principle of cultural difference also serves as a guide in examining cultural variables that intervene in individual or intergroup interactions and account for different responses to a communicative act. The dimensions of cultural difference necessitate examining the complex interrelatedness of culture and communication. The treatment of the concept of "cultural difference" and of the critical link between communication and culture is what distinguishes intercultural communication from other areas of communication study.

Conceptual Elements of Intercultural Communication

The study of intercultural communication requires an understanding of its conceptual foundations, *culture* and *communication*. Various scholars have made attempts to define culture (Kroeber & Kluckhohn, 1972). It has proved to be a complex concept. Intercultural-communication scholars have also tried to define culture. Their definitions reflect a heterogeneity of perspectives, approaches, and concerns. Nevertheless, a generally accepted working definition refers to culture as a system of shared symbols, beliefs, and practices created by a group of people as an adaptive mechanism for their survival and development and then transmitted to succeeding generations as part of their communicable knowledge. Each culture is unique. Members of a particular culture develop their own special mechanisms to adapt to the circumstances in which they find themselves. These mechanisms are formalized and become part of the group's traditions, beliefs, and practices.

Culture provides people with a general cognitive framework for an understanding of and for functioning in their environment. This cognitive framework, or worldview, as it is generally referred to, enables the members of a given culture to make predictions and interpretations of each member's behaviors.

Culture is a means through which activities of life an be hierarchically ordered by importance and immediacy. The needs of a culture may vary, as may priorities attached to certain groups of behavior. A matter that has importance in one culture may not in another.

Culture gives persons the symbols and the contexts with which to communicate something about themselves to others. The ability to communicate about themselves has enabled groups to maintain and survive in their own cultures, as well as to make contact with others.

Culture has been likened to an iceberg in the sense that a small portion of it can be seen on the surface, while a larger portion is hidden underneath (Ruhly, 1976). The hidden portion of our culture generally remains out of our awareness, though its pervasive effects on our behavior, perception, or attitude can be realized, especially in situations where we come in contact with people who do not share our cultural code. The way we encode our nonverbal messages, for example, is so automatic that we are quite unconscious of the categories we make. Then when we use these categories in an intercultural encounter, we founder, because what we generally have taken for granted is not necessarily shared by the participant from another culture. A task for intercultural communication, therefore, is to raise the hidden portion of our culture to a level of awareness that makes corrective influences possible and keeps us from tripping over invisible cultural "ropes" (Smith, 1966).

It is evident from our discussion of culture that communication does not exist in a vacuum. Culture provides the context for communication to take place. But communication is what allows a culture to develop, maintain, and perpetuate itself. Communication is the process of conveying messages and sharing meanings by means of symbols. The symbols may be linguistic, nonverbal, pictorial, ideographic, notational, or other forms. Such symbols are part of the content and form of a culture.

Culture affects how messages are sent, how they are received, and how they are interpreted. Cultural similarity in the encoding, decoding, and transmission of messages renders the sharing of meanings workable. The way we communicate, the symbols we use, and our interpretations of messages are all prescribed by our culture. As cultures vary, the manner, the form, and the style of communication also differ. An understanding of the complex interrelatedness of culture and communication is, therefore, critical in the study of intercultural communication.

Defining Intercultural Communication

Intercultural communication means many things to many people. The variety of interpretations reflects the interdisciplinary nature of the subject as well as its multifarious beginnings. It demonstrates the need to pull together related research on cross-cultural interactions from various disciplines and integrate them into a unified approach for theory building.

Intercultural communication embraces the traditions and contemporary concerns of both the social sciences and the humanities. The core of its subject matter shows contributions from the insights of cultural anthropology, linguistics, cross-cultural and social psychology, sociology, and speech communication. This multidisciplinary base has been a rich resource for its development. Unfortunately, the potential strength of such a base has been diluted by the variety of approaches and emphases that have been employed in the study of the field. What are needed at this juncture are a redefinition of the area of study and a limitation of the focus of intercultural communication study to make this subject more manageable.

A popular definition of intercultural communication found in early writings is "communication between peoples of different cultures" (Condon & Yousef, 1975; Dodd, 1977; Prosser, 1978a; Sitaram & Cogdell, 1976). The authors then proceed to describe cultural variables affecting communication. There are two problems with this approach: (1) The definition is too inclusive to make it meaningful. One cannot draw precise boundaries between where intercultural communication begins and ends. (2) The descriptions of cultural phenomena portray static elements rather than the dynamic phenomenon of intercultural communication. Intercultural communication is an ongoing, ever-changing process.

A typical research report on intercultural communication is the following one: Participant A interacts with Participant B who is from another culture. Both participants are surprised by, embarrassed by, angered by, or uncertain of the other person's behavior. This may lead to a termination of the encounter. The incident is then attributed to "cultural differences." This interpretation is supported by a listing of the cultural differences, and the report concludes that "culture affects communication."

Some recent studies on intercultural communication have broken away from the traditional approach, which has focused mainly on the cultural aspects of cross-cultural contacts. Newer studies are starting to focus on the process of communication and on the application of intercultural-communication principles to the intercultural context (Kim, 1984; Sarbaugh & Asuncion-Lande, 1983).

In keeping with the change of emphasis in the study of intercultural communication, we offer this definition: Intercultural communication refers to the process of symbolic interaction involving individuals or groups who possess recognized cultural differences in perception and behavior that will significantly affect the manner, the form, and the outcome of the encounter. The participants in an intercultural encounter bring with them their own cultural precepts, which act to screen the messages they send and receive. The cultural frameworks in which the communicators interpret messages may vary from maximal to minimal differences. Some of these differences may be obvious, others may be more subtle. The success or failure of the interaction will depend to a large extent on the participants' familiarity with each other's background, their perceptions of the differences separating them, and their mutuality of purpose (Cushman & Cahn, 1985; Samovar, Porter, & Jain, 1981). If they perceive themselves to be so different that communication will require some extra effort on their part, they may nevertheless decide to continue with the communication to achieve complementary or mutual goals. But they may also terminate it because it is not worth the effort (Gudykunst & Kim, 1984a). This perspective considers communica-

tion a "shared" experience rather than an individual act with individual performers. It recognizes the process nature of communication, and demonstrates that cultural difference is the matrix of communication.

Cultural Variables in Communication

Scholars and practitioners of intercultural communication have arrived at a consensus that the encoding and decoding of messages in cross-cultural contexts require a recognition and an understanding of the cultural variables in communication. Some of the most critical of these variables include language, nonverbal codes, worldview, role relationships, and patterns of thinking (Argyle, 1982; Asuncion-Lande, 1981; Condon & Yousef, 1975; Dodd, 1977; Gudykunst & Kim, 1984a; Samovar & Porter, 1976; Sarbaugh, 1979; Sitaram & Cogdell, 1976).

Language Language is the most obvious and most enduring difficulty in intercultural communication. Individuals gather, give, and receive information through language. As language has developed in the context of a particular culture, of necessity it reflects that culture. For example, the significant objects in a culture are specifically labeled, whereas the less important ones are given generalized names. Kinship ties are very important in social relationships in the Philippines. The term *cousin* in Philipino will include ten or more specific words to illustrate the degree of blood relationship within an extended family system. The American, on the other hand, will use the general term *cousin* to designate varying degrees of kinship. The Asian will have more than ten words for *rice,* which is his primary food. The Arab will have many words to designate *camel,* which is an important element of survival in the desert. These examples illustrate that a connection exists between the vocabulary of a given culture and the objects and ideas that are significant in the culture.

The link between language and culture also poses difficulties in translating from one language to another. A translation is not merely a substitution of word for word. It involves conveying whole contexts (Bickley, 1982). Misunderstandings caused by inadequate translation have run the gamut from funny to tragic. A sensational but erroneous news report related by Bickley involved the mistranslation of an Italian expression into English. According to the news report, the Capuchin monks were abandoning their traditional vows of celibacy. A superintendent of the Capuchin College in Washington had stated that 29.6 percent of the monks had said that they wanted to have *intimo rapporto* ("closer friendship") with women. International wire services translated the Italian phrase to mean "sexual relations."

The Nonverbal Code The nonverbal code is another potential difficulty for intercultural communication. Its effects on communicative behavior are not as readily observed as the verbal code, for nonverbal messages operate primarily out of awareness. Because they are largely unconscious, nonverbal codes are more prone to misinterpretations and are less conducive to corrective influences.

Scholars have disagreed on the definitional limit of nonverbal communication, but they seem to have reached a consensus on its general functions. Nonverbal behavior is usually used to communicate feelings, attitudes, and preferences. Nonverbal codes may reinforce or contradict the verbal message or provide feedback.

Opinions vary concerning the classification of nonverbal behaviors. A review of the literature, however, shows recurring items such as body motions, including postures, gestures, facial expressions, and eye movements; space zoning, which includes physical distances between individuals in private and public places, and the positioning of objects in the physical environment; paralanguage, which includes auditory cues that accompany linguistic signals; temporal orientations; and silence.

The nonverbal code, like the linguistic code, is subject to cultural influence. Specific nonverbal behaviors that are symbolic in one culture may not elicit any response in another culture, or they may elicit different reactions. For example, eye contact is an important aspect of interpersonal communication between two white American speakers. To a Navajo, eye contact means aggression, especially when the participants in a communication act have different status or ages. Thus in normal social encounters, eye contact is avoided.

Another example of cultural difference is in the use of silence. In American culture, silence can be a cause for apprehension, especially if it is prolonged, while in an Indian culture, silence can mean intense, pleasurable, or meditative communication. The use of space is another confounding problem in intercultural communication. Latinos prefer to stand very close to the person with whom they are conversing. The Thai would prefer them to be four feet apart. Finally, cultures vary in their conceptualization of temporal orientation. Pennington (1975) observed that blacks differ from whites in their concept of appropriate waiting period to call on a new neighbor. Another cultural contrast on time conceptualization is the future orientation of white Americans. In Navajo, there are no words for future time.

Worldview Worldview is another potential problem in intercultural communication. It is considered to be one of the most important cognitive mechanisms influencing communication. Worldview is the representation of the internal view of an individual or a group, which is molded and organized according to cultural preconceptions reflecting basic values, beliefs, and attitudes (Dodd, 1981, 1987). One's worldview encompasses the sum total of one's experience and knowledge.

The concept of worldview contains three dimensions: the purpose of life, the nature of life, humanity's relation to the cosmos (Sarbaugh, 1979). The purpose of life for one cultural group may be to control the environment; for another it may be to live in harmony with it. The nature of life for some people may be a continual process of change, of discovery, or of pleasure and excitement. For another group it may be an acceptance of what fate offers, be it joy or sorrow, contentment or suffering. The relation of humanity to the cosmos may be one of dependence on a supreme being or on nature; one of interdependence between a person, God, and the universe; or it may be a harmonious balance between nature and humanity. The importance of worldview in intercultural communication is that it serves as a perceptual screen for incoming messages, and as a basis for interpreting observed events and activities.

Role Relationship The concept of role relationship is another possible problem for communication. Role relationships provide insights into the ways a culture maintains social order and control among its members. Role relationships are organized according to age, sex, social status, kinship, power, wealth, knowledge, and experience. Some cultures may exhibit all these types of relationships. Others may not. Furthermore, the behavioral manifestations of each of these relationships may vary from culture to culture. Sex roles, for example, have been found to differ between Papua New Guinean and American cultures. In Papua New Guinea, males hunt and they clear land for small farming, females plant and harvest food, care for small children, and do household chores. In American culture, traditional sex roles, though changing, still dictate that females are to do household chores while males are the primary breadwinners.

Another manifestation of role relationship can be observed in hierarchical divisions of status and horizontal divisions of exclusion and inclusion. For example, Japanese culture is status oriented. Each member of a status hierarchy, whether in an organizational or a social context, acts according to well-defined roles within these settings. An American, on the other hand, though aware of status distinctions in an organizational

setting, may not necessarily recognize such distinctions in a social context. Americans are more accustomed to treating individuals as equals and behave accordingly. The important point for intercultural communication is that Americans are not used to status differences, and their tendency to treat others as equals regardless of their cultural background often creates barriers to effective communication in intercultural situations.

Thought Patterns Differences in patterns of thought pose another potential difficulty in intercultural communication. Thought patterning refers to the processing of data from impressions and experiences in one's daily life. It involves encoding and decoding information or reasoning. Thought patterning indicates how individuals form fundamental concepts, organize ideas, and define sources of knowledge. Americans are known to rely heavily on analytical thought. When they reason, they follow some sort of "logical" system in which consistencies and relationships of elements are delineated, enabling them to form "valid" conclusions. In analytic thought, a conscious step-by-step process takes place. An incident is taken apart, the elements are identified in sequence, the relationship of the elements is examined, new possibilities are generated, and then the elements are put back together to yield an "obvious" conclusion (Howell, 1982).

The Japanese, on the other hand, favor "holistic" data processing, in which everything about an incident is absorbed in its totality without the person consciously thinking about it. The subconscious or inner out-of-awareness resources process the information, and after a period when nothing seems to be happening, there is a flash of insight and an idea is born (Howell, 1982). Still another mode of thinking has been identified as purely intuitive data processing, or Gestalt thinking. This mode is known to be favored in Asian and African cultures. Intuitive thinking is different from holistic thinking in the sense that the process is nonsymbolic, nonquantitative, and totally random (Condon & Yousef, 1975; Howell, 1982).

Differences in thought patterns may be the most serious of all obstacles to communication because of the participants' tendency to screen out perceived distortions in each other's message. The significance of the concept of thought patterns to communication is that differences in patterns are not absolute. Although certain cultures may show a predominance of one pattern, other modes of thinking may be present, and may be employed in different situations. Americans may use intuitive thinking when they make decisions on who to marry, for example.

The cultural factors sketched above provide a framework in which cultural differences can be assessed, and where basic communication principles can be applied in the interaction process between culturally diverse participants.

RESEARCH ISSUES IN INTERCULTURAL COMMUNICATION

Issues in Theory Development

Communication scholars have made some significant contributions toward the conceptualization of intercultural communication. But the pervasive influence of earlier formulations, emphasizing cultural rather than communicative aspects, has impeded theory development. What should be done now is to integrate the cultural and communicative approaches in order to arrive at a more accurate description of the intercultural process of communication.

Degree of Difference Perhaps one of the most promising developments in intercultural communication research is the proposition that intercultural communication differs from other forms of human communication *only* in the degree of difference between the communicants (Dodd, 1981, 1987; Gudykunst & Kim, 1984b; Samovar, Porter, & Jain, 1981; Sarbaugh, 1979). A critical problem in intercultural communication study is specifying the degree of difference that

would make one communication event intercultural and another not. The following example should illustrate this problem: A native of East Germany and an American know that they are from different cultures and therefore expect problems of intercultural communication. But what about communication between an American and a (non-French) Canadian? Their language and nonverbal codes are quite similar. Both are inclined to assume that they share a common culture. They may therefore be unable to accept the fact that there are cultural differences between them to which they must be sensitive.

Sarbaugh's (1979) conceptual scheme of a homogeneity-heterogeneity continuum offers a starting point for a discussion of this definitional problem. He explains heterogeneity and homogeneity as follows: If two circles represent the life experiences of two persons (or groups), and the circles have minimal overlap (represent minimal similarity of experience), the two persons would be near the heterogeneous end of the continuum. If the circles have maximum overlap, the two would be near the homogeneous end of the continuum. Sarbaugh labels the heterogeneous end of the continuum "intercultural" and the homogeneous end of the continuum "intracultural." He concedes that there are no completely heterogeneous or homogeneous pairs, but he claims that the heterogeneity of participants in an interpersonal encounter can be plotted through points along the continuum. These points are labeled "levels of interculturalness." Sarbaugh's basic assumption is that communication becomes increasingly difficult and decreasingly efficient as the heterogeneity of the participants increases.

Let us go back to the example of the American and the East German. Their life experiences would normally have minimal overlap, and they would recognize that fact. They are close to the heterogeneous end of the continuum. Thus their communication would be labeled intercultural. In the American-Canadian example, the classification of their communication as inter- or intracultural will depend on their perceptions of the degree of homogeneity of their experiences. Sarbaugh identifies key variables on which the participants can be expected to differ, and where the heterogeneity-homogeneity continuum can be assessed. Among the variables on which participants in a communicative act can be expected to differ are: language or code systems; worldviews; perceived relationships between participants; perceived intent of each participant.

The amount of difference will increase as we move from the most intracultural (homogeneous) to the most intercultural (heterogeneous) act. The more homogeneous the participants, the more similar their perceptions and interpretations following a communicative act; the more heterogeneous participants, the more dissimilar their perceptions and interpretations. The main strengths of Sarbaugh's proposed scheme are: (1) its attention to the operations of basic communication principles at the different levels of intra-interculturalness, and (2) its classification of events according to the different levels of intercultural communication. Some empirical efforts are needed, however, to test his categories.

Uncertainty Reduction Another interesting approach toward the conceptual refinement of intercultural communication, proposed by Gudykunst (1980; Gudykunst & Kim, 1984a), starts with the premise that communication is a transactional symbolic activity that involves making predictions and reducing uncertainty. Gudykunst claims that the greatest amount of uncertainty exists when strangers communicate with each other. Strangers are people who are unknown and unfamiliar, and are in an environment they don't know too well. Whenever we encounter a stranger, our primary concern is to increase our ability to predict our behavior and that of the other person (Gudykunst & Kim, 1984a). This conceptualization of uncertainty reduction when communicating with strangers is not original with Gudykunst (Berger & Calabrese, 1975; Miller & Steinberg, 1975). But he is the first to adapt this notion as a framework for delineating intercultural communication.

Gudykunst believes that in communication between strangers, the participants are influenced by their conceptual filters. The categories of conceptual filters that influence communication are identified as: cultural (such as worldview and value orientations), sociocultural (such as group membership and role relationships), psychocultural (such as cognitive processes and attitudinal influences), and environmental (such as the physical and psychological environments) (Gudykunst & Kim, 1984a). Each of these filters influences our interpretation of strangers' messages and our predictions about their behaviors. If we do not understand the strangers' filters, we cannot make accurate predictions or interpretations of their behavior.

Gudykunst's proposed framework specifies that the process of intercultural communication is not unique, but reflects the basic processes of human communication. In this he reinforces Sarbaugh's proposition that the variables and the underlying processes operating in any communicative act are the same. The value of this model lies in its refinement of the conceptual boundaries of intercultural communication. It is another step toward conceptual clarification and simplification. Its apparent limitation is in its failure to explain what is taking place in the encounters between strangers.

Methodological Issues

Definitional and conceptual issues still dominate research activity in intercultural communication. But an increasing number of studies have begun to deal with methodological concerns. The most recent comprehensive review of research methodologies in intercultural communication took place in 1981 at the Speech Communication Association annual convention. Ten core participants were asked to write papers on research methodologies in intercultural communication. These papers served as resources for the discussions that followed. Some of the papers were published in a volume of the *International and Intercultural Communication Annual* entitled

"Methods for Intercultural Communication Research" (Gudykunst & Kim, 1984b). Among the questions discussed at the seminar: (1) What methodological approaches are most useful and appropriate for the study of intercultural communication phenomena? (2) What are the relative merits of qualitative and quantitative methodologies for studying intercultural communication? (3) Are the analytic tools for the study of general communication identical for intercultural communication? (4) How can we determine the reliability and validity of instruments for examining intercultural communication phenomena?

The seminar produced no definitive conclusions, but it spotlighted the pervasive issues and research trends. The conclusions of the seminar were:

1. Research methods employed in intercultural communication are patterned after those employed in general and interpersonal communication research. The intercultural context is an excellent ground for hypothesis testing and for developing innovative methodologies.

2. Both quantitative and qualitative methods of research are employed in studying intercultural phenomena. However, quantitative research methods appear to have a slight edge over qualitative research methods, as shown in the number of articles and research reports that have been published in interculturally oriented professional journals. Earlier studies of intercultural communication were predominantly descriptive.

3. Quantitative research methods are employed for examining relationships between different cultural variables among various cultural groups. Qualitative research approaches explain the structure and the interpretation of messages.

4. Some quantitative techniques include content analysis, network analysis, and spatial modeling. Some qualitative techniques include ethnographic analysis, naturalistic observations, metaphor analysis, discourse analysis, rhetorical analysis, constructivism, rules-structure and meaning-structure analysis. These techniques are also employed in general communication studies.

5. There is no one "appropriate" method for studying intercultural communication. Any scientific tool used in general communication study can also be used for intercultural communication study.

6. The validity and reliability of instruments for intercultural study depend on several factors: the nature of the phenomena being tested, the comparability of samples and cultures, the translatability and transferability of research tools, and the researcher's competence. These factors are all interrelated, but each one will be considered individually.

We know from preceding discussion that the core variables of intercultural communication are the "cultural differences" that affect interactions. If we want to know, for example, some of the major values, beliefs, and attitudes of the culture being represented in a recorded communication, content analysis may furnish some clues. By providing us with a way of quantifying terms, phrases, and themes that stand for underlying values, content analysis can increase our knowledge of and insight into a given cultural group. If our subject of inquiry is the identification of normative patterns of behavior, ethnomethodology may be a useful tool to adapt. Ethnomethodologists examine the subjects' perception of social order to discover the interpretative practices by which the habitual aspects of daily life are rationalized.

Similar acts may have different implications in various cultures. For example, the act of reciprocity is necessary for the functioning of *all* societies. But it differs in its importance and ramifications from one culture to another. Philippine society values close stable relationships of mutual aid. Any favor given is seen as part of the process of building such relationships. The immediate return of a favor is not necessary and may in fact not be desired since it could imply a wish not to become involved in a stable relationship. But a long-term obligation is nevertheless created. In American society, it is assumed that all individuals are available for mutual cooperation. Indeed, that mutual aid, if it is not costly, should be given to all individuals without thought of forming special relationships. Small favors do not create an obligation, but merely require a "thank you." In short, Americans are expected to help others by virtue of being members of a larger society. In the Philippines, favors are viewed as part of the process of building special relationships.

A previous section of this chapter mentioned that intercultural communication is a testing ground for theory and methods in communication research. But the researcher should be aware of the following caveats: The research tools employed in one culture should be translated exactly so that they test the same phenomena in the other cultures. There should be equivalent terms for the same phenomena in the language of the culture under study. Consider the following: The term *delicadeza* in Spanish is difficult to translate into English or Pilipino because of the several nuances in its use by Spanish speakers. And some words in the original research instrument may not have the same experiential domain in other cultures. The word *snow,* for example, can be translated into several languages, but it is doubtful whether people in many cultures can conjure the reality of what it actually connotes.

Some Unanswered Questions

As the study of intercultural communication continues to develop, issues continue to emerge.

One issue is the ethical dimensions of intercultural communication. What is ethically responsible behavior in an intercultural encounter? Should we impose our own standards of communication behavior, even if it is alien to the other participant? Can we and should we develop an ethical code that could be used as a guideline for communication between cultures? Finally, toward what ends should scholarship in intercultural communication be directed?

A second issue is the development of instructional materials and innovative methods of instruction that will reflect the changing nature of education in an interdependent world. What teaching methods should we use to develop cultural sensitivity and empathy? What kinds of materials should we use to teach competence in intercultural communication? How do we define competence in intercultural communication?

A third issue deals with the practical applications of intercultural research. How can researchers make their findings readily available to practitioners? How can we facilitate collaborative efforts between researchers, practitioners, and subjects to achieve the same ends?

A final question deals with the value of research to the subjects and to the cultures under study. How can we as intercultural-communication scholars make our research valuable to the subjects of our study? What types of research should be undertaken that would be useful to their cultures?

Solutions to these questions may not come easily. We need a coordinated effort of intercultural scholars and practitioners from diverse cultures and a variety of viewpoints to attempt to solve them. The first prerequisite for meeting this goal is for intercultural specialists to practice what they preach.

PRACTICING INTERCULTURAL COMMUNICATION

Guidelines for Improving Intercultural Communication Skills

It is almost impossible to confine one's own communication to one's cultural, racial, ethnic, or social group. At work, at play, in the marketplace, at school, or in various public areas where people congregate, one is certain to come in contact with someone who is from a different background. People are now traveling more frequently, and they are going to more distant places than ever before, thereby being exposed to more culturally diverse societies. As they encounter peoples from different cultures, their communication skills are severely tested. Their ability to communicate in unfamiliar surroundings and with strangers may make a difference as to whether their sojourn or their interpersonal encounters are enjoyable or stressful.

Self-Awareness A first requirement for becoming interculturally skilled is to know one's own culture. When one becomes aware of one's cultural assumptions, they become less of a stumbling block to effective communication (Barna, 1985). Most individuals identify with a particular culture, but a great number of them are not consciously aware of the cultural precepts that govern their behaviors. Most assume that their own way of life is the "correct" way. They then are surprised or disturbed when they encounter people who also have their own unique ways of interpreting reality.

Cultural self-awareness enables one to be sensitive to cultural identities different from one's own. This awareness may lead participants to mutually work toward a resolution of the differences, especially if they want to maintain their communication.

Open-Mindedness Another requirement for becoming interculturally skilled is to avoid making generalizations about other cultures unless one is thoroughly familiar with them. In cross-cultural encounters, it is almost impossible to avoid making stereotypes about others. A stereotype is a form of generalization that involves the name of a group of people and statements about them (Brislin, 1981). Because stereotypes are categorizations of individual elements, they mask the differences between these elements. Since intercultural communication is mainly concerned with cultural differences, it is necessary to look beyond surface generalizations about them and note the complexity of these diversities.

Another requirement for intercultural skills is an acceptance of the principle of cultural relativ-ism. According to this principle, every culture is unique, and its premises are as valid as those of other cultures. A cultural relativist avoids being trapped by his or her ethnocentrism, which refers to the belief that one's cultural practices are superior to those of other cultures. To be proud of one's own culture is a positive attribute, but this pride should be accompanied by a recognition and a respect for other cultures.

Flexibility and Creativity Another requirement for becoming interculturally skilled is to have a healthy attitude toward change. One goes through life expecting that some changes in attitudes and values toward existence, relationships, and standards of living will take place. But when one has to suddenly confront alterations to habitual practices or familiar surroundings, one usually experiences confusion, discomfort, frustration. The phenomenon of confusion or discomfort when faced with sudden change has been labeled "culture shock." Originally conceptualized by Oberg (1958), culture shock, or what is now increasingly known as "transition shock" (Asuncion-Lande, 1980), is the anxiety caused by unfamiliar surroundings and the inability to adjust to new environments.

There has been much speculation about the causes of culture shock. Some of the more plausible assumptions: (1) It arises from the experience of dealing with others from very different backgrounds (Brislin, 1981). (2) It is a lack of knowledge about other cultures (Furnham & Bochner, 1982). (3). It is a lack of experience in dealing with cultural diversities (Taft, 1977). (4) It is personal rigidity (Harris & Moran, 1979). The phenomenon of culture shock has parallels to other responses to critical situations occasioned by sudden changes in one's life. It underscores the need to be receptive to new experiences and new challenges in everyday life.

Finally, one must be creative and experimental to become interculturally skilled. Intercultural communication requires quick responses, constant adaptations, and spontaneous adjustments to the needs of the communicative act. The processes involved are more intuitive than analytical and result in what Howell (1979) has termed "flashes of insight" that resemble artistic creativity. To foster such creativity, one needs to be open to new and different experiences that may arise in the course of an intercultural encounter.

These guidelines are general and interrelated. They are meant to serve as starting points for serious thinking about goals and consequences of one's communication behavior, especially in cross-cultural or multicultural contexts. It is hoped that these guidelines will have particular relevance to the student and to the practitioner of intercultural communication who are concerned with interpersonal relationships in an increasingly interdependent world.

Approaches to Becoming Interculturally Skilled

The growing recognition of intercultural communication's importance has led to the proliferation of academic courses and training programs on the subject. Although the programs may differ in methods and assumptions, their main purpose is to prepare individuals to function effectively in intercultural contexts. The most widely used training methods reflect either of two generally recognized approaches: the culture-general training approach and the culture-specific training approach (Ruhly, 1976). Other training approaches gaining increasing acceptance among cross-cultural trainers, especially in management contexts, are experiential learning and cultural synergy.

The Culture-General Approach The culture-general approach focuses on the individual's knowledge of his or her own culture. Its main purpose is to train the individual for interaction in a variety of cultures. The emphasis is on cultural self-awareness, based on the assumption that to function effectively in another culture one must first understand one's own culture. One must also be able to understand oneself first before one can understand a person from another

culture. The culture-general approach has several advantages for those who want to develop intercultural skills: (1) It enhances the ability to diagnose problems in intercultural interactions. (2) It fosters tolerance for "unusual" behaviors. (3) It motivates people to learn more about their own and other cultures (Harris & Moran, 1979). The major disadvantages of this approach are that it is time consuming, and it requires skilled supervision. Some of the techniques used in connection with this approach include role playing, critical incident analysis, and group discussion.

The Culture-Specific Approach The culture-specific approach to training in intercultural skills focuses on knowledge of a specific culture. Its main objective is to prepare students to respond to unfamiliar situations in a particular culture by familiarizing them with its basic values, beliefs, attitudes, motivations, and behaviors. Learning a specific culture has several advantages. It enhances an appreciation of the unique characteristics of the culture. Familiarity with the patterns of behavior of a given culture can help prevent inadvertent blunders, and may also facilitate the adjustment of the individual to that culture. The main drawbacks of the culture-specific approach to training are that one cannot possibly learn everything that needs to be known about a particular culture and generalizations about particular behaviors do not usually take individual idiosyncrasies into account. Some forms of culture-specific training activities include area study courses at universities and colleges, simulation exercises, the use of informants from the target culture, and field experiences.

Experiential Learning Experiential techniques in teaching and training in intercultural communication have gained increasing acceptance among educators and trainers. Some experiential learning techniques are simulation exercises, games, role playing, internships, and field trips.

Experiential learning refers to the process of learning by doing. The student is expected to be an active participant in his or her own instruction. The knowledge comes from the individual's insights and reactions to the learning situation. The primary objectives of experiential learning in intercultural communication are: (1) to increase one's understanding of other cultures; (2) to develop skills for effective cross-cultural interaction; and (3) to promote intercultural communication.

Two of the most widely used simulation exercises are BaFa BaFa and Culture Contact. BaFa BaFa is a game that involves 15 to 20 players. Two groups are formed representing two different cultures. The members visit back and forth to experience and to attempt to understand the other culture. Culture Contact is a role-play game designed to focus on the types of misunderstandings and potential conflict that can arise when a trading expedition docks at an island inhabited by a preindustrial society. After each game, a discussion follows to pinpoint the problem areas and to process the experience.

The simulated games are designed to help students explore, expand, and deepen their knowledge of intercultural interaction. When the students perform these exercises, they may experience almost all the full range of thoughts and feelings they would if they were to visit other cultures and participate in the daily activities of the inhabitants. They may also experience the difficulty of being objective as they listen to ideas they do not share, or as they are confronted with behaviors they cannot comprehend. When the students become aware of potential conflicts, they are taught skills for managing them.

The students are aided in their efforts by the facilitator or instructor in an atmosphere that is more supportive and less threatening than an actual foreign experience. In the discussion that follows the exercise, students can reflect on the explanations of their behaviors and experiment with new ways of practicing intercultural communication. The challenge of discovering what they are expected to learn often results in students taking considerably greater initiative and responsibility in attaining their objectives.

Another advantage of experiential learning is that it can be easily combined with other methods of instruction and enhance learning on the subject. The major disadvantage of this method is that it is culture bound—that is, most of the exercises, and their underlying principles, reflect American values and patterns of thinking, which cannot be easily transferred into the context of other cultures. Experiential learning is biased toward individual expression and assertiveness in articulating strong emotions. These values are not so common in other cultures.

Cultural Synergy This approach, which is gaining popularity in multinational management training, is designed to create a collaborative perspective in international business operations (Adler, 1980). Its goal is to promote an atmosphere of cooperation among members and clients of a transnational organization in order to facilitate coordination, information flow, and continuity in the organization. It emphasizes the building of trust and good feelings, encourages authenticity and clear intent, promotes reciprocity and interdependence, and seeks to foster creativity and excellence (Harris & Moran, 1987). Computer-aided instruction is an essential part of the training process, as is the use of cognitive (lectures, seminars, conferences) and experiential modes of learning. The advantages of cultural synergy are that it prepares the trainee to cope with a rapidly changing organizational environment and it is in tune with the trend toward global interdependence. Its main drawback is that it may be very difficult to implement.

Cross-cultural programs are now becoming a regular part of personnel training in government, business, and industry (Harris & Moran, 1987). The realities of a multicultural society and the interdependence among nations make cross-cultural training a necessity. Regardless of the training approach adopted, there is a similarity in the major objectives, which are to prepare individuals to live in foreign cultures and to develop skills for appropriate, sensitive, and consistent behavior in intercultural interactions.

CONCLUSION

No person can communicate as a "free agent." The influence of culture on behavior is ever present. Culture affects how messages are sent, how they are received, and how they are interpreted. Thus when persons from different backgrounds interact, they are more likely to respond differently to the same message because of the filtering effect of their cultures. Their differing responses can cause problems in communication.

Communication is important for the survival of culture. It is through communication that cultural components are transmitted to succeeding generations. Communication helps shape culture, while culture gives it substance and direction. This interdependent relationship is vividly illustrated in the process of intercultural communication.

Intercultural communication is defined as the process of symbolic interaction between individuals and groups who possess recognized cultural differences in perceptions and modes of behavior that will significantly affect the manner and the outcome of the encounter.

The concept of difference is an important dimension of intercultural communication. The critical aspect is the degree of difference that exists between the participants.

Some cultural variables in which the degree of difference can be assessed include language, nonverbal code, role relationships, worldview, and thought patterns. They can influence the manner, direction, and outcome of the intercultural encounter.

Research on intercultural communication in the past ten years has led to the formation of common basic concepts that can explain the nature of communication in cross-cultural contexts. But though some significant advances in theory development have been made, notably in the delineation of the focus of study, there is a need for empirical testing and for refinement of the various approaches that have been developed so far.

Recognition of the usefulness of intercultural training in professional education is growing. This recognition has led to various training programs for developing and improving intercultural skills. Four identifiable approaches for training and teaching include culture-general, culture-specific, experiential, and cultural synergy. Evaluative research on these approaches has given no indication as to which of these four would be the most effective. However, experiential techniques that combine culture-general and culture-specific approaches are gaining wide acceptance among teachers and trainers.

There are no simple guidelines for intercultural effectiveness. But it has been demonstrated that an understanding of the impact of culture on communication behavior can help improve interaction skills in cross-cultural or multicultural contexts.

SUMMARY

As contact among different world cultures has become more frequent and more important, interest in intercultural communication has increased. Cultural differences can exist not just from nation to nation but also within a single territorial boundary.

Intercultural communication is influenced by a number of cultural differences, from language and nonverbal differences to different worldviews. Research in intercultural communication has been difficult, but important theoretical distinctions among cultures are now being identified.

The practice of effective intercultural communication involves several basic principles. Effective intercultural communicators must know their own culture, avoid generalizations while accepting cultural relativism, have a healthy attitude toward change, and be willing to be creatively experimental. Some of the best techniques for learning to communicate interculturally are experiential techniques for hands-on practice.

REVIEW AND DISCUSSION QUESTIONS

1. Cultural differences are sometimes a matter of absolute differences (as when a different language is spoken) and sometimes matters of degree (such as the amount of deference shown to authority figures). Which kind of cultural difference, absolute or relative, would be the source of more communication difficulties? Which type of difference would be easier to detect or learn about? Which kind would be easier for intercultural communicators to adapt to?

2. Cultural differences can exist within a nation or geographic region as well as between countries. Would this mixing of cultures make it easier or harder for someone to communicate with one of the groups? Are persons who come from such multiculture areas more likely to be good intercultural communicators, and why?

3. The chapters on interpersonal communication (Chapter 5) and on language (Chapter 2) discussed the idea that significant differences existed between individuals in the way they perceive and interpret the world. This difference is similar to the differences between cultures discussed here. Is it fair to say that good intercultural communication skills are the same skills needed by any good communicators, or that, vice versa, a good interpersonal communicator already has the skills necessary to communicate effectively across cultures? Are there any unique communication skills in either setting that are not applicable in the other?

4. The guidelines provided for practicing effective intercultural communication mainly deal with promoting a flexible and nonjudgmental attitude in the communicator. What are some specific communication behaviors that would reflect this commitment to openness?

REFERENCES

Adler, N. (1980). Cultural synergy: The management of cross-cultural organizations. In W. W. Burke & D. Goldstein (Eds.), *Trends and issues in O.D.* (pp. 163–184). San Diego, CA: University Associates.

Argyle, M. (1982). Intercultural communication. In S. Bochner (Ed.), *Cultures in contact: Studies in cross-cultural interaction* (pp. 61–80). New York: Pergamon.

Asuncion-Lande, N. (Ed.). (1980). *Ethical perspectives and critical issues in intercultural communication.* Annandale, VA: Speech Communication Association.

Asuncion-Lande, N. C. (1981). An overview of intercultural communication. In N. Asuncion-Lande & E. M. Pascasio (Eds.), *Building bridges across cultures* (pp. 1–10). Manila, Philippines: Solidaridad Press.

Barna, L. (1985). Stumbling blocks to intercultural communication. In L. Samovar & R. Porter (Eds.), *Intercultural communication: A reader* (pp. 330–337). Belmont, CA: Wadsworth.

Berger, C., & Calabrese, R. (1975). Some explorations in initial interactions and beyond. *Human Communication Research, 1,* 99–112.

Bickley, V. C. (1982). Language as the bridge. In S. Bochner (Ed.), *Cultures in contact* (pp. 99–126). New York: Pergamon.

Bochner, S. (Ed.). (1982). *Cultures in contact: Studies in cross-cultural interaction.* New York: Pergamon.

Brislin, R. W. (1981). *Cross-cultural encounters: Face-to-face interaction.* New York: Pergamon.

Condon, J., & Saito, M. (Eds.). (1976). *Communicating across cultures for what?* Tokyo: Simul Press.

Condon, J., & Yousef, F. (1975). *An introduction to intercultural communication.* New York: Bobbs-Merrill.

Cushman, D., & Cahn, D. D., Jr. (1985). *Communication in interpersonal relationships.* Albany, NY: SUNY Press.

Dodd, C. H. (1977). *Perspectives on cross-cultural communication.* Dubuque, IA: Kendall/Hunt.

Dodd, C. H. (1981, 1987). *Dynamics of intercultural communication.* Dubuque, IA: Wm. C. Brown.

Furnham, A., & Bochner, S. (1982). Social difficulty in a foreign culture: An empirical analysis of culture shock. In S. Bochner (Ed.), *Cultures in contact* (pp. 161–198). New York: Pergamon.

Gudykunst, W. (1980). Toward a "model" of intercultural relationship development. Paper presented at the Speech Communication Association convention, New York.

Gudykunst, W., & Kim, Y. (1984a). *Communicating with strangers.* Reading, MA: Addison-Wesley.

Gudykunst, W., & Kim Y. (Eds.). (1984b). *Methods for intercultural communication research.* Beverly Hills: Sage.

Harris, P. R., & Moran, R. T. (1979, 1987). *Managing cultural differences.* Houston: Gulf.

Howell, W. S. (1979). Theoretical directions for intercultural communication. In M. Asante, E. Newmark, & C. Blake (Eds.), *Handbook of intercultural communication* (pp. 23–41). Beverly Hills: Sage.

Howell, W. S. (1982). *The empathic communicator.* Belmont, CA: Wadsworth.

Kim, Y. (1984). Searching for creative integration. In W. Gudykunst & Y. Kim (Eds.), *Methods for intercultural communication research* (pp. 13–30). Beverly Hills: Sage.

Korzenny, F., & Griffis Korzenny, B. A. (1980). Teaching intercultural communication in the 1980's: Philosophy, methods, and evaluation research. Paper presented at the Speech Communication Association convention, New York.

Kroeber, A., & Kluckhohn, C. (1972). *Culture: A critical review of concepts and definitions*. New York: Vintage Books.

Miller, G. R., & Steinberg, M. (1975). *Between people*. Chicago: Science Research Associates.

Oberg, K. (1958). *Culture shock and the problem of adjustment to new culture environments*. Washington, DC: Department of State, Foreign Service Institute.

Pennington, D. (1975). Temporality among black Americans: Implications for intercultural communication. Unpublished doctoral dissertation, University of Kansas, Lawrence.

Prosser, M. H. (Ed.). (1973). *USIA intercultural communication course: 1978 proceedings*. Washington, DC: United States Information Agency.

Prosser, M. H. (1978a). *The cultural dialogue: An introduction to intercultural communication*. New York: Harper & Row.

Prosser, M. H. (1978b). Intercultural communication theory and research: An overview of major constructs. In B. D. Ruben (Ed.), *Communication Yearbook 2* (pp. 335–344). New Brunswick, NJ: ICA-Transaction Books.

Rogers, E., & Chaffee, S. (1983). Communication as an academic discipline: A dialogue. *Journal of Communication, 33,* 18–30.

Ruben, B. (1985). Human communication and cross-cultural effectiveness. In L. A. Samovar & R. Porter (Eds.), *Intercultural communication: A reader* (pp. 338–346). Belmont, CA: Wadsworth.

Ruhly, S. (1976). *Orientations to intercultural communication*. Chicago: Scientific Research Associates Modcom Series.

Samovar, L. A., & Porter, R. (Eds.). (1976, 1985). *Intercultural communication: A reader*. Belmont, CA: Wadsworth.

Samovar, L. A., Porter, R. E., & Jain, N. C. (1981). *Understanding intercultural communication*. Belmont, CA: Wadsworth.

Sarbaugh, L. (1979). *Intercultural communication*. Rochelle Park, NJ: Hayden.

Sarbaugh, L., & Asuncion-Lande, N. (1983). Theory building in intercultural communication: Synthesizing the action caucus. In W. Gudykunst (Ed.), *Intercultural communication theory: Current perspectives* (pp. 45–62). Beverly Hills: Sage.

Schramm, W. (1983). The unique perspective of communication: A retrospective view. *Journal of Communication, 33,* 6–17.

Sitaram, K. S., & Cogdell, R. T. (1976). *Foundations of intercultural communication*. Columbus, OH: Charles E. Merrill.

Smith, A. G. (Ed.). (1966). *Communication and culture: Readings in the codes of human interaction*. New York: Holt, Rinehart & Winston.

Taft, R. (1977). Coping with unfamiliar cultures. In N. Warren (Ed.), *Studies in cross-cultural psychology* (Vol. 1, pp. 121–151). London: Academic Press.

PART THREE

Persuasive Functions of Communication

The study of persuasive communication is as old as recorded history and cuts across many academic disciplines. Formal writing and research on the subject continue to proliferate, partially because persuasion and social influence are so pervasive in our daily lives. Doctors, lawyers, merchants, teachers, salespeople, politicians, arbitrators, business executives, stockbrokers, and bartenders are only a few of the practitioners who must rely heavily on their ability to persuade. Indeed, anyone who has ever made a serious request of a reluctant benefactor or been asked to deliver a weighty personal favor understands the significance of being able to influence human behavior successfully. We are all persuaders and persuadees in everyday social intercourse. We all have our arsenals of defensive and offensive weaponry designed for persuasive warfare.

Because persuasion is common to virtually every communication context, Part Three is devoted entirely to it. Chapter 10, "Communication and Influence," is designed to help the reader understand fundamental persuasion processes and analyze the persuasive efforts of others. The authors provide a comprehensive conceptual framework explaining what persuasion is, how it works, and what outcomes it can produce. On the practical side, key variables associated with the persuader (source), the persuadee (receiver), and the message are discussed in detail to inform the reader how to become a more persuasive communicator. This review is unique with regard to its analysis of how persuasion can be used to create resistance to change, as well as change itself.

The other chapters in Part Three focus on two pivotal functions of persuasion at a societal and international level. Everett Rogers examines old and new approaches to the diffusion of technological innovation for purposes of economic development in Chapter 11, "Communication and Social Change." Earmarks of the new paradigm are emphases on: an equitable distribution of benefits, direct participation in decision making by the citizenry, and self-help in the developmental process. Persuasive strategies for achieving these outcomes in a society at large are addressed in considerable detail. The chapter closes with a discussion of how information flows between nations, creating (or reinforcing) as many global problems as it resolves, such as dependency cycles for weaker countries and media imperialism by the strong.

These topics provide an appropriate entree to Chapter 12, where Chaffee and Hernandez-Ramos probe principles of and perspectives on political communication. The perceptive reader will recognize in this highly informative article an international breadth that rises above partisan loyalties. Theory and research regarding the organization of national political and communication systems are reviewed from three angles. First, major types of mass media–government relationships in operation around the world are identified and explained. Second, the dominant model espoused by Western democracies such as the United States is critically examined. Third, for purposes of comparison, the authors explore the intellectual, philosophical, and political traditions of Latin America, as representative of many underdeveloped countries of the Third World regarding political communication. The breadth and depth of this chapter provide insights into the current world order, the cross-national impact of mass media on economic development, and the ongoing debate between modernization and dependency theorists.

10

Communication and Influence

Michael Burgoon
University of Arizona

Michael D. Miller
University of Hawaii

Michael Burgoon is Professor and Head of Communication and Professor of Family and Community Medicine at the University of Arizona. His main areas of interest are persuasion, public opinion, and mass media effects. Dr. Burgoon is actively engaged in consulting for a number of media organizations in the United States. For the past several years, he has conducted research on communication patterns including media use of Hispanics now living in the United States. He is an author of Mexican Americans and the Mass Media. *Recently, Dr. Burgoon's research interests have focused on compliance in health care contexts.*

Michael D. Miller is Associate Professor and Graduate Faculty Chair of Speech at the University of Hawaii. He received a Ph.D. degree in communication studies from the University of Florida. Dr. Miller's research and teaching interests include persuasion, interpersonal influence, and physician–patient relationships.

LEARNING OBJECTIVES

After studying this chapter you should be able to:

- Draw all the major distinctions between communication and persuasion.
- Define the three major components of attitudes.
- List the potential types of outcomes of persuasion.
- Discuss the major components of source credibility.

- Describe the three major factors in interpersonal attraction.
- Explain how similarity can enhance persuasion.
- Summarize the various types of power and their influence on persuasion.
- Discuss the demographic variables related to persuadability.
- Give examples of personality variables influencing persuadability.
- Summarize Toulmin's theory on three basic elements of an argument.
- List the major factors related to the persuasiveness of evidence.
- Identify characteristics of organization that aid persuasion.
- Explain two language factors that influence persuasiveness.
- Give two examples of sequential strategies of persuasion.
- Discuss factors affecting the selection and use of persuasion strategies in various situations.
- Review inoculation theory and the two mechanisms by which it induces resistance to persuasion.

People often talk about the power of certain communicators. They refer to dynamic speakers as powerful in promoting a charismatic image, to political orators as powerful in "moving the masses," and to successful negotiators as powerful in their control and use of information. When we speak of the power of the spoken word or of an individual speaker, we are simply recognizing what scholars and teachers have recognized for thousands of years: Communication that influences others is a powerful tool. Persuasive communication is a tool to be used for either good or bad ends, but a powerful tool it is. Although communication serves many other functions for people, as the preceding chapters have suggested, this chapter is going to take a more detailed look at one function of communication: effecting change in others and getting others to comply with your requests, demands, and arguments.

We will begin by attempting to sort out communication that is persuasive in nature from communication people use for other functions. That task should lead us to a useful definition of just what constitutes persuasion. But before we define persuasion, it is important to discuss some of our assumptions about the general process of communication, not just communication designed to influence others. Not surprisingly, there are numerous definitions of communication. People tend to agree that communication is a dynamic process, that this process is a transaction affecting both the producer of messages and those who hear the messages, and that communication is a personal, symbolic code of abstractions. Beyond these basic assumptions, communication scholars disagree on how to define communication.

COMMUNICATION AND INTENT

The primary disagreement centers on the notion of intent. When we talk about intent, we are really raising the basic question of whether or not a source has to *intentionally* perform a speech act designed to produce some *effect* before it can be called communication. Such a position has been called a source-oriented definition of communication. G. R. Miller and Steinberg (1975) argue strongly for such an intentional definition:

We have chosen to restrict our discussion of communication to intentional symbolic transactions: those in which at least one of the parties transmits a message to another with the intent of modifying the other's behavior (such as getting him to do or not do something or to believe or not believe something). By our definition, intent to communicate and intent to influence are synonymous. If there is no intent, there is no message.

Such a definition leads one to view all communication as persuasive. It also focuses attention on certain variables in the communication process, such as the content of a message, the way it is delivered, and its persuasive impact.

Another way of viewing communication, with some very different assumptions, has been called by some a receiver-oriented view of communication. Advocates of this perspective suggest that communication occurs any time a receiver responds to a stimulus. Cronkhite (1976), once a proponent of a strict receiver orientation, claimed that communication can be produced intentionally or unintentionally and responded to in an intentional or unintentional manner; a decade later, he recanted this position and now claims that such a definition of communication is simply too broad and encompassing (Cronkhite, 1986).

We also find such a broad definition of communication to be less than useful for our purposes, because such general definitions suggest that anything people do can be called communication, a view that makes it difficult to study communication in any systematic manner. M. Burgoon and Ruffner (1978) attempt to deal with the question of intent and the issue of a source versus receiver orientation to communication by analyzing the grid in Figure 10.1. They suggest that there is no problem in labeling Cell A communication; when one person intends to direct symbolic behavior toward another person and the target of the behavior perceives such an intent, most, if not all, would agree that this is communication. Burgoon and Ruffner, unlike others who have written about defining characteristics, also had no trouble dismissing Cell D as noncommunication behavior. When behaviors occur that have no symbolic meaning to either party in the transaction and are not seen as communication by them, they are of little concern to the communication scholar.

The other two cells in the grid present more of an analytical challenge. Cell B graphically illustrates a problem that many of us have had at one time or another. We had absolutely no intent to communicate our feelings or anything else to another person, yet he or she perceived us as attempting to communicate something. For example, if I pass you in the hall and do not make eye contact with you, you might perceive that I am trying to communicate my dislike for you when I simply did not see you and meant no such thing by my behavior. A receiver-oriented advocate would say that, in fact, communication did occur because you responded to some symbolic meaning in my behavior. A source-oriented advocate would say that no communication occurred because the source intended nothing by what he or she did.

Although it is not crucial for us to take either point of view in this discussion, we would suggest

	Source has an intent to communicate	Source does not have an intent to communicate
Receiver perceives an intent to communicate	A. Communication	B. Ascribed communication
Receiver does not perceive an intent to communicate	C. Communication attempt	D. Behavior

Figure 10.1 The question of intent.

that certainly there is *ascribed communication* in this situation. In addition, there is a *lack of understanding* of how behaviors affect others. We will argue in this chapter that successful persuaders must minimize those behaviors that unintentionally affect others in ways that make the would-be persuaders less successful. Successful persuaders will attempt to intentionally control all their behaviors so that unintentional acts do not reduce their ability to influence others.

Cell C also presents some difficulties. In this case, I was intentionally sending a message to you, but you did not perceive that I was. Shall we call such situations communication? It is probably more useful to say that a *communication attempt* was made, but there was a *failure to be understood*. Clearly, people interested in persuasion need to study this issue of intentionality and learn strategies for using communication for instrumental purposes—that is, to get what they want from others. Successful persuaders must be especially sensitive to using such instrumental communication to make sure that their intentions to communicate are understood by other people.

Intent and Persuasion

Whereas the general question of whether intent must be present for any symbolic activity to be considered communication is hotly contested,

there is more agreement about the specific role of intent in the process of persuasion (G. R. Miller, Burgoon, & Burgoon, 1984). Bettinghaus (1968) defines persuasion as a conscious attempt by one individual to change the behavior of another individual or group of individuals through the use of some message. Central to that definition are the notions of conscious intent, behavioral change, and message transmission. Brembeck and Howell (1952) view persuasion as the conscious attempt to modify thought and action by manipulating people's motives toward predetermined ends. Like Bettinghaus, these authors stress the importance of conscious intent in the persuasion process. We concur with these authors that the term *persuasion* should be reserved for those situations in which one party consciously intends to influence another. The grid in Figure 10.2 modifies the Burgoon-Ruffner approach, depicting only those situations in which people perceive or do not perceive another's attempt to influence them via symbolic messages.

The communication grid in Figure 10.1 did not require that either party in the transaction agree on the *nature* of the intent to communicate. The persuasion grid requires that there be some agreement between source and receiver on the general nature of the intent behind the communication. Cell A is obviously persuasion commu-

	Source has an intent to persuade	Source does not have an intent to persuade
Receiver perceives an intent to persuade	A. Persuasion (possible forewarning)	B. Not persuasion (possible conformity)
Receiver does not perceive an intent to persuade	C. Persuasion (possible deception)	D. Ruled out as persuasion

Figure 10.2 Intent and persuasion.

nication, because the source has every intention to influence the receiver, and the receiver understands that he or she is the target of a persuader's attempt. Billboards shout out product slogans, broadcast media try to sell us all kinds of goods and services, and a trip to the local shopping mall provides examples of communication transactions where people would agree that persuasion is being attempted.

Although in many of our communication transactions those involved are keenly aware of the fact that an attempt to influence is being made, such knowledge can present problems for the potential persuader. Research has uncovered something called the forewarning effect: Some people become more resistant to influence attempts when they are aware that a source is attempting to influence them. Later in this chapter, we will deal with inducing and overcoming such resistance to persuasion, but it should be noted here that the potential for a boomerang effect exists when receivers become aware that a communicator is attempting to manipulate them. In some cases, people will actually change their attitudes in the direction opposite to that advocated by a speaker; in other cases, persuaders will be seen as more credible and honest when they openly admit that an influence attempt is the major purpose of their communication. If such a credibility change occurs as the result of such open expression of intent, forewarned people may actually be more persuadable.

In Cell B the source has absolutely no intent to influence receivers but, in fact, they are persuaded by what the source says or does. Though some might argue that we ought to be interested in any communication transaction in which receivers are influenced, for the purposes of this analysis, we reject such arguments. As we have said, if the source does not have the *intent* to influence, we will not consider such situations legitimate persuasion. For example, an esteemed professor might find that students are imitating his or her speech mannerisms, political views, or even dress. We acknowledge that such changes are interesting to some social scientists, but in the study of persuasion we deny their import. When a receiver or group of people conform to the attitudes and/or behaviors of someone who had no intent to produce such conformity, including such behaviors under the general rubric of persuasion makes little sense. We therefore exclude mere pressures toward conformity from our discussion. We prefer to deal with those situations where the source clearly has an intent to influence or persuade.

The situations represented by Cell C clearly fit our view of the process of persuasion. Even though a receiver may not precisely know that a source intends to influence, we are willing to grant that many situations require concealing that intent from receivers. As we said earlier, forewarning of an intent to influence can produce the opposite of the desired effect. If, in fact, a clear intention to influence is likely to prompt a defensive response, the communicator may be wise to hide this intention.

Concerning Cell C, it is often the case that what has been called "deception" may be a shrewd strategy for a persuader to use. Sometimes a source desires to influence audience members but is best served by making them think the true purpose of the communication transaction is to inform or educate. Some research has suggested that people are more likely to be influenced by "overheard conversations," in which they are supposedly not the targets of persuasion (Walster & Festinger, 1962). If people hear things they think were not meant for their ears, they may be less defensive and may be changed by the force of arguments they perceive to be aimed at others or to be lacking the intent to persuade.

We feel obligated to offer a caveat about the use of deception in persuasive communication. Too many people feel that all persuasion attempts mandate the use of deception. They have internalized the notion that, in all cases, they are better served by keeping the target audience unaware of their intent to influence. Communication scholars have pointed out the fallacy of such assumptions, but we think it wise to review some of the pitfalls of relying exclusively on deception as part of one's persuasion repertoire (Ekman & Friesen, 1974; Knapp & Comadena, 1979).

First, as we have already said, speakers can *increase* their credibility in some situations just by admitting that they want to influence their listeners. They are seen as honest and straightforward. Second, any communicator who is caught deceiving an audience runs a great risk of being derogated when his or her intent is made apparent. In fact, when a communicator relies on deceptive practices to persuade, a later speaker may use this information to discredit the deceiver and as a means of converting the audience to his or her way of thinking. Although some people do not like to be influenced, probably even more resent being deceived. Finally, the notion that people prefer to resist change for the sake of resisting change is unfounded. Some people enjoy being influenced by good arguments (Roberts, 1924). Thus, rather than devising elaborate schemes for keeping target audiences "in the dark" about just why you are persuading them, setting a tone that the most rational course of action *is to be influenced* might pay off. We are arguing that deception, like all strategies of persuasion, has its costs and benefits, and that the wise persuader will carefully consider what will work best in each situation rather than blindly applying one single strategy to all communication transactions.

It should come as no surprise that we are willing to rule out Cell D as important to this discussion of persuasion. When there is no attempt to influence, and target audiences correctly perceive that the communicator has no intent to exert influence, obviously something other than persuasion is going on.

In summary, although there may be no need to invoke a strict source-oriented perspective in our view of the general nature of communication, we opt for a more constricted definition of those behaviors we are willing to label persuasive communication. In fact, we accept an exclusively source-determined position on persuasion. We want to examine situations in which source and receiver are aware that they are involved in a persuasion attempt as well as those in which, for whatever reason, the source has an intent to persuade that is unrecognized by the target. Our argument that mere conformity behaviors are not to be considered persuasion should make it clear that the *intent* of the source supersedes any outcome measure (that is, whether change actually occurred or not). Given this limited view of persuasion, the remainder of the chapter is devoted to those situations in which a person wishes to influence others.

We now turn our attention to making you aware of variables in the process of communication that are likely to enhance or inhibit attempts at persuasion. Moreover, we shall focus on message variables and the development of overall message strategies for those of you who have decided that your goal is to become a more skilled persuader.

INFLUENCE ATTEMPTS

After reading the first part of this chapter, if you believe that persuasion is almost synonymous with changes in overt behavior and/or attitude, we have not been successful influence agents. Many treatises on persuasion do rely on an overt expression of attitude or behavior change as an index of influence. However, we want to make a crucial distinction between the way we will use the term *influence attempt* in this chapter and the way it is often used by others. The notion of influence does not necessarily imply modifying or reversing an overt, nonverbal behavior, nor does it always indicate changing the direction or relative attractiveness of an attitude statement.

If a person was moderately in favor of moving to the Southwest, and, after hearing us speak about the merits of such a move, left the communication transaction even more in favor of a move, we would view the influence attempt as successful. We obviously have not changed the direction (valence) of the attitude, nor did we even attempt to do so, but we did achieve what we set out to do in our influence attempt:

strengthen an already existing positive attitude. Moreover, if we can make people more resistant to counterpropaganda (messages seeking to promote changes in their attitudes at a later time), then we will have been successful in our influence attempt. Inducing resistance to future persuasion is often an important goal of persuasion that is neglected in our rather myopic concern with only the effects of attempts to change people.

In order to clearly articulate how communication can operate to influence others, we will now examine the components of influence attempts. Figure 10.3 graphically displays the process of

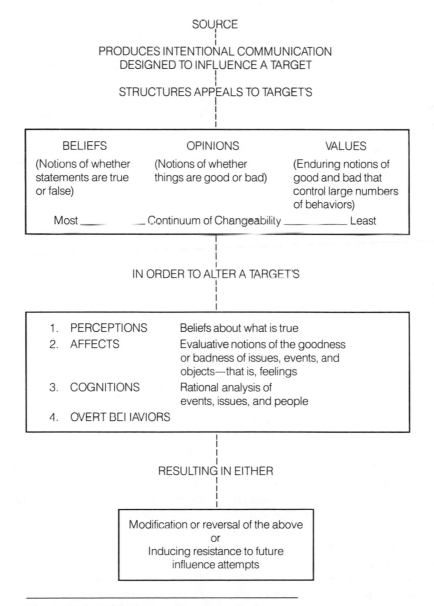

SOURCE

PRODUCES INTENTIONAL COMMUNICATION
DESIGNED TO INFLUENCE A TARGET

STRUCTURES APPEALS TO TARGET'S

BELIEFS	OPINIONS	VALUES
(Notions of whether statements are true or false)	(Notions of whether things are good or bad)	(Enduring notions of good and bad that control large numbers of behaviors)

Most _____ _____ Continuum of Changeability _____ _____ Least

IN ORDER TO ALTER A TARGET'S

1. PERCEPTIONS   Beliefs about what is true
2. AFFECTS   Evaluative notions of the goodness or badness of issues, events, and objects—that is, feelings
3. COGNITIONS   Rational analysis of events, issues, and people
4. OVERT BEHAVIORS

RESULTING IN EITHER

Modification or reversal of the above
or
Inducing resistance to future
influence attempts

Figure 10.3 Model of persuasive communication.

persuasion as we view it. It suggests a very source-oriented view of influence attempts, which recognizes that we are dealing with appeals aimed at different psychological processes. Further, this expanded view of persuasion recognizes that multiple outcomes define the success or failure of any given attempt. This graphic display of the process of persuasion lays the foundation for the remainder of our discussion.

Attitudes

This model suggests there are at least three different components of attitudes that merit attention.

Belief Systems and Opinion Statements

First, every individual has a system of beliefs that represents his or her view of reality. Belief systems consist of a series of statements to which any target can respond on the basis of his or her notion of truth or falsity. The statement that poverty exists in the Third World is a statement of belief. A person believes that statement is either true or false.

Accepting a statement into our belief system says nothing about our evaluation of that belief. We can either evaluate poverty to be a serious problem needing the attention of the developed world, or we can believe that even though poverty exists, it is not a bad thing. When we make evaluative statements about the goodness or badness of some event, issue, or remark, we have moved to the second level of our model: opinion statements. Opinion statements are merely our evaluative reactions—our own statements about what is good or bad, desirable or undesirable.

Communicators seeking to persuade often make the mistake of attempting to alter opinions or evaluative responses when the belief system is not present to support such altered evaluative responses. For example, some people living in the United States may have had no direct experience with poverty in the Third World and therefore may have no basis for even believing that such a situation exists. It would be a mistake to begin by arguing with them that poverty is awful in some nations and that the United States ought to do more about this problem if they are unconvinced that widespread poverty exists. We would be better off to first alter their belief system by providing information to clearly demonstrate the existence of widespread poverty and attack their underlying false beliefs, then proceed to arguments in an attempt to alter their opinions. We may not be able to convince such people of the wisdom of certain policy options designed to improve the lot of people around the world, but we would certainly increase the probability of a successful modification of opinions if the beliefs about reality were altered first.

Values Values, the third component of our model, represent more enduring notions of goodness and badness that guide our behavior in a variety of contexts. They have been inculcated over a number of years and are usually resistant to change attempts. For example, our religious values are probably very resistant to change and guide many of our actions in dealing with other people. Since our values control so many of our opinions and behaviors, a change in one value might dictate a change in a large number of beliefs, opinions, and behaviors. Although values resist most change attempts, when we are successful in changing such enduring traits we have probably produced a very permanent change in people. If someone has had an enduring faith in capitalism as a guiding force in the organizing of governments and goes through a value change in which he or she endorses socialism or communism, one can expect a very committed convert. We would also expect many other changes in behaviors, beliefs, and opinions to accompany such a conversion in a major value system.

Concerning susceptibility to change, beliefs are probably the cognitive component most easily changed. We can often change people's beliefs by just providing them with additional information about the nature of things. Changing their opinions or evaluative responses to events, issues, and people is more difficult. Just providing information may or may not change the way they feel about things. However, since opinions usually control more limited ranges of behaviors than do more enduring values, opinions are usually more susceptible to influence attempts than are values. On the other hand, if we do succeed in changing people's more enduring value systems, we have probably achieved a change that will last a long time and control many other of their opinions and behaviors.

Other Areas of Change

The next stage in our model identifies other possible alterations in receivers that persuasion produces. When we attack belief systems, we can alter *perceptions* about what is true and false in the world. We also might be satisfied with changing people's feelings toward our positions. When we appeal to *affect,* we rely on emotional responses toward events, issues, and people (Roberts, 1924). At other times, we appeal to the more rational side of people and we change their *cognitions,* or the way they analyze problems. Finally, we may be less interested in perceptions, affect, or cognition and may be merely concerned with whether we can obtain overt behavioral compliance with our requests. In other words, we care about what people do, not what they think or how they feel. Any of the above can be considered successful outcomes of a given persuasion attempt. Some persuasion attempts are aimed at changing just one component; others may attempt multiple changes in people, as in affect *and* behavior. Again, success can be defined only in relation to the original intent of the persuasion transactions.

Finally, two end results are possible. As the model depicts, we are willing to let persuasion success be defined as *either* the modification or reversal of previously held opinions, beliefs, and values or changes in overt behaviors, *or* the induction of resistance to future persuasion attempts.

The Three Phases of Influence

All of this taken together indicates that the influence process has three distinct phases: *discontinuance, conversion,* and *deterrence.* Each phase represents very different goals for a persuader, and each mandates a different communication strategy.

Discontinuance In this phase, a persuader is usually dealing with target audiences who are hostile toward the position being advocated. The persuader is advocating "Y," and the audience believes "X" or at least "Not Y." The communication strategy most useful is one of hostility reduction. Possible goals are reducing overt opposition (getting people to at least listen to your position); creating doubts about the correctness of the target's present beliefs, opinions, and values; or creating ambivalence about the desirability of specific outcomes in the minds of target receivers. Often, when advertisers introduce a new product, they face the task of convincing people that they should give up their present products and try something new. At least at the initial stages of such a campaign, the potential persuader might be satisfied if the message is attended to and people begin to question the wisdom of their present buying behavior.

Conversion One strategy of this second phase in the influence process is to convert disbelievers, which requires modifying or reversing previously held attitudes or behaviors. Another strategy is to educate those who have no attitudes on the issue—the uninformed. This requires the shaping of an attitude or behavior rather than reversing some already established attitude or behavior. A third strategy relates to the apathetic. Such people really have no initial interest in the issue of concern to the persuader. The goal of the persuader in this case is to make the issue relevant to the audience with the hope that they will then adopt the position or behaviors being advocated. Obviously, converting disbelievers, informing the uninformed, and motivating the apathetic require very different message strategies. Each of these tasks must be dealt with differently to ensure that the end result is acceptance of the stance being taken by the speaker.

Deterrence   This final phase is the opposite of the discontinuance phase, because the persuader is talking with people who already hold the attitudes or are presently behaving in ways that are consistent with his or her goals. The objective is to deter or discourage any change. The communication strategy most appropriate is reinforcing and intensifying previously held attitudes and/or behaviors (L. K. Miller, 1980). This might take the form of getting target audiences to view something more favorably or to increase their behavioral commitment to an issue. Deterrence would be used by a politician to persuade people to change their commitment from private support to public commitment by actively working as a volunteer. Many campaigns also attempt to increase commitment by asking those who have already given time and money to the candidate to give even more. All of this is done to prevent attitudinal and behavioral reversals so that the persuader can be confident that the discontinuance strategies of other persuaders will be ineffective with people who are currently supportive.

Many long-term persuasion campaigns require the balancing of strategies to deal with different audience subsets who are at different points of commitment at any given time. For example, product advertising requires reinforcing those people who are currently buying the product while at the same time trying to convince others to switch or at least consider switching to it. At times political and advertising campaigns fail because they direct their attention solely to conversion and ignore important strategies designed to keep the already converted in the fold.

We have argued that the process of persuasion can result in many different outcomes, all of which can be called successful depending on the goals of the individuals engaged in such commu-

nication. We think such a view allows the potential persuader to better analyze any given situation and more clearly tailor his or her strategies to a target audience. Now we will turn to specific variables in the persuasion process that affect the potential outcomes. We will begin by examining characteristics of both the source and receiver that either inhibit or enhance persuasion success.

PEOPLE VARIABLES IN THE PERSUASION PROCESS

The Source

Some people just seem to be better at persuading than others. We listen to what they have to say and often end up acting or thinking in ways consistent with their advocated positions. When we can find no other explanation for their persuasion successes, we tend to invent labels to describe such people. For example, we say that certain television evangelists are "charismatic" because they raise enormous amounts of money and convert the masses to a way of thinking or behaving. Unfortunately, such a label is of minimal use to the student of persuasion, for it has little to say about what any source does in order to be successful. We simply have no general guidelines about what it takes to be a charismatic leader. Communication research, however, provides some suggestions on how to enhance persuasion abilities by centering on specific variables. In this section we will deal with source credibility as an important determinant of the success or failure of persuasion messages and specifically focus on attraction between source and receiver, source-receiver similarity, power, and persuasion outcomes.

Source Credibility   For thousands of years, scholars have known that we make judgments about the effectiveness of speakers that affect whether they influence us or not (Anderson & Clevenger, 1972; McCroskey & Young, 1981). Aristotle said that *ethos,* or what we call credibility, is one of the most potent, if not *the* most potent, means of persuasion. More-contemporary communication research evidence supports this notion that source credibility may be the single best predictor of persuasion success (Lashbrook, 1971). An extremely important point to anyone interested in becoming more persuasive is that no communicator possesses an inherent trait called credibility. Source credibility, in fact, is conferred by the receiver. This means that unless a receiver perceives credibility exists, it does not. Just as credibility is given by the audience, it can be taken away by the audience. Although many factors, such as age, sex, and race, affect the way audiences perceive speakers, evidence is clear that communicators can exert control over the way they will be perceived. The wise persuader will be aware of the many techniques available to manipulate perceptions of this important source variable.

Communication researchers (McCroskey, Holridge, & Toomb, 1974; McCroskey, Jensen, & Todd, 1972; McCroskey, Jensen, Todd, & Toomb, 1972; McCroskey, Jensen, & Valencia, 1973) have systematically analyzed what constitutes a credible speaker. They found that people make at least five *independent* decisions about a source, all of which contribute to their definition of source credibility. These dimensions of source credibility are:

- *Competence,* or the source's knowledge of the subject.
- *Character,* or the extent to which the source can be trusted to speak honestly.
- *Composure,* the ability to remain calm and collected, especially in stress-producing situations.
- *Sociability,* the basic likableness of the communicator.
- *Extroversion,* a judgment of whether the source is outgoing or timid in communication transactions.

These decisions by receivers are said to be independent in that making a positive judgment on one dimension does not predict judgments on other dimensions. We may think a communicator is extremely competent and sociable but not believe he or she is honest or of high character.

The dimension of competence is obviously crucial in many persuasion situations. If you are not perceived to be competent or to at least have an adequate level of knowledge on the topic being discussed, your trustworthiness or likability may make little difference to the receiver. Overall, the speaker who is perceived to be competent has a higher probability of being effective in a variety of influence attempts.

An important question for the student of persuasion is just what a communicator can do to increase the audience's perception of his or her competence on a given issue. First, it is not uncommon in many public speaking situations for speakers to be introduced by another individual. Often, such introductions enhance the perceived competence of the upcoming speaker by referring to titles, accomplishments, and previous experience (Ostermeier, 1967). Speakers themselves can also manipulate perceived competence by referring to their experience with the topic or by associating themselves with other competent people, by carefully preparing the message, or by selecting good evidence to support their claims (McCroskey, 1969). In most persuasion situations, it is probably impossible to be perceived as "too competent." In other words, an ideal source would rank very high on this dimension. Moreover, it would be expected that to the extent you are successful in increasing your perceived competence, you will be more effective in influencing others.

When people consider a source to be low in character or trustworthiness, they are less likely to even listen to, let alone be influenced by the content of, the message. In fact, many people will actively avoid communicating with someone who does not meet their personal standards of character. Such judgments are obviously highly personal in nature but may be based on direct experience with the source or perhaps hearsay evidence provided by others. There is no simple answer to the question of how you go about building perceptions of character in target audiences. Obviously, any prior history that brings your integrity into question may hinder future persuasion attempts. Moreover, people who are known for continually shifting their positions over time will often be seen as less trustworthy than those who appear more consistent in their attitudes and behaviors. As mentioned earlier in this chapter, a source caught attempting to deceive an audience, even in the case of merely hiding the intent to persuade, may be seen as a less than trustworthy communicator. Obviously, the ideal source would do everything possible to be seen as honest and of good character. Once the character dimension is questioned, rebuilding trust and rapport with receivers is extremely difficult.

Research by G. R. Miller and Hewgill (1964), among others, indicates that a communicator who appears nervous and lacks composure will be seen as less credible and less able to persuade others. Many people we call "good public speakers" are not more competent or of higher character but merely more at ease when speaking to an audience—no matter how large or small. To increase your perceived composure, an obvious first step is to practice until you become a more effective speaker (Addington, 1971; Apple, Streeter, & Krauss, 1974; Beebe, 1974; Delia, 1972; Kleinke, 1975; Mehrabian, 1969; N. Miller, Maruyama, Beaber, & Valone, 1976; Pearce & Brommel, 1972; Widgery, 1974). In many cultures, showing too much emotion, either through verbal choices or nonverbal behaviors, is seen as inappropriate in many communication contexts. Obviously, some communication contexts call for more intense displays of emotion, but clearly, the speaker who is seen as being in control of his or her emotions is going to be the most able to influence others (Burgoon & Saine, 1978; Schneider, Hastorf, & Ellsworth, 1979).

Communicators who project likableness to their audiences are more effective in a variety of situations. We tend to like those people who indicate they like and respect us, and thus we spend more time communicating with such people. Ob-viously, as we spend more time communicating with such people, they become a more influential part of our lives. A person who approaches others in a friendly, even cheerful manner is much more likely to gain their attention and keep their interest in the topic of discussion than someone who makes no attempt to show concern for and liking of them.

Finally, the communicator who is not timid, but rather outgoing and energetic in communication situations, is going to be viewed as extroverted. We like extroverts to a degree, but people can be so outgoing that they completely dominate others and make receivers feel like a negligible part of the communication transaction. A balance must be struck between appearing to be too extroverted, and therefore too dominant, and being too introverted, and therefore boring (Burgoon, 1976).

Taken together, all five of these dimensions represent the judgments we make about other communicators. It is true that we often make snap judgments about people on each of these dimensions very early in our relationships. Therefore, it is important for the persuasive communicator to understand that his or her actions will influence such perceptions by others and to carefully tailor strategies to ensure that he or she is viewed positively along these evaluative dimensions of source credibility.

Attraction Personal attraction is similar to credibility, but there are enough differences to warrant a brief discussion of the bases on which people become attracted to others. Attraction is an important variable, for research has clearly demonstrated that we spend more time communicating with people we are attracted to and become similar to them in beliefs, opinions, values, and behaviors (McCroskey & McCain, 1974). Also, the more time we spend with others, the more we become attracted to them. So a cycle develops between attraction and influence that merits our attention.

Apparently, at least three different factors determine our attraction to other people. The first is a *social* factor, which is very similar to the sociability dimension of credibility. We are attracted to people whom we feel could be our friends and thus are more likely to be influenced by them. A second dimension is *physical* attraction. Whether we think that this is the way things should be or not, it is often the case that physically attractive people are often more successful persuaders in a variety of influence attempts. The final factor is *task* attraction. We often choose to interact with people because we respect their ability to get the job done. That respect gives such people a certain amount of influence over our attitudes and behaviors.

Similarity The question of whether opposites attract or whether like attracts like has been considered throughout the ages. A question of most concern to us is whether people who possess attributes similar to those of their target audiences will be more or less effective than communicators who are clearly different from the people they are attempting to persuade. Like credibility, similarity does not exist unless people involved in the transaction perceive it to exist. Attributes that may lead to perceived similarity include demographic characteristics such as age, education, sex, cultural or ethnic identity, and socioeconomic status. Also included may be beliefs, opinions, and values (Alpert & Anderson, 1973; McCroskey, Richmond, & Daly, 1975).

The similarity-dissimilarity relationship between source and receiver has an important impact on persuasion. When we have a choice about who we will communicate with, we tend to choose someone like ourselves (Rogers & Bhowmik, 1970). As might be expected, a certain amount of source-receiver similarity leads to more effective, satisfying communication in that people who share common interests have more to communicate about.

However, total similarity is probably not the optimum state when the purpose of the communication transaction is to influence others. Total similarity produces a static state, since people in total agreement have little to talk about on any

topic. There seems to be an optimum level of dissimilarity. We often desire to get information on a variety of topics from a communicator who is slightly dissimilar from us and who, we hope, is more competent on the subject of discussion than we are.

Of course, it cannot hurt if we perceive a source to be even more trustworthy than we see ourselves. We tend to be influenced most by people we can look up to on certain attributes, whose competence and expertise we respect. In some cultures, people who are dissimilar in age (older) are sought for advice because they are different and have lived longer, and therefore know more than we do. Such people are often very influential within their cultures. Obviously, the optimum level of dissimilarity varies from situation to situation, but it is fair to say that some identifiable differences between source and receiver will lead to more success in influence attempts.

If source and receiver are too dissimilar, the would-be persuader might have to compensate for those differences in order to be optimally influential. One way to compensate is to simply communicate more with the dissimilar receiver, which can increase attraction and demonstrate more similarities than had previously been perceived. Another way to compensate for differences is to develop empathy for the receiver, learn to take the perspective of the receiver, and tailor messages to better suit that target person. A skilled communicator will work toward reducing dissimilarity when it inhibits his or her ability to influence others, while at the same time pointing out, when appropriate, differences in knowledge or competence favoring him or her so that the target audience will adopt the advocated position or suggested behavior.

Power Too little attention has been paid to the power that certain people hold over others (French & Raven, 1968). With this power comes the ability to control behaviors, gain compliance, and often to change beliefs, opinions, and values. Some power is real (for example, the man with a gun at your head), and some is only perceived by receivers but becomes real because they believe it to be so. In any given influence situation, receivers have certain unique physical, psychological, and social needs. A communicator's ability to satisfy those needs forms the motive bases from which power may operate in influence attempts (Madson, 1974). Motive bases are the reasons we have for allowing people to exert control over us. Although the bases of power are contingent on the needs of the target audience in any given situation, five general types of power have been identified that tend to operate in compliance-gaining situations.

The power of a source to provide positive reinforcement is called *reward power*. For reward power to be effective in gaining compliance, receivers have to both perceive that the rewards a source can give are worthwhile and believe that the source has the ability to deliver those rewards. Sources with great ability to provide rewards, monetary or social, often have great power to influence others. To the extent that sources can continue to deliver such rewards, they will probably continue to have power over other individuals. When the targets' perceptions of the value of the rewards or their belief that people exercising reward power will continue to reward them diminish, this base of power becomes ineffective in influencing behavior.

Coercive power is the mirror image of reward power. It is the ability of sources to punish people if they do not comply with requests. Since most people know that they can use either reward or coercive power in many situations, the question becomes which is more effective. People can react very negatively to coercive power, resulting in significantly lower levels of attraction and credibility for a communicator who relies on it. Moreover, people will comply only when they know they are being watched by the person who can dole out punishment. Coercive power can often be used to get people to *stop* doing things you do not want them to do, but it is not very effective as a means of getting people to continue to behave as you desire in the long run.

We are using *referent power* when we ask people to do something "for me." In this case, we are asking the receiver to identify with the source and do things to please him or her (Bandura, 1976). Referent power works well when the source is well liked or highly respected. Most of us will do things for our friends and others we respect. However, a communicator can overuse this base of power and find, at some point, that he or she has simply asked for too much on the basis of referent power alone. The well will some day run dry. If the communicator is wise, he or she will reciprocate on occasion and do things for the receiver. This will replenish the reservoir of goodwill and rebuild the base of referent power for future influence attempts.

Expert power is similar to the dimension of competence discussed in the section on source credibility. People who have superior knowledge tend to have the power to influence. This is not only because they can provide us with data and evidence that will change our opinions, but because their reputation as an expert precedes them and gives them a great ability to influence.

Legitimate power comes from the belief that the source has the right to influence or control behaviors. People holding certain positions in organizations, institutions, and societies may be accorded the right to prescribe other people's behavior. A judge has the right to sentence a prisoner, a teacher the right to assign homework, and a boss the right to supervise employees. All these examples of power come not from personal characteristics of the source, but from the position he or she holds. Because we respect specific positions and traditions, we would comply with any person who held that particular position. That is a formidable source of power in most cultures.

There are three conditions that will maximize the use of power in influence attempts. First is *perceived control,* or the receiver's decision as to whether the source can actually apply negative or positive reinforcement. If a source is not perceived to be a person who could actually reward or punish, then he or she will have little power to control behaviors or influence others.

The second decision centers on whether the receiver believes the source to have *perceived concern*. Many times, people make requests of others that they really do not expect to be fulfilled; in fact, they do not care whether receivers comply. Often, sources are just behaving in a way prescribed to them by others. For example, a manager may be forced to communicate with employees about specific company policies while having no personal interest in whether subordinates comply with the policies. When such a state of affairs is perceived by target audiences, little compliance is gained.

Finally, there is the question of *perceived scrutiny*. The receiver must make a decision as to whether the communicator will even know whether compliance was obtained or not. If the base of power is coercive, it is clear that people will not comply if they think the source will not even know whether they did what they were told. Many managers spend a great deal of their time scrutinizing employees to make sure they do comply with requests. They have to do this because they have given no other reasons for the employees to work hard, or do well, other than they will be punished if they do not and paid if they do. Without constant scrutiny in such situations, power to control behaviors is limited, because no attempts have been made to create more positive attitudes about work and about management. What all this may say is that the ability to give reasons to others to get their compliance may be the most important power base of all.

The Receiver

Having discussed at some length the source variables that enhance or inhibit persuasion, we should now briefly review some receiver variables that have received research attention. Skilled persuaders will understand that an accurate analysis of the audience will allow them to better adapt to given communication situations and that the following are just generalizations which may or may not be useful in any given situation. We will begin by examining some demographic variables in receivers and then briefly review some research on the relationship between selected personality variables and persuadability.

Demographic Analysis   Some research indicates that as age increases, a person's susceptibility to persuasion decreases (Janis & Rife, 1959; Marple, 1933). It may be that the older one gets, the more pragmatic and cautious one becomes. There is also considerable evidence that the sex of the receiver is an important predictor of persuadability. Specifically, females have been found to be more persuadable, or to put it another way, males are more resistant to change (Apsler & Sears, 1968; Cronkhite, 1969; Dean, Austin, & Watts, 1971; Hovland, Janis, & Kelley, 1953; Rosenfeld & Christie, 1974; Stone, 1969). One explanation advanced for this finding is that in many cultures, males are taught to be aggressive and dominant, whereas females are taught to be passive and submissive to others (M. Burgoon & Ruffner, 1978). Finally, some attempts have been made to uncover the relationships between general intelligence and persuadability. The fairest conclusion from that research would be that intelligence alone is not a very good predictor of susceptibility to influence. The intelligence of receivers simply does not predict how they will respond to a given message or allow generalizations across influence attempts.

Personality Analysis   Demographic analysis of an audience may be useful to a source in many situations, but it is also useful to view receivers as unique individuals possessing a personality that will affect their response to influence attempts. Although a lot of research has been done in the area of personality, we will discuss three personality traits that seem to be related to susceptibility to influence in predictable ways: dogmatism, self-esteem, and anxiety (Apsler & Sears, 1968; Cronkhite, 1969; Dean, Austin, & Watts, 1971; Hovland, Janis, & Kelley, 1953; Rosenfeld & Christie, 1974; Stone, 1969).

Dogmatism has been defined as a closed system of beliefs or disbeliefs about reality (Cronkhite & Goetz, 1971; Hunter, Levine, & Sayers, 1976). Dogmatic people are authoritarian, narrow, opinionated, and closed-minded. They can be unbending, because they always believe they are right and are intolerant of others they believe to be wrong. Therefore, in many cases, dogmatic individuals are very difficult to persuade (Cronkhite & Goetz, 1971; Kaminski, McDermott, & Boster, 1977). However, in at least one case dogmatics are easier to persuade than less authoritarian people: when the source is in a position of power and authority. Dogmatics will bow to people in positions of authority. The power of the position is more important to highly dogmatic people than the content of the message (Cronkhite & Goetz, 1971).

Each individual has a concept of self, formed partially from his or her own perceptions and partially by feedback from others. People with low *self-esteem* are conformists by nature; they have limited confidence in their own opinions and thus are easily persuaded by the communication of others (Gelfand, 1962; Gollob & Dittes, 1965; Lehmann, 1970). Individuals with high self-esteem have greater confidence in their own opinions and find it easier to challenge the opinions of would-be persuaders (Cox & Bauer, 1964; Gelfand, 1962; Gollob & Dittes, 1965). This makes them less susceptible, in general, to influence attempts.

Finally, *anxiety* in receivers is also a predictor of reactions to influence attempts. People who are chronically anxious tend to avoid messages that will produce more anxiety (Cialdini, Petty, & Cacioppo, 1981; Harris & Jellison, 1971; Janis & Feshback, 1953; McGuire, 1968, 1969; Millman, 1965; Niles, 1964). They actively block out messages that might frighten or worry them. Therefore, any persuasion message that attempts to frighten people into taking certain actions will most likely be ignored by chronically anxious people. On the other hand, people who are chronically low in anxiety are actually stimulated by fear appeals. Such people pay more attention to the communicator and, therefore, become more susceptible to social influence. The best advice to a communicator is to beware of attempting to use scare tactics when the audience is already frightened about the issue (Janis & Feshback, 1953; Leventhal, 1970; McGuire, 1968, 1969; Millman, 1965; Niles, 1964). Messages about such topics as health, war, and family should not attempt to scare those people who are already most worried about the future, for they will just ignore the speaker in many cases.

MESSAGE VARIABLES IN THE PERSUASION PROCESS

The Structure of Persuasive Messages

This section will consider the dynamics of information influence, how messages are selected, structured, and optimally utilized in the process of influencing others. Toulmin (1959) has suggested that all persuasive arguments contain three components: (1) a claim, (2) a warrant, and (3) data. A *claim* is any statement, either implicit or explicit, that the persuader wants an audience to accept. There are three types of claims that encompass the different alterations in receivers discussed earlier. A *policy claim* calls for a specific course of action (designed to produce changes in overt behavior). A *fact claim* asserts the existence or nonexistence, truth or falsity of some state of affairs (designed to modify perceptions or cognitions). A *value claim* addresses the evaluation of a concept or action (intended to modify affect). Although the three types of claims differ in their desired outcomes, any claim, regardless of type, must be supported with both a warrant and data.

A *warrant* is a general belief or attitude stated in support of a claim. In other words, a warrant is a general reason the claim should be accepted by the audience. To be effective, the warrant must be implicitly accepted by the audience. It is highly unlikely that an audience will accept a claim if the general justification for the claim has already been rejected.

The third component of a persuasive argument is *data*. Data are specific facts or beliefs stated in support of a claim and are linked to the claim via the warrant. In one sense, the components of an argument (claim, warrant, and data) can be viewed as the three components of a syllogism. The warrant is the major premise, a datum is the minor premise, and the claim is the proposition or conclusion. Consider this example:

1. Increasing crop yields is desirable (major premise or warrant).

2. Using Brand X fertilizer increases yields (minor premise or data).

3. Thus you should use Brand X fertilizer (conclusion or claim).

Three types of data can be used in persuasive arguments. *First-order data* are beliefs or facts the persuader and an audience hold in common. Since these data are already accepted as valid by the audience, the crucial aspect in supporting a claim with first-order data is the advocate's ability to find a warrant compelling enough to lead the audience to accept the claim, given the assumed validity of the data. *Second-order data* are beliefs advanced by the persuader but not previously held by the audience. The process of using second-order data is often called source assertion, since the audience is being asked to accept the validity of the data entirely on the word of the source. Thus to use second-order data successfully, the advocate must not only find a compelling warrant, but must also be seen as credible enough for the audience to accept his or her assertions without recourse to other information. *Third-order data* is often called evidence. Evidence is any belief or information that comes from a party outside the immediate communication transaction. For example, citing government statistics in support of a claim is using evidence.

Constructing Messages to Influence Others

Evidence As indicated earlier in this chapter, the mere presentation of objective information about a topic will often result in a change in the beliefs of one's audience (Cathcart, 1953; McCroskey, 1972; Reynolds & Burgoon, 1983). Unfortunately for the persuader, these changes in belief do not always occur, and even when belief changes are evident, attitude change or changes in overt behavior do not always follow. Thus including evidence in a persuasion message does not guarantee success. Indeed, early reviews of the role of evidence in persuasion effectiveness concluded that it has little systematic influence. However, in many situations the judicious use of evidence can enhance the persuasive impact of the communicator (McCroskey, 1969, 1972; McCroskey & Mehrley, 1969).

To be effective, evidence must be new to the audience (Anatol & Mandel, 1972; McCroskey, 1972). If the audience is already aware of the information, the evidence has probably been previously accepted or rejected and is unlikely to have further impact on the audience's attitudes or behaviors. This suggests that evidence can be especially effective when used on those with no prior knowledge about the topic. Almost any objective information would then be new and potentially effective. A second consideration is that the evidence must be "good" evidence in the sense that it is pertinent to the claim. "Bad," or irrelevant, evidence will probably be ineffective in changing the audience's attitudes toward the claim, and may reduce the credibility of the advocate (McCroskey, 1972).

Two different types of credibility are pertinent to the use of evidence. First is source credibility in the sense used earlier in this discussion, judgments of such attributes as competence and trustworthiness made by the audience about the advocate. If source credibility is high, the communicator has less need to rely on evidence—source assertion is likely to suffice in persuading the audience. On the other hand, if source credibility is more moderate, the effective use of evidence becomes more crucial, since the clear citation of evidence will increase success in persuasion, as well as potentially increase perceptions of the advocate's credibility (McCroskey, 1972; McCroskey & Mehrley, 1969; G. R. Miller & Baseheart, 1969).

A second type of credibility that must be considered is the credibility of the sources of evidence cited by the advocate. Citing information from what the audience believes to be dubious sources can be counterproductive. One tactic that can be used to reduce the negative impact of relying on low-credibility sources of evidence is to avoid revealing the identity of the source until after the evidence has been presented. Assume, for example, an advocate wanted to convince his or her audience to use Brand X fertilizer and wanted to cite statements made by a Brand X salesperson to support the claim. Our advocate could cite the source of the evidence before revealing the data ("According to a Brand X salesperson, Brand X is the most effective fertilizer available."), or the advocate could reveal the data and then cite the source ("Brand X is the most effective fertilizer available today. This information is from a Brand X salesperson."). Research has indicated that the latter method leads to increased persuasion success when the evidence source is considered to be low in credibility. This probably occurs because when an audience is forewarned that information from what they consider to be a dubious source is forthcoming, they develop a negative response set which results in immediate rejection of the information. If the audience is not aware of the source of information, the evidence is processed without bias and has a chance to produce the desired impact. One has only to examine print advertisements using movie reviews to see that this practice is widely used by advertising strategists. A quote from a review appears prominently, with the name and affiliation of the reviewer following it in smaller print.

Message-Sidedness Persuasion typically deals with "issues." The term *issue* implies that conflicting views may be present. For each argument you advance, there can be counterclaims, opposing warrants, and perhaps conflicting data. You must decide whether to acknowledge these arguments or not. A one-sided message simply ignores opposing arguments. You present claims, warrants, and data without acknowledging any opposing views or arguments. A two-sided message presents arguments from both points of view but leads to the conclusion that your claim is the more desirable.

A careful analysis of the goals of the persuader and the characteristics of the audience is important in deciding on a one-sided or two-sided message. A one-sided message can be effective if you are operating in the deterrence phase of the persuasion process (Hass & Linder, 1972; Hovland, Lumsdaine, & Sheffield, 1949; Lumsdaine & Janis, 1953). If the audience initially is in general agreement with the claim, and the desired outcome is to reinforce present attitudes or to increase the commitment of the audience, a two-sided message may be unnecessary. If, however, you are attempting discontinuance or conversion, some initial hostility is likely and a two-sided message might be more effective (Hovland, Lumsdaine, & Sheffield, 1949; Lumsdaine & Janis, 1953).

Another factor to consider is the education level of the audience. In general, people who have more formal education tend to be more influenced by two-sided messages, regardless of their initial attitudes or the persuader's goal. Similar effects are found when the audience has previously been exposed to opposing arguments; people knowledgeable of opposing arguments are more readily influenced by two-sided than by one-sided messages (Lumsdaine & Janis, 1953; McGuire, 1968). Several factors may explain one-sided messages' lack of effectiveness in this type of situation. First, people aware of opposing arguments may feel that these arguments must be refuted or shown to be unimportant before they are willing to adopt the position advocated by the persuader. Other possibilities are that the failure to acknowledge opposing arguments may raise questions about a source's competence ("Isn't this person intelligent enough to realize there is another side to this issue?") or trustworthiness ("I know there are arguments for the other side, so why isn't this person acknowledging them?").

Message Organization Although many teachers of speech and composition seem to believe that highly organized messages are the most persuasive, there is actually little research evidence to support this contention. A number of structural characteristics can, however, be manipulated to increase the persuasiveness of influence attempts.

One-sided messages typically offer a solution to some problem as the central claim of the communication. This raises the question as to which should be presented first, the problem or the solution. Generally, it is more effective to demonstrate that a problem does indeed exist before offering the solution (Cohen, 1957; McCroskey & Mehrley, 1969; Seligman, Bush, & Kirsch, 1976).

With two-sided messages, the structure is usually more complex: You have to deal not only with your own arguments, but with the counterarguments of the opposition. Which arguments should you present first, the ones you wish to have accepted or the ones you wish to refute? The most effective structure is to first present the arguments you wish to have accepted and then refute opposing arguments (Gillig & Greenwald, 1974; N. Miller & Campbell, 1959). To present the opposing arguments first runs the risk of unintentionally influencing the audience to accept these undesirable arguments. Presenting the desirable arguments first may allow the receiver to be persuaded by the "good" arguments before he or she is exposed to opposing claims.

Another factor to consider when structuring persuasion appeals is when to emphasize the points on which you and the audience initially agree or disagree. When your goal is deterrence, there will obviously be many points of agreement and few points of disagreement between you and the audience. Even when your goal is discontinuance or conversion, there will usually be some points of common agreement along with disagreement. Whatever your goal, the wisest strategy is to begin the message by emphasizing the points of agreement before attempting to sway the audience on the points of contention. Early emphasis on points of agreement may increase perceptions of similarity between the audience and you, thus increasing your persuasive impact. Conversely, early emphasis on points of disagreement may exaggerate the disparities between the outcomes you desire and the initial position of the audience, leading the audience to see your position as more discrepant from their own position than it actually may be.

Fear Appeals An ages-old yet still often used persuasion tactic is to attempt to sway an audience through the use of fear-inducing messages. Fear appeals are messages designed to convince receivers that some great harm will befall them or someone important to them if your claim is not adopted. "Stop smoking or you will be dead within a year," "This country faces economic ruin if my fiscal policies are not adopted," and "If you don't buy enough life insurance your family will suffer after you are gone" are all examples of appeals based on fear.

Even though a number of studies have reported conflicting results, moderately strong fear appeals are generally more effective than weak ones (Baron & Byrne, 1977; Higbee, 1969; Leventhal & Niles, 1965). A number of explanations for the relative superiority of strong fear appeals have been put forward, but one of the more parsimonious is a drive-reduction explanation (Baron & Byrne, 1977). The drive-reduction model assumes that strong fear appeals lead to an increased state of arousal in the receiver. Accompanying recommendations on how the threatened outcomes can be avoided (acceptance of the claim) reassure the receiver and reduce the negative arousal. This reduction in negative forms of arousal is reinforcing and strengthens acceptance of the claims and recommendations of the advocate, thus inducing attitude and/or behavior change.

Several factors have been found to add to the effectiveness of strong fear appeals. For example, fear appeals that point out immediate and severe consequences of noncompliance are more effective than those that focus on more long-term or delayed effects. Also, strong fear appeals supported by evidence are more likely to be effective than those without evidence. Not surprisingly, highly credible communicators can effectively use fear appeals when less credible communicators cannot. Finally, fear appeals that indicate noncompliance will result in harm befalling a loved one of the receiver are likely to be more effective than appeals that threaten only the receiver. However, it should be noted that fear appeals often lead to undesired results when used in real-life situations. Harsh fear appeals can actually produce boomerang effects when the variables necessary to make them effective are missing (such as immediate effects or highly credible sources). Thus the person considering using strong fear appeals will want to carefully weigh the risks involved if any variable necessary to enhance rather than inhibit change is missing from the specific situation.

Language Intensity   Language intensity is the degree to which a persuasion message deviates from being a neutral statement (Bowers, 1964). For example, the statement "That is a very good idea" is more intense than the statement "That is a good idea." It has become almost a cultural truism that effective speakers are those who passionately defend their ideas, and we have come to believe that the intense speaker is usually effective in gaining compliance and changing attitudes.

The perceived intensity of a message can be manipulated in several ways. One of the more common ways is through the use of qualifiers that indicate the extremity of one's position, as in the example above. Similarly, the use of qualifiers that indicate certainty also influences perceptions of intensity (McEwen & Greenberg, 1970). "This is certainly the best course of action" is a more intense statement than "This is probably the best course of action." Also, messages using metaphor, especially those with sexual or violent connotations, are perceived to be highly intense. The statement "Current economic policies in the United States are raping the poor" is an example of a highly intense metaphor.

Research on the effectiveness of appeals varying in the use of intense language indicates that highly intense messages are generally less persuasive than messages relying on more moderate levels of language intensity (Bowers, 1964; Bradac, Bowers, & Courtwright, 1979; Chase & Kelly, 1976; M. D. Miller & Burgoon, 1979). Some sources of communication, however, seem to have more options in the levels of language intensity they can effectively use. Highly credible speakers, for example, can typically use very strongly worded messages and retain or even increase their impact.

Further, one key determinant of the level of intensity that should be used is what is considered *appropriate* by one's audience. Burgoon and his associates have demonstrated in several studies that using unexpectedly or inappropriately intense language is highly detrimental to one's effectiveness (M. Burgoon & Chase, 1973; M. Burgoon, Jones, & Stewart, 1974; M. Burgoon & Stewart, 1974). For example, females in this culture are expected to use less intense language, and when they violate such expectations, they are ineffective in influence attempts. The same is true of sources, of either sex, who are perceived to be low in credibility.

Opinionated Language   Closely related to the use of intense language is the use of opinionated language. Opinionated statements actually convey two messages: the source's attitude toward the topic and his or her attitude toward those people who agree or disagree with the position being advocated. The statement "Arizona is a beautiful state and anyone who thinks otherwise is an idiot" would be considered opinionated, since it conveys the persuasion claim ("Arizona is a beautiful state") and the source's attitude toward those who would disagree with the claim (". . . is an idiot"). Because it derogates those who disagree, the statement about Arizona is an opinionated rejection statement. An opinionated statement that praises those who agree ("Any intelligent person would agree that Arizona is a beautiful state") is an opinionated acceptance statement.

Not surprisingly, opinionated language is perceived to be more intense than nonopinionated statements (G. R. Miller & Lobe, 1967). As such, the strictures concerning the use of intense language also apply to the use of opinionated statements. When the audience is highly involved in the topic under discussion and when it already holds strong opinions about the issue, nonopinionated language is more effective than opinionated language. However, if the audience is neutral on the topic, opinionated rejection statements can actually be more effective than statements that contain no opinionated language.

Because the findings are so similar to those suggesting contrast effects for highly intense language, opinionated language should be considered a subset of possible high-intensity language options. Some general conclusions can be offered from the combined research efforts on language intensity and opinionatedness. When the audience thinks the source is highly credible, more intense language of all kinds can be used to support the claim. But when the communicator is unsure of his or her credibility or knows it to be low and is advocating a position that is counter to beliefs or opinions important to the receiver, the communicator should, as a matter of strategy, choose less intense language. All of this suggests a need for reconsideration of the intuitive assumption that a passionate speaker is the most persuasive; research evidence clearly suggests that this is not always the case.

COMPREHENSIVE MESSAGE STRATEGIES TO SUCCEED

Although the previously discussed research dealt with the manipulation of one variable (such as evidence or language intensity) in a single persuasion message, many if not most influence attempts are sequential in nature. That is, they take on the form of a campaign, with multiple persuasion attempts carried out over time. Two of these sequential compliance-gaining strategies have received significant attention in the research literature.

The Foot-in-the-Door Technique

This technique is based on the premise that we are often forced to attempt to gain compliance using some pressure (DeJong, 1979; Dillard, Hunter, & Burgoon, 1984; Foss & Dempsey, 1979; Seligman, Bush, & Kirsch, 1976; Snyder & Cunningham, 1975). The basic foot-in-the-door strategy is for the persuader to make a relatively small initial request, to which he or she is certain the target will agree. Sometime later the target is again approached, this time with a larger request, which is what the persuader really desires. A number of studies have indicated that those people who comply with a small initial request are more likely to comply with the second, larger request than are people who are merely approached with a single large request (DeJong, 1979; Dillard, Hunter, & Burgoon, 1984).

Presumably, this effect results from a change in the way the target sees himself or herself after complying with the first request. Freedman and Fraser (1966) explain the phenomenon this way:

Once he has agreed to a request, his attitude may change. He may become in his own eyes a person who does this sort of thing, who agrees to requests made by strangers, and who takes actions on things he believes in, who cooperates with good cause. (p. 201)

The experimental procedure used in one of Freedman and Fraser's experiments illustrates the foot-in-the-door technique and its effect. The large request put to a group of homeowners was that they install big signs in their front yards that read "DRIVE CAREFULLY." Of the homeowners approached without a first small request, fewer than 17 percent were willing to comply. But of those approached with a small request first (either to sign a petition or to put up a small sign), 50 to 76 percent were willing to comply with the second request and put the sign in their front lawn.

Perhaps the most crucial aspect of the foot-in-the-door technique is determining the size of the initial request. The first request must be small enough that the receiver complies, since failure to gain compliance with the small request eliminates the chance of the sequential request strategy succeeding. However, the initial request cannot be so small as to be seen as trivial. For foot-in-the-door to work, compliance with the first request must be a significant enough act that the receiver comes to see himself or herself as the type of individual committed to similar types of actions (M. Burgoon & Bettinghaus, 1980).

One interesting aspect of the foot-in-the-door technique is that an astute persuader can actually turn someone else's prior success in gaining compliance with a particular target to his or her own advantage. A person might, for example, be in the position of attempting to gain compliance from an individual who has recently acceded to a similar yet smaller request from another persuader. A foot-in-the-door strategy would suggest that this target is now more vulnerable to the appeals of the second advocate.

The Door-in-the-Face Technique

Though also sequential in nature, this technique takes a very different approach to gaining compliance (Cann, Sherman, & Elkes, 1975). In door-in-the-face, the target is first approached with a very large request that the persuader assumes will be *refused*. Later the target is approached with a second, more moderate request. The action requested in the second message is actually the response the persuader desires. Although more than one explanation for the effectiveness of door-in-the-face strategy has been advanced (Cann, Sherman, & Elkes, 1975; Snyder & Cunningham, 1975), the research seems to support an explanation based on the norm of reciprocity. Cialdini, Vincent, et al. (1975) suggest that people feel obligated to make concessions to those who have made concessions to them. Thus if a persuader concedes the legitimacy of a target's rejection of an initial request by making a smaller, less demanding request, the target presumably feels some pressure to likewise make a concession by agreeing to the second, more reasonable appeal.

Several conditions are necessary for the door-in-the-face technique to be successful. First, the initial request must be refused. Since this initial request asks for even more from the target than is actually needed or desired, failure to meet this necessary condition could be seen as being overly successful, which is not likely in most influence attempts. Further, the size of the initial, or "throwaway," request must be carefully considered. The first request must not be so large as to be absurd, yet it should be large enough to ensure its rejection will not lead to the target beginning to see himself or herself as the kind of person who refuses all requests of this type. In other words, the very mechanism (self-attribution) that leads to the effectiveness of foot-in-the-door must be prevented from becoming a motivational factor when trying to use door-in-the-face. Finally, the second request must be unambiguously smaller than the first so that the persuader will be seen as making a significant concession in the appeal. Also, since door-in-the-face depends on the target feeling that he or she has an obligation to make some type of reciprocal concession to the persuader, it is evident that successful use of door-in-the-face requires that the same person make both of the requests (M. Burgoon & Bettinghaus, 1980).

Compliance-Gaining Strategies

1.	Promise	If you will comply, I will reward you.
2.	Threat	If you do not comply, I will punish you.
3.	Expertise (positive)	If you comply, you will be rewarded because of "the nature of things."
4.	Expertise (negative)	If you do not comply, you will be punished because of "the nature of things."
5.	Liking	Actor is friendly and helpful to get target in a "good frame of mind" so that he will comply.
6.	Pre-giving	Actor rewards target before requesting compliance.
7.	Aversive stimulation	Actor continuously punishes target, making cessation contingent on compliance.
8.	Debt	You owe me compliance because of past favors.
9.	Moral appeal	You are immoral if you do not comply.
10.	Self-feeling (positive)	You will feel better about yourself if you comply.
11.	Self-feeling (negative)	You will feel worse about yourself if you do not comply.
12.	Altercasting (positive)	A person with "good" qualities would comply.
13.	Altercasting (negative)	Only a person with "bad" qualities would not comply.
14.	Altruism	I need your compliance very badly, so do it for me.
15.	Esteem (positive)	People you value will think better of you if you comply.
16.	Esteem (negative)	People you value will think worse of you if you do not comply.

Figure 10.4 The Marwell and Schmitt typology.

Source: Gerald Marwell and David R. Schmitt, "Dimensions of Compliance-Gaining Behavior: An Empirical Analysis," *Sociometry* 30(1967): 357–358. Used by permission.

Strategy Selection and Effectiveness

In addition to dealing with specific variables in persuasion messages and with the effectiveness of sequential requests, much recent research has explored the selection and use of broad general types of persuasion messages. Although a number of typologies of persuasion strategies have been developed, perhaps the most comprehen-sive and widely used was compiled by Marwell and Schmitt (1967). Their typology (Figure 10.4) contains 16 compliance-gaining strategies identi-fied in the earlier work of persuasion theorists.

Most of the research on these comprehensive persuasion strategies has centered on how likely they are to be used in persuasion situations rather than on their efficacy (Cody & McLaughlin, 1980). Marwell and Schmitt's initial study found that two higher-order dimensions of judgment underlie decisions to use or not use particular strategies. One of these dimensions was defined by techniques generally high in social acceptability, the other by techniques low in social acceptability. Subsequent research has demonstrated that the likelihood of use of the strategies varies widely across populations and greatly depends on the persuasion situation, such as whether the relationship between the source and target is personal or impersonal and whether the target is of higher or lower power than the source (G. R. Miller, Boster, Roloff, & Seibold, 1977; M. D. Miller, 1982). Preference for particular strategies varies with the cultural background and sex of the persuader (M. Burgoon, Dillard, & Doran, 1983; M. Burgoon, Dillard, Doran, & Miller, 1982).

In one of the few studies to examine strategy effectiveness rather than strategy selection, M. Burgoon, Dillard, and Doran (1983) found that people expect men and women to use different strategies. Males were expected to use more verbally aggressive (antisocial) persuasion strategies, whereas females were expected to use more prosocial message strategies. The results of this study further indicated that when either men or women deviated from social expectations by using "inappropriate" strategies, their persuasive impact was reduced.

THE OTHER SIDE OF THE COIN: INOCULATING PEOPLE AGAINST PERSUASION

As indicated earlier in this chapter, many influence attempts are designed to lead people to maintain their present attitudes, beliefs, or values in the face of forthcoming persuasion attacks. Although a number of approaches to inducing resistance to persuasion have been tried (McGuire, 1961; Papageorgis & McGuire, 1961; Tannenbaum & Norris, 1965), the most consistently tested and supported hypotheses have been generated by *inoculation theory*. As outlined by McGuire (1964), inoculation theory is based on a biological analogy. In the biological situation,

the person is typically made resistant to some attacking virus by pre-exposure to a weakened dose of the virus. This mild dose stimulates his defenses so that he will be better able to overcome any massive viral attack to which he is later exposed. (p. 200)

In the persuasion situation, the analogous method would be to expose the target to a weakened form of the forthcoming persuasion effort in order to stimulate his or her defenses against the full-strength argument. This inoculation is most effectively accomplished through the use of refutational messages (Festinger & Maccoby, 1964; McGuire, 1961, 1962; McGuire & Papageorgis, 1961, 1962). Refutational messages first warn of arguments that might be used in attempts to change the receiver's current attitudes or behaviors, and then indicate why these arguments are not valid. Returning to the fertilizer example, imagine that local farmers are currently using Brand X fertilizer and are satisfied with it. Our Brand X advocate is aware, however, that these farmers are likely to come into contact with a Brand Z salesperson. Our advocate has reason to believe that the salesperson may claim Brand Z leads to increased crop yields when compared to Brand X. In order to inoculate his or her audience against this argument, the Brand X advocate might use a message similar to this: "Some people may try to tell you that Brand Z is more effective in increasing crop yields than Brand X. However, that is not the case in this region of the country. With the soil and climate conditions we have, Brand X is still more effective."

Notice that the inoculation message exposes the audience to a potential argument for Brand Z and then tells why this argument is not a valid reason for changing one's current attitudes or behaviors.

In this example, the inoculation message refutes the same argument to be used in the subsequent counterpropaganda. Often, it is not possible to know exactly what arguments future counterpropaganda will contain. Suppose the advocate for Brand Z had not mentioned crop yields in his attempt to convince people to turn away from Brand X and had relied instead on arguments stressing the easier application and cheaper price of Brand Z compared to Brand X. Would our advocate's inoculation message still be effective against this type of counterpropaganda? According to inoculation theory, it should be.

Inoculation theory assumes that refutational messages are effective because they supply two factors necessary for resistance (Anderson & McGuire, 1965; Dean, Austin, & Watts, 1971; McGuire, 1961, 1962, 1970). First, the exposure to arguments that could be used against the receiver's current attitudes or behaviors is threatening to the receiver and stimulates the recall of arguments against change that he or she might already have. Further, the receiver is motivated to generate new arguments with which to resist forthcoming attacks. Thus a refutational strategy should be effective in inducing resistance to persuasion whether or not the subsequent counterpropaganda relies on arguments refuted in the inoculation attempt.

Another strategy often used by advocates hoping to induce resistance to persuasion is the supportive message strategy (Anderson & McGuire, 1965; McGuire, 1961, 1962, 1970; Tannenbaum, Macaulay, & Norris, 1966; Tannenbaum & Norris, 1965). This strategy attempts to induce resistance by isolating the receiver from contact with counterpropaganda while providing him or her with information consistent with currently held attitudes or behaviors. For example, "Brand X Fertilizer is easy to use, inexpensive, and increases crop yields" is a supportive message. It supplies only information consistent with the receiver's beliefs and does not acknowledge any arguments that might be used for Brand Z. Although this type of supportive strategy is likely to be effective in

maintaining attitudes as long as the receiver is not exposed to counterpropaganda, it provides little defense when the receiver is made aware of opposing arguments (M. Burgoon, Cohen, Miller, & Montgomery, 1978; Dean, Austin, & Watts, 1971; Hollander, 1974; McGuire, 1961; Papageorgis & McGuire, 1961; Tannenbaum & Norris, 1965). This lack of effectiveness is presumably attributable to the receiver's lack of motivation and practice in defending his or her beliefs.

CONCLUSION

We have attempted in this chapter to analyze just what persuasion is and how it can work to provide a variety of outcomes for the would-be persuader. We have also discussed source, receiver, and message variables to provide practical information on how one can more effectively communicate in a persuasive manner. We have examined the various goals that any given communicator can have in terms of changing other people or making audiences more resistant to the persuasion attempts of others. As we said at the beginning of this chapter, persuasive communication can be a powerful tool used for good or bad. Although some might question whether we indeed should provide people with the knowledge to influence others, we feel quite comfortable in engaging in such an effort, for we believe that the more we all know about how communication works, the more able we will be to either produce change or resist change when others attempt to persuade us of things not in our best interest. Whatever the problems involved with the study of and potential use of these persuasion techniques, such communication is preferable, in our minds, to attempts to force people to believe and behave in specific ways.

SUMMARY

Communication frequently is used with the purpose of influencing others. A wide range of possible effects can

result from an effort to persuade, including changes in perception, affect, cognition, and behavior.

Characteristics of both the source and the receiver in a persuasion situation can influence the outcome.

Source characteristics such as credibility, attraction, similarity, and power are integral to persuasion. The persuadability of receivers often differs depending on their demographic or personality characteristics.

The persuasiveness of a message is influenced by the choices made in its construction. The general structure of persuasive arguments has been discussed extensively by Toulmin and others. Some individual factors in the message that have been studied extensively include evidence, organization, fear appeals, and various language choices. Additional strategies for persuasion include serial strategies such as foot-in-the-door and door-in-the-face. The study of the choice of particular strategies in particular situations has begun only comparatively recently.

Resistance to persuasion has also not attracted as much attention as it deserves. Approaches to inducing resistance include both supportive messages and inoculation.

REVIEW AND DISCUSSION QUESTIONS

1. Which is more important to determining the success of persuasion: the characteristics of the receiver or the characteristics and message strategies of the persuader? Can a skillful persuader eventually find a method of persuading almost any receiver?

2. The source characteristics that enhance persuasion all depend on the perceptions of the receiver for their effectiveness. What, if anything, can persuaders do in their communication to enhance the likelihood that they will be perceived as being: credible, attractive, similar, or powerful?

3. Persuasion is sometimes attacked as being manipulative or deceptive, as preventing the receiver from making a logical and voluntary decision. Which of the message factors discussed in this chapter can be described as using logic or reason, and which do not appeal to reason? Specifically, are the language strategies in message construction based in logic or in some kind of unconscious reaction (see Chapter 2)?

4. Much less attention is devoted to research on resistance to persuasion than to research on persuasion. How easy is it to produce persuasive effects in real life? Is it true that most individual persuasion efforts are relatively ineffective unless they are part of a larger campaign or unless they are repeated frequently?

REFERENCES

Addington, D. (1971). The effects of vocal variations on ratings of source credibility. *Speech Monographs, 38,* 242–247.

Alpert, M. I., & Anderson, W. T. (1973). Optimal heterophily and communication effectiveness: Some empirical findings. *Journal of Communication, 23,* 328–343.

Anatol, K. W. E., & Mandel, J. E. (1972). Strategies of resistance to persuasion: New subject matter for the teacher of speech communication. *Central States Speech Journal, 23,* 11–17.

Anderson, K., & Clevenger, T. (1972). A summary of experimental research in ethos. In T. D. Beisecker & D. W. Parson (Eds.), *The process of social influence* (pp. 223–247). Englewood Cliffs, NJ: Prentice-Hall.

Anderson, L. R., & McGuire, W. J. (1965). Prior reassurance of group consensus as a factor in producing resistance to persuasion. *Sociometry, 28,* 44–56.

Apple, W., Streeter, L., & Krauss, R. (1974). Effects of pitch and speech rate on personal attributions. *Journal of Personality and Social Psychology, 37,* 715–737.

Apsler, R., & Sears, D. O. (1968). Warning, personal involvement, and attitude change. *Journal of Personality and Social Psychology, 9,* 162–166.

Bandura, A. (1976). *Social learning theory.* Englewood Cliffs, NJ: Prentice-Hall.

Baron, R. A., & Byrne, D. (1977). *Social psychology: Understanding human interaction.* Boston: Allyn & Bacon.

Beebe, S. A. (1974). Eye contact: A nonverbal determinant of speaker credibility. *Speech Teacher, 23,* 21–28.

Bettinghaus, E. P. (1968). *Persuasive communication.* New York: Holt, Rinehart & Winston.

Bowers, J. W. (1964). Some correlates of language intensity. *Quarterly Journal of Speech, 50,* 415–420.

Bradac, J., Bowers, J. W., & Courtwright, J. (1979). Three language variables in communication research: Intensity, immediacy, and diversity. *Human Communication Research, 5,* 257–269.

Brembeck, W. L., & Howell, W. S. (1952). *Persuasion.* Englewood Cliffs, NJ: Prentice-Hall.

Burgoon, J. K. (1976). The ideal source: A reexamination of source credibility measurement. *Central States Speech Journal, 27,* 200–206.

Burgoon, J. K., & Saine, T. (1978). *The unspoken dialogue.* Boston: Houghton Mifflin.

Burgoon, M., & Bettinghaus, E. P. (1980). Persuasive message strategies. In M. E. Roloff & G. R. Miller

(Eds.), *Persuasion: New directions in theory and research* (pp. 141–170). Beverly Hills: Sage.

Burgoon, M., & Chase, L. J. (1973). The effects of differential linguistic patterns in messages attempting to induce resistance to persuasion. *Speech Monographs, 40,* 1–7.

Burgoon, M., Cohen, M. M., Miller, M. D., & Montgomery, C. L. (1978). An empirical test of a model of resistance to persuasion. *Human Communication Research, 5,* 27–29.

Burgoon, M., Dillard, J., & Doran, N. E. (1983). Friendly and unfriendly persuasion: Effects of violations of expectations by males and females. *Human Communication Research, 10,* 283–294.

Burgoon, M., Dillard, J., Doran, N. E., & Miller, M. D. (1982). Cultural and situation influences on the process of persuasive strategy selection. *International Journal of Intercultural Relations, 4,* 85–100.

Burgoon, M., Jones, S. B., & Stewart, D. (1974). Toward a message-centered theory of persuasion: Three empirical investigations of language intensity. *Human Communication Research, 1,* 240–256.

Burgoon, M., & Ruffner, M. (1978). *Human communication* (2nd ed.). New York: Holt, Rinehart & Winston.

Burgoon, M., & Stewart, D. (1974). Empirical investigations of language intensity: The effects of sex of source, receiver, and language intensity on attitude change. *Human Communication Research, 1,* 244–248.

Cann, A., Sherman, S. J., & Elkes, R. (1975). Effects of initial request size and timing of a second request in compliance: The foot-in-the-door and the door-in-the-face. *Journal of Personality and Social Psychology, 32,* 774–782.

Cathcart, R. S. (1953). An experimental study of the relative effectiveness of selected means of handling evidence in speeches of advocacy. Unpublished doctoral dissertation, Northwestern University, Evanston, Il.

Chase, L. J., & Kelly, C. W. (1976). Language intensity and resistance to persuasion: A research note. *Human Communication Research, 3,* 82–85.

Cialdini, R. B., Petty, R. E., & Cacioppo, J. T. (1981). Attributions and attitude change. *Annual Reviews of Psychology, 32,* 357–404.

Cialdini, R. B., Vincent, E. J., Lewis, K. S., Catalan, J., Wheeler, D., & Darby, L. (1975). Reciprocal concessions procedure for inducing compliance: The door-in-the-face technique. *Journal of Personality and Social Psychology, 31,* 206–215.

Cody, M. J., & McLaughlin, M. L. (1980). Perceptions of compliance-gaining situations: A dimensional analysis. *Communication Monographs, 47,* 132–148.

Cohen, A. R. (1957). Need for cognition and order of communication as determinants of opinion change. In C. I. Hovland (Ed.), *The order of presentation in persuasion* (pp. 79–97). New Haven, CT: Yale University Press.

Cox, D. F., & Bauer, R. A. (1964). Self-confidence and persuasibility in women. *Public Opinion Quarterly, 28,* 453–466.

Cronkhite, G. (1969). *Persuasion: Speech and behavioral change.* Indianapolis: Bobbs-Merrill.

Cronkhite, G. (1976). *Communication and awareness.* Menlo Park, NJ: Cummings.

Cronkhite, G. (1986). On the focus, scope, and coherence of the study of human symbolic activity. *Quarterly Journal of Speech, 72,* 231–246.

Cronkhite, G., & Goetz, E. (1971). Dogmatism, persuasibility, and attitude. *Journal of Communication, 21,* 342–352.

Dean, R. B., Austin, J. A., & Watts, W. A. (1971). Forewarning effects in persuasion: Field and classroom experiments. *Journal of Personality and Social Psychology, 18,* 210–221.

DeJong, W. (1979). An examination of self-perception mediation of the foot-in-the-door effect. *Journal of Personality and Social Psychology, 37,* 2221–2239.

Delia, J. (1972). Dialects and the effects of stereotypes on impression formation. *Quarterly Journal of Speech, 58,* 21–25.

Dillard, J., Hunter, J. E., & Burgoon, M. (1984). A meta-analysis of two sequential request strategies for gaining compliance: Foot-in-the-door and door-in-the-face. *Human Communication Research, 10,* 461–488.

Ekman, P., & Friesen, W. V. (1974). Detecting deception from the body or face. *Journal of Personality and Social Psychology, 29,* 288–298.

Festinger, L., & Maccoby, N. (1974). On resistance to persuasive communication. *Journal of Abnormal and Social Psychology, 68,* 359–366.

Foss, R. D., & Dempsey, C. B. (1979). Blood donation and the foot-in-the-door technique: A limiting case. *Journal of Personality and Social Psychology, 37,* 580–590.

Freedman, J. L., & Fraser, S. C. (1966). Compliance without pressure: The foot-in-the-door technique. *Journal of Personality and Social Psychology, 4,* 195–202.

French, J., & Raven, B. (1968). The bases of social power. In D. Cartwright & A. Zander (Eds.), *Group dynamics* (pp. 259–269). New York: Harper & Row.

Gelfand, D. M. (1962). The influence of self-esteem on the rate of verbal conditioning and social matching behavior. *Journal of Abnormal and Social Psychology, 65,* 259–265.

Gillig, P. M., & Greenwald, A. G. (1974). Is it time to lay the sleeper effect to rest? *Journal of Personality and Social Psychology, 29,* 132–201.

Gollob, H. G., & Dittes, J. E. (1965). Different effects of manipulated self-esteem on persuasibility depending on the threat and complexity of the communication. *Journal of Personality and Social Psychology, 2,* 195–201.

Harris, V. A., & Jellison, J. M. (1971). Fear-arousing communications, false physiological feedback, and the acceptance of recommendations. *Journal of Experimental and Social Psychology, 7,* 269–279.

Hass, R. G., & Linder, D. E. (1972). Counterargument availability and the effects of message structure on persuasion. *Journal of Personality and Social Psychology, 23,* 219–233.

Higbee, K. L. (1969). Fifteen years of fear arousal: Research of threat appeals, 1953–1968. *Psychological Bulletin, 72,* 426–444.

Hollander, S. W. (1974). Effects of forewarning factors on pre and post communication attitude change. *Journal of Personality and Social Psychology, 30,* 272–278.

Hovland, C. I., Janis, I. L., & Kelley, H. H. (1953). *Communication and persuasion.* New Haven, CT: Yale University Press.

Hovland, C. I., Lumsdaine, A. A., & Sheffield, F. D. (1949). *Experiments on mass communication.* Princeton, NJ: Princeton University Press.

Hunter, J. E., Levine, R. L., & Sayers, S. E. (1976). Attitude change in hierarchical belief systems and its relation to persuasibility, dogmatism, and rigidity. *Human Communication Research, 3,* 3–28.

Janis, I. L., & Feshback, S. (1953). Effects of fear-arousing communications. *Journal of Abnormal and Social Psychology, 48,* 78–92.

Janis, I. L., & Rife, D. (1959). Persuasibility and emotional disorder. In C. I. Hovland & I. L. Janis (Eds.), *Personality and persuasibility* (pp. 121–140). New Haven, CT: Yale University Press.

Kaminski, E., McDermott, S., & Boster, F. (1977). The use of compliance-gaining strategies as a function of Machiavellianism of situations. Paper presented at the Central States Speech Association convention, Southfield, MI.

Kleinke, C. (1975). *First impressions.* Englewood Cliffs, NJ: Prentice-Hall.

Knapp, M. L., & Comadena, M. E. (1979). Telling it like it isn't: A review of theory and research on deceptive communications. *Human Communication Research, 5,* 270–285.

Lashbrook, V. J. (1971). Source credibility: A summary of experimental research. Paper presented at the Speech Communication Association convention, San Francisco.

Lehmann, S. (1970). Personality and compliance: A study of anxiety and self-esteem in opinion and behavior change. *Journal of Personality and Social Psychology, 15,* 76–86.

Leventhal, H. (1970). Findings of theory in the study of fear communications. In L. Berkowitz (Ed.), *Experimental social psychology* (Vol. 5, pp. 119–186). New York: Academic Press.

Leventhal, H., & Niles, P. (1965). Persistence of influence for varying durations of exposure to threat stimuli. *Psychological Reports, 16,* 223–233.

Lumsdaine, A. A., & Janis, I. L. (1953). Resistance to "counterpropaganda" produced by one-sided and two-sided "propaganda" presentations. *Public Opinion Quarterly, 17,* 311–318.

Madson, K. B. (1974) *Modern theories of motivation.* New York: Wiley.

Marple, C. (1933). The comparative susceptibility of three age levels to the suggestion of group versus expert opinion. *Journal of Social Psychology, 4,* 176–186.

Marwell, G., & Schmitt, D. R. (1967). Dimensions of compliance-gaining behavior: An empirical analysis. *Sociometry, 30,* 350–364.

McCroskey, J. C. (1969). A summary of experimental research on the effects of evidence in persuasive communication. *Quarterly Journal of Speech, 55,* 169–176.

McCroskey, J. C. (1972). A summary of experimental research on the effects of evidence in persuasive communication. In T. D. Beisecker & D. W. Parson (Eds.), *The process of social influence* (pp. 318–324). Englewood Cliffs, NJ: Prentice-Hall.

McCroskey, J. C., Holridge, W., & Toomb, J. K. (1974). An instrument for measuring the source credibility of basic speech communication instructors. *Speech Teacher, 23,* 26–33.

McCroskey, J. C., Jensen, T., & Todd, C. (1972). The generalizability of source credibility scales for public figures. Paper presented at the Speech Communication Association convention, Chicago.

McCroskey, J. C., Jensen, T., Todd, C., & Toomb, J. (1972). Measurement of the credibility of organization sources. Paper presented at the Western Speech Communication Association Convention, Honolulu.

McCroskey, J. C., Jensen, T., & Valencia, C. (1973). Measurement of the credibility of peers and spouses. Paper presented at the International Communication Association convention, Montreal.

McCroskey, J. C., & McCain, T. A. (1974). The measurement of interpersonal attraction. *Communication Monographs, 41,* 261–266.

McCroskey, J. C., & Mehrley, R. S. (1969). The effects of disorganization and nonfluency on attitude change and source credibility. *Speech Monographs, 36,* 13–21.

McCroskey, J. C., Richmond, V. P., & Daly, J. A. (1975). The development of a measure of perceived homophily in interpersonal communication. *Human Communication Research, 1,* 323–332.

McCroskey, J. C., & Young, T. J. (1981). Ethos and credibility: The construct and its measurement after three decades. *Central States Speech Journal, 32,* 24–34.

McEwen, W. J., & Greenberg, B. S. (1970). The effects of message intensity on receiver evaluation of source, message, and topic. *Journal of Communication, 20,* 340–350.

McGuire, W. J. (1961). The effectiveness of supportive and refutational defenses in immunizing and restoring beliefs against persuasion. *Sociometry, 24,* 184–197.

McGuire, W. J. (1962). Persistence of the resistance to persuasion induced by various types of prior belief defenses. *Journal of Abnormal and Social Psychology, 64,* 241–248.

McGuire, W. J. (1964). Inducing resistance to persuasion: Some contemporary approaches. In L. Berkowitz (Ed.), *Advances in experimental social psychology* (Vol. 1, pp. 191–229). New York: Academic Press.

McGuire, W. J. (1968). Personality and susceptibility to social influence. In E. F. Borgatta & W. W. Lambert (Eds.), *Handbook of personality theory and research* (pp. 1130–1187). Chicago: Rand McNally.

McGuire, W. J. (1969). The nature of attitudes and attitudinal change. In G. Lindzey & E. Aronson (Eds.), *The handbook of social psychology* (Vol. 3, pp. 136–314). Reading, MA: Addison-Wesley.

McGuire, W. J. (1970, February). A vaccine for brainwash. *Psychology Today, 3,* pp. 36–39, 63–64.

McGuire, W. J., & Papageorgis, D. (1961). The relative efficacy of various types of prior belief-defenses in producing immunity against persuasion. *Journal of Abnormal and Social Psychology, 62,* 327–337.

McGuire, W. J., & Papageorgis, D. (1962). Effectiveness of forewarning in developing resistance to persuasion. *Public Opinion Quarterly, 26,* 24–34.

Mehrabian, A. (1969). Significance of posture and position in the communication of attitude and status relationships. *Psychological Bulletin, 71,* 359–372.

Miller, G. R., & Baseheart, J. (1969). Source trustworthiness, opinionated statements and response to persuasive communication. *Speech Monographs, 36,* 1–7.

Miller, G. R., Boster, F., Roloff, M. E., & Seibold, D. (1977). Compliance-gaining message strategies: A typology and some findings concerning effects of situational differences. *Communication Monographs, 44,* 37–51.

Miller, G. R., Burgoon, M., & Burgoon, J. K. (1984). Communication and compliance: An overview of the research on the process of persuasion. In C. Arnold & J. W. Bowers (Eds.), *Handbook of rhetorical and communication theory* (pp. 400–474). Boston: Allyn & Bacon.

Miller, G. R., & Hewgill, M. A. (1964). The effects of variation in nonfluency on audience ratings of source credibility. *Quarterly Journal of Speech, 50,* 36–44.

Miller, G. R., & Lobe, J. (1967). Opinionated language, open- and closed-mindedness and responses to persuasive communications. *Journal of Communication, 17,* 333–341.

Miller, G. R., & Steinberg, M. (1975). *Between people: A new analysis of interpersonal communication.* Chicago: Science Research Associates.

Miller, L. K. (1980). *Principles of everyday behavior analysis* (2nd ed.). Monterey, CA: Brooks/Cole.

Miller, M. D. (1982). Friendship, power, and the language of compliance-gaining. *Journal of Language and Social Psychology, 1,* 111–121.

Miller, M. D., & Burgoon, M. (1979). The relationship between violations of expectations and the induction of resistance to persuasion. *Human Communication Research, 5,* 301–313.

Miller, N., & Campbell, D. T. (1959). Recency and primacy in persuasion as a function of the timing of speeches and measurement. *Journal of Abnormal and Social Psychology, 59,* 1–9.

Miller, N., Maruyama, G., Beaber, R. J., & Valone, K. (1976). Speed of speech and persuasion. *Journal of Personality and Social Psychology, 34,* 615–624.

Millman, S. (1965). The relationship between anxiety, learning, and opinion change. Unpublished doctoral dissertation, Columbia University, New York.

Niles, P. (1964). The relationship of susceptibility and anxiety to acceptance of fear-arousing communications. Unpublished doctoral dissertation, Yale University, New Haven, CT.

Ostermeier, T. H. (1967). Effects of and type and frequency of reference upon perceived source credibility and attitude change. *Speech Monographs, 34,* 137–144.

Papageorgis, D., & McGuire, W. J. (1961). The generality of immunity to persuasion produced by pre-exposure to weakened counterarguments. *Journal of Abnormal and Social Psychology, 62,* 475–481.

Pearce, W. B., & Brommel, B. (1972). Vocalic communication in persuasion. *Quarterly Journal of Speech, 58,* 298–306.

Reynolds, R. A., & Burgoon, M. (1983). Belief processing, reasoning, and evidence. In R. Bostrom (Ed.), *Communication Yearbook 7* (pp. 49–82). Beverly Hills: Sage.

Roberts, W. R. (1924). Aristotle on public speaking. *Fortnightly Review, 122–116,* 201–210.

Rogers, E., & Bhowmik, D. (1970). Homophily-heterophily: Relational concepts for communication. *Public Opinion Quarterly, 34,* 523–538.

Rosenfeld, L., & Christie, V. (1974). Sex and persuasibility revisited. *Western Speech, 38*(4), 224–253.

Schneider, D., Hastorf, A., & Ellsworth, P. (1979). *Person perception.* Reading, MA: Addison-Wesley.

Seligman, C., Bush, M., & Kirsch, K. (1976). Relationship between compliance in the foot-in-the-door paradigm and size of first request. *Journal of Personality and Social Psychology, 33,* 517–520.

Snyder, M., & Cunningham, M. R. (1975). To comply or not comply: Testing the self-perception explanation of the "foot-in-the-door" phenomenon. *Journal of Personality and Social Psychology, 37,* 64–67.

Stone, V. A. (1969). Individual differences and inoculation against persuasion. *Journalism Quarterly, 46,* 267–273.

Tannenbaum, P. H., Macaulay, J. R., & Norris, E. L. (1966). Principle of congruity and reduction of persuasion. *Journal of Personality and Social Psychology, 2,* 233–238.

Tannenbaum, P. H., & Norris, E. L. (1965). Effects of combining congruity principle strategies for the reduction of persuasion. *Sociometry, 28,* 145–157.

Toulmin, S. (1959). *The uses of argument.* Cambridge: Cambridge University Press.

Walster, E., & Festinger, L. (1962). The effectiveness of overheard persuasive communications. *Journal of Abnormal and Social Psychology, 65,* 395–402.

Widgery, R. N. (1974). Sex of receiver and physical attractiveness of source as determinants of initial credibility perception. *Western Speech, 38*(1), 13–17.

11

Communication and Social Change

Everett M. Rogers
University of Southern California

Everett M. Rogers is Janet M. Peck Professor of International Communication in the Institute for Communication Research at Stanford University. He teaches and conducts research on the diffusion of innovation, development communication, and new communication technology. Dr. Rogers's recent books include Silicon Valley Fever: Growth of High-Technology Culture *(with Judith K. Larsen) and* Television Flows in Latin America *(with Jorge Reina Schement).*

LEARNING OBJECTIVES

After studying this chapter you should be able to:

- Explain the assumptions of the traditional view of development and social change in the Third World.

- Discuss reasons the traditional view of development has not worked as predicted.

- Outline the three basic characteristics of the new development paradigm.

- Define diffusion of innovation.

- Recall five characteristics of an innovation that directly relate to its rate of adoption.

- Tell what types of communication work best for different parts of the diffusion-of-innovation process.

- Sequence the five categories of adopters in order of their innovativeness.

- Identify the different types of consequences of innovation.

- List eight strategies for narrowing information gaps in diffusion.

- Discuss the use of new media technologies in development and diffusion.
- Explain the relationship between dependency theory and the concept of media imperialism.

Twenty years ago, there were high hopes for the role of mass communication in bringing about development in Latin America, Africa, and Asia. The media, particularly radio, were penetrating the mass audience in Third World countries. These mass communication channels seemed capable of acting like "magic multipliers" in quickly conveying useful information about development opportunities to the people.

Now, two decades later, we can assess the actual accomplishments of development communication. The mass media have indeed reached large audiences, putting villagers and urban poor in touch with the rest of the world. New communication technologies like broadcast satellites are being used by many Third World nations. Government officials in Latin America, Africa, and Asia have heeded the advice of communication scientists and have sought to employ mass communication for development purposes.

But the resulting rate of actual development has generally been disappointing. Why? What lessons can we learn from the experience to date with development communication that can lead to greater success in the future? How can we gain from development failures in the past so as to advance our theoretical understanding of the crucial issues of communication and social change?

We define *social change* as the process by which alteration in the structure and function of a social system occurs (Rogers, 1983, p. 6). When innovations are invented, diffused, and adopted or rejected, certain consequences result and social change takes place. Such change can occur in other ways, such as through a political revolution or a natural disaster, like an earthquake. Some types of social change are planned and managed; others happen spontaneously.

One kind of planned social change that is especially important in the Third World is development. In fact, the highest priority of most national governments in these countries is to advance the socioeconomic development of their people. What is development? *Development* is defined as a widely participatory process of social change in a society, intended to bring about both social and material advancement (including greater equality, freedom, and other valued qualities) for the majority of the people through gaining greater control over their environment (Rogers, 1976).

Diffusion is the process by which an innovation is communicated through certain channels over time among the members of a social system (Rogers, 1983, p. 5). Thus diffusion is one type of communication, in that the messages are concerned with new ideas. *Communication* is a process in which participants create and share information with one another in order to reach a mutual understanding (Rogers & Kincaid, 1981). We think of communication as a two-way process of convergence. Such convergence (or divergence) occurs as two or more individuals move toward each other (or further apart) in the meanings they ascribe to certain events.

In the case of diffusion, the main contents of communication messages deal with innovations. An *innovation* is an idea, practice, or object that is perceived as new by an individual or other unit of adoption (Rogers, 1983, p. 35). Many of the innovations leading to social change are technological, but nontechnological ideas like a new religious movement or a political ideology may also be important. *Technology* is a design for instrumental action that reduces the uncertainty in cause-effect relationships involved in achieving a desired outcome.

TOWARD A NEW PARADIGM OF DEVELOPMENT

The definition of development has changed in recent years. The way that this fundamental intellectual shift occurred is a fascinating example of the interplay between world events, on one hand, and academic thinking, on the other. Here we trace this passing of the dominant conception of development.

Every field of scientific research must make certain simplifying assumptions about the complex realities that it studies. Such assumptions are built into the intellectual paradigm that guides a field of research. A *paradigm* is a conceptual structure that is shared by a community of scholars and that provides model problems and solutions for research (Kuhn, 1970).

Often, the assumptions in a paradigm are not fully recognized, even if they affect such important matters as what is studied and what is ignored, and which research methods are favored and which are rejected. When a scientist follows a certain theoretical paradigm, he or she puts on a set of intellectual blinders that blocks out much of reality. Scientists in any field always face the problem of their "trained incapacity"—that is, the more we know about how to do something, the more difficult it is to learn to do it differently. To a certain extent, such trained incapacity is necessary. Otherwise, a scientist could not cope with the vast uncertainties of the research process in his or her field.

The advance of a scientific field is a gradual, puzzle-solving process through which important research questions are identified and eventually answered. Scientific progress is aided by recognizing the many assumptions, biases, and weaknesses of a scientific field. That is why the intellectual criticism of development communication made in recent years is a healthy sign of progress.

The Dominant Paradigm of Development

The most influential book about development communication is Wilbur Schramm's *Mass Media and National Development* (1964). It brought together much of the thinking of the day about the potential role of the media in development. The 1960s were an upbeat period of thinking about development. Radio audiences in the Third World were expanding tremendously, partly because of the low-cost receivers made possible by the electronic transistor. Expectations were high for the role of mass communication in facilitating development.

Many Third World nations, especially in Africa and Asia, had gained their independence from European colonial powers during the 1950s and 1960s, and their national governments then turned to domestic issues like bringing about rapid development. United Nations agencies and the aid programs of the United States and other industrialized countries stood by to assist Third World nations in their development activities. The post–World War II success of the Marshall Plan in European recovery seemed to imply that rapid development of a country was possible, given certain forms of international assistance.

Schramm's book was widely read by government officials and scholars in the Third World, who set out to follow the path to development that it generally outlines At that time, we thought of development communication as mainly a one-way transfer of information from a national development agency (agriculture, health, nutrition, family planning, and so on) to the people. That role fit well with the one-way nature of broadcasting media like radio.

In the mid-1960s, definitions of development centered on the criterion of economic growth. The measure of national development at a given point in time was the gross national product (GNP), or, when divided by the total population of a nation, per capita income. Bankers and economists were in charge of development programs in most countries. They defined the problem of development mainly in economic terms. Five-year development plans were created to guide the development activities of national governments. Individuals, it was assumed, would respond directly to economic incentives, and the profit motive was thought to be sufficient to engender the large-scale behavior changes necessary for development to occur.

Development planners thought that economic growth could be infinite. Bigger was thought to be better, and the belief that technology was at the heart of development was unquestioned. Much of the technology came from the industrialized nations of Europe and America, but its applicability to Third World conditions was not considered problematic. The technologies transferred to the Third World through international development programs were mainly capital intensive and labor reducing, enabling heavy industrialization to occur via hydroelectric plants and steel mills.

Rapid industrialization was accompanied by urbanization as factory workers were drawn from farming villages to the city. Many Third World cities, like Bangkok, Mexico City, and Lagos, began to face severe social problems related to crowding as millions of rural citizens migrated to the cities. Once this flow got under way, it seemed impossible to slow down, even when jobs, adequate housing, and other services could not be provided to the new urbanites. The Third World city often offered a poorer quality of life than the villages from which people migrated.

Finally, the 1960s conception of development assumed that the main causes of underdevelopment lay within the Third World countries, rather than in their trade and other economic relationships with industrialized nations. Blame for underdevelopment was placed on (1) peasant villagers, who seemed fatalistic and unresponsive to technological innovation, and (2) such social structural problems as a tangled government bureaucracy, a top-heavy land tenure system, and graft and corruption by officials and business people. Development models created by Western intellectuals (and by Western-trained intellectuals from the Third World) were less likely to recognize the great importance of external constraints on a nation's development, the economic imperialism of multinational corporations, or the dependence that international technical assistance programs might create. Only later was it recognized that the causes of underdevelopment lay outside a Third World nation as well as within it.

So the main elements in the dominant paradigm of development were industrialization, urbanization, capital-intensive technology, centralized development planning, a focus on economic growth, and an overemphasis on internal causes of underdevelopment.

Reasons for the Passing of the Development Paradigm

About 1970, the conception of development that we have just described began to be questioned and supplanted with alternative models. The dominant paradigm had not worked very well, even by the previously accepted criterion of economic growth. During the 1960s, the typical Third World nation achieved a rate of growth in per capita income of 2 or 3 percent per year, far lower than had been planned and expected. Even in nations like Taiwan, Korea, and Mexico (which were then considered development success stories because of their growth rate of 5 to 10 percent), troublesome questions were raised about the unequal distribution of the economic growth that had occurred. Most of the advance was in the hands of a relatively small number of urban, educated elites, usually living in the nation's capital city. The mass population of rural villagers and urban poor was only slightly better off in an absolute sense than it had been, and in a relative sense it was often worse off.

However one measured development in most of Latin America, Africa, and Asia during the 1960s, not a great deal had occurred. Instead, most development programs in education, health, agriculture, and industrialization brought economic stagnation, a concentration of incomes, high unemployment, overurbanization, and food shortages. If these past development programs represented any kind of test of the intellectual paradigm on which they were based, the model was found to be seriously wanting.

Emerging Alternatives: The New Development

By the mid-1970s, the dominant paradigm had passed, at least as the main model for development in Latin America, Africa, and Asia. A single, integrated paradigm has not replaced it. Different Third World nations now follow somewhat different models of development, even though the following elements are usually found.

Equality   The distribution of the benefits of development, such as income, education, and information, became a major consideration after the early 1970s. If the average per capita income in a nation increased, but only because the elites were much richer, was this real development? Development policies that would close the gaps of inequality between the more advanced and less advanced sectors of a Third World nation were emphasized. The implications of these egalitarian policies for development communication were profound; for example, they meant that radio was more likely to be used than television. "Little" media (usually understood to include radio and less complicated channels) were given priority over the "big" media (such as film and television). We detail the equality aspects of the new development communication in a later section of this chapter.

Participation   A major shift in thinking about development happened when it was realized that development was not something that a central government did *to* its people, but rather something that the people did for themselves. Government assistance was still a necessary ingredient in development, but government was not solely in charge of all aspects of development. Popular participation in development planning and execution was given much more emphasis in the 1970s and since. In the 1980s, video productions by villagers and urban poor were used to communicate needs for development projects to government officials.

Self-development   Many types of development, it came to be realized, could best be carried out by people in a village or an urban neighborhood. Self-reliance or independence from a national government, encouraging the use of local resources and the people's initiative, were emphasized. This decentralization of development meant that the role of development communication was quite different than previously envisioned. Now it was intended to encourage self-development by informing a population about successful models of local self-reliance that they could emulate.

Basic to emerging alternatives to the dominant paradigm was a new definition of development. Such valued ends as equality, freedom, independence, and social advancement, rather than purely materialistic ends, were emphasized. Previously in this chapter, we defined development as a widely participatory process of social change in a society, intended to bring about both social and material advancement (including greater equality, freedom, and other valued qualities) for the majority of the people through their gaining greater control over their environment. The implications of this new definition of development began to be reflected in actual development programs in the Third World.

DIFFUSION OF INNOVATIONS

We defined *diffusion* as the process by which an innovation is communicated through certain channels over time among the members of a social system. The main elements in the diffusion of new ideas are: (1) an *innovation* (defined as an idea, practice, or object perceived as new by an individual or other unit of adoption), (2) *communicated* through certain *channels* (3) over *time* (4) among the members of a *social system*. It is the relative newness of the idea being communicated that sets off diffusion from other types of human communication. This newness means that a certain degree of uncertainty for individuals is always involved in the diffusion of an innovation.

Uncertainty is the degree to which a number of alternatives are perceived with respect to the occurrence of an event and the relative probabilities of these alternatives. This uncertainty is reduced when an individual seeks information. So the diffusion behavior of individuals consists of their searching for information that allows them to cope with the uncertainty involved in ideas that are perceived as new.

Over 4,000 research studies have been completed on the diffusion of innovations in the past 45 years. Out of this vast body of research has come a series of generalizations about (1) the characteristics of individuals and other adopter units who are relatively early and late to adopt a new idea, (2) the communication channels through which innovations diffuse, and (3) the characteristics of innovations that lead to a relatively rapid rate of adoption.

Diffusion research began in the United States, where a general theoretical model of diffusion was formulated. Beginning about 1960, this diffusion model was transferred to Third World nations, initially without adequate questioning of how appropriate this model was to the new context. Only in the 1970s did scholars begin to critically assess the issue of the distinctiveness of diffusion under Third World conditions. The diffusion model was frequently incorporated into development programs in Latin America, Africa, and Asia, where it fit well with the desire of national governments to convey new ideas in agriculture, health, family planning, and education to their people.

The rate of adoption of an innovation is positively related to the following characteristics of the innovation (as perceived by the members of the system in which the innovation is diffusing): (1) relative advantage, the degree to which the innovation is perceived as superior to the idea that it replaces, (2) compatibility, (3) complexity, (4) triability, and (5) observability. An innovation that is relatively advantageous, compatible with past experiences, low in complexity, available for trial, and observable will be adopted relatively more rapidly.

Mass media channels are more effective than interpersonal channels in creating knowledge of innovations. However, interpersonal channels are more effective in forming and changing attitudes toward an innovation, and thus in influencing the individual's decision to adopt or reject the inno-

vation. Most individuals evaluate an innovation not on the basis of scientific research by experts, but on the basis of the subjective evaluations of "near-peers" who have already adopted the innovation. These network peers serve as social models, whose innovation behavior is often imitated by others in their system. Person-to-person imitation and social modeling are thus essential elements in the diffusion process.

Certain individuals in a social system play an especially important role in the interpersonal diffusion of innovations; they are called opinion leaders. *Opinion leadership* is the degree to which an individual is able to informally influence others' attitudes or overt behavior in a desired way with relative frequency. Development programs in the Third World have often sought to identify opinion leaders in a community in order to ask their assistance in diffusing innovations to others in the system.

Innovativeness is the degree to which an individual or other unit is relatively earlier than their peers in adopting new ideas. The variable of innovativeness is often broken up into five adopter categories: (1) innovators, the first to adopt, (2) early adopters, (3) early majority, (4) late majority, and (5) laggards, the last to adopt. One of the most common topics for diffusion research is to determine the characteristics of the adopter categories for agricultural, health, and family planning innovations.

CONSEQUENCES OF INNOVATIONS

Consequences are the changes that an individual or a social system experiences as a result of adopting or rejecting an innovation (Rogers, 1983). An innovation obviously has little effect until it is put into use by the individuals in a system. In spite of the importance of consequences of innovations, this topic has received relatively little attention from researchers. Nor have development officials paid the consequences of innovations much heed; they have usually assumed that a given innovation will produce only beneficial results for its adopters. Unfortunately, this has often not been so.

Classifications of Consequences

Consequences are not one-dimensional; they can take various forms and be classified into one or more taxonomies. Here we categorize consequences as (1) desirable or undesirable, (2) direct or indirect, and (3) anticipated or unanticipated.

Desirable consequences are the functional effects of an innovation to an individual or to a social system; *undesirable consequences* are the dysfunctional effects. Every system has certain qualities that an innovation should not destroy if the welfare of the system is to be maintained: respect for human life and property, maintenance of individual dignity, and appreciation of others. Other sociocultural elements can be modified, discontinued, and supplanted with little impact.

Most innovations cause both desirable and undesirable consequences. Understandably, individuals want to enjoy the functional consequences of an innovation (like increased effectiveness, efficiency, or convenience) and to avoid the dysfunctional effects (such as changes in social values and institutions). But the desirable and undesirable consequences often cannot be separated. The erroneous assumption of separability was expressed by the Ayatollah Khomeini of Iran a few years ago; he wanted such Western technology as television, air conditioning, and the telephone, but rejected Western music, clothing, and values on female equality.

We conclude that it is usually difficult or impossible to manage the effects of an innovation so as to separate the desirable from the undesirable consequences.

Another classification of consequences turns on whether they are direct or indirect. *Direct consequences* are the changes to an individual or a social system that occur in immediate response to an innovation. *Indirect consequences* are the changes to an individual or a social system that occur as a result of the direct consequences of an innovation.

For example, one direct result of semiconductors that are used in microcomputers is improved data handling and thus more effective management of information. This direct consequence of semiconductors is likely to be accompanied by many indirect consequences, such as increased unemployment, socioeconomic inequality, and possible threats to individual privacy (Rogers & Larsen, 1984).

The indirect consequences of an innovation are often especially difficult to plan for, as they are often unanticipated. *Anticipated consequences* are changes resulting from an innovation that are recognized and intended by the members of a social system. *Unanticipated consequences* are changes that are neither intended nor recognized by the members of a social system. A system is like a bowl of marbles. Move any one of its elements and the positions of all the others are changed. In certain nations like India, where a communication satellite was launched in the early 1980s mainly to facilitate television broadcasting, a relative surprise was the tremendous increase in the long-distance telephone calls transmitted by satellite.

The undesirable, indirect, and unanticipated consequences of innovations usually go together, as do the desirable, direct, and anticipated consequences.

EQUALITY IN THE CONSEQUENCES OF INNOVATION

The importance of equality in the distribution of an innovation's consequences was first realized in the early 1970s. Until that time, most diffusion programs simply ignored the equality issue, generally trusting in the "trickle-down" theory to cancel out the gap-widening results of innovation diffusion in the long run. The passing of the dominant paradigm of development led to questioning whether real development had occurred if socioeconomic inequality had increased. Certainly the major change in thinking about development in recent years has been a new emphasis on equality in the distribution of consequences of innovation.

A concern with studying equality was also taking hold among communication scientists. The main research question pursued in past communication research had been, What are the effects? With more concern with equality issues came an additional research question: Has the communication activity had a greater effect on certain individuals than on others?

Once Tichenor, Donohue, and Olien (1970) called for this new emphasis in communication research, and development programs began to focus on socioeconomic equality among their beneficiaries, we began to learn more about how to diffuse innovations in ways that could be more equalizing. These studies showed that the consequences of the adoption of innovations usually tend to widen the socioeconomic gap between the earlier and later adopting categories in a system, and between the population segments previously high and low in socioeconomic status.

An illustration of diffusion research concerned with equality is Havens's (1975) study of the diffusion of two coffee varieties among Colombian farmers over an eight-year period. Of the original sample of 56 coffee growers, 17 adopted the new varieties, which considerably increased their yields. These farmers also adopted chemical fertilizers and herbicides along with the new coffee varieties. As a result, eight years later, the adopters had earned much higher incomes than the nonadopters; one consequence of the coffee varieties was a wider gap between the already well-to-do farmers (who adopted the varieties) and those less well-off. The smaller farmers could not afford to adopt because they could not secure credit to tide them over during the three years required for the new coffee trees to begin producing.

Here we see an example of how a system's social structure partly determines the degree of equality of an innovation's consequences. When the structure is already very unequal, the consequences of an innovation often lead to greater inequality. In Latin America, Africa, and Asia, the social structure of a local community or of a nation is often in sharp contrast to that of Europe and America. Wealth, power, and information are usually concentrated in a few hands. Significantly, it was in the Third World in the 1970s that equality consequences of innovation began to receive research attention. Today a concern with the equality of mass media communication effects is also found in the United States.

Strategies for Narrowing Information Gaps

What can a development agency do if it wishes to decrease the degree of inequality resulting from the diffusion of innovations?

- *Use lower socioeconomic focus.* Provide messages that are redundant to people of higher socioeconomic status, but appropriate to the needs of lower classes. An illustration of this strategy comes from a study by Shingi and Mody (1976) in India. Agricultural television programs were developed that focused on topics already familiar to larger farmers but of interest to smaller farmers. The result of this "ceiling effect" was to close the agricultural knowledge gap between the larger and smaller farmers.

- *Focus on late majority and laggards.* Concentrate development program attention on the late majority and laggards, instead of innovators and early majority. The later adopters tend to place less credibility in government programs and are seldom active in searching for information about technological innovations. To reach later adopters and achieve effects similar to those recognized with early adopters, government officials will have to expend greater effort.

- *Tailor messages to audience.* Develop communication messages especially for those of lower socioeconomic status in terms of their particular characteristics like education, attitudes, communication habits, and so forth.

- *Use high-access media channels.* Use communication channels that are particularly able to get through to those of lower socioeconomic status, so that access is not a barrier to their gaining information about innovations. This strategy might entail using radio instead of television to contact villagers in a Third World country, for example.

- *Select appropriate innovations.* Give priority to developing and diffusing innovations that are especially appropriate for those of lower socioeconomic status. Agricultural research in Latin America has often been directed mainly at crops that are grown and exported by large commercial farmers. Such research seldom leads to innovations that are useful to small farmers who grow primarily subsistence crops.

- *Use the personal element.* Organize those of lower socioeconomic status in small groups in which they can learn from each other about innovations and share their resources in order to speed the adoption process.

- *Use opinion leaders.* Identify the opinion leaders among those of lower socioeconomic status, and concentrate development efforts on them so as to activate peer networks about an innovation. Roling, Ascroft, and Chege (1976) reported success in closing information gaps with this opinion leadership strategy in Kenya, where small-scale farmers were given training in corn-growing innovations.

- *Use participative planning.* Provide a means for those of lower socioeconomic status to participate in the planning and execution of diffusion programs.

When development agencies follow these communication strategies, they can narrow, or at least not widen, socioeconomic information gaps in a social system. In other words, greater inequality is not an inevitable consequence of diffusion of innovations through development programs.

COMMUNICATION TECHNOLOGY AND SOCIAL CHANGE

In recent decades the United States, Japan, and most Western European nations have become "information societies"; more than half their work force and gross national product are involved in the input, processing, or output of information. Examples of information occupations are teaching, social work, journalism, computer programming, and secretarial work. The transition of society from an industrial to an information society is driven by such communication technologies as computers, satellites, and cable TV, often combined in various types of communication systems.

A special aspect of recent communication technologies is their interactive nature, made possible by the inclusion of a computer as one element in a communication system. The newer interactive technologies like videotext, teletext, and cable television systems represent a basic change from the one-way nature of television, radio, print, and film of the past. The interactive nature of new communication technologies means that the difference between mass media and interpersonal communication may become much less important.

Microcomputers

Undoubtedly the most important recent technological change has been the increasingly widespread use of computers, especially microcomputers. To date, microcomputers are used mainly in information societies and have had only rather limited applications in the Third World.

There are both an optimistic and a pessimistic view of the future impact of new communication technologies in the Third World. Illustrative of the optimistic position is Servan-Schreiber (1981), who argues that microcomputers can help the Third World catch up to Europe and America by jumping over the industrial era and moving directly into the information era. Because of their relatively low cost and simplicity, microcomputers may become practical for linking a peasant village to urban centers and to government development agencies. This link has been formed by various development agencies, which use microcomputers for management information strategies.

Some Third World countries like Mexico, Brazil, and India have established national policies to encourage their indigenous microcomputer industries. Such policies recognize the crucial importance of a domestic microcomputer industry in becoming an information society. Brazil is the most successful example of this approach, with 40 Brazilian microcomputer companies.

Malaysia, the Philippines, Indonesia, Singapore, Korea, Taiwan, and Mexico have become major sites for the production of semiconductor chips and microcomputers. But these microelectronics operations are typically owned by U.S. or Japanese firms; they employ thousands of Third World women at relatively low wages to perform monotonous, assembly-line work (Rogers & Larsen, 1984). However, several Third World nations in the 1980s have sought to create their own microelectronics production centers.

A pessimistic view of the future impact of these new communication technologies on Third World development notes that microcomputers have not yet been very widely applied to development problems in the Third World (although they have the potential to make an important contribution to development). Unfortunately, the main impacts of the new communication technologies may be widened socioeconomic gaps and increased inequality, at least in the immediate future.

Satellites

Perhaps the one bright spot for communication technology's role in development is satellites. Here the spectacular case is India, where the SITE (Satellite Instructional Television Experiment) project was carried out in the mid-1970s. About 2,400 Indian villages received direct broadcasts from the SITE satellite for one year; the programs conveyed useful information to village families about agriculture, health and family planning, education, and nationalism. In the 1980s, the Indian government launched an enthusiastic plan to provide television broadcasting to the entire nation. Similarly, satellite broadcasting systems were mounted in Indonesia, the five nations of Southeast Asia, the Arab states, and in Brazil. In addition to television, such satellite systems typically provide telephone links at low cost across great distances.

INTERNATIONAL NEWS FLOW

Besides development communication, the other main issue in international communication is international news flow. There is a long tradition of scholarly studies of news flow between nations, most of which show an imbalance between Euro-America and the Third World. The major news agencies (like the Associated Press, United Press International, Reuters, and Agence-France Presse) are Western-owned and -operated, and carry news that reflects a Western viewpoint. The distribution of television and films, the ownership of advertising agencies, and the control of newspapers and magazines are also concentrated in Euro-America.

During the 1970s and 1980s, this media imbalance became the topic of a major world debate, centered in UNESCO, about what could be done to correct the imbalance and thus bring about a new world information order (MacBride Commission, 1980). Communication researchers played an important role in this policy discussion, documenting how serious the imbalance was and suggesting policy alternatives. Varis and Nordenstreng (1975) found that a rather high percentage of television broadcast hours were imported from the United States, ranging to 85 percent in some of the smaller Latin American nations.

Dependency theory is the viewpoint that Third World countries are less developed mainly because of their inferior economic relationships with developed nations (Schement & Rogers,

1984). Dependency theorists look for the causes of underdevelopment in the trade and other economic relations of a Third World country with industrialized nations. When applied to the case of media flow, dependency theorists would look for the economic and cultural dependence created by the sale of media products to a Third World nation.

Media imperialism occurs when the mass media are used as ideological and economic tools of the world capitalistic system, serving to lock Third World economies and cultures into subservient roles as markets and suppliers of raw materials. TV flow in Latin America is one example of media imperialism. Do the imported television series and other media products detract from national goals of development? The imported programs may deflect the media from their priority use for development, but little is actually known, on the basis of research, about this issue.

Antola and Rogers (1984) found that by 1982 the share of Latin American television broadcast hours imported from the United States had substantially decreased. Commercial television systems in Mexico and Brazil rose from 1972 to 1982; they produced most of their own nations' TV fare and exported it to other Latin American nations. Most of this Latin American television programming consisted of *telenovelas* (something like U.S. soap operas), which are extremely popular in Latin America. So imported U.S. television series are much less important in Latin America today than a decade ago. However, U.S.-style commercial television broadcasting has been adopted throughout Latin America. Most of these television systems were partly owned or assisted by the three U.S. networks in their early days. These relationships have now ended, but their influence continues in that Latin American TV systems are mainly privately owned, commercially operated, and mainly dedicated to providing entertainment programming for the largest possible audience. Thus the direct influence of U.S. ownership of television systems in Latin America and of imported U.S. TV programming is now much diminished.

A pattern similar to that just described for Latin America has also occurred in other nations recently, although the details differ. The trends are toward a decrease in imported television series and other media products, to greatly increased media audiences (especially for television in the 1980s), to entertainment (rather than instructional) media content, and to greater commercialization of television broadcasting. Unfortunately, these trends mean that the mass media systems in Third World nations have not yet contributed very directly to national development. The media are predominantly entertainment- and urban-oriented, containing little content that is instrumental to reaching development goals. But the potential exists, and promising combinations of entertainment with development contents were being broadcast in the late 1980s in Mexico, India, Kenya, and other nations.

CONCLUSION

The mass media of communication have the potential to make important contributions to desired social change in the Third World nations of Latin America, Africa, and Asia, but to date this potential has not been very fully realized.

One way social change occurs is through the diffusion of innovations. Diffusion is the process by which an innovation is communicated through certain channels over time among the members of a social system.

The type of social change most desired in Third World nations is development, defined as a widely participatory process of social change in society, intended to bring about both social and material advancement (including greater equality, freedom, and other valued ideals) for the majority of the people through their gaining greater control over their environment. During the 1950s and 1960s, most Third World nations followed a model of development that entailed heavy industrialization, urbanization, capital-intensive technology, centralized development planning, a focus on economic growth, and an emphasis on internal causes of underdevelopment.

This dominant paradigm of development began to be questioned in the 1970s and various alternatives to it were explored. One of the most important intellectual changes was to recognize the role of socioeconomic equality in development. Unfortunately, one of the frequent consequences of diffusion is a widening of the gap between the socioeconomic elites and the masses in a system. But recent communication research indicates that such increased inequality is not inevitable; if certain strategies of social change are followed, it is possible to close socioeconomic gaps (or at least not to widen them).

SUMMARY

The role of the mass media in the development of the Third World has not proceeded as originally expected. The traditional view of development predicted that the diffusion of technological innovations would bring socioeconomic development. But development was not always beneficial to the Third World; it seldom progressed at the rate predicted, and its benefits did not go equally to all citizens. Today a new approach to development emphasizes equality, participation, and self-development.

Diffusion of innovations has been extensively researched. The speed of adoption of innovations is directly related to the characteristics of the innovation, such as its advantage or its complexity. The type of media used to diffuse information about innovations influences the rate of adoption, as does the innovativeness of the various members of the target audience.

Consequences of innovation can be classified in many ways. One of the consequences that has been of great interest is the desire to narrow rather than widen the socioeconomic gap within developing societies. A number of information strategies for narrowing the gap in development by focusing on poor target audiences have been developed.

New media technologies are being developed that have the potential to assist in the development of Third World countries. But dependency theory raises the concern that the new media, especially to the extent that they bring in greater outside media influences, may actually impede development by facilitating a form of media imperialism which subverts indigenous development.

REVIEW AND DISCUSSION QUESTIONS

1. Discuss the differences between the traditional view of development and the new development paradigm. How would these development paradigms differ on the most appropriate forms of communication for introducing innovations to developing societies?

2. How does the study of diffusion of innovation compare to the study of persuasion (Chapter 10) or organizations (Chapter 7)? To what extent is the research on persuasion applicable in Third World development settings? To what extent is research on diffusion of innovation in developing nations useful to someone interested in persuasion, such as an advertiser selling a new product?

3. Which concepts of intercultural communication (Chapter 9) would be applicable in analyzing diffusion-of-innovation research? What principles of effective intercultural communication may have been violated by the traditional approach to development?

4. Although the emphasis of the new development paradigm is on social equality, the study of political communication in developing nations (Chapter 12) suggests that such actions may also have political consequences. How much responsibility should the communication scholar or consultant have for these indirect political consequences of development? Can these consequences be controlled through the diffusion strategies chosen, if that were desirable?

REFERENCES

Antola, L., & Rogers, E. M. (1984). Television flows in Latin America. *Communication Research, 11*(2), 183–202.

Havens, A. E. (1975). Diffusion of new seed varieties and its consequences: A Colombian case. In R. E. Dumett & L. J. Brainard (Eds.), *Problems of rural development: Case studies and multidisciplinary perspectives* (pp. 93–111). Leiden: E. J. Brill.

Kuhn, T. S. (1970). *The structure of scientific revolutions*. Chicago: University of Chicago Press.

MacBride Commission (1980). *Many voices, one world: Report by the International Commission for the*

Study of Communication Problems. London: Kogan Page; New York: Unipub.

Rogers, E. (1976). Communication and development: The passing of the dominant paradigm. *Communication Research, 3*(2), 213–240.

Rogers, E. M. (1983). *Diffusion of innovations.* New York: Free Press.

Rogers, E. M., & Kincaid, D. L. (1981). *Communication networks: A new paradigm for research.* New York: Free Press.

Rogers, E. M., & Larsen, J. K. (1984). *Silicon Valley fever: Growth of high-technology culture.* New York: Basic Books.

Roling, N. G., Ascroft, J., & Chege, F. W. (1976). The diffusion of innovations and the issue of equality in rural development. *Communication Research, 3*(2), 155–170.

Schement, J. R., & Rogers, E. M. (1984). Media flows in Latin America. *Communication Research, 11*(2), 305–320.

Schramm, W. (1964). *Mass media and national development.* Stanford, CA: Sage.

Servan-Schreiber, J. (1981). *The world challenge.* New York: Simon & Schuster.

Shingi, P. M., & Mody, B. (1976). The communication effects gap: A field experiment on television and agricultural ignorance in India. *Communication Research, 3*(2), 171–190.

Tichenor, P. J., Donohue, G. A., & Olien, C. N. (1970). Mass media flow and differential growth in knowledge. *Public Opinion Quarterly, 34,* 159–170.

Varis, T., & Nordenstreng, K. (1975). *Television broadcasting as a one-way street.* Paris: UNESCO.

12

Political Communication

Steven H. Chaffee
Stanford University

Pedro F. Hernandez-Ramos
The University of Pennsylvania

Steven H. Chaffee is Professor and Director of the Institute for Communication Research at Stanford University. He is former director of the School of Journalism and Mass Communication at the University of Wisconsin–Madison. His research has included areas such as election campaigns, adolescent socialization and family communication, co-orientational models, and the social effects of television and other mass media.

Pedro F. Hernandez-Ramos is assistant editor of the International Encyclopedia of Communication *at the University of Pennsylvania. He holds a B.A. (Lic.) degree in communication from Universidad Iberoamericana in Mexico and a Ph.D. degree in communication from Stanford University. His research has focused on the role of television in child development and theories of public communication campaigns applied to topics such as smoking and family planning.*

The authors thank Diana C. Mutz for her thoughtful comments on an earlier draft of this chapter.

LEARNING OBJECTIVES

After studying this chapter you should be able to:

- Distinguish between authoritarian and libertarian approaches to government relations with the media.
- Identify the limited-effects theory of political effects.

- Describe the weaknesses in the selective-exposure principle with respect to political communication.

- Discuss changes in media ownership and competition patterns that have affected the political content of the media.

- Outline the evidence for and against the agenda-setting function of the media.

- Trace changes in partisanship in media coverage of debates and campaigns.

- Summarize the kinds of uses voters make of the media.

- Explain what is meant by a transactional approach to political communication.

- Distinguish between modernization theory and dependency theory with respect to developing nations.

- State the assumptions of research under modernization theory.

- List the major political functions of the mass media that are recognized by modernization theory.

- State the assumptions of research under dependency theory.

- Discuss the relationship between national communication policies and political and economic development.

- Define cultural imperialism.

- Provide examples of alternative communication.

- Explain how alternative communication would influence politics.

No field of communication research is so controversial, or so different from one country to another, as political communication. The very words *political* and *communication* take on quite different meanings in different social, economic, and government contexts. We will outline the assumptions and viewpoints that have informed a number of different traditions in the study of political communication, in the United States and elsewhere. Our purpose is to help the reader appreciate the intellectual value, and recognize some of the shortcomings, of major contemporary approaches.

Most research on political communication has been conducted in countries that share distinct cultural and political characteristics: electoral democracies with well-developed mass media industries, widespread literacy, and some unity of language, literature, and religion. Most of these nations are in the Americas and Western Europe. These countries usually have strong universities and public policies that foster and reward scholarly research. In this hospitable setting, one can study such problems as the role the press plays in political decision making, how control of media is related to other forms of power in the society, and ways to organize effective communication campaigns on behalf of a political cause. In other countries, research is much more difficult to undertake, both because of its expense relative to other pressing societal needs and because it may be perceived as threatening to economic, political, or intellectual elites. Our outline of the field must rely on research examples from countries where strong traditions of inquiry about political communication have already developed. Our hope is that this chapter will help stimulate new directions in political communication research that are appropriate to other settings as well.

This chapter reviews research and theory regarding communication and politics from three broad points of view. The first is comparative, and consists of brief sketches of the major ideal models of media-government relations that are to be found in different nations and political traditions around the world. The second is the predominant perspective in the United States and similar Western democracies, in which communication institutions are analyzed in terms of how they serve the political process. The third draws heavily from Latin American intellectual traditions, concentrating on political criticism of media institutions. To draw the contrast between the latter two perspectives, we refer to them generically as, respectively, "the communication of politics" and "the politics of communication."

IDEAL TYPES OF MEDIA-GOVERNMENT RELATIONSHIPS

Human values and normative ideals shape both the structure of political communication and scholarly investigation of it. For purposes of comparing different countries, scholars usually refer to a few distinct "ideal types." No nation is a pure example of any of these types; they are ideal, not real. Over time, a nation may move away from one and toward another model. To the extent that conscious attempts are made to develop media-government relationships in terms of these types, then these ideals are real in their consequences.

The Authoritarian-Libertarian Distinction

One idealized distinction was outlined in an influential book by Siebert, Peterson, and Schramm (1956). Siebert contrasted two extreme images of the relationship between government and press that he called "authoritarian" and "libertarian." Historically, he argued, what today are called "the mass media" emerged in a context of absolute government authority. This was most obvious in Europe, where printing developed rapidly in the 16th and 17th centuries in countries ruled by powerful monarchs whose authority was based on lineage and an assumption of "divine right." Military and ecclesiastical authority also provided a basis of censorship and prohibition of publication; as printing proliferated, punishment of outspoken critics of the established order became common practice. In most countries today, royal and ecclesiastical authority have diminished, but military and secular power have not. Authoritarian control over the press continues to be exercised with varying degrees of severity in many nations.

The traditional authoritarian model of press-government relationships is one of separate political and communication systems, the latter privately owned but subordinate to government. Control is exercised negatively via censorship, licensing, or punishment of "seditious" statements. The mass media, like other institutions in society, are subject to established authority; their most prudent path is to avoid any act that might be perceived as undermining that authority. McQuail (1983) points out that this general conservatism extends beyond the political to the moral realm as well. In authoritarian systems, the media are not to offend the dominant moral values of society, and censorship and the criminal justice system may be used both to enforce social conformity and to protect those in authority.

The libertarian ideal grew out of a reaction against authoritarian practices in the era of colonial revolution against European domination. The United States, the first "new nation" to break free from colonial rule in the New World, prohibited its own government from abridging "freedom of speech, or of the press" in the U.S. Constitution's famous First Amendment. This guarantee of freedom of communication was an attempt to create a new kind of political system, one in which the media become an integral part of the political process. It assumes that the central problem is determining which of various alternative policies will provide "the greatest good for the greatest number" and that this judgment can best be reached by letting everyone consider all the possibilities. As the poet John Milton (1644) put it in defending his own attack on ecclesiastical authority (he had defied his Roman Catholic government by divorcing his first wife so he could remarry): "Who ever knew truth put to the worse, in a free and open encounter?"

In practice, unfortunately, encounters among competing political interests are rarely free and open, and "truth" often takes a beating in the media. The assumption that there is a single, optimum political outcome ("truth"?) that will be the best choice for most people is an idea much more widely believed in the affluent United States than in most other countries. The view of politics as a struggle among different classes or sectors of society, where one interest succeeds at the expense of the others, is not so compatible with the simplest version of the libertarian ideal of political communication. Countries attempting to put libertarian principles into practice have had to adopt a number of compromise policies. In modern society, it is simply impossible to guarantee everyone the opportunity to publish (or broadcast) his or her opinions. No one's attempt to communicate is to be interfered with, but this "freedom from" control is mainly enjoyed by established media institutions such as newspapers, magazines, film producers, and broadcasting stations. Little "freedom for" communication is available to most of us as individuals (Schramm, 1957). McQuail (1983) argues that the libertarian approach ought to be called simply "free press theory," because it essentially amounts to that.

The libertarian prohibition on censorship also has been compromised to protect people from statements that may do them personal harm. Just as there can be no constitutionally protected freedom to yell "Fire!" in a crowded theater, civil laws regarding slander and libel have to be defined carefully to protect victims of (individual or media) carelessness and malice. The role of government is more limited than that of ordinary citizens. The U.S. government, for example, may not exercise "prior restraint" over any publication, and statements that attack the government or its officials are not punishable—even though they might otherwise be libelous. Perhaps most fundamental to the libertarian ideal—and most difficult to accept for those unfamiliar with it—is the principle that publication of error or falsehood—is protected just as firmly as is truth. Because it is assumed that "truth will out," inherent in libertarian theory is a sort of "freedom to lie," or at least freedom to print irresponsible criticisms of the government.

Authoritarian and libertarian concepts are what we might call *normative theories*. They specify what the relationship between the political system and the communication media *ought* to be. They represent extremes, and although examples of both can be found among the countries of the world today, probably no pure case of either is to be found. Rigid authoritarian regimes that suppress all opposition tend to relax their controls over the press after a few years in power—or else they are overthrown. Conversely, although one can find traces of libertarian rhetoric in almost any political system, in only about two dozen nations is even the reduced "free press" version of libertarianism outlined above established practice. These tend to be relatively affluent nations with market economies, as the ideologies of free trade and free press are closely linked. They are also mostly electoral democracies, because the clash of competing opinions in a free press derives most of its presumed value from the "enlightment" it provides for the electorate. Where most people do not vote for and against policies, or at least choose among alternative parties and leaders, a free press can contribute little to the functioning of the political system.

The Agency Approach

The authoritarian model, in which the communication system is defined as outside of (and subordinate to) the political system, and the libertarian model, in which the communication system is protected as part of the political system but independent of the formal government, are by no means the only alternatives. It is obviously possible to incorporate a communication system into a government, on the assumption that the political system will then operate more effectively in pursuing its goals. This premise requires the prior assumption that the government represents all the people and their collective interest. In libertarian terms, this would mean that "the truth" has already been determined and is embodied in the policies of those who are currently in power. On these assumptions, nations have tended with increasing frequency in the 20th century to convert the mass media into agencies of the government.

Although its philosophical basis can be traced to numerous earlier writers, this agency approach was first put into practice on a large scale by the Soviet Union after the Russian revolution of 1917. Thus it is often referred to as the "Soviet-Communist theory of the press" (Schramm, in Siebert et al., 1956) or "Soviet media theory" (McQuail, 1983). It is not, however, peculiar to Soviet-bloc nations nor even to countries with socialized economies. Examples of the agency approach can be found practically everywhere, since anyone in a position of authority (or responsibility) to carry out policy will be inclined to use the power of modern mass media in achieving his or her goals. Even within a strong libertarian tradition, this will be the case to some extent. The U.S. government rarely interferes with the work of reporters who cover its activities, but it employs hundreds of times as many professional journalists on its own behalf in public affairs offices throughout the Pentagon and other government bureaucracies.

At a political level below that of the state, one routinely finds controlled communication agencies, such as teacher-supervised student newspapers in schools, the publication of "house organs" in large businesses, and the production of media materials urging innovations in agriculture and family planning by government "change agents."

What distinguishes the Soviet approach is the *exclusive* control the state exercises over communication. Here again, we must draw a distinction between the ideal and actual practice, because no nation has ever exercised complete control over the media of all its citizens for an extended period of time. Still, many try—and they are as often regimes of the right (such as Nazi Germany) as of the left. Communication media are not, in such a system, to be privately owned; this principle is, of course, most compatible with the assumptions of a socialized economy in which all means of production *ought to be* owned and operated by the state. The goals of society are to be ascertained by political leaders without widespread public debate of alternatives;

these goals are then pursued through communication of various types (persuasion, agitation, education), using the media where appropriate and controlling them (via censorship, criminal punishment, and so on) so they will serve the predetermined needs of the state. Within these constraints, the media are expected to support progressive movements, to serve the needs of their audiences, and to provide an accurate portrayal of events as defined by the ruling ideology of the society.

Unlike the press in an authoritarian system, then, agency media have a defined positive role in the political process. Because they are the major communication institutions within the society, agency media carry a much heavier responsibility for providing needed messages than those operating under libertarian assumptions, which allow any single medium a wide latitude for error and falsehood.

Modifications of Libertarianism

The 20th-century advent of the news magazine, radio, film, and television has led to various limitations on libertarian principles. This is due in part to changes in the newspaper industry, for which the free press doctrine was originally formulated. In the United States today, each urban center typically has only one or two newspapers, and increasingly they are under the management of one of a very few chain owners. As technological development of communication media continues, control tends to be in the hands of a few, very large media organizations. Satellite and computer technologies, for example, are changing the news industry, through giant institutions such as Televisa in Mexico, Reuters in Europe, and the Gannett newspaper chain in the United States. The libertarian ideal, born before the electronic media, when many small, independent newspapers were being published across Europe and the United States, has been adapted to the realities of a world of proliferating channels and concentrated ownership.

Social-Responsibility Theory The first major critique of libertarian press institutions in the United States grew out of general disenchantment with laissez-faire policies during the Great Depression of the 1930s. A blue ribbon commission headed by University of Chicago president Robert M. Hutchins was funded by Time Inc., itself one of the great media baronies of this century. Its report, *A Free and Responsible Press,* marks the first major exposition of what has come to be called the social-responsibility theory of the press (Hutchins et al., 1947; Siebert et al., 1956). More than any of the other ideal perspectives we have discussed, social responsibility is a normative theory, an outline of what a communication system ought to contribute to society rather than an empirical description of what it actually does. Oddly, perhaps, it is also more of a compromise "solution" than the other theories.

Social-responsibility theory is usually seen as a product of U.S. experience and thought. It takes as given most of the conditions that have developed in the United States under the First Amendment: private ownership of almost all mass media, the assumption that competing voices in the free "marketplace of ideas" will produce the best solutions to political and other societal problems, and the principle that government should not exercise prior restraint over communication. (The most notable exception is that radio and television broadcasting frequencies must be allocated through government authority because of the limited number of channels available.) These assumptions alone have obviously not been sufficient to guarantee that the news media today will perform the tasks for which they were originally granted their precious and remarkable freedom. Public communication institutions, in accepting press freedom under libertarian theory, incur a concomitant responsibility to the society that protects them from interference by its government.

There is no single list of obligations that all who argue for social responsibility would impose on the media. But prominent in the Hutchins Commission's report and later syntheses are such concepts as accuracy, objectivity, fairness, and professional standards in news reporting. The media are expected somehow to regulate themselves in these respects so that government will not have to step in. Such a normative argument implies an evident paradox: The "free" press should regulate itself lest it be regulated by government and thus cease to be free. The leading media powers in the United States argue that this amounts to no freedom at all (in libertarian terms), and have made rather little progress toward self-regulation since Hutchins's day.

In reaction to this unresponsive position, social-responsibility adherents have sometimes proposed that an independent body be established to monitor press performance, hear complaints, or otherwise to help foster media responsibility. In the United States this has been done in minor ways through government bodies that mildly regulate broadcasting (Federal Communications Commission) and advertising (Federal Trade Commission), or through bodies created by and for the media themselves (often called press councils). Occasionally, the monitoring function is assigned to blue-ribbon bodies modeled after the Hutchins Commission, which included educators, successful businessmen, a poet, and other people of accomplishment—but no journalists and no one holding public office.

In countries that stay close to the libertarian ideal with respect to print media, public broadcasting systems are usually operated according to social-responsibility principles. This is the case, for example, in the government-operated television systems of the Federal Republic of Germany, Britain's BBC, and the public television system (NHK) in Japan.

One inherent difficulty has been the problem of defining precisely what "socially responsible" media performance is. For example, it is widely accepted in academic and policymaking circles that television violence strengthens some viewers' tendencies toward aggressive behavior (Comstock, Chaffee, Katzman, McCombs, & Roberts, 1978), and perhaps also increases people's fear of violence and crime (Gerbner, Gross, & Signorielli, 1980). Violence on television has been restricted by government policy, however, much more in Canada and European countries than in the United States, where most of the relevant research has been conducted. Many people also think that heavy media emphasis on sexual activity—especially illicit, extramarital, dehumanizing, or criminal sex—strengthens some people's propensity toward such behavior and the perception by others that it is commonplace. Attacks on the media as socially irresponsible and in need of regulation with regard to violence and sex tend to come from politically opposite directions: violence from the liberal side, sex more often from conservatives. But in any case, attempts to reform an essentially libertarian media-government system from within are not easily carried out. Sex and violence remain staples of popular entertainment.

Access and Pluralism Several other lines of modification of libertarianism deserve note, in part because they probably represent trends that will grow in coming years. One is the "access" movement. With modern media systems characterized by "bigness and fewness" (Schramm, 1957), freedom of the press is no longer so much a civil right enjoyed by all citizens as it is a special privilege of a few people who sit atop huge media organizations. Many attempts to increase people's access to the channels of communication have been undertaken, although a general right of public access to private media has never been established in a libertarian context.

More general is the concept of "pluralism," which takes many forms. The press is expected, as part of its social responsibility, to represent the interests and concerns of the various racial, religious, and other groups that make up the total community. This may be accomplished by giving minority representatives access (for example, running a newspaper column by a minority leader), by offering opportunity for reply to an editorial to anyone with an opposing perspective, or by hiring minority reporters (Kerner et al., 1968).

The Democratic-Participant Approach Another trend toward "reformed libertarianism" is what McQuail (1983) calls "democratic-participant media theory." This is a form of critique rooted in disillusionment with established political processes and parties, as well as with the media, including both commercial and the "elitist" publicly controlled media. The argument is that big, centralized media tend to reflect the perspective of the powerful, the established, the metropolitan, or at best the "average" taste. The call is for less professional, more personal and local opportunities for people to use media. The democratic-participant approach is far from a coherent "theory"; it consists of a loosely related set of "ought to" demands.

Communication technology may facilitate attempts to respond to this participant perspective. For example, computer-based interactive systems are being developed for television, so that viewers can send messages back to the communication source. Satellite transmission can free people of the need to be located in a central metropolis in order to engage in the business of the day. Optimistic futurists see great possibilities in these user-controlled communication systems. To date, however, it is powerful elites such as the financial community, law enforcement agencies, and bureaucratic work organizations (medicine, the military, scientists) who have enjoyed most of the advantages of new communication technologies. Whether technology *could* bring about the widespread access desired by democratic-participant theorists is not in question; whether it *will* is.

Development Theory

Most countries in the world today have not yet developed economically to the stage where political communication systems modeled after those of European, Soviet, or North American nations become feasible. In many Third World countries, the technological state of communication media remains largely preindustrial (except for radio), at least partly because there is not a sufficient audience of affluent, literate "consumers" to justify a technologically advanced media system. Where hunger and disease are prevalent, public health and the development of agriculture understandably take precedence over cultural and even political concerns. The place of political communication research in such an economic environment is necessarily a matter of compromise.

It is difficult to generalize about the practices of developing nations, since more than 100 countries could be so described. From a broad menu of alternatives, developing nations have chosen many different paths (Katz & Wedell, 1977). Some operate under fairly strict authoritarian or agency principles, but most Third World countries—particularly those "new nations" that were once colonies of European powers—have been attracted to features of the libertarian ideal. For example, the constitutions of most newly independent countries include some variant of freedom of the press. But this libertarian principle is more clearly recognized as an ideal, or a goal toward which the nation will strive, than as a near-absolute guarantee in the manner of the U.S. Constitution. The achievement of press freedom takes its place alongside other long-term societal goals, which are political, social, and cultural—but first, economic.

A kind of "development theory" is, however, emerging from the many compromises among competing values that less-developed nations have made in their political communication systems. Economic development implies social change, and even where press freedom is seen as a major goal, it must be subordinated to economic priorities and other development needs of society (McQuail, 1983). This may mean, on occasion, imposing either authoritarian constraints (such as censorship) or agency-type constraints (such as required publication) on the media.

It also implies that journalists and others in the media should be "part of the team," devoted to helping the established political leadership carry out its policies of national development. Often, this may mean not reporting certain events or not expressing antiestablishment opinions, and it almost invariably means emphasizing the content

and symbolism of nationhood: the language, culture, and news of the country and those most like it, rather than news and culture from remote Western powers. It is in this area of international communication that development theory has staked out its clearest position.

A major document expressing political communication concerns of developing nations is *Many Voices, One World,* the report of UNESCO's International Commission for the Study of Communication Problems (MacBride et al., 1980). These concerns are made the more urgent by satellite broadcasting, rapid world news flow, and transfers of communication technologies to less-developed countries (Rogers & Schement, 1984). In Third World settings, social stratification tends to be severe; the economic distance between elites and the very poor is several times greater than in the West. Not surprisingly, then, concepts of social class and rural-urban differentiation enter much more centrally into the emerging development model of political communication. The politics of the use of communication in Third World nations is discussed later in this chapter.

The Value of Normative Theories

We have discussed a variety of normative ideals or theories of what the relationship between a society's communication system and its political system ought to be. What is the value of this intellectual exercise, especially in a book devoted to the "social science" of communication? Our answer is threefold:

1. Understanding what a political communication system ought to be doing is a necessary first step in assessing whether it is in fact doing what it is supposed to do. For example, the next section will review at some length the empirical social research dealing with political communication in the United States and, to a lesser extent, in other countries that share roughly the same assumptions about the role of the media in politics. This research, and the rationale for choosing particu-

lar topics of study, can be understood only in light of those assumptions. The United States views its media in essentially libertarian terms, with room for various kinds of modifications and reforms in the service of a competitive electoral democracy.

Thus our intent is not to mechanically review the literature on political communication in the United States. Rather, we will use that literature to evaluate communication institutions within the context of that country's libertarian-democratic tradition. "Is communication institution 'X' serving the society well or not?" is the type of valuative question that stimulates most research on political communication. The social science of political communication is neither value-free nor apolitical.

2. Elaboration of normative theory is itself a major form of academic scholarship. A later section of this chapter will examine in detail several leading concepts and intellectual traditions that have occupied some of the best minds among Latin American, U.S., and European scholars. Although normative discourse is not usually considered "social science" (as ordinarily defined in the United States), it is generally regarded as an acceptable form of scholarship. Examining the role communication institutions play in a particular society and proposing an alternative set of arrangements involves awareness of many idealized options—not just the reality being confronted and the specific direction of reform advocated. Much of what is written about communication institutions cannot be read in isolation, because it is part of an ongoing dialectic among many normative viewpoints.

3. Conditions considered theoretically desirable often shape social reality. Human beings have an incredible capacity to transform their social institutions, and they usually do so most effectively when striving to meet a global ideal—even though that ideal may never be fully realized. Normative theories possess, each by its own internal logic and prescriptions, the power to direct the activities of millions of people—in the cases of some theories, literally billions of people.

As a case in point, even though no single news story may ever be fully objective, the normative goal of objectivity in journalism is a powerful factor in determining why the press of the United States covers news as it does. And even though no single national policy can be absolutely identified as moving a society in the direction of development, the goal of development is widely shared in most countries, and the activities of the press are often expected to be subordinated to it.

THE COMMUNICATION OF POLITICS

Political communication in any society is at least as old as the political system itself. In the case of the United States, it goes back to the founding of the republic more than 200 years ago, and back even further to the origins of the British traditions of the press and politics.

The study of political communication as a social science, on the other hand, is quite recent. It is essentially a product of our own time, resulting from the introduction of new conceptual ideas and methods of research, combined with real change—even within a few decades—in our institutions of political communication. The outline that follows is partly historical, partly conceptual, and of necessity highly condensed. It focuses on the way politics is communicated in modern society. This theme is most often described in terms of the political effects of mass communication, although it could also be viewed as the way media are used to conduct political activities.

The Lazarsfeld Tradition: Limited Effects

Early in the presidential election year of 1940, a team of researchers from Columbia University traveled to Erie County in northern Ohio to study "the influence of mass communication in an election campaign." Under the leadership of Paul F. Lazarsfeld, a marketing psychologist who had left his native Vienna in the early years of Nazi domination, these researchers brought to their groundbreaking study a vague sense that the mass media wielded awesome power over people's minds. Their survey, for which commercial pollster Elmo Roper was the leading consultant, led them to a conclusion quite opposite to their expectations. Instead of finding evidence of massive media manipulation in the manner of the press systems of Germany and the Soviet Union, they were told by the people they questioned that (1) most of them had made up their minds on how to vote before the campaign even started, and (2) the newspapers and radio provided some relevant information, but as a rule they voted the same as other people with whom they talked.

The People's Choice (Lazarsfeld, Berelson, & Gaudet, 1948), the slim monograph reporting their survey, had a powerfully sobering impact on academic thought concerning mass media effects; it is still one of the most regularly cited empirical studies in the entire mass communication field. Out of this study and a replication in Elmira, New York, in 1948 (Berelson, Lazarsfeld, & McPhee, 1954) came what is now called the "limited-effects model" or "law of minimal consequences" (Klapper, 1960). Until the mid-1970s this was the dominant view regarding political mass communication (Gitlin, 1978), that the impact of media is ordinarily quite limited because people's party loyalties and social ties intervene to counteract media messages. The news media seem not nearly so trustworthy as one's family, friends, and co-workers. Information does not flow directly from the media to the individual, but instead is delivered to most people through a smaller number of opinion leaders, informed peers who filter the news for everyone else.

Because Lazarsfeld's was the first major study on the subject, its conclusions hold an enduring position in the scholarly literature, one that has long outlived the empirical import and relevance of the survey itself. Current research, which often provides clear-cut evidence of political influence of mass communication, is typically reported in the context of the Lazarsfeld results, almost as if "limited effects" was the basic rule and differing conclusions merely isolated exceptions to it. The

limited-effects model was both a valuable synthesis of early research and a healthy antidote to the apocalyptic fears of mass media and propaganda that pervaded the Depression of the 1930s, World War II (1939–45), and the early Cold War period (1945–50). But it is far from an adequate analysis of the status of political communication in the United States today.

The Demise of Selective Exposure

One of the most popular tenets of the limited-effects model was the concept of selective exposure. Klapper (1960) emphasized that people have a tendency to expose themselves to media messages that will reinforce beliefs that they already hold. In the Erie County and Elmira studies, it was noted that people who intended to vote Republican mostly read newspapers that opposed the Democratic president, whereas those who were voting Democratic relied more on radio (which was nonpartisan) for their news.

This media-party relationship could have been explained in several ways, including an effect of the partisan bias in the newspapers or as a reflection of socioeconomic differences (for example, newspapers and Republicans were both more instrumental for the white-collar middle class). But the explanation favored among academics was that people sought out media content that was congenial to their political beliefs. This conception accorded with the more general image of people as self-deluding, a popular academic view stimulated by Freudian psychology, among other influences. The idea of selective exposure based on partisan predispositions is still to be found in many textbooks on mass communication.

Selective exposure is an example of a concept in social science that survives beyond its time. Sears and Freedman (1967) reviewed a number of surveys and experimental studies and concluded that there was no evidence that people actively seek information to support a political position they already hold. They did note that people do indeed receive messages compatible with their political values, a phenomenon they called "de facto selective exposure," but they could not attribute this to the exercise of preference or motivated activity on the part of media audience members.

Just as products for housewives are advertised on daytime television and just as life insurance salespeople contact newly married couples, it is good business to provide an upper-middle-class audience with material about conservative politicians, a working-class audience with labor-oriented news, and so on. Planners of political campaigns know this as well as any other communication professional. A commercial radio station, for example, features a distinctive style of music that attracts an audience with highly specific age, sex, and socioeconomic characteristics. Newspapers that are delivered to homes in the morning are likely to be read by white-collar and professional workers; blue-collar and factory workers typically go to work an hour or two earlier in the day and arrive home earlier in the afternoon, when an evening newspaper is delivered. It should not be surprising, then, to find that labor-oriented dailies in cities like Cleveland and Cincinnati were delivered in the afternoon. (It should also not be surprising that these liberal afternoon newspapers have almost totally disappeared from major U.S. cities, as factories have closed and the labor force has become progressively more white-collar.) Successful media planners try to ensure selective exposure of the "target audience," even if audience members do not themselves seek it.

Regardless of why it might occur, the question of effects of selective exposure remains. Is the effect of overexposure to the side already favored one of "reinforcement," as Klapper (1960) asserted? In bipartisan politics, selective exposure may involve the strengthening either of one's liking for the preferred candidate ("positive reinforcement") or of disliking of the opposition candidate ("negative reinforcement"), or both. Chaffee and Miyo (1983) could find no clear evidence of either process, however, in a study of the 1980 presidential election campaign, in which

they measured people's evaluations of the candidates both prior to and again near the end of the campaign, and their exposure to messages of both candidates during the campaign.

Decline in Partisanship

Not only has research refuted the major hypotheses regarding both the presumed cause (motivation) and effect (reinforcement) of Klapper's proposition concerning selective exposure, but the phenomenon itself is in historical decline. Newspapers in the United States are much less partisan than at the time of Lazarsfeld's studies, and today's reader has far fewer newspapers to choose among, so that it is hard to be "selective" at all. The alternatives to newspapers for political communication are television and radio, neither of which is partisan in any consistent way. As more people rely on these nonpartisan electronic media, selective exposure inevitably declines.

U.S. newspapers shift from deep partisanship toward political independence and a blurring of liberal-conservative ideologies can be traced over the last few decades. When the First Amendment was adopted, the press consisted of many small, politically partisan papers that carried rather little "news" in our 20th-century sense. In each major city, one could find a newspaper to suit practically every political taste. Many papers adopted names that clearly indicated their political affiliations: the *Democrat,* the *Union,* the *Republican,* and so on. It was from this multitude of partisan voices that the libertarian ideal promised "truth" would emerge. Early in this century, however, the number of newspapers in the United States began to shrink, and by the 1940s the one-newspaper city was becoming the rule.

An overwhelming majority of U.S. newspapers, which are of course businesses, support the business-oriented Republican party (except in the South, where that party scarcely existed until recent decades). Countless content analyses of the "one-party press" showed that newspapers consistently opposed Franklin D. Roosevelt and his Democratic successor, Harry S Truman. By the

1950s the popular Republican president Dwight D. Eisenhower enjoyed highly favorable press coverage. But something of far greater historical importance to political communication came to the United States during that period: television. Eisenhower became a familiar figure in millions of homes as he held casual press conferences and delivered his homely yet authoritative speeches. The demands of this new medium, which puts a premium on personality, have certainly had an impact on the selection of candidates and the ways they campaign. But even more consequential for political communication has been the impact of television, as a competing medium, on the newspaper.

Media Competition Television took away from the newspaper a good share of people's time and attention and, not coincidentally, a considerable amount of advertising revenue as well. The strain on newspapers was not immediately so severe as it was on the film and radio industries, because television was primarily an entertainment medium. But the newspaper industry did have to redefine its niche in this new competitive environment. Newspapers had always had a political role, but competition from television created a need to redesign that role. By the end of the 1960s, more people were telling Roper Poll interviewers that they got most of their news from television rather than newspapers.

Moreover, people were (and still are) saying they believe television more than they do newspapers. Professional journalists recognize but are confused by this assertion, because they know that far more reporting resources go into newspapers than into television, and that newspapers carry much more information on their many pages than a television newscast can possibly transmit. Television news, by and large, comes from newspaper-based sources such as the Associated Press. Yet when polls ask the hypothetical question "If you received conflicting reports from television and the newspaper, which would you believe?", most Americans answer "Television." Why?

A number of reasons for the higher credibility attached to television are advanced; most of them have to do with either the personal nature of a live newscaster (Carter & Greenberg, 1965) or the thought that "on television, you can actually see what happened" (even though it is very rare to literally see a politically relevant news event occurring on television). Still another reason is to be found in the lingering partisan bias of newspapers, which overwhelmingly continue to support Republican presidential candidates. Television, like radio, has been forced through government regulation to operate under the social-responsibility theory of the press, at least insofar as political balance and fairness are concerned. This has turned out to be good business as well.

In the era of television, the U.S. newspaper has become much less partisan than it was traditionally. Newspapers still endorse candidates and take political positions, but these expressions of partisanship are today almost entirely confined to the editorial page, a section inside the paper that typically includes signed columns representing a variety of political positions. The front page and most of the news sections of today's newspapers are produced by reporters and editors who subscribe to high professional standards of fairness and objectivity. In short, the U.S. newspaper of today is closer than ever before to meeting the normative demands of social-responsibility theory.

Economic conservatism is still the political ideology that dominates commercial media hierarchies, just as in any major businesses. The daily newspaper is one of the largest manufacturing industries in the United States, and newspapers in most U.S. cities have no direct competition. A "monopoly" publisher in a one-newspaper town is likely to feel a strong urge to propagandize local readers on behalf of business interests. The fact that this only occasionally occurs nowadays is due, at least in part, to the ubiquitous presence of nonpartisan television.

Newspaper reporters, like rank-and-file workers in most industries and like other college-educated professionals in the United States, tend to be politically liberal. Until the coming of television, however, U.S. journalists harbored mostly liberal sentiments but produced mostly conservative newspapers because that is what their employers wanted. Today those employers, locked in competition with another medium, are more often acquiescing to the professional demands of their journalists and the criticisms of social-responsibility advocates.

This diminished partisanship of the newspaper means that policies developed in some countries to provide balance among newspapers representing different parties could not be easily applied in the United States. In Norway, for example, the government subsidizes partisan newspapers to ensure that the voices of differing ideologies will continue to compete in the "marketplace of ideas." In the United States these contrasting voices are more often found within a single publication, rather than across competing publications (if they are found at all).

What has been lost from our less partisan media are the political extremes. The press has gradually become centrist, perhaps a bit Republican (because of the publishers) and a bit liberal (because of the journalists), but these are not radical viewpoints of right or left. Visitors from European countries often complain that the press in the United States is too bland, lacking the vigorous debate to which they are accustomed among the partisan newspapers of Paris, London, or Rome.

Television has carried its nonpartisanship to a further extreme. Its content in the United States today is largely nonpolitical. During an election campaign, national news programs provide pictures of the candidates and reports of where they have spoken, but very little of what the candidates have said regarding public policy is repeated (Patterson & McClure, 1976). Public affairs analysis on commercial television has largely disappeared from the air, or is confined to time slots unlikely to attract wide audiences. Public television, which once featured a number of public affairs reporting and discussion programs, has become mainly a medium for the performing arts. The blocks of nightly news programs, previously dominated by national networks with their large bureaus in Washington, D.C., have increasingly concentrated on local news (accidents, fires, homicides, but little politics except in capital cities). This is mostly because a television station can keep all advertising revenues from its own local news shows, whereas it must share with the network its proceeds from commercials sponsoring national news.

Under social-responsibility theory, political balance—in the U.S. context this means bipartisanship—is a major goal. But in the face of pressure to balance its political content, U.S. television has found a simple solution: reduce it to a minimum. By broadcasting very little partisan political material, television has avoided running afoul of such government regulatory policies as "equal time," which requires giving political candidates comparable treatment, and the "fairness doctrine," which requires a relatively balanced treatment of issues. This outcome is just the opposite of the intention of social-responsibility theory, of course, and recently a virtual "deregulation" of commercial television has taken place, which is to say a shift toward libertarian principles.

Debates and Issues

An important innovation television has brought to political communication is the televised debate between candidates. In 1960 John F. Kennedy and Richard M. Nixon appeared together on live television, each behind a podium, with a moderator and a panel of journalists who asked questions. In that election and again when Gerald Ford and Jimmy Carter met in 1976, these debates attracted huge television audiences. Although not everyone who tuned in paid close attention, there is evidence that many voters sought and gained from the debates a clarification of the differences between the two candidates on various policy issues (Katz & Feldman, 1962; Sears & Chaffee, 1979). Those watching learned as much from the candidate they opposed as from the one they favored (Carter, 1962). These findings are quite contrary to the selective-exposure hypothesis that people seek only supportive messages.

By the 1970s, U.S. voters were much more strongly determined by specific policy issues than by party affiliation or candidate images (Nie, Verba, & Petrocik, 1976). Lacking strong partisan predispositions, many voters no longer made up their minds in advance of a national election (Chaffee & Choe, 1980). They often turn today for enlightenment to television news—a medium through which selective exposure would be very difficult to accomplish. Unfortunately, television news ordinarily does not provide much information about candidates' issue positions and policy proposals. The electorate is probably much better prepared to vote intelligently when there have been televised debates such as those of 1960 and 1976, because the debates force issue-related content onto the screen, even though the television industry itself avoids partisan conflict as a rule. More recently, issue voting appears to have declined. In 1984 Ronald Reagan won a landslide reelection, even though most TV viewers thought he "lost" his debates with Walter Mondale and most voters agreed more with Mondale on major public issues. Television brings voters both information and personalities, and it is difficult to predict which will prevail in a specific instance.

Agenda Setting

In a time when the limited-effects model was still given wide credence, a political scientist (Cohen, 1963) analyzing the relationship between the press and foreign policy asserted that "the press . . . may not be successful much of the time in telling people what to think, but it is stunningly successful in telling its readers what to think about" (p. 13).

This proposition was first put to empirical test by McCombs and Shaw (1972), who called it the "agenda-setting function" of mass media. They found relatively high correlations between the frequency with which a topic (such as "inflation" or "taxes" or "war") was mentioned by people as "the most important problem facing the country"

and the prominence with which those topics were featured in newspaper articles. They concluded that the news media, by choosing to emphasize certain problems but not others, "set the agenda" of public concern and thus presumably of political action. If so, this would seem to be a powerful, if subtle, form of political influence.

Agenda setting is a specific example of what Lasswell (1948) called the "correlation function" of communication in a social system. Among other macrosocial functions, communication correlates the different components of a society so that they can work in concert on a common task or problem. An agenda for a meeting is a list of topics that the members of a group are to take up; an issue that is not on the agenda is usually not dealt with, and in political bodies, control over the agenda (such as what bills a legislature will consider, and when) can be a highly significant source of power. McCombs, Shaw, and their colleagues argue that the news media do indeed serve this function for U.S. society, and offer elaborate bodies of evidence to support their claim (McCombs, 1981; Shaw & McCombs, 1977; Weaver, Graber, McCombs, & Eyal, 1981).

However, other researchers have not produced such consistently supportive evidence. McLeod, Becker, and Byrnes (1974) tested the agenda-setting hypothesis in a two-newspaper city. During the election campaign of 1972, they found that the more liberal of the two (which gave more emphasis to the then-rumored Watergate conspiracy) also had readers who were more likely to list "honesty in government" as a major issue in the election campaign. It may be that this newspaper's heavier coverage of Watergate moved the honesty issue to a prominent position on the political agenda. The liberal newspaper's readers did indeed vote strongly against President Nixon's successful reelection bid, but they almost certainly would have done so anyway. Causation is difficult to infer from these correlational studies.

Becker et al. (1979) used monthly Gallup Poll results on the "most important problem" question in an attempt to test the agenda-setting effect of the Ford-Carter debates of 1976. They found that the issues emphasized in the debates were, as expected, highly correlated with the public's agenda of problems throughout the year. But the correlations were strongest between the content of the debates and the public's agenda several months before the debates were held, rather than after them (as a media-effects hypothesis would have predicted). It was as if the public's concerns, manifested in the published Gallup Poll results, had set the agenda for the debates, rather than the reverse. This is highly plausible, because political candidates and their campaign staffs carefully monitor public opinion polls and tailor their communication plans to the popular mood. Polls have themselves become a medium of political communication, a major channel for messages to the government from the governed.

In addition, the principle that emphasis in the news media shapes the audiences' priorities regarding public problems has been demonstrated in field experiments (Iyengar, Peters, & Kinder, 1982). People were paid to watch only one television news program for a week while the programs on that channel were systematically varied so that different economic problems were emphasized. When viewers were exposed to more news featuring a certain problem, they were more likely to say that it was a major problem facing the country. They were also more likely to use the issue in question as a basis for evaluating candidates for office. This is much stronger causal evidence than the correlations obtained in other studies, which could be explained by a number of alternative hypotheses aside from direct media effects.

The idea of a broad agenda-setting function, beyond a simple content-specific effects hypothesis, is more intriguing still. Just where does the press's own agenda, or ordering of public problems, originate? Is it established by political interest groups, candidates for office, or the public, or is it driven by events and problems in the "real world" that news media are supposed to cover? Probably all these factors, and others, play some part.

To speak of "media influence," for example, suggests that there is a large element of discretion in journalistic circles about which issues to emphasize. As a rule, this is not the case. Given the same facts and contexts, different journalists tend to produce approximately the same reportage. The weekly issues of the competing news magazines *Time* and *Newsweek* are often strikingly similar. So are stories on major political events filed by the Associated Press and United Press International, and, derivatively, most newspaper front pages across the United States. Principles of professional journalistic practice are closely followed, and they produce predictable coverage of unpredictable news events.

These conventional practices raise another question about agenda setting as a general function for the political system. It is quite difficult for a new topic or issue to break into the news. Shoemaker (1982) has shown that political interest groups perceived as extreme or deviant by the press are less likely to be covered, and that constricted coverage affects people's evaluation of such "deviants." News media are institutions largely operated by and for the middle class (or at least the literate sectors of society), not the poor and the uneducated. Thus middle-class agenda setting via the media can be successful at diverting public attention away from the problems of the poor.

Lazarsfeld and Merton (1971) suggested that "status conferral" is an important social function of mass communication. What they meant was that simply being mentioned in the press confers a degree of high status on a person or public issue, regardless of the nature of the coverage. Even criminals and other notorious figures can become celebrities, and politicians are fond of saying that "the worst thing the papers can do is to ignore you." Political candidates are often drawn from other fields that attract media publicity (such as the military, acting, professional athletics), carrying over their high status to the electoral arena. Agenda setting can be viewed as the process of conferring status on an issue or public problem. This may be a more important political function than personal status conferral; political actors on whom the media confer status usually come and go in relatively brief periods of time, whereas political issues tend to endure on the public agenda much longer.

Covering Campaigns

The fact that professional journalists largely agree on how to cover politics makes them vulnerable to political manipulation. Political offices are often staffed with ex-journalists who understand conventional practice quite well and are skilled at arranging events so that the politicians they serve can "use" the press to maximum advantage. Several studies have examined the interplay between politicians and journalists, with particular emphasis on election campaigns (Barber, 1978; O'Keefe & Atwood, 1981; Patterson, 1980).

The most thorough empirical analysis of campaign coverage to date is a study by Clarke and Evans (1983) of reporters and candidates for 82 seats (randomly sampled) in the U.S. Congress in 1978. They compared three kinds of candidates: incumbents, challengers to incumbents, and contestants for open seats (that is, in districts where there was no incumbent). The latter, the authors reasoned, pose the greatest journalistic opportunity, because they are "new faces" in politics. Incumbents, who because of the power of their office find it easy to raise money, reported about twice as much campaign spending as the challengers facing them, but only about half as much as the spending of candidates for open seats. No matter. In terms of paragraphs of coverage in the newspapers, the open-seat contestants got only a small fraction of the coverage given to incumbents and even challengers.

Open-seat candidates, seemingly frustrated in their efforts to break into print through their publicity campaigns, must turn to a different method, the paid advertisement. A strong correlation exists between the amount of money a candidate for an open seat spends on newspaper and television advertising and the amount of information people have about the candidate (Clarke & Evans,

1983). Patterson and McClure (1976) note that candidate advertisements on television contain considerable information about policy issues; they credit these advertisements with a major informational role (see also Kaid, 1981).

"Journalism loses again," Clarke and Evans (1983) comment ruefully on the paltry press coverage of open-seat candidates; the opportunity for the press to introduce new political faces to the public seems to be almost entirely passed by, so great is the attention to incumbents and their challengers. They also point out that in each open race "an incumbent was born" who will enjoy "all the journalistic perquisites" of incumbency in future races. Once elected, members of Congress are rarely unseated by the voters.

Uses of Mass Media

Although much research since Lazarsfeld's early work has focused on what mass media might be doing to people (media effects), there has recently been a resurgence of interest in what people do with mass media (media uses). What has come to be called "uses-and-gratifications research" was given a strong boost by an Israeli study of "the use of mass media for important things" (Katz, Gurevitch, & Haas, 1973), a British national election study (Blumler & McQuail, 1969), and a review volume coedited by the principal investigators on these seminal projects (Blumler & Katz, 1974). Their lead has been followed by a number of productive political communication researchers in the United States (reviewed in McLeod & Becker, 1981).

It is doubtful that mass media are essential to the satisfaction of basic human needs, but several generic kinds of needs can be met satisfactorily through use of mass communication. This is especially the case with politics, which for most people is not a particularly urgent concern most of the time but which regularly confronts people with demands for opinion and decision.

Democratic systems, with their frequent elections, place an especially heavy burden of decision on voters. In the United States, a given citizen is represented by dozens of elected officials (a president, two U.S. senators, a congressional representative, a long list of state, county, and municipal officers, and various judges) and is regularly called on to choose among rival candidates for these offices. Voters also pass directly on legislation through initiative and referendum processes. Given these numerous decision requirements, it should not be surprising that the most common reasons people give for reading newspapers or watching televised debates include "to help me make up my mind," "to see what the candidates are like," and "to find out what they would be like in office."

Other uses of political mass communication that people mention with some frequency bespeak a spectator's perspective on politics: "to judge which candidate is likely to win" and "to give me something to talk about with others in political discussions." Exposure to political content in the media, then, becomes integrated with people's lives in more ways than one. There are probably other motivations for using mass media that people do not necessarily recognize in themselves or do not express in survey interviews.

The gratifications a person seeks from mass media are much more a property of the individual's personal situation than of the medium or the social structure. Responding to criticisms that they have neglected the impact of social class and other demographic variables, McLeod and Becker (1981) point out that empirical studies have found at best weak relationships between a person's location in the social structure and the gratifications sought from mass media.

Situational factors do, however, enter in. Students preparing for an examination on current events, for example, are much more likely to consult the newspaper and watch news on television than those who are not faced with this temporary information need. Similarly, during the final weeks before an election, voters are much more likely to attend closely to political broadcasts and news articles than those same people would a year earlier or later.

Seeking and finding gratifications for one's needs are two different matters. As a rule, considerably more people report using mass media in pursuit of a specific gratification than say that their efforts succeeded. McLeod, Bybee, and Durall (1979) examined the 1976 Ford-Carter debates on television from this perspective. With regard to learning where the candidates stood on the issues, 86 percent of those surveyed said they sought this gratification "a lot" and only 1 percent "a little." By contrast, only 31 percent said the debates had been "very helpful" in this way; 25 percent said the debates had been "not at all helpful" in learning "stands on issues." Perhaps these voters' expectations for the debates were too high. Other studies showed that many people did gain considerable clarification of issue differences between Ford and Carter as a result of the debates (Sears & Chaffee, 1979).

The discrepancy between what people say they want, what they feel they get, and what they actually do want or get from their use of mass media presents a methodological poser. To determine what people "feel inside," there is usually no alternative to simply asking them; for the most part, researchers have to accept people's self-reports as reasonably valid.

One should, of course, be very skeptical of self-reports, because people may not want to admit to others—sometimes not even to themselves—what their true motivations are. Further, they may not know, and may not even have strong motivations; the survey question presumes that media use is directed behavior, but much of it may take place rather mindlessly. People are also not always good judges of the effects messages have had on them or of the gratifications they have received. Researchers have been quite active in seeking external validation of measurements used in the uses-and-gratifications tradition. Among the most important of these has been validation by examining the relationship between uses and effects, which constitutes both a method of research and a theoretical approach of growing importance.

Transactional Models

In political communication analysis, there is a tendency to think of messages as flowing in one direction only: from the political system to its members, from media to audience. In practice, of course, politically relevant messages flow in all directions, although not equally in terms of amount or political import. Even when we limit our consideration to mass communication, a form of interaction does take place between the receiver and the medium. Use of mass media is, after all, volitional. People may or may not read a particular book or go to see a new film, and not everyone reads a newspaper or watches television. Even when they do, there is a wide variety of choices from which each person selects only a few. Viewed from the receiver's perspective, expectations may be thought of as "gratifications sought" (in the sense of the previous section). But from the perspective of the source, they might be seen as "effects." Perhaps they are best characterized as "effects sought."

In an influential paper encouraging marketing researchers to look at the communication process from the audience's point of view, Bauer (1964) pointed out that communication is a "transactional process in which two parties each expect to give and take from the deal approximately equitable value." This transactional model is easy enough to imagine when analyzing interpersonal communication; each person gives something to the conversation in the hope of gaining something in return, and an interaction can be evaluated in terms of the extent to which it has met the expectations of each party. Bauer proposed that this kind of thinking be extended to mass communication; a transactional approach has been strongly advocated in the area of political communication by Kraus and Davis (1976).

Orientation One way to study political mass communication processes transactionally is to make an explicit connection between uses-and-gratifications measures and independent measures of communication effects. In a study of the agenda-setting effects of the televised 1973 hearings of the U.S. Senate on the Watergate scandals, Weaver, McCombs, and Spellman (1975) found that the effects hypothesis held up only among those viewers who had a strong need for political "orientation." It is as if, seeking order, they got it; others, who did not share this need, did not exhibit this effect. That is only one side (the viewer's) of a transactional picture; on the other side were political actors (the investigating senators, the defensive Nixon White House, and the media themselves), each attempting to extract some advantage from the total political process of which the media events were only a small, although essential, component.

The concept of a need for orientation that is required for agenda-setting effects to occur is an example of what is called a "contingent condition" in social research. Because this kind of variable is a characteristic of the individual in a specific situation, it is sometimes called a "contingent orientation" (Chaffee, 1975). Many contingent conditions that govern media effects are not psychological orientations specific to individuals or situations. Structural factors, such as censorship or other constraints on media, may account for differential effects. A person seeking information about candidates' stands on policy issues who relies on television for news is unlikely to gain much information if this kind of content does not appear in television newscasts (Patterson & McClure, 1976). A person who is blind or deaf or illiterate will be affected very little by certain media, for reasons that obviously have nothing to do with motivations or needs. But research has uncovered a number of transactional relationships that are based on contingent orientations.

Two types of contingent orientation analyses have been developed within the uses-and-gratifications tradition in political communication. One is global, the other more specific. The global approach is exemplified by Blumler and McQuail (1969), who simply summed up measures of the strength of each specific motivation in a single index of overall "strength of motivation." This was not a very satisfactory approach, however, since they could find no general pattern of overall motivation strengthening the effects of exposure to political campaign messages. So they—and most researchers since—have focused on specific motivations and have tried to match them to specific effects. Voters who seek clarification of candidates' positions on issues are likely to exhibit increased retention of information as a result of exposure to campaign communication, whereas other people are not.

McLeod, Luetscher, and McDonald (1980) found that the contingent orientation of seeking excitement and something to talk about was related to "blaming a variety of sources for inflation." Those who make their voting decisions prior to an election campaign do not later increase their communication activity, whereas those who make their decisions during the course of the campaign do. The latter group was particularly reliant on television in 1976, the year of the Ford-Carter debates (Chaffee & Choe, 1980), but not in 1980, when Carter and Reagan met only once on television just a few days before the election (Whitney & Goldman, 1985).

Overview

Political communication in the United States is obviously not a fixed or unitary matter. Simple statements about how it operates are subject to many sources of variation: what the political issue is, what the media do about it, what people's orientation toward it is, and so forth. For a general model, we might think of a triangle whose three corners represent the political system, the communication system, and the electorate. The sides of the triangle represent lines of communication. Messages flow in both directions along each side of the triangle, and each corner also provides an indirect route through which communication might pass between the other two. Indirect interaction is most obvious where the communication media are interposed between the political sys-

tem and the electorate. Government policies, and proposed modifications of them, are examples of messages that flow to citizens via the media. Public opinion polls are one example of "messages" flowing from people to their government. There are other indirect flows as well. People who need information put demands on the media for it, as do people who want more entertainment, less violence, or some other change in the communication system, and they often bring political pressure—usually via the government—on the media.

Political communication around this imaginary triangle linking the worlds of politics, media, and ordinary citizens occurs not because it is desirable but because it is inevitable. The press in the United States exists in its present form because it discharges a political function. It is difficult to conceive of an electoral democracy without a parallel media system. Just as the press needs politics—which accounts for some 40 percent of newspaper content—politics needs an audience to which its "product" can be sold. The audience consists of many people with varied information and opinion needs imposed on them by the political system their forebears created, and which they continue to support. In all, while relationships in the grand triangle we have been discussing are not always harmonious, they are decidedly symbiotic. Variations will evolve further as our political and communication institutions change. But interactions between them will continue, and promise a rich variety of research opportunities for social scientists.

THE POLITICS OF COMMUNICATION AND NATIONAL DEVELOPMENT

When it first evolved in the 1950s and early 1960s, the concept of development was linked to a presumed process of "modernization"; those two words were used almost interchangeably. In this chapter we have been using *development* more broadly, to include the entire set of social, economic, and political problems facing underdeveloped nations. We will restrict the term *mod-*

ernization to the particular set of assumptions about the role of communication that were made by early development scholars; the reader should remember, though, that other writers may call this development theory instead.

Two theories dominate this area of study. Modernization theory is mainly the work of social scientists from the United States who have worked in underdeveloped countries of the Third World (for example, Lerner, 1958; Schramm, 1964). Because of the unbalanced relationship between the United States and Third World countries—an imbalance that includes communication flow—a broad critique of the modernization theory of development has been constructed, called dependency theory. It too is a theory of development, but it proceeds from very different assumptions. As we present these competing conceptions of communication and development, it will become apparent how each leads naturally to a definition of different issues as "problems" and, consequently, as research topics.

Modernization Theory

A general model of development put forth by economists such as Rostow (1960) has had enormous impact on the thinking and research of communication scholars in the United States. In essence, it assumes that all not-yet-developed nations are involved in a process of modernization, which means developing in the same way the United States and other industrialized nations have developed, in the direction of "Westernization." The United States and Western Europe, this approach assumes, represent developed or modern nations; they are the model toward which less-developed countries should and will progress. Among numerous development programs the United States has initiated on the basis of these assumptions, the best known is the Alliance For Progress of the Kennedy administration.

In addition to the teleological image of development as progressive Westernization, modernization theory evaluates nations as having achieved one or more in a series of stages, begin-

ning with "traditional" society and culminating in a "modern" society. Accompanying this unidirectional process is a shift from traditional, predominantly interpersonal means of communication to heavy reliance on modern mass media (Lerner, 1967; Schramm, 1964), and from authoritarian political institutions to libertarian arrangements (Inkeles & Smith, 1974). The communication process through which this transformation occurs is called diffusion (see Chapter 11).

In practice, modernization programs frequently ran into difficulty. Communication, it was soon learned, might be necessary to bring about certain social changes, but it is certainly not sufficient. A method of farming, say, or of infant care suitable in the United States might nevertheless be inappropriate in a different culture. The history of the development-through-modernization movement is replete with instances of innovations that people decided not to adopt, and of attitudes about their relationship to the world that they declined to change.

One of the most salient of these instances for communication scholars was the devotion to work and desire for personal achievement that many saw as the enduring basis for development in the Western industrial nations (Schramm, 1964). As Lerner (1967) put it, the developing nations needed the functional equivalent of Weber's Protestant ethic or what Schramm (1964) called more directly "the work ethic." Modernization theory is in disrepute among some U.S. scholars and is widely rejected today in many Third World settings. But its basic tenets persist among many other scholars and, more important, in many governments as well, as for example in the Reagan administration's approach to Central American problems.

Elguea, a Mexican scholar, considers that there are just two "hard-core", unchallengeable assumptions essential to the theory we are calling modernization:

(1) . . . development was thought to be a unilinear succession of general stages . . . [to] an evolved, 'modern' society. (2) Second . . . is what

*has been called 'diffusionism.' [D]evelopment oc-
curs through the spread of cultural patterns, attitudes, capital, technology, etc., from the modern
or 'developed' countries to the traditional or
'underdeveloped' ones" (1984, p. 60).*

These beliefs, once the basis for what seemed
a promising program of nation-building, have become highly controversial. Some former devo-
tees of the modernization approach have more
recently found it less suitable than they had
thought. For example, Rogers (1976) has written
that the "dominant paradigm" of modernization
theory has become obsolete. He proposes an approach that is more in keeping with the peoples
and perspectives of underdeveloped countries.
But leaders in the intellectual movement against
modernization theory have mostly been scholars
in Latin America and other regions that have a
different viewpoint on what it means to a nation
to be underdeveloped. Before we examine in detail research that has grown out of modernization
theory, we will outline the main features of this
alternative approach.

Dependency Theory

Many theories have developed in reaction to
modernization theory. Elguea (1984) finds that
they share a common core of beliefs, which lead
to testable propositions quite different from
those of scholars working within the framework
of modernization programs. The two most important shared assumptions, Elguea says, are:

*(1) The notion of "dependency" as a determi-
nant of national development and underdevelopment; and its corollary, development and
underdevelopment are not independent
processes, but two aspects of the same process of
capitalist expansion. (2) The notion of a single
world system as necessary to understand development and underdevelopment. (p. 93)*

Dependency theory puts primary emphasis on
economic, political, and historical factors, and
on the structure of society in its analysis of the
relationship between development and underdevelopment. One implication for the study of
communication is that the focus shifts from the
behavior of the individual to structural relations
among major social institutions. For example, it
becomes important to examine in detail the economic organization of the mass media, particularly ownership and its effect on media operation
and content. Dependency theorists are much
more concerned with these large and powerful
media institutions—their historical origins and
their relationships to other sources of power in
society—than they are with the role of communication in people's daily social life. In general,
social and political factors are seen as dependent
on economic and historical-structural factors,
much more than the reverse.

Communication researchers working within
the dependency framework are concerned with,
and deeply critical of, the communication relationships between their own predominantly
underdeveloped countries and the more industrialized nations of North America and Western
Europe. The economic imbalance between these
two sets of countries is mirrored by a communication imbalance that is all too obvious in advertising and news. As noted in Chapter 11,
communication flows from the United States to
Latin America much more than in the reverse direction, for example (Rogers & Schement, 1984).
This imbalance, and its negative implications for
development and preservation of autonomous
political systems and cultures in Latin America, is
the dominant issue in political communication
research in that region.

**Communication Research Under Moderni-
zation Theory** Focusing on the individual as
the unit of analysis led modernization theorists
to frame their research questions in particular
ways and to prefer certain methods over others.
For the most part, only research questions ad-
dressable at the individual level were considered;
political implications of the mass media and of
communication interventions, for example,
tended to be ignored, in favor of specific effects

on individuals. Although modernization researchers noted political entanglements of communication programs in passing, they made little of them, perhaps partly out of fear that those in power would not cooperate with researchers opening up political questions (Hornik, 1980).

From the perspective of modernization theory, the researcher may accept as given that the country of interest may be labeled "underdeveloped." Some of the defining characteristics of underdevelopment include: economic reliance on agriculture and extraction industries; insufficient production for manufactured exports; importing of manufactured goods; low levels of technological and industrial development; low educational levels and widespread illiteracy; little political participation; increasing concentration of people in urban areas with insufficient housing. Some of these problems can be addressed through communication to individuals, but many cannot. For example, mass media may be used in a literacy campaign, or in a program designed to foster new agricultural practices among farmers, or to promote political participation, but communication cannot remedy housing or public service deficiencies.

With the individual as the unit of analysis, problems have to be formulated in terms of how individuals think, react, and function. It is through aggregation of individual actions and behaviors that social change comes about. In other words, "societies" per se do not change, but rather each individual (though probably not all) will do so, and thus the social system as an aggregate is changed.

The researcher, then, sees a problem whose solution requires that many individuals change in a specific way. In terms of modernization theory, individuals need to move from traditional to modern values, attitudes, beliefs, and practices. Usually, the problem is defined from a top-down perspective. A government, for example, reaches the conclusion that farm practices are inadequate to meet national goals, which means that traditional ways of farming need to be modified or dropped altogether. But the definition of "inade-

quate" comes from above, rather than from the farmers. Often, traditional practices are the only ones a person knows; the farmer may be mystified, fearful, or antagonistic toward attempts to force modernization.

The issue of who defines what a problem is has been largely ignored in communication studies within the modernization framework. Researchers have valiantly tackled the problems handed down to them, trying as best they could to assess the role communication media had played or could play in development. Among the more salient problems these researchers confronted were education (Arnove, 1980; May, Hornik & McAnany, 1976), political participation (Abreu Sojo, 1980; Pye, 1963), agricultural innovations (Rogers, 1965), social integration (Mathiason, 1967), value and attitude formation and change (Kahl, 1973), family planning (Rogers, 1973), and the use of health services and related health practices (Foote, Parker, & Hudson, 1976).

Mass Media and Politics

When trying to analyze the political roles of the media, researchers have asked two broad questions: First, how have the mass media been used to channel and control the political activity of a country's people? Second, how have the mass media been (or could they be) used to create support for existing regimes in which they operate? The first question has been addressed in terms of "political participation"; the second corresponds to "political socialization."

Mass Media and Political Participation   Public participation in government processes is considered necessary in all democracies, including countries that consider themselves "in transition" to democracy. Low political participation of the civilian population is one of the indicators commonly used to suggest underdevelopment. In the modernization perspective, the mass media are assigned a dual role: information disseminator and participation motivator. Development is believed to be possible only when broad sectors of society are politically involved, when people are "developing themselves" rather than passively being developed.

In most Third World countries, development plans generally fail to involve or benefit all levels of society. Existing elites have been strengthened in their power, an unintended consequence of most development efforts. In addition, the mass media—owned and operated by those same elites in most cases—have not played the roles modernization theorists expected. Instead, the media have by conveying images from the affluent West built a "revolution of rising expectations" that many observers fear is degenerating into a "revolution of rising frustrations."

Abreu Sojo (1980) argues for mass media that would be open to all ideologies and to the opinions and ideas of all social groups. His central statement is that "a better use of the mass media can increase people's critical conscience and activate it" (p. 10). This is, from his perspective, exactly the opposite of what the media accomplish now: preservation of the status quo. According to Chaffee and Izcaray (1974), "The effect of the media is to correlate the parts of society strictly by bringing the thinking of the less educated into line with that of the upper educational strata" (p. 392).

Not all mass media exert the same type of influence, Abreu Sojo notes. He sees a general correlation between media exposure and political participation, television being "the only medium that does not present this relationship." Rather, "heavy exposure to television is related to a lower participation index" (pp. 109–110). The opposite is true for newspapers; heavier readers exhibit higher participation levels. These patterns hold in the United States as well.

That newspapers have greater political impact than television, in terms of being positively associated with participation, should surprise no one. Dillon Soares (1971) examined Brazilians' voting behavior, newspaper use, and occupational and socioeconomic status ("class situation"). He concluded that "political propaganda, newspaper reading, and agreement with a newspaper's polit-

ical orientation do influence, without determining, the individual's political attitudes, his electoral tendencies, his vote" (p. 188). In accord with Abreu Sojo, Dillon Soares found that frequent newspaper reading and the tendency to vote for the candidate backed by the newspaper were consistently associated, but noted that the reverse statement could be as easily made: "The less discrepancy between the opinions and political preferences of the readers and the political orientations of the newspaper, the higher the frequency of reading" (p. 188). This interpretation amounts to selective exposure, an audience pattern that may require (1) sufficient political development for a multiparty situation, (2) sufficient media development for multiple communication sources, each identified with a different party, and perhaps (3) a level of education sufficient to enable people to select media sources on the basis of partisan slant, but not so high that they easily arrive at political opinions independently.

Dillon Soares distinguishes further the influence of the mass media on political matters and, in a broader sense, their "formative power" toward a "class conscience." He points out that during elections, almost all information available to the voter originates directly or indirectly in the mass media. But the formation of a class conscience—the realization that one's low economic, political, or social situation need not be as it is—may emerge from a critical appraisal of one's environment, and media impact will be less. Others (such as Reyes Matta, 1981) would disagree, arguing that such an appraisal comes only after deliberate efforts by community organizers or other external agents.

Mass Media and Political Socialization
Political socialization refers to the process by which new members of a society acquire information about the political system. Most political socialization studies look at ways that children develop cognitions about their country's political characteristics. Socialization processes in most societies work in the direction of maintaining the

status quo, by instilling in people the notion that an individual can do little to influence the political process. Young people tend to learn that they are helpless against the political system and machinery. The same is probably the case for immigrants to developed countries, who also must be "socialized" into the new political system in which they find themselves. Rarely are they presented with much opportunity for political action.

This feeling of limited efficacy is not limited to research subjects; it is also common among communication researchers themselves. Hornik (1988) comments:

Communication technology projects, as with most development projects, will rarely succeed without prior commitment to change in the sector by substantial political forces . . . Four decades of experience have taught us that the technologies, awesome as they may be, are under the control of those interests. Project failure often is not merely a technical failure or a failure of management, rather, technical and management failings may be symptoms of the distribution of power in a society. Communication interventions should be undertaken when concrete evidence of commitment to change in the sector is present. (pp. 24–25) . . . Placing communication within the substantive agency concerned recognizes that communication must complement a broader intervention. It serves to accelerate change, not instigate it. (p. 22)

This topic marks a major point of disagreement between researchers working within the modernization and dependency frameworks. One certainly cannot say that politics is ignored in the modernization approach. It is clear, however, that researchers of this stripe are willing to take the political system as it is, and not worry about changing that system as a direct consequence of the communication intervention. Communication is effective, from a modernization perspective, only when the political system is willing to tolerate change. Dependency theory, by contrast, sees political changes as essential to other kinds of social change.

Communication Research Under Dependency Theory In an assessment of the state of modernization theory, Rogers (1976) declared:

Most "development" efforts have brought further stagnation, a greater concentration of income and power, high unemployment, and food shortages in these [underdeveloped] nations. If these past development programs represented any kind of test of the intellectual paradigm on which they were based, the model has been found rather seriously wanting. (p. 130)

As Elguea (1984) points out, dependency theories are "a response to the theoretical and empirical failure of modernization" theory (p. 90). Dependency theory has criticized modernization theory along three main lines: (1) the distinction between a traditional and a modern society; (2) the role that agro-commercial elites play in development processes; and (3) the lack of empirical corroboration for some of the predictions of modernization.

The "new dependency" (Chilcote, 1974) or "media imperialism" (Fejes, 1981) perspective begins with an openly critical attitude toward existing economic, political, and social structures in which to study communication. Beltrán (1976a) has written that "questioning the present structures of Latin American society is an attitude shared by all researchers using this new approach" (p. 36). The "criticism of the existing order" tenet was put forth by Pasquali (1963, 1972), who tied studies of media content (in Venezuela) to the concept of "cultural industries." Advances in dependency theory were related to theories regarding imbalances between the "central" and "peripheral" countries in world markets and proposals for a new world economic order (Hamelink, 1983).

A 1972 international seminar on the sociopolitical role of mass media (Textual, 1973) advocated a research agenda for dependency theorists:

In defense of the ideologies and behavior patterns imposed by the dominant classes, the mass

media play a role of first importance that be-
comes even more critical in the present moment,
at which a confrontation between the old and
the new forces has become particularly acute
and the majority of Latin American societies are
pushing for an authentic take-off [despegue].
That is why the analysis of the power structure
of the mass media is extraordinarily relevant.
(p. 77)

Topics for research in this approach include ownership structures, the communicator as intermediary between senders and receivers, international news agencies, advertising agencies, production and distribution of media materials, foreign investments in the mass media, media power structures, and ideological functions of the mass media.

National Communication Policies

During the late 1960s, UNESCO began organizing conferences around the concept of a new world information order to accompany the proposed new world economic order (Hamelink, 1983). By the 1970s, it was urging formulation of "national communication policies" in Third World countries and creation of a regional news service that would be an alternative to the wire services based in the United States and Europe. The suggestion of government involvement in press services in turn gave UNESCO itself "a bad press" in Western journalistic circles, and paved the way for withdrawal of the United States from UNESCO in the 1980s.

Beltrán (1976b) defines a national communication policy as "a lasting, explicit, and integrated set of fragmentary communication policies, which are integrated as a coherent body of norms and principles intended as guides of behavior for the specialized institutions involved in the general communication process within a country" (p. 4). What Beltrán calls "fragmentary communication policies" are the more specific guidelines aimed at regulating actions of specific parts of the social communication system. These would

include, for example, the television, radio, advertising, cinema, and newspaper industries. A directive state role in national communication policy is understandable, because owners of the media, professionals working in them, and government officials who try to write or carry out these fragmentary policies often experience conflicts.

The perceived need in the Third World for greater government control of communication flow across national borders stems from the conclusion that the free flow of information does not benefit, and in fact does harm to, these countries. From a U.S. perspective, there is no conflict between the information needs of developing countries and the free flow of information, which moves predominantly from the United States to Latin American nations. Nations at the receiving end do not share this viewpoint, and much has been written on negative effects of "free" flow.

The most frequent reaction to the new-order proposals in the United States, Western Europe, and the centers of power in Latin American nations has been one of strong opposition (see, for example, "Freedom at Issue," 1976). One common argument in the United States is that its foreign policy cannot be understood by those living in other countries unless they have available to them the image of the world that is available to U.S. citizens. This argument is played in a slightly different way in Latin America, where those with capitalist ideals say that the process of development will be accelerated by contact with the U.S. perspective on all issues.

A second argument relates the notions of freedom of information, censorship, and the "democratic ideal." On the one hand, the libertarian critique says that national communication policies represent efforts by the state to gain control over the lives of private individuals, particularly media entrepreneurs. Local elites argue that just as controls would damage democratic institutions in the United States, they would wreak havoc with democratic institutions and conscience in countries where those traditions are not so well established.

According to Hamelink (1983), the proposal for national communication policies calls for some key changes: greater government involvement in the mass media (which does not imply suppression of private enterprise); regulations for activities of the mass media; less reliance on international news agencies; and increased attention to development of national and regional news services. The proposal also addresses the need to ensure that mass media fulfill their public service role even when operated as private enterprises, and that broadcasting respect the national culture. In the short run, the likelihood of most Third World nations defining such policies is low. The general trend, however, is for the state to develop its own broadcast media and through them attempt to fulfill the promise of culture and education that commercial media do not deliver. At least for the present, decisions *not* to nationalize commercial media will probably continue to be the rule.

Cultural Imperialism

The scores of studies that have appeared over the past 20 years dealing with cultural (or ideological) imperialism indicate the considerable appeal this issue has among communication scholars in Latin America, Europe, and even the United States. The scholarship in this area involves analyzing external factors of the power structure that influence or control the mass media in underdeveloped countries. Domination of dependent countries by the metropolitan powers continues to receive a great deal of attention.

Beltrán and Fox de Cardona (1980) have added a few topics to this research agenda. Their work centers on official international propaganda organizations (such as the U.S. Information Agency) and security and intelligence organizations (such as the Central Intelligence Agency). The cultural-imperialism contention is that the powerful nations are capable of "no longer destroying the cultural products themselves, but based on a very clever ideological penetration, of neutralizing the capacity of the people to go on reproducing, and, therefore, developing their own culture" (Urrutia Boloña, 1973, p. 4).

Several studies analyze the content of different media through which this undermining is thought to be practiced: comic books (Dorfman & Mattelart, 1980), television (Romano, 1979), advertising (Arriaga, 1980), children's programming (Mattelart, 1973), radio programming (Rogoff, 1980), and news (*Crisis*, 1975). Their conclusions are the subject of considerable debate. The central, though often unstated, premise guiding this type of study is that cultural "homogenization" is important to metropolitan powers, to ensure continued expansion of systems of production, distribution, and consumption under their control (Dagnino, 1973). Elimination of sociocultural differences takes place both internally—to align the ideas of the underprivileged with those of the elites—and externally, to maintain the international hierarchy between dependent and dominant nations.

The line between media (cultural-ideological) imperialism and economic imperialism is often hazy (Paz, 1977), especially since critiques of media imperialism rely so heavily on the assumptions and concepts of economic imperialism. Consequently, the media-imperialism school has had difficulty achieving recognition as a theoretical framework in its own right (Boyd-Barret, 1981; Dagnino, 1973).

There has also been some confusion regarding the intellectual roots of this line of thinking. Fejes (1981) suggests:

In one sense, the research on media imperialism can be situated within the broad tradition of a Marxist critique of capitalism in that in the global growth of Western communication media researchers see a reflection of the general imperialist expansion of Western capitalist societies. Yet it is a mistake to label this approach Marxist in any detailed and precise sense of the word.
(pp. 282–283)

The latter point is especially important because a common criticism of Third World communication scholarship is its supposed Marxist character. Why else (it is argued) would they criticize "free enterprise"? (To some, *Marx* is indeed a four-letter word!) But at the same time it is unwise to ignore the fact that many acknowledged Marxist critics (such as Esteinou, 1981) consider themselves part of the dependency tradition, at least in trying to identify historical and economic elements of capitalism's worldwide expansion.

Recently, the cultural-imperialism perspective has receded somewhat in the face of evidence that market factors, rather than some conspiratorial intention, lie behind the control over Third World culture that Western cultures seem to exercise. Rogers and Schement (1984) provide a good deal of evidence that the north-to-south direction of mass communication flow in the Americas is better seen as a matter of business than as attempted cultural domination. Indeed, such Latin American transnationals as Televisa of Mexico not only provide a substantial amount of the Spanish-language television for the rest of Latin America, but have invested heavily in media outlets in the United States as well. The empirical inadequacy—and to some extent theoretical weaknesses—of the cultural-imperialism view have led Mattelart and others to reappraise some of its central concepts (Mattelart, 1983; Mattelart, Delcourt, & Mattelart, 1984).

[*The*] *notion of cultural imperialism, and its corollary, "cultural dependence," is clearly no longer adequate. The increasing commercialization of the cultural sector and the parallel development of the new technologies of communication have projected culture into the theatre of industrial and political structures. . . . The relationship between culture and industry is gradually being added to a debate formerly centered on that between culture and the state. (Mattelart et al., 1984, pp. 25, 27)*

Overall, then, the vociferous media-imperialism critique is beginning to subside. There is little empirical evidence of either the imperialist conspiracy that is supposed to lie behind it nor of the attitude effects it is thought to engender. On the other hand, there is evidence that when market conditions are right, international communication will flow *from,* not just toward, less-developed countries. For many, though, this is cold comfort, as market conditions continue to be highly unfavorable to most developing countries.

Alternative Communication and Other Proposals

Communication scholars in Latin America have proposed several models for work in the field that depart—sometimes drastically—from traditional ways of conceiving communication research. One model goes under the broad label of "alternative communication," which, according to Reyes Matta (1981), stands in direct opposition to the development ideal of modernization theory. Reyes Matta suggests that the latter is marked by individualism, consumerism, and (in terms of communication) a vertical relationship between source and receiver.

Paiva (1983) identifies two main classes of actors in alternative communication. The first consists of groups that have been victims of discrimination or domination, such as slum dwellers, ethnic minorities, women, labor unions, neighborhood associations, and church-based groups. The second class Paiva labels "mediators." It includes individuals or groups with socioeconomic or education backgrounds different from those in the first class but with similar political goals. Collaborations between these two sets of actors take the form of joint projects in three areas of activity: information, education, and organization. Their central goals are promotion of intra- and intergroup cohesiveness and of political participation. Conscious and organized participation is thought to be possible through provision of adequate levels of information; through getting people to understand their plight and to express their needs; and through development of power-sharing forms of participation in a democratic society.

The proposal for alternative communication, like many coming from Latin America, builds on ideas advanced by Brazilian educator Paulo Freire (1971, 1975). His work has attracted a wide following due principally to two concepts. One is "conscientization," as opposed to the modernization ideal of information; the other is communication, as opposed to the modernization notion of extension in rural development.

Freire (1971) proposes a kind of development that is highly respectful of the traditions, culture, and goals of the individual and the community. He holds that an "informed" society is not necessarily any more democratic or egalitarian than an uninformed, totalitarian society. Freire argues for a development ideal that tries to bring about conscientization, implying that individuals should be able to recognize the global structure of society, its major deficiencies, their position in it, and what can be done to change an unjust society.

The notion of conscientization is closely tied to Freire's idea of communication as a dialog between equals. Conscientization may come about only when those who are "ahead" are willing to deal on an equal footing with those who are still "behind"—without trying to impose their own frames of reference and with respect for the latter's characteristic ways of thinking, organization, and so on. Freire argues that modernization's extension work does not respect traditions and attempts to impose external patterns foreign to the individual and the community, so that people are constrained to change according to the wishes of a governing body far removed from them rather than of their own volition.

But how can one bring about this type of development, a more just society where the communication media benefit all members of society and not just a small minority? Diaz Bordenave and Martins de Carvalho (1978) set out to answer this question, mainly through exploration of the notion they call *planificación* (roughly, "planning"). They sought a different way of using this concept, one that does not correspond to its use in the modernization literature. From their perspective, the media as presently organized do not clear the way for social communication but, quite the contrary, present obstacles to it. Diaz Borden-ave and Martins not only propose ways to overcome such obstacles but also suggest other functions that the media could perform in society, such as: (1) an expressive function; (2) a relational function; (3) an identity function; (4) a conscientization function; and (5) the function of catalyzers of social change. Whereas functions 1 through 3 reflect the more humanistic bent in this approach, functions 4 and 5 make clear the political awareness of the researchers and their recognition of the political power of the media. They see that those who own the media have power and that if the social structure is to change, alternative approaches will first have to gain political power.

Scholars adopting this approach try to rid themselves of commonly used concepts, theories, and methodologies in order to make a fresh start. But a clear break from past ideas is difficult. Diaz Bordenave and Martins deal with this problem by taking a specific concept and practice, in this case *planificación,* and "rewrite the book" on it. What they have called "planning without a plan" summarizes their core ideas: a planning action that is less manipulative and allows the public to participate in decisions about planned actions; the "derationalization" of the overall planning process; reflection beginning from basic facts and conditions close to large sectors of the population; elimination of centralism in the decision-making process; and elimination of technocratic attitudes in the planning process.

As could be expected, the idea of planning without a plan entails a different kind of communication research, one that places a whole new set of expectations on researchers. Under the label "militant research," proponents of this approach (such as Bonilla, 1978) suggest that there can be no distinction between the researcher and the research methodology; that methodology itself should not be alien to social groups with whom the researcher is working; that methodology evolves according to political and social pressures; and that methodology depends in large measure on strategies for social change that have been adopted by relevant social groups. Briefly stated, militant research implies that the researcher becomes part of the community under study and should let the group define problems, propose solutions, suggest ways of studying the problems, and recommend methods of collecting and processing information. The ideal is for the researcher to become more of an educator and community organizer, rather than remain an outsider. Dervin (1981) has expressed similar ideas in the U.S. context.

Despite the romantic appeal of such an approach, it has serious practical and epistemological problems. At a practical level, the very presence of the researcher in a community represents an intervention, no matter how benign the intention. Its first purpose is to motivate the people toward some form of action (such as to become critical of their own reality), which would be less likely to happen if they were left on their own. There is also the problem of political power. The community may become aware, thanks to the militant research experience, that its situation has to change, but without political power—which is often the case—changes are hard to come by, while repression, either direct (as through police or military intervention) or indirect (as in ignoring demands), is frequently the result.

At an epistemological level, the criterion of action (praxis) as the basis for knowledge presents difficult problems, particularly when the requirement is that knowledge arise from the concrete situation of the population. Specifically, the criteria for distinguishing between knowledge and ignorance become confused. If action is to be the decisive element, any concept or hypothesis may be considered "knowledge" so long as it proves useful "in the hands of the key sectors and groups for the formation and development of their class conscience, and according to the organizational force that they are capable of generating" (Diaz Bordenave & Martins, 1978, p. 298). In this case, a statement would be considered true only if it promotes the betterment of the particular group with which the researcher is involved. This point, however, ignores the fact that "knowledge of how repressive social structures can be changed may spring, not from an 'emancipatory interest,' but from the very opposite motive—the desire of, say, an authoritarian regime to ward off such changes" (Lessnoff, 1974, p. 153).

Overview

Enzensberger (1981) lists six major issues confronting researchers in communication who attempt to change the structure of the mass media. These issues can be outlined against the principles to which they are opposed (see Table 12.1).

It is quite understandable for communication researchers in the Third World to have taken such an interest in the political, economic, cultural, and social factors influencing operation and use of communication media. Intellectual traditions, which make communication researchers part of the educated elites, have produced two distinct views of intellectual work: whether the intellectual should, or should not, be involved politically in society. Each intellectual tradition answers in a different way, which in turn generates a different approach to conceptualizing, defining, studying, and proposing solutions to social problems as well as to the role of the researcher.

As Elguea (1984) points out, the debate in the sociology of development between modernization and dependency theories has been fruitful for two reasons. One is that it has exposed the weaknesses of each position. The other is that both camps have benefited from the competition (with or without their acknowledgment), because they have been forced to confront problems and inconsistencies that otherwise might have gone unquestioned. Elguea sees the debate as very much alive, and not likely to subside for some time. We doubt that everything has been said regarding the role of communication media in development. We do believe, however, that our thinking on these development issues has much to gain from cross-examination within the context of the larger debate.

Table 12.1 Major Issues Confronting Researchers in Communication.

Repressive Use of the Media	Emancipatory Use of the Media
Program of central control	Decentralized programs
One source (transmitter), many receivers	Each receiver a potential source (transmitter)
Immobilization of isolated individuals	Mobilization of the masses
"Passive attention" behavior toward consumption	Interaction between participants, feedback
Process of depolitization	Process of political learning
Production by specialists	Socialized control by self-governing organizations

CONCLUSION

Perhaps the most important point of our discussion is that the nature of the political system in a country is bound to influence political communication research there. Certain features of the political system, when it is linked to the social communication system, are considered to be more worthy of research than others by scholars in each country. One important difference between Latin American and U.S. scholarship in political communication stems from the different ways in which the interaction between the communication and political systems is expected to influence larger societal outcomes. Whereas in the United States the two systems—communication and political—are perceived to be relatively independent of each other, in Latin America a different set of conditions has made the interlock between the two systems a major source of concern and study. The fact that political and economic elites are frequently the same people, who also often control the mass media in Latin American countries, gives researchers a working hypothesis that the mass media are being used to further the political and economic interests of those elites. A different ownership structure has made this type of question seem less urgent to communication researchers in the United States.

A second major difference comes from the attention paid to transnational factors affecting the operation of mass media. This is one area in which Latin American researchers have much more to study than their U.S. counterparts, since communication tends to flow from north to south, from "central" to "peripheral" countries. The influence of U.S. multinational corporations over the mass media systems of Latin American nations through advertising, direct investments, program sales, and news services has been a motivating factor behind research areas like cultural imperialism and the development of national communication policies. New communication technologies, particularly computer-based applications and satellites, provide researchers both in the United States and Latin America with new areas for research. Once again, they must deal with the implications of such technologies (their intended uses, by whom, and for what purposes) regarding the economic, political, social, and cultural development of Latin American nations.

A third variation stems from the intellectual traditions influencing political communication research. The failure of development programs based on modernization theory fostered an alternative approach, dependency theory. The ensuing debate is highly relevant for several academic disciplines, national governments, and media policymakers.

One final consideration concerns the roles of political communication researchers. It is always difficult not to embrace specific research topics, as well as commitments, based on one's political preferences or ideals. Researchers may or may not choose to be directly involved in carrying out the implications of their research results. They may play a strictly scientific role, where their political involvement stops with the research itself, or they may occupy a more critical role, where communication research and political activism go hand in hand (as in militant research). Although these are certainly not the only alternatives, they seem to represent the two extremes between which most of us must find a place.

SUMMARY

Theoretical models of media-government relations are an important framework for any discussion of the mass media and politics. Nations can adopt either an authoritarian or a libertarian approach to media relations. Nations vary widely in how they mix these two opposite positions. The two basic approaches may not be implemented anywhere in pure form, but they provide a view of the two extremes to which media-government relations can go.

Research on the effect of the media on politics in the United States and other Western democracies was at one time heavily influenced by the findings of the limited-effects theorists. More recently, this approach has been challenged, as the introduction of television, changes in competition, and the decline of partisanship among newspapers have altered the consumption patterns and the content of the mass media consumed by the average voter. Such concepts as selective exposure and agenda setting, which grew out of the limited-effects approach, are being reexamined in light of more current and less supportive evidence. Coverage of political candidates and debates has also changed in recent years. Theories to explain these new patterns of political communication include uses-and-gratification theories and transactional theories.

Another area of research on media and politics is the cross-national study of the impact of the media on development. Modernization theory has suggested a diffusion of technological innovations to less-developed countries, and focused its research on individual adopters of innovation. In the political sphere, the mass media are assumed to disseminate information and to motivate participation in the political process. Dependency theory, by contrast, suggests that the structure of society, and indeed the world order, reflects political and economic forces that keep some nations inherently underdeveloped. Dependency research focuses on larger social units, and is concerned with communication issues such as national communication policies, cultural imperialism, and alternative communication.

REVIEW AND DISCUSSION QUESTIONS

1. Exactly where is the United States today on the spectrum of authoritarian versus libertarian policies toward the media? Give examples of government policies toward the media that reflect each of these approaches.

2. The chapter suggests that many of the early findings of the limited-effects theorists either may have been in error or are no longer applicable. How much of this change can be accounted for simply by changes in society and changes in the media over time? How long will current research findings and theories remain valid? How will scholars know when to discard or update these findings, as they are now updating the limited-effects theories?

3. The research traditions represented by modernization theory and dependency theory are based on totally different assumptions about the economic conditions in the Third World. Are these traditions in conflict, or do they represent two parallel aspects of the same problem, both of which must be dealt with before social change or modernization can come about?

4. Modern U.S. politicians have been accused of using the techniques of advertising and mass media manipulation to distort the electoral process. What would the general research available about the mass media (Chapter 8) and about persuasion (Chapter 10) say about this claim? Based on the research reported in this chapter as well as those, in what areas of politics are the mass media most likely to have a significant effect, and how?

REFERENCES

Abreu Sojo, I. (1980). *Los medios de difusion masiva y la estratificación social en la participación y comunicación politica.* Barquisemeto, Venezuela: FUDECO.

Arnove, R. F. (1980). Education policies of the national front. In R. A. Berry, R. G. Hellman, & M. Solaun (Eds.), *Politics of compromise: Coalition government in Colombia* (pp. 381–411). New Brunswick, NJ: Transaction.

Arriaga, P. (1980). *Publicidad, economia y comunicación masiva.* Mexico City: CEESTM/Nueva Imagen.

Barber, J. D. (1978). *Race for the presidency: The media and the nominating process.* Englewood Cliffs, NJ: Prentice-Hall.

Bauer, R. A. (1964). The obstinate audience: The influence process from the point of view of social communication. *American Psychologist, 19,* 319–328.

Becker, L., Weaver, D., Graber, D., & McCombs, M. (1979). Influences on public agendas. In S. Kraus (Ed.), *The great debates: Carter vs. Ford, 1976* (pp. 418–428). Bloomington: Indiana University Press.

Beltrán, L. R. (1976a). Alien premises, objects, and methods in Latin American communication research. In E. M. Rogers (Ed.), *Communication and development: Critical perspectives.* Beverly Hills: Sage Contemporary Social Science Issues 32.

Beltrán, L. R. (1976b). Politicas nacionales de comunicación en America Latina: Los primeros pâsos. *Nueva Sociedad,* Julio-Agosto, pp. 1–9.

Beltrán, L. R., & Fox de Cardona, E. (1980). *Comunicación dominada: Estados unidos en los medios de America Latina.* Mexico City: ILET/Nueva Imagen.

Berelson, B., Lazarsfeld, P., & McPhee, W. N. (1954). *Voting: A study of opinion formation in a presidential campaign.* Chicago: University of Chicago Press.

Blumler, J. G., & Katz, E. (Eds.). (1974). *The uses of mass communications: Current perspectives on gratification research.* Beverly Hills: Sage.

Blumler, J. G., & McQuail, D. (1969). *Television in politics: Its uses and influence.* Chicago: University of Chicago Press.

Bonilla, V. D. (1978). Causa popular, ciencia popular: Una metodologia del conocimiento cientifico a traves de la acción. In J. Diaz Bordenave & H. Martins de Carvalho, *Planificación y comunicación.* Quito, Ecuador: Don Bosco.

Boyd-Barret, O. (1981). El imperialismo de los medios: Hacia un marco internacional para el analisis de los sistemas de medios. In J. Curran, M. Gurevitch, & J. Woollacott (Eds.), *Sociedad y comunicación de masas.* Mexico City: Fondo de Cultura Economica.

Carter, R. F. (1962). Some effects of the debates. In S. Kraus (Ed.), *The great debates: Carter vs. Ford, 1976* (pp. 173–223). Bloomington: Indiana University Press.

Carter, R. F., & Greenberg, B. S. (1965). Newspapers or television: Which do you believe? *Journalism Quarterly, 42*(1), 29–34.

Chaffee, S. H. (Ed.). (1975). *Political communication: Issues and strategies for research.* Beverly Hills: Sage.

Chaffee, S. H., & Choe, S. Y. (1980). Time of decision and media use during the Ford-Carter campaign. *Public Opinion Quarterly, 44,* 53–69.

Chaffee, S. H., & Izcaray, F. (1974). Mass communication functions in a media-rich developing society. *Communication Research, 2,* 367–395.

Chaffee, S. H., & Izcaray, F. (1976). *Modelos de comunicación de masas para una sociedad en desarrollo rica en medios de comunicación social.* Barquisemeto, Venezuela: FUDECO.

Chaffee, S. H., & Miyo, Y. (1983). Selective exposure and the reinforcement hypothesis: An intergenerational panel study of the 1980 presidential campaign. *Communication Research, 10,* 3–36.

Chilcote, R. (1974). A critical synthesis of the dependency literature. *Latin American Perspectives, 1*(1), 4–29.

Clarke, P., & Evans, S. (1983). *Covering campaigns: Journalism in congressional elections.* Stanford, CA: Stanford University Press.

Cohen, B. (1963). *The press and foreign policy.* Princeton, NJ: Princeton University Press.

Comstock, G., Chaffee, S. H., Katzman, N., McCombs, M. E., & Roberts, D. F. (1978). *Television and human behavior.* New York: Columbia University Press.

Crisis: Los medios de comunicación. Un pais multimillonario en una nación extranjer. (1975, November), 12–18.

Dagnino, E. (1973). Cultural and ideological dependence: Building a theoretical framework. In F. Bonilla & R. Girtling (Eds.), *Structures of dependency.* E. Palo Alto, CA: Distributed by Nairobi Bookstore.

Dervin, B. (1981). Mass communicating: Changing conceptions of the audience. In R. Rice & W. Paisley (Eds.), *Public communication campaigns* (pp. 71–87). Beverly Hills: Sage.

Diaz Bordenave, J., & Martins de Carvalho, H. (1978). *Planificación y comunicación.* Quito, Ecuador: Don Bosco.

Dillon Soares, G. A. (1971). La dictadura de la propaganda. *Revista Latinoamericana de Sociologia, 7*(2–3), 175–192.

Dorfman, A., & Mattelart, A. (1980). *Para leer el pato donald: Comunicación de masa y colonialismo* (21st ed.). Mexico City: Siglo Ventiuno.

Elguea, J. (1984). Sociology of development and philosophy of science: A case study in contemporary scientific growth. Unpublished doctoral dissertation, Stanford, CA.

Enzensberger, H. M. (1981). *Elementos para una teoria de los medios de comunicación* (3rd ed.). Barcelona: Anagrama.

Esteinou, J. (1981). *Medios de comunicación y acumulación de capital.* Mexico City: Universidad Iberoamericana, Cuadernos del Centro de Servicio y Promoción Social.

Fejes, F. (1981). Media imperialism: An assessment. *Media, Culture and Society, 3,* 281–289.

Foote, D., Parker, E., & Hudson, H. (1976). *Telemedicine in Alaska: The ATS-6 satellite biomedical demonstration.* Stanford, CA: Institute for Communication Research.

Freedom at Issue: Governmental control of press advanced by UNESCO conference. September–October 1976, No. 37.

Freire, P. (1971). *Conciencia critica y liberación.* Bogota, Colombia: Ediciones "Camilo."

Freire, P. (1975). *Que es la concientización y como funciona?* Lima, Peru: Editorial Causachun.

Gerbner, G., Gross, L., Morgan, M., & Signorielli, N. (1980). The "mainstreaming" of America: Violence profile No. 11. *Journal of Communication, 30,* 10–27.

Gitlin, T. (1978). Media sociology: The dominant paradigm. *Theory and Society, 6,* 205–253.

Hamelink, C. J. (Ed.). (1980). *Communication in the eighties: A reader on the "MacBride Report."* Rome: IDOC International.

Hamelink. C. J. (1983). *Cultural autonomy in global communication.* New York: Longman.

Hornik, R. (1980). Communication as complement in development. *Journal of Communication, 30*(2), 10–240.

Hornik, R., with E. B. Parker, E. Contreras-Bunge, D. Foote, D. Goldschmidt, & B. Searle (1979). *Communication as complement: An overview of communication in development.* Stanford, CA: Institute for Communication Research.

Hornik, R. (1988). *Development communication: Information, agriculture, and nutrition in the third world.* New York: Longman.

Hutchins, R. et al. (Commission on Freedom of the Press). (1947). *A free and responsible press.* Chicago: University of Chicago Press.

Inkeles, A., & Smith, D. H. (1974). *Becoming modern: Individual change in six developing countries.* Cambridge, MA: Harvard University Press.

Iyengar, S., Peters, M. D., & Kinder, D. R. (1982). Experimental demonstrations of the "not-so-minimal" consequences of television news programs. *American Political Science Review, 76,* 848–858.

Kahl, J. A. (1973). *The measurement of modernism.* Austin: University of Texas Press.

Kaid, L. L. (1981). Political advertising. In D. D. Nimmo & K. R. Sanders (Eds.), *Handbook of political communication* (pp. 249–271). Beverly Hills: Sage.

Katz, E., & Feldman, J. (1962). The debates in light of research: A survey of surveys. In S. Kraus (Ed.), *The great debates: Carter vs. Ford, 1976* (pp. 173–223). Bloomington: Indiana University Press.

Katz, E., Gurevitch, M., & Haas, H. (1973). On the use of television for important things. *American Sociological Review, 38,* 164–181.

Katz, E., & Wedell, G., with M. Pilsworth & D. Shinar (1977). *Broadcasting in the Third World: Promise and performance.* Cambridge, MA: Harvard University Press.

Kerner, O. et al. (1968). *Report. U.S. national advisory commission on civil disorders.* Washington, DC: U.S. Government Printing Office.

Klapper, J. T. (1960). *The effects of mass communication.* Glencoe, IL: Free Press.

Kraus, S. (Ed.). (1962). *The great debates: Carter vs. Ford, 1976.* Bloomington: Indiana University Press.

Kraus, S., & Davis, D. (1976). *The effects of mass communications on political behavior.* University Park: Pennsylvania State University Press.

Lasswell, H. (1948). The structure and function of communication in society. In L. Bryson (Ed.), *The communication of ideas.* New York: Institute for Religious and Social Studies.

Lazarsfeld, P., Berelson, B., & Gaudet, H. (1948). *The people's choice* (2nd ed.). New York: Columbia University Press.

Lazarsfeld, P., & Merton, R. (1971). Mass communication, popular taste and organized social action (Original work published 1948). In W. Schramm & D. F. Roberts (Eds.), *The process and effects of mass communication.* Urbana: University of Illinois Press.

Lerner, D. (1958). *The passing of traditional society.* New York: Free Press.

Lerner, D. (1967). Communication and change in developing countries. Honolulu: East-West Center.

Lessnoff, M. (1974). *The structure of social science. A philosophical introduction.* London: George Allen and Unwin.

MacBride, S. et al. (1980). *Many voices, one world: Report by the International Commission for the Study of Communication Problems.* Paris: UNESCO. London: Kogan Page. New York: Uniport.

Mathiason, J. R. (1967). The Venezuelan campesino: Perspectives on change. In F. Bonilla & J. A. Silva Michelena (Eds.), *A strategy for research on social policy* (pp. 120–155). Cambridge, MA: MIT Press.

Mattelart, A. (1973, September). El imperialismo en busca de la contrarrevolución cultural. "Plaza sesamo:" Prologo a la telerepresión del ano 2000. *Comunicación y Cultura,* No. 1 [Buenos Aires].

Mattelart, A. (1983). *Transnationals and the Third World: The struggle for culture.* (D. Buxton, Trans.). South Hadley, MA: Bergin and Garvey.

Mattelart, A., Delcourt, X., & Mattelart, M. (1984). *International image markets: In search of an alternative perspective.* (D. Buxton, Trans.). London: Comedia.

Mayo, J. K., Hornik, R. C., & McAnany, E. G. (1976). *Educational reform with television: The El Salvador experience.* Stanford, CA: Stanford University Press.

McCombs, M. (1981). The agenda setting approach. In D. D. Nimmo & K. R. Sanders (Eds.), *Handbook of political communication* (pp. 121–140). Beverly Hills: Sage.

McCombs, M., & Shaw, D. L. (1972). The agenda-setting function of mass media. *Public Opinion Quarterly, 36*(2), 176–187.

McLeod, J., & Becker, L. B. (1981). The uses and gratifications approach. In D. D. Nimmo & K. R. Sanders (Eds.), *Handbook of political communication* (pp. 67–99). Beverly Hills: Sage.

McLeod, J., Becker, L. B., & Byrnes, J. E. (1974). Another look at the agenda setting function of the press. *Communication Research, 1*(1), 131–166.

McLeod, J. M., Bybee, C., & Durall, J. A. (1979). Equivalence of informed political participation: The 1976 debates as a source of influence. *Communication Research, 6,* 463–487.

McLeod, J. M., Luetscher, W., & McDonald, D. (1980). Beyond mere exposure: Media orientations and their impact on political processes. Paper presented to the Association for Education in Journalism, Boston.

McQuail, D. (1983). *Mass communication theory: An introduction.* London: Sage.

Milton, J. (1951). *Areopagitica.* (G. H. Sabine, Ed.). New York: Appleton-Century-Crofts. (Original work published 1644)

Nie, N., Verba, S., & Petrocik, J. (1976). *The changing American voter.* Cambridge, MA: Harvard University Press.

Nimmo, D. D., & Sanders, K. R. (Eds). (1981). *Handbook of political communication.* Beverly Hills: Sage.

O'Keefe, G. J., & Atwood, L. E. (1981). Communication and election campaigns. In D. D. Nimmo & K. R. Sanders (Eds.), *Handbook of political communication* (pp. 329–357). Beverly Hills: Sage.

Paiva, A. (1983). La comunicación alternativa: Sus campos de influencia, sus limitaciones y sus perspectivas de desarrollo. In F. Reyes Matta (Ed.), *Comunicación alternativa y busquedas democraticas* (pp. 29–156). Mexico City: ILET/Friedrich Ebert Stiftung.

Pasquali, A. (1963). *Comunicación y cultura de masas: La masificación de la cultura por medios audiovisuales en las regiones subdesarrolladas.* Caracas: Universidad Central de Venezuela.

Pasquali, A. (1972). *Comunicación y cultura de masas* (2nd ed.). Caracas: Monte Avila.

Patterson, T. E. (1980). *The mass media election.* New York: Praeger.

Patterson, T. E., & McClure, R. D. (1976). *The unseeing eye.* New York: G. P. Putnam's.

Paz, I. (1977). *Medios masivos, ideologia y propaganda imperialista.* La Habana, Cuba: Cuadernos de la Revista Union.

Pye, L. (Ed.) (1963). *Communications and political development.* Princeton, NJ: Princeton University Press.

Reyes Matta, F. (1981, September 4). La comunicación alternativa como respuesta democratica. Mexico City: *El Dia* [newspaper].

Rogers, E. M. (1965). Mass media exposure and modernization among Colombian peasants. *Public Opinion Quarterly, 29*(4), 614–625.

Rogers, E. M. (1969). *Modernization among peasants.* New York: Holt, Rinehart & Winston.

Rogers, E. M. (1973). *Communication strategies for family planning.* New York: Free Press.

Rogers, E. M. (1976). Communication and development: The passing of the dominant paradigm. *Communication research, 3,* 213–240.

Rogers, E. M. (1983). *Diffusion of innovations* (3rd ed.). (Original work published 1964) New York: Free Press.

Rogers, E. M., & Schement, J. (1984). Media flows in Latin America. *Communication Research, 11*(2) (entire issue).

Rogoff, E. (1980). Comunicación de masas y dominación cultural en America Latina. *Revista de Ciencias Sociales, 22,* 1–2, 103–126.

Romano, S. (1979). Radio, televisión y enajenación en Mexico. *Revista Mexicana de Ciencias Politicas y Sociales, 25,* 95–96, 111–121.

Rostow, W. W. (1960). *The stages of economic growth.* Cambridge: Cambridge University Press.

Schramm, W. (1957). *Responsibility in mass communication.* New York: Harper & Row.

Schramm, W. (1964). *Mass media and national development: The role of information in the developing countries.* Stanford, CA: Stanford University Press.

Sears, D., & Chaffee, S. H. (1979). Uses and effects of the 1976 debates: An overview of empirical studies.

In S. Kraus (Ed.), *The great debates: Carter vs. Ford, 1976.* Bloomington: Indiana University Press.

Sears, D. O., & Freedman, J. L. (1967). Selective exposure to information: A critical review. *Public Opinion Quarterly, 31,* 194–213.

Shaw, D. L., & McCombs, M. E. (Eds.). (1977). *The emergence of American political issues.* St. Paul, MN: West Publishing.

Shoemaker, P. J. (1982). Deviance of political groups and media treatment. *Communication Research, 9,* 249–286.

Siebert, F., Peterson, T., & Schramm, W. (1956). *Four theories of the press.* Urbana: University of Illinois Press.

Textual [Peru]. (1973). No. 8, Diciembre, 77–79.

Urrutia Boloña, C. (1973). Comunicación masiva y agresión cultural. *Textual* [Peru], No. 8.

Weaver, D., Graber, D., McCombs, M. E., & Eyal, C. (1981). *Media agenda-setting in a presidential election: Issues, images, interest.* New York: Praeger.

Weaver, D., McCombs, M. E., & Spellman, C. (1975). Watergate and the media: A case study of agenda-setting. *American Politics Quarterly, 3,* 458–472.

Whitney, D. C., & Goldman, S. B. (1985). Media use and time of vote decision: A study of the 1980 presidential election. *Communication Research, 12,* 511–529.

Wright, C. R. (1959). *Mass communication: A sociological perspective.* New York: Random House.

PART FOUR

Methods of Communication Inquiry

Literally hundreds of reference citations dot the preceding pages. The majority identify published reports of communication research, studies that represent the finished product of an arduous and complex investigative process. These citations are a kind of academic pedigree; they report this book's intellectual bloodlines. Indeed, the knowledge claims contained in a textbook of this type are only as credible as the body of literature used to support them. But the supportive literature, however extensive, is virtually valueless to the reader who lacks an understanding of research methodology with which to retrieve, analyze, and appraise it firsthand. Given the nature and number of methods available to communication researchers today, the uninformed reader's quandary cannot be resolved entirely in the balance of this book. The two chapters of Part Four, "Methods of Communication Inquiry," are designed to minimize the immediate problem while providing a foundation for future growth in the area of research expertise.

Although there are no real shortcuts to learning research methods, we believe Chapters 13 and 14 provide a relatively clear and simple framework into which the complexities of methodology can be assimilated over time. Chapter 13, "Basic Types of Communication Research," begins with an effort to stimulate the reader's interest by arguing the practicality of studying the research process. Four fundamental types of communication inquiry are then identified and examined in terms of their goals, basic structure, typical location (or setting), methods of observation, and appropriate approaches to data analysis. The final chapter, "A General Model of the Research Process," focuses more directly on the actual conduct of communication research. Short of hands-on experience, we believe Chapter 14 comes as close as possible via the printed page to walking the reader step by step through the research process. Moreover, the model presented can be readily adapted to meet the objectives of each of the four types of research discussed in Chapter 13. Similar to other chapters in this volume, the main advantage of Chapters 13 and 14 is their synthesis of a rather large body of information for which the student is typically required to search through many sources.

13

Basic Types of Communication Research

Gordon L. Dahnke
Michigan State University

Katherine I. Miller
Michigan State University

Gordon L. Dahnke *is Assistant Professor of Communication at Michigan State University, where he received a Ph.D. degree in communication studies. His teaching and research interests include interpersonal, nonverbal, and small group communication as well as research methodology. Dr. Dahnke recently served a Fulbright Fellowship sponsored by the U.S. International Communication Agency at Anáhuac University in Mexico City.*

Katherine I. Miller *is Assistant Professor of Communication at Michigan State University. She received her Ph.D. from the Annenberg School of Communications at the University of Southern California. Dr. Miller's research on organizational and health communication has been published in a wide range of communication and management journals. Her current research interests center on the development of stress and burnout among human service workers and the role of supportive and participative communication systems in coping with these phenomena.*

LEARNING OBJECTIVES

After studying this chapter you should be able to:

• List three reasons for the study of research methods.

• Define communication inquiry.

• Explain the relationship among the three goals of theory construction.

• Identify the four basic types of communication inquiry.

- State the primary purpose of each type of communication inquiry.
- Discuss the structure of each type of communication inquiry.
- Tell the typical setting for each type of communication inquiry.
- List the observational technique options for each type of communication inquiry.
- Describe the analytical tools employed with each type of communication inquiry.

Communicating well enough to get by in most ordinary situations is mainly a matter of common sense, is it not? Why then should students of communication concern themselves with methods of inquiry? Would it be prudent to ask what the term *communication inquiry* means conceptually to the opinion leaders of our discipline? Can we divide and conquer the territory associated with this scholastic interest by means of a typology? That is, would it expedite the learning process to identify the most common types of communication inquiry and to compare their distinguishing characteristics? The following discussion provides relatively straightforward answers to these questions, beginning with why we are prone to ask them in the first place.

From birth to death, across culture, climate, and class, human beings are tireless interrogators. Perhaps our natural inclination to ask questions is reason enough to examine methods of inquiry. The study of research processes is simply an effort to learn how to ask large, more important questions in pursuit of more reliable, meaningful answers.

If scientific inquiry is not a panacea for all problems, those familiar with modern history will not dispute its formative impact on public and private life in this century. Whether your interests lie in preparing a scholastic term paper, persuading a potential buyer to make a deal, convincing a member of the opposite sex to share an evening, motivating the masses to get out and vote, changing your employer's mind regarding a raise in pay, or simply learning to think more productively about any nagging problem, your exposure to methods of inquiry will be difficult to overdo. The advantages of understanding scientific inquiry are worth discussing in greater detail.

First, regarding careers that involve direct contact with the social science enterprise (or its output) in any substantive area addressed in this volume, the need to understand research processes is self-evident. Less obvious is the fact that many students who do not plan or prepare themselves to conduct research eventually end up occupying positions that demand a basic knowledge of this area. Others who aspire to hold more prestigious, profitable positions downstream are unable to secure them without additional training in research methodology. At the risk of repeating an argument you may already have conceded, college diplomas quickly become obsolete without regular consumption of new information generated by ongoing research in virtually every social science discipline and related profession.

Second, practitioners in business administration, public relations, industrial psychology, organizational development, advertising, education, medicine, law, politics, mass media (radio, television, and newspapers), government, and social services are already finding it difficult to survive without the ability to *read, evaluate,* and *apply* results of social science (particularly communication) research.

Third, as a result of relentless media exposure, citizens in our society are compelled to make daily (if not hourly) decisions in response to a barrage of claims and questions raised in the name of research. Nonprofessionals who understand the basic tenets of science are better prepared to evaluate available evidence bearing on these day-to-day issues. When different studies investigating the same phenomena produce conflicting results, it requires an informed person to decide which conclusion merits his or her confidence. Error in this regard can be extremely costly! And all indications are that the need for knowledge of research methods will continue to increase at an inordinately rapid rate.

DEFINING CHARACTERISTICS OF COMMUNICATION INQUIRY

Respected writers on methods of social science (such as Kerlinger, 1973) sometimes avoid any attempt to define science per se because an adequate, comprehensive definition of the term is difficult to provide. Yet it seems necessary at this point to offer at least a working definition of what we have been calling scientific communication research: It is a systematic method for conducting and recording observations of intentional, symbolic human transactions. These observations are made by human observers and recorded systematically so they can be compared across observers and over time, primarily for purposes of explanation, prediction, and control.

All the particulars of this definition need not concern us now. Three pivotal ideas are important at this juncture. First, observation is the sine qua non method of science; no less of the scientific approach to any type of research. Strictly speaking, that which is unobservable via one or more of the five human senses cannot be subjected to communication research according to the definition above. For example, aggressive attitudes, hostility, or motivations of long-term marriage partners may interest the communication scientist intensely, but such "inside-the-head" constructs, as they are often called, cannot be observed directly (Kerlinger, 1973). Their use in communication research depends on our ability to observe external behaviors from which these invented attitude constructs can be inferred; no one has ever "seen" an attitude.

Second, though observability is a necessary condition for scientific research, our definition does not consider *all* observable behavior relevant for purposes of communication research; it restricts the domain or range of eligible observations to communicative events of the intentional, symbolic, and transactional type (Miller & Steinberg, 1975). The term *intentional* specifies that communication minimally requires a source making a conscious effort (intending) to send a message. For instance, there is no end to the number of different, *unintended* meanings a self-appointed receiver could impose on the behavior of an unsuspecting (involuntary) source. Moreover, there is no end to the different types of behavior and nonbehavior that can be assigned meaning in this manner. In other words, if I can impose whatever meaning I choose on head-scratching activity, I can also arbitrarily assign meaning to inactivity; for example, a silent, motionless stare into space could be interpreted to mean someone is uninterested, bored, tired, in love, concentrating intensely, fantasizing, and so on. Thus *communication* would be little more than a synonym for anything people do or do not do; it would refer to everything about human behavior in general, but nothing in particular. Such loose definitions are virtually useless for scientific purposes.

Communicative events, as defined above, necessarily involve the use of symbols. A symbol can be any figure, cluster of alphabetic letters, gesture, facial expression, body movement, object—indeed, anything that stands for or represents some meaning beyond itself. In addition, symbols must represent shared meanings; that is, their meanings must be established by conventional use or prior agreement so that they are interpretable by people other than the symbol source.

Finally, given our working definition, the domain of relevant observation in communication research is further delineated by the term *transaction*. To say that such events are transactional underscores the dynamic, ongoing, interdependent relationship between participants engaged in ordinary communicative acts.

A third feature of our working definition needs clarification here. It says that we systematically observe and record our observations primarily for purposes of explanation, prediction, and control. The first and foremost objective of social science is *explanation*. An explanation is a theory that answers "why" questions about the way things work.

In science, theory development takes precedence over specific problems, whether they concern newlyweds at an interpersonal level or nuclear arms at an international level, because such problems are rarely (if ever) solved efficiently apart from analyzing them in terms specified by relevant general theory. The only alternative to problem solving through application of theory is a haphazard, hit-or-miss, trial-and-error approach.

A general theory, then, explains those operations common to a whole class of objects, people, or events; because of this one-to-many relationship, theory development is the most efficient means of solving specific problems. In short, any attempt to solve specific problems has a greater probability of success at minimal cost when the solver applies general knowledge, such as a theory or an explanation of how the phenomenon of interest works. Likewise, one good theory, once it has been "born and raised," is capable of generating a large number of cost-effective solutions to the same problem under different circumstances, different problems under similar circumstances, and perhaps even different problems under different circumstances.

Little has been said thus far about the subsidiary aims of science included in our definition of communication research: prediction and control. But, as Kurt Lewin has said, nothing is more practical than a good theory, because such theories provide our *only* explanations (knowledge and understanding) of communicative phenomena or any other natural event we may wish to alter.

Scientific inquiry aims to harness formal logic and empirical evidence in pursuit of *more probable* explanations, which, in turn, increase our predictive accuracy. Because the propositions with which theories are built invariably express probable relationships, our explanations are themselves predictive in nature. That is, each proposition predicts a more or less probable relationship. The predictive power of a formal theory depends on how general it is (as sug-

gested above) and the degree of probability associated with the *least probable* proposition in the explanation.

The prior discussion of explanation and prediction—indeed, all of science—would be dispensable if human beings had no interest in controlling their physical and social surroundings. In situations where the actual course of natural events cannot as yet be altered, such as tornados, our concern is to predict their outcomes. But prediction is not an end in itself; we make predictions about events in the real world and test them repeatedly in order to control their effects on human life. To the extent that our predictions are confirmed by observation, they afford knowledge *in advance* of what has not yet occurred. Thus increasingly reliable prediction implies increased opportunity to successfully influence our future state and circumstance. On these accounts, we come full circle back to the notion that explanation is the primary aim of science; the entire process stands or falls on theory. With that end in mind, we next consider various ways in which observations can be made.

TYPES OF COMMUNICATION RESEARCH

The wide range of topics considered in this textbook is a clear indication of the breadth of the field of communication. Communication scholars explore issues ranging from nonverbal behavior to the mass media, from friendship formation to political persuasion. Given this range of interests among communication scholars, it is not surprising that the research tools and strategies used are just as varied. In the balance of this chapter, we will consider four major types of communication research: exploratory research, descriptive research, correlational research, and experimental research. We will consider five aspects of each type of research: (1) the purpose and goals of the research, with an eye toward discovering the types of questions that can best be answered through different types of communication research; (2) the structure of each type of research;

(3) the typical settings (laboratory or field) of the research types in our typology; (4) the observational techniques researchers use, from participant observation to questionnaires to unobtrusive measures; (5) the analytical tools employed in various types of research, including the wide range of statistical and reporting options available to communication researchers.

Exploratory Communication Research

Purpose and Goals   As a general statement of purpose, Selltiz, Jahoda, Deutsch, and Cook (1959) assert that the major emphasis in formulative or exploratory research "is on discovery of ideas and insights" (p. 50). Kerlinger (1973) adopted some additional distinctions in stating that exploratory studies "have three purposes: to discover significant variables in the field situation, to discover relations among variables, and to lay the groundwork for later, more systematic, and rigorous testing of hypotheses" (p. 406). For our purposes in the field of communication, it is perhaps most useful to consider two major types of exploratory research: (1) inquiry designed to aid in the formation of research problems and hypotheses, and (2) inquiry designed to aid in the discovery and investigation of important communication variables.

Exploratory research designed to aid in forming research questions and hypotheses can run the gamut from "scouting expeditions" in relatively unexamined territories of human communication to more formal experiments designed to disclose promising relationships among key variables for theory-building ends. As a case in point, researchers have considered the impacts of doctor-patient communication on the end results of medical care, but communication in home health-care settings is still virgin territory in terms of research attention. A researcher interested in developing hypotheses or "grounded theory" about human communication in these settings would need to use relatively flexible re-

search techniques in a scouting expedition on the topic of interest.

The second general type of exploratory research involves the discovery and investigation of variables that may be important in the communication process. Often, this type of research involves the investigation of a general typology of communication variables or development of instruments for their measurement. For example, researchers interested in how people gain compliance from others began with exploratory research into the typical communicative strategies individuals use in persuasive situations (Marwell & Schmitt, 1967; Wiesman & Schenck-Hamlin, 1981). Similarly, researchers interested in why some people are more anxious in communicative situations than others began their program of research by developing measures of communication apprehension (McCroskey, 1970). This kind of exploratory research into the nature of the variables we study is an important precursor to the study of how these variables relate to other outcomes of interest.

Structure   Research designed to discover new variables and to explore the relationships among variables both have minimal structure. Because of the newness of the area being investigated, an exploratory researcher has few initial research questions or hypotheses. Rather, such research is typically guided by the data as the research progresses. For example, Quinn (1977), noting the influx of women into the workplace, was interested in the effects of romantic relationships in organizations. There was no past research on this topic, and Quinn could do little but speculate about what the important precursors and ramifications of such relationships were. Thus in designing his research, he began with a large number of unstructured interviews asking individuals about office romances they had observed. This led Quinn to formulate some more focused questions about the motives of individuals in office romances, the effect of such a relationship on their performance, and the ways co-workers reacted to participants in the romance. Had Quinn begun his research with a structured questionnaire, he may not have included issues that emerged as important during the initial interviews.

Setting Most exploratory studies in communication take place outside the research laboratory. As noted above, the major goals of exploratory research are the discovery of crucial communication variables and the potential relationships among these variables. Typically, such discovery will take place in a natural environment, where we can look at how people actually communicate in their day-to-day lives. The control gained in the laboratory is also typically unnecessary in exploratory studies, because the researcher does not have a clear idea of what variables should be manipulated and controlled in order to answer research questions or test hypotheses.

Observations Exploratory research is characterized by the use of a wide range of observational methods; it often begins with the observation of natural behavior. For example, Whyte's classic study of "street corner society" (1955) explored street-life social structure and involved direct observation by participating in the social structure. Exploratory research could also involve unstructured interviews (as described in the Quinn study above), or a more wide-ranging questionnaire approach. For example, G. R. Miller, Mongeau, and Sleight (1986) were interested in deception among individuals in intimate relationships. Although they had no specific hypotheses, a questionnaire study of a number of married couples led them to some initial conclusions about "fudging to friends and lying to lovers."

The consideration of artifactual data is also a potent avenue for the discovery of communication variables and relationships. For example, in an exploratory investigation of organizational culture, K. I. Miller, Zook, and Mack (1987) coded the content of company newsletters in order to consider the ways communication artifacts rep-

resent organizational values. In short, the data for exploratory research can be collected with a wide variety of observational techniques. The best guiding principle is to let the nature of the communication phenomenon guide the researcher to the appropriate observational system.

Analysis The kind of analyses performed on exploratory data varies with the purpose of the research. For the first purpose considered above, development of research questions and hypotheses, the method of analysis is often a qualitative assessment of the data collected. For example, a researcher might examine interview transcripts to look for the patterns in which important concepts are linked in individual cases. Quantitative methods of data analysis are also available to the exploratory researcher, detailed in Tukey (1977). Many of these techniques can be performed through simple paper-and-pencil calculations; they are often designed to help the researcher get a clearer visual and numerical picture of the relationships in the data.

For the second purpose of exploratory research, the discovery and development of communication concepts, both qualitative and quantitative methods of analysis are helpful. For instance, an in-depth look at the content of proposed measures and variable typologies is always the first step of analysis in this type of study. The researcher should carefully consider whether the important dimensions and attributes of the communication concept are adequately represented in the measure or typology proposed. Following this qualitative assessment, a wide variety of quantitative techniques is available for assessing the reliability and validity of a developed scale. Some of the more commonly used methods of this type are exploratory factor analysis, confirmatory factor analysis, and q-sort analysis. Specific discussion of these methods is impossible given the scope of this chapter (see Fishbein, 1967; Hunter & Gerbing, 1982; and Nunnally, 1967, for more detailed treatment). In general, all of these techniques are concerned with the ways items in a scale or typology group together mathematically to form dimensions and subdimensions of communication concepts.

Descriptive Communication Research

Descriptive communication research, unlike exploratory research, typically considers variables with which the investigator is familiar. The emphasis in descriptive research is on accurate measurement that can provide a complete and detailed assessment of the behavior or phenomenon under investigation. Descriptive research is so commonplace that we are often unaware of its persistent influence on daily life. The U.S. Census, for example, is a descriptive endeavor; it serves to describe important characteristics of county, state, and national populations by means of systematic observation and analysis. Many commercial, political, and education decision makers rely routinely on this information. Similarly, TV ratings compiled regularly by the A.C. Nielsen Company describe viewing behaviors and demographic characteristics relative to various segments of the national audience. Ratings of this type largely determine the extent to which advertisers are willing to sponsor particular media networks and programs. In short, descriptive research has a steady impact on our lives and is an important tool for learning about communication phenomena.

Purpose and Goals Most social scientists would agree that description is an important function of the research process (for example, Babble, 1986; Kerlinger, 1973; Kidder, 1981). Description is necessary for the explanation and prediction of social events; indeed, description is the foundation on which social science research rests. The precise purpose of descriptive research, per se, is more difficult to define. However, it is reasonable to consider three primary goals of descriptive research:

1. To characterize communication processes and events. That is, we are interested in gaining an accurate and detailed picture of what makes up our communication behavior.

2. To predict present or future events from single-variable data. An example of this type of research is the Nielsen ratings discussed above, in which a description of the viewing audience is used to make predictions and decisions about the allocation of advertising dollars.

3. To serve as a foundation for the building of communication theory. That is, an accurate description of communication behavior may disclose promising variables and relationships for future explanatory inquiry.

Structure Like exploratory research, descriptive research typically involves a relatively low level of structure in that research hypotheses are rarely established in advance. However, descriptive research is more structured than exploratory research in terms of a priori definitions for the phenomena being studied. In exploratory research, the investigator is always open to considering outside variables that may shed light on the phenomenon in question. In descriptive research, by contrast, the premium is on obtaining an accurate and complete description of the phenomenon. Given this objective, the researcher must develop in advance a clear definition of what is being studied and develop a research design with sufficient structure to ensure a complete description of that phenomenon.

Setting Descriptive research almost always takes place in the field, as descriptions of behavior in natural settings will typically be more useful than descriptions of behavior in the constrained environment of the laboratory. For example, a topic of great concern in many organizations is the manner in which employees are socialized to an understanding of the values and practices of the company (Jablin & Krone, 1987). Clearly, a description of the stages of the socialization process and the communication strategies companies use to facilitate this process must come from the workplace, as laboratory studies of this process would have little resemblance to the experiences of organization newcomers.

Observation The type of observation used in descriptive research depends largely on the specific goals of the researchers. Often, descriptive research will involve extensive surveys of many people on a given set of variables. A great deal of research on the mass media takes this form. For instance, a research project on the use of the media by Spanish-speaking Americans (Greenberg, Burgoon, Burgoon, & Korzenny, 1983) involved the study of Hispanic Americans in six southwestern U.S. communities. The goal of the study was to describe the mass communication behavior of Hispanics and Anglos, the amount of media coverage allocated to Hispanic-American concerns, and perceptions held by both local newspaper publishers and Hispanic community leaders. In short, this was a broad descriptive study requiring careful measurement and a broad sample. This study was typical of descriptive research, particularly in the area of mass communication.

Not all descriptive studies involve such a broad effort, however. One important kind of description is the case study, in which one example of a phenomenon is studied intensively. The goal of the case study is to provide a finely detailed description that might serve to either refute a theory on a given issue or lead to the refinement of research questions in the area. Redding (1970) discusses this type of descriptive research, saying "Even the much maligned one-shot descriptive case study can indeed yield valuable scientific conclusions if it is planned with reference to specified theoretical constructs. A single study— or better yet a series of studies—can at least provide sound evidence that a given theory does not apply to specified situations" (p. 147). A good example of such research is Stern's (1979) study of the development of the communication network linking intercollegiate athletics. His case study of the history of the National Collegiate Athletic Association (NCAA) produced a detailed picture of the process of network emergence that could be captured only in an intensive case analysis.

Analysis As was the case with exploratory research, the type of analysis employed in descriptive research will depend to a large extent on the goals of the researcher. If the purpose of the study is a relatively straightforward characterization of communication events, the researcher will typically use relatively simple quantitative statistics such as means, variances, and percentages. When appropriate, statistical tests may be used to determine whether differences among groups being described are statistically significant. In descriptive research, however, the emphasis is not on *explaining* differences among groups, but rather on merely identifying them. Different research goals may lead the descriptive researcher to very different data analysis techniques. Data from case studies, for example, do not lend themselves to quantitative methods of analysis; they are more amenable to qualitative analysis in the mode of anthropological research. For instance, Trujillo (1983) examined the managerial communication patterns of the owner of a car dealership. His detailed consideration of the actual conversations and behavior of the individual led Trujillo to an interesting description of the ways different leadership roles were enacted in this organization.

Correlational Communication Research

Most elementary discussions of quantitative methods for social research will tell you that the first step toward *explaining* any event is to establish an empirical association between two or more seemingly relevant variables. Finding such associations is the general goal of correlational research. Two variables are said to be associated empirically when statistical evidence has been found indicating that variations in each of the two variables occur side-by-side in some systematic pattern.

Such evidence is found by using valid and reliable measures of communication variables that allow for the assignment of numbers to quantify changes within each variable. Commonly used correlational techniques can then indicate the *direction* of change in one set of numerical values relative to co-occurring changes in the other set, as well as the *magnitude* of their joint variation. Assuming that a joint pattern of change does emerge and its magnitude is sufficiently large (by conventional standards), social researchers of the quantitative stripe are willing to infer a similar pattern of variation among the original variables the abstract number purportedly represent.

For example, assume that a researcher was interested in the relationship between employee participation in decision making and satisfaction with work. To study this phenomenon, the researcher could develop or adopt measures of both participation and work satisfaction and administer a questionnaire incorporating these measures to a large number of employees. Correlational analysis would then tell the researcher the extent to which people who participated in decisions also tended to be satisfied with their work.

Several issues about such research should be noted, however. First, the statistical procedure of correlation is at least one step removed from the "real world" arena where the variables of interest actually operate; the size of this step depends on the quality of the measurement we use. Second, even if we obtain a sizable correlation between the variables of interest—that is, we find that increases in participation are typically accompanied by increases in job satisfaction—we cannot conclude that participation "causes" satisfaction with work. Indeed, just the opposite could be the case: perhaps people who like their work are more likely to voluntarily participate in decisions. Or perhaps both of these outcomes are caused by a third variable such as the type of job an individual holds or level in the organization's hierarchy.

In short, researchers should use caution with correlational research, because the value of its output largely depends on both the quality of measurement and the strength of the theory (or reasoning process) linking the communication variables at the outset.

Purpose and Goals With the foregoing cautions in mind, we can set forth several goals of correlational research. Clearly, the most basic goal is the discovery of association between two or more variables of interest. This basic purpose can then aid in achieving two other goals: (1) the prediction of present and future events from bivariate or multivariate data, and (2) the discovery of potential (and we stress potential) cause-effect explanations of communication processes. For example, a researcher may have an interest in whether the variables *communication overload* and *job stress* covary with each other. If such a relationship is confirmed, further theory and research might investigate the existence of a causal link between load and stress and possibly look for ways to predict stress from levels of communication overload. The first step in this type of research is always to determine the covariation between the variables of interest.

Structure Because the researcher is now moving into the area of explanation, correlational research typically involves specifying precise research questions, and perhaps even hypotheses. Predictions in this kind of research typically take the form of predictions about covariation (for example, predicting that participation in decision making will be related to job satisfaction) rather than predictions about causes (that is, participation would typically not be hypothesized to be the "cause" of job satisfaction). In addition to the explicitness of predictions, correlational research also involves a greater degree of structure in terms of measurement and sampling.

Settings Correlational research almost always takes place in the field rather than in the laboratory. The researcher is interested in the covariation of naturally occurring communication phenomena, and these phenomena must be measured in the most natural setting possible. For example, mass media researchers investigating the relationship between socioeconomic status and the viewing of soap operas could not conduct their research in a laboratory setting. Rather, they would be required to conduct their research in such a way as to gather information about people's day-to-day television viewing behavior and correlate information about that behavior with socioeconomic indicators.

Observation Correlational research typically deals with quantitative data gathered through questionnaire measures or with artifactual quantitative data. Typically, the researcher tries to gather data from a large number of people, as the level of confidence a researcher has in his or her conclusions depends on the size of the sample. As noted above, the researcher is also concerned with the quality of measures used in correlational research. Valid and reliable measurement scales are essential. A *reliable* scale is one that, applied repeatedly to the same object, will yield the same result every time. A *valid* scale is one that adequately represents the "real" meaning of a concept under consideration.

The reliability and validity of measurement instruments are of paramount importance in correlational research. For example, K. I. Miller and Monge (1987) were interested in worker participation, knowledge about the workplace, and satisfaction as these variables may influence perceptions of equity and organizational commitment. The first step in their research was to find or develop scales for the relevant variables that appeared to have a high level of validity. Then, before considering correlations among the variables, they tested the empirical quality of their measurement scales with confirmatory factor analysis. Only after the quality of measurement was determined did they move on to examining the relationships among the variables by means of correlational techniques.

Analysis Data in correlational research are analyzed with statistics that rely on the "general linear model." The most straightforward member of this family of statistics is the Pearson product-moment correlation. As noted earlier, the correlation coefficient allows the researcher to investigate the covariation between two sets of numbers. For example, consider the relationship between the nonverbal cue of eye contact in a dyad and the degree of attraction between the members of this dyad. If more eye contact was typically accompanied by more attraction in dyads, we would say that there was a positive correlation between these two variables. If more eye contact was typically accompanied by less attraction in dyads, we would say that there was a negative correlation between these two variables. If no meaningful pattern of shared variation between these two variables was found, we would say that the correlation between them was zero.

A number of other statistical techniques based largely on the correlational model allow the researcher to learn even more about the relationships among variables. For example, *multiple regression* can be used to look at the relative impact of two or more independent variables on a single dependent variable. Other regression techniques allow the researcher to consider multiple independent and dependent variables. *Path analysis* is a more complex technique that provides a means for the researcher to make causal inferences about correlational data. In short, a wide variety of analytical techniques are available to the researcher that are based on the general notion of investigating the ways a set of variables covary with each other.

Experimental Communication Research

Purpose and Goals It was noted earlier that the first step toward reaching the conclusion that variables are causally related is to establish the covariation between these variables. The correlational research discussed above concentrates on this notion of covariance among variables. However, it takes more than covariance between two variables to establish causality. In order to establish causality, the researcher must also establish time ordering among the variables (that is, show that the cause preceded the effect) and rule out the possibility that other variables might be entering into the causal relationship.

For example, it can be demonstrated that covariation exists between the human use of umbrellas and the emergence of earthworms from underground. If covariance was all we needed to establish causality, we might conclude that raising umbrellas draws worms out of the ground or vice versa. However, when we add the two other requirements for causality, we would not be so quick to reach this conclusion. First, it would be difficult for us to determine that the umbrellas always came out before the worms (or vice versa). And it would be virtually impossible for us to rule out a third variable—rain, for instance—that could explain both the raising of umbrellas and the emergence of earthworms.

Experimental research attempts to establish causal relationships by looking for covariation among the variables of interest while fixing the time ordering of these variables and attempting to control for the influence of extraneous variables. To continue with our whimsical example, an experimental researcher interested in the effect of umbrella use on the emergence of earthworms could design a study in which the opening of umbrellas was under the control of the researcher; this would be the manipulated, independent variable. The researcher would also attempt to maintain outside influences at a constant level for different umbrella-opening (experimental) conditions. For example, the researcher could assure that there was *no* rain accompanying the opening of umbrellas, that there was *always* rain accompanying the opening of umbrellas, or that the occurrence of rain was *randomly distributed* among umbrella-opening conditions. With a tightly controlled experiment of this type, the researcher could be confident of his or her decision about the effect of umbrella opening on earthworm emergence.

Structure The search for causal relationships among communication variables requires the re-

searcher to conduct tightly structured inquiry. Experimental research involves the *manipulation* of one or more independent variables. One or more dependent variables are then *measured* to determine the impact of the independent variables. The manipulation of the independent variable thus assures that it precedes the dependent variable in time—a necessary requirement for causality.

The experimental researcher is also concerned with structuring the research in such a way as to rule out alternative explanations for changes in the dependent variable. In general, the researcher wants to maximize the impact of the independent variable on the dependent variable, and control for the impact of other variables on the dependent variable. When a design is successful in doing this, it is said to have a high level of internal validity. For example, participants in an experiment are often randomly assigned to experimental groups. This structure helps assure the researcher that the two groups are likely to be equivalent. The researcher might also want to order the manipulations and measurements in an experiment in such a way as to rule out the possibility that other variables caused observed changes in the dependent variable. (For more detail on the use of experimental design to enhance internal validity, see Campbell & Stanley, 1963.)

Setting As noted above, experimental research requires the researcher to exert a great deal of control over study procedures. Thus experimental research must be conducted in a setting that will allow the researcher to manipulate the relevant variables and measure their effect on other variables. This degree of experimental control is most easily obtained in a laboratory setting. For example, consider Stiff and Miller's (1986) research on deception. Their hypotheses required them to manipulate the situation in such a way that experimental participants would be motivated to deceive and would believe that the person they were talking to did not know that they were deceiving. Constructing such a situation in the field could be extremely difficult, but a laboratory setting allowed these researchers the control required to manipulate the necessary variables.

This is not to suggest, however, that experimental research requires a laboratory setting. Field experiments that allow for the manipulation and control of relevant variables without sacrificing the generalizability which can be gained from a natural setting are extremely valuable. For example, a researcher interested in the effect of the communication style of elementary-school teachers on student learning would be well advised to conduct a tightly designed field experiment. In such an experiment, the researcher could train teachers in varying styles of communication and measure the impact of these styles on the learning of students in the classroom. In this way, the independent variable would be manipulated and other relevant variables could be controlled, allowing the researcher to make causal statements about the relationship between communication style and student learning. At the same time, the natural classroom setting would enhance the researcher's confidence in the applicability of research claims to the "real world" of the elementary school.

Observation   In experimental research, the independent variables are manipulated by the experimenter and the dependents are measured. Thus the observation of the dependent variable allows many of the same measurement options noted for exploratory, descriptive, and correlational research. The dependent variable in experimental research might be measured through a questionnaire or through observation of behavior, depending on the research question under investigation. The fact that the independent variable is manipulated, however, does not relieve the researcher of the burden of measurement. Rather, experimental research, in addition to the measurement of the dependent variables, should include a *manipulation check* to determine whether the researcher was successful in manipulating the independent variable.

For example, persuasion researchers interested in the effect of source credibility on attitude change might attempt to manipulate the credibility of the source delivering a message. A message advocating national health insurance might be portrayed as delivered by a leading expert on the medical industry (high-credibility source) and a high school senior (low-credibility source). However, manipulating credibility in this way does not ensure that experiment participants actually *perceive* the two sources as differing in credibility. Thus an experimental researcher should measure perceptions of credibility to serve as a check on the quality of the experimental manipulation.

Analysis   Analysis of experimental data requires the researcher to determine whether the manipulated independent variable had an impact on the dependent variable. For example, a persuasion researcher might be interested in whether source credibility (the manipulated independent variable) has an impact on attitude change (the measured dependent variable). Thus analysis in experimental research typically requires the comparison of scores on the dependent variable between several groups of respondents (such as a group who heard a high-credibility source and a group who heard a low-credibility source). The general model used to test for these differences is analysis of variance (ANOVA), a form of the general linear model (see Keppel, 1982, for a complete description of the use of ANOVA in experimental research). Experimental researchers also use many of the descriptive and correlational analytical techniques described in earlier sections of this chapter.

CONCLUSION

Exploratory, descriptive, correlational, and experimental research are all valid and important ways of generating knowledge about human communication. The choice of research technique depends on the nature of the phenomenon under investigation, the particular research questions or

Table 13.1 A Comparative Summary of Typical Features of Nonexperimental and Experimental Types of Communication Inquiry.

Type of Communication Inquiry	Primary Purpose	Typical Degree of Structure	Typical Settings	Typical Observation/ Design Options	Typical Analysis	Goals
NONEXPERIMENTAL						
exploratory studies	discovery, insight	minimum	natural	observation interview questionnaire	primarily qualitative	1. formulation of research problems 2. may suggest promising research hypotheses 3. discovery of important communication variables
descriptive studies	accurate measurement	low	natural or seminatural	survey case study	qualitative or quantitative	1. objective characterization of communicative events 2. prediction of present/future events 3. may disclose promising variables for theory construction
correlational studies	measurement of association	moderate	natural or seminatural	survey or other measurement of multiple variables	quantitative	1. objective measures of association between communication variables 2. prediction of present/future events from 3. may disclose potential cause-effect relations
EXPERIMENTAL						
experiments	tests of general and concrete quasicausal relationships	high	structured (laboratory or field)	controlled conditions, manipulation of variables, and preferably random assignment of subjects	quantitative	1. assessment of quasicausal relations 2. assessment of time order among variables 3. control of effects of extraneous variables

hypotheses being addressed, and the resources available to the researcher. These four types of research vary greatly in terms of goals, structure, setting, observational techniques, and analytical techniques; these contrasts have been discussed extensively in this chapter and are highlighted in Table 13.1. Clearly, these kinds of research address different needs—each kind of research will answer some questions and leave others unanswered. For example, though exploratory research might be useful in helping the social scientist form hypotheses about the relationships among variables, it will not be useful in providing a test of possible causal relationships among those variables. Similarly, though experimental research provides the control necessary to allow a researcher to make causal inferences, that very control inhibits the researcher from discovering previously unsuspected relationships. Thus communication researchers should be cognizant of the tradeoffs inherent in choosing a method of doing research: The control of the laboratory typically requires the sacrifice of generalizing to a wide range of settings, the breadth of descriptive research requires the sacrifice of finely tuned causal explanations, and so on.

However, an awareness of the tradeoffs and sacrifices inherent in the choice of a research method should not discourage communication researchers. Rather, a knowledge of the strengths and weaknesses of a wide range of research methods should encourage communication scientists to engage in programs of research that incorporate many research methods. This will allow the researcher to capitalize on each method's strengths and minimize each method's weaknesses.

Consider, for example, a researcher interested in the ways spouses resolve marital conflict. The researcher might begin with exploratory research in which couples were observed in a variety of situations. This type of unstructured observation could lead the researcher to a number of hypotheses about the strategies and tactics used in resolving marital conflict. Using this information, the researcher might conduct a large-scale survey to draw a more finely tuned description of when and how couples use various modes of conflict resolution. This description could be correlated with other variables, such as marital satisfaction, socioeconomic status, and education, in subsequent investigations. The causal nature of relationships discovered in this research could be investigated in experimental research, or perhaps the researcher might want to go back into the field to observe more couples in natural settings to further develop the explanation of marital conflict resolution. In short, the use of all types of communication research can provide us with richer knowledge of human communication than any particular research method on its own.

SUMMARY

The scientific study of communication provides systematic procedures for the observation and analysis of communicative behavior. The goal of scientific investigation is the construction of theories for explanation, prediction, and control of communicative behaviors.

Communication inquiry methods are the specific research techniques that generate this scientific knowledge. There are four basic methods of communication inquiry, from exploratory studies through laboratory experiments. Each method of research provides different types of information for different circumstances. Each method of research has its individual strengths and weaknesses, depending on the type of question to be answered.

Each of the four methods of communication research has its own goals or purpose. The methods differ in their degree of structure, in the typical setting in which they are used, and in the observational techniques used to collect information. Finally, the findings of each method of inquiry must be analyzed, and the appropriate analytical techniques will vary from method to method.

REVIEW AND DISCUSSION QUESTIONS

1. Each method of communication inquiry has strengths and weaknesses. For each method, describe a practical communication research situation appropriate for that method and a research situation in which it would be totally inappropriate to use that method.

2. For each of the earlier chapters, identify the type of inquiry method that seems to be used most often.

3. Does there appear to be a logical temporal sequence in the types of communication inquiry as listed in this chapter? For example, which types of research would be most appropriate early in the investigation of a communication phenomenon and which types of inquiry would only be useful later in the research process?

4. Choose a chapter from this text and design an imaginary research project for that area of communication, using each of the four methods of inquiry. Discuss the strengths and weaknesses of your design, in the context of other research in that chapter.

REFERENCES

Babbie, E. (1986). *The practice of social research* (4th ed.). Belmont, CA: Wadsworth.

Campbell, D. T., & Stanley, J. C. (1963). *Experimental and quasi-experimental designs for research*. Chicago: Rand McNally.

Fishbein, M. (Ed.) (1967). *Readings in attitude theory and measurement*l. New York: Wiley.

Greenberg, B. S., Burgoon, M., Burgoon, J., & Korzenny, F. (Eds.). (1983). *Mexican Americans and the mass media*. Norwood, NJ: Ablex.

Hunter, J. E., & Gerbing, D. W. (1982). Unidimensional measurement, second order factor analysis, and causal models. *Research in Organizational Behavior, 4,* 267–320.

Jablin, F. M., & Krone, K. J. (1987). Organizational communication and organizational assimilation: An intra- and inter-level analysis. In C. Berger & S. H. Chaffee (Eds.), *Handbook of communication science*. Newbury Park, CA: Sage.

Keppel, G. (1982). *Design and analysis: A researcher's handbook* (2nd ed.). Englewood Cliffs, NJ: Prentice-Hall.

Kerlinger, F. N. (1973). *Foundations of behavioral research* (2nd ed.). New York: Holt, Rinehart & Winston.

Kidder, L. H. (1981). *Research methods in social relations*. New York: Holt, Rinehart & Winston.

Marwell, G., & Schmitt, D. R. (1967). Dimensions of compliance-gaining behavior: An empirical analysis. *Sociometry, 30,* 350–364.

McCroskey, J. C. (1970). Measures of communication bound anxiety. *Speech Monographs, 37,* 269–277.

Miller, G. R., Mongeau, P. A., & Sleight, C. (1986). Fudging with friends and lying to lovers: Deceptive communication in personal relationships. *Journal of Social and Personal Relationships, 3,* 495–512.

Miller, G. R., & Steinberg, M. (1975). *Between people: A new analysis of interpersonal communication*. Chicago: Science Research Associates.

Miller, K. I., & Monge, P. R. (1986). Participation, satisfaction, and productivity: A meta-analytic review. *Academy of Management Journal, 29,* 727–753.

Miller, K. I., & Monge, P. R. (1987). The development and test of a system of organizational participation and allocation. In M. McLaughlin (Ed.), *Communication Yearbook 10* (pp. 431–455). Beverly Hills: Sage.

Miller, K. I., Zook, E., G., & Mack, L. J. (1987, November). Communication artifacts and organizational culture: An investigation of internal company newsletters. Paper presented at the annual meeting of the Speech Communication Association, Boston.

Nunnally, J. (1967). *Psychometric theory*. New York: McGraw-Hill.

Quinn, R. E. (1977). Coping with Cupid: The formation, impact, and management of romantic relationships in organizations. *Administrative Science Quarterly, 22,* 30–45.

Redding, W. C. (1970). Research setting: Field studies. In P. Emmert & W. D. Brooks (Eds.), *Methods of research in communication* (pp. 105–159). Boston: Houghton Mifflin.

Selltiz, C., Jahoda, M., Deutsch M., & Cook, S. W. (1959). *Research methods in social relations*. New York: Holt, Rinehart & Winston.

Stern, R. N. (1979). The development of an interorganizational control network: The case of intercollegiate athletics. *Administrative Science Quarterly, 24,* 242–266.

Stiff, J. B., & Miller, G. R. (1986). "Come to think of it . . ." Interrogative probes, deceptive communication, and deception detection. *Human Communication Research, 12,* 339–357.

Trujillo, N. (1983). "Performing" Mintzberg's roles: The nature of managerial communication. In L. Putnam and M. Pacanowsky (Eds.), *Communication and organizations: An interpretive approach* (pp. 73–97). Beverly Hills: Sage.

Tukey, J. W. (1977). *Exploratory data analysis*. Reading, MA: Addison-Wesley.

Whyte, W. F. (1955). *Street corner society: The social structure of an Italian slum.* (rev. ed.). Chicago: University of Chicago Press.

Wiseman, R. L., & Schenck-Hamlin, W. (1981). A multi-dimensional scaling validation of an inductively-derived set of compliance gaining strategies. *Communication Monographs, 48,* 251–270.

14

A General Model of the Research Process

Gordon L. Dahnke
Michigan State University

Katherine I. Miller
Michigan State University

Gordon L. Dahnke *is Assistant Professor of Communication at Michigan State University, where he received a Ph.D. degree in communication studies. His teaching and research interests include interpersonal, nonverbal, and small group communication as well as research methodology. Dr. Dahnke recently served a Fulbright Fellowship sponsored by the U.S. International Communication Agency at Anáhuac University in Mexico City.*

Katherine I. Miller *is Assistant Professor of Communication at Michigan State University. She received her Ph.D. from the Annenberg School of Communications at the University of Southern California. Dr. Miller's research on organizational and health communication has been published in a wide range of communication and management journals. Her current research interests center on the development of stress and burnout among human service workers and the role of supportive and participative communication systems in coping with these phenomena.*

LEARNING OBJECTIVES

After studying this chapter you should be able to:

- List five guidelines for a good research idea.
- Identify five kinds of research questions.
- Distinguish among primary, secondary, and tertiary sources in a literature review.
- Explain the role of a theoretical perspective in the research process.

- Define scientific hypothesis.
- Distinguish between concepual definitions and operational definitions.
- Differentiate between reliability and validity.
- Give examples of threats to internal validity.
- Relate the concepts of sample and population to each other.
- List various types of sampling available to a researcher.
- Define replicability of research.
- Outline the major steps in writing a research report.
- Describe the 12-step process of communication research.

In Chapter 13, we discussed a number of types of communication research in terms of their goals and purposes, the structure and setting of the research, the nature of observation, and the nature of analysis. These types of research are quite distinct. However different these types of research might be, though, they share a concern for a systematic and careful approach to communication inquiry. An exploratory researcher may be flexible, but such a researcher is not sloppy. A descriptive research may measure a broad range of variables, but he or she does not choose those variables haphazardly. In short, communication researchers, regardless of the type of research they do, pride themselves on producing verifiable knowledge about the process of communicating. The results of research are verifiable because the researcher is systematic.

This chapter will outline the nature of the research process that leads the communication researcher to verifiable statements about human communication. Obviously, steps of this process are more or less important depending on the type of research being conducted, but this does not mitigate the importance of a systematic investigative process for all types of inquiry.

A WORKING MODEL OF THE RESEARCH PROCESS

Hypotheses and research questions are explored and tested through a series of component steps that function together as a unified system. These components are interdependent in the sense that the first step largely determines and is determined by the last step as well as all intervening steps. "A mechanically consecutive sequence of procedures, in which one research step is entirely completed before the next is begun, is rarely, if ever, the experience of social scientists" (Selltiz, Jahoda, Deutsch, & Cook, 1959, p. 8). Thus the reader must remember that each step of the research process is part of a larger system. As we focus attention momentarily on Step 1 of the research process (and each succeeding step), the perceptive reader will keep one eye on the larger model, remembering the interdependence of all elements in the system.

Step 1: The Very Idea!

Most students are familiar with the intellectual pains one often endures in bringing forth an idea. There is no substitute for a good idea, nor a foolproof formula for generating one. To date, no one has been able to observe the human mind "creating" an idea, so we know perhaps less about how ideas originate than any other aspect of the research process. However, successful inventors of productive ideas suggest the following criteria:

1. *Good research ideas puzzle, prod, and excite the researcher personally.* Like choosing a mate, one should select an idea with which one can live for some time. As Wood (1974) suggests, "A person who is highly motivated to solve a problem is likely to make more attempts to reach a solution and be more tolerant of failure; she/he is likely to generate ideas and to continue generating ideas even if the first several attempts are not very fruitful" (p. 16).

2. *Good research ideas are not necessarily new.* Particularly for the neophyte, it is not a bad idea

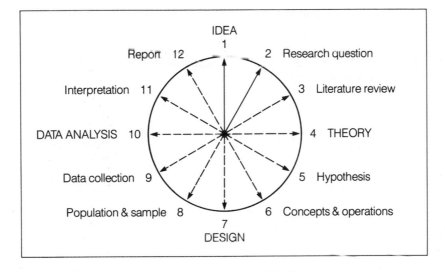

Figure 14.1. A model of interdependent steps in experimental research designed to test hypotheses.

to begin with an old idea. Science is a repetitive, self-correcting process; observations of the same phenomena must be compared across observers and over time. Published reports are an excellent source of new and "used" ideas generated from prior research.

3. *Good research ideas have predictable, intellectual roots.* Good ideas do not simply pop into the heads of certain gifted, superintelligent people. More likely, good ideas are spawned by minds immersed in current knowledge, past research, and hard reflective thinking. The average intellect, gnawing at current communication problems, is fertile soil for fruitful ideas. Better-read researchers have a better idea of what constitutes a good idea.

4. *Good research ideas have potential theory-building, problem-solving capability.* Underwood (1966) cautions against the premature labeling of a research idea as either uninteresting or unimportant. Yet if a reasonable argument cannot be made for the eventual application of theoretical ideas to practical problems, then their signifi-

cance is in serious question ((; R. Miller & Nicholson, 1976).

5. *Good research ideas envision testable relationships.* This criterion is not crucial in exploratory and descriptive research. However, for correlational and experimental research, ideas that cannot be translated into relationships between observable variables are virtually useless. This is where thinking ahead to subsequent steps in the research process becomes important.

Step 2: Formulate a Research Question

Kerlinger (1973), relying on John Dewey's well-known analysis of reflective thinking, suggests that ideas begin with a lack of understanding, a vague unrest regarding some phenomenon, a curiosity about why things are as they are. Accordingly, Kerlinger argues that it is extremely important for the researcher

to get the idea out in the open, to express the problem in some reasonably manageable form. Rarely or never will the problem spring full-

blown at this stage. He must struggle with it, try it out, live with it . . . . Sooner or later, explicitly or implicitly, he states the problem, even if his expression of it is inchoate and tentative . . . . Without some sort of statement of the problem, the scientist can rarely go further and expect his work to be fruitful. (pp. 11–12)

People ask at least five basic types of questions involving issues of fact, definition, value, policy, and implementation (Tubbs, 1984). Consider, for example, the following questions about pornography:

- What are the long-range effects of pornography on attitudes toward women? (fact)

- What is pornography? (definition)

- Is the sale of pornography right or wrong, ethical or unethical? (value)

- What position should the state adopt toward the sale of pornography? (policy)

- What measures should the state adopt to enforce its policy regarding pornographic sales? (implementation)

Questions of fact are most germane to scientific inquiry—factual information is science's stock-in-trade. At this stage of the research process, then, the abstract idea must be pared down to a concrete, researchable question of fact. It should be noted that this question might be more or less specific, depending on whether the research is exploratory, descriptive, correlational, or experimental. For example, an exploratory researcher may ask a somewhat broad question such as, "What differentiates the content of 'soft-core' and 'hard-core' pornography," whereas an experimental researcher may consider a more narrow question such as, "Is the effect of pornography on aggressive attitudes different for men and women?" Differences in specificity notwithstanding, though, it is crucial that the researcher begin with a clear question to guide the subsequent steps of the study.

Step 3: Review the Literature

It is estimated that human knowledge doubles every seven years; information in the field of communication may be increasing even more rapidly. Investigators who are not abreast of current knowledge run the risk of "rediscovering South America"—making a costly research effort to uncover what is already known. Therefore, it is vital at the outset to review theoretic and empirical developments in any proposed area of inquiry. Records of existing information on a particular topic are collectively known as its *literature;* an effort to retrieve such records is called a *literature search.* Competent work in either laboratory or field research, then, requires informed use of the library. Specific instructions on using local library facilities are impractical for a diverse readership. Rather, we will distinguish three basic types of literature and suggest ways these resources can be used.

Primary sources are the ultimate aim of a literature search; they provide access to firsthand information. For present purposes, these sources include original reports of communication research found in periodicals, monographs, theses and dissertations, government documents, and conference proceedings. Competent reports of research present sufficient detail to permit critical evaluation and replication of the research by the scientific community. These resources are extremely useful to both novice and experienced researchers, for they provide information both on what we know and on the methods that were used to generate that knowledge. A number of journals publish primarily communication research, though researchers in communication often publish their work in the journals of psychology, sociology, and other social sciences as well. Journals specifically devoted to communication research include *Human Communication Research, Communication Monographs,* the *Journal of Broadcasting, Communication Research,* and the *Journal of Communication.*

Secondary sources contain "repackaged" information such as reviews of research conducted in a given area, commentaries, and abstracts (brief summaries) compiled from primary sources. Secondary sources can serve to acquaint a researcher with a given topic area, provide a review of the current state of our knowledge about that area, and direct the inquirer to original documents. Textbooks and handbooks can often serve as useful introductions to a research area, and in the field of communication, a number of secondary sources are often useful, including *Communication Abstracts, Psychological Abstracts,* and *Broadcasting/Cablecasting Yearbook.*

Tertiary sources, still further removed from original works, aid access to both primary and secondary sources. They also serve to locate nondocumentary sources, such as professionals, industries, and organizations that support or conduct research in a given field. Conventional tertiary sources as well as computerized retrieval systems are increasingly available in modern libraries around the world. Some tertiary sources of particular use to communication researchers include: *Social Science Citation Index, Readers' Guide to Periodical Literature, International Television Almanac,* and *Dissertation Abstracts International.*

These examples only skim the surface of literature sources available to the communication researcher. Because the body of available literature in any subdivision of our discipline is so vast, it may be advantageous to refine the research question (Step 2 above) following a literature search. Newcomers may even choose to review the literature in a particular area to generate ideas (Step 1). However, it should be apparent that a clearly specified research question will focus and facilitate the literature search considerably.

Step 4: Develop a Theoretical Perspective

The purpose of the literature review is to discern whether existing theory and prior research suggest an answer, a partial answer, or a direction to follow in seeking an answer to the research question (Step 2). In a well-established area of communication research, relevant literature may reveal a full-blown, general theory with strong empirical support. Such a clearly articulated, established theory is defined by Kerlinger (1973) as "a set of interrelated constructs (concepts), definitions, and propositions that present a systematic view of phenomena by specifying relations among variables, with the purpose of explaining and predicting the phenomena" (p. 9).

For example, consider a research question regarding the effect of individual communicative characteristics on small-group interaction. A review of the literature might disclose Hopkins's (1964) work on the exercise of influence in small groups. Hopkins's theory is quite well developed in that it lists a number of specific propositions interrelating five key variables in the form of "If . . . , then . . . " statements. For example, Hopkins includes propositions that suggest if an individual has a high rank in a group, he or she will be central in a group, and if a person is central in a group, he or she will be influential in the group.

It is somewhat unusual, though, to find a complete and well-articulated theory in communication research, for the field of communication is relatively young. More typically, a literature search will yield bits and pieces of theory with limited support. Such a tentative "mini-theory" might aid the researcher in considering important variables or considering the possible relationship among variables, but it will rarely provide definitive statements regarding the operation of the phenomenon. When confronted with a literature of this type, the researcher must integrate the pieces of theory, make carefully reasoned arguments, and provide supportive results from prior research diffused throughout the literature.

As a concrete example, K. I. Miller and Monge (1986) asked a research question about the influence of participation in decision making on the satisfaction and productivity of individuals in the workplace. Their literature review led then to voluminous research on the topic, but no clear theoretical position on the causal relationships among key variables. At this point, they proposed several models that integrated the positions of past scholars. These were an *affective* model of participation, which suggested that the primary outcome of participation was the satisfaction of higher-order needs; a *cognitive* model, which suggested that the primary outcome of participation is a better pool of information and increased productivity; and a *contingency* model of participation, which proposed that the effects of participation would depend to a large extent on the situation in which participation was used.

Finally, it is also possible—though somewhat unusual—that a literature review will lead only to unresearched insights and ideas loosely related to the question of interest. This will most often be the case for an individual embarking on exploratory research. In this case, it is incumbent on the researcher to reason with the evidence available, and perhaps search literatures in related areas, in order to refine the research questions and guide the research effort. For example, researchers considering the effects of the introduction of cable television in the early 1980s had little to draw on in terms of specific research, for the technology was a new one. However, these investigators could look to research on the introduction of television, radio, and other new media technologies for direction.

Step 5: Generate Explicit Hypotheses

A hypothesis is a prediction about relationships between variables. As part of ordinary life, we all have hunches about the way people will behave and communicate. For example, through observing our friends' dating behavior over a period of time, we might hypothesize that the success of a romantic relationship depends on the quality of "first impressions." Or after observing children watching Saturday-morning cartoons, we might hypothesize that watching violent cartoons will lead to aggressiveness. These hypotheses that we make about everyday life are not unlike the hypotheses that social scientists make. Both "naive" and "scientific" hypotheses speculate about the relationships between variables, and typically these speculations specify the causal relationships between variables (such as violent cartoons "cause" aggressiveness).

Scientific hypotheses differ from naive hypotheses in several important ways, however. First, scientific hypotheses are typically grounded in past theory and research rather than in casual observation; the literature review (Step 3) can often provide important insights that will lead to our predictions about the relationships between variables. In contrast, a naive hypothesis will usually be based on our observations of the behavior of friends and acquaintances. A second difference between scientific hypotheses and naive hypotheses is the way the hypothesis is confirmed or disconfirmed. Naive hypotheses are often investigated through casual observation. In contrast, a scientist, in testing a hypothesis, works from a system that will eliminate (or at least minimize) biases from the testing process. The entire research process as discussed in this chapter is designed to maximize objectivity for testing scientific hypotheses.

The importance of generating specific research hypotheses varies with the type of research being performed. In exploratory research, hypotheses may not even be presented. This is because the researcher is unsure of the relationships among variables of interest and the research is designed to shed light on possible relationships rather than to test the precise form of those relationships. In descriptive research, too, hypotheses are often not advanced by the researcher. The descriptive researcher is seeking to draw an exact and detailed picture of communication phenomena. The relationship among variables is not as important to this researcher as the precise description of the variables themselves. In correlational research, though, it is typical to advance hypotheses. These hypotheses usually take the form of specifying the covariance of variables rather than a precise causal relationship. For example, typical hypotheses in correlational research might be:

Hypothesis 1A: As the level of self-disclosure in a relationship increases, the level of satisfaction with the relationship will increase.

Hypothesis 2A: There is a negative relationship between television viewing and sociability such that high levels of television viewing will be associated with low levels of sociability.

These hypotheses explicitly define the variables of interest and the expected covariation between them. However, these hypotheses for correlational research do not specify the causal relationships among the variables. An experimental researcher would take this final step to specify the exact nature of the hypothesized relationship, as an experiment will allow the researcher to manipulate the independent variable to aid in assessing causal relationships. Hence, an experimental researcher might test the following hypotheses:

Hypothesis 1B: High levels of self-disclosure will lead to satisfaction with a relationship.

Hypothesis 2B: Television viewing causes people to be low in sociability.

Step 6: Define the Concepts and Operations

The next step of the research process is to define all important components of the research. The definitional stage will take on different forms in different types of research. For example, exploratory researchers may not develop strict definitions of the concepts under study, for it is hoped that the nature of these concepts will become clearer through the research. However, even exploratory researchers need to define terms to some extent in order to know what to look for, and the definitional phase of research is even more crucial in descriptive, correlational, and experimental research.

Definitions are extremely important for at least two reasons. First, the researcher necessarily shuttles back and forth between two radically different worlds: the theory-hypothesis-concept domain and the observation-numbers-analysis domain. We begin with abstract sets of ideas and end up analyzing concrete sets of raw data. As intimated earlier, relationships identified in the data are unintelligible unless they can be translated back into the precise meaning of the original ideas. Second, the scientific community must be able to retrace our steps from theory to results so as to assess how efficiently the original concepts were actually measured and tested and to possibly replicate our research (G. R. Miller & Nicholson, 1976). The bridge between the world of ideas and the world of data and numbers is built with conceptual and operational definitions.

A *conceptual definition* assigns precise verbal meaning to each variable (concept) entered in hypothesized relations; it is a denotative description much like an ordinary dictionary provides. Scientific concepts, however, because of their base in theory, often have a meaning beyond our common sense dictionary definitions. Concepts devised to serve scientific purposes in this manner are called *constructs*. For example, Hopkins (1964) needed to define *centrality* and *conformity* in his research on small-group communication. He conceptually defined these terms as follows:

Centrality. closeness to the "center" of the group's interaction network; this refers simultaneously to the *frequency* with which a member participates in interaction with other group members and the *range* of other members with whom he or she interacts.

Conformity: degree of congruence between a member's actual belief in relation to a norm and the group position on that norm (the average of other members).

Each variable also requires an *operational definition,* which specifies the exact procedures or operations used to measure it. In general, operational definitions spell out precisely what procedures will be used to measure a given concept. This could involve the specification of a scale used to measure a concept, or perhaps, in experimental research, a specification of how an independent variable will be manipulated by the researchers. The critical feature of any operational definition is its connection with the conceptual variable it purports to measure. That is, the operational definition must provide a valid and reliable means of measuring a particular variable as that variable (construct) has been defined conceptually.

For example, to test a hypothesis positing centrality as the independent variable and conformity as the dependent variable (such as "group members who are more central will be more conforming"), measures must be devised for centrality and conformity that will relate to the conceptual definitions given above. Since centrality was conceptually defined as both the range and frequency of participation, an operation must measure how many people each individual communicates with and how often the communication occurs. Given the conceptual definition of conformity, an operation would measure individual beliefs relative to one or more salient group norms and compare the individual beliefs to the collective group beliefs on those norms.

The import of valid and reliable operational definitions is difficult to overstate. As we noted in Chapter 13, a measuring instrument or procedure is *valid* to the extent that different scores obtained from its use reflect "true" differences in the variable it is designed to measure. An instrument is *reliable* to the extent that it produces consistent scores for a particular variable across repeated applications under the same (or highly similar) conditions. If an instrument is valid, it is also reliable; that is, it measures the characteristic of interest with minimal distortion from other factors in the environment. Conversely, an instrument may be reliable but not valid; that is, it may consistently measure something other than that for which it was designed.

Step 7: Design the Study

The object of research design is to provide the best test possible for the hypotheses or, in exploratory research, the best method to uncover relevant variables and relationships in the phenomena under investigation. The importance of careful research design is never as obvious as in experimental research. The goal of experimental design is to maximize *internal validity,* the extent to which the research design permits the experimenter to reach causal conclusions about the effect of the independent variable on the dependent variable. This is done by eliminating alternative explanations for the results of experiments. These alternative explanations are called *threats* to internal validity.

There are a number of threats to internal validity and a variety of experimental designs that will minimize these threats. Campbell and Stanley (1963) provide the classic treatment on minimizing threats to internal validity through careful experimental design, and the interested reader is referred to this text for greater detail on this issue. For the sake of illustration, however, it is useful to consider a specific research hypothesis, possible alternative explanations for that hypothesis, and ways experimental design could control for these threats. Consider the following research hypothesis:

Hypothesis: The use of positive verbal feedback by elementary-school teachers will lead to higher levels of student performance.

A researcher testing this hypothesis might train elementary teachers at School A in the use of positive verbal feedback and ask them to use this kind of feedback for a year. Instructors at School B receive no special training or instructions. After a year, the researcher reviews performance measures of students in each school. Because students in School A perform better than students in School B, the researcher concludes that positive verbal feedback has a positive impact on student performance.

The question of the internal validity of this research design rests on the degree to which alternative explanations for this result could be plausibly proposed. We will consider three possible alternative explanations.

1. *Selection* as a threat to internal validity. It is possible that even before the introduction of positive feedback, students in the first school were higher performers than students in the second. Thus the selection of certain kinds of individuals for the experiment provides an alternative explanation for the findings. Designing the experiment to include a test of performance beforehand or randomly assigning classrooms from both schools to the two experimental conditions would have helped control for this threat.

2. *History* as a threat to internal validity. It is possible that other events at School A (such as the introduction of a new reading program) could account for the performance increases rather than the introduction of positive verbal feedback. Thus a historical event provides an alternative explanation for the findings. Again, randomly assigning classrooms from both schools to the experimental conditions would have controlled for this threat.

3. *Instrumentation* as a threat to internal validity. It is possible that student performance is measured differently at School A and School B. If this is the case, the difference in measurement instruments could provide an alternative explanation for the findings. The use of standard instruments for measurement would control for this threat.

These are only three of many possible threats to internal validity that a communication researcher must consider in designing research. These threats are the easiest to see (and control for) in experimental research, but they also must be considered when conducting exploratory, descriptive, and correlational research. The general goal for research design in all these instances should be to increase the researcher's level of confidence in the research findings. This can be achieved only through careful consideration of the structure of the research and the specific procedures used to carry out the research.

Step 8: Define the Population and Sample

Rarely is an investigator interested exclusively in information obtained from the behavior of the participants in a specific research project. Typically, our objective is to generate general knowledge claims about the communication behavior of people who have *not* participated in the research. For example, if we are interested in learning about the effects of media campaigns on the success of political candidates, it is virtually impossible to interview all relevant voters. However, we can assess voting preferences for an entire country by interviewing a representative sample of the population. Similarly, in conducting other communication research, be it exploratory, descriptive, correlational, or experimental, we are trying to generalize from the communication behavior of the individuals observed in the research to the communication behavior of many other similar people. The individuals we study in our research are known as the *sample*. The set of people we are attempting to generalize to is known as the *population*.

Membership in the population under study must be clearly defined. In the political research mentioned above, the population we are interested in consists of American voters. A study of communication in health-care settings might define the population as "attending physicians." Once the researcher has explicitly defined the population of interest, it is possible to select a sample for the research that approximates all known and unknown characteristics of the population. If the sample is indeed representative of the population, the researcher can draw inferential conclusions about the nature of the population from the experimental results.

Random sampling procedures increase the probability of obtaining samples that actually represent a condensed version, or microcosm, of the population from which they are drawn. Most social scientists define a random sample as one in which every member of the population has an equal chance of being selected. The mechanics of selecting such a sample are usually quite simple. For example, one may use dice, numbers drawn out of a hat, or tables of random numbers to select subjects from a gross list, perhaps a directory of the population membership. Most statistics texts provide useful tables of computer-generated random numbers for this purpose. The reader should also consult such a source regarding the technical question of sample size.

Researchers strive to obtain a randomly selected sample, because it enhances our ability to make generalizations about the population under investigation. As Kerlinger (1973) notes:

Since, in random procedures, every member of a population has an equal chance of being selected, members with certain distinguishing characteristics—male or female, high or low intelligence . . . and so on and on—will, if selected, probably be counterbalanced in the long run by the selection of other members of the population with the "opposite" quantity or quality of the characteristic. We can say that this is a practical principle of what usually happens; we cannot say it is a law of nature. (p. 123)

Obtaining a random sample of the population is not always possible, however. Thus a variety of other sampling alternatives are available to the communication researcher. For example, *quota sampling* seeks to assure that the sample represents the population by choosing "quotas" of people who have the characteristics that represent the sample. For example, the researcher might be careful to include people with less than high school, high school, college, and postgraduate education to be sure the sample represents all possible levels of educational achievement. In quota sampling, however, the individuals representing these various population subgroups are not chosen randomly. A researcher might choose to use *stratified random sampling,* in which in-

dividuals are chosen randomly from population subgroups for inclusion in the sample. Or a researcher might choose to use a *convenience sample,* in which individuals who are readily available are chosen for the research. Obviously, a convenience sample means a much lower level of confidence regarding the representativeness of the sample, but the savings in time and money can sometimes be worthwhile, particularly in exploratory stages of research.

Step 9: Conduct the Study and Collect the Data

As folk wisdom puts it, "The road to hell is paved with good intentions." In science, quality designs are necessary but not sufficient. The best-laid plans can be rendered useless through faulty execution. Our goal in conducting research is to assure that we are in a position to gather the type of data we need and that our hypotheses (if they have been proposed) receive a valid test. The roadblocks that can hamper us in this objective vary with the type of research being conducted. In general, careful attention to developing and implementing standardized procedures in data collection will help the researcher maintain confidence in the quality of data collected. For illustrative purposes, we will consider some potential problems in conducting two types of research: the problem of "confounding" in experimental research and the problems that can accompany observation in exploratory research.

Confounding in experimental research occurs when any factor capable of influencing subject performance (except the independent variable) varies systematically from one experimental condition to another. We considered several possible confounds (such as history, selection, and instrumentation) in our discussion of research design. There are also a number of confounds that researchers should be wary of when actually conducting the research. Any variation in procedure, the physical environment, or characteristics of the experimenter could confound the effects of the independent variable on the dependent variable. Salient variables of this type are: time of day, room temperature, nonstandard or ambiguous instruction of subjects, multiple laboratories, group versus individual testing, multiple observers (or research assistants), physical attraction between the sexes, and inconsistent nonverbal communication.

Unless care is taken to minimize and distribute these potential influences equally across all experimental conditions, they are capable of inflating or deflating effects attributable to the independent variable. Moreover, in lieu of adequate controls, such unwanted effects become inseparable from the effects of the independent variable.

Exploratory research rarely considers strictly causal relationships, and thus confounding is not a crucial issue in this kind of research. However, this does not mitigate the need to take extreme care in the actual procedures used in research. Consider, for example, exploratory research on the nature of communication in doctor-patient dyads. The quality of the research in this case will depend on the quality of the observation of the dyads. This will require careful consideration of a number of factors, including: (1) the training of observers to ensure consistency across observation; (2) the degree to which the observer influences the nature of interaction between doctor and patient; and (3) consistency in recording interactional events. Inconsistency in the method of data collection can lead to muddled or incorrect interpretations in exploratory research as much as in the more controlled experimental setting.

In all types of research, the most dependable insurance against recognized and unforeseen contamination problems encountered in data collection is a *pilot study*. A pilot study serves as a "dress rehearsal" to test the reliability of procedures, instructions, measurements, observer performance, and mechanical equipment *before* authentic data are collected. Wood (1974) offers an excellent introductory chapter on basic issues of this type surrounding the conduct of social science research. More detailed discussion of this area is found in Underwood (1966).

Step 10: Analyze the Data

This operation is not the researcher's first thought about data analysis. Which statistical techniques are capable of providing an answer to the research question (Step 2) and a valid test of relevant hypotheses (Step 5) will have been largely determined by one's choice of measuring instruments (Step 6) and the appropriate research design (Step 7). Certain hypotheses, measurement techniques, and designs require specific types of analysis, and vice versa. Moreover, sophisticated statistical tools cannot compensate for weak design, inadequate sampling (Step 8), or sloppy execution (Step 9). Social scientists use a somewhat trite but pointed expression to summarize these concerns: "garbage in, garbage out." In other words, the quality of output resulting from data analysis cannot exceed that of the input data.

As was noted in Chapter 13, the specific types of analysis used will depend to a large degree on the type of research being conducted. In exploratory research, analysis might involve a qualitative assessment of the content of interviews or interactions. Descriptive research would require the computation of statistics considering the central tendency and dispersion of the measured variables among subjects. Correlational research and experimental research will typically employ statistics based on the general linear model such as regression, correlation, and analysis of variance. Ultimately, any data analysis should culminate in the assessment of empirical evidence to support the research hypothesis or to answer the research question. The reader interested in a more detailed introduction to statistics typically used in social science research should consult a basic text such as Runyon and Haber (1984).

Step 11: Interpret the Findings

Statistical analyses begin and end with numbers. At this point the researcher has little more than a set of abstract symbols. Our ultimate concern is with the meaning of these numbers, both within and beyond the study that produced them.

The goal of interpretation is to draw unequivocal conclusions regarding a plausible answer to the research question (Step 2). If results of the research consistently support our hypothesis, that answer will be straightforward. Interpretation of nonsignificant or mixed results, however, is more troublesome. If our analysis does not support our hypothesis, there are a number of explanations. The theory that generated the hypothesis might be in error, our reasoning deriving the hypothesis may have been flawed, or the research test of the hypothesis may have been inadequate in some way. There is no foolproof or even standard method for determining a "proper" interpretation for equivocal results. In practice, researchers tend to revise or ultimately give up their theories as a last resort only after repeated testing fails to produce support. Typically, the conduct and validity of the experiment are questioned first.

In brief, when problems of interpretation arise, it is highly advisable to: (1) consult informed experts in the research area for their objective evaluation, and (2) allow the data to speak for themselves—accept the findings at face value until they are superseded by more definitive evidence. In this regard, it is important to note that results which do not support the hypothesis, when they are consistent and clear-cut, can be as informative and important as supporting results to the scientific community.

Finally, when firm conclusions (positive or negative) can be drawn from a given study, we seek to relate this information to the larger body of existing theory and relevant knowledge in the field of communication. This is done by comparing results and inferences drawn from the data with those of previous research reported in the literature. (Step 3 returns to haunt us.) Of greatest concern at this point is the extent to which implications of the present study contradict, confirm, or extend existing theory; do they increase or decrease our current ability to explain communication phenomena? Ultimately, that judgment belongs to our peers.

Step 12: Report the Research

The purpose of the research report is to provide public access to knowledge generated by the research. The report should inform other scholars and practitioners about the problem investigated, the method used to address the problem, and the results of the investigation. Kerlinger (1973) suggests a single criterion for assessing the quality of the written report:

Can another investigator replicate the research by following the research report? If he cannot, owing to incomplete or inadequate reporting of methodology or to lack of clarity in presentation, then the report is inadequate. (p. 694)

To achieve replicability and publishability, the report seeks a delicate balance between brevity that includes necessary detail and clarity that excludes subjective "sell" tactics. Its outline essentially parallels the research process under review here:

I. THE PROBLEM
   A. Research question
   B. Literature review
   C. Theory and hypotheses
   D. Conceptual definitions

II. THE METHOD
   A. Operational definitions
   B. Research design
   C. Population and sampling method
   D. Research procedures
   E. Methods of analysis

III. THE RESULTS
   A. Sample description
   B. Manipulation checks (if appropriate)
   C. Reliability tests (if appropriate)
   D. Tests of hypotheses and research
      questions

IV. THE DISCUSSION
   A. Interpretation and conclusions
   B. Theoretic implications
   C. Methodological limitations
   D. Directions for future research

One final thought. Wood (1974) draws a useful distinction between the *statistical* versus the *psychological* significance of scientific research. Psychological significance refers to the value of a particular study as a contribution to human knowledge; it is "determined by the quality of the idea, the adequacy of the test, and the clarity of the results" (p. 239). Though all three criteria are important, the quality of a good idea will tend to live on despite the measure of a single study. Thus we come full circle back to the genesis (Step 1) of the research process modeled in Figure 14.1. First and foremost, the scientific community will judge the merit of our ideas.

SUMMARY

The process of conducting communication research can be described as a cycle with 12 basic steps. This chapter traces these 12 steps, indicating what should happen at each stage and how that stage builds to the next logical step.

The researcher must first have a research idea, from which a research question is formulated. After a review of the literature on the subject, a theoretical perspective on the problem is adopted and explicit research hypotheses are generated.

In order to conduct a study to test the research hypothesis, the concepts in the hypothesis must be converted to operations necessary to measure or carry out the hypothesis. An appropriate research design is then selected, along with a sample of subjects to test the hypothesis.

The study is then conducted and data are collected. The data are analyzed and interpreted, concluding with a reporting of the research to the scientific community. This cycle of research repeats back to the first step from this point, in a process of replication.

REVIEW AND DISCUSSION QUESTIONS

1. Each of the 12 steps in the research cycle is part of the process for a reason. Explain the purpose of each step. What does each step uniquely add to the research process that helps improve the final product?

2. Which steps in the research process seem the most prone to error? In which steps is it most difficult to assure the accuracy or correctness of the researcher's actions?

3. Explain the importance of the cycle of research described in this model of the research process. Compare the idea that a research design should be changed and improved each time through the cycle with the concept of replicating studies exactly as they were conducted before. Give the values and drawbacks of improving the design each time versus replicating previous designs exactly.

4. Choose a topic from a previous chapter and design an imaginary study for an aspect of it that interests you. At each stage of the process, check to see that you are following the procedures described in this chapter.

REFERENCES

Campbell, D. T., & Stanley, J. C. (1963). *Experimental and quasi-experimental designs for research.* Chicago: Rand McNally.

Hopkins, T. K. (1964). *The exercise of influence in small groups.* Totowa, NJ: Bedminster Press.

Kerlinger, F. N. (1973). *Foundations of behavioral research* (2nd ed.). New York: Holt, Rinehart & Winston.

Miller, G. R., & Nicholson, H. E. (1976). *Communication inquiry: A perspective on a process.* Reading, MA: Addison-Wesley.

Miller, K. I., & Monge, P. R. (1986). Participation, satisfaction, and productivity: A meta-analytic review. *Academy of Management Journal, 29,* 727–753.

Runyon, R. P., & Haber, A. (1984). *Fundamentals of behavioral statistics.* New York: Random House.

Selltiz, C., Jahoda, M., Deutsch, M., & Cook, S. W. (1959). *Research methods in social relations* (rev. ed.). New York: Holt, Rinehart & Winston.

Tubbs, S. L. (1984). *A systems approach to small group interaction* (2nd ed.). Reading, MA: Addison-Wesley.

Underwood, B. J. (1966). *Experimental psychology* (2nd ed.). New York: Appleton-Century-Crofts.

Wood, G. (1974). *Fundamentals of psychological research.* Boston: Little, Brown.

Index of Names

Flavell, J. H., 42
Florence, B. J., 102
Follett, M. P., 162
Foote, D., 293
Foss, K. A., 1
Foss, R. D., 249
Fourment, C., 126
Fox de Cardona, E., 297
Fox, J. C., 126
Frank, F., 145
Fraser, S. C., 249, 250
Freedman, J. L., 249, 250, 281
Freire, P., 299
French, J., 241
French, J. R. P., 160
Friedlander, B. Z., 30
Friedlander, F., 147
Friedrich, G. W., 64
Friesen, P. H., 173
Friesen, W. V., 53, 56, 62, 234
Fry, C. L., 42
Fulk, J., 74, 174
Funk, F. E., 166
Funkhouser, G. R., 190
Furnham, A., 220

Galbraith, J., 174
Gallupe, R. B., 140
Gantz, W., 190, 192
Gardner, B. J., 33
Gardner, R. A., 33
Gardner, R. R., 106, 107, 108
Garfinkel, H., 38
Garramone, G., 200
Garvey, C., 41
Gatti, F. M., 60
Gaudet, H., 281
Gebel, A. S., 130
Geertz, C., 14
Gelfand, D. M., 244
Gelman, R., 39, 40
Genova, B. K., 192
Gerbin, D. W., 314
Gerbner, G., 11, 277
Gergen, K. J., 4
Gerson, L. W., 138
Gerth, H. H., 159
Gerwirtz, J. L., 126
Gibb, J. R., 166
Gibson, J. W., 157
Giddens, A., 172
Gilbert, S. J., 112
Gilchrist, J. C., 140
Gillespie, D. L., 138
Gilmour, R., 51
Giltin, P., 194
Gioia, D. A., 173
Gitlin, T., 281
Glucksberg, S., 29
Goethals, C. R., 126
Goetz, E., 244
Golden, J. L., 17
Goldhaber, G. M., 157, 171
Goldman, M., 133
Goldman, S. B., 290
Goldman-Eisler, F., 53
Gollob, H. G., 244

Goodacre, D. M., III, 133
Gootman, J. M., 58
Gouldner, A. W., 107
Gouran, D. S., 88, 123, 131, 134, 136, 138, 143
Graber, D., 285
Graen, G. B., 173
Graham, J. A., 63
Grassi, E., 6
Green, S. G., 173
Greenberg, B., 78, 89, 194, 196, 197
Greenberg, B. S., 183, 190, 191, 192, 196, 200, 201, 248, 283, 316
Greenfield, P. M., 30
Greenwald, A. G., 247
Greenwood, R., 172
Greer, F. L., 131
Gregory, D., 133
Greiner, L. E., 168
Griffis, Korzenny, B.A., 209
Griffitt, W., 126
Gross, E., 133
Gross, L., 277
Gross, N., 136
Grossberg, L., 37
Gudykunst, W. B., 174, 175, 213, 216, 217, 218
Guetzkow, H., 139, 165
Gunter, B., 193
Gurevitch, M., 287

Haas, H. 207
Haber, A., 335
Hackman, J. R., 144, 145
Halamaj, J., 174
Hall, E. R., 134
Hall, E. T., 51, 53, 97
Hall, J. A., 53, 57, 60
Halliday, M. A. K., 29, 30
Hamelink, C. J., 197, 295, 296
Hamilton, V. L., 138
Hamon, C. M., 137
Haney, W. F., 166
Hare, A. P., 132
Harland, C., 137
Harnack, R. G., 137
Harre, R., 102
Harris, A. M., 137
Harris, H. J., 137
Harris, L., 173
Harris, P. R., 209, 210, 220, 221, 222
Harris, V. A., 244
Harrison, R. P., 62, 147
Hart, R. P., 64
Harvey, J. B., 145
Harvey, M. G., 78
Hass, R. G., 246
Hastorf, A., 240
Hausman, H. J., 133
Havens, A. E., 266
Haviland, S. E., 29
Hawkins, W. C., 130
Hawthorn, W., 131
Heeter, C., 78, 196
Heilman, M. E., 52
Heintz, R. K., 142
Hemphill, J. K., 132

Henderson, L., 194
Henley, N., 60
Hephill, J. K., 133
Herden, R., 172
Hernandez-Ramos, P. F., 272
Hess, E. H., 53
Hewgill, M. A., 240
Hewitt, J., 138
Hiemstra, G., 74
Higbee, K. L., 247
Higgins, E. T., 29, 30
Hill, D., 78
Hill, R. J., 191
Hill, T. A., 126, 133, 141
Hiltz, S. R., 73, 74, 174
Hinings, R., 172
Hirokawa, R. Y., 131, 136, 143, 175
Hodges, K. K., 194
Hodgetts, R. M., 157
Hoel, W., 173
Hoffman, L. R., 134
Hoffman, M., 195
Hoffman, R. L., 168
Hofstede, G., 174
Hogan, R., 41
Holdridge, U. E., 141
Hollander, E. P., 130, 136, 141, 143
Hollander, S. W., 253
Holley, W. H., 167
Holridge, W., 239
Homans, G., 124
Hoogstraten, J., 133
Hooven, J., 166
Hooven, J. L., 160
Hopkins, T. K., 329, 331
Hopson, J. L., 65
Horai, J., 63
Hornik, R. C., 293, 295
Hovland, C. I., 9, 243, 246
Howell, W. S., 215, 221, 232
Hudson, H. E., 70, 73, 82, 293
Hunt, E., 7
Hunt, J. G., 143
Hunter, J. E., 244, 249, 314
Hutchins, R., 277
Hymes, D., 28, 29, 31
Hymovitch, B., 137

Ickes, W., 130
Indik, B. P., 132
Ingram, E., 167
Inkeles, A., 291
Ittleson, W. H., 53
Iverson, M. A., 131
Iyengar, S., 286
Izcaray, F., 294

Jablin, F. M., 89, 156, 157, 164, 167, 168, 169, 170, 171, 172, 173, 315
Jackson, D. D., 117
Jackson, J., 166
Jacobson, E. H., 165, 265
Jacobson, L., 57
Jahoda, M., 313, 326
Jain, N. C., 211, 213, 216
Janis, I. L., 133, 243, 244, 246

Volterra, V., 35
Von Bertalanffy, L., 162, 167
Vorst, H. C. M., 133
Vroom, V., 168

Wahrman, R., 138
Walker, L. C., 140
Walster, E. H., 53, 233
Walters, R. H., 200
Walton, E., 168
Wapner, S., 38
Ware, J. R., 147
Waterman, D., 79
Waterman, R. H., Jr., 173
Watts, W. A., 243, 253
Watzlawick, P., 12, 117
Weaver, C. H., 168
Weaver, D., 285, 289
Weaver, W., 10, 11
Weaver-Lariscy, R., 191
Webber, R. A., 171
Weber, M., 158, 159
Webster, J., 78
Wedell, G., 279
Weick, K. E., 174
Weigel, R. H., 132
Weinstein, E. A., 31

Weiss, R. S., 165
Wells, G., 28
Wells, W., 60
Welsh, C. A., 40
Werner, H., 38, 42
Westley, B., 9
Whately, R., 7
Wheeler, D., 250
Wheeler, L., 130
Wheelwright, P., 15
White, L. L., 172
White, R. K., 142, 160
Whiting, G., 102
Whitney, D. C., 290
Whorf, B. L., 35
Widgery, R. N., 63, 240
Wiemann, J. M., 65
Wiesman, R. L., 313
Wiley, M. G., 130
Willerman, B., 127
Williams, E., 73
Williams, F., 70, 73, 76
Williams, L., 126
Williams, M., 51, 62
Willis, F. N., 138
Willis, R. H., 126
Winans, J., 7
Winch, R. F., 106

Windahl, S., 79
Wittgenstein, L., 12
Wood, G., 326, 335, 337
Woodward, J., 163
Woolbert, C., 7
Woolfolk, A. W., 52
Worchel, P., 126
Wright, J. W., 42
Wurster, C. R., 130
Wurtzel, A. H., 75
Wyden, P., 92

Yalom, I. D., 147
Young, P. C., 130
Young, T. J., 238
Yousef, F., 212, 213, 215

Zajonc, R. B., 166
Zander, H., 127
Ziller, R. C., 145
Zillman, D., 201
Zimmer, J. L., 138
Zlatchin, C., 62
Zook, E. G., 314
Zuckerman, M., 59, 63

Index of Subjects

Ability, group composition and, 130–131
Access movement, government-media relationship, 278
Adaptors, in nonverbal communication, 56
Affect displays, in nonverbal communication, 56
Age, group composition and, 130
Agency model, government-media relationship, 275–276
Agenda setting and mass media, 285–286, 289
Alternative communication model, political communication, 298–300
Anxiety, influence attempts and, 244
Aristotelian approach, study of communication, 5
Attitudes, persuasive influence and, 236, 237
Authoritarian-libertarian model, government-media relationship, 274–275

BaFa BaFa game, 222
Boundary spanners, organizations, 171
Bullet theory, 13
Bureaucracy, Weber's theory, 159–160

Cable television, 76–77, 188
Campaign coverage, 287
Chimpanzees, sign-language learning, 33
Chirologia (Bulwer), 2, 7
Claims, in persuasive messages, 244
Clarity and communication, 15
Classical theory, of management, 158–159
Climate studies, organizations, 166, 167–168, 169, 171, 172
Coercive power, 242
Cognitions, persuasive influence and, 237
Cognitive approach, 38
organizational communication, 173
Communication
intent and, 231–232

language as communicative action, 29–32
receiver-oriented definition, 231
source-oriented definition, 230
study of
Aristotelian approach, 5
Cornell school, 7–9
elocutionists, 7
future perspective, 10–15
humanists, 6
mass communication theories, 9
Middle Ages, 5–6
Midwestern school, 7–9
Platonic approach, 4–5
scientific age, 6–7
Sophist approach, 4
speech-communication discipline, 9
Communication of Affect-Receiving Ability Test (CARAT), 57
Communication networks
centralized versus decentralized networks, 139, 140
independence in, 139
in organizations, study of, 165–166, 168, 171–172
saturation in, 140
Communication research
characteristics of, 311–312
correlational communications research, 316–317
descriptive communications research, 315
experimental communications research, 318–320
exploratory communications research, 313
See also Research process.
Communication technologies
cable television, 76–77
computers, 72
effects of, 73, 82
electronic mail, 74
meaning of, 71–72
satellites, 79–80

teleconferencing, 74–75, 81
telephone, uses of, 75
text services, 73–74
videocassettes, 79
Communications networks, in organizations, study of, 165–166, 168, 171–172
Complementarity, in interpersonal attraction, 106
Complementary relationships, 117–118
Compu-Serve, 73
Computers, 72
and social change, 267–268
Conceptual Frontiers in Speech-Communication (Kibler and Barker), 9
Conflict, role, 136
Conformity, group norms, 136, 137
Confounding, in experimental research, 334–335
Conjunctive task, of group, 144
Conscientization concept, 299
Consequences, of innovations, 264–265
Constantine, Emperor, 5
Contingency model
of leadership effectiveness, 142–143
of management, 162–164
Convenience sample, 334
Conversation of gestures, 32
Conversion, in influence process, 237–238
Coordination in communication, 13–14
Coorientation model, 14
Cornell School, study of communication, 7–9
Correlational communications research, elements of, 316–317
Correlational function, of communication, 285
Creativity, intercultural communication and, 220–221
Credibility
dimensions of, 239, 240
hindrances to, 239–240
increasing audience perception of, 239